2006-2007
EVANGELICAL
SUNDAY SCHOOL LESSON
COMMENTARY

FIFTY-FIFTH ANNUAL VOLUME
Based on the
Evangelical Bible Lesson Series

Editorial Staff
Lance Colkmire — Editor
Tammy Hatfield — Editorial Assistant
Bill George — Editor in Chief
M. Thomas Propes — General Director of Publications

Lesson Exposition Writers

Lance Colkmire	Joshua Rice
Jerald Daffe	Glenda Walter
Rodney Hodge	Richard Keith Whitt

Published by

PATHWAY PRESS   Cleveland, Tennessee

* To place an order, call 1-800-553-8506.
* To contact the editor, call 423-478-7597.

Lesson treatments in the *Evangelical Sunday School Lesson Commentary* for 2006-2007 are based upon the outlines of the Pentecostal-Charismatic Bible Lesson Series prepared by the Pentecostal-Charismatic Curriculum Commission.

Copyright 2006

PATHWAY PRESS, Cleveland, Tennessee

ISBN: 1-59684-150-8

ISSN: 1555-5801

Printed in the United States of America

TABLE OF CONTENTS

SPRING QUARTER LESSONS

UNIT ONE THEME—THE TEACHINGS OF JESUS (Matthew)

UNIT TWO THEME—THE CHRISTIAN FAMILY

SUMMER QUARTER LESSONS

UNIT ONE THEME—GOD'S PROVIDENCE IN SALVATION HISTORY

UNIT TWO THEME—PRAYERS AND EXHORTATIONS IN THE PSALMS

INTRODUCTION TO THE 2006-2007 COMMENTARY

The *Evangelical Sunday School Lesson Commentary* contains in a single volume a full study of the Sunday school lessons for the months beginning with September 2006 and running through August 2007. The 12 months of lessons draw from both the Old Testament and the New Testament in an effort to provide balance and establish relationship between these distinct but inspired writings. The lessons in this 2006-2007 volume are drawn from the first year of a seven-year cycle, which will be completed in August 2013. (The cycle is printed in full on page 15 of this volume.)

The lessons for the *Evangelical Commentary* are based on the Evangelical Bible Lesson Series Outlines, prepared by the Pentecostal-Charismatic Curriculum Commission. (The Pentecostal-Charismatic Curriculum Commission is a member of the National Association of Evangelicals.) The lessons in this volume, taken together with the other annual volumes of lessons in the cycle, provide a valuable commentary on a wide range of Biblical subjects. Each quarter is divided into two units of study.

The 2006-2007 commentary is the work of a team of Christian scholars and writers who have developed the volume under the supervision of Pathway Press. All the major writers, introduced on the following pages, represent a team of ministers committed to a strictly Evangelical interpretation of the Scriptures. The guiding theological principles of this commentary are expressed in the following statement of faith:

1. WE BELIEVE the Bible to be the inspired, the only infallible, authoritative Word of God.

2. WE BELIEVE that there is one God, eternally existing in three persons: Father, Son, and Holy Spirit.

3. WE BELIEVE in the deity of our Lord Jesus Christ, in His virgin birth, in His sinless life, in His miracles, in His vicarious and atoning death through His shed blood, in His bodily resurrection, in His ascension to the right hand of the Father, and in His personal return in power and glory.

4. WE BELIEVE that for the salvation of lost and sinful men, personal reception of the Lord Jesus Christ and regeneration by the Holy Spirit are absolutely essential.

5. WE BELIEVE in the present ministry of the Holy Spirit by whose cleansing and indwelling the Christian is enabled to live a godly life.

6. WE BELIEVE in the personal return of the Lord Jesus Christ.

7. WE BELIEVE in the resurrection of both the saved and the lost—they that are saved, unto the resurrection of life; and they that are lost, unto the resurrection of damnation.

8. WE BELIEVE in the spiritual unity of believers in our Lord Jesus Christ.

USING THE 2006-2007 COMMENTARY

The *Evangelical Sunday School Lesson Commentary* for 2006-2007 is presented to the reader with the hope that it will become his or her weekly companion through the months ahead.

Quarterly unit themes for the 2006-2007 volume are as follows:

• Fall Quarter—Unit One: "Message of the Old Testament"; Unit Two: "Message of the New Testament"

• Winter Quarter—Unit One: "Beginnings" (Genesis 1—11); Unit Two: "Basic Christian Doctrines"

• Spring Quarter—Unit One: "The Teachings of Jesus" (Matthew); Unit Two: "The Christian Family"

• Summer Quarter—Unit One: "God's Providence in Salvation History"; Unit Two: "Prayers and Exhortations in the Psalms"

The lesson sequence used in this volume is prepared by the Pentecostal-Charismatic Curriculum Commission. The specific material used in developing each lesson is written and edited under the guidance of the editorial staff of Pathway Press.

INTRODUCTION: The opening of each week's lesson features a one-page introduction. It provides background information that sets the stage for the lesson.

CONTEXT: A time and place is given for most lessons. Where there is a wide range of ideas regarding the exact time or place, we favor the majority opinion of conservative scholars.

PRINTED TEXT: The printed text is the body of Scripture designated each week for verse-by-verse study in the classroom. Drawing on the study text the teacher delves into this printed text, exploring its content with the students.

CENTRAL TRUTH and FOCUS: The central truth states the single unifying principle that the expositors attempted to clarify in each lesson. The focus describes the overall lesson goal.

DICTIONARY: A dictionary, which attempts to bring pronunciation and clarification to difficult words or phrases, is included with many lessons.

EXPOSITION and LESSON OUTLINE: The heart of this commentary—and probably the heart of the teacher's instruction each week—is the exposition of the printed text. This exposition material is organized in outline form, which indicates how the material is to be divided for study.

QUOTATIONS and ILLUSTRATIONS: Each section of every lesson contains illustrations and sayings the teacher can use in connecting the lesson to daily living.

TALK ABOUT IT: Questions are printed throughout the lesson to help students explore the Scripture text and how it speaks to believers today.

CONCLUSION: Each lesson ends with a brief conclusion that makes a summarizing statement.

GOLDEN TEXT CHALLENGE: The golden text challenge for each week is a brief reflection on that single verse. The word *challenge* is used because its purpose is to help students apply this key verse to their life.

DAILY BIBLE READINGS: The daily Bible readings are included for the teacher to use in his or her own devotions throughout the week, as well as to share with members of their class.

SCRIPTURE TEXTS USED IN LESSON EXPOSITION

Genesis

1:1-3	September 3
1:1-5, 20	December 3
1:24-31	September 3
1:25-31	December 3
2:1-3	December 3
2:7-9, 18, 21-25	December 3
2:18-23	April 29
2:25	December 3
3:1-19	December 10
3:14-19, 22-24	September 3
3:22-24	December 10
6:1-8	December 17
6:5-8	September 3
6:11-19, 22	December 17
7:1	September 3
7:1, 7, 11-16	December 17
7:17, 21	September 3
7:23, 24	December 17
8:1	September 3
8:1-4	December 17
8:15, 16	September 3
8:15-22	December 17
8:20-22	September 3
9:1, 2, 11-13, 15-17	December 17
12:1-8	September 3
46:1-7	September 3
49:8-10	September 3

Exodus

1:22	June 3
2:23-25	September 10
3:1, 2, 7-10	September 10
3:7-10, 12-15	June 3
12:40-42	September 10
13:20-22	September 10
15:26	February 18
16:4, 5	June 3
17:5, 6	June 3
24:3-7	December 31

Leviticus

19:1, 2, 37	September 10

Numbers

9:21, 22	September 10

Deuteronomy

2:1-3, 7, 14	September 10
4:1, 2, 5, 6, 9, 10	May 6
5:1-3, 22, 32, 33	September 10
6:4	January 7
6:1-9	April 29

Deuteronomy (con't)

8:3	June 3
34:4, 10-12	June 3

Joshua

1:1-5	June 3
1:1-6	September 17

Judges

2:7-10, 15, 16	September 17

Ruth

1:14-22	June 10
2:5-12	June 10
4:13-17	June 10

1 Samuel

7:13-17	September 17
16:1, 2, 4, 5, 11-13	June 17
17:33-40, 45-47	June 17

2 Samuel

5:1-5	September 17
7:8-13	June 17

1 Kings

2:1-4	September 17
9:1-3	September 17

2 Chronicles

9:30, 31	September 17
10:16-19	September 17
36:14-21	September 17

Ezra

1:1-8	September 24
2:68-70	September 24
3:1-3, 10-13	September 24
6:14, 15	September 24

Nehemiah

8:1-3, 5, 6, 9, 10	September 24
9:1-3, 38	September 24

Esther

3:8, 9	June 24
4:1, 4, 13-16	June 24
5:1, 2	June 24
7:1-6	June 24
8:3, 11, 18, 19, 27, 28	June 24

Job

1:1, 8-12, 20-22	October 8
2:4-10	October 8

Job (con't)

13:15, 16	October 8
42:5, 6, 10	October 8

Psalms

13:1-6	October 1
18:1-6, 16-19, 28-36, 43-50	July 22
22:1-11, 19-31	July 29
27:1-14	August 5
29:1-11	August 5
37:1-8, 11-20, 34-40	August 12
40:1-17	August 19
68:1-6, 18-22, 28-35	August 26
78:1-7	October 1
103:3	February 18
127:1-5	May 6
128:1-6	April 29
148:1-14	October 1

Proverbs

3:9, 10	May 13
8:1-11	October 8
18:13	May 20
22:6	May 6
23:13-16	May 6

Ecclesiastes

1:2, 3	October 8
5:1-3	May 20
8:12, 13	October 8
12:13, 14	October 8

Isaiah

1:2-4, 16-20	October 15
5:1-3	May 20
7:14	July 8
11:1, 2	October 15
11:6-9	February 25
40:3-5	July 1
45:5, 6	January 7
53:4, 5	February 18

Jeremiah

7:3-7	October 15
23:5	October 15
25:8-11	October 15

Ezekiel

14:12-14	October 15

Micah

5:2	October 15
7:18-20	October 15

Zechariah

9:9	October 15

Malachi

3:8-11	May 13

Matthew

1:18-25	December 24
2:1-12	December 24
3:1-3	July 1
3:11	January 28
3:16, 17	January 7
5:13-32	March 4
5:33-48	March 11
6:1-18	March 18
7:1-20, 24-27	March 25
8:16, 17	February 18
9:14, 15	March 18
10:16-42	April 1
18:1-9, 15-27, 35	April 15
19:3-6	April 29
24:1-9, 21-31, 34-42	April 22
25:31-36, 41-46	October 22
28:19, 20	February 11

Mark

10:13-16	May 6
10:35-45	October 22
16:16	January 21
16:18	February 18

Luke

1:13-17	July 1
1:26-38, 46-50	July 8
3:1-6, 15-18	July 1
9:18-27	October 22
12:13-21	May 13
22:19, 20	January 21
24:49	January 28

John

1:1-14	October 29
3:3-7	January 14
7:37-39	January 28
13:4-17	January 21
14:16, 17	January 7
17:14-19	February 4
20:1-23	April 8

Acts

1:4-8	January 28
1:4-8	May 27
1:15-17	December 31
2:1-4	November 5
2:1-4	January 28

Acts (con't)

2:1-8, 12-18	May 27
2:14-18	November 5
2:37-39	May 27
2:38, 39	January 28
2:41	November 5
2:42-47	February 11
2:46, 47	November 5
3:1-10	February 18
4:10-12	January 14
4:29-31	February 18
4:31-33	January 28
8:1-8	November 5
8:4-8	February 18
8:36-39	January 21
9:1-5, 10-17	July 15
10:44-48	January 28
13:1-5	November 5
13:46-49	July 15
19:1-7	January 28
28:16, 30, 31	November 5

Romans

5:9-11	January 14
6:3-5	January 21
6:23	December 10
10:8-13	January 14
11:13-16	July 15
12:1, 2	February 4
12:4, 5	February 11
12:9-21	May 20

1 Corinthians

3:11	February 11
6:9-11	February 4
10:16, 17	January 21
11:23-26	January 21
12:12, 13, 26, 27	February 11
16:1-3	May 13

2 Corinthians

5:17	January 14
7:1	February 4
9:6-8	May 13
13:14	January 7

Galatians

1:1-10	November 12

Ephesians

1:22	February 11
2:1-10	January 14
2:20	February 11
4:11-13	February 11
4:25-29	May 20
6:1-4	May 6

Colossians

1:18	February 11
2:16, 17	December 3

1 Thessalonians

4:3-8	February 4
4:13-18	February 25

2 Thessalonians

3:1-15	November 12

1 Timothy

6:6-10	May 13

2 Timothy

2:20, 21	February 4
3:15-17	December 31
5:9, 10	January 21

Titus

3:5-7	January 14

Philemon

8-21	November 12

Hebrews

2:1-10	November 19
4:6-11	December 3
4:12, 13	December 31
9:14	January 7
9:15	July 8
12:14	February 4
13:5, 6	May 13
13:12	February 4

James

1:19-21	May 20
5:14-16	February 18

1 Peter

1:2	January 7
1:13-16	February 4
1:22, 23	December 31
2:1-10	November 19
2:24	February 18
3:18	January 7

2 Peter

1:20, 21	December 31
3:10-14	February 25
3:15, 16	December 31

1 John

1:1-7	October 29
3:1-3	February 4

2 John

7-11	October 29

3 John
2-4, 9-11   October 29

Jude
1-4, 17-25   November 19

Revelation
1:1-3, 10-20   November 26

Revelation (con't)
3:10	February 25
6:15-17	February 25
12:1-12	November 26
19:11-16	February 25
20:4-6, 11-15	February 25
21:1-4	February 25
22:1-5	November 26

SCRIPTURE TEXTS USED IN GOLDEN TEXT CHALLENGE

Genesis
1:1   December 3

Exodus
3:8   June 3

Joshua
24:15   April 29

Ruth
4:14   June 10

1 Samuel
16:7   June 17

1 Chronicles
29:11   September 17

Esther
4:14   June 24

Psalms
18:2	July 22
22:24	July 29
27:1	August 5
37:5, 6	August 12
40:17	August 19
68:20	August 26
126:1, 2	September 24

Isaiah
7:14   December 24

Matthew
3:2	July 1
5:17	March 4
5:44	March 11
5:48	March 18
6:33	May 13
7:12	April 15
7:24	March 25
16:24	April 1
24:30	April 22

Mark
1:11	October 22
16:6	April 8

Luke
24:49   January 28

John
20:31   October 29

Acts
1:8	November 5
2:39	May 27
2:46, 47	January 21
13:47	July 15

Romans
1:16	November 12
6:23	December 10

1 Corinthians
12:27   February 11

2 Corinthians
13:14   January 7

Ephesians
4:29	May 20
6:4	May 6

Colossians
1:27	July 8
3:16	October 1

2 Timothy
3:16   December 31

Titus
2:14	September 10
3:5	January 14

Hebrews
12:14   February 4

James
1:5	October 8
5:15	February 18

2 Peter
1:21	October 15
2:5	December 17

Jude		**Revelation**	
1:3	November 19	4:11	September 3
		22:12	November 6
		22:20	February 25

ACKNOWLEDGMENTS

Many books, magazines and Web sites have been used in the research that has gone into the 2006-2007 *Evangelical Commentary*. The major resources that have been used are listed below.

Bibles
King James Version, Oxford University Press, Oxford, England
Life Application Study Bible, Zondervan Publishing House, Grand Rapids
New American Standard Bible (*NASB*), Holman Publishers, Nashville
New International Version (*NIV*), Zondervan Publishing House, Grand Rapids
New King James Version (*NKJV*), Thomas Nelson Publishers, Nashville
The Nelson Study Bible, Thomas Nelson Publishers, Nashville
Word in Life Study Bible, Thomas Nelson Publishers, Nashville

Commentaries
Adam Clarke's Commentary, Abingdon-Cokesbury, Nashville
Barnes' Notes, BibleSoft.com
Commentaries on the Old Testament (Keil & Delitzsch), Eerdmans Publishing Co., Grand Rapids
Ellicott's Bible Commentary, Zondervan Publishing House, Grand Rapids
Expositions of Holy Scriptures, Alexander MacLaren, Eerdmans Publishing Co., Grand Rapids
Expository Thoughts on the Gospels, J.C. Ryle, Baker Books, Grand Rapids
Hebrews: Finding the Better Way, Ron Phillips, Pathway Press, Cleveland, TN
Jamieson, Fausset and Brown Commentary, BibleSoft.com
Life Application Commentary, Tyndale House, Carol Stream, IL
Matthew Henry's Commentary, BibleSoft.com
The Bible Exposition Commentary: New Testament, Warren Wiersbe, Victor Books, Colorado Springs
The Expositor's Greek Testament, Eerdmans Publishing Co., Grand Rapids
The Interpreter's Bible, Abingdon Press, Nashville
The Pulpit Commentary, Eerdmans Publishing Co., Grand Rapids
The Wesleyan Commentary, Eerdmans Publishing Co., Grand Rapids
The Wycliffe Bible Commentary, Moody Press, Chicago
Zondervan NIV Bible Commentary, Zondervan Publishing House, Grand Rapids

Illustrations
A-Z Sparkling Illustrations, Stephen Gaukroger and Nick Mercer, Baker Books, Grand Rapids
ChristiansQuoting.org
Knight's Master Book of New Illustrations, Eerdmans Publishing Co., Grand Rapids

Notes and Quotes, The Warner Press, Anderson, IN
1,000 New Illustrations, Al Bryant, Zondervan Publishing Co., Grand Rapids
Quotable Quotations, Scripture Press Publications, Wheaton
The Encyclopedia of Religious Quotations, Fleming H. Revell Co., Old Tappan, NJ
Sermon Illustrations.com
The Speaker's Sourcebook, Zondervan Publishing House, Grand Rapids
3,000 Illustrations for Christian Service, Eerdmans Publishing Co., Grand Rapids
Who Said That?, George Sweeting, Moody Press, Chicago

General Reference Books

Biblical Characters From the Old and New Testament, Alexander Whyte, Kregel
     Publications, Grand Rapids
Harper's Bible Dictionary, Harper and Brothers Publishers, New York
Pictorial Dictionary of the Bible, Zondervan Publishing House, Grand Rapids
Pronouncing Biblical Names, Broadman and Holman Publishers, Nashville
The Interpreter's Dictionary of the Bible, Abingdon Press, Nashville

Fall Quarter September, October, November	Winter Quarter December, January, February	Spring Quarter March, April, May	Summer Quarter June July, August
Fall 2006 1 • Message of the Old Testament 2 • Message of the New Testament	**Winter 2006-07** 1 • Beginnings (Genesis 1-11) 2 • Basic Christian Doctrine	**Spring 2007** 1 • The Teachings of Jesus (Matthew) 2 • The Christian Family	**Summer 2007** 1 • God's Providence 2 • Prayers and Exhortations in Psalms
Fall 2007 1 • Abraham (Genesis 12—25) 2 • Women Who Changed Their World	**Winter 2007-08** 1 • Isaac, Jacob & Joseph 2 • Spiritual Living 3 • Ecclesiastes	**Spring 2008** 1 • Romans & Galatians 2 • Discipleship	**Summer 2008** 1 • God Delivers His People (Exodus) 2 • Great Hymns of the Bible
Fall 2008 1 • The Early Church (Acts, Part 1) 2 • Job (Faithfulness) 3 • Proverbs	**Winter 2008-09** 1 • 1 & 2 Corinthians 2 • Faith for Living	**Spring 2009** 1 • Mark* (The Servant Messiah) 2 • Practical Christian Living (James)	**Summer 2009** 1 • Prayers in the Psalms 2 • Joshua and Judges
Fall 2009 1 • The Expanding Church (Acts, Part 2) 2 • The Gospel Fulfills the Law (Leviticus–Deuteronomy)	**Winter 2009-10** 1 • Major Prophets (Isaiah, Jeremiah & Ezekiel) 2 • Bible Answers to Crucial Questions	**Spring 2010** 1 • Ephesians: Understanding God's Eternal Purposes 2 • Commended by Christ	**Summer 2010** 1 • 1 & 2 Samuel 2 • Sin and Holiness
Fall 2010 1 • Hope Through Christ (1 & 2 Peter) 2 • The Person and Work of the Holy Spirit	**Winter 2010-11** 1 • Godly Kings of Judah (1 & 2 Kings; 1 & 2 Chronicles) 2 • Christian Ethics	**Spring 2011** 1 • Luke* 2 • Ruth and Esther	**Summer 2011** 1 • Partnership in the Gospel (Philippians) 2 • Wholeness in Christ (Colossians) 3 • Great Friendships of the Bible
Fall 2011 1 • Justice and Mercy (Minor Prophets) 2 • Priorities and Values	**Winter 2011-12** 1 • 1, 2, 3 John & Jude 2 • Growing Spiritually	**Spring 2012** 1 • Return From Exile (Ezra and Nehemiah) 2 • Gifts of the Spirit	**Summer 2012** 1 • 1 & 2 Thessalonians (The Second Coming) 2 • Redemption and Spiritual Renewal
Fall 2012 1 • Hebrews 2 • Who Is God? (The Nature of God)	**Winter 2012-13** 1 • Pastoral Epistles (1 & 2 Timothy, Titus, Philemon) 2 • Prayer	**Spring 2013** 1 • John* (The Son of God) 2 • The Church	**Summer 2013** 1 • Daniel and Revelation (Triumph of Christ's Kingdom) 2 • Help for Life's Journey

*Unit themes subject to revision
**Emphasize the uniqueness of each Gospel.

Introduction to Fall Quarter

M essage of the Old Testament" is the theme of the first seven lessons, presenting an overview of these inspired writings. Expositions were written by the Reverend Dr. Jerald Daffe (B.A., M.A., D.Min.).

Dr. Daffe earned his degrees from Northwest Bible College, Wheaton College Graduate School, and Western Conservative Baptist Seminary. An ordained minister in the Church of God, Dr. Daffe has served in the pastoral ministry for 10 years and has been a faculty member at Northwest Bible College and Lee University for 30 years. Dr. Daffe received the Excellence in Advising Award (1999) at Lee University. His three latest books are *Speaking in Tongues*, *Life Challenges for Men*, and *Revival: God's Plan for His People*.

The second unit is an overview of the 27 New Testament books, grouped as follows: synoptic Gospels, writings of John, Acts of the Apostles, letters of Paul, general letters, and the Revelation. Expositions were written by the Reverend Rodney Hodge (A.B.).

Reverend Hodge is an ordained minister who has served as minister of music for 31 years at Northwood Temple Pentecostal Holiness Church in Fayetteville, North Carolina. He holds degrees from Emmanuel College and the University of Georgia and did graduate studies in history at the University of Georgia.

Reverend Hodge has written numerous Bible study programs, as well as dramas and music productions, and has produced an entire series of theater productions for church use.

History Is God's Story (Genesis)

Genesis 1:1-31; 3:1-24; 6:1 through 9:29; 12:1-8; 46:1-7; 49:8-10

INTRODUCTION

Do you like history? This question evokes two opposite responses. There are those who thoroughly enjoy the *who*, *what*, *where* and *when* details of people and events. They can't seem to get enough of the pictures of the past and the impact on future generations. On the other side are those who find history either boring or confusing. Some people say, "If you had my history teacher, you wouldn't like it either!"

Consider a second question: Do you have a *philosophy* of history? Many people will respond in the negative, especially those who do not like the subject or have done little study in the area. Others may not be sure, thinking that a philosophy requires some complicated system of thought. But wait a minute! Anyone who is a Bible-believing Christian *does* have a philosophy of history. And here's how. By definition, a philosophy is a study of truth or principles which underlie the universe. Applied to history, one's philosophy includes how history began, what are its controlling principles, and when it will end.

For believers these major questions are answered in the Scriptures. We know history began through God's creative work. He brought everything into being through His power. We know history continues within the framework of God's sovereign purpose. He continues to be involved in the affairs of humankind, though not dictating every action or thought. We know history will end when God deems time ended with Christ's return. He chooses the time span for human occupation of the earth.

The goal of this lesson is for us to first acknowledge God as the Creator of all that is. All the wonders of life stem from His creativity and not from an evolutionary process of millions of years. As the Creator, God exerts sovereignty over all. He is in charge. With that in mind, our goal is to be in submission to Him while cultivating a close relationship through Jesus Christ, the means of our salvation.

Unit Theme:
Message of the Old Testament

Central Truth:
God the Creator is the Sovereign Lord of history.

Focus:
Acknowledge that God is the Creator, and submit to His good will for our lives.

Context:
Genesis was written between 1450 and 1400 B.C. Scholars believe it was revealed to Moses on Mount Sinai.

Golden Text:
"Thou art worthy, O Lord, to receive glory and honour and power: for thou hast created all things, and for thy pleasure they are and were created" (Revelation 4:11).

Study Outline:
I. God Creates Everything (Genesis 1:1-3, 24-31)
II. God Gives New Beginnings (Genesis 3:14-19, 22-24; 6:5-8; 7:1, 17, 21; 8:1, 15, 16, 20-22)
III. God Chooses a Nation (Genesis 12:1-8; 46:1-7; 49:8-10)

I. GOD CREATES EVERYTHING (Genesis 1:1-3, 24-31)

Today's lesson spans events from the entire book of Genesis—Creation to the blessing of Judah. The exact period of time isn't known. Some would suggest it to be a little over 2,000 years. Others believe it to be much longer. But length of time isn't the important issue. Our emphasis must be on the process of history as God creates and then continues to be involved in the events of human history.

A. Creation Initiated (vv. 1-3)

1. In the beginning God created the heaven and the earth.

2. And the earth was without form, and void; and darkness was upon the face of the deep. And the Spirit of God moved upon the face of the waters.

3. And God said, Let there be light: and there was light.

Talk About It:
1. What is meant by "the beginning" (v. 1)?
2. How did God bring light into the world, and why is this significant?

The first sentence of the Bible begins with a definite statement. It introduces us to God and His creative work. Notice the absence of any explanation, or even apology, for such a statement without any details. Of importance is the existence of God and His relationship to the universe as the divine Creator of all which exists. No dating or time period appears, which again indicates the importance lies in the *who* and *what*—namely, God creates.

Verse 2 causes some difficulty since here we see an earth already in existence. Its condition can also be described as "formless and empty" (*NIV*). This chaotic condition seems contradictory to the description of the laying of the foundation as described in Job 38:1-7. The angels shout for joy at this time of creation. Why would there be rejoicing at the establishment of such a dismal planet? For that reason the "gap theory" is suggested. This supposes an initial perfect earth brought to ruin by some catastrophic event—specifically, Satan's rebellion. In that case, the events described would be a restoration.

Though this theory may be of interest, one can become so sidetracked with what we are *not* told that we minimize what God wants us to know. One of those items is the hint of His Trinitarian being. The latter portion of verse 2 points to the Spirit of God. And in verse 26, God speaks in the plural when creating human life.

In the verses following the introduction, we read of God's creative work during a period of six 24-hour days. Some have suggested these are really geological ages in an attempt to explain the concept of earth being hundreds of thousands of years old; however, a geological age doesn't have a morning nor an evening. Also, keep in mind that God rested on the seventh day. If that were a geological age, it could mean God is still resting and not involved in human affairs!

"The world embarrasses me, and I cannot dream that this watch exists and has no watchmaker."
—**Voltaire**

History Is God's Story

The orderliness of God's creative work stands out so clearly. He moves from the simple to the complex in a process which lays the foundations for the next level. On day one, there is light and darkness. On day two, He creates the earth's atmosphere. On day three, He creates vegetation. On day four, the sun, moon and stars come into existence. On day five, the lower forms of life such as fish and fowl are created. On day six, land creatures and humans are created.

Within these six days God created everything which He intended for the fulfillment of the divine purpose.

B. Creation Complete (vv. 24-31)

24. And God said, Let the earth bring forth the living creature after his kind, cattle, and creeping thing, and beast of the earth after his kind: and it was so.

25. And God made the beast of the earth after his kind, and cattle after their kind, and every thing that creepeth upon the earth after his kind: and God saw that it was good.

26. And God said, Let us make man in our image, after our likeness: and let them have dominion over the fish of the sea, and over the fowl of the air, and over the cattle, and over all the earth, and over every creeping thing that creepeth upon the earth.

27. So God created man in his own image, in the image of God created he him; male and female created he them.

28. And God blessed them, and God said unto them, Be fruitful, and multiply, and replenish the earth, and subdue it: and have dominion over the fish of the sea, and over the fowl of the air, and over every living thing that moveth upon the earth.

29. And God said, Behold, I have given you every herb bearing seed, which is upon the face of all the earth, and every tree, in the which is the fruit of a tree yielding seed; to you it shall be for meat.

30. And to every beast of the earth, and to every fowl of the air, and to every thing that creepeth upon the earth, wherein there is life, I have given every green herb for meat: and it was so.

31. And God saw every thing that he had made, and, behold, it was very good. And the evening and the morning were the sixth day.

These verses concentrate on God's creative work during the sixth day of the process. God in His greatness could have accompanied everything in a single event, but He chose a systematic process. More than likely, it was for our benefit in attempting to understand what took place rather than for God's necessity.

Talk About It:
1. What did God give humanity dominion over? Why?
2. What does it mean to be made "in the image of God" (v. 27)?

The final part of creation includes all the land animals and humankind. God began with the "living creatures." This means mammals and reptiles as well as the insects and various worms. Though we might wish some would have been left out due to our dislike for them, our Creator knows the entire scheme and all the necessary parts. Notice how verse 25 points out the distinctiveness of each species.

God's final creative act was to bring people into existence. Verse 26 shows humans to be the most important of all God's creatures. He created us in His own image. We know this doesn't mean physical shape since God is invisible and has no defined form (see John 4:24; 1 Timothy 1:17). "His image" means we were given intelligence, a will and a moral nature. We have the ability to analyze, make choices, and recognize the impact of what we say and do.

A second distinction of humanity is being given dominion over all the other creatures. Adam and Eve were not to be subservient to any of them. They were to rule. Both Adam and Eve were created on the same day, though the specifics of Eve's creation are recorded in chapter 2.

From the beginning God created two genders within humanity (1:27). They were sexual beings with the ability to reproduce and continue the human race. In fact, they were told to reproduce and fill the earth with their offspring (v. 28). Human sexuality was not a result of their sin as some have concluded. Rather, it becomes a fulfillment of being one flesh and obeying the directive of continuing humanity.

Having created an environment for life, sea and land creatures and then the first two humans, God stopped the creative action. But He did not end His involvement and sovereignty.

II. GOD GIVES NEW BEGINNINGS (Genesis 3:14-19, 22-24; 6:5-8; 7:1,17, 21; 8:1, 15, 16, 20-22)

A. Life Outside the Garden (3:14-19, 22-24)

14. And the Lord God said unto the serpent, Because thou hast done this, thou art cursed above all cattle, and above every beast of the field; upon thy belly shalt thou go, and dust shalt thou eat all the days of thy life:

15. And I will put enmity between thee and the woman, and between thy seed and her seed; it shall bruise thy head, and thou shalt bruise his heel.

16. Unto the woman he said, I will greatly multiply thy sorrow and thy conception; in sorrow thou shalt bring forth children; and thy desire shall be to thy husband, and he shall rule over thee.

17. And unto Adam he said, Because thou hast hearkened unto the voice of thy wife, and hast eaten of the tree,

> "The higher the mountains, the more understandable is the glory of Him who made them and who holds them in His hand."
> —**Francis Schaeffer**

History Is God's Story

of which I commanded thee, saying, Thou shalt not eat of it: cursed is the ground for thy sake; in sorrow shalt thou eat of it all the days of thy life;

18. Thorns also and thistles shall it bring forth to thee; and thou shalt eat the herb of the field;

19. In the sweat of thy face shalt thou eat bread, till thou return unto the ground; for out of it wast thou taken: for dust thou art, and unto dust shalt thou return.

22. And the Lord God said, Behold, the man is become as one of us, to know good and evil: and now, lest he put forth his hand, and take also of the tree of life, and eat, and live for ever:

23. Therefore the Lord God sent him forth from the garden of Eden, to till the ground from whence he was taken.

24. So he drove out the man; and he placed at the east of the garden of Eden Cherubims, and a flaming sword which turned every way, to keep the way of the tree of life.

Here we see God pronouncing judgment for Adam and Eve's sin. At this point, they are still in the Garden of Eden while hearing of their future. This new beginning would be far different than their initial life. First, there would be a different relationship between the animals and humans, beginning with an overall fear and hatred of snakes. In addition, Eve would find sorrow and pain in the process of childbirth. Apparently this was not how God had initially intended for the birth process to function. Next, making a living would not be easy. Thistles and thorns would grow and hinder productivity. In reality, it often seems that weeds grow far better than the intended crop. From seedtime to harvest would be a time of hard work and perspiration in order to grow the necessary food.

Adam and Eve's sin made it impossible for them to continue living in the special garden. A primary cause for concern is the presence of the Tree of Life there. If they continued to eat its fruit, it would make them live forever in their sinful state. That would be inconsistent with God's judgment for sin which includes physical death. Verse 19 indicates that when they die they will return to the dust from which they were made.

A sad picture is painted in verse 24. Adam and Eve, the epitome of God's creation, are expelled from the wonderful garden of bliss which was made for them. They probably did not want to leave, but God forced them out into the rest of the world.

B. Life Dominated by Sin (6:5-8; 7:1, 17, 21)

6:5. And God saw that the wickedness of man was great in the earth, and that every imagination of the thoughts of his heart was only evil continually.

6. And it repented the Lord that he had made man on the earth, and it grieved him at his heart.

Talk About It:
1. Describe the curse God put on the serpent.
2. Why did God expel Adam and Eve from Eden?

7. And the Lord said, I will destroy man whom I have created from the face of the earth; both man, and beast, and the creeping thing, and the fowls of the air; for it repenteth me that I have made them.

8. But Noah found grace in the eyes of the Lord.

7:1. And the Lord said unto Noah, Come thou and all thy house into the ark; for thee have I seen righteous before me in this generation.

17. And the flood was forty days upon the earth; and the waters increased, and bare up the ark, and it was lift up above the earth.

21. And all flesh died that moved upon the earth, both of fowl, and of cattle, and of beast, and of every creeping thing that creepeth upon the earth, and every man.

Talk About It:
1. Explain the phrase "God repented," and why He did so.
2. What does "grace" (6:8) mean?
3. What was different between Noah and his peers?
4. Why did God wreak total destruction on the earth?

Left to itself, sin doesn't diminish or die away. It perpetuates itself and grows. No wonder yeast is symbolic of sin (1 Corinthians 5:8). The sin initiated in the garden through the actions of Adam and Eve continues. Cain kills his brother, Abel. Murder continues through the actions of Lamech (Genesis 4:23). Also, we see him becoming the first recorded polygamist. Even though a godly line exists through Seth, sin so dominates the world that God determines drastic action to be the only solution. Verse 5 of our text points to sin's having engulfed the human race on every level.

What should be done? God is grieved at the changed relationship between Himself and His creation. Those whom He previously desired to protect must now be destroyed. Sin always brings eventual destruction, though for the moment it appears to be pleasurable. God doesn't change His mind about the rightness of having created humankind. The creation of Adam and Eve in their holiness still stands as a positive action. But now the human race's decision to serve self demands drastic action that will impact all life on earth.

In this abyss of spiritual darkness, one pinpoint of light shines through in the person of Noah. In marked contrast, God sees a man who continues to live righteously and influence his family in the same way. Unbowed by the lifestyles of those around him, Noah walks with God. He becomes God's chosen vessel to preserve a remnant of the human race and the animals which had been created. By faith he builds a huge boat on dry land because floodwaters were going to inundate the whole earth. Only the dimensions of the ark are given along with several construction specifics (see vv. 14-22). How long it took to construct, and who did all the work isn't given. When everything is ready, God instructs Noah to stock the ark with an established number of mated animals, enter the ark with his family and expect rain within seven days (7:1- 4). Keep in mind

"The first chapters of the Bible tell us of the sin of man. The guilt of that sin had rested upon every single one of us, its guilt and its terrible results; but it also tells us of something greater still; it tells us of the grace of the offended God."
—J. Gresham Machen

they had never experienced rain prior to this time (see 2:5, 6).

God unleashes the floodwater. It rains for 40 days and nights. The vast amounts of water under the earth burst upward (see 7:11). When the surge of water stops, the highest points on earth are covered with a minimum of 22 feet of water. This amount of depth is necessary so the ark could float without any danger of striking the bottom.

Verse 21 states so clearly the result of a life dominated by sin. Everything on the earth perishes!

C. Life Preserved by God (8:1, 15, 16, 20-22)

1. And God remembered Noah, and every living thing, and all the cattle that was with him in the ark: and God made a wind to pass over the earth, and the waters asswaged;

15. And God spake unto Noah, saying,

16. Go forth of the ark, thou, and thy wife, and thy sons, and thy sons' wives with thee.

20. And Noah builded an altar unto the Lord; and took of every clean beast, and of every clean fowl, and offered burnt offerings on the altar.

21. And the Lord smelled a sweet savour; and the Lord said in his heart, I will not again curse the ground any more for man's sake; for the imagination of man's heart is evil from his youth; neither will I again smite any more every thing living, as I have done.

22. While the earth remaineth, seedtime and harvest, and cold and heat, and summer and winter, and day and night shall not cease.

God preserves the remnant of humankind and animal life so the earth can be replenished. After residing in the ark for 371 days, Noah is instructed to take his family and creatures out of the ark. They are to multiply and restore that which had been destroyed (v. 17).

Noah's first action upon leaving the ark is worship. He builds an altar and offers a burnt sacrifice. This action pleases God, who then chooses to offer a self-imposed covenant. He recognizes the possibility of the human race once again being dominated by sin to the same extent as before. However, God chooses to never curse the earth or bring mass destruction on all life. The continued maintenance of the sequence of seasons is guaranteed (vv. 21, 22). Other provisions include human supremacy over animal life, provisions of animal flesh for food provided the blood is drained from it, and human authority over other humans to administer judgment in the case of murder (9:2-6).

God then institutes a continuing visible seal of His covenant which will continually be evident when rain clouds deliver their

Talk About It:
1. What did God "remember" (v. 1), and what was the result?
2. Explain the promises God made in verses 21 and 22.

water. Each time a rainbow appears, it speaks of God's covenant with Noah which continues even today (vv. 12, 13).

As a side note, this is the first of three covenants in the Old Testament—God's covenants with Noah, Abraham and David. Each was given to a specific person with impact for a larger group of people.

III. GOD CHOOSES A NATION (Genesis 12:1-8; 46:1-7; 49:8-10)

A. Founded in Abraham (12:1-8)

1. Now the Lord had said unto Abram, Get thee out of thy country, and from thy kindred, and from thy father's house, unto a land that I will shew thee:

2. And I will make of thee a great nation, and I will bless thee, and make thy name great; and thou shalt be a blessing:

3. And I will bless them that bless thee, and curse him that curseth thee: and in thee shall all families of the earth be blessed.

4. So Abram departed, as the Lord had spoken unto him; and Lot went with him: and Abram was seventy and five years old when he departed out of Haran.

5. And Abram took Sarai his wife, and Lot his brother's son, and all their substance that they had gathered, and the souls that they had gotten in Haran; and they went forth to go into the land of Canaan; and into the land of Canaan they came.

6. And Abram passed through the land unto the place of Sichem, unto the plain of Moreh. And the Canaanite was then in the land.

7. And the Lord appeared unto Abram, and said, Unto thy seed will I give this land: and there builded he an altar unto the Lord, who appeared unto him.

8. And he removed from thence unto a mountain on the east of Bethel, and pitched his tent, having Bethel on the west, and Hai on the east: and there he builded an altar unto the Lord, and called upon the name of the Lord.

This third new beginning of our lesson provides the background for the establishment of the nation of Israel through whom the Savior would come, providing redemption for all people. The last verses of chapter 11 give some biographical details and the setting for God's initiating a covenant which makes Abraham the father of a new nation that would spring from his descendants.

How Abraham made the transition from an idol worshiper to a servant of God isn't recorded. Its completeness is evident; otherwise, no such covenant with God would have been made.

Haran (v. 5)—A city located in northern Mesopotamia, it was a center of worship for the moon-god, Sin.

Canaan (v. 5)—The old name for Palestine

Bethel (v. 8)—A town in Canaan, its name means "house of God."

Talk About It:
1. Where did God tell Abram to go? Why?
2. Why did Abram build two altars?

History Is God's Story

God's offer is monumental—a new land, a great nation descending from him, God's blessings, a famous name, and protection from those who would curse him. With these wonderful promises came some requirements—break family ties, leave the cultured city of Ur and go to an unnamed, unseen location.

Comparing 11:31 and 12:4 lifts up an important part of the story in view of the Oriental culture. The eldest male stands as the authority with all members of the family following his leadership. Terah, Abraham's father, led his family from Ur to Haran. But it is at Haran (after Terah's death) where Abraham moved outside of the cultural framework and took initiative to move on in order to fulfill God's plan.

Upon arriving in Canaan, Abraham sees it is occupied by another group of people. God moves to answer the normal question or bring assurance by promising this land will be owned by Abraham's offspring. Though still childless, Abraham built an altar to the Lord and then proceeded to settle in this promised land.

B. Expanded in Jacob (46:1-7)

1. And Israel took his journey with all that he had, and came to Beersheba, and offered sacrifices unto the God of his father Isaac.

2. And God spake unto Israel in the visions of the night, and said, Jacob, Jacob. And he said, Here am I.

3. And he said, I am God, the God of thy father: fear not to go down into Egypt; for I will there make of thee a great nation:

4. I will go down with thee into Egypt; and I will also surely bring thee up again: and Joseph shall put his hand upon thine eyes.

5. And Jacob rose up from Beersheba: and the sons of Israel carried Jacob their father, and their little ones, and their wives, in the wagons which Pharaoh had sent to carry him.

6. And they took their cattle, and their goods, which they had gotten in the land of Canaan, and came into Egypt, Jacob, and all his seed with him:

7. His sons, and his sons' sons with him, his daughters, and his sons' daughters, and all his seed brought he with him into Egypt.

Having been confronted with the joyous news of Joseph's still being alive, Jacob (Israel) decides to go to Egypt and see his son prior to death. Prior to doing so, he offers sacrifices to God. Apparently he is seeking guidance and protection. In the night God responds in a vision with several specific statements:

Beersheba (v. 1)— A town in southern Canaan

Talk About It: Note how many times the word *I* is used in verses 3 and 4. Why is this important?

(1) He isn't to fear going to this foreign country. (2) During the time Jacob's family resides in Egypt, they will expand and become a nation separate from the Egyptians. (3) When Jacob dies, his favorite son, Joseph, will be with him.

Consider how this promise confirms the covenant made to Abraham. It not only continues but will be fulfilled in a land other than Canaan. Through the events surrounding Joseph's rise to a position of rulership, God provides an environment where Jacob's family will flourish. The 12 sons' families will multiply until, some 400 years later, they may number near 3 million.

C. Fulfilled in Judah (49:8-10)

8. Judah, thou art he whom thy brethren shall praise: thy hand shall be in the neck of thine enemies; thy father's children shall bow down before thee.

9. Judah is a lion's whelp: from the prey, my son, thou art gone up: he stooped down, he couched as a lion, and as an old lion; who shall rouse him up?

10. The sceptre shall not depart from Judah, nor a law-giver from between his feet, until Shiloh come; and unto him shall the gathering of the people be.

From the last two verses of chapter 48, it is apparent that Jacob's life is about to end. He calls for all of his sons to gather around with the intent of blessing them regarding their futures. Jacob's prophetic words are not limited to just his 12 sons' lifetimes but include their descendants. Most of his words would not come to place for hundreds of years.

The key issue here was who would receive the blessing as the birthright son and be given recognition as the head of the extended family. Normally the honor was reserved for the first-born son.

Jacob speaks to his sons in their birth order, beginning with the oldest, Reuben. Each of the three oldest sons are bypassed for previous actions that disqualify them from being the head of the family from which the Messiah would come. Reuben's sleeping with his father's concubine, Bilhah, not only dishonored his father and the family but showed his turbulent personality (35:22). In the case of Simeon and Levi, they are disqualified for their cruel murders after having given their word to allow their sister to marry the man who had violated her (ch. 34).

Then Jacob comes to Judah. The father declared that the leadership of the new nation would be from the descendants of Judah. Using the description of a lion indicated the strength of the tribe of Judah. Not only would it become the largest numerically, but it would have a strong military presence. In verse 8, the sons' bowing down speaks of the time when all would give their allegiance to a ruler from this tribe. This happened some

Shiloh (v. 10)— either a compound word meaning "whose it is" or a reference to the town in central Palestine where Joshua placed the Tabernacle after the conquest of Canaan

Talk About It: Describe the promises God gave to Judah.

Unbroken Covenant
The progress of tiny Israel as a nation continues to perplex and frustrate her foes. In the first seven years of existence, its trade deficit was $175 billion. Yet through loans, gifts and German reparations, the economy survived. The unbelievable victory in the Six Days' War of 1967 reunited the city of Jerusalem and wrecked havoc on its enemies' forces.

600 years later when David became king over all the tribes.

Verse 10 points to the authority of rulership, with the scepter being the sign. Initially we see this fulfilled in David and his descendants. A descendant of David remained on the throne until the nation's captivity in 586 B.C.

The ultimate fulfillment of verse 10 is in Christ. Both of the New Testament genealogies (Matthew 1; Luke 3) show Christ being in the lineage of Judah. Christ would not be just the king of the Jews; He would rule over all nations.

CONCLUSION

As we dwell on the truths revealed in the Book of Genesis, our faith should be strengthened. We are reminded our existence isn't a chance happening of fate.

As we've seen from Abraham through Judah, it's interesting to see how God unfolds His plan one step at a time. This reminds us to be patient as He unfolds His plan for our lives.

GOLDEN TEXT CHALLENGE

"THOU ART WORTHY, O LORD, TO RECEIVE GLORY AND HONOUR AND POWER: FOR THOU HAST CREATED ALL THINGS, AND FOR THY PLEASURE THEY ARE AND WERE CREATED" (Revelation 4:11).

Here the final book of the Bible refers to God's creative acts recorded in the first book and says God is worthy to be worshiped because He is the Creator. We should worship Him because of His glory, which we witness every day in His glorious creation. We should honor Him because He is the Creator of "all things," and Genesis says they were all "good" or "very good." We should worship Him because of His power, which He displayed by simply speaking the world into existence.

Since we "exist and were created" (*NKJV*) by the will of God, we must give Him glory and honor by doing His will, which includes making worship a life practice.

Large areas of formerly desolate land now grow acres of vegetables and fruits. Though 2,000 years passed from the time of the Roman takeover of Palestine in 66 B.C. until the reinstitution of Israel as a free independent nation in 1948, God's covenant for this nation still remains intact.

Daily Devotions:
M. God Created Our World
Genesis 2:1-7
T. God Is Most Excellent
Psalm 8:1-9
W. God Rules Over All
Daniel 4:28-37
T. God Became a Human
John 1:1-14
F. God Revealed in Nature
Romans 1:18-25
S. God Revealed in Christ
Colossians 1:12-20

Redemption and Law (Exodus to Deuteronomy)

Exodus 1:7-14; 2:23-25; 3:1-10; 12:40-42; 13:20-22; Leviticus 19:1-37; Numbers 9:15-23; Deuteronomy 2:1-15; 5:1-32

Unit Theme:
Message of the Old Testament

Central Truth:
God redeems us from sin to be His people.

Focus:
Recognize in God's dealings with Israel His care for His people, and trust Him.

Context:
The events recorded in Exodus, Leviticus, Numbers and Deuteronomy probably took place in the 15th century B.C.

Golden Text:
"[Christ] gave himself for us, that he might redeem us from all iniquity, and purify unto himself a peculiar people, zealous of good works" (Titus 2:14).

Study Outline:
I. God Redeems His People
(Exodus 2:23-25; 3:1-10; 12:40-42)
II. God Leads His People
(Exodus 13:20-22; Numbers 9:15-22; Deuteronomy 2:1-3, 7, 14)
III. God Commands His People
(Leviticus 19:1, 2, 37; Deuteronomy 5:1-3, 22, 32, 33)

INTRODUCTION

DNA is a wonderful weapon for crime fighting. Through this scientific discovery those who otherwise might escape conviction and punishment are brought to justice. Just a droplet of blood, strand of hair or particle of skin can prove a person's presence and participation in a crime.

The wonder of DNA extends beyond convicting criminals to vindicating those who are innocent. Over the past several years a number of imprisoned individuals have been released after many years behind bars. Mistaken witnesses and faulty investigative methods stood in the way of being declared innocent of the charges. They had no hope until the blessing of DNA was applied to their cases.

Today's lesson gives an account of being hopelessly imprisoned without just cause. In this case it isn't one or two individuals who are in bondage, but rather an entire nation. It demonstrates how God doesn't bring a nation into existence and then leave them to fend for themselves. Instead, He brings freedom and salvation. God redeems them from the situation. Through His power the price of freedom is paid.

Conservative scholars place the events of our study in the 15th century B.C. (1400s). Geographically the lesson text begins with the Hebrews in Egypt and ends with their being at Mount Sinai, which was their stopping place for about 13 months. Here God gives them the Law, the Tabernacle is built, and the Hebrews become a nation.

In God's dealings with Israel, He showed His care for His people. In return He expected their trust and obedience. This concept remains the same today for us who have become God's people. Though we have never been slaves in a foreign land, we all have been in the prison of sin. As believers we stand redeemed and cleansed. As a people purified from original sin, it then becomes our responsibility to lead a life that honors God and fulfills His will.

I. GOD REDEEMS HIS PEOPLE (Exodus 2:23-25;
   3:1, 2, 7-10; 12:40-42)
A. The Bondage (2:23-25)

23. And it came to pass in process of time, that the king of Egypt died: and the children of Israel sighed by reason of the bondage, and they cried, and their cry came up unto God by reason of the bondage.

24. And God heard their groaning, and God remembered his covenant with Abraham, with Isaac, and with Jacob.

25. And God looked upon the children of Israel, and God had respect unto them.

had respect (v. 25)
—was concerned

What a difference several centuries can make in the fortunes of a people! At the closing of the Book of Genesis, the Hebrews are the extended family of Joseph—the ruler whose actions saved them from the destruction of an extended famine. But at the beginning of the Exodus account they are a slave nation. The fading memory of Joseph combined with the Hebrews' expansive population growth causes the fear that they may take over the Egyptian nation. Seeing them as potential workforce, the new king had them enslaved and put into construction and field service (1:11). However, the population continues to grow in spite of repeated efforts to curb it (vv. 12, 15-17).

Talk About It:
1. What do sighing and crying (v. 23) and groaning (v. 24) have to do with prayer?
2. What did God "remember," and why was this important?

Under the heavy load of physical labor and attempted population restriction, the Hebrews cry out to God for help. No, God isn't oblivious to their situation. He knows all along what is taking place. He understands the load they bear. Now comes a point in time when their intense seeking for God's help and His timetable intersect. "God remembered His covenant" points to God's choosing at this time to fulfill His promise to Abraham, Isaac and Jacob (2:24).

Abraham, father of the Hebrews, received the covenant first (Genesis 12; 13; 15; 17). Then God renewed it with his descendants (Genesis 26; 35). Note the words God spoke to Abraham in Genesis 15:13. Here God foretold how his descendants would be aliens in a foreign country for 400 years, where they would be afflicted and enslaved.

"Perhaps one reason God delays His answers to our prayers is because He knows we need to be with Him far more than we need the things we ask of Him."
—Ben Patterson

B. A Leader (3:1, 2, 7-10)

1. Now Moses kept the flock of Jethro his father in law, the priest of Midian: and he led the flock to the backside of the desert, and came to the mountain of God, even to Horeb.

2. And the angel of the Lord appeared unto him in a flame of fire out of the midst of a bush: and he looked, and, behold, the bush burned with fire, and the bush was not consumed.

7. And the Lord said, I have surely seen the affliction of

Midian (v. 1)—land lying mostly east of the Jordan River and Dead Sea

Horeb (v. 1)—the mountain where God commissioned Moses

my people which are in Egypt, and have heard their cry by reason of their taskmasters; for I know their sorrows;

8. And I am come down to deliver them out of the hand of the Egyptians, and to bring them up out of that land unto a good land and a large, unto a land flowing with milk and honey; unto the place of the Canaanites, and the Hittites, and the Amorites, and the Perizzites, and the Hivites, and the Jebusites.

9. Now therefore, behold, the cry of the children of Israel is come unto me: and I have also seen the oppression wherewith the Egyptians oppress them.

10. Come now therefore, and I will send thee unto Pharaoh, that thou mayest bring forth my people the children of Israel out of Egypt.

Talk About It:
1. Why do you suppose God spoke to Moses from a burning bush?
2. What had God "seen" and "heard" (v. 7), and what was His plan (v. 8)? What was Moses' role to be (v. 10)?

As chapter 3 begins, we find Moses working as a shepherd. This has been his occupation for 40 years after fleeing for his life from Egypt. He left the plush and pleasure of the palace for a nomadic shepherd's tent.

While tending to his duties one day, Moses experiences an unusual phenomenon. A bush bursts into flame but burns without being consumed. When Moses turns aside to view this sight, he has a divine encounter that alters the rest of his life.

After identifying Himself as the God of Moses' ancestors, the Lord reveals the purpose for this encounter. He has heard the cries of His people and knows the sorrow they are experiencing because of their harsh taskmasters. In contrast to the present is God's intention for their future. Not only does He intend to deliver them from Egypt, but He will take them to a place which has everything needed for their livelihood. The specific location is clearly defined in verse 8 as Canaan. The people now occupying the Promised Land are going to be replaced by the Hebrews.

God further emphasizes His having heard the Hebrews' cry of despair and pain (v. 9). He knows all the details of the oppression. Now is where Moses comes in. He is to be God's representative going to Pharaoh and securing the people's release. No details as to how this will be accomplished are given. The issue at hand is Moses' call to leadership.

As always, God not only sees the problem but has the solution and the people needed to accomplish it.

C. The Release (12:40-42)

40. Now the sojourning of the children of Israel, who dwelt in Egypt, was four hundred and thirty years.

41. And it came to pass at the end of the four hundred and thirty years, even the selfsame day it came to pass, that all the hosts of the Lord went out from the land of Egypt.

42. It is a night to be much observed unto the Lord for bringing them out from the land of Egypt: this is that night of the Lord to be observed of all the children of Israel in their generations.

The process which leads to the Hebrews escaping the bondage of Egypt includes 10 plagues over a period of about one year (see chs. 7-11). Each one of them attacks one of the polytheistic worship practices of the Egyptians, who worshiped some 70 gods. The plagues also progress in intensity. The first three are merely bothersome, while the second three inflict pain and loss. The next set of three demonstrates abnormal upheavals of nature. The last one sets the stage for the institution of the Passover. All firstborn of humans and beasts would die unless they were covered by blood sacrifice. The Hebrews are instructed to select a perfect lamb, kill it and then sprinkle its blood on the doorframe (see 12:1-13).

This last plague provides a night for both Hebrews and Egyptians to remember. One can only attempt to imagine the horror of that evening for the Egyptians. Besides being the heir of a double portion, the firstborn son represented the hope, support and leadership for the family in the future.

No wonder God intended for His people to annually commemorate this night. It represented their being redeemed from the death angel and bondage as a nation. This included both an individual and corporate dimension.

II. GOD LEADS HIS PEOPLE (Exodus 13:20-22;
 Numbers 9:15, 16, 21, 22; Deuteronomy 2:1-3, 7, 14)
A. Clear Direction (Exodus 13:20-22; Numbers 9:15, 16, 21, 22)
 (Numbers 9:15, 16 is not included in the printed text.)
Exodus 13:20: And they took their journey from Succoth, and encamped in Etham, in the edge of the wilderness.

21. And the Lord went before them by day in a pillar of a cloud, to lead them the way; and by night in a pillar of fire, to give them light; to go by day and night:

22. He took not away the pillar of the cloud by day, nor the pillar of fire by night, from before the people.

Numbers 9:21. And so it was, when the cloud abode from even unto the morning, and that the cloud was taken up in the morning, then they journeyed: whether it was by day or by night that the cloud was taken up, they journeyed.

22. Or whether it were two days, or a month, or a year, that the cloud tarried upon the tabernacle, remaining thereon, the children of Israel abode in their tents, and journeyed not: but when it was taken up, they journeyed.

Imagine what it would have been like to be part of the Hebrew nation and daily see the visible presence of God's

Talk About It:
What was different about this night than all the nights of the previous 430 years?

Already Paid
During the 1960's and '70s, stamp redemption was a large business. Grocery stores and gas stations commonly distributed stamps in proportion to one's purchase. Carefully gluing them in the stamp books eventually resulted in having a sufficient number to make a purchase at a redemption store. No money was exchanged, so it appeared to be free. However, the cost of the redemption had already been paid at the time of the original purchase.

Talk About It:
1. What did the Lord teach the Israelites through the pillar of cloud and the fire?
2. What was the purpose of the Tabernacle, and how did God honor it?

"We often ask God for too little. We know what we need—a yes or no answer, please, to a simple question. Or perhaps a road sign. Something quick and easy to point the way. What we really ought to have is the Guide himself. Maps, road signs, a few useful phrases are things, but infinitely better is someone who has been there before and knows the way."
—Elisabeth Elliot
(A Slow and Certain Light)

Kadesh-barnea (v. 14)—the place from which the 12 spies were originally sent to explore Canaan (Numbers 32:8)
Zered (v. 14)—a camping place of Israel at the end of their wilderness journeys

divine direction. In jest, some suggest it would be nice if God were to write in the sky today or send an e-mail providing the guidance we need each day. Can you imagine what it would be like as a nation to know our leaders weren't the ultimate ones responsible for its directions?

God chose the exact route and the timetable for the Hebrews' movement. From a geographic standpoint, the shortest journey to the Promised Land was about 200 miles using the *Via Maris*—"the way of the sea." However, this would necessitate going through the warlike Philistines. This fledgling nation had no army and lacked the organization that would come later. For their protection and development, God took them on the southern route known as the "pilgrim's way."

So there would be no doubt as to when to move and so all could see, God led through the symbols of a pillar of cloud by day and a pillar of fire by night. This indicated the people would march some during the day and some during the night, when the temperatures would be cooler.

These constant symbols reminded the people of God's continuing presence. He did not leave them at any point of the day nor at any place in the journey. Tragically, the Hebrews overlooked His provision and quickly turned to grumbling and complaining. Of course, we can be guilty of the same. The constant direction of the Scripture and the communing presence of the Holy Spirit provide guidance which we must be careful not to neglect.

B. Desert Wandering (Deuteronomy 2:1-3, 7, 14)

1. Then we turned, and took our journey into the wilderness by the way of the Red sea, as the Lord spake unto me: and we compassed mount Seir many days.

2. And the Lord spake unto me, saying,

3. Ye have compassed this mountain long enough: turn you northward.

7. For the Lord thy God hath blessed thee in all the works of thy hand: he knoweth thy walking through this great wilderness: these forty years the Lord thy God hath been with thee; thou hast lacked nothing.

14. And the space in which we came from Kadesh-barnea, until we were come over the brook Zered, was thirty and eight years; until all the generation of the men of war were wasted out from among the host, as the Lord sware unto them.

As Moses reaches the end of his life and leadership, he reminds the Israelites through a series of addresses of the events through which they have come. The word *wilderness* (v. 1) usually causes us to think of the rebellion which kept them wandering in a literal "death march" for some 38 years.

Numbers 13 and 14 give the specific story of their refusal to enter the promised land of Canaan after hearing of the strength of the people and their cities. As a result, their punishment was for a generation to die before the nation could inherit their promised homeland (Deuteronomy 2:14). "Forty years" (v. 7) appears to either be a rounded number or to include their time traveling to Mount Sinai and their years staying there. Thirty-eight years likely is the time of punishment mercifully shortened by God from the punishment of one year for each of the 40 days the Hebrew spies had explored the land of Canaan (Numbers 13:25).

Now it is time to move—a second opportunity to enter Canaan. On this occasion, God directs them to move in a easterly path rather than enter from the south. However, God carefully instructs them not to attempt to take any land from Edom (the descendants of Esau), for it belonged to them by divine covenant (Deuteronomy 2:4). The Hebrews also were not to pillage for needed supplies. Instead, they were to buy whatever was required, even drinking water (v. 6).

A key principle is how God continued to be with the Hebrews throughout the years of their sin and punishment. His love continued, and His provisions were there without fail. Neither their clothes nor sandals wore out (29:5), and six of the seven days of every week, manna appeared. God always protected them even though they frequently were in the territory of peoples with armies far stronger than themselves.

In the lives of God's people today, no matter where God leads, He is there with us. Our heavenly Father doesn't discard us because of doubt or failure. Even during times of discipline He continues to be there desiring for us to repent, change, and grow in His grace and love.

III. GOD COMMANDS HIS PEOPLE (Leviticus 19:1, 2, 37; Deuteronomy 5:1-3, 22, 32, 33)
A. The Principle of Holiness (Leviticus 19:1, 2, 37)
1. And the Lord spake unto Moses, saying,
2. Speak unto all the congregation of the children of Israel, and say unto them, Ye shall be holy: for I the Lord your God am holy.
37. Therefore shall ye observe all my statutes, and all my judgments, and do them: I am the Lord.
The concept of holiness provides a challenge for many believers. Some feel it overly restricts their freedom and fulfillment of personal desire. Others struggle with the concept of holiness for fear of being bound by legalism. Each struggles unnecessarily. For when we come to a Biblical understanding of Christ's holy nature and the relationship He desires with us,

Talk About It:
1. How specifically did God guide Moses?
2. Since God was leading the Israelites, why did they stay in the wilderness 38 years?

Talk About It:
Why does God demand holiness and obedience from His people?

we see the beauty of holiness. Relationship to Christ is always submission to Him rather than fulfillment of self. True relationship with Christ is not the robotic following of a set of rules, but seeking to follow His teachings and example.

When discussing or studying holiness, Leviticus 19 is often overlooked. Consequently, the holy nature of God is not adequately seen in light of the Old Testament as holiness translates itself in the specifics of daily living.

In this chapter we see God directing Moses to communicate to the people the principle of personal holiness. Without apology or extensive explanation, the message is simple and clear. They are to strive to be holy. That is the nature of God. As His children, it is only logical for the offspring to be like the parent. It is reasonable for a righteous God to require righteousness, the opposite of sin.

The admonitions in chapter 19 remind the Israelites of a standard which they are to live by. It permeates all aspects of their inner beings and outer activities. For the Israelites we see the directives including both the ceremonial law and ethical requirements. Being a follower of God does not allow for a compartmentalization of one's life. No area can be restricted from His prescribed standards of holiness.

Some of the many specific commands were distinct requirements for the ancient Israelites, like those found in verses 19 and 23. However, the majority are directly applicable to living a life of holiness in the 21st century. In verses 11-18 we find not only a repeat of some of the basic laws of God from the Old Testament but also principles which are of a New Testament nature. For example: Do not steal or lie; do not spread gossip nor misuse God's name; love your neighbor as yourself.

When studying a passage such as this, our desire should be for a fulfillment of the principle of holiness. When believers become so preoccupied with personal freedom and fear of legalism, they quickly lose sight of what God both desires and requires—holiness of the heart, mind and body we should live by.

Hebrews 12:14 admonishes us: "Make every effort to live in peace with all men and to be holy; without holiness no one will see the Lord" (*NIV*).

> "The first duty of every soul is to find not its freedom but its Master."
> —Peter T. Forsythe

B. The Commandments for Living
   (Deuteronomy 5:1-3, 22, 32, 33)
   1. And Moses called all Israel, and said unto them, Hear, O Israel, the statutes and judgments which I speak in your ears this day, that ye may learn them, and keep, and do them.
   2. The Lord our God made a covenant with us in Horeb.
   3. The Lord made not this covenant with our fathers,

Redemption and Law

but with us, even us, who are all of us here alive this day.

22. These words the Lord spake unto all your assembly in the mount out of the midst of the fire, of the cloud, and of the thick darkness, with a great voice: and he added no more. And he wrote them in two tables of stone, and delivered them unto me.

32. Ye shall observe to do therefore as the Lord your God hath commanded you: ye shall not turn aside to the right hand or to the left.

33. Ye shall walk in all the ways which the Lord your God hath commanded you, that ye may live, and that it may be well with you, and that ye may prolong your days in the land which ye shall possess.

Talk About It:
1. Describe the covenant God made with Israel.
2. How would God bless His people if they kept His covenant?

Here Moses tells Israel's new generation the events of God's giving the Commandments at Mount Sinai nearly 40 years before. Moses' time of leadership is about to end due to his disobedience when Israel needed water (see Numbers 20:1-12). As he prepares to leave, there are specific items Moses wants God's people to remember in the future. One of those is the dramatic giving of the Law with its guidelines for all dimensions of life. He wants them to not only hear these laws repeated, but to "learn them, and keep, and do them" (Deuteronomy 5:1). Little value comes from hearing unless God's laws become implanted in individual hearts and in the corporate heart of the nation.

In verse 22, Moses reminds those who were alive at the time how God spoke directly to them with a tremendous display of phenomena (see Exodus 19:18). He also points out the people's response. Dominated by fear, they asked for Moses to hear future words from the Lord and convey them. He became the go-between (Exodus 20:19-21; Deuteronomy 5:5).

After this brief introduction, Moses restates the Ten Commandments (vv. 6-21). Then he spends time in a return look at the people's response when they first received those commands (Exodus 20). They recognized being in the presence of God and being witnesses of His glory, impressing on them the reality of their God being alive. Keep in mind they had already seen a great number of miracles that should have already convinced them of God's reality.

The Israelites who stood at the base of Mount Sinai were witnesses to the 10 plagues, the opening of the Red Sea, manna from heaven, bitter water turned sweet, and much more. Yet, instead of reveling in the power and might of God, they allowed fear to invade when God displayed His glory at Mount Sinai. They said, "We have heard His voice from the midst of the fire. . . . If we hear the voice of the Lord our God anymore, then we shall die" (Deuteronomy 5:24, 25, *NKJV*).

"I find that doing the will of God leaves me with no time for disputing about His plans."
—**George Macdonald**

God gave the people what they wanted, even though it may not have been what He wanted or in their best interest. They offered a sense of commitment to His will, if God would just do things their way.

In verse 31, we see the people's loss became Moses' gain. He had the privilege of standing by God, communing with Him face-to-face, and then conveying it to the people. This reminds us that anytime we individually or corporately want to do anything other than how God designs it, we are the losers.

Moses then offers a conclusion which isn't optional or negotiable. God's commandments are to be followed without variations! It can't be stated any clearer than that. In the final verse of the chapter, the importance of their lifestyle becomes very plain. Their lives depend on it—both spiritually and physically. They would possess the Promised Land, but they would have to "walk in all the ways . . . God hath commanded" in order to "prolong" their days in Canaan (v. 33).

CONCLUSION

"On this very important verse [Deuteronomy 5:33] we may remark, a long life is a great blessing, if a man lives to God, because it is in life, and in life alone, that a preparation for eternal glory may be acquired," wrote Adam Clarke. "Those who wish to die soon have never yet learned to live, and know not the value of life or time. Many have a vain hope that they shall get either in death, or in the other world, a preparation for glory. This is a fatal error. Here, alone, we may acquaint ourselves with God, and receive that holiness without which none can see Him."

GOLDEN TEXT CHALLENGE

"[CHRIST] GAVE HIMSELF FOR US, THAT HE MIGHT REDEEM US FROM ALL INIQUITY, AND PURIFY UNTO HIMSELF A PECULIAR PEOPLE, ZEALOUS OF GOOD WORKS" (Titus 2:14).

When Christians are called a *peculiar people*, we are not called strange or odd, as some have imagined, but "particular." We are to be a people made fit for the Lord himself. In this life we shall be *zealous of good works*—active in the spread of the gospel by our example and our words.

The world cannot understand this kind of people any more than they could understand Jesus when He was alive on the earth. He was *peculiar*—"one of a kind." He says the same is true of us. Jesus gave Himself so we might be redeemed from the things of this world and consecrated to Him as His people and His witnesses on the earth.

Daily Devotions:
M. Assurance of
   Redemption
   Exodus 6:1-8
T. Thank God for
   Redemption
   Psalm 107:1-9
W. The Redeemer
   Promised
   Isaiah 59:16-21
T. Jesus, the
   Messiah-
   Redeemer
   Luke 2:25-38
F. Redeemed by
   God's Grace
   Romans 3:23-
   26
S. Redeemed by
   Christ's Blood
   Ephesians 1:3-9

A Nation Under God (Joshua to 2 Chronicles)

**Joshua 1:1-9; Judges 2:7-16; 1 Samuel 7:13-17;
2 Samuel 5:1-5; 1 Kings 2:1-4; 9:1-9;
2 Chronicles 9:30, 31; 10:1-19; 36:14-21**

INTRODUCTION

If you are a United States citizen, the words "one nation under God" have a special significance. It's part of our Pledge of Allegiance. Inserted by an act of Congress in the 1950s, this phrase recently became a point of contention. Those in opposition to its placement in our pledge see it as a breech of the separation of church and state. Such secularists have a constant opposition to any spiritual or religious inclusion in the public life.

Since the intent of this lesson goes far beyond the framework of one country's pledge to its flag, let's consider what it means to be "under God." When God established Israel as a nation at Mount Sinai (Horeb), it was as a theocracy. God stood as the head of the nation and made His will known through selected leaders. First was Moses. Second came Joshua. Later God used the various judges. Closely correlated to their leadership stood God's revealed law. The Ten Commandments and other laws provided guidelines for all aspects of the nation's corporate and individual lives.

Eventually the people requested a king so they could be like other nations (1 Samuel 8:5). God granted their request. Now they were subject to taxation, conscription and loss of choice lands. At the head of the nation was a king whom God selected by divine appointment in the initial years of Israel's history. Though under the leadership of a king, they were still to be a nation in which God's will and law reigned supreme. It sounded so simple except for the human factor. Choosing the roads of self-indulgence and personal preference turned the nation as a whole against God. Then, instead of enjoying the blessings of obedience, the nation suffered the punishment of disobedience.

Today's lesson spans some 800 years of Israel's history as a nation. Regretfully, Israel's history appears to be a better example of failure than service to God. Though the promises were superior, the people's inferior relationship with God produced failure. The people repeatedly chose to live like the citizens of a pagan god instead of like a nation living under the umbrella of God's directions and provisions.

Unit Theme:
Message of the Old Testament

Central Truth:
God calls us to live as citizens of His kingdom.

Focus:
Learn from Israel's history that God rewards obedience and punishes disobedience.

Context:
Eight centuries of Israel's history

Golden Text:
"Thine, O Lord, is the greatness, and the power, and the glory, and the victory, and the majesty: for all that is in the heaven and in the earth is thine" (1 Chronicles 29:11).

Study Outline:
I. Living in the Promised Land (Joshua 1:1-6; Judges 2:7-16; 1 Samuel 7:13-17)
II. A United and Blessed Kingdom (2 Samuel 5:1-5; 1 Kings 2:1-4; 9:1-9)
III. A Divided and Lost Kingdom (2 Chronicles 9:30, 31; 10:1-19; 36:14-21)

I. LIVING IN THE PROMISED LAND (Joshua 1:1-6; Judges 2:7-16; 1 Samuel 7:13-17)

A. The Promise (Joshua 1:1-6)

1. Now after the death of Moses the servant of the Lord it came to pass, that the Lord spake unto Joshua the son of Nun, Moses' minister, saying,

2. Moses my servant is dead; now therefore arise, go over this Jordan, thou, and all this people, unto the land which I do give to them, even to the children of Israel.

3. Every place that the sole of your foot shall tread upon, that have I given unto you, as I said unto Moses.

4. From the wilderness and this Lebanon even unto the great river, the river Euphrates, all the land of the Hittites, and unto the great sea toward the going down of the sun, shall be your coast.

5. There shall not any man be able to stand before thee all the days of thy life: as I was with Moses, so I will be with thee: I will not fail thee, nor forsake thee.

6. Be strong and of a good courage: for unto this people shalt thou divide for an inheritance the land, which I sware unto their fathers to give them.

Talk About It:
1. What was God's first command to Joshua, and why was it such a challenge (vv. 1, 2)?
2. List the promises God gave to Joshua in verses 3-5.
3. Compare Joshua 1:6 with Philippians 4:13. Why should we be "of good courage"?

"The world has no room for cowards. We must all be ready somehow to toil, to suffer, to die. And yours is not the less noble [calling] because no drum beats before you when you go out into your daily battle fields, and no crowds shout about your coming when

Moses died and then was buried by the archangel Michael (see Jude 9). It was time for the new leader, Joshua, to take charge and lead the nation into the land of Canaan. He was a mature man (80 years old), a military leader, the right-hand man of the previous leader, and, most importantly, a man of faith. Yet he faced a daunting task of filling the shoes of Moses, with whom God spoke face-to-face (Exodus 33:11). Joshua had to lead a nation of people who tended to be fickle and conquer a land with peoples who were militarily stronger than themselves. Would they be a people of faith or fright? That was the unknown factor.

Knowing this, God provided tremendous encouragement along with the directive to cross the Jordan River and begin the invasion. He began with the promise of the land of Canaan. They were being given ownership. All they had to do was pick up their feet and walk on the soil within its borders. If they would be courageous and obedient, God would fulfill the promise given to Abraham several centuries before (Genesis 12). So there would be no doubt as to the extent of the land, God provided the boundary lines (Joshua 1:4).

In verse 5 God promised them victory. No one in the land would be able to withstand them. It's interesting how God placed a provision there—all the days of Joshua's life. At the end of the book it becomes apparent how influential Joshua's life was even after his death. The nation would continue to follow the Lord under the elders who served with Joshua (Joshua

24:31). God emphasizes His being with Joshua in the same way He was with Moses. There would be no failing nor forsaking on His part.

All God required of Joshua was for him to be strong in his commitment and not fear. As a result, he would have the privilege of dividing the land among the tribes.

God intended for His people to live in Canaan. He desired victory for them. He wanted Joshua to be successful. Both he and the people could have everything God offered. All He required was their obedient involvement.

B. The Failure (Judges 2:7-16)
(Judges 2:11-14 is not included in the printed text.)

7. And the people served the Lord all the days of Joshua, and all the days of the elders that outlived Joshua, who had seen all the great works of the Lord, that he did for Israel.

8. And Joshua, the son of Nun, the servant of the Lord, died, *being* an hundred and ten years old.

9. And they buried him in the border of his inheritance in Timnath-heres, in the mount of Ephraim, on the north side of the hill Gaash.

10. And also all that generation were gathered unto their fathers: and there arose another generation after them, which knew not the Lord, nor yet the works which he had done for Israel.

15. Whithersoever they went out, the hand of the Lord was against them for evil, as the Lord had said, and as the Lord had sworn unto them: and they were greatly distressed.

16. Nevertheless the Lord raised up judges, which delivered them out of the hand of those that spoiled them.

Joshua's 30 years as the leader of Israel influenced the people for another generation of time. These people also were eyewitnesses of God's miraculous works on their behalf. However, they did fail in one area: they chose to enslave and tax the people who were to be destroyed (see 1:28). Then, when a new generation arose who were not committed to the Lord and had not experienced His miraculous provision and intervention, they became idolaters. They followed the very gods of the heathens whom God intended to be destroyed for their sins.

God's punishment strikes swiftly. Instead of being the conquerors, the Israelites become the conquered and oppressed. Instead of being victorious, they are beaten. Marauding bands of their enemies come at harvest time to strip them of their precious harvests. As a nation, they reap the consequences of sin.

you return from your daily victory or defeat."
—**Robert Louis Stevenson**

Timnath-heres—
(TIM-nath-HE-reez)—
v. 9—a village in Ephraim *(EE-fray-um)*

Ashtaroth *(ASH-tuh-rath)*—v. 13—statues of the fertility goddesses of the ancient Near East

Talk About It:
1. What was different between the "Joshua generation" and the one immediately following (vv. 7-13)?
2. How did this generation suffer as a result of their sin (vv. 14, 15)?
3. Describe the purpose of the judges God raised up (v. 16).

Yet, even in the middle of Israel's disobedience, God's mercy becomes evident. After the Israelites cry out to the Lord and humbly recognize their sins, He sends "judges" who will lead them out of their dilemma. "The judges were tribesmen in Israel upon whom the Lord laid the burden of Israel's apostate and oppressed state. They were the spiritual ancestors of the prophets" (*Scofield Reference Bible*).

C. The Victory (1 Samuel 7:13-17)

13. So the Philistines were subdued, and they came no more into the coast of Israel: and the hand of the Lord was against the Philistines all the days of Samuel.

14. And the cities which the Philistines had taken from Israel were restored to Israel, from Ekron even unto Gath; and the coasts thereof did Israel deliver out of the hands of the Philistines. And there was peace between Israel and the Amorites.

15. And Samuel judged Israel all the days of his life.

16. And he went from year to year in circuit to Bethel, and Gilgal, and Mizpeh, and judged Israel in all those places.

17. And his return was to Ramah; for there was his house; and there he judged Israel; and there he built an altar unto the Lord.

Talk About It:
Describe the success Samuel had as the leader of Israel. What was the key?

The era of the judges closed with this statement: "Every man did that which was right in his own eyes" (Judges 21:25). However, under the godly leadership of the prophet Samuel, Israel returns to her God. Though they fear the military might of the Philistines, they must fight. As the Philistine armies advance, the Israelites ask Samuel to continue seeking for God's intervention (1 Samuel 7:8). The Lord answers his prayer and miraculously intervenes in the battle. The Israelites then pursue the fleeing Philistine soldiers. Not only does Israel retake cities previously captured by the enemy, but so beaten are the Philistines that they no longer invade Israel during Samuel's leadership.

Here we again see the impact a leader can have on an entire nation. Samuel's predecessor, Eli and his sons, had allowed Israel to enter a period of spiritual decline. In contrast is Samuel, who put God and His law first. As he travels a regular circuit holding court and influencing the people toward righteousness, Israel reaps the spiritual and physical blessings.

II. A UNITED AND BLESSED KINGDOM (2 Samuel 5:1-5; 1 Kings 2:1-4; 9:1-9)

A. United Under David (2 Samuel 5:1-5)

1. Then came all the tribes of Israel to David unto

Hebron, and spake, saying, Behold, we are thy bone and thy flesh.

2. Also in time past, when Saul was king over us, thou wast he that leddest out and broughtest in Israel: and the Lord said to thee, Thou shalt feed my people Israel, and thou shalt be a captain over Israel.

3. So all the elders of Israel came to the king to Hebron; and king David made a league with them in Hebron before the Lord: and they anointed David king over Israel.

4. David was thirty years old when he began to reign, and he reigned forty years.

5. In Hebron he reigned over Judah seven years and six months: and in Jerusalem he reigned thirty and three years over all Israel and Judah.

God always fulfills His Word. We have the obligation to be patient and allow His process and timetable to be fulfilled. David provides an excellent example. While still a boy herding sheep, he was anointed to be the second king of Israel. His age is not given, but it appears he probably was no older than his mid-teens. Though he was marvelously used of God in defeating Goliath, the mighty champion of the Philistines, the years following were difficult. Repeatedly Saul, his king and father-in-law, allowed jealousy to drive him to attempted murder. Finally, David became a fugitive surrounded by a band of men who also were outcasts from the kingdom. David's righteousness kept him from killing Saul on two occasions when unknowingly the king placed himself in easy striking distance.

After Saul's death only one tribe, Judah, aligned themselves with David and made him their king. The others pledged allegiance to Saul's one surviving son, Ishbosheth. David waited. There was no political campaign nor military excursion to further his right as the anointed of God to rule over all 12 tribes.

Seven and one-half years later (v. 5), tragedy strikes the other kingdom. Two rebels, Rechab and Baanah, rise against King Ishbosheth and assassinate him as he lies in bed. Assuming David will reward them for their actions, they take the head of their king to David's residence in Hebron. Instead, David responds by ordering their deaths (see ch. 4).

At this point (ch. 5) the other tribes come to Hebron to ask David to be their king as well. They offer several reasons why he is qualified to serve in this position. First, by blood they are one people. They are Israelites as he is. Second, they point to his feats while Saul was king. More than likely, the account of David's slaying Goliath and their routing the Philistine army remains fresh in their thinking though it occurred some 20 years earlier.

David responds positively. They "close the deal," so to speak, and he is anointed king over the entire nation. At last the

Talk About It:
1. The word *all* is used three times in these five verses. Why is this important?
2. Describe the role of Israel's king, as seen in verse 2.

"Coming together is a beginning; keeping together is progress; working together is success."

—Quotable Quotes

12 tribes are again united under a single monarch. He is now the 37-year-old king of the whole nation of Israel.

During the first seven and one-half years as king of Judah, Hebron was David's capital city. With the tribes united, a more suitable capital city needed to be secured. This led to the capture of Jerusalem from the Jebusites and the establishment of his capital there. This fulfilled God's Word of a specific place which the Lord would choose (Deuteronomy 12:5).

B. Conditional Promises to Solomon (1 Kings 2:1-4; 9:1-9)
(1 Kings 9:4-9 is not included in the printed text.)
2:1. Now the days of David drew nigh that he should die; and he charged Solomon his son, saying,

2. I go the way of all the earth: be thou strong therefore, and shew thyself a man;

3. And keep the charge of the Lord thy God, to walk in his ways, to keep his statutes, and his commandments, and his judgments, and his testimonies, as it is written in the law of Moses, that thou mayest prosper in all that thou doest, and whithersoever thou turnest thyself:

4. That the Lord may continue his word which he spake concerning me, saying, If thy children take heed to their way, to walk before me in truth with all their heart and with all their soul, there shall not fail thee (said he) a man on the throne of Israel.

9:1. And it came to pass, when Solomon had finished the building of the house of the Lord, and the king's house, and all Solomon's desire which he was pleased to do,

2. That the Lord appeared to Solomon the second time, as he had appeared unto him at Gibeon.

3. And the Lord said unto him, I have heard thy prayer and thy supplication, that thou hast made before me: I have hallowed this house, which thou hast built, to put my name there for ever; and mine eyes and mine heart shall be there perpetually.

Talk About It:
1. What did David mean by telling Solomon, "Show yourself a man" (2:2, *NIV*)?
2. What promise had God made to David (v. 4), and what was the condition of that promise (v. 3)?

Solomon had some big shoes to fill as he succeeded his father, David, on the throne. During his reign David expanded the kingdom, defeated many foes, and provided a stable life for millions of Israelites as well as subservient peoples. Before his death, David gave a straightforward charge to his son. First, Solomon was to stand up and be a man (2:2). He was to demonstrate manhood consistent with the position and opportunity before him. Keep in mind Solomon was about 20 years old—some 10 years younger than David when he took the throne over a single tribe, Judah.

The second part of the charge was spiritual. If he would fulfill the specifics of the law of Moses, prosperity would come

A Nation Under God

(v. 3). This necessitated keeping the Ten Commandments as well as the other laws which were relational and ceremonial. Even the king did not have the right to be selective as to which part of God's laws he would keep.

3. What was God's response to the Temple built by Solomon (9:3)?
4. What warning did God issue (vv. 6-9)?

In verse 4 David's charge to Solomon reflects a personal reason for wanting Solomon to follow the laws. Years previously God promised David that his descendants would remain on the throne forever (2 Samuel 7:13). David wanted this promise to be fulfilled. But he also understood God's desire for obedience from those who sat on the throne.

The events in 1 Kings 9 occur after the dedication of the Temple. Solomon has been on the throne for at least 11 years, possibly even 14, when God appears to him for a second time. The first appearance is recorded in 1 Kings 3, when God offered Solomon anything he wanted. His wise choice of wisdom resulted in other blessings. The second divine encounter contains the same opportunity for blessings; however, it also includes a sobering warning.

God acknowledges hearing Solomon's dedicatory prayer (ch. 8) and accepts the Temple as His place forever. He then makes some conditional promises (9:4, 5). If Solomon will be a man of integrity and righteousness evidenced by observing the whole Law, the promise to David will be fulfilled through him as well.

Then comes the other side. Turning away from God and turning to other gods will have horrible consequences (vv. 6-9). Not only will the people be removed from the land, but this beautiful Temple will become a location of ridicule and scoffing. This does come true when the armies of Babylon destroy the Temple in 586 B.C. during their third invasion of the land.

It is easy to forget the precious promises God continues to offer to each one of us as believers. Besides the future rewards, we have the promise of His Holy Spirit's guidance and comfort. We know God wants to continue to work in us and fulfill His will. All of these are conditional upon our obedience and continual seeking to follow our Lord.

III. A DIVIDED AND LOST KINGDOM (2 Chronicles 9:30, 31; 10:1-19; 36:14-21)

A. Division of the Kingdom (9:30, 31; 10:1-19)
  (2 Chronicles 10:1-15 is not included in the printed text.)
  9:30. And Solomon reigned in Jerusalem over all Israel forty years.

  31. And Solomon slept with his fathers, and he was buried in the city of David his father: and Rehoboam his son reigned in his stead.

  10:16. And when all Israel saw that the king would not hearken unto them, the people answered the king, saying,

Rehoboam (*REE-huh-BOW-uhm*)—9:31—Solomon's son and successor on the throne

Jeroboam (*JER-uh-BOW-uhm*)— **10:2**—a public official under Solomon who founded the northern kingdom when the nation divided

the tribute (v. 18)—forced labor

Talk About It:
1. What request was made of Rehoboam?
2. Whose counsel did he accept, and whose did he reject (10:8)? Why?
3. What resulted from Rehoboam's decision (vv. 16-19)?

"Men and nations behave wisely once they have exhausted all the other alternatives."
—**Abba Eban**

What portion have we in David? and we have none inheritance in the son of Jesse: every man to your tents, O Israel: and now, David, see to thine own house. So all Israel went to their tents.

17. But as for the children of Israel that dwelt in the cities of Judah, Rehoboam reigned over them.

18. Then king Rehoboam sent Hadoram that was over the tribute; and the children of Israel stoned him with stones, that he died. But king Rehoboam made speed to get him up to his chariot, to flee to Jerusalem.

19. And Israel rebelled against the house of David unto this day.

After 40 years as king of Israel, Solomon died at the age of 60. His failure to obediently follow the laws of God resulted in his not receiving the promise of long life. However, the splendor of his kingdom cannot be underestimated in light of the Queen of Sheba's comments (1 Kings 10:6, 7). But, as Solomon's reign came to a close, apparently the economics of the nation were not good. Solomon's huge political and military government took their toll. At best the nation's treasury was empty and at worst the nation was bankrupt. Into that setting came Rehoboam, heir to the throne.

Rehoboam's first test comes when the 10 northern tribes request a lighter load in terms of taxation and conscripted labor (2 Chronicles 10:1-15). For such a concession, they offer their loyalty. Rehoboam's request for time before giving an answer allows him to consult with two sets of counselors. The elder council of his father's reign advises kindness and favorable response. In marked contrast is the advice of his friends with whom he had grown up. Apparently they have visions of grandeur and reject reality. They advise the king to say, "My father laid on you a heavy yoke; I will make it even heavier" (v. 11, *NIV*).

As soon as Rehoboam states his position, the northern tribes return home and disavow any allegiance to him (v. 16). Besides, they have one of their own—Jeroboam—to become their new king. Some years previously Jeroboam attempted to overthrow Solomon after the prophet Ahijah said he would rule over 10 tribes in the future. Jeroboam fled to Egypt after his rebellion failed, returning only upon hearing of Solomon's death (1 Kings 11:27-40).

The division of the kingdom resulted from the sin of Solomon. Out of respect for his father, David, God did not allow it to happen during his lifetime (1 Kings 11:12). The sad aspect of this part of Solomon's life is how age with its resulting experience did not cause him to make spiritual decisions that honored God. Instead he allowed his many wives to gradually lead him to the worship of gods other than Jehovah.

A Nation Under God

B. Destruction of the Kingdom (36:14-21)

14. Moreover all the chief of the priests, and the people, transgressed very much after all the abominations of the heathen; and polluted the house of the Lord which he had hallowed in Jerusalem.

15. And the Lord God of their fathers sent to them by his messengers, rising up betimes, and sending; because he had compassion on his people, and on his dwelling place:

16. But they mocked the messengers of God, and despised his words, and misused his prophets, until the wrath of the Lord arose against his people, till there was no remedy.

17. Therefore he brought upon them the king of the Chaldees, who slew their young men with the sword in the house of their sanctuary, and had no compassion upon young man or maiden, old man, or him that stooped for age: he gave them all into his hand.

18. And all the vessels of the house of God, great and small, and the treasures of the house of the Lord, and the treasures of the king, and of his princes; all these he brought to Babylon.

19. And they burnt the house of God, and brake down the wall of Jerusalem, and burnt all the palaces thereof with fire, and destroyed all the goodly vessels thereof.

20. And them that had escaped from the sword carried he away to Babylon; where they were servants to him and his sons until the reign of the kingdom of Persia:

21. To fulfil the word of the Lord by the mouth of Jeremiah, until the land had enjoyed her sabbaths: for as long as she lay desolate she kept sabbath, to fulfil threescore and ten years.

betimes (v. 15)—
"again and again"
(*NIV*)

God's plans for His people were thwarted by their sin, and He had to punish them. In 722 B.C. the northern kingdom fell to the invading forces of the Assyrians. The southern kingdom of Judah continued for another century. But they too failed to serve God, and eventually the worst scenario took place.

The pitiful spiritual condition of God's people was evident. Even the priests neglected God and turned to the worship of the pagan gods of surrounding nations. Defiling of the Temple took place not only from their unfaithfulness, but apparently from the inclusion of other gods in the sacred place of worship. Their commitment to the other gods was so strong that when God sent prophets with words of warning, they simply rejected the messengers and mocked their message.

Finally, God could not allow their actions and attitudes to continue. His holiness and justice demanded their disobedience to be punished. These disobedient people falsely assumed their

Talk About It:
1. What happened to Israel's priests (v. 14)?
2. How did the Israelites treat the many prophets God sent them (vv. 15, 16)?
3. Describe God's judgment against His people (vv. 17-21).

self-sufficiency, but now God chose to fulfill His words of the past. His warning of their being displaced from their land for disobedience began coming to pass. God used Nebuchadnezzar and the Babylonians as the chosen instrument. Several years prior to the invasion, God warned the people through the prophet Habakkbuk (1:6) of the Babylonians coming, but to no avail. They failed to listen and change their ways.

The forces of Nebuchadnezzar came on three separate occasions. In 605 B.C., King Jehoiakim of Judah was taken prisoner and a number of the brightest young men were taken into exile, including Daniel. In 597 B.C., Nebuchadnezzar and his army returned, took King Jehoiachin (Jehoiakim's son) captive, removed the Temple treasures, and took 10,000 captives including the prophet Ezekiel. Finally, in 586 B.C., Nebuchadnezzar marched against rebellious King Zedekiah. After a siege of about 18 months, the city of Jerusalem fell. The walls and all the important buildings of the city were destroyed, including Solomon's temple (see 2 Kings 23:36–25:21).

CONCLUSION
Disobedience brought the demise of the nation of Israel. Most of the population was killed or taken captive. Those who remained in the land were poor and living in desolate conditions. Why? How could this be?

The answer rests in their choosing to no longer remain a nation under God's law and direction. Their independent pursuit of self-determination brought His judgment and the destruction of a chosen nation.

Daily Devotions:
M. Promise of
   Nationhood
   Genesis 46:1-7
T. The Kingdom
   Belongs to God
   1 Chronicles
   29:10-14
W. Trust in God
   Brings Blessing
   Psalm 33:12-22
T. The Gospel for
   All Nations
   Romans 1:1-5,
   14-16
F. A Holy Nation
   1 Peter 2:9-12
S. The Saved
   From All Nations
   Revelation 7:9-17

GOLDEN TEXT CHALLENGE
"THINE, O LORD, IS THE GREATNESS, AND THE POWER, AND THE GLORY, AND THE VICTORY, AND THE MAJESTY: FOR ALL THAT IS IN THE HEAVEN AND IN THE EARTH IS THINE; THINE IS THE KINGDOM, O LORD, AND THOU ART EXALTED AS HEAD ABOVE ALL" (1 Chronicles 29:11).

The order of this verse's beginning—where David prays, "Thine, O Lord, is the greatness"—places the emphasis on the Lord, as if to say, "It is You, O Lord, who is great; not I, nor even Solomon."

The list of qualities are appropriate for a mighty king: "power" is the might of a warrior; "glory" is the ornamental magnificence of a Louis XIV; "victory" and "the earth is thine" are the ambition of every autocrat. The climax, "thine is the kingdom," summarizes what David was saying. Any human greatness which fancies that it is self-existent is a delusion and an offense to God (adapted from *The Daily Bible Study Series*).

God Restores His People (Ezra and Nehemiah)

Ezra 1:1-8; 2:64-70; 3:1-13; 6:1-22; Nehemiah 8:1 through 9:38

INTRODUCTION

Things get scratched, chipped, broken and worn out. When that happens, it leaves us with three choices—keep them as they are, throw them away or attempt restoration.

Isn't it amazing how some people are so skilled in restoration? Someone finds a dilapidated, rusting car stored in a barn or even hidden in a junk yard. After hundreds of painstaking hours of work and hunting for parts coupled with thousands of dollars, eventually it's as though a new vehicle sits in the garage. The paint is the color of the original. The chrome shines. The upholstery is the same fabric. Before us stands an antique model as good as new.

Another fascination of restoration takes place with paintings. They become discolored from various pollutants as hundreds of years pass. Then along comes a skilled restorer who takes off the darkening discolorations, allowing the bright, beautiful colors of the past to shine again. Occasionally, even tears in the canvas are repaired and pigments applied so expertly it appears as though the original artist applied them.

Individuals who like antique clothing frequently find garments that appear to be faded and even stained. Yet, after soaking them in a special solution, the stains lift and the true color(s) appear. A dingy white suddenly is seen to be a soft pink or yellow. What once appeared to be an aging, worthless garment becomes a restored piece of greater value and use.

Of course, it isn't only things that need restoration. Relationships can also be scratched, chipped and broken. They too need restoration. Sometimes, through intense efforts of the people involved, it can be accomplished. Other times the intervention of a third person becomes necessary. In some cases a relationship can be restored only through divine intervention.

The nation of Israel frequently found themselves in a strained relationship with their God. Their repeated disobedience and disregard eventually severed it to the point God brought severe punishment. He allowed their enemies to enter, disrupt life and take many prisoners. Yet, even as God was judging His people, He was promising their return and restoration.

Today's lesson shows the fulfillment of God's promise. Miraculously He brought some of the Jews back to Canaan. They rebuilt the Temple. God and His people renewed the covenant.

Unit Theme:
Message of the Old Testament

Central Truth:
God restores those who repent.

Focus:
Observe that God restores those who repent, and give thanks for His mercy.

Context:
Ezra and Nehemiah lead in restoring Jerusalem in the fifth century B.C.

Golden Text:
"When the Lord turned again the captivity of Zion, we were like them that dream. Then . . . said they among the heathen, The Lord hath done great things for them" (Psalm 126:1, 2).

Study Outline:
I. Reestablished in the Promised Land (Ezra 1:1-8; 2:64-70)
II. God's House Rebuilt (Ezra 3:1-13; 6:1-17)
III. Covenant With God Renewed (Nehemiah 8:1-12; 9:1-3, 32-38)

I. REESTABLISHED IN THE PROMISED LAND
(Ezra 1:1-8; 2:64-70)

A. Cyrus' Decree (1:1-8)

1. Now in the first year of Cyrus king of Persia, that the word of the Lord by the mouth of Jeremiah might be fulfilled, the Lord stirred up the spirit of Cyrus king of Persia, that he made a proclamation throughout all his kingdom, and put it also in writing, saying,

2. Thus saith Cyrus king of Persia, The Lord God of heaven hath given me all the kingdoms of the earth; and he hath charged me to build him an house at Jerusalem, which is in Judah.

3. Who is there among you of all his people? his God be with him, and let him go up to Jerusalem, which is in Judah, and build the house of the Lord God of Israel, (he is the God,) which is in Jerusalem.

4. And whosoever remaineth in any place where he sojourneth, let the men of his place help him with silver, and with gold, and with goods, and with beasts, beside the freewill offering for the house of God that is in Jerusalem.

5. Then rose up the chief of the fathers of Judah and Benjamin, and the priests, and the Levites, with all them whose spirit God had raised, to go up to build the house of the Lord which is in Jerusalem.

6. And all they that were about them strengthened their hands with vessels of silver, with gold, with goods, and with beasts, and with precious things, beside all that was willingly offered.

Sheshbazzar (*shesh-BAZE-er*)—v. 8—The governor of Judah appointed by Persia's King Cyrus, he laid the foundation of the Temple.

7. Also Cyrus the king brought forth the vessels of the house of the Lord, which Nebuchadnezzar had brought forth out of Jerusalem, and had put them in the house of his gods;

8. Even those did Cyrus king of Persia bring forth by the hand of Mithredath the treasurer, and numbered them unto Sheshbazzar, the prince of Judah.

The significance of Cyrus' decree is emphasized from a variety of perspectives. First, here we see the fulfillment of prophecies. Some 200 years previously Isaiah prophesied this event: "[God] saith of Cyrus, He is my shepherd, and shall perform all my pleasure: even saying to Jerusalem, Thou shalt be built; and to the temple, Thy foundation shall be laid" (44:28). The prophet Jeremiah on two occasions indicated how, after 70 years of captivity, the Babylonian Captivity would end and a restoration would occur (25:12; 29:10).

Second, this action is uncharacteristic of a ruler of this era. It's unheard of to not only allow a captive people to return home, but to also assist them in a building project in their capital city. Even

God Restores His People

though the city continued to be an area of ruin, its history and potential would be seen as a possible threat in the future.

Third, here we see the sovereign hand of God in the rise and fall of nations. Cyrus' rise to leadership and guiding the Medes and Persians to overthrow the Babylonians followed the exact pattern seen in Nebuchadnezzar's dream (Daniel 2) and Daniel's two visions of nearly half a century later (chs. 7, 8).

Fourth, the significance of this event can be further seen by the repetition. The last verse of 2 Chronicles and the first verses of Ezra describe the same event. Repetition such as this emphasizes the attention which needs to be given to Cyrus' actions. The specifics of how God moved in Cyrus' heart are not shared. Some suggest Daniel might have been an instrument in this process, but no evidence of this exists.

When Belshazzar knew the Medes and Persians were coming closer, he collected the gods from the other cities hoping their collective powers would protect him. This effort failed (Daniel 5:30). After Cyrus' victory he returned the gods to the home cities, much to the appreciation of the inhabitants. Within this environment God moved Cyrus to take actions of restoration for the Jews and their temple.

In Ezra 1:3 we see how Cyrus opened the door for anyone who desired to return to Jerusalem for the purpose of building the Temple. Also, he directed the Jews' heathen neighbors to assist those choosing to return with precious metals as well as animals needed for the trip (v. 4). Besides these gifts, freewill offerings were to be sent for construction of the Temple. Verse 6 shows how the people complied with Cyrus' directive.

The completeness of God's moving on Cyrus is evident in the final action of bringing out all the vessels of the Temple which Nebuchadnezzar had taken from Jerusalem. They were given to the Jews who were returning for placement in the Temple upon its reconstruction (vv. 7, 8).

B. Restoration Fulfilled (2:64-70)
(Ezra 2:64-67 is not included in the printed text.)
68. And some of the chief of the fathers, when they came to the house of the Lord which is at Jerusalem, offered freely for the house of God to set it up in his place:

69. They gave after their ability unto the treasure of the work threescore and one thousand drams of gold, and five thousand pound of silver, and one hundred priests' garments.

70. So the priests, and the Levites, and some of the people, and the singers, and the porters, and the Nethinims, dwelt in their cities, and all Israel in their cities.

This last section of chapter 2 provides a statistical picture of

Talk About It:
1. What do verses 1-4 reveal about the sovereignty of God?
2. Explain the phrase "whose spirit God had raised" (v. 5). How and when does God do this today?
3. What would be restored to Jerusalem (v. 7)? Why was this significant?

"In the total expanse of human life there is not a single square inch of which the Christ, who alone is sovereign, does not declare, 'That is mine!'"

—Abraham Kuyper

drams (v. 69)— gold coins

the Nethinims (v. 70)—Temple servants

Talk About It:
1. In the first return of people to Jerusalem, why are the specific numbers of people and various animals given (vv. 64-67)? Why is the specific amount given to the treasury shown?
2. After 70 years in another land, what challenges did the people face in resettling "in their cities" (v. 70)?

the group that accepted this God-given opportunity to return to their homeland and be the instruments of restoration. The corporate group numbered slightly less than 50,000. Though this may appear to be a sizeable party, this was a small percentage of the number of Jews living after 70 years in captivity. These people had been moved by the Spirit of God to return in the same manner Cyrus had been prompted to initiate this unusual action. Otherwise, they may have been content to stay in their adopted land with its current comforts and established lifestyle.

Of interest is the number of animals taken—a total of 8,136. This number was needed to carry materials for the Temple, personal belongings and the basic supplies for the trip. Imagine the logistics of this 500-mile trip in view of the people and animals!

Scripture records no detail or summary of the trip. It simply picks up with their arrival in Jerusalem. Immediately the people contributed from their personal funds to the "building account." This does not include the monies contributed by their Babylonian neighbors prior to leaving. Now they were in Jerusalem and had the necessary funds. All that remained for them to do was begin the actual project.

II. GOD'S HOUSE REBUILT (Ezra 3:1-13; 6:1-17)
A. Rebuilding the Temple (3:1-13)
(Ezra 3:4-9 is not included in the printed text.)

Jeshua (v. 2)—a priest who returned to Jerusalem

Zerubbabel (zeh-RUB-uh-buhl)—v. 2—The governor of Judah who led the completion of the Temple; he may have been the same person as Sheshbazzar (1:8).

1. And when the seventh month was come, and the children of Israel were in the cities, the people gathered themselves together as one man to Jerusalem.

2. Then stood up Jeshua the son of Jozadak, and his brethren the priests, and Zerubbabel the son of Shealtiel, and his brethren, and builded the altar of the God of Israel, to offer burnt offerings thereon, as it is written in the law of Moses the man of God.

3. And they set the altar upon his bases; for fear was upon them because of the people of those countries: and they offered burnt offerings thereon unto the Lord, even burnt offerings morning and evening.

10. And when the builders laid the foundation of the temple of the Lord, they set the priests in their apparel with trumpets, and the Levites the sons of Asaph with cymbals, to praise the Lord, after the ordinance of David king of Israel.

11. And they sang together by course in praising and giving thanks unto the Lord; because he is good, for his mercy endureth for ever toward Israel. And all the people shouted with a great shout, when they praised the Lord, because the foundation of the house of the Lord was laid.

12. But many of the priests and Levites and chief of the

fathers, who were ancient men, that had seen the first house, when the foundation of this house was laid before their eyes, wept with a loud voice; and many shouted aloud for joy:

13. So that the people could not discern the noise of the shout of joy from the noise of the weeping of the people: for the people shouted with a loud shout, and the noise was heard afar off.

After arriving in Palestine, this first group of immigrants took a short period of time to establish the daily life of their families. In the seventh month of their first year the people gathered in Jerusalem. In a unified effort they anticipated the reestablishment of sacrificial worship. Under the leadership of Jeshua, construction of the altar for sacrifice began. Verse 3 indicates they worked in spite of the fear of attack by those who did not want to see the Jews reestablish their worship and way of life. As soon as the altar was completed, the regular morning and evening sacrifices commenced and the people were able to commemorate the Feast of Tabernacles.

Only after the establishment of worship did they proceed with constructing the Temple. Verse 7 says the workmen were paid upfront to begin the construction activities. Also, the trade goods of food, drink and oil were paid in advance for the cedar logs which would be delivered.

Supervision of the construction became the responsibility of the Levites. The usual age for service in the Temple was from 30 to 50; however, the supervisory work was given to the Levites who were as young as 20.

The laying of the foundation became the occasion for a major celebration. The priests were garbed in their sacred vestments. The trumpets and symbols were ready to be used when the people offered their praise and thanksgiving to the Lord. Verse 11 describes the atmosphere as resounding with the praises of the people. They had a reason to rejoice. They had been without a temple for about 71 years. But that would soon be changed. At least that was their perspective at the time.

Mingled with the shouts of praise was *weeping*. While the younger men rejoiced, the "old men who had seen the first Temple, wept with a loud voice" (v. 12, *NKJV*). Why? One reason might be they were mourning for the sins of the past which resulted in the destruction of the original Temple. A second reason might be their realizing this Temple would not have the magnitude nor magnificence of the one constructed by Solomon.

With all the mingling of joy and sorrow, there was a tremendous amount of noise. This wasn't a quiet, somber celebration! All of the people expressed themselves freely with no inhibition of sound.

Talk About It:
1. Why was the altar built before the Temple foundation was laid?
2. Describe and explain the different responses to the dedication of the Temple's foundation (vv. 11-13).

"More tears are shed in our theaters over fancied tragedies than in our churches over real ones."
—**Frank C. Rideout**

(Ezra 6:1-13, 16, 17 is not included in the printed text.)

Darius (duh-RYE-us)—v. 1—the king of Persia following the reign of Cyrus

14. And the elders of the Jews builded, and they prospered through the prophesying of Haggai the prophet and Zechariah the son of Iddo. And they builded, and finished it, according to the commandment of the God of Israel, and according to the commandment of Cyrus, and Darius, and Artaxerxes king of Persia.

15. And this house was finished on the third day of the month Adar, which was in the sixth year of the reign of Darius the king.

Talk About It:
1. What decree did Darius make regarding the continued building of the Temple (vv. 7-10)? What would happen to those who opposed it (v. 11)?
2. What appeal did Darius make to God on the Temple's behalf (v. 12)?
3. What was set in place after the Temple was finished (v. 18)?

After the foundations of the Temple were laid, the enemies of the Jews created legal problems with the Persian king (Artaxerxes). After being refused the opportunity to help build the Temple, they falsely accused the Jews of rebuilding the city wall with the purpose of rebelling and refusing to pay taxes (4:12-16). When Artaxerxes ordered construction in Jerusalem to stop, they complied. Instead of pleading their case and telling how the deceased former emperor, Cyrus, had authorized the rebuilding, they rationalized how this may not be the right time to build the Lord's house (Haggai 1:2). And, in place of working on God's house, they constructed their own houses (v. 4).

About 15 years of inactivity on the rebuilding, the prophets Haggai and Zechariah appeared on the scene (Ezra 5:1). Immediately the people began to rebuild again as directed (v. 2). This time when neighboring leaders challenged their efforts, the Jews responded differently. They sent a letter to King Darius outlining the events of the past years (vv. 7-16). The letter included a request for a search of the records in order to find Cyrus' decree (v. 17).

An extensive search revealed the decree to be exactly as the Jews recorded in their letter. Ezra 6:3-5 records the original decree. Then, beginning with verse 6 is the following decree by King Darius in view of the discovery. Those who were in opposition to the building project needed to stop. Goods and money for the construction were to be provided. Also, the animals needed for the daily sacrifice were to be provided. Of special interest is the penalty for anyone who would attempt to interfere with the project. Materials from his own house were to be used for a hanging platform (v. 11). When the king projected a capital punishment such as this, you can be sure there would be compliance.

"If you're ever tempted to give up, just think of Brahms, who took seven long years to compose his famous Lullaby. He kept falling asleep at the piano."
—Robert Oren

Verse 13 shows how Tatnai, the governor who previously stirred up the opposition, now changed directions quickly. He complied with the king's decree and became a provider and ready assistant.

The result of obediently fulfilling the directions of the prophets

God Restores His People

Haggai and Zechariah are emphasized in verse 14. As the people worked on the Temple, they experienced prosperity. Four years after restarting the project, the Temple was completed (516 B.C.). Its dedication became a time of great joy. Unlike the laying of the foundation nearly 20 years before, there were no people mourning.

This portion of our lesson reminds us how people can become sidetracked from God's intended purpose. We see how good projects may necessitate our struggling and fighting for truth so God's will can be fulfilled.

III. COVENANT WITH GOD RENEWED (Nehemiah 8:1-12; 9:1-3, 32-38)
A. Reading the Law (8:1-12)
(Nehemiah 8:4, 7, 8, 11, 12 is not included in the printed text.)
1. And all the people gathered themselves together as one man into the street that was before the water gate; and they spake unto Ezra the scribe to bring the book of the law of Moses, which the Lord had commanded to Israel.

2. And Ezra the priest brought the law before the congregation both of men and women, and all that could hear with understanding, upon the first day of the seventh month.

3. And he read therein before the street that was before the water gate from the morning until midday, before the men and the women, and those that could understand; and the ears of all the people were attentive unto the book of the law.

5. And Ezra opened the book in the sight of all the people; (for he was above all the people;) and when he opened it, all the people stood up:

6. And Ezra blessed the Lord, the great God. And all the people answered, Amen, Amen, with lifting up their hands: and they bowed their heads, and worshipped the Lord with their faces to the ground.

9. And Nehemiah, which is the Tirshatha, and Ezra the priest the scribe, and the Levites that taught the people, said unto all the people, This day is holy unto the Lord your God; mourn not, nor weep. For all the people wept, when they heard the words of the law.

10. Then he said unto them, Go your way, eat the fat, and drink the sweet, and send portions unto them for whom nothing is prepared: for this day is holy unto our Lord: neither be ye sorry; for the joy of the Lord is your strength.

This portion of our lesson involves a "fast-forward" in time. Nehemiah came to Jerusalem in 444 B.C. as the governor with

Talk About It:
1. Who attended the reading of the Scriptures, and for how long (v. 3)?
2. How did the people respond to the reading and teaching, and why (v. 9)?

the purpose of rebuilding the walls of the city. In the seven decades between the completion of the Temple and Nehemiah's coming was a second population of restoration. Under the leadership of Ezra the scribe, some 6,000 Jews returned to their homeland in 458 B.C. (Ezra 7:1–8:36).

Through the "on task" leadership of Nehemiah, the walls of the city were raised in 52 days. He didn't allow the tactics of Sanballat and Tobiah to delay their work in the slightest (see Nehemiah 4; 6). Now that the physical structures were in place, it became vital to consider the people's spirituality and relationship to God. Chapter 8 describes the beginning of one of the most unusual revivals in history.

A side emphasis deserves our attention here. Too frequently when speaking of revival, we have a limited perception. Our ideas are often built on a tradition or a narrow historical event. A true understanding of spiritual renewal comes when we are able to see the breadth of revival beginning in the Scriptures and continuing through our day.

From a physical standpoint, the Jews had made tremendous strides. Once again they had a temple, and now the city was secure with the city walls rebuilt. Yet, to obtain wholeness, they still needed to recommit to their covenant with God. Having settled, now special attention to spiritual matters became the priority.

Unlike what we might expect as the pattern for spiritual renewal, they gathered to hear the reading of the Law. Men, women and children who could understand what would be read and discussed gathered. A wooden platform provided the stage for Ezra. It enabled the people to see him and allowed the sound to carry throughout this large audience. From dawn until noon they stood to hear the Law read and explained. Verse 4 lists individuals who stood on either side of Ezra on the platform. Not only does this give us some idea of the size of the stage, but it suggests these men must have assisted in the process. This is confirmed in verses 7 and 8.

Worship flows in the process of hearing the Scripture read. Ezra verbally praised the Lord. The people responded by saying "Amen," lifting their hands, and then bowing in worship. The people, recognizing their sinful disobedience to God's law, began weeping. However, Nehemiah, Ezra and the Levites asked the people to stop their mourning. Instead, they asked the congregation to hold this as a sacred day and recognize God's strength as a source of joy.

Yes, there would be a time for mourning, confession and repentance. That would follow. Now they were to eat and rejoice. They were privileged to be standing in the Promised Land. God's prophetic promises of bringing His people back from captivity had become a reality. They could trust in Him to

"A readiness to believe every promise implicitly, to obey every command unhesitatingly, to stand perfect and complete in all the will of God, is the only true spirit of Bible study."
—Andrew Murray

fulfill His promises. Also, having heard the Law read and explained could be a source of joy since they now understood it (v. 12). This day stood as another new beginning.

This passage of the story reminds us of the importance that should be given to the reading of the Word of God as part of our individual and corporate spiritual renewal and commitment to God. Too frequently our modern worship pattern consists of singing, praying and preaching with very little reading of the Bible. And many Christians spend little time reading God's Word in their private devotions.

B. Confessing Their Sins (9:1-3, 32-38)
(Nehemiah 9:32-37 is not included in the printed text.)

1. Now in the twenty and fourth day of this month the children of Israel were assembled with fasting, and with sackclothes, and earth upon them.

2. And the seed of Israel separated themselves from all strangers, and stood and confessed their sins, and the iniquities of their fathers.

3. And they stood up in their place, and read in the book of the law of the Lord their God one fourth part of the day; and another fourth part they confessed, and worshipped the Lord their God.

38. And because of all this we make a sure covenant, and write it; and our princes, Levites, and priests, seal unto it.

A few days pass after the completion of the people's celebration of the Feast of Tabernacles. Then, on the 24th day of this same month, they gather again for some deep soul-searching. Now is the time for the mourning which was restrained on the first day of hearing the Law. Their seriousness quickly becomes apparent. They express their sorrow in three ways. First, they fast. Second, they clothe themselves with sackcloth—material made of coarse goat hair. Third, they throw dust on their heads. Each act alone speaks of sorrow, but together they demonstrate the people's genuine commitment to the task of spiritual renewal and reestablishing the covenant.

Once again Ezra reads the Law. This occurs for three hours, and then this is followed by the people confessing their sins for the next three hours. As they confess their sins, it is evident they understand why their nation had suffered so greatly. The sins of their fathers and mothers of previous generations were the result of personal choices, which resulted in divine judgment. They recognize how mercifully God had responded regardless of their despicable action. They declared God's justice in all His actions toward them (v. 33).

At the end of this time of confession, the people committed

Talk About It:
1. Describe the "revival service" depicted in verses 1-3.
2. Why did the people make a covenant with the Lord (v. 38)?

themselves to loyalty by signing a written covenant (v. 38). The specifics of it are recorded in chapter 10. What is so significant about their action? First, it indicates this was not just an emotional experience which would quickly fade. Second, by putting the commitment in writing, it would always be there to refresh their memory.

CONCLUSION
Reality TV programs are a major attraction to viewing audiences. Extreme makeovers of homes and bodies enable families and individuals to enjoy comforts and feel better about themselves. Crowded homes are refitted to feature spacious, theme-centered rooms adapted to family needs. Reshaped noses, capped teeth and new hairstyles change appearance and perspective. All of these have benefit; however, they are all external changes and do not bring about a total change of the family's or individual's true being. It is God's desire to restore individuals, families and churches from the inside out.

GOLDEN TEXT CHALLENGE
"WHEN THE LORD TURNED AGAIN THE CAPTIVITY OF ZION, WE WERE LIKE THEM THAT DREAM. THEN WAS OUR MOUTH FILLED WITH LAUGHTER, AND OUR TONGUE WITH SINGING: THEN SAID THEY AMONG THE HEATHEN, THE LORD HATH DONE GREAT THINGS FOR THEM" (Psalm 126:1, 2).

During the 70 years the Jews were in captivity, they must have often wondered if God's promise to bring them back to their homeland would ever be realized. When it finally came to pass—when God supernaturally opened the door for them to return home—it seemed like a dream. But this was reality! They were awake, and God's promise was alive!

These people who had left their homeland with their heads down, their hearts broken and their feet chained could now return "with rejoicing" (v. 6). Their hearts were filled with joy, and this joy was expressed through laughter and singing.

As people from other nations saw the Jews returning to Jerusalem, they had to admit, "The Lord hath done great things for them" (v. 2). There was no other explanation for their miraculous return. God's people responded, "The Lord has done great things for us, and we are glad" (v. 3, *NKJV*).

Psalm 126 should remind us that God's promises to us are not mere dreams or wishes. Instead, they are realities that will materialize in His time and way. Remember this: "They that sow in tears shall reap in joy" (v. 5).

Daily Devotions:
M. Restoration Promised
   Deuteronomy 30:1-8
T. Repentance Brings Restoration
   1 Kings 8:33-40
W. Restoration Celebrated
   Psalm 126:1-6
T. Restoration of a Son
   Luke 15:11-24
F. Restoration of a Disciple
   John 21:14-22
S. Reconciled to God by Christ
   2 Corinthians 5:14-21

God Restores His People

God-Inspired Poetry (The Psalms)

Psalms 13:1-6; 78:1-72; 148:1-14

INTRODUCTION

The popularity of the Book of Psalms can hardly be over-estimated. These writings provide comfort and direction to many believers. When teaching from Psalms, it is interesting to ask individuals which chapter is special to them. The responses are amazing. They reveal again and again how this divinely inspired writing speaks to us in a variety of ways.

In *Eerdman's Handbook to the Bible*, the introduction to the discussion on the Book of Psalms reads: "The Psalms express the whole range of human feeling and experience, from dark depression to exuberant joy. They are rooted in particular circumstances, yet they are timeless, and so among the best-loved, most-read, parts of the Bible. In our modern age we are stirred by the same emotions, puzzled over the same fundamental problems of life, cry out in need or worship, to the same God, as the psalmists of old. We find it easy to identify with them. And we find their sheer, dogged faith, the depth of their love for God, both a tonic and a rebuke."

This previous description is important, since we can easily assume the major characteristic of the Psalms to be praise. However, in actuality there appears to be more lamenting and questioning which eventually turns to praise. This reflects the human dilemma of living in a world surrounded by sin and not knowing why we are in certain situations. At the same time we are able to see how God intervenes. He brings assurance and rescue. This total picture enables us to trust in God and boldly sing the songs of praise.

The Book of Psalms served as a worship book/hymnal for the Jews. Its 150 separate psalms or poems are divided into five separate books/sections. Each ends with a special praise to God. Though we do not have the notation to know the melody for how they would have been sung, it is amazing how many portions have been set to music, and we sing them even today. Many praise choruses, as well as some hymns, are built on the Psalms.

To fully appreciate these psalms, it is important to remember they are poems. The poetic style isn't one of rhyme. Instead, there are patterns of reiteration (repetition, but in different words) and contrast. Many different authors contributed to this divinely inspired book. David was the majority writer, with 73 psalms credited to his authorship.

Our lesson demonstrates the variety of experience and content which comprises the psalms.

Unit Theme:
Message of the Old Testament

Central Truth:
The Psalms inspire us to love and worship God.

Focus:
Appreciate the Psalms as divinely inspired writings, and be instructed and edified by them.

Context:
An overview of the Jewish worship book—the Psalms

Golden Text:
"Let the word of Christ dwell in you richly in all wisdom; teaching and admonishing one another in psalms and hymns and spiritual songs, singing with grace in your hearts to the Lord" (Colossians 3:16).

Study Outline:
I. Songs of Prayer (Psalm 13:1-6)
II. Songs of Godly Instruction (Psalm 78:1-7)
III. Songs of Praise to God (Psalm 148:1-14)

I. SONGS OF PRAYER (Psalm 13:1-6)

A. Despair (vv. 1-4)

1. How long wilt thou forget me, O Lord? for ever? how long wilt thou hide thy face from me?

2. How long shall I take counsel in my soul, having sorrow in my heart daily? how long shall mine enemy be exalted over me?

3. Consider and hear me, O Lord my God: lighten mine eyes, lest I sleep the sleep of death;

4. Lest mine enemy say, I have prevailed against him; and those that trouble me rejoice when I am moved.

When up seems down and the clouds block even the slightest ray of light, waves of despair may buffet even the strongest believer. In those moments when all hope seems lost, a multitude of questions may arise reflecting our feeling of being alone and without anyone caring. Even God, our loving heavenly Father, appears distant and uninvolved in our situation. Although we may know that to be untrue, our emotions initially dominate and some heavy questions arise.

Psalm 13, as well as the previous one, is thought to have been written during the extended period of David fleeing from the wrath of King Saul. Jealousy drove Saul to seek the death of his own son-in-law. On earlier occasions David escaped Saul's javelin; however, now David was a fugitive with a band of men. They had to work to avoid the posted lookouts who would reveal their location (see 1 Samuel 24:1). Eventually in an attempt to have some sense of peace, David even enters the territory of the Philistines, Israel's enemy (1 Samuel 27).

In the questions David raises in Psalm 13, some make assumptions of being rejected at worst or forgotten at best. Others contain a glimmer of hope even in the distress. Verse 1 seems to be an example of the former. He expresses a hopelessness due to God's apparently being inattentive to his plight. Keep in mind David's time as a fugitive was not measured in days, weeks or months, but in years! In verse 2 David asks, "How long must I wrestle with my thoughts?" (*NIV*). It reflects a battle between the flesh and the spirit. The flesh saw only hopelessness and defeat, while the spirit held on to hope in spite of the circumstances.

To further understand the struggle, we must remember that as a teenage boy David received the anointing to be the next king of Israel. A decade or more had passed and, instead of progressing toward this position, it appeared death was more likely. As a result, his eyes were dimmed with sorrow. Can you imagine the constant stress he and the others were under as they worked to stay alive and keep their families safe?

Also, there was the frustration of thinking how the enemy

God-Inspired Poetry

must be rejoicing at his discomfort brought about by Saul's hatred. Regardless of the depressing circumstance, David did not take the situation into his own hands when he could have killed Saul on two separate occasions. Even when David's trusted men encouraged him to do so, he refrained (1 Samuel 24:1-7; 26:7-11).

B. Assurance (vv. 5, 6)

5. But I have trusted in thy mercy; my heart shall rejoice in thy salvation.

6. I will sing unto the Lord, because he hath dealt bountifully with me.

How does a person move from despair to assurance in such a short time? Easy? Well, yes and no. For some It is difficult since they do not have the guidance of where to look. Others make the transition rather quickly as they stop and begin to reflect on God's grace and mercy. Past experiences demonstrate God's great care. Once we remember, it becomes a source of trust and a stimulus for rejoicing. Because of God's extended mercy we enjoy salvation. *Salvation* indicates deliverance from bondage of various types. Usually we think first of spiritual deliverance from the bondage of sin, and rightly so. It also may be applied to deliverance from the wiles of Satan and life situations.

The usual David stories come to mind. As a shepherd boy he successfully killed a lion and a bear (1 Samuel 17:34-36). What a feat when you remember it was "paw-to-hand" combat. There was no high-powered rifle, only the rod, similar to a "billy club" but with metal bits lodged in the knobby head. A major feat was the challenge of champions in which Goliath was defeated by David's slingshot. The women sang his praises much to the chagrin of King Saul.

In light of these and other examples of God's providential preservation, David could now move from the darkness to light. No, he didn't know how God would work in his circumstances. But his trust level enabled him to sing to the Lord instead of offer questions. What a transition! David's experience wasn't an isolated one in which a selected servant received the blessing of salvation. It applies to each of us as well. When we become a believer we are freed from the darkness and death of sins' bondages. We too have the joy of experiencing His direction in our lives. On occasions we may be delivered or protected from devastating circumstances, some unknown to us. Some may even be able to remember events where if it had not been for the hand of God, who knows what would have occurred.

A practical activity for all of us, especially in gloomy circumstances, is to count our blessings. This may be done in silent

> "It is strange that in our praying we seldom ask for a change of character, but always a change of circumstances."
> —***Bits and Pieces***

Talk About It:
1. What caused the turnaround in David's feelings?
2. Explain the phrase "He hath dealt bountifully with me" (v. 6).

> "If you can't be thankful for what you have received, be thankful for what you have escaped."
> —***Quotable Quotes***

recollection; however, why not allow others to be blessed by testifying of God's faithfulness?

II. SONGS OF GODLY INSTRUCTION (Psalm 78:1-7)

A. The Task (vv. 1-4)

1. Give ear, O my people, to my law: incline your ears to the words of my mouth.

2. I will open my mouth in a parable: I will utter sayings of old:

3. Which we have heard and known, and our fathers have told us.

4. We will not hide them from their children, showing to the generation to come the praises of the Lord, and his strength, and his wonderful works that he hath done.

Psalm 78 is the longest of a group of psalms often referred to as the "historical psalms." They speak of various events which significantly touched Israel's history. The first eight verses of Psalm 78 establish principles/directives which indicate the value of reviewing the past. It's easy to lose the past simply by not taking the time to discuss it with succeeding generations.

As you read Moses' speeches to the Israelites or Stephen's last exhortation to the crowd prior to his martyrdom (Deuteronomy 29; Acts 7), the importance of seeing the present through the lens of the past is emphasized. The past warns the conscientious to avoid its pitfalls and to practice what is right.

Speaking as God's representative, the writer of Psalm 78 exhorts God's people to give obedient attention to his instruction. The emphasis isn't on future revelation. Rather, it is an initiation to look at what God has already revealed. This includes both the Law and the Prophets. Another important aspect is the rehearsal of God's mighty acts on the behalf of Israel, including miracles of provision and protection. But there also were the times when God brought judgment on Israel for their unfaithfulness.

The task God now calls them to is transferring the knowledge of God from generation to generation. Parents are to transfer this knowledge of God to their children. Verse 4 says they are to hear the wondrous works of God so they too can rejoice. It is important for them to know what a powerful God they are serving.

It is easy to study these verses and see them as an encounter or requirement of the past. To do so is totally missing the point. We too are to be the promoters of what God has done, not only in the historical past, but also in our own lives. Our children need to hear the faith stories of their grandparents. Equally important is for them to know what He has done and is doing in our lives. We must keep the testimony alive!

Talk About It:
1. What should we do with our ears (v. 1)? With our mouth (vv. 2, 3)?
2. According to verse 4, what must we pass on to the next generation? Why is this important?

"Children are not casual guests in our home. They have been loaned to us temporarily for the purpose of loving them and instilling a foundation of values on which their future lives will be built."
—James C. Dobson

God-Inspired Poetry

B. The Results (vv. 5-7)

5. For he established a testimony in Jacob, and appointed a law in Israel, which he commanded our fathers, that they should make them known to their children:

6. That the generation to come might know them, even the children, even the children which should be born; who should arise and declare them to their children:

7. That they might set their hope in God, and not forget the works of God, but keep his commandments.

From the beginning of the nation of Israel, God's intention was for the fathers and mothers to pass on to their children the marvelous mercies and works of God. The verbal transmission of spiritual truth and experience was to continue from generation to generation (Deuteronomy 4:9, 10; 6:6, 7; 11:18, 19).

There are two specific results which this testimony of the past should produce. First, each generation should receive it and transmit it to the next. No generation will then be missed and be ignorant of the God they are to serve. This verbal transmission can accurately share the details of the past though traveling through many generations. Alex Haley's book *Roots* shows how this is accomplished.

Second is the spiritual impact on the generation hearing the testimony. It enables them to make a commitment to serve this great God who loves and cares for those who commit their lives to Him. This means maintaining a steadfast obedience to God's commandments rather than viewing them as options or suggestions. His commandments are absolutes which are to become the framework for our lifestyles.

III. SONGS OF PRAISE TO GOD (Psalm 148:1-14)
A. Call for Praise (vv. 1-12)

1. Praise ye the Lord. Praise ye the Lord from the heavens: praise him in the heights.

2. Praise ye him, all his angels: praise ye him, all his hosts.

3. Praise ye him, sun and moon: praise him, all ye stars of light.

4. Praise him, ye heavens of heavens, and ye waters that be above the heavens.

5. Let them praise the name of the Lord: for he commanded, and they were created.

6. He hath also stablished them for ever and ever: he hath made a decree which shall not pass.

7. Praise the Lord from the earth, ye dragons, and all deeps:

8. Fire, and hail; snow, and vapours; stormy wind fulfilling his word:

9. Mountains, and all hills; fruitful trees, and all cedars:

Talk About It:
1. Describe the continuing process explained in verses 5 and 6.
2. According to verse 7, what is the goal of this process?

"What children need most are a congregation that fully receives them into the family of God, pastors and teachers that serve as models and guides in discipleship, and families that nurture them into the covenant of Jesus Christ through example and instruction. Our task is to pass on our faith in a manner that will enable them to pass it on to others."
—**Jackie Johns**

10. Beasts, and all cattle; creeping things, and flying fowl:

11. Kings of the earth, and all people; princes, and all judges of the earth:

12. Both young men, and maidens; old men, and children:

The occasion for this psalm is not given. A review of the content causes one to speculate it must have been truly significant for such an expansive, expressive call for praise. It is universal. Every aspect of God's creation is called upon to praise the Creator who brings all into existence.

It is understood how, by their nature, some parts of creation do not have the will nor intellect, much less the means to initiate and continue the action of praise. However, from a poetical, symbolic perspective, the universe is presented as having the ability to praise the One who sovereignly created and governs.

Keep in mind this is a poem with parallel repetition. Imagine how the words would flow while being sung.

It may seem a strange question to ask, but it is necessary to do so. What does it mean to praise the Lord? Here the statement "Praise ye the Lord" means "Hallelujah." The latter three letters are the word *Yah*, which is a frequent contraction of *Yahweh*, one of the names of God. It is the personal name of the living God. In the first 12 verses of this chapter, all of creation is called to offer Him the highest praise. The psalmist begins with the angels, but quickly moves to the many dimensions of creation. Verse 5 points to God as the Creator of all. It is only reasonable to ask for all to praise the One who brought everything into existence.

After summoning those items in the heavens to praise, he turns his attention to the earth. He begins with the great sea creatures of the deep and progresses to different types of weather. Then the poet moves to the various topographic features, trees and animals. All are to join in this call to praise. After having covered the many inanimate forces, the psalm turns to God's highest creation, the human race.

Note the various groups of humans who are included. Verse 11 specifically names kings, princes and judges, but generally names "all people." Verse 12 makes this call gender- and age-inclusive. Even children are to praise God. In fact, children sometimes set the example in worship (Matthew 21:14-16).

The bottom line is very clear. God, our Creator, is worthy of praise from the entire creation. The practical application includes each one of us. We too are to be a part of this symphony of praise.

B. Reason for Praise (vv. 13, 14)

13. Let them praise the name of the Lord: for his name

Talk About It:
1. What do the heavens reveal about the Lord (vv. 1-6)?
2. According to verses 11 and 12, who should praise God? Is anyone left out?

Not Haphazard
Ask the astronomer if God is a haphazard God. He will tell you that every star moves with precision in its celestial path. Ask the scientist if God is a haphazard God. He will tell you that His formulas and equations are fixed, and that to ignore the laws of science would be a fool's folly.
—Billy Graham

alone is excellent; his glory is above the earth and heaven.

14. He also exalteth the horn of his people, the praise of all his saints; even of the children of Israel, a people near unto him. Praise ye the Lord.

Why should we praise the Lord with exuberance and continuity? Seems like an unusual question to ask in view of everything He has done for us. But, that is the very reason we need to ask! Our foremost reason to offer praise to God stems from, first and foremost, who He is. His nature alone provides sufficient reason for us to be a people involved who regularly offer praise.

When we begin to list the characteristics and attributes of God, we are confronted with His incomparable nature. He is *omnipotent* (all-powerful), *omniscient* (all-knowing), and *omnipresent* (all-present). Then consider His holiness, mercy and justice. Also, God never changes. Unlike the many aspects of our life and culture which seem to change with little or no notice, our God is the same in the years past, the present, and in the future. What a blessing!

Verse 14 points to another action of our God. He involves Himself in the lives of His people. It is possible this verse refers to some event in which God intervenes and brings victory. Anytime, regardless of the size of the intervention, God works in our behalf and He deserves our praise!

Nowhere in Psalm 148 is there any suggestion of our praising God with the hope of God changing our situation. That's what petition in prayer is for. We ask for what we need. However, prior to that, let's not forget to offer praise simply for who God is and all He has already done.

Talk About It:
1. Why does God's character call for our praise (v. 13)?
2. How do God's actions call for our praise (v. 14)?

"You don't have to be afraid of praising God too much; unlike humans, He never gets a big head."
—Paul Dibble

CONCLUSION

Music is a vital part of every culture. It provides a medium for sharing stories, expressing inner feelings, entertaining and worship. Though the styles vary greatly from one people group to another, there is a universal appreciation for this art form. Ironically, music also becomes a point of division between age groups and within families.

In the worship renewal movement, which began in the 1960s, music in the church became a divisive issue. Different styles of worship music sometimes separated the body of Christ, and this is still happening today. But it should not. When our focus is one of glorifying God whether or not the musical style is our favorite, we will lift Him up and help unify His body.

GOLDEN TEXT CHALLENGE

"LET THE WORD OF CHRIST DWELL IN YOU RICHLY IN ALL WISDOM; TEACHING AND ADMONISHING ONE ANOTHER IN PSALMS AND HYMNS AND SPIRITUAL

SONGS, SINGING WITH GRACE IN YOUR HEARTS TO THE LORD" (Colossians 3:16).

Christian worship has always been characterized by the Word and music. Paul mentioned three aspects of music that bring variety and joy to the church:

Psalms refers to the Old Testament liturgy that belonged to the church. The Book of Psalms contains the ancient songs of God's people. Many reformed churches used the Psalter as their primary hymnal, and today the psalms are being redis-covered in praise choruses.

Hymns are songs reflecting the great theological truths of Christianity. Philippians 2:5-11 is a New Testament example. These songs continue to be written and express the deep beliefs of the Christian community.

Spiritual songs are the "new songs" of the Spirit expressed in choruses of praise and worship. Spiritual songs can also be the music of the Spirit as we sing in other tongues in praise to the Lord.

Note that this verse closed with a qualifier about how we sing to the Lord: "with grace in your hearts." This means singing is actually a gift of praise from the Lord.

God-Given Wisdom
(Job, Proverbs and Ecclesiastes)

Job 1:1 through 2:13; 13:13-16; 42:1-17; Proverbs 8:1-11; Ecclesiastes 1:1-11; 8:12, 13; 12:13, 14

INTRODUCTION

Isn't it amazing how a person can be smart and yet be so stupid! A person who has a high IQ or is highly knowledgeable in many areas might, when it comes to the practical aspects of life, make decisions as though they were still in elementary school. That is due to there being a great difference between wisdom and intelligence or information. Also, there is the issue of using the wisdom one possesses.

King Solomon provides us with an excellent example. When God appeared to him in a dream offering whatever he wanted, this young man described himself as being a child. Wow! There's not too many 20-year-old males who admit to that. For that reason, Solomon asked for and received wisdom (1 Kings 3:5-14). Years later, when visited by the Queen of Sheba, she said, "Your wisdom and prosperity exceed the fame of which I heard" (10:7, *NKJV*). But, as we know from the Scriptural record, Solomon's wisdom didn't keep him making right decisions. In his old age, Solomon's many wives turned his heart toward their gods (11:2-6).

The result of Solomon's choosing personal pleasure over wisdom was far-reaching. The entire kingdom did not remain under the leadership of his heirs (vv. 9-13). This in turn set the stage for the leader of the other nation to push his people toward idolatry. Jeroboam worked to separate his people from their allegiance to Jerusalem and the worship of God in the Temple. He initiated two new worship sites, Dan and Bethel, with golden calves. He also initiated a non-Levitical priesthood.

This lesson strives to have us grasp the importance of applying the wisdom of God's Word to our daily lives. As humans utilizing natural gifts, we may become adept in our personal lives as employers, employees, parents and friends. Even then, the Scriptures provide wisdom for each of these areas of our lives and, more importantly, for our spiritual relationships.

Today's golden text, James 1:5, teaches that not one of us has to wander through life without wisdom. It's attainable without price or purchase. All we need to do is ask God for wisdom. Simple? Yes! However, it doesn't happen without our being proactive. Attaining wisdom includes our reaching out to the Book which contains it, the Bible.

Unit Theme:
Message of the Old Testament

Central Truth:
God imparts wisdom through His Word.

Focus:
Affirm the supreme wisdom of God's Word and govern our lives by it.

Context:
Seeing the necessity of wisdom from three of the Old Testament's Books of Wisdom

Golden Text:
"If any of you lack wisdom, let him ask of God, that giveth to all men liberally, and upbraideth not; and it shall be given him" (James 1:5).

Study Outline:
I. Wisdom to Trust God
(Job 1:1—2:10; 13:13-16; 42:1-10)
II. Wisdom to Live Right
(Proverbs 8:1-11)
III. Wisdom to Know Life's Purpose
(Ecclesiastes 1:1-11; 8:12, 13; 12:13, 14)

I. WISDOM TO TRUST GOD (Job 1:1—2:10; 13:13-16; 42:1-10)

A. In All Situations (1:1—2:10)

(Job 1:1-7, 13-19; 2:1-3 is not included in the printed text.)

perfect (v. 1)—
without blame

eschewed (v. 1)—
shunned

1:8. And the Lord said unto Satan, Hast thou considered my servant Job, that there is none like him in the earth, a perfect and an upright man, one that feareth God, and escheweth evil?

9. Then Satan answered the Lord, and said, Doth Job fear God for nought?

10. Hast not thou made an hedge about him, and about his house, and about all that he hath on every side? Thou hast blessed the work of his hands, and his substance is increased in the land.

11. But put forth thine hand now, and touch all that he hath, and he will curse thee to thy face.

12. And the Lord said unto Satan, Behold, all that he hath is in thy power; only upon himself put not forth thine hand. So Satan went forth from the presence of the Lord.

20. Then Job arose, and rent his mantle, and shaved his head, and fell down upon the ground, and worshipped,

21. And said, Naked came I out of my mother's womb, and naked shall I return thither: the Lord gave, and the Lord hath taken away; blessed be the name of the Lord.

22. In all this Job sinned not, nor charged God foolishly.

2:4. And Satan answered the Lord, and said, Skin for skin, yea, all that a man hath will he give for his life.

5. But put forth thine hand now, and touch his bone and his flesh, and he will curse thee to thy face.

6. And the Lord said unto Satan, Behold, he is in thine hand; but save his life.

7. So went Satan forth from the presence of the Lord, and smote Job with sore boils from the sole of his foot unto his crown.

8. And he took him a potsherd to scrape himself withal; and he sat down among the ashes.

9. Then said his wife unto him, Dost thou still retain thine integrity? curse God, and die.

10. But he said unto her, Thou speakest as one of the foolish women speaketh. What? shall we receive good at the hand of God, and shall we not receive evil? In all this did not Job sin with his lips.

Talk About It:
1. What was the key to Job's character?

As we begin this study of a well-known Old Testament character, one principle needs to be foundational. This account isn't a relating of God's testing Job. It stands on a completely different concept. Here God presents Job to Satan as an example of a righteous, God-fearing man. Notice how God describes

God-Given Wisdom

Job in the same terms on two occasions (1:8; 2:3). His wisdom is initially evident in his character. Here is a man who refuses evil. He chooses the good. It's the description of a person who understands the need to avoid what would be spiritually fatal.

Satan's response points us to one of the blessings of being a servant of God. He cares for us. In the case of Job, Satan suggests his prosperity stems from God's protection over his family and possessions. Why wouldn't Job be such a wonderful example of commitment to righteousness? But what would happen if all this were to be stripped from him? Wouldn't he simply curse God?

With confidence, God willingly put Job to the test of Satan, with one exception—all Job possessed was fair game, except for his person.

When Satan struck Job, it came quickly and forcefully against his family and his possessions (1:13-17). On a given day, Job received messenger after messenger who brought news of disaster. First, all his donkeys and oxen were stolen, servants were killed, and only one escaped to share the news. Second, fire from heaven destroyed all his sheep and servants, save one who escaped. Third, word came of all his camels being stolen and servants killed, except for one. Finally, Job learned all his sons and daughters had been killed when a storm destroyed the house where they were eating together.

As would be expected, Job responded with all the signs of great sorrow. He tore his outer mantle, and then went a step further by shaving his head. Some individuals of the ancient Orient saw the hair of the head as sacred. Shaving it occurred only in the deepest sorrow, time of humiliation, or at the completion of a vow.

Job did not just demonstrate sorrow; he followed with worship. With wisdom, he spoke of the sovereignty of God, saying it was just as easy and right for God to take as it was for Him to give. Job knew he had been the recipient of God's blessings previously, so how could he protest what was being taken from him? Sorrow, yes! Rail against God, never! Everyone comes into the world with nothing and will leave in the same manner.

This response of righteousness in the face of death and loss definitely raised the stakes. After an unknown interlude of time, Satan once again joined himself to a heavenly council meeting (2:1-3). In a repeat performance, God once again called attention to Job's condition of righteousness. Though stripped of family and possessions, he continued to be a person of righteous character and godly wisdom.

In verse 4, Satan suggested that afflicting a person's health would provide a totally different test. He believed that if Job were attacked physically, his blessing of God would turn to cursing. God's confidence in Job was so secure that He allowed

2. Why do you suppose God allowed Satan to test Job so severely?
3. Why was it so important to Job to maintain his integrity?

"A talent is formed in stillness, a character in the world's torrents."
—Goethe

Satan to inflict physical problems. The only exception was to not bringing about Job's death. Immediately Satan inflicted Job with painful boils covering his whole body. There is one type of boil that literally causes swelling over one's entire body to the point of disfigurement, making it painful to sit, lay or stand.

In this pitiful state, Job sat in ashes scraping his body with broken pottery. His wife could not understand why he continued to hold to his integrity before God. Her suggestion was simple: "Curse God and die!" (v. 9). That would end the misery.

Once again Job wisely trusted in God. In the past, good things were their lot. Why turn from Him just because they now were experiencing very difficult circumstances? Job rebuked his wife and resisted her suggestion. Once again Job demonstrated to Satan the type of spiritual man he was, and God knew it all along.

B. To the Point of Death (13:13-16)

(Job 13:13, 14 is not included in the printed text.)

15. Though he slay me, yet will I trust in him: but I will maintain mine own ways before him.

16. He also shall be my salvation: for an hypocrite shall not come before him.

Talk About It:
1. Describe the depth of Job's confidence in God.
2. What did Job mean by saying, "I take my flesh in my teeth" (v. 14)?
3. What can a "hypocrite" not do (v. 16)? Why not?

In this section of Scripture, Job and his friends are discussing the cause of his situation. He is responding to Zophar, who suggested Job must be lying by refusing to admit his own sins had brought this suffering upon him (ch. 11). Job is in the middle of his reply when he declares, "Though He slay me, yet will I trust Him" (13:15, *NKJV*). Even if this series of events would progress to the point of death, Job would seek vindication. He knew his own spiritual condition and would continue to plead his case even before the face of God.

Notice the confidence expressed in verse 16. Job believed all of this would turn out positively. He would be delivered because of righteousness. No sinful person could ever successfully plead his or her case before the presence of God.

Many centuries later we see the apostle Paul expressing the same hope of deliverance. Though a prisoner in Rome chained to a 24-hour guard and seemingly at the disposition of ruthless Nero, Paul confidently expects his situation to be positive. He too faces death with no guarantee of life. He writes, "For to me to live is Christ, and to die is gain" (Philippians 1:21).

C. In Repentance (42:1-10)

(Job 42:1-4, 7-9 is not included in the printed text.)

5. I have heard of thee by the hearing of the ear: but now mine eye seeth thee.

6. Wherefore I abhor myself, and repent in dust and ashes.

10. And the Lord turned the captivity of Job, when he prayed for his friends: also the Lord gave Job twice as much as he had before.

Can a person live righteously and speak ignorantly? Absolutely yes! Job serves as a positive example of such behavior.

Beginning in chapter 38, God speaks directly to Job. He immediately points to the problem of Job's attempting to speak to a situation without seeing the picture of God's sovereignty over all. God wants Job to understand his ignorance in dealing with the circumstances which have stripped him of material goods, health, and the support of his spouse. It's not an issue of having or having not sinned.

Without condemning Job nor declaring his innocence, God asks dozens of diverse questions, such as "Hast thou entered into the springs of the sea?" and "Have the gates of death been opened unto thee?" (38:16, 17). To each question Job realizes either his ignorance or inability.

In 42:5, Job indicates his growth in knowledge and understanding of God. His new perspective unveils his lowly position versus God's greatness. Thus he repents "in dust and ashes" (v. 6) for making judgments and speaking about things he did not comprehend (v. 3).

Notice the chronology. After Job recognizes his true position before God and repents, God rewards him greatly. God gives him twice as much wealth as before, prolongs his life, and gives him 10 more children. This reminds us of the need to remain spiritually close to our Lord and Master, Jesus Christ. Only when we maintain the proper spiritual relationship with Him can we expect His blessings.

While none of us are promised material wealth because of our spirituality, we can count on the riches of salvation and security in His promises.

Talk About It:
1. Through his suffering, what did Job discover about God?
2. Why did Job repent?
3. When did God restore Job's losses? Why then?

"Wisdom resists group pressures, thinks for itself, and is reconciled to the use of its own judgment."
—Selected

II. WISDOM TO LIVE RIGHT (Proverbs 8:1-11)
A. Listening (vv. 1-5)

1. Doth not wisdom cry? and understanding put forth her voice?

2. She standeth in the top of high places, by the way in the places of the paths.

3. She crieth at the gates, at the entry of the city, at the coming in at the doors.

4. Unto you, O men, I call; and my voice is to the sons of man.

5. O ye simple, understand wisdom: and, ye fools, be ye of an understanding heart.

Talk About It:
1. How does wisdom *cry out* to people today?
2. Who can receive "an understanding heart" (v. 5)?

The writer of this section of Proverbs presents wisdom as a person calling out and inviting people to follow her ways. This is in contrast to the appealing voice of the deceiver presented in the previous chapter. Instead of succumbing to worldly lust which eventually destroys in spite of its current pleasures, wisdom calls for people to seek after an understanding heart.

The "high places" in verse 2 speaks to the custom of a messenger finding a high place in a city to deliver official directives so everyone could hear. Verses 2 and 3 also point to the practice of making announcements near the major routes into a city. This happened because business often took place at the city gates where there would be a gathering of the town elders.

These verses remind us that wisdom can be found, if one chooses to listen as it is being given. Though communication means were limited in the culture of this writing, wisdom still made itself known. How fortunate we are to have a broad spectrum of methods to hear the truth of wisdom. The challenge continues to be discerning between competing voices and choosing to restrict immediate pleasure for long-term reward.

"There is no lock on the door of wisdom."
—*Quotable Quotes*

B. Speaking (vv. 6-9)

6. Hear; for I will speak of excellent things; and the opening of my lips shall be right things.

7. For my mouth shall speak truth; and wickedness is an abomination to my lips.

8. All the words of my mouth are in righteousness; there is nothing froward or perverse in them.

9. They are all plain to him that understandeth, and right to them that find knowledge.

Wisdom shows the contrast between her words and the words from other sources. Wisdom elevates truthful principles, brought to light so individuals can know what is right.

Verse 8 shows how wisdom offers words that are just rather than words that are crooked or twisted. The words of wisdom are never marked by deception or error. The word *crooked* ("froward") refers to threads, cords, or ropes that are twisted over and over; it also can refer to the twisting of limbs. Liars and deceivers twist words and concepts for their own benefits. But wisdom speaks in straight words without bending to the right or the left.

Talk About It:
1. What words does wisdom speak? What words does it not speak?
2. Who is able to understand words of wisdom? Why?

Unless we have a discerning heart and mind, the faultless presentation of wisdom may be missed. If we have been filled with wrong information and faulty ideas, the truth may not sink in. That is why the ministry of the Holy Spirit continues to be so important in each of our lives. He will lead us in truth (John 14:16, 17; 16:13).

C. Choosing (vv. 10, 11)

10. Receive my instruction, and not silver; and knowledge rather than choice gold.

11. For wisdom is better than rubies; and all the things that may be desired are not to be compared to it.

Possessing the wisdom to live right boils down to one issue—our choice. No one can be forced to follow the principles of wisdom. It becomes a matter of choosing what is most important to us.

These verses emphasize the struggle which frequently takes place within us humans, presenting the power of materialism as represented by silver, gold and rubies. They stand as the precious possessions which many strive for at the expense of truth. The writer says wisdom and possessions do not belong in the same class for comparison. We know how possessions can be lost, stolen or destroyed. Wisdom remains forever. It cannot be taken from us by anyone.

No one should interpret these verses as opposing the possession of material goods or working toward accumulating some. The issue is understanding their place in our value system. Wisdom always needs to be seen as the higher item of value. It is to be greatly desired!

III. WISDOM TO KNOW LIFE'S PURPOSE (Ecclesiastes 1:1-11; 8:12, 13; 12:13, 14)

A. Repetition of Events (1:1-11)

(Ecclesiastes 1:1, 4-11 is not included in the printed text.)

2. Vanity of vanities, saith the Preacher, vanity of vanities; all is vanity.

3. What profit hath a man of all his labour which he taketh under the sun?

The opening theme of Ecclesiastes is that life is meaningless as expressed by the author, Solomon. Though he has "had it all" as described in chapter 2, he still lacks purpose in life. Regardless of all his material gain and personal accomplishments, there is that empty feeling. Solomon recognizes the mortality of each generation, with life on earth continuing even as people fade away in death (1:4).

Next, Solomon addresses the repetition of events. Within nature the sun continues its pattern. (Even though we know it is the earth that revolves, we too speak of the sun rising and setting.) The wind blows and whirls while rivers continue to flow, emptying into the ocean but never filling it. In human relationships we see repeated patterns of love, anger, separation and reunion. When new ideas are projected, close scrutiny reveals they are simply modification or revisions of those of a previous time. That should not keep us from creating or developing.

Talk About It:
What makes instruction, knowledge and wisdom so valuable?

"It is better to weep with wise men than to laugh with fools."
—**Spanish proverb**

vanity (v. 2)—emptiness or nonsense

Talk About It:
1. Answer the question in verse 3: "What profit has a man from all his labor in which he toils under the sun?" (*NKJV*).
2. Explain Solomon's statement about the eye and ear in verse 8.
3. From an earthly perspective, are the issues in verses 9-11 true? Are they true from a heavenly, eternal perspective?

However, while doing so, we must not think too highly of ourselves.

The conclusion of this segment pushes us to recognize the temporariness of life. This, in turn, should provide a foundation for seeking the purpose of life.

B. Reverence to God (8:12, 13)

12. Though a sinner do evil an hundred times, and his days be prolonged, yet surely I know that it shall be well with them that fear God, which fear before him:

13. But it shall not be well with the wicked, neither shall he prolong his days, which are as a shadow; because he feareth not before God.

These two verses are a brief reminder of the difference between the end of the wicked and the righteous. Wisdom understands the length of a person's life isn't necessarily a stamp of approval on their beliefs and lifestyle. What makes the difference continues to be the condition of one's heart, and his or her attitude and relationship with God.

This reminds us of the fallacy behind someone's reasoning when they assume their health and material prosperity are a sign of their being right with God. The final accounting comes from one's reverent attitude toward God, not from one's possessions.

Sometimes here on earth it appears the righteous experience what the wicked deserve. In turn, the ungodly may be living a life we would expect to be the just due of the righteous. But such inconsistencies are part of living in a world dominated by sin. We must remember that life on earth is only a passing moment compared with eternity. Reverent service to God brings rewards far beyond the short, temporary years of life on earth.

C. Keeping God's Commandments (12:13, 14)

13. Let us hear the conclusion of the whole matter: Fear God, and keep his commandments: for this is the whole duty of man.

14. For God shall bring every work into judgment, with every secret thing, whether it be good, or whether it be evil.

Solomon ends his discourse with these famous words. They're the bottom line for life. You may try every philosophy of life, attempt the breadth of pleasurable experiences, and strive to accumulate vast possessions. When you have attempted everything, there is no fulfillment and lasting impact such as found in fulfilling the commandments of God.

Besides, our entire lives will be scrutinized. Even the secret items now hidden to everyone else will be revealed. Our eternal future depends on what God sees.

God-Given Wisdom

CONCLUSION

The wise person understands the greatest fulfillment in this life is to reverently serve God. And this person knows the Bible reveals how to serve God. Most importantly, the wise person regularly reads God's Word and lets God's Spirit apply it to his or her life.

GOLDEN TEXT CHALLENGE

"IF ANY OF YOU LACK WISDOM, LET HIM ASK OF GOD, THAT GIVETH TO ALL MEN LIBERALLY, AND UPBRAIDETH NOT; AND IT SHALL BE GIVEN HIM" (James 1:5).

Wisdom is not merely knowing—it is knowing how; it is effectiveness in life; it is living. Wisdom is productive. There is a fleshly wisdom by which one "gets ahead," but which produces "confusion and every evil work" (3:16). But there is also a divine wisdom whose product is like the fruit of the Spirit; it is "pure, peaceable, gentle, easy to be entreated, full of mercy and good fruits" (see v. 17).

This divine wisdom is personal, not abstract. Solomon depicted wisdom as crying out to the simple ones, as having been with God when He made the worlds (Proverbs 8). Wisdom is not summoned by the payment of tuition (17:16). It evades the proud and scorning (14:6). It is brought near by godly reverence: "The fear of the Lord is the beginning of wisdom" (9:10). This wisdom is inseparable from God and Christ. Paul declares that Christ is "made unto us wisdom" (1 Corinthians 1:30). Hence, God, who upbraids not, gives to the believing seeker Himself in Christ—the basic life, breath and wisdom of the Christian.

Daily Devotions:
M. The Allure of False Wisdom
   Genesis 3:1-13
T. Wisdom Comes From God
   Job 28:20-28
W. Value and Benefits of Wisdom
   Proverbs 3:13-22
T. Wise and Foolish Builders
   Matthew 7:21-27
F. Spirit-Filled and Wise
   Acts 6:1-7
S. Wisdom for Salvation
   2 Timothy 3:14-17

God's Messengers, the Prophets (Isaiah to Malachi)

Isaiah 1:1-20; 11:1-5; Jeremiah 7:3-7; 23:5; 25:8-11; Ezekiel 14:12-14; Micah 5:2; 7:18-20; Zechariah 9:9

Unit Theme:
Message of the Old Testament

Central Truth:
God inspired the prophets to speak His Word.

Focus:
Consider the words of the prophets and believe the Bible.

Context:
An overview of the Prophetic Books

Golden Text:
"For the prophecy came not in old time by the will of man: but holy men of God spake as they were moved by the Holy Ghost" (2 Peter 1:21).

Study Outline:
I. Prophecies of Warning and Judgment (Isaiah 1:1-20; Jeremiah 25:8-11; Ezekiel 14:12-14)
II. Prophecies of Exhortation and Comfort (Jeremiah 7:3-7; Micah 7:18-20)
III. Prophecies About the Messiah (Isaiah 11:1-5; Jeremiah 23:5; Micah 5:2; Zechariah 9:9)

INTRODUCTION

It is regrettable that so many believers neglect the richness of the Old Testament. They may utilize some of the psalms and a few choice verses; however, most of their attention centers on the New Testament.

We must remember that the two testaments as a whole make up the Holy Scriptures. Many items in the New Testament cannot be properly understood without the foundational perspectives of the Old Testament. Also, we cannot rejoice appropriately at many of the events in the New Testament without knowing them to be the fulfillment of prophecy.

This brings us to the ministry of the prophets. Some have their names attached to the books of their utterances. Others are mentioned only in the historical books. The writing prophets are the emphasis for this lesson. Our golden text emphasizes the means by which they become the messengers of God. Through the Holy Spirit, God communicated to them the messages which the selected audiences needed to hear. Some of their prophecies had a narrow time focus, while others are still to be fulfilled.

Before continuing into the lesson, let's look briefly at the office of prophet/prophetess. Once Israel became a monarchy under the reign of Saul, God chose to regularly communicate His will and word through the means of chosen human messengers. Prior to this there were prophets, but now there would be a continuous succession of them bringing His word to Israel and other nations.

By definition, *prophets/prophetesses* are men/women whom God calls to announce and illuminate His will and work in history. Their task is one of forthtelling and foretelling. The first is a repeating of truths that are already known. The latter is the predicting of future events.

Prophets/prophetesses functioned as the "spokespersons" of God and two criteria: *faithfulness* and *fulfillment*. True prophets served God in word and deed (Deuteronomy 13), and their predictions came true within the conditions allowed (ch. 18).

With this introduction in mind, let's consider the prophetic words of five individuals.

I. PROPHECIES OF WARNING AND JUDGMENT
(Isaiah 1:1-20; Jeremiah 25:8-11; Ezekiel 14:12-14)

A. Choice to Make (Isaiah 1:1-20)
(Isaiah 1:1, 5-15 is not included in the printed text.)

2. Hear, O heavens, and give ear, O earth: for the Lord hath spoken, I have nourished and brought up children, and they have rebelled against me.

3. The ox knoweth his owner, and the ass his master's crib: but Israel doth not know, my people doth not consider.

4. Ah sinful nation, a people laden with iniquity, a seed of evildoers, children that are corrupters: they have forsaken the Lord, they have provoked the Holy One of Israel unto anger, they are gone away backward.

16. Wash you, make you clean; put away the evil of your doings from before mine eyes; cease to do evil;

17. Learn to do well; seek judgment, relieve the oppressed, judge the fatherless, plead for the widow.

18. Come now, and let us reason together, saith the Lord: though your sins be as scarlet, they shall be as white as snow; though they be red like crimson, they shall be as wool.

19. If ye be willing and obedient, ye shall eat the good of the land:

20. But if ye refuse and rebel, ye shall be devoured with the sword: for the mouth of the Lord hath spoken it.

stricken (v. 5)—beaten

revolt (v. 5)—rebel

cottage (v. 8)—booth

lodge (v. 8)—hut

In the last half of the eighth century B.C., God commissioned Isaiah to be His prophetic voice to the people of Judah. In the opening chapter of this prophesy they were being confronted with a major choice: Change their ways or face future destruction.

The prophet Isaiah described the pitiful condition of the people in view of how well they had been treated by the Lord. Verses 2 and 3 state it succinctly. Though God nourished them and brought them to maturity, there was no love or loyalty. In fact, just the opposite occurred. They were in complete rebellion while appearing to show a form of obedience to His directives. Isaiah declared them as not even being on the level of cattle or donkeys! These animals know who is the master and come to the feeding trough. But not the people of Judah! They disregarded and rejected the One who was watching over and providing for them.

In verses 4-7 the Lord describes Judah as a sinful people who had forsaken God to the point of kindling His anger against them. Their pitiful moral and spiritual condition is described in terms of human illnesses and injury. Their whole being was sick—head and heart. They were covered with wounds and bruises which had received no care.

Talk About It:
1. How were the people of Israel worse than oxen and donkeys (vv. 2, 3)?
2. Describe the people's wounded condition (vv. 5, 6).
3. How did God show mercy to Israel (v. 9)?
4. What warning did God give (v. 20)?

hissing (v. 9)—a sound of scorn and mocking

The physical nation of Judah also reflected this illness and brokenness. As a result of foreign invaders, the cities and countryside were filled with ruins. Except for the mercy of God, all of the cities could have suffered the same total destruction as Sodom and Gomorrah.

Beginning with verse 10 we see how contemptible these people had become. They appeared to be following the guidelines for worship in terms of the various offerings, celebrations and sacrifices. But it was all an outward act without repentance and daily obedience. Verse 15 says they prayed with uplifted hands, but sin covered them.

For churchgoers today, just saying the right words and going through outward forms of worship without love and commitment to God places us in the same predicament. We too may cause God's anger to rise against us.

God calls His people to make the choice of repenting, changing our lifestyles, and experiencing the blessings of God. God desires our love and loyalty. He wants us to be obedient in all areas of our lives. In turn, we will be the recipients of His choice blessings.

B. Consequences of Disobedience (Jeremiah 25:8-11)

8. Therefore thus saith the Lord of hosts; Because ye have not heard my words,

9. Behold, I will send and take all the families of the north, saith the Lord, and Nebuchadrezzar the king of Babylon, my servant, and will bring them against this land, and against the inhabitants thereof, and against all these nations round about, and will utterly destroy them, and make them an astonishment, and an hissing, and perpetual desolations.

10. Moreover I will take from them the voice of mirth, and the voice of gladness, the voice of the bridegroom, and the voice of the bride, the sound of the millstones, and the light of the candle.

11. And this whole land shall be a desolation, and an astonishment; and these nations shall serve the king of Babylon seventy years.

Can you imagine being the prophet Jeremiah and serving as the messenger of *how* judgment would come? It's one thing to say judgment is coming. But it is completely different when a prophet identifies the nation God has chosen as the instrument of judgment. Coming from the north, King Nebuchadnezzar and the forces of Babylon (Chaldeans) would execute terrible judgment not only against Judah but also the surrounding nations. The description of Nebuchadnezzar as God's servant (v. 9) does not mean he was righteous. His commitment to other gods and needing to be humbled before the true God is seen clearly in the Book of Daniel. Yet God would use Nebuchadnezzar for His purposes.

So there would be no mistake concerning the impact this invading force would have, verse 9 gives the description of utter destruction, while verse 10 brings it down to personal dimensions. The sounds of joy would be gone. No longer would there be extended wedding celebrations. Gone would be the sounds of daily work and the lights in homes at night. Desolation would reign. People would be dead or in captivity with those remaining living in a depressed condition.

Jeremiah declared the length of the captivity would be 70 years. This reveals God's sovereignty over all events, including judgment.

C. Hand of Judgment (Ezekiel 14:12-14)

12. The word of the Lord came again to me, saying,

13. Son of man, when the land sinneth against me by trespassing grievously, then will I stretch out mine hand upon it, and will break the staff of the bread thereof, and will send famine upon it, and will cut off man and beast from it:

14. Though these three men, Noah, Daniel, and Job, were in it, they should deliver but their own souls by their righteousness, saith the Lord God.

Ezekiel prophesied from Babylon, where he was taken as a captive. His purpose was "to keep before the generation born in exile the national sins which had brought Israel so low [and] to sustain the faith of the exiles by predictions of national restoration" (*Scofield Reference Bible*).

In the prophecy of Ezekiel 14, Jerusalem had not fallen, though many Jews had already been deported. Amazing, Jerusalem's residents still were not even considering changing their ways! God must bring judgment on them to eventually bring the nation back to righteousness. He wanted them to be His people, and He wanted to be their God (v. 11). But at this point other idols filled their hearts.

Due to their grievous sin, God was allowing His judgment to decimate their country. Jerusalem would not stand. Since bread played such a dominant part of the people's diet, the Lord spoke of breaking its supply. Famine would stalk the city. The armies of Babylon had already entered Judah and taken captives. Cutting off the food supply of the capital city would be part of Babylon's siege against it.

The surety of the judgment and the sinfulness of the people were described further through an unusual illustration. Ezekiel named Noah, Daniel and Job as excellent examples of righteousness and commitment to God. While Noah and Job had

trespassing grievously (v. 13)—being persistently unfaithful

staff (v. 13)—supply

Talk About It:
1. When might God allow famine to come upon a nation?
2. Whose righteousness brings deliverance during judgment?

been deceased for many centuries, Daniel was a contemporary example of commitment to God. He had been transported to Babylon in the first deportation. Even while being trained for government service in idolatrous Babylon, he held to the standards of his faith in God and the required standards of Judaism.

Ezekiel's prophecy pointed how even if these three men were now present in Jerusalem, it would not change the city's sinful condition and the coming judgment. "They could save only themselves by their righteousness, declares the Sovereign Lord. . . . They could save neither son nor daughter" (vv. 14, 20, *NIV*).

II. PROPHECIES OF EXHORTATION AND COMFORT
(Jeremiah 7:3-7; Micah 7:18-20)

A. Call for Change (Jeremiah 7:3-7)

3. Thus saith the Lord of hosts, the God of Israel, Amend your ways and your doings, and I will cause you to dwell in this place.

4. Trust ye not in lying words, saying, The temple of the Lord, The temple of the Lord, The temple of the Lord, are these.

5. For if ye throughly amend your ways and your doings; if ye throughly execute judgment between a man and his neighbour;

6. If ye oppress not the stranger, the fatherless, and the widow, and shed not innocent blood in this place, neither walk after other gods to your hurt:

7. Then will I cause you to dwell in this place, in the land that I gave to your fathers, for ever and ever.

Have you ever wondered how frustrating it must be for God to love us so much, yet see us persist in living life the way we want regardless of His warnings? Because of God's great love for His children, He offers the opportunity to change our ways and be restored. This is clearly seen in Jeremiah's prophetic words.

The call in verse 3 is for the people to change their ways. If they would, God offered them the opportunity to remain in the land. This would seem like a simple choice to most people. But when a person or a nation is entrenched in sin, truth may not appear as truth. That is why God asked them to stop trusting in the lies which had been heaped on them. Leading people kept saying the city of Jerusalem was safe from any attack. It was the location of the Temple—surely God wouldn't allow judgment to come on this holy place! But how wrong they were!

Jeremiah pointed out four distinctive sins that were at the root of Judah's problem. The first was the mistreatment of

Talk About It:
1. Why did God say not to trust "the temple of the Lord" (v. 4)?
2. Why is the word *thoroughly* used twice in verse 5?
3. What did God want to do for His people (v. 7)?

neighbors. Instead of selfishly seeking their own personal benefit, concern and care should be extended to those around.

Second was the oppression of those who were less fortunate. Three different people groups are mentioned. "Strangers" could be Gentiles living in the land or those traveling through. Orphans and widows with their limited finances had no one to rise to their defense unless the common people committed to protect them.

Third was the issue of murdering the innocent—the ultimate means of oppressing people.

Fourth, Jeremiah named idolatry. Its being listed last by no means says it was a lesser sin. The Ten Commandments, as recorded in Exodus 20 and Deuteronomy 5, place worship of God and Him alone to be the foundation for all the guidelines which follow.

The prophetic word was clear: "Reform your ways and your actions, and I will let you live in this place" (Jeremiah 7:3, *NIV*). The Abrahamic covenant, passed down from generation to generation, promised the land of Canaan as an everlasting possession. God wanted to bless Judah by allowing their residence in the Promised Land to continue without interruption.

> "It is much easier to repent of sins we have committed than to repent of those we intend to commit."
> —Josh Billings

B. God's Compassion (Micah 7:18-20)

18. Who is a God like unto thee, that pardoneth iniquity, and passeth by the transgression of the remnant of his heritage? he retaineth not his anger for ever, because he delighteth in mercy.

19. He will turn again, he will have compassion upon us; he will subdue our iniquities; and thou wilt cast all their sins into the depths of the sea.

20. Thou wilt perform the truth to Jacob, and the mercy to Abraham, which thou hast sworn unto our fathers from the days of old.

Micah prophesied nearly a century before Jeremiah. The last three verses of his prophecy are a tremendous source of comfort. They describe dimensions of God that some overlook while others attempt to exploit. Within Christianity there are those who perceive God as a harsh disciplinarian just waiting to pounce on anyone for the smallest sin. On the opposite side are those who view God as a loving heavenly Father who always blesses all humankind regardless of their actions. Micah strikes the truthful balance.

In these verses we see the depth of the Father's compassion toward His people. However, there is a point where there is no choice but to judge a persistently sinful people. But even then, God's anger does not continue forever. When people repent, He forgives and restores. Their sins are buried in His

Talk About It:
1. According to verse 18, what makes God incomparable?
2. What two things does God do with a repentant person's sins (v. 19), and what does this mean?

forgetfulness instead of accumulating against them. The picture of burying sins in the sea reflects a time when recovery of anything sunken in the ocean's depths was an impossibility.

Verse 20 speaks to God's fulfilling His promises regardless of when they were made. Abraham was the father of the nation of Israel through the promised son, Isaac, while Jacob's sons became the founding fathers of the various tribes of Israel. God's covenant was continuing in Micah's day, even though both Abraham and Jacob had been deceased for many centuries.

The question in verse 18 deserves our consideration: "Who is a God like you?" (v. 18, *NIV*). Its structure indicates there is no other who offers such comfort and compassion. And His mercy still applies to every believer today! We are so blessed! How can we not continue to serve a God who, even in times of discipline, loves us and seeks our best?

III. PROPHECIES ABOUT THE MESSIAH (Isaiah 11:1-5; Jeremiah 23:5; Micah 5:2; Zechariah 9:9)

Though these verses are commonly recognized and some repeated during the Christmas season, we need to be reminded not only of the content but the means of their coming to us. These prophets willingly spoke by the inspiration of the Holy Spirit events which we now look back at in history.

A. Family Lineage (Isaiah 11:1-5; Jeremiah 23:5)
(Isaiah 11:3-5 is not included in the printed text.)

Isaiah 11:1. And there shall come forth a rod out of the stem of Jesse, and a Branch shall grow out of his roots:

2. And the spirit of the Lord shall rest upon him, the spirit of wisdom and understanding, the spirit of counsel and might, the spirit of knowledge and of the fear of the Lord.

Jeremiah 23:5. Behold, the days come, saith the Lord, that I will raise unto David a righteous Branch, and a King shall reign and prosper, and shall execute judgment and justice in the earth.

These two portions of prophetic verse lay a distinct family lineage from which the Messiah would come. Isaiah's prophecy indicated the family (Jesse's) while Jeremiah pointed to the son of the family (David) from which the Messiah would appear. Anyone not from the tribe of Judah could not make such a claim (see Genesis 49:8-10).

Jeremiah's prophecy also said the Messiah would be a King. This prophecy was fulfilled as the Magi came seeking the newborn "King of the Jews" (Matthew 2:2).

Now consider the other characteristics prophesied by Isaiah, all of which came to pass (or will come to pass) in Jesus Christ:

Talk About It:
1. How would the judgments made by Jesus Christ be different than those made by earthly judges (Isaiah 11:3-5)?
2. Why would His judgments be perfect (vv. 1, 2)?

God's Messengers, the Prophets

- The Spirit of the Lord would rest upon Him, giving Him wisdom and understanding, knowledge and power.
- His judgments about people's character would be perfect.
- He would judge the earth.
- His righteousness and faithfulness would stand out.

B. Birthplace (Micah 5:2)

2. But thou, Bethlehem Ephratah, though thou be little among the thousands of Judah, yet out of thee shall he come forth unto me that is to be ruler in Israel; whose goings forth have been from of old, from everlasting.

A small town several miles southwest of Jerusalem was selected by God for the birthplace of the Messiah. This event alone brought historical acclaim to a small village, and now, in the 21st century, thousands of tourists visit Bethlehem annually. No reason is given for God's selection. To us, however, it represents the humility Christ demonstrated in taking on human flesh and living like us. He identified with common people.

The fulfillment of the Bethlehem prophecy came as a result of Caesar Augustus' decree requiring heads of families to return to their home city for a census. It reminds us again how God uses a variety of people, regardless of their position or lifestyle, to fulfill His purpose.

Talk About It:
Contrast the town of Bethlehem with the One who would be born there.

C. King's Entry (Zechariah 9:9)

9. Rejoice greatly, O daughter of Zion; shout, O daughter of Jerusalem: behold, thy King cometh unto thee: he is just, and having salvation; lowly, and riding upon an ass, and upon a colt the foal of an ass.

This one verse of Zechariah's prophecy details a particular event which was fulfilled in Matthew 21. Upon the directive of Jesus, two disciples went into Jerusalem and secured a donkey for Him to ride while entering the city (vv. 6, 7). The crowds rejoiced when they saw Him shouting, "Hosanna to the son of David. . . . Hosanna in the highest" (v. 9).

It wasn't just a king who rode into Jerusalem, but "thy King" who "is just" (Zechariah 9:9). The Messiah was free from bias or prejudice. And He entered the city "having salvation"—providing freedom from bondage and a future of life eternal with the Father.

Talk About It:
When Jesus made His triumphal entry to Jerusalem, what was He riding, and why? What was He bringing, and why?

CONCLUSION

The book *The World's Worst Predictions* lists some of history's all-time prophetic goofs:
- King George II said in 1773 that the American colonies had little stomach for revolution.

- An official of the White Star Line, speaking of the firm's newly built flagship, the *Titanic*, launched in 1912, declared that the ship was unsinkable.
- In 1939 *The New York Times* said the problem of TV was that people had to glue their eyes to a screen, and that the average American wouldn't have time for it.
- An English astronomy professor said in the early 19th century that air travel at high speed would be impossible because passengers would suffocate.

While predictions and prophecies generated by humans often fail, not so with prophecies that come from God. We see this in the scores of Old Testament prophecies that have already been fulfilled, and we will continue to see God's words fulfilled in the future, both on earth and in eternity.

Daily Devotions:
M. Prophetic Office Established
Deuteronomy 18:15-22
T. God Sent the Prophets
2 Chronicles 36:14-21
W. False Prophets Condemned
Jeremiah 23:25-32
T. John the Baptist, a Prophet
Matthew 11:1-10
F. God's Prophets Rejected
Matthew 23:29-39
S. Prophets Foretold Christ's Coming
1 Peter 1:10-13

GOLDEN TEXT CHALLENGE

"FOR THE PROPHECY CAME NOT IN OLD TIME BY THE WILL OF MAN: BUT HOLY MEN OF GOD SPAKE AS THEY WERE MOVED BY THE HOLY GHOST" (2 Peter 1:21).

Bible prophecy did not proceed from the prophet's own knowledge or invention, nor was it the result of the prophet's calculation or conjecture. The prophecies of the Bible did not originate in the minds of people, but in the heart and mind of God.

"Holy men of God" were chosen to be the mouthpieces to reveal the words of God to humanity. God is particular about the character of the people who work for Him. He chooses those who are sincere and sanctified.

The prophecies which the "holy men of God" gave were God-inspired. The prophets were moved upon by the Holy Spirit to deliver divine messages.

No wonder Christians can have complete confidence in the Scriptures! God's Word is the highest authority in matters of doctrine and behavior. The people who penned the Bible did so under the direction of God's Spirit.

Let us be thankful for the Word of God. Let us study it, live by it, and teach it to others.

Synoptic Gospels (Matthew, Mark and Luke)

Matthew 25:31-46; Mark 10:32-45; Luke 9:18-27

INTRODUCTION

Matthew, Mark and Luke are known as the synoptic Gospels. The Greek word *synoptikos* means "seeing things together," or having a common viewpoint. These three writings essentially tell a story of the days of Jesus' life on earth. This is in contrast to John, who picks only a few important signs to prove that Jesus is the Son of God. While the synoptic letters have common materials and generally agree chronologically, they each contain unique episodes and details. However, the fact they are in such overall harmony can only be attributed to the Holy Spirit's overseeing.

Matthew's Gospel might be summarized as a Jew writing to Jews about a Jew. He uses the phrase "kingdom of heaven" 33 times and the term "kingdom of God" four times. He sets about to show Jesus as the fulfillment of Old Testament prophecies of the messianic King. He even opens with a genealogy to prove Jesus' credentials as a descendant of David. It is interesting that Matthew himself was a social outcast among his own people. A tax collector when Jesus called him, he was so ostracized by Jewish society that he could dissect his own religious/cultural heritage with clear objectivity.

Mark's Gospel is not nearly so biographical. Instead, his letter is concentrated on action—the things Jesus did. Jesus is seen as a conquering Savior-King, constantly casting out demons, healing diseases, overcoming death. Moving like a fast-paced adventure movie, Mark gives the reader an eye-witness view of events, including the crowds' reaction. He gives attention to detail, though his is the shortest of the Gospels. This is because he omits the longer teaching discourses Jesus gave. Mark's style was well-suited to the Gentile Roman world, a people who had little interest in Jewish heritage or Greek intellectualism.

We come next to Luke's Gospel. Luke never met Jesus nor witnessed His ministry firsthand. Not only that, he was Greek and not Jewish. Still, Luke chose to follow the Lord. His writing is unique for several reasons. First, his letter has a sequel—the Book of Acts. Next, he includes the Lord's ascension. Third, Luke is the longest of the Gospels, and records such a variety of the Lord's teaching, parables and miracles that it is the fullest single portrait of His ministry. Finally, Luke's writing is the only one addressed to a single individual—someone named Theophilus, who was likely a Gentile believer.

Unit Theme:
Message of the New Testament

Central Truth:
Jesus Christ came as King, Suffering Servant, and Son of Man.

Focus:
Recognize the Synoptic Gospels as sources of knowledge about the earthly life of Christ and discern the unique message of each Gospel.

Context:
Overview of the Synoptic Gospels

Golden Text:
"There came a voice from heaven, saying, Thou art my beloved Son, in whom I am well pleased" (Mark 1:11).

Study Outline:
I. Matthew: Christ the King (Matthew 25:31-46)
II. Mark: Christ the Servant (Mark 10:35-45)
III. Luke: Christ, Son of Man (Luke 9:18-27)

I. MATTHEW: CHRIST THE KING (Matthew 25:31-46)

The Gospel of Matthew uses the term *kingdom* 56 times, the first and second instances being both John the Baptist and Jesus making the same declaration, "Repent: for the kingdom of heaven is at hand" (3:2; 4:17). If the Kingdom was at hand, then accessibility to it must have been forthcoming. The purpose of the Lord's earthly ministry was to restore to humanity what had been stolen by Satan in the Garden of Eden. Adam and Eve were originally given the earth to rule in God's behalf, and had been commanded to "have dominion" (Genesis 1:28). Psalm 115:16 declares God has given the earth "to the children of men." Earth was meant for people to rule. This was, and is, the eternal plan of God.

Jesus said of Himself, "For the Son of man is come to seek and to save that which was lost" (Luke 19:10). What was lost? Yes, it was men and women's souls, but it was much more. It was that lost dominion over the earth! Through Satan's deception, Adam forfeited his position of honor. Jesus told Peter (and every believer to follow) prophetically that He was giving back to humanity the keys to the Kingdom (Matthew 16:19). When He died on the cross, He descended into hell (Hades) and took the keys from Satan (Revelation 1:18). After resurrecting from the grave, He offered humanity the potential to rule again. He said, "All power is given unto me in heaven and in earth. Go ye therefore . . ." (Matthew 28:18, 19). Just after this Great Commission, He ascended back to heaven. That is where He has been until He returns in His glory, and thus we come to our present text.

A. Returning for His Kingdom (v. 31)

31. When the Son of man shall come in his glory, and all the holy angels with him, then shall he sit upon the throne of his glory.

Talk About It:
1. Why is Jesus Christ sometimes called "the Son of Man"?
2. How will Christ's second coming to earth differ from His first coming?

Several hundred years before Jesus ascended to glory, Daniel saw in a vision His arrival back there. Excerpts from Daniel 7:13, 14 paint the picture: "I saw . . . and, behold, one like the Son of man came with the clouds of heaven, and came to the Ancient of days. . . . And there was given him dominion, and glory, and a kingdom, that all people, nations, and languages, should serve him . . . and his kingdom . . . shall not be destroyed." Now, if Jesus is in heaven, whom did He leave in charge of the earth? None other than faithful believers who take up the Great Commission. The Kingdom is in the invisible realm, but it is to be manifest into the visible by servants who fulfill their commission. The full manifestation will not come until He returns, but by faithful obedience we can bring major aspects of the Kingdom into the visible realm.

Manifesting the Kingdom is possible through stewardship over what has been put in our hands. This was perfectly illustrated by the Lord when He gave the parable of the pounds (or *minas*) as told in Luke 19:11-27. The disciples were wondering when the Lord would restore the Kingdom. However, they had the wrong kingdom in mind. Jesus' purpose was not to restore the political/religious entity of the state of Israel, but something far greater. In response to their question, He gave them a simple lesson on stewardship. The nobleman in the parable is Jesus himself (the *far country* being the heavenly throne where He ascended). What the servants each did with the pound they were given was paramount in determining both their reward and how much of the Kingdom would be manifest from the invisible to the visible.

> "If Christ were coming again tomorrow, I would plant a tree today."
> —**Martin Luther**

B. Nations Judged for Their Stewardship (vv. 32, 33)

32. And before him shall be gathered all nations: and he shall separate them one from another, as a shepherd divideth his sheep from the goats:

33. And he shall set the sheep on his right hand, but the goats on the left.

Not only are individuals judged for their stewardship, but nations as well. Those with free access to the gospel (and the resources to spread the Word) will be judged with a far steeper judgment than poorer nations. A nation like the United States will be judged as far more responsible than a destitute country in Africa. Though by far the greatest missionary activity comes from the United States, have American Christians done enough, based on their vast resources? Only God is the judge.

The Kingdom is manifest through believers as they are energized and empowered by the Holy Spirit to be witnesses to "the uttermost part of the earth" (Acts 1:8). As we approach the end of the age, believers will be greatly empowered to demonstrate the Kingdom. This is indicated by the promise of the early and latter rains as seen in James 5:7, 8. The early rain of the Holy Spirit was seen in the first-century church. Soon to come, however, will be the latter rain of the Holy Spirit, where believers will be empowered to do "greater works"—in quantity, not quality— than those Jesus did (see John 14:12).

The judgment of nations will be a universal court. Peoples of the earth will be separated into two categories, much like a shepherd separates sheep and goats. Every nation will have heard the preaching of the "gospel of the kingdom" (Matthew 24:14), which means that everyone will have seen some manifestation of the Kingdom in their land. The Lord's judgment is a righteous one. No one will have the excuse of ignorance.

Talk About It:
How can the peoples of all nations and languages be divided into only two groups?

C. A Kingdom Prepared From the Foundation of the Earth (vv. 34-46)

(Matthew 25:37-40 is not included in the printed text.)

34. Then shall the King say unto them on his right hand, Come, ye blessed of my Father, inherit the kingdom prepared for you from the foundation of the world:

35. For I was an hungred, and ye gave me meat: I was thirsty, and ye gave me drink: I was a stranger, and ye took me in:

36. Naked, and ye clothed me: I was sick, and ye visited me: I was in prison, and ye came unto me.

41. Then shall he say also unto them on the left hand, Depart from me, ye cursed, into everlasting fire, prepared for the devil and his angels:

42. For I was an hungred, and ye gave me no meat: I was thirsty, and ye gave me no drink:

43. I was a stranger, and ye took me not in: naked, and ye clothed me not: sick, and in prison, and ye visited me not.

44. Then shall they also answer him, saying, Lord, when saw we thee an hungred, or athirst, or a stranger, or naked, or sick, or in prison, and did not minister unto thee?

45. Then shall he answer them, saying, Verily I say unto you, Inasmuch as ye did it not to one of the least of these, ye did it not to me.

46. And these shall go away into everlasting punishment: but the righteous into life eternal.

Even though the devil tricked Adam out of his rightful place of dominion, God's plan was never sidetracked. From the very foundation of the earth, God planned a kingdom where humanity and God would work and fellowship together. However, because man was given a free will, the chance had to be taken that he would fall—and fall he did. In His infinite knowledge, God knew exactly what would happen. So, after many millennia of humanity's failure and ultimate redemption through Christ's sacrifice, the Kingdom is still intact and strong. It is manifest in this age through believers by the power of the Spirit dwelling in them, and it will be fully visible when Christ returns in power.

In these verses we see that Gentiles are included by the mention of nations. "This kingdom Messiah is establishing will include the Gentiles, and not as a last-minute adjustment to God's plan but determined from the very foundation of the world. The messianic kingdom, therefore, was predetermined, before the world was put into operation, to be a place for the human race to experience the divine kingship of God's Anointed" (*Moody Gospel Commentary—Matthew*).

We further see here that the Jews, including the Lord's

Talk About It:
1. What are the "sheep" called, and what will they receive (v. 34)?
2. Whom does Jesus identify Himself with in this teaching (v. 40)? Why?
3. What are the "goats" called, and what will they receive (v. 41)?
4. Compare and contrast the fate of the blessed and the cursed (v. 46).

disciples, were too limited in their vision of the Kingdom. It was never meant to be the exclusive right of the Jews. This does not detract from the covenant with David, where his "Son" would rule over the earth. Israel will head the many nations, but all nations are included.

II. MARK: CHRIST THE SERVANT (Mark 10:35-45)

Mark wrote primarily to strengthen believers who were facing persecution and martyrdom (which was at the time under Nero). Readers could see that Jesus also suffered, but triumphed over that suffering and death as well. Mark wrote after the death of Peter and other eyewitnesses, thus proving a great encouragement to the next generations of believers. Both Matthew and Mark had firsthand knowledge of Jesus. Matthew was a disciple, while Mark likely witnessed much of Jesus' ministry in and around Jerusalem. His widowed mother's home was an early-church meeting place. Mark is also thought to have been the youth wearing a linen cloth at Jesus' arrest (Mark 14:51, 52). In chapter 10, Mark reveals what it means to be the Lord's servant—a theme in his book (see 9:35).

A. A Self-Centered Request (vv. 35-40)

35. And James and John, the sons of Zebedee, come unto him, saying, Master, we would that thou shouldest do for us whatsoever we shall desire.

36. And he said unto them, What would ye that I should do for you?

37. They said unto him, Grant unto us that we may sit, one on thy right hand, and the other on thy left hand, in thy glory.

38. But Jesus said unto them, Ye know not what ye ask: can ye drink of the cup that I drink of? and be baptized with the baptism that I am baptized with?

39. And they said unto him, We can. And Jesus said unto them, Ye shall indeed drink of the cup that I drink of; and with the baptism that I am baptized withal shall ye be baptized:

40. But to sit on my right hand and on my left hand is not mine to give; but it shall be given to them for whom it is prepared.

Though this appears to be purely the working of the two ambitious disciples, Matthew's account of the story indicates their mother was very much involved in the plot (Matthew 20:20). To ask to be seated at a monarch's right hand was to request the most prominent position in government. To be seated at the left hand ranked just below that. Jesus responded by questioning their ability to handle the tests that would come with such

Serving People

We find it encouraging to think of ourselves as God's servants. Who would not want to be a servant of the King? But when it comes to serving other people, we begin to question the consequences. We feel noble when serving God; we feel humble when serving people. Serving God receives a favorable response; serving people, especially those who cannot repay, has no visible benefit from anyone—except from God!
—**Charles Swindoll**

Talk About It:
1. Put James' and John's statement in verse 35 in your own words.

2. What was the motive behind the two disciples' request in verse 37?
3. Explain Jesus' use of the words *cup* and *baptism*.

> "Pride will push you to seek places you think you deserve rather than where God has chosen you to serve."
> —C. Gene Wilkes

Talk About It:
Explain the reaction of the other 10 disciples.

Talk About It:
1. In verse 42, how does Jesus describe the world's idea of authority?

positions. In their ignorance they answered "yes." This is hard for us to conceive, since Jesus had been giving constant reminders that He would face death shortly. By now the crowds had quit following, and the notion of a grand earthly kingdom was fading fast. Why, then, would these two make such an ambitious request? Did they still believe Jesus would defeat the Romans and restore Israel? To think such would require a great stretch of imagination. All we conclude is that all the disciples were blind to the meaning and fast approach of the Cross. Jesus was still the center of their imagination, and for that they can be commended. Their selfishness, however, cannot be so applauded. Also, we would have to conclude that if such a brash request were granted, there would eventually arise jealousy between the two brothers over the higher "right" position.

Jesus compared His coming suffering to drinking a cup and experiencing a baptism. Little did the disciples realize what it would cost to go through such horror. Ironically, they would themselves face the same tests. James was the first disciple to be martyred, and John would be greatly persecuted, as well as exiled to a deserted island.

B. Ten Angry Men (v. 41)

41. And when the ten heard it, they began to be much displeased with James and John.

Just how did the other 10 disciples hear about James and John's request? Were they in earshot? Or had the two been brash enough to make their plan known to them? Either way, it did not set well with the rest. Though not mentioned by name, their closest friend Peter probably led the verbal assault on the two brothers. "No doubt the men were unhappy because they had not thought of asking first!" (*The Bible Exposition Commentary*).

C. A Servant's Heart (vv. 42-44)

42. But Jesus called them to him, and saith unto them, Ye know that they which are accounted to rule over the Gentiles exercise lordship over them; and their great ones exercise authority upon them.

43. But so shall it not be among you: but whosoever will be great among you, shall be your minister:

44. And whosoever of you will be the chiefest, shall be servant of all.

Jesus is not seen in the Gospel of Matthew as a servant. In fact, the term is never used. However, the presentation of Jesus by Mark is that of a suffering servant. We see this first in Mark 9, where the disciples are arguing over who is the greatest among them. Jesus answers by saying, "If any man desire to be first, the same shall be last of all, and servant of all" (v. 35). In chapter 10 Jesus compares servanthood with greatness. Those who desire to be great must first be the servant of others.

All the disciples were guilty of choosing the wrong role models to follow. All around them were Roman officials, military officers, ranking priests at the Temple, and so on. These were worldly models who all loved position and authority. Jesus was telling the men to view greatness from an opposite perspective. True greatness is accomplished not by exercising lordship and authority over people, but rather by listening to them, being sensitive to their needs, and serving them. In other words, to be great, one must minister to others.

2. From the heavenly perspective, who is greatest, and why?

D. Jesus, the Example of Servanthood (v. 45)

45. For even the Son of man came not to be ministered unto, but to minister, and to give his life a ransom for many.

Jesus had already said many times that He would have to die, and that His death would be a sacrificial one (for people's sins). Here He showed the disciples that He did not come to earth to *demand* from His followers, but rather to *minister* to them. Verse 45 is the dividing point for the Gospel of Mark. Up to this point the book has emphasized Christ's servanthood. For the remainder, Mark concentrates on the account of His death and resurrection. The word *ransom* indicates an amount of money paid to free slaves or hostages. It is found only two other times in the New Testament (Matthew 20:28; 1 Timothy 2:6). The Lord's life was given for others so they would not have to die.

Talk About It: How did Jesus describe His earthly mission?

III. LUKE: CHRIST, SON OF MAN (Luke 9:18-27)

Luke portrays Jesus as the full-packaged answer to people's problems. He is the promised Messiah, the Son of God, the Servant, and the Lord who sits at God's right hand. Luke emphasizes the availability of this redeeming Lord to everyone, Gentile and Jew alike.

"Service must be preceded by surrender. Somewhere between salvation and maturity in Christ our prayers should turn from 'give me' to 'use me.' Until then, we are quite useless to God."

—Ron Dicianni

A. A Question Posed (vv. 18, 19)

18. And it came to pass, as he was alone praying, his disciples were with him: and he asked them, saying, Whom say the people that I am?

19. They answering said, John the Baptist; but some say, Elias; and others say, that one of the old prophets is risen again.

In Mark's Gospel we identified a turning point. Our text here also gives the turning point for Luke's Gospel. Until now Luke has been recording the reactions of people to Jesus' message and miracles, as well as their questions about His identity. Now we see that the

Talk About It:
1. Why do you suppose Jesus asked His disciples the question in verse 18?
2. Name some common ideas about Jesus' identity.

logical deduction to all that has happened thus far is proclaimed by Peter—Jesus is the Christ, the promised Messiah.

The setting for this passage is one of the moments when Jesus escaped from the crowds to be alone. He likely would have enjoyed total solitude in order to commune with the Father, but the disciples "joined Him" (v. 18, *NKJV*). Why was Jesus praying? Because His entire ministry was carried out as a human under the guidance of the Holy Spirit. He had laid down His deity in order to live totally as a man. Had He done all that He did as God, His ministry would not be miraculous at all; but carrying it out as a man led by the Spirit, we can identify with and reach for the same heights.

The initial reaction to Jesus' question brought the typical responses. Instead of answering from the heart, the disciples answered what they heard others say. Perhaps they were wondering why He would pose such a question. "If any of us asked our friends what people were saying about us, it would be an evidence of pride, but not so with Jesus Christ. People had better know who He is, because what we think about Jesus determines our eternal destiny. It is impossible to be wrong about Jesus and right with God" (*The Bible Exposition Commentary*).

"He was God and man in one person, that God and man might be happy together again."
—**George Whitefield**

B. The Question Posed Again (v. 20)
20. He said unto them, But whom say ye that I am? Peter answering said, The Christ of God.

As He began His ministry, Jesus had prayed all night in choosing His disciples (see Luke 6:12, 13). Perhaps now He had foreseen through prayer that it was time for them to come to a clear understanding of who He was. They must express what they felt, not what others said. There is power in speaking. Thoughts do not become embedded in the will until they are spoken. There were plenty of itinerant rabbis who went about teaching, and these had disciples who followed them. Though Jesus had already performed great miracles at this time, still the disciples needed to see themselves as following Someone greater than ever walked the earth before. If He was not the Messiah, then they were simply following some great miracle-working teacher. But if He was the Messiah, then their destinies, as well as the destiny of all humanity to follow, was at stake.

When Jesus used the word *ye,* it was in the plural form. Though it would be Peter who spoke, he was speaking for all. Peter "did not understand the exact nature of Jesus' ministry, but he knew one fact for sure—Jesus was the Messiah, the Christ" (*Life Application Bible Commentary*). The word *Christ* in Greek (*Messiah* in Hebrew) means "the Anointed One," indicating the central figure whom all of the Old Testament had anticipated.

C. A Warning Issued (vv. 21, 22)

21. And he straitly charged them, and commanded them to tell no man that thing;

22. Saying, The Son of man must suffer many things, and be rejected of the elders and chief priests and scribes, and be slain, and be raised the third day.

Jesus knew the true role of the Messiah was far different from that which the people believed. Every Jew had the expectation that the Messiah would be a political leader who would free Israel from the bonds of the Romans. As said in our earlier discussions on Matthew, they simply had the wrong kingdom in mind. Jesus was not so interested in Israel as He was in a universal kingdom, though Israel will ultimately be at the center of it. Also, the people would not comprehend the element of suffering that the Messiah would have to go through, even though many Old Testament prophecies indicated such (see Isaiah 53). The disciples themselves would have to be reoriented as events moved toward the Cross. Even though history shows they still were unprepared for what happened at Calvary, can you imagine their reactions had they not had some warning? Likely, none would have stayed in Jerusalem. None would have been near when the Resurrection occurred. Thus, the Lord's messiahship could not be openly proclaimed until His true nature and path of suffering was revealed.

Talk About It:
1. Why did Jesus issue the charge to "not to tell this to anyone" (v. 21, *NIV*)?
2. How specifically did Jesus describe His upcoming suffering, and why?

D. Self-Denial Required (vv. 23-26)

23. And he said to them all, If any man will come after me, let him deny himself, and take up his cross daily, and follow me.

24. For whosoever will save his life shall lose it: but whosoever will lose his life for my sake, the same shall save it.

25. For what is a man advantaged, if he gain the whole world, and lose himself, or be cast away?

26. For whosoever shall be ashamed of me and of my words, of him shall the Son of man be ashamed, when he shall come in his own glory, and in his Father's, and of the holy angels.

If Jesus was going to have to die through a cruel crucifixion, then His followers would have to be prepared for the same. To "take up" one's cross meant a march toward death. Every disciple understood the cross to be the cruelest form of execution. They had seen it used many times under the oppressive Roman rule. They heretofore had seen themselves as playing glorious roles in a grand kingdom Jesus would establish after defeating the Romans. They perhaps even envisioned themselves as ranking officers, ready to carry out military exploits in

Talk About It:
1. According to verse 23, what three things must Christ's followers do, and what do they mean?
2. In what sense must every Christian "lose his life"?

3. How do we show we are not ashamed of Christ and His words?

"There are no crown-wearers in heaven who were not cross-bearers here below."
—**Charles Spurgeon**

Talk About It:
What is the kingdom of God, and when does a person receive it?

His behalf. Having seen the miracles He had performed, they could easily picture Him empowering them to do great exploits. What they didn't understand was they would have to humble themselves with the same humility that He expressed. They would have to be willing to die to themselves. Jesus did add the hope of a future glory, indicating there would be a resurrection. The disciples were perplexed by such words. Only later as events played out would they understand the implications of what Jesus was now saying.

This was the first time in Luke's Gospel that Jesus began to impress on the disciples what would take place. From then on He taught clearly and specifically what they could expect to happen. He would not be a conquering Savior until He had first been a suffering One.

E. Seeing Into the Kingdom (v. 27)

27. But I tell you of a truth, there be some standing here, which shall not taste of death, till they see the kingdom of God.

Jesus said some of the disciples would not die until they had seen a manifestation of the Kingdom. This would occur just eight days later when Jesus took Peter, James and John up on the mountain and was transfigured (vv. 28-36). The three disciples were privileged to see marvelously into another realm where Jesus was in His resplendent glory. He became like lightning, shining white, and what had been invisible was now visible. Moses represented the Law, while Elijah represented the Prophets. The Law and the Prophets were fulfilled as Jesus came visibly in His kingdom.

CONCLUSION

The Jews expected the Messiah to restore the kingdom of Israel. After all, the rule of David's line was to be forever. Thus, throughout His earthly ministry Jesus was plagued with the question, "When will You restore the Kingdom?" Once, Jesus answered this question by saying, "The kingdom of God is within you" (Luke 17:21).

Just before His ascension, the disciples again asked when a kingdom would be restored to Israel (Acts 1:6). They still didn't grasp that the Kingdom was far more than one nation's destiny. Jesus answered, "It is not for you to know the times or the seasons, which the Father hath put in his own power. But ye shall receive power, after that the Holy Ghost is come upon you: and ye shall be witnesses unto me . . ." (vv. 7, 8).

Like the disciples, theologians have been puzzled through the centuries as to what form the Kingdom has been established on the earth, and how much is yet to be seen when

Jesus returns. Perhaps we have all missed the point. Jesus gave a simple answer. He was sending Someone to empower believers to bring the Kingdom into manifestation in His absence. How much of the Kingdom we see on the earth right now is directly dependent on how much we allow the Holy Spirit's power to work through us.

GOLDEN TEXT CHALLENGE

"THERE CAME A VOICE FROM HEAVEN, SAYING, THOU ART MY BELOVED SON, IN WHOM I AM WELL PLEASED" (Mark 1:11).

In the first verse of Mark's Gospel, he calls Jesus Christ "the Son of God." Ten verses later, after John baptizes Jesus, God the Father declares, "You are My beloved Son, in whom I am well pleased."

In this baptism scene, God the Holy Spirit likewise authenticated Jesus' identity by "descending upon Him like a dove" (v. 10, *NKJV*). Immediately afterward, the Holy Spirit led Jesus into the wilderness.

Through the Spirit's inspiration, the synoptic writers each painted a portrait of God's Son from a different angle. Matthew presented Him as the King of kings; Mark portrayed Him as the Suffering Servant; Luke depicted Him as the perfect Man—a sinless Savior. He is Jesus Christ, the Son of God.

Daily Devotions:
M. Suffering Servant
   Isaiah 53:1-8
T. Son of Man
   Daniel 7:9-14
W. Coming King
   Zechariah 9:9-12
T. Beloved Servant
   Matthew 12:14-21
F. Holy One of God
   Mark 1:23-28
S. Mighty Prophet
   Luke 24:18-27

Writings of John
(Gospel of John and 1, 2 and 3 John)

John 1:1-14; 1 John 1:1-7; 2 John 1-13; 3 John 1-14

Unit Theme:
Message of the New Testament

Central Truth:
The life and teachings of Christ are foundational for Christian living.

Focus:
Discover and apply truths about Christ and Christian living in John's writings.

Context:
An overview of John's Gospel and his three epistles

Golden Text:
"These are written, that ye might believe that Jesus is the Christ, the Son of God; and that believing ye might have life through his name" (John 20:31).

Study Outline:
I. Gospel: The Son of God
   (John 1:1-14)
II. Exhortations for Christian Living
   (1 John 1:1-7)
III. Fellowship in Christ
   (2 John 1-13; 3 John 1-14)

INTRODUCTION

The Gospel of John states its purpose more clearly than any other book of the Bible. John writes, "But these are written, that ye might believe that Jesus is the Christ, the Son of God; and that believing ye might have life through his name" (20:31). Most scholars believe this Gospel letter was written between A.D. 85 and 95, well after the three synoptic Gospels had been in circulation for years. John never intended to pen another biography of the Lord's life and ministry. Instead, he wrote to show exactly who Jesus was, and is—the Son of God. Every chapter and verse is a presentation of His deity. The case is laid out much like a lawyer would present in a courtroom, using signs and statements to verify Jesus' identity.

Matthew focused on a Jewish audience, while Mark wrote for a busy Roman world, and Luke beautifully penned a long letter for the reflective Greek mind. So, who was John's intended audience? His letter is addressed to all—Jews and Gentiles alike. He frequently interprets Jewish words and customs to help Gentile readers, and he emphasizes to Jews that Jesus was the fulfillment of Old Testament prophecies, as well as the symbolic types given in the Old Testament.

More than anything else, John wanted people to see Jesus as the answer to their needs. He is the Son of God, and all who commit themselves to Him will be given eternal life. In chapter 1, John identifies seven names and titles that portray Jesus as eternal God come in the flesh: the Word (vv. 1-3, 14), the Light (vv. 4-13), the Son of God (vv. 15-28, 34, 49), the Lamb of God (vv. 29-36), the Messiah (vv. 37-42), the King of Israel (vv. 43-49), and the Son of Man (vv. 50, 51). No wonder this is the first place any potential new believer should start his journey in studying the Bible. John lays out all that is necessary to help one believe on the Son and find life.

The three letters of John were written in direct response to problems arising in churches. By the latter decades of the first century, false teachers and false doctrines were quickly spreading in various churches, especially in Asia. Gnosticism would later become a full-blown heretical theological system, but was now in its early stages, basically teaching that all matter is evil, while all things spiritual are good. Thus, if God is truly good, He could not have created the physical universe.

I. GOSPEL: THE SON OF GOD (John 1:1-14)

A. The Living Word (vv. 1-5)

1. In the beginning was the Word, and the Word was with God, and the Word was God.

2. The same was in the beginning with God.

3. All things were made by him; and without him was not any thing made that was made.

4. In him was life; and the life was the light of men.

5. And the light shineth in darkness; and the darkness comprehended it not.

There is a great similarity between the first verses of Genesis and the first verses of John. One begins the story of the old covenant, while the other begins the story of the new covenant. Genesis starts with the moment of Creation and moves toward the creation of humanity. John starts with creation of "all things" and looks back at eternity past to see who was the Creator.

The *Word* that John speaks of is Jesus. He was with God, meaning a direct relationship of equality with His Father. "The Word was of the very quality of God, while still retaining His personal distinction from the Father" (*The Nelson Study Bible*). John 1:1 is possibly the strongest assertion of the deity of Christ in the New Testament. However, we must understand that He is not a God separate from the Father. Such a view would be polytheistic.

Verses 1 and 2 tell us that Jesus has always existed. He is God, and was with God. Verse 3 identifies Him as the creative force behind all things that have come into being. Paul reiterates this when he says, "For by him were all things created, that are in heaven, and that are in earth, visible and invisible, whether they be thrones, or dominions, or principalities, or powers: all things were created by him, and for him" (Colossians 1:16). John 1:4 speaks of Him as creating not only things, but life. Life is the very theme of John's Gospel, being used 36 times. All the essentials for life were also created by Him—light, air, water and food. Literally, everything that exists traces its source to Jesus.

One way to illustrate the Trinity is to see the Father as the sun, Jesus as the light the sun emits, and the Holy Spirit as the warmth produced by the sun. A similar metaphor is the following: The Father compares to the heat rays of the sun—His love can be felt but not seen. The Son compares to the light rays of the sun—these are what make the sun visible. The Holy Spirit corresponds to the chemical action that is produced by the sun—He is the power of the sun. Neither the heat, light, nor chemical action is a full explanation of the sun. It takes all three. In the same sense, it takes the Father, the Son, and the Holy

Talk About It:
1. Why is Jesus Christ called "the Word"?
2. How was Jesus involved with the creation of the world?
3. What is the *darkness* (v. 5), and what can it not do? Why not?

"Whoever thinks God is most freely revealed in the impersonal movements of the stellar galaxies must reckon yet with Jesus Christ as the incarnation of righteousness, goodness and love, and with the well-nigh irresistible impression that the eternal God is best seen in His personality and life."
—Carl F.H. Henry

Spirit to complete the triune God. John's Gospel was written to show the role of the Son in the cosmic scheme of eternity.

B. John the Baptist (vv. 6-8)

6. There was a man sent from God, whose name was John.

7. The same came for a witness, to bear witness of the Light, that all men through him might believe.

8. He was not that Light, but was sent to bear witness of that Light.

The coming of one who would herald the appearance of the Messiah had been predicted by Old Testament prophets. Isaiah spoke of him: "The voice of him that crieth in the wilderness, Prepare ye the way of the Lord, make straight in the desert a highway for our God" (Isaiah 40:3). Malachi said that this forerunner would have the character of Elijah (Malachi 4:5, 6). He would turn the hearts of the people, or prepare them, for the coming of the Messiah. If we trace the people who heard and believed the message of repentance that John the Baptist preached, we see it was generally those people who ultimately received Jesus. Those who refused John hated Jesus. We know that John was full of the Holy Spirit before his birth (Luke 1:15), and that the angel confirmed to Zacharias that this child would fulfill the prophecy of Malachi (v. 17).

We might ask why John the apostle would jump from the lofty heights of describing the Word to suddenly stating simply that a man was sent from God named John [the Baptist]. It appears to be a radical change of thought. "Actually, the startling shift in time dramatically illustrates the eternal light suddenly shining in the darkness" (*Life Application Commentary*). Also, some think the mention of John here was to show that he was not the Messiah, nor had illusions of such. The fact was, however, that John made many disciples, and some of those missed the Messiah. Acts 19:1-6 records an incident where Paul met a pocket of such disciples in Ephesus who had not heard of Christ. To their credit, they did believe when Paul witnessed to them, they were baptized, and they received the Holy Spirit right then and there. One commentator said, "It is not improbable that there might have been many others who adhered to John, and perhaps many who supposed that he was the Messiah. On these accounts it was important for the evangelist to show that John 'was not the Christ,' and . . . was an important 'witness' to prove that Jesus of Nazareth was the Christ" (*Barnes' Notes*).

C. The Light (vv. 9-11)

9. That was the true Light, which lighteth every man that cometh into the world.

Talk About It:
1. Describe the ministry of John the Baptist.
2. How are all believers to be like John?

End-Time Anointing
John the Baptist carried an "Elijah" anointing. Malachi had said, "Behold, I will send you Elijah the prophet before the coming of the great and dreadful day of the Lord" (Malachi 4:5, *NKJV*). The angel told Zacharias that his son, John, would "turn many of the children of Israel to the Lord their God. He will also go before Him in the spirit and power of Elijah" (Luke 1:15-17, *NKJV*).
Jesus said, "Elijah is coming first and will restore all things. But I say to you that Elijah has come already" (Matthew 17:11, 12, *NKJV*). John the Baptist had already been beheaded at this

10. He was in the world, and the world was made by him, and the world knew him not.

11. He came unto his own, and his own received him not.

The first creative act of Genesis was the production of light, for without light there can be no life. There are four things necessary for life—light, air, water and food. Without light, none of the others matter. Jesus is the source of all light. Throughout John's Gospel we see the conflict between light and darkness. When Lucifer was cast out of heaven (Isaiah 14:12), he landed on "the ground"—that is, earth. Yet, this was before the Genesis story of man's creation began. Thus, Satan lived in darkness on the earth. He was already here when Adam was placed in the Garden of Eden. He didn't have to come from elsewhere. The invasion of light by Jesus coming to earth set the stage for the great battle between light and darkness.

It is interesting that John does not identify Jesus as the Light until verse 17, but rather first describes His nature. That nature is one of light replacing darkness everywhere it shines. John uses the term *light* 24 times. Verse 9 says the Light gives light to every person on earth—Jew and Gentile alike. This indicates that God's love and plan of redemption is for everyone. The Jews were looking for a nationalistic leader, but God sent instead a Savior for the entire world. Sadly, the nation that was supposed to be the herald of the Light was the very people who refused the Light. "In spite of the rejection described here, John steers clear of passing sentence on the world. Instead, he turns our attention on those who did welcome Christ in sincere faith" (*Life Application Commentary*).

D. Believers (vv. 12, 13)

12. But as many as received him, to them gave he power to become the sons of God, even to them that believe on his name:

13. Which were born, not of blood, nor of the will of the flesh, nor of the will of man, but of God.

The word *receive* means "to accept with favor." It implies a welcoming heart. Initially Jesus was received by the masses, but by the time He began His march toward Calvary, nearly everyone had forsaken Him. "Believe on his name" occurs three times in John. It was not His name specifically, but what His name stood for that was important. Those who did believe accepted Him as the Christ, the Anointed One of God. John points out great extremes, such as the vast difference between light and darkness. The same case is made between rejection and reception. Those who received Jesus were given the power to become children of God. The word *become* "indicates clearly that people are not the spiritual children of God by natural

time. He was the one Jesus referred to as "has come already." Malachi said Elijah will appear before the "great and dreadful day of the Lord." This indicates that as we approach the end of the age, someone, or more likely a great group of believers, will carry a powerful anointing to preach and prepare the earth for the second coming of Christ.

Talk About It:
1. Describe the irony found in verse 10.
2. Who were Jesus' "own" people, and why did they not receive Him?

Talk About It:
Describe the authority Christ gives to those who receive Him.

birth, for we cannot become what we already are" (*Zondervan NIV Bible Commentary*). Instead, there is a change in nature, a new relationship that is spiritual in nature, not biological.

E. The Word Made Flesh (v. 14)

14. And the Word was made flesh, and dwelt among us, (and we beheld his glory, the glory as of the only begotten of the Father,) full of grace and truth.

Talk About It:
1. Why did the Word take on human flesh?
2. What is Jesus "full of," and why is this important?

Jesus laid aside His attributes of deity to become a man—*flesh.* He came to dwell among those very beings He had created, to walk as they walked, live as they lived, and restore them to the life that had been planned for them. John returns to the term he used at the beginning of the letter—*the Word.* A heresy of the first century said Jesus did not truly become human, but only seemed human. John refutes this, and does so again in 1 John 4:3, where he says, "And every spirit that confesseth not that Jesus Christ is come in the flesh is not of God: and this is that spirit of antichrist, whereof ye have heard that it should come; and even now already is it in the world." Jesus was not part man and part God; rather, He came fully as man and fully as God. He laid aside His powers of deity. He said He could only do what He saw the Father doing (John 5:19). The power to do these things came by the fact that He was full of the Holy Spirit (Luke 4:1).

II. EXHORTATIONS FOR CHRISTIAN LIVING (1 John 1:1-7)

A. Fellowship With the Word of Life (vv. 1-3)

1. That which was from the beginning, which we have heard, which we have seen with our eyes, which we have looked upon, and our hands have handled, of the Word of life;

2. (For the life was manifested, and we have seen it, and bear witness, and shew unto you that eternal life, which was with the Father, and was manifested unto us;)

3. That which we have seen and heard declare we unto you, that ye also may have fellowship with us: and truly our fellowship is with the Father, and with his Son Jesus Christ.

Talk About It:
1. What qualified John to testify about Jesus Christ?
2. According to verse 3, why did John *declare* this message?

John began his Gospel letter by describing the Word. Here he does the same, but concentrates on the personal relationship that he and the other apostles had with the Lord. No doubt the memory of those days of walking with Jesus on earth were burned into his mind, though he also recognized there is continued fellowship with the Lord by the Holy Spirit dwelling in the believer. The eternal Son of God, who had lived in intimate fellowship with the eternal Father, had taken on the form of humanity and walked with John and the others. John remains awestruck at what he experienced, but he is also aware that this special relationship gives him authority to speak to believers who never saw the Lord in physical person. Though he humbly doesn't mention it, John was one of the three disciples who had an even more personal friendship. John was known as "the disciple whom Jesus loved" (John 21:20). "Word of Life" (1 John 1:1) is used frequently today, especially as names for churches. It describes "the Son of God as the personal expression of the invisible God and the giver of divine, eternal life to the believers" (*Life Application Commentary*).

The word *manifest* (v. 2) means "to make apparent, uncover" or simply "to bring from the invisible to the visible." God was made manifest to man as He came to earth as the Son—Jesus Christ. When Jesus entered into time, His fellowship with the Father did also. So, to hear Jesus speak was to hear direct communication from the eternal God to His Son. The word *life* (v. 2) is the Greek word *zoe*, which means "divine, eternal life from God." In other words, Jesus is the One who is pure life from God, and John and the other disciples witnessed this life in person. John's was no second-hand religious experience. He knew Jesus face-to-face.

Does this mean that later believers are at a disadvantage? Certainly not. Even Jesus himself said, "It is to your advantage that I go away; for if I do not go away, the Helper will not come to you" (John 16:7, *NKJV*). It was not the physical presence of Jesus that was so important, but the relationship through the Holy Spirit. That relationship began by putting complete trust in Jesus. It was, however, during the time of the Lord's physical presence on earth that the disciples were introduced to the Father and initiated into fellowship. The Greek word used here for *fellowship* is *koinonia,* which means a living relationship and partnership, both spiritual and eternal. John recorded the words of Jesus in his Gospel: "And this is eternal life, that they may know You, the only true God, and Jesus Christ whom You have sent" (17:3, *NKJV*). Knowing the Son means knowing the Father. The apostles had been the first to experience this relationship, and were also commissioned to preach the gospel. We are to follow their example.

> "A Christian is not one who is *seeking* God's favor and forgiveness—he is one who has *found* them."
>
> —T. Roland Phillips

B. Fellowship With One Another (vv. 4-7)

4. And these things write we unto you, that your joy may be full.

5. This then is the message which we have heard of him, and declare unto you, that God is light, and in him is no darkness at all.

6. If we say that we have fellowship with him, and walk in darkness, we lie, and do not the truth:

7. But if we walk in the light, as he is in the light, we have

fellowship one with another, and the blood of Jesus Christ his Son cleanseth us from all sin.

There can be no real joy unless one is in proper relationship with God and others. Walking in the light brings joy because Jesus cleanses us from sin. As we walk in the light of Jesus' love, fellowship with the Father and other believers is made available to us. The word *fellowship* means "to have in common." Sinners have nothing in common with God, but by believing on Jesus, we become members of God's family. We become "partakers of the divine nature, having escaped the corruption that is in the world through lust" (2 Peter 1:4). The word for *partaker* is the same word used here for *fellowship.* In other words, we now have a way of relating to the Father—that way being through His Son Jesus, who came to earth as a human and gave Himself as a sacrifice to bring restoration of humanity back to the Father. In other words, "Jesus Christ took on Himself the nature of man that by faith we may receive the very nature of God!" (*The Bible Exposition Commentary*). John was frustrated because false ideas and doctrines (which were lies about the nature of God) were infiltrating churches. If believers were deceived, then they would not be able to maintain a unity of faith, and thus lose fellowship.

III. FELLOWSHIP IN CHRIST (2 John 1-13; 3 John 1-14)
A. Beware of Deceivers (2 John 1-13)

(2 John 1-6, 12, 13 is not included in the printed text.)

7. For many deceivers are entered into the world, who confess not that Jesus Christ is come in the flesh. This is a deceiver and an antichrist.

8. Look to yourselves, that we lose not those things which we have wrought, but that we receive a full reward.

9. Whosoever transgresseth, and abideth not in the doctrine of Christ, hath not God. He that abideth in the doctrine of Christ, he hath both the Father and the Son.

10. If there come any unto you, and bring not this doctrine, receive him not into your house, neither bid him God speed:

11. For he that biddeth him God speed is partaker of his evil deeds.

All three of John's letters were corrective in nature. This second letter was addressed to the "elect lady and her children" (v. 1). This was either a figurative name for a church body or a specific person. Most likely it was a group of believers dealing with false doctrines. Like Paul's letters, John constantly had to deal with some sort of schism. The question at stake here was the identity and nature of Jesus. A heresy called *Docetism* was teaching that Christ did not actually come in the flesh—that is,

---

Talk About It:
1. What makes a person's joy *full,* or complete?
2. Explain the lie mentioned in verse 6.
3. What are the benefits of walking "in the light" (v. 7)?

"God calls us not to solitary sainthood but to fellowship in a company of committed men."
—David Schuller

---

abideth in (v. 9)—continue in

Talk About It:
1. What brought John "great joy" (v. 4, *NIV*)? Why? Is there anyone who brings you such joy for a similar reason?

Writings of John

He didn't have a real human body, but only had the appearance of such. Thus, He really didn't die on the cross for people's sins. John was adamant for the truth. After all, he had been witness to the Lord's life. He saw Him in the flesh. He lived with Him, talked and ate with Him—and even watched Him die on the cross!

To deny the Incarnation is to deny God's plan of redemption. Those who promote such heresy are not Christian, but rather are antichrists. For a believer to become deceived by such false doctrine makes him liable to lose "a full reward" from God (v. 8). At Christ's return, John's readers hoped to receive "full and complete salvation, but there was no absolute guarantee of their reward. Therefore, they must guard themselves against the dangerous teaching held by false teachers, lest the gift of eternal life be lost," wrote French Arrington. To fall into the trap of false doctrine leaves one open to further works of the devil, which then leads to complete deception—and even the loss of heaven.

False teaching is just as big a problem today as it was in the first century. John viewed this as a serious threat to the church. We presently see so much of it that we are numbed by it and turn the other way. However, we should realize the danger it poses, and how easily it can infiltrate the lives of the most sincere believers. It is so dangerous that John said welcoming a false teacher into one's home brings condemnation unto that home.

B. Walk in Truth (3 John 1-14)

(3 John 1, 5-8, 12-14 is not included in the printed text.)

2. Beloved, I wish above all things that thou mayest prosper and be in health, even as thy soul prospereth.

3. For I rejoiced greatly, when the brethren came and testified of the truth that is in thee, even as thou walkest in the truth.

4. I have no greater joy than to hear that my children walk in truth.

9. I wrote unto the church: but Diotrephes, who loveth to have the preeminence among them, receiveth us not.

10. Wherefore, if I come, I will remember his deeds which he doeth, prating against us with malicious words: and not content therewith, neither doth he himself receive the brethren, and forbiddeth them that would, and casteth them out of the church.

11. Beloved, follow not that which is evil, but that which is good. He that doeth good is of God: but he that doeth evil hath not seen God.

This third letter of John was addressed to a faithful church member named Gaius. This giving man had opened his home

---

2. How must Christians "walk" (v. 6)? Why is this critical?

3. How do we know if a teacher is a "deceiver" (v. 7)?

4. What must believers *continue in*, and why (vv. 8, 9)?

"Our Lord told His disciples that love and obedience are organically united. The final test of love is obedience."
—A.W. Tozer

after a godly sort (v. 6)—"in a manner worthy of God" (*NIV*)

prating (v. 10)—raising false accusations

Talk About It:
1. What was the condition of Gaius' soul (v. 2)? How did John know this (v. 3)?
2. What spiritual gift did Gaius have, and how was he using it (vv. 5-8)?
3. How do we know if someone is "of God" (v. 11)?

many times to itinerant preachers and teachers. Such people were the means of the day for spreading the gospel message to various congregations.

John's third letter had two purposes. The first was a commendation to Gaius for his hospitality. The various teachers had nothing but good things to say about his generosity. Likely, too, Gaius was an example of what the writer of Hebrews exhorts: "Be not forgetful to entertain strangers: for thereby some have entertained angels unawares" (13:2). John wished for Gaius both physical and spiritual prosperity, because he walked in truth. He was humble, giving, and a lover of all that was right. The truth he walked in was the "body of truth given to the church through the apostles and the prophets, that is, the Scripture" (*Nelson Study Bible*).

The second purpose of the letter was a warning against a power-hungry leader named Diotrephes. This individual had asserted control over a local congregation, refusing to let legitimate traveling teachers minister. "His love of power and authority has led him not only to defy the authority of the elder but also to convince others to follow his defiance or be excommunicated" (*Life Application Commentary*). John was encouraging Gaius to not be influenced by such a selfish example. It appears that John was planning to come himself and deal with Diotrephes. Like Paul, he was willing to use his apostolic authority when required. Paul made similar threats in 2 Corinthians 10:2 and 13:1, 2.

"Of two evils, choose neither."
—Charles Spurgeon

CONCLUSION

If you will read John's Gospel and his three epistles together, you will see that John was passionate about the truth. In John 14:6, he quoted Jesus' self-description as "the way, the truth, and the life." In 1 John 3:19, he said "we are of the truth"; in 2 John 2, he said the truth "dwelleth in us, and shall be with us for ever"; in 3 John 4, he said his greatest joy was hearing that his converts "walk in truth."

In our contemporary society which argues that there is no definite standard of truth, we must hold on to truth, first by believing Jesus is *the Truth* and committing our lives to Him. Then we will be people *of the truth*, God's truth will *dwell in us*, and we will be able to help others *walk in truth*.

GOLDEN TEXT CHALLENGE

"THESE ARE WRITTEN, THAT YE MIGHT BELIEVE THAT JESUS IS THE CHRIST, THE SON OF GOD; AND THAT BELIEVING YE MIGHT HAVE LIFE THROUGH HIS NAME" (John 20:31).

To be true New Testament believers, we must press what

we believe into experience; otherwise, we don't really believe it. John could testify to a personal eyewitness relationship with Christ. He had experienced the Lord. His relationship was not secondhand, nor wishful thinking. He and the other disciples had lived with Christ for three years. They had been personal witnesses to all He did.

So what is your experience? Do you know with certainty that Jesus lives in you? Have you heard Him speak to you? Do you have fellowship with Him? A living faith is one of continual relationship. We cannot let ourselves be content to hear about the experiences of others. We must experience Jesus for ourselves.

Daily Devotions:
M. Faith Assures Success
2 Chronicles 20:15-20
T. Faith Brings Triumph
Job 19:23-27
W. Faith Dismisses Fear
Psalm 118:1-8
T. Faith Secures Salvation
John 3:14-18
F. Faith Comes From God's Word
Romans 10:13-17
S. Faith Provides Defense
Ephesians 6:13-18

Expansion of the Church (Acts of the Apostles)

Acts 2:1-47; 8:1-8; 13:1-52; 28:16-31

Unit Theme:
Message of the New Testament

Central Truth:
The church began and grows through the power of the Holy Spirit.

Focus:
Explore the expansion of the church in the Book of Acts and implement Biblical patterns of church growth.

Context:
Luke wrote the Book of Acts around A.D. 61 or 62.

Golden Text:
"Ye shall receive power, after that the Holy Ghost is come upon you: and ye shall be witnesses unto me both in Jerusalem, and in all Judaea, and in Samaria, and unto the uttermost part of the earth" (Acts 1:8).

Study Outline:
I. Inauguration of the Church
(Acts 2:1-4, 14-18, 37-47)
II. Extension of the Church
(Acts 8:1-8)
III. Into All the World
(Acts 13:1-5; 28:16, 30, 31)

INTRODUCTION

The Book of Acts is the story of the birth and development of the church, the background for all the New Testament epistles. It is Volume 2 of Luke's writing to an unknown individual named Theophilus. This man was possibly a Roman official, his name meaning "friend of God." After a proper salutation to his friend, Luke picks up the story where His Gospel letter left off, and moves quickly to the Lord's ascension back to heaven. One could begin reading Acts after any of the Gospel letters and not feel lost. However, to jump from the Gospels to any other New Testament letter would be confusing. Acts bridges the gap between the life and ministry of Christ and the growth of the church through the first century.

Acts is primarily a historical narrative, but it also provides the framework for much of Christian theology and doctrine. Our faith rests on the facts of Jesus' life—His death, resurrection, and sending of the Holy Spirit. Those facts are then manifest in experiences and events. The growth of the church was directly based on the resurrection of Jesus from the grave, and the empowerment of believers by the Holy Spirit to proclaim this message. Jesus was no dead revolutionary. He was a living Savior who could turn everything in life upside down.

Though it is titled "The Acts of the Apostles," this is really the story of the work of the Holy Spirit in and through the church. The Gospels record what Jesus did while on earth, while Acts tells us what He continued to do through the Spirit. Chapter 1 wraps up all the "old business" to get the believers ready for Pentecost. It summarizes what happened during the 40 days of appearances the believers had with the risen Lord, His ascension, and then the waiting in the Upper Room. Then—all heaven breaks loose with chapter 2.

I. INAUGURATION OF THE CHURCH
(Acts 2:1-4, 14-18, 37-47)

A. Birth of the Church (vv. 1-4)

1. And when the day of Pentecost was fully come, they were all with one accord in one place.

2. And suddenly there came a sound from heaven as of a rushing mighty wind, and it filled all the house where they were sitting.

3. And there appeared unto them cloven tongues like as of fire, and it sat upon each of them.

cloven (v. 3)—
divided into parts

4. And they were all filled with the Holy Ghost, and began to speak with other tongues, as the Spirit gave them utterance.

Like he had been during the Lord's ministry, Peter was still the leader of the disciples at the beginning of Acts. After a disastrous denial of Jesus at the Crucifixion, he was broken by his personal failure. However, during the days after the Resurrection, Jesus reaffirmed the fisherman. By the time of the waiting in the Upper Room, Peter had regained a confidence, but this time not in himself but rather in the Lord.

Talk About It:
1. What is the significance of the word *one* being used twice in verse 1?
2. What does "gave them utterance" mean?

Pentecost was one of three major festivals that brought Jews to Jerusalem. Derived from the Greek word for *fifty*, it occurred 50 days after the Day of Firstfruits. The Day of Firstfruits always took place on the Sabbath following Passover, so Pentecost (50 days later) always occurred on a Sunday, the first day of the week. Thus, the birth of the church occurred on a Sunday, and this is one reason Christians through the centuries have worshiped on this day (not to mention the fact that Jesus rose on a Sunday morning).

In the Jewish traditions of the Law, a priest waved a sheaf of grain on the Day of Firstfruits, but presented two loaves of bread on the Day of Pentecost. Unknown to them, this would represent the uniting of Jew and Gentile into the body of the Lord through the Holy Spirit's outpouring. "The Jewish believers received this [Spirit] baptism at Pentecost, and the Gentile believers in the home of Cornelius" (*The Bible Exposition Commentary*).

Jesus had told the believers present at His ascension to wait in Jerusalem for the "Promise of the Father" (Acts 1:4, *NKJV*). As a result, 120 believers were together in one place and in one accord. Though we generally think of them as being in the Upper Room, they might have been meeting in one of the open areas of the Temple. For so many to quickly gather in reaction to what was happening is hard to imagine in the narrow side streets of Jerusalem where the Upper Room was located.

The 10 days spent together likely provided good opportunity to heal wounds between the disciples. They could express their sorrow for arguing as to who was the greatest. Also, they presumably reviewed many of the things Jesus had said, especially as relating to the Comforter He had spoken of on the night of the Last Supper (see John 14–16).

What happened on Pentecost morning was Spirit-directed. First, the 120 were praying together in unity. Next, they all spoke in tongues as the Spirit gave utterance. Unbelievers heard what was happening. The Spirit convicted these unbelievers. As a result, many people were saved.

B. Peter's Sermon (vv. 14-18)

14. But Peter, standing up with the eleven, lifted up his voice, and said unto them, Ye men of Judaea, and all ye that dwell at Jerusalem, be this known unto you, and hearken to my words:

the third hour (v. 15)—9 o'clock in the morning

15. For these are not drunken, as ye suppose, seeing it is but the third hour of the day.

16. But this is that which was spoken by the prophet Joel;

17. And it shall come to pass in the last days, saith God, I will pour out of my Spirit upon all flesh: and your sons and your daughters shall prophesy, and your young men shall see visions, and your old men shall dream dreams:

18. And on my servants and on my handmaidens I will pour out in those days of my Spirit; and they shall prophesy.

Talk About It:
1. Why did some people think the believers were drunk?
2. What does "pour out of my Spirit" mean?

Peter stood up to speak in response to the wild speculations that were taking place in the crowds. There were both local Jews and Jews from other lands present. The visitors heard believers speaking in their native tongues and dialects, and were amazed. The local Judeans heard only gibberish and thought the believers were drunk with wine. The fact that visiting Jews had come to Jerusalem from all around the known world indicates a hunger in their hearts. The local Jews, having been around the Temple and the "things of God" all their lives, were callous. Most had no desire for what God might be doing in their midst.

A fresh move of God always seems to bring a negative reaction from those already established spiritually. It has been said that the greatest enemy to a fresh move of God are the leaders of the last move. "Moves of God usually come with a stigma—something that is unappealing and considered repulsive by some. Tongues became the 20th-century stigma that many were unwilling to bear" (Bill Johnson, *When Heaven Invades Earth*).

Peter's sermon proves to be one of the greatest of all time, though he likely had no idea of all that would come from his mouth when he stood before the crowd. He used a passage

Expansion of the Church

from Joel 2 to explain what had just occurred. It is amazing that he could quote such a remote reference from a minor prophet. His uneducated Galilean-fisherman background cannot explain such knowledge. This had to be the working of the Holy Spirit.

Joel 2 speaks of an outpouring of the Holy Spirit that includes prophecy, dreams and visions. It is intriguing that what had just happened showed none of those manifestations, but rather was distinguished by wind, fire and tongues. Does this mean Peter misinterpreted Scripture? No, because it is obvious God chose the passage for him. The manifestations mentioned by Joel would come in God's time. Bill Johnson said, "The Word does not confine God—it reveals Him. Joel 2 revealed the nature of God's work among man. Acts 2 was an illustration of what God intended by that prophecy."

C. The Spirit at Work (vv. 37-47)
(Acts 2:37-40, 42-45 is not included in the printed text.)

41. Then they that gladly received his word were baptized: and the same day there were added unto them about three thousand souls.

46. And they, continuing daily with one accord in the temple, and breaking bread from house to house, did eat their meat with gladness and singleness of heart,

47. Praising God, and having favour with all the people. And the Lord added to the church daily such as should be saved.

The crowds were stunned by the anointed power of Peter's sermon. How could an uneducated fisherman speak like this? They asked the question that anyone sharing the gospel is anxious to hear: "What shall we do?" (v. 37). It is not enough just to be convicted of sin. There must be a responsive action that shows abandonment of sin.

C.S. Lewis said, "Christianity tells people to repent and promises forgiveness. It therefore has nothing to say to people who do not know they have done anything to repent of, and who do not feel that they need any forgiveness" (quoted in *Life Application Commentary*). Revealed truth must bring transformation or, put another way, revelation must result in experience. Peter's response was for the people to repent and be baptized in the name of Jesus for the cleansing of their sins. He also said they, too, would receive the gift of the Holy Spirit. He could have only said these words by the power of the Spirit. How otherwise could he know that the Holy Spirit would fall on the masses?

It is interesting that Peter directed the new converts to be baptized. There had not been a great deal of this practice during the Lord's ministry. It was more associated with John the Baptist. John, in his Gospel, tells us that Jesus' disciples carried out the

Talk About It:
1. List the things in which the early believers "continued steadfastly" (v. 42). Is our church following their example?
2. What caused *fear* or *awe* to grip "every soul" (v. 43)? How does this compare to our day?
3. Describe four or five characteristics of the first church (vv. 44-47).

baptisms, not Jesus himself (4:2). Why, then, is this rite so important? Baptism is a visible witness to the world of an inward work that has taken place. It is a proclamation of commitment to follow Jesus.

In summary, Peter asked for a fourfold response from the people who were ready to be saved (Acts 2:38):

1. *Turn from sin*, that is, repent. *Repent* means "to go back to God's view of things." It is a change of mind that results in new purpose and direction.

2. *Look to Jesus.* Jesus is the way to God. There is no other way (John 14:6).

3. *Be baptized.* Show the world your change of heart.

4. *Receive the Holy Spirit.* There is a measure of the Holy Spirit that comes upon every believer at salvation. In His first appearance to the disciples after the Resurrection, Jesus "breathed on them, and saith unto them, Receive ye the Holy Ghost" (20:22). Yet, we know they didn't receive the Holy Spirit in power until Pentecost. Peter was urging every new believer to press on and receive this power.

The reality of the believers' new life in Christ was seen both in the symbolic act of baptism and in their corporate life. Not only were they in *one accord* on Pentecost, but also in their daily worship gatherings in the Temple courtyard. They gladly worshiped and fellowshipped together, giving them favor with people and causing the church to multiply (Acts 2:41-47).

II. EXTENSION OF THE CHURCH (Acts 8:1-8)
A. Persecution of the Church (vv. 1-4)

1. And Saul was consenting unto his death. And at that time there was a great persecution against the church which was at Jerusalem; and they were all scattered abroad throughout the regions of Judaea and Samaria, except the apostles.

2. And devout men carried Stephen to his burial, and made great lamentation over him.

3. As for Saul, he made havock of the church, entering into every house, and haling men and women committed them to prison.

4. Therefore they that were scattered abroad went every where preaching the word.

haling (v. 3)—
dragging off

Talk About It:
1. What was the immediate result of the "great persecution" against Christians (v. 1)?

The stoning of Stephen had just occurred, and blame for this could easily be laid upon Saul. He was the instigating force that stirred hatred among the Jews for Christians. He led the first major persecution of the church. Men and women were beaten, imprisoned and, now with Stephen, put to death. Yet, Saul thought he was obeying God. In his mind he was protecting the truth.

Expansion of the Church

Verse 1 is a turning point in the book. Here we are introduced to the man who, though now was persecuting the church, would soon become its greatest proponent and defender. Luke heightens the drama of the story by introducing Saul here, though it will be another chapter before we see his conversion.

Persecution has always proved to be the means of growth for the church. "Persecution does to the church what wind does to seed: it scatters it and only produces a greater harvest" (*The Bible Exposition Commentary*). Had there been no persecution, few believers would have ventured far from Jerusalem. The message of the gospel was never meant to be contained by a small number in a specific setting. The Great Commission was to go to all nations (Matthew 28:19). Quickly after the Day of Pentecost, the thousands who had visited Jerusalem were already scattering to every nation, but this was not enough. God allowed persecution as a means to keep the church from settling down to respectability. Initially, the apostles had the favor of the masses in Jerusalem. Acts 5:13 says "the people esteemed them highly" (*NKJV*). We can easily tolerate some opposition when we know public opinion is behind us, but that can lead to complacency.

B. Philip's Anointed Preaching (vv. 5-8)

5. Then Philip went down to the city of Samaria, and preached Christ unto them.

6. And the people with one accord gave heed unto those things which Philip spake, hearing and seeing the miracles which he did.

7. For unclean spirits, crying with loud voice, came out of many that were possessed with them: and many taken with palsies, and that were lame, were healed.

8. And there was great joy in that city.

The Kingdom is manifested when it is preached in power with a demonstration of mighty works. Many of the visitors to Jerusalem who were converted on the Day of Pentecost soon headed back to their home countries. Yes, they were carrying the gospel with them, but they had not seen the demonstration of the gospel through powerful miracles. We don't see wonders and signs until Acts 2:43. However, when believers were dispersed after the stoning of Stephen, we see mighty things happening wherever the believers went. This was especially true with Philip. It was this powerful display of the gospel that caused the church to explode into the world.

Philip, along with Stephen, was among the deacons chosen to serve widows. From our perspective today, this might seem like a lowly task. However, the qualifications for this ministry were set at a high standard—"good reputation, full of the Holy

2. How did God turn something bad into something good (v. 4)?

palsies (v. 7)—
paralyses

Talk About It:
1. What was significant about Philip, a Jew, preaching in Samaria?
2. Why was there *great joy* in Samaria?

Spirit and wisdom" (Acts 6:3, *NKJV*). We should never scoff at what appears to be small beginnings for ministry. We must do what our hands have been given to do, and, being full of the Spirit, should precede anything we attempt. Philip, like Stephen, quickly grew in ministry and soon became an evangelist.

Some of the believers escaping Jerusalem scattered in Judea and farther away to distant fields. Philip chose to go to Samaria. The Samaritans were a half-breed people (a mixture of Jew and Gentile) and were openly despised by Jews. Still, Philip felt called and laid aside prejudice. What resulted was a bridge between two peoples, and a step toward bringing the church to the realization that the gospel was meant for all people. Though the disciples had originally heard the call to go into all the world, they had not had their eyes opened to just what this meant. Philip helped open the church's eyes.

III. INTO ALL THE WORLD (Acts 13:1-5; 28:16, 30, 31)
A. The Church at Antioch (13:1-5)

1. Now there were in the church that was at Antioch certain prophets and teachers; as Barnabas, and Simeon that was called Niger, and Lucius of Cyrene, and Manaen, which had been brought up with Herod the tetrarch, and Saul.

2. As they ministered to the Lord, and fasted, the Holy Ghost said, Separate me Barnabas and Saul for the work whereunto I have called them.

3. And when they had fasted and prayed, and laid their hands on them, they sent them away.

4. So they, being sent forth by the Holy Ghost, departed unto Seleucia; and from thence they sailed to Cyprus.

5. And when they were at Salamis, they preached the word of God in the synagogues of the Jews: and they had also John to their minister.

Here we see that the focal center of the early church had shifted from Jerusalem to Antioch, a city in Syria. Notice from the names listed that this was an international church. Barriers were being broken down, although these people were still Hellenist Jews (Acts 11:20). The Antioch church was birthed through the scattering of believers after the stoning of Stephen. Some had come to Antioch with a powerful witness, and many received the gospel. When word of this got to Jerusalem, the apostles sent Barnabas to check it out. Seeing something powerful, Barnabas went to Tarsus and found Paul (see vv. 21-25).

Though Barnabas and Paul were the leading teachers for the thriving church, we see others rising here. It was also in Antioch that believers were first called "Christians" (v. 26).

The church at Antioch was well-equipped. Good leadership

"The world is far more ready to receive the gospel than Christians are to hand it out."
—George W. Peters

Simeon (*SIM-ee-un*), Lucius (*LEW-she-us*), and Manaen (*MAN-uh-en*), along with Barnabas and Paul (v. 1), were leaders at the church in Antioch.

Seleucia (*see-LEW-she-uh*)—v. 4—a seaport of Syrian Antioch

Salamis (*SAL-uh-mis*)—v. 5—a town on the east coast of the island of Cyprus

Talk About It:
1. What were the leaders doing when the Holy Spirit gave them guidance, and what did they do after the Spirit spoke?
2. What is the significance of laying on of hands (v. 3)?

Expansion of the Church

was begetting new leaders, including some prophets (13:1). Prophets in the New Testament, and today as well, are simply "forth-tellers" of God's word. They may have predictions of the future, or they may have revelations of the meanings of events, times and specific scriptures. Since the Antioch church no longer needed Barnabas and Paul as teachers, these two could be freed for other works in the Kingdom. We see also a perfect pattern for sending out missionaries. First, God chooses those to be sent. Second, the church certifies and stands behind the call on the missionary's life. Third, the Spirit and the church send out the missionary, with proper prayer and support. Every missionary needs the backing of a church family.

B. Paul in Rome (28:16)

16. And when we came to Rome, the centurion delivered the prisoners to the captain of the guard: but Paul was suffered to dwell by himself with a soldier that kept him.

By the time we reach this passage, Paul had completed three major missionary journeys, established many churches, and evangelized a great portion of the known world. The story of his long journey to Rome (including two years' incarceration in Caesarea) is recorded in Acts 21–28. God had promised Paul that he would minister in Rome, and even shipwreck and serpent bites could not stop him. In the verses prior to verse 16, we see that Paul received a grand welcome from believers in Italy. This encouraged him greatly, although we hear no more of his intermingling with them. Paul's ministry in prison would be primarily to the churches he had established, Jews in Rome who had not yet believed, and the Gentile world he had not yet visited.

Talk About It:
1. Why was Paul now a prisoner?
2. How was he shown favor?

C. Ministry From Prison (vv. 30, 31)

30. And Paul dwelt two whole years in his own hired house, and received all that came in unto him,

31. Preaching the kingdom of God, and teaching those things which concern the Lord Jesus Christ, with all confidence, no man forbidding him.

Luke ends his history of the early church here. What happened to Paul in the years afterward has to be surmised through his letters to various churches and individuals. He was in this first imprisonment for two years, and during that time was able to receive friends and visitors regularly. He also wrote the Prison Epistles—letters to the Ephesians, Philippians, Colossians and to Philemon. Likely in A.D. 63 he was released, and returned to his travel ministry. He may have traveled as far as Spain. During this time he wrote 1 Timothy and Titus. He was arrested again in A.D. 67 and returned to a cell in Rome. Here he wrote his last letter—2 Timothy. He was soon executed (beheaded) by Nero.

Talk About It:
1. How did Paul take advantage of his incarceration?
2. Why did Paul have such confidence in the Lord despite his ongoing imprisonment?

Daily Devotions:
M. The Church Is Precious
Deuteronomy 32:9-13
T. The Church Is Loved
Isaiah 62:1-5
W. The Church Is Chosen
Malachi 3:16-18
T. The Church Established on Christ
Matthew 16:16-19
F. The Church Multiplies
Acts 5:12-16
S. The Church Is Christ's Bride
Revelation 21:1-5

Sadly as this ends, we cannot underrate the power of Paul's ministry. His letters provide a framework for Christian doctrine, church government and personal conduct. Though Paul never met Jesus in person during the Lord's earthly ministry, no one had a greater personal revelation of the Savior.

CONCLUSION

The church at Antioch, where believers were first called "Christians," was the model for all churches to follow. They were not close-minded, but reached out to other peoples. They developed strong leaders, including prophets and teachers. Not high-minded, they respected the godly overseers sent to them by the apostles in Jerusalem. In addition, this was the first church to send out missionaries. Paul and Barnabas were commissioned there by the laying on of hands. Following their first journey, Paul and Barnabas returned to Antioch, and part of their news was that the gospel had been extended to Gentiles. To their credit, this church accepted the radical concept without question (Acts 14:27).

How does our congregation compare with the Antioch church? Are we open-minded toward people who are different from us? Are we developing godly leaders? Do we respect those who are over us in the Lord? Are we a mission-minded church, in word and deed?

GOLDEN TEXT CHALLENGE

"YE SHALL RECEIVE POWER, AFTER THAT THE HOLY GHOST IS COME UPON YOU: AND YE SHALL BE WITNESSES UNTO ME BOTH IN JERUSALEM, AND IN ALL JUDAEA, AND IN SAMARIA, AND UNTO THE UTTERMOST PART OF THE EARTH" (Acts 1:8).

The primary reason God pours out His Spirit is so His church will "be witnesses unto [Christ] both in Jerusalem [our town], and in all Judaea [our nation], and in Samaria [to people we've held prejudice against], and unto the uttermost part of the earth."

The Book of Acts is far more than just a historical record of how Christ's church once operated; it also shows how believers of all ages can be Spirit-empowered witnesses.

Letters of Paul the Apostle (Romans through Philemon)

Galatians 1:1-24; 2 Thessalonians 3:1-18; Philemon 1-25

INTRODUCTION

The Great Commission mandated that Christians go into all the world, forgetting ethnic, racial, cultural or national barriers, and make disciples of all people. If there was one man who attempted to carry out this mandate, it was Paul. Though raised as a strict Jew (a Pharisee no less), he quickly was transformed after his Damascus-road experience, and set about to spread the Word. He had once been the greatest opponent of Christianity, but soon became its greatest champion.

Immediately upon conversion, Paul started preaching in Damascus and Arabia. Years later, he and Barnabas were sent out by the church at Antioch as missionaries, and soon he became known as the apostle to the Gentiles.

In our lesson we deal with three letters Paul wrote. The first one is addressed to the Galatians. These were churches that he and Barnabas had founded on their first missionary journey—in Derbe, Lystra and Iconium. The occasion for the letter was his frustration at Judaizers who came behind him and insisted no one could be saved without first ascribing to Jewish law and tradition, especially the rite of circumcision.

The second letter we will examine is 2 Thessalonians. Thessalonica was one of the first cities to be evangelized by Paul and Silas on the second missionary journey after they landed in Europe. This letter was written to clarify confusion that developed as to the second coming of Christ.

In the third letter we see that Paul made converts to the gospel from all walks of life—some poor and some wealthy. One was a man named Philemon, a successful businessman. Like most affluent citizens of the Roman world, he owned slaves. For reasons we do not know, one of those slaves—Onesimus—had escaped and made his way to Rome. After a period of time, Philemon had likely given up hope of finding the slave and had written him off as a loss. The slave found his way to Paul's door, became a convert to Christianity, and now Paul was caught in the dilemma of what to do with him.

Unit Theme:
Message of the New Testament

Central Truth:
Paul's letters teach us what to believe and how to live.

Focus:
Examine Paul's letters as sources of doctrine and counsel and apply these truths to the needs of today's church.

Context:
Selected passages from Paul's letters

Golden Text:
"For I am not ashamed of the gospel of Christ: for it is the power of God unto salvation to every one that believeth" (Romans 1:16).

Study Outline:
I. Provide Christian Teachings (Galatians 1:1-10)
II. Offer Solutions to Problems (2 Thessalonians 3:1-18)
III. Give Personal Counsel (Philemon 1-25)

I. PROVIDE CHRISTIAN TEACHINGS (Galatians 1:1-10)
A. The Gospel in a Nutshell (vv. 1-5)

1. Paul, an apostle, (not of men, neither by man, but by Jesus Christ, and God the Father, who raised him from the dead;)

2. And all the brethren which are with me, unto the churches of Galatia:

3. Grace be to you and peace from God the Father, and from our Lord Jesus Christ,

4. Who gave himself for our sins, that he might deliver us from this present evil world, according to the will of God and our Father:

5. To whom be glory for ever and ever. Amen.

Talk About It:
1. How did Paul identify himself and his calling? Why was this important?
2. What is God's will for us (v. 4)?

Paul was living proof of the transforming power of Jesus Christ. Christ had died for the sins of humanity, was buried, and had risen on the third day as Christ himself had predicted. The resulting good news was that because of what Jesus did on the cross, the free gift of salvation was now available to all—without baggage. This was the simple message Paul had preached when he came to the Galatians. It had changed his life and their lives as well. Paul began his letter reiterating this good news, because this was what was being attacked among the believers in Galatia. Developing here was the debate that would touch nearly every church and believer in the first century.

Soon after Paul and Barnabas had returned to Antioch at the end of the first missionary journey, Judaizers from Jerusalem complained that they had diluted the gospel to fit the ears of Gentile prospects. Not only that, they questioned Paul's qualifications as an apostle, since he had not personally been among the Lord's 12 disciples. Their chief interest was in keeping Christianity as a sect of Judaism. Some of the Judaizers took it upon themselves to go to the Galatian churches and change their thinking. They insisted that Gentiles had to first be circumcised, and then follow Jewish laws and customs in order to be saved. Paul was furious when he saw what was happening. This letter was his response.

"Redemption requires that radical evil and radical atonement collide."
—Patricia Hampl

B. Another Gospel (v. 6)

6. I marvel that ye are so soon removed from him that called you into the grace of Christ unto another gospel.

Talk About It:
What does the grace of Christ have to do with the gospel of Christ?

Paul was amazed that the Galatian Christians could be so easily deceived. They were exchanging the good news of the gospel for the bad news the Judaizers had impressed upon them. They had believed a lie instead of the truth. In his subsequent letters to churches and individuals, Paul began by praising the faith of the recipients of the letter. Not so here. He immediately rebuked his readers for having been so easily swayed from the faith he had brought them. He saw their actions as an apostasy.

Besides the false teaching itself, Paul was astonished at the speed with which the Galatian believers had been taken in. They had "become infatuated with the religion of the Judaizers, just the way little children follow a stranger because he offers them candy" (*The Bible Exposition Commentary*). Not only that, they had not bothered to consult with him, the very one who had shown them the faith.

Salvation by faith in Jesus alone is the theme of Galatians, but Paul had to impress on his readers first that they were not simply modifying what they had been initially taught. No, they were abandoning God's grace toward them and replacing it with an impossible legalism. We wonder why the Judaizers were so anxious to go to these cities and "correct" Paul's doctrine. They had not earlier been so interested in evangelism. We must believe that they had a vendetta against Paul himself. Paul had upset the entire Jewish system. Even Jews who had accepted Jesus were still steeped in their traditions.

> "The gospel is neither a discussion nor a debate. It is an announcement."
> —**Paul S. Rees**

C. No Other Gospel (vv. 7-10)

7. Which is not another; but there be some that trouble you, and would pervert the gospel of Christ.

8. But though we, or an angel from heaven, preach any other gospel unto you than that which we have preached unto you, let him be accursed.

9. As we said before, so say I now again, If any man preach any other gospel unto you than that ye have received, let him be accursed.

10. For do I now persuade men, or God? or do I seek to please men? for if I yet pleased men, I should not be the servant of Christ.

Paul would not allow men with false doctrines to put believers in bondage. The Christian life is one of fellowship with Christ, not one of rules and rites. The Judaizers were perverting the gospel, mixing legalistic rules with the free gift of salvation. This doesn't work. Also, grace is involved in more than initial salvation. We are saved by grace, but we also have to live by grace. We do not please God by trying to do good works. Yes, works are the result of grace, but they do not grant us grace. Paul wrote to the Corinthians: "But by the grace of God I am what I am: and his grace which was bestowed upon me was not in vain; but I laboured more abundantly than they all: yet not I, but the grace of God which was with me" (1 Corinthians 15:10). Paul could credit to himself more good works than anyone, but he knew it wasn't his works that saved and sustained him.

Paul went on to make his case even stronger by saying that

Talk About It:
1. Why do some people twist the gospel of Christ? How serious is this perversion?
2. Why can people pleasers not be servants of Christ?

Total Transformation
Paul's frustration at the fickleness of the Galatian believers is understandable. No one could have

even an angel appearing with a different doctrine should be cursed. In other words, it didn't matter how "spiritual" someone might seem in presenting a case for his teachings; if the doctrines being taught were contrary to the free grace found in Christ, let him be condemned. We note that this passage strongly stands against Mormonism, with its teaching that an angel appeared to Joseph Smith.

II. OFFER SOLUTIONS TO PROBLEMS
(2 Thessalonians 3:1-18)
A. An Appeal for Prayer (vv. 1-5)

1. Finally, brethren, pray for us, that the word of the Lord may have free course, and be glorified, even as it is with you:

2. And that we may be delivered from unreasonable and wicked men: for all men have not faith.

3. But the Lord is faithful, who shall stablish you, and keep you from evil.

4. And we have confidence in the Lord touching you, that ye both do and will do the things which we command you.

5. And the Lord direct your hearts into the love of God, and into the patient waiting for Christ.

The first letter to the Thessalonian church had been written only about six months after Paul's brief stay there on the second missionary journey. Because of persecution he had been forced to leave the city. As soon as he could, he sent Timothy back there to establish the new believers in the faith. Timothy returned with all their questions, and thus the initial correspondence, written from Corinth. In that first letter Paul reviewed the tenets of the faith and challenged the believers to stand faithful despite the persecution they were enduring. He also attempted to clarify confusion about the Lord's return. Apparently some believers had already died at Thessalonica, and there was question as to their participation in Jesus' second coming. Paul explained to them the resurrection of the saints that happens in conjunction with His return (1 Thessalonians 4:13-18). He then exhorted the believers to always be ready and watching.

When this second letter was written only a few months later, there was apparently still confusion in the church, though the people were faithful. Some claimed that the Great Tribulation and the Day of the Lord had already begun. Some had quit working and spent all their time simply waiting for the Lord. Perhaps the persecution they were enduring fueled their extreme hopes for such an immediate return. In this letter, Paul gives a clear explanation of the rise of the "man of sin" (2:3) and the conditions that would exist at the end of the age just prior to the Lord's return.

By the time we reach chapter 3, Paul has finished correcting the church and now appeals for prayer. They were to pray for the advancement of the gospel to all people, and also for Paul's deliverance from human opposition. He also expressed his confidence in the Thessalonians' strength to stand firm in the faith, despite persecution, through the Lord's power.

B. Commands Against Idleness (vv. 6-12)

6. Now we command you, brethren, in the name of our Lord Jesus Christ, that ye withdraw yourselves from every brother that walketh disorderly, and not after the tradition which he received of us.

7. For yourselves know how ye ought to follow us: for we behaved not ourselves disorderly among you;

8. Neither did we eat any man's bread for nought; but wrought with labour and travail night and day, that we might not be chargeable to any of you:

9. Not because we have not power, but to make ourselves an ensample unto you to follow us.

10. For even when we were with you, this we commanded you, that if any would not work, neither should he eat.

11. For we hear that there are some which walk among you disorderly, working not at all, but are busybodies.

12. Now them that are such we command and exhort by our Lord Jesus Christ, that with quietness they work, and eat their own bread.

In the first letter Paul had exhorted the people, "Study to be quiet, and to do your own business, and to work with your own hands, as we commanded you" (1 Thessalonians 4:11). Paul himself was industrious, and was likely by nature impatient with lazy people. Here, however, he addresses a specific problem caused by people believing the Lord's return was so near that there was no need to work. The resultant idleness and "living off the church" was creating a hardship on those who were working. "They may have considered work too menial or unspiritual, equivalent to laying up treasures on earth rather than in heaven" (*Life Application Commentary*). Paul is firm to say that they are not honoring the Lord with such behavior. While he had been in Thessalonica, he had imposed the rule—if you don't work, you don't eat. He now goes further to say that the faithful, hardworking people should stay away from these lazy individuals. This doesn't indicate excommunication, but rather a withdrawal from fellowship. In other words, support was to be cut off so they would have to work.

In verse 9, Paul speaks of not wanting to use his authority to demand financial backing for himself. Rather, he wants to be

can free us, and the Light who can lead us."
—**William A. Ward**

Talk About It:
1. Whom do Christians need to "withdraw" from (v. 6)? Why?
2. Describe the lifestyle Paul led before the Thessalonians (vv. 7-10).
3. What's a *busybody*? How should he or she change?

an example for others to follow by his own industriousness. "The fact that he worked would also cut off any opportunity to accuse him of greed. He wanted nothing to hinder the spread of the Gospel" (*Nelson Study Bible*). Paul was adamant in proclaiming that salvation is by faith alone, and not by works. At the same time, he recognized that salvation should produce good works, personal industriousness, and a willingness to work in order to help others.

C. An Encouraging Appeal (vv. 13-18)

(2 Thessalonians 3:16-18 is not included in the printed text.)

13. But ye, brethren, be not weary in well doing.

14. And if any man obey not our word by this epistle, note that man, and have no company with him, that he may be ashamed.

15. Yet count him not as an enemy, but admonish him as a brother.

Having admonished the idle, Paul encourages the faithful, hardworking saints. They should continue their "well doing." Despite the hard times they were facing, there was reward to be gained. He had said almost the same words to the Galatians, adding, "In due season we shall reap, if we faint not" (6:9). He also notes again that those who do not heed what he had commanded should be ostracized from fellowship. Paul did not want these souls lost, but simply reprimanded. The goal of church discipline must always be restoration, not excommunication.

III. GIVE PERSONAL COUNSEL (Philemon 1-25)

A. A Personal Letter (vv. 1-7)

(Verses 1-7 are not included in the printed text.)

At the time of Paul's writing this letter, there were approximately 60 million slaves in the Roman Empire. Many of these were becoming Christians, but still had pagan owners. One exception was Onesimus. He was a runaway slave who belonged to a Christian master named Philemon. It was after his escape that the slave himself became a believer. Under Roman law, any slave who ran from his master's household was subject to punishment, even the death penalty. The letter to Philemon is Paul's appeal that Onesimus no longer be viewed as a runaway, but rather as a Christian brother who has seen the error of his past ways and now wants to rectify it. This intensely personal letter is carefully worded and appeals to Philemon's sense of Christian love and responsibility. It contains a message of reconciliation as taught in another of Paul's letters, 2 Corinthians: "All things are of God, who hath reconciled us to himself by Jesus Christ, and hath given to us the ministry of reconciliation" (5:18).

We don't know what caused Onesimus to seek out Paul in Rome. He may simply have come to Paul out of a guilty conscience. Their meeting did prove to be providential, with the slave giving his life to Christ and making himself available to the apostle for service. As he was being mentored in the faith, his guilt for having abandoned his master likely surfaced. By law, Paul was required to return him to his master, or at least report his whereabouts to local authorities. Paul had to handle this delicately, for word would eventually reach Philemon of what had happened.

B. Boldness Empowered by Love (vv. 8-10)

8. Wherefore, though I might be much bold in Christ to enjoin thee that which is convenient,

9. Yet for love's sake I rather beseech thee, being such an one as Paul the aged, and now also a prisoner of Jesus Christ.

10. I beseech thee for my son Onesimus, whom I have begotten in my bonds.

Paul staked his friendship with Philemon on his request to receive the runaway slave. To understand the significance of what he was asking Philemon to do, we must understand slavery as it existed at that time. It was as common as any employer-employee relationship. Though they might have hated their personal status, most slaves accepted their lot in life. While not showing his disapproval for the institution, Paul still shed light of the gospel on the subject. Under the Law of Moses, Jews could own slaves, but their time of servitude was limited, and certain rights were guaranteed them. But Philemon was a Roman. There were no Roman laws against treating slaves harshly.

Though he was a Roman, Philemon had become a Christian. Paul pleaded to the fact that he had undergone an internal transformation. No matter what the prevailing culture might say, Paul hoped Philemon would receive the reformed slave with love. Paul appealed to Philemon as a brother in Christ. In verses 1 and 9 he called himself a "prisoner of Jesus Christ."

C. The Unprofitable One (vv. 11-16)

11. Which in time past was to thee unprofitable, but now profitable to thee and to me:

12. Whom I have sent again: thou therefore receive him, that is, mine own bowels:

13. Whom I would have retained with me, that in thy stead he might have ministered unto me in the bonds of the gospel:

14. But without thy mind would I do nothing; that thy benefit should not be as it were of necessity, but willingly.

15. For perhaps he therefore departed for a season, that thou shouldest receive him for ever;

> "As iron sharpens iron, so one man sharpens another" (Proverbs 27:17, *NIV*).

that which is convenient (v. 8)—"what you ought to do" (*NIV*)

Onesimus (*oh-NES-ih-mus*)—v. 10—Philemon's slave, his name meant "profitable."

Talk About It:
Why did Paul speak on behalf of Onesimus?

bowels (v. 12)—heart

16. Not now as a servant, but above a servant, a brother beloved, specially to me, but how much more unto thee, both in the flesh, and in the Lord?

Paul used a play on words here to emphasize a point. The name *Onesimus* means "useful," yet the runaway had been anything but that. However, the former unprofitable servant would now be profitable to his master. Paul admitted that he would have liked Onesimus to stay with him (for he was of great help in the ministry), but he recognized Philemon's priority in the case. Neither did Paul want to pressure Philemon into sending the slave back to Rome to serve the apostle. Most importantly, the slave had undergone a transformation of the heart. Paul hoped Philemon would see this and judge accordingly.

Was there a hidden reason for Onesimus to run away and later return? Perhaps God was working providentially on behalf of everyone involved so that Philemon would now have not only a slave, but a Christian brother as well. Paul's appeal takes on a spiritual quality. Not only would Onesimus now be a good servant on a human level, but also a good worker in the kingdom of God. There is a far deeper principle here. Christ calls for a higher standard, as seen in the story of the Prodigal Son (Luke 15:11-32). Paul hoped Philemon would treat Onesimus just as the father treated the Prodigal.

D. Partners in Christ (vv. 17-25)
(Verses 22-25 are not included in the printed text.)

17. If thou count me therefore a partner, receive him as myself.

18. If he hath wronged thee, or oweth thee ought, put that on mine account;

19. I Paul have written it with mine own hand, I will repay it: albeit I do not say to thee how thou owest unto me even thine own self besides.

20. Yea, brother, let me have joy of thee in the Lord: refresh my bowels in the Lord.

21. Having confidence in thy obedience I wrote unto thee, knowing that thou wilt also do more than I say.

Paul entreated Philemon to receive Onesimus just as he would receive Paul. Paul not only interceded for the slave, he also identified with him. Paul also takes into account that the slave might have stolen from his master. He was himself willing to restore any such debt. This action by the apostle reminds us of the truth that Christ paid the debt for our sins with His own blood. Paul had probably questioned Onesimus thoroughly as to any wrongs that might need restitution. He was absolutely assured of the man's newfound integrity in Christ.

Talk About It:
1. How had Onesimus become *profitable*?
2. How had the identity of Onesimus changed (v. 16)?

"A valuable friend is one who'll tell you what you should be told, even if it offends you."
—Frank A. Clark

Talk About It:
1. What offer did Paul make in verse 18? How is this like Christ's offer on our behalf?
2. What did Philemon owe Paul (v. 19)? Why?
3. Describe the confidence Paul had.

CONCLUSION

The passages selected in this overview of Paul's epistles demonstrate the power of Scripture.

In Galatians 1 we see there is no other source of truth available to humanity that can bring people into the saving grace of God. The Book of Mormon, the Koran, the corrupted Bible of the Jehovah's Witnesses, and all other holy books present "other gospels" that lead to destruction.

In 2 Thessalonians 3 we see that God's Word shows us how to live and how not to live. It is powerful in its divinely inspired practicality.

Paul's letter to Philemon demonstrates that Scripture is personal. It speaks to us as individuals, challenging us to walk in God's love.

GOLDEN TEXT CHALLENGE

"FOR I AM NOT ASHAMED OF THE GOSPEL OF CHRIST: FOR IT IS THE POWER OF GOD UNTO SALVATION TO EVERY ONE THAT BELIEVETH" (Romans 1:16).

In the golden text, Paul told us why he was ready to preach the gospel at Rome—because he was unashamed of the gospel, for it was the power of God to effect salvation; and why the gospel was the power of God to effect salvation—because therein the righteousness of God had been revealed (v. 17).

Paul was "not ashamed of the gospel." The somewhat negative way in which the apostle expressed himself here may seem inconsistent with his more usual confident and positive posture on other occasions. But we must recall that Rome was the seat of world empire and the epitome of world power. Paul's undertone of assurance disavowed any insecurity or intimidation. Absence of shame, when confronted with the pretensions of human wisdom and might, is proof of faith, while any emotion of shame betrays unbelief in the truth of the gospel.

The gospel is "the power of God" to effect "salvation." The Greek word for *power* focuses attention upon source rather than demonstration, although the latter is included in the thought. God's power is a principle operating on a vast and continually enlarging scale, taking effect in a countless number of individuals.

It is clear that the power of God unto salvation is operative only conditionally. Only those who believe are, by that grace of acceptance, benefited, for salvation has neither reality, validity, nor meaning apart from faith.

Daily Devotions:
M. Wise Counsel
   Exodus 18:17-21
T. Multitude of Counsel
   Proverbs 11:10-14
W. Warning Counsel
   Daniel 4:24-27
T. Redemptive Counsel
   Ephesians 1:7-11
F. Immutable Counsel
   Hebrews 6:16-19
S. Divine Counsel
   Revelation 3:15-19

General Letters
(Hebrews through 2 Peter and Jude)

Hebrews 2:1-18; 1 Peter 2:1-10; Jude 1-25

Unit Theme:
Message of the New Testament

Central Truth:
God's Word provides instruction, encouragement and challenge for godly living.

Focus:
Survey the General Letters for insights into Christian living.

Context:
Overview of Hebrews, 1 Peter and Jude

Golden Text:
"Beloved, when I gave all diligence to write unto you of the common salvation, it was needful for me to write unto you, and exhort you that ye should earnestly contend for the faith which was once delivered unto the saints" (Jude 3).

Study Outline:
I. Words of Admonition and Encouragement (Hebrews 2:1-18)
II. Words of Exhortation (1 Peter 2:1-10)
III. Words of Challenge (Jude 1-25)

INTRODUCTION

Suppose you run a family business that has been making a special kind of basket for hundreds of years. Then, suddenly one day you're walking through the markets and see a stack of baskets that look just like yours. You pick one up to examine it, and yes, it's made just as well as yours, maybe even a little better. You look at the tag and see that it was mass-produced in China, and sells for only a fraction of what your baskets sell for. You know you can't produce baskets that cheap! What are you going to do?

This story illustrates how some Jewish believers felt when the church developed and grew. Their heritage was threatened. At first all believers had been Jewish. Jesus was a Jew, His disciples were all Jewish, and everyone met at the Temple and the various synagogues to worship. Christianity was an exciting new "branch" of Judaism. Pretty soon, however, tensions began to mount as the freedom that came with Christianity butted up against the strict forms, dietary laws and traditions that the Jews had worked so hard to maintain.

Hebrews is a letter written to Jews who were struggling with these issues. The writer begins by showing that the old covenant (Judaism) and the new (Christianity) are both revealed by God, but that the new is absolutely superior to the old. No longer was the blood sacrifice of animals required. The moral aspects of the Mosaic Law were certainly still valid, but the rituals were not. It was a giant step to make in leaving traditions behind, but Christ was worth it.

Our second letter in this lesson is 1 Peter. Whereas Hebrews was written to ambivalent Jewish believers tempted to turn back to Judaism because of growing opposition and persecution, the people Peter addresses are crushed, overwhelmed and caught in the middle of it. Yet, Peter encourages them with the promise of a "living hope" found in Jesus. Despite their circumstances, his readers are living with the fulfilled promise of salvation, something the prophets of old never had.

The short letter of Jude is our last assignment. Written most likely by the half-brother of Jesus, Jude lays a harsh assault on false teachers. Both he and James, though not believing their brother to be the Messiah during His earthly ministry, later became great defenders and proponents of the faith.

I. WORDS OF ADMONITION AND ENCOURAGEMENT
(Hebrews 2:1-18)

A. Take Heed (v. 1)

1. Therefore we ought to give the more earnest heed to the things which we have heard, lest at any time we should let them slip.

Hebrews was addressed to Jewish believers who were having doubts over having left their traditional heritages to become Christians. The writer makes a case to prove they had made the right decision. The word *better* is used 13 times to show Christ as superior, His sacrifice a better sacrifice, the new covenant a better covenant. Under the Levitical system of sacrifices, an individual could never quite know if he had done everything necessary for his sins to be pardoned. Only the blood of Christ was fully atoning.

Two other words frequently used in Hebrews are *eternal* and *perfect.* The redemption achieved by animal sacrifice was only temporary, but the salvation achieved through Christ is everlasting and perfect. In other words, the life promised through Christ is "*better* because these blessings are *eternal* and they give us a *perfect* standing before God" (*The Bible Exposition Commentary*).

Why was this *earnest heed*, or personal soul-searching, so important at this time? Because the church was going through hard times, with persecution sprouting up everywhere. These were second-generation believers. They had not personally witnessed the ministry of Jesus. They had been faithful, but their experience was not as strong as that of the earlier believers. Thus it was easier for them to be seduced by false teaching.

The phrase "lest at any time we should let them slip" is translated in the *New King James Version* as "lest we drift away." This is the first of five admonitions made in the book. One commentary lists the admonitions as follows: Drifting from the Word (neglect), Hebrews 2:1-4; Doubting the Word (hard heart), 3:7—4:13; Dullness toward the Word (sluggishness), 5:11—6:20; Despising the Word (willfulness), 10:26-39; and Defying the Word (refusing to hear), 12:14-29 (*The Bible Exposition Commentary*). Notice there is a progression from bad to worse to worst. Simple drifting often results in defiance to God, and with that comes frightening discipline. Thus, we should always keep ourselves in self-examination. Like a woman who regularly checks herself for the first sign of cancer (a small lump), we should ever check our spiritual thermometers.

B. Don't Neglect (vv. 2-4)

2. For if the word spoken by angels was stedfast, and every transgression and disobedience received a just recompence of reward;

Talk About It:
How can we give *more earnest heed* to God's Word?

"Come to the Bible, not to study the history of God's divine action, but to be its object; not to learn what it has achieved throughout the centuries and still does, but simply to be the subject of its operation."
—Jean-Pierre de Caussade

3. How shall we escape, if we neglect so great salvation; which at the first began to be spoken by the Lord, and was confirmed unto us by them that heard him;

4. God also bearing them witness, both with signs and wonders, and with divers miracles, and gifts of the Holy Ghost, according to his own will?

God manifested Himself in mighty ways in the Old Testament. To the Israelites He was a pillar of fire by night and a cloud by day. He also showed Himself in the Tabernacle and the Temple. He sometimes sent angels to deliver messages. Now, if those people did not heed the word given with such powerful displays, and were justly punished, then how much more responsibility do Christians have after having received the glorious Son of God himself! "If disregard of Moses' law brought punishment, then disregard of the gospel would bring even far greater punishment" (*Life Application Commentary*). To reject the new covenant and regress to something of lesser value would ultimately bring terrible consequences.

The writer lists three witnesses to confirm the strength of salvation through Christ. First, there was Jesus himself. He announced the new plan when He said about Zacchaeus, "This day is salvation come to this house" (Luke 19:9). He also said, "For salvation is of the Jews" (John 4:22). He valued the Jewish heritage, but it was incomplete. He said, "Do not think that I came to destroy the Law or the Prophets. I did not come to destroy but to fulfill" (Matthew 5:17, *NKJV*). Second, there were those who heard and received Jesus' message personally. Third, those same people saw the signs, wonders and miracles Jesus did, and themselves were given the power to do signs, wonders and miracles.

The readers addressed here were second-generation believers who apparently had not themselves experienced great wonders. Their faith was influenced by the testimonies of others. Yet, all the way through the Book of Acts we see the gospel confirmed by the miraculous. It has been said that a person with a testimony is never at disadvantage to someone with only an argument. If signs and wonders were living proof of the power of the gospel, should we not be praying for the reoccurrence of the same today?

C. Christ Restores (vv. 5-18)

(Hebrews 2:11-18 is not included in the printed text.)

5. For unto the angels hath he not put in subjection the world to come, whereof we speak.

6. But one in a certain place testified, saying, What is man, that thou art mindful of him? or the son of man, that thou visitest him?

Talk About It:
1. What kind of *reward* (v. 2) do we *not* want to receive?
2. Who first spoke the message of salvation, and who confirmed it (v. 3)?
3. How did God verify the truth of the gospel (v. 4)?

"We are saved to know God, to enter His wonder-filled Presence through the new and living way and remain in that Presence forever. We are called to an everlasting preoccupation with God."
—A.W. Tozer

7. Thou madest him a little lower than the angels; thou crownedst him with glory and honour, and didst set him over the works of thy hands:

8. Thou hast put all things in subjection under his feet. For in that he put all in subjection under him, he left nothing that is not put under him. But now we see not yet all things put under him.

9. But we see Jesus, who was made a little lower than the angels for the suffering of death, crowned with glory and honour; that he by the grace of God should taste death for every man.

10. For it became him, for whom are all things, and by whom are all things, in bringing many sons unto glory, to make the captain of their salvation perfect through sufferings.

Since Jesus' humanity might be a stumbling block in proving His superiority, the writer quotes Psalm 8 to show how the Father temporarily made the Son lower than the angels in order to achieve His purposes. Yet, the Son would have all things under His subjection, including the angelic world. This refers to the original plan for people. The psalmist said, "The heaven, even the heavens, are the Lord's: but the earth hath he given to the children of men" (Psalm 115:16). Adam was created to have dominion over the earth, but he lost it when he was tricked out of his dominion by Satan. It took another man, a perfect One, to restore that dominion. We don't yet see that full dominion (Hebrews 2:8) because there is still sin on the earth (v. 15), but we will one day. Christ has regained what Adam lost, "the original calling for human beings to rule over God's creation" (*Nelson Study Bible*).

Talk About It:
1. According to verses 5-8, what is the position of humanity?
2. In what sense is Jesus a *captain* (v. 10)?
3. What is Jesus not *ashamed* to call us, and why not (vv. 11-13)?
4. Why is Jesus able to deliver us from temptation (vv. 14-18)?

II. WORDS OF EXHORTATION (1 Peter 2:1-10)
A. All Forms of Evil (v. 1)

1. Wherefore laying aside all malice, and all guile, and hypocrisies, and envies, and all evil speakings.

The recipients of Peter's letter were all strangers on the earth. The old song "This World Is Not My Home" well describes them. They were citizens of heaven through faith in Christ and, like Abraham, they had their eyes focused on their eternal home (Hebrews 11:8-16). As Jesus said, "They are not of the world, even as I am not of the world" (John 17:16). Because they were strangers, they lived by a different code. Their standards and values were different from the world's. Yet, because of this, they were experiencing great trials and persecutions. Though many of them were Jews scattered from out of Palestine, many were Gentiles. Peter was writing to encourage them to stand strong in their faith, be good witnesses to their

Talk About It:
What will happen if a Christian does not *lay aside* the things in verse 1?

persecutors, and remember that their suffering would ultimately lead them to glory.

Peter likely had a sense that persecutions were about to intensify. Believers, then, must bolster their faith and be ready to stand. Here he gave the path to follow. *Laying aside* means to remove just like taking off an old garment. *Malice* means evil done despite the good one has received. *Guile* means deliberate evil or lying. *Hypocrisy* is saying one thing but doing something else. *Envy* means wanting something that belongs to someone else. *Evil speaking* means slander. All of these are part of the old life, and must be put away.

B. The Milk of the Word (vv. 2, 3)

2. As newborn babes, desire the sincere milk of the word, that ye may grow thereby:

3. If so be ye have tasted that the Lord is gracious.

Talk About It:
What is necessary for Christian growth? Why?

Whereas Paul was frustrated at believers who had failed to mature and still needed the milk of the Word (1 Corinthians 3:2), Peter here admonished his readers to feed on the milk. Milk nourishes and helps one grow to maturity. He was not implying that his readers were infants in the faith, for many had been Christians for years. Instead, he was saying they should always crave more and more of God's Word. They had already tasted of the goodness found in salvation. That sweet taste should heighten their appetite for more.

C. Living Stones (vv. 4-8)

4. To whom coming, as unto a living stone, disallowed indeed of men, but chosen of God, and precious,

5. Ye also, as lively stones, are built up a spiritual house, an holy priesthood, to offer up spiritual sacrifices, acceptable to God by Jesus Christ.

6. Wherefore also it is contained in the scripture, Behold, I lay in Zion a chief corner stone, elect, precious: and he that believeth on him shall not be confounded.

7. Unto you therefore which believe he is precious: but unto them which be disobedient, the stone which the builders disallowed, the same is made the head of the corner,

8. And a stone of stumbling, and a rock of offence, even to them which stumble at the word, being disobedient: whereunto also they were appointed.

Talk About It:
1. Why is Jesus called the "living Stone"?
2. What "spiritual sacrifices" (v. 5) does God require from believers?
3. How do some people *stumble* over the Word of God (v. 8)?

Peter identifies his readers as living stones, ready to be used in God's building project. They had already been hewn from natural rock into shapes that were prepared to put in place. Christ is described as "the living Stone" (v. 4, *NIV*). Jesus said of Himself, "The stone which the builders rejected, the same is become the head of the corner" (Matthew 21:42). The cornerstone is most important in a building. Peter had referred to Jesus this same way in his sermon before the Sanhedrin in Acts 4. Both Jesus and Peter were quoting from Psalm 118:22 in describing how most Jewish people rejected Jesus, the Cornerstone.

When Peter refers to Psalm 118:22 in his first epistle, he says Jews and Gentiles alike who believe in Christ are *living stones*—people made alive in Christ. However, for those who reject Him, Christ is "a stone that causes men to stumble and a rock that makes them fall" (v. 8, *NIV*).

D. A Chosen Priesthood (vv. 9, 10)

9. But ye are a chosen generation, a royal priesthood, an holy nation, a peculiar people; that ye should shew forth the praises of him who hath called you out of darkness into his marvellous light:

10. Which in time past were not a people, but are now the people of God: which had not obtained mercy, but now have obtained mercy.

Believers are not only stones, but they now make up a new holy priesthood. They are both the temple (1 Corinthians 6:19) and the priests of the temple. Peter's reference in verse 9 comes from Exodus 19:6, where God portrays Israel as "a kingdom of priests and a holy nation" (*NKJV*). As opposed to Old Testament priests (who could enter God's presence only at prescribed times and with specific ceremonial cleansing), believers can enter God's presence at any time. Hebrews 4:16 says, "Let us therefore come boldly unto the throne of grace, that we may obtain mercy, and find grace to help in time of need."

Old Testament priests offered the blood of animals. New Testament Christians instead offer spiritual sacrifices, which are "your bodies as living sacrifices, holy and pleasing to God—this is your spiritual act of worship" (Romans 12:1, *NIV*). This is done by giving our lives, our wills, our desires, and our time to God.

III. WORDS OF CHALLENGE (Jude 1-25)
A. Contend for the Faith (vv. 1-3)

1. Jude, the servant of Jesus Christ, and brother of James, to them that are sanctified by God the Father, and preserved in Jesus Christ, and called:

2. Mercy unto you, and peace, and love, be multiplied.

3. Beloved, when I gave all diligence to write unto you of the common salvation, it was needful for me to write unto you, and exhort you that ye should earnestly contend for the faith which was once delivered unto the saints.

Jude's letter was likely written between A.D. 60 and 64. At

> "One of the many divine qualities of the Bible is that it does not yield its secrets to the irreverent and the censorious."
> **—James Packer**

Talk About It:
1. What four terms does Peter use to describe believers? What does each one mean?
2. Why do we need the mercy of God to become the people of God?

Talk About It:
1. How can God's "mercy . . . peace, and love, be multiplied" (v. 2) in believers' lives?
2. What was the main purpose for Jude writing this letter (v. 3)? Why can this letter be valuable to us?

least it was before the fall of the Temple in A.D. 70, for he would surely have mentioned that as having been a form of God's judgment against those trying to destroy the Christian faith. In his second letter, Peter had predicted that apostates would come. Jude declared they had already arrived.

There is a striking parallel between this letter and 2 Peter, and both were apparently intended for the same readership. Jude addressed his readers as those who have been *called.* Paul used this term for believers in Romans 8:28, saying, "And we know that all things work together for good to them that love God, to them who are the called according to his purpose." Other New Testament words that describe the saints include *elect, chosen* and *predestined.* No matter which term is used, the reference is to those who have found "common salvation" through Jesus (Jude 3).

Jude's great concern was the impending danger of false teachers. Perhaps he meant to write purely as an encouragement, but his urgency over this matter changed the tone of his writing. He addressed the readers as *beloved,* a term indicating one with authority. Certainly the brother of the Lord would have had strong standing among the Christian body. The only time the word *contend* appears in the New Testament is here. Contending for the faith "would not be easy; it called for hard work, diligent study, willingness to stand against society's desire to water down the gospel, speaking up for the truth and bearing the burden of interpreting the timeless truth to a changing society" (*Life Application Commentary*).

"God's Word is pure and sure, in spite of the devil, in spite of your fear, in spite of everything."
—R.A. Torrey

Believers could not afford to be complacent. They must defend the faith just as they would their most prized possession. The *faith* included the body of teaching and doctrines passed down through the apostles in the years just after Pentecost. Faith can only stand as it stands on truth. Whatever is true has power. Diluted doctrine meant diluted power.

lasciviousness (v. 4)—immorality

dignities (v. 8)—authorities

B. Do Not Be Deceived (vv. 4-19)

(Jude 5-16 is not included in the printed text.)

4. For there are certain men crept in unawares, who were before of old ordained to this condemnation, ungodly men, turning the grace of our God into lasciviousness, and denying the only Lord God, and our Lord Jesus Christ.

17. But, beloved, remember ye the words which were spoken before of the apostles of our Lord Jesus Christ;

18. How that they told you there should be mockers in the last time, who should walk after their own ungodly lusts.

19. These be they who separate themselves, sensual, having not the Spirit.

What are the essential doctrines that must be defended? They include the deity of Christ; the Trinity; the resurrection of Christ from the dead; salvation by faith alone through Christ's atoning blood; the fact that Jesus walked on the earth as a human, yet fully God; the second return of Christ; the Holy Spirit in dwelling the believer. Nonessential things can be left to individual choice, but these truths cannot be sacrificed.

In verse 8, Jude speaks of the arrogance of false teachers. They had not been commissioned by the church, nor commissioned by the Holy Spirit (remember Paul and Barnabas' commission by the Holy Spirit when they left on their first missionary journey—Acts 13:2). They also rebelled against all authority—they "despised dominion" (Jude 8). "The false teachers even rejected those who were placed in positions of authority in local congregations. They not only preferred error to truth but also demeaned and rejected those who taught the truth" (*Nelson Study Bible*).

Authority is one of the greatest principles taught in the New Testament. God's kingdom is a kingdom, and He works through delegated authority. Paul exhorted Timothy to pray "for kings, and for all that are in authority; that we may lead a quiet and peaceable life in all godliness and honesty" (1 Timothy 2:2). To place oneself above authority was to put oneself outside the realm of the Kingdom.

In verse 11 of the text we see that, like Cain, these people did not put their trust in the Lord, but rather in their own pride and self-righteousness. Like Balaam, they were greedy. Like Korah ("Core"), they resented the prominent positions others occupied as God's representatives.

Jude urged his readers to remember how the apostles had warned that scoffers following their own ungodly desires would come (v. 18). They would be characterized by grumblings, faultfinding, boasting and flattery (v. 16). Their goal would be to divide the church (v. 19).

C. Build Yourself Up (vv. 20-25)

20. But ye, beloved, building up yourselves on your most holy faith, praying in the Holy Ghost,

21. Keep yourselves in the love of God, looking for the mercy of our Lord Jesus Christ unto eternal life.

22. And of some have compassion, making a difference:

23. And others save with fear, pulling them out of the fire; hating even the garment spotted by the flesh.

24. Now unto him that is able to keep you from falling, and to present you faultless before the presence of his glory with exceeding joy,

Talk About It:
1. What should we learn from the examples of unfaithful Israelites (v. 5), fallen angels, (v. 6) and Sodom and Gomorrah (v. 7)?
2. What can we learn from the archangel Michael about resisting Satan (v. 9)?
3. According to verses 16-18, what are common characteristics of false teachers? What is leading them, and who is not leading them (v. 19)?

25. To the only wise God our Saviour, be glory and
majesty, dominion and power, both now and ever. Amen.

After venting all his frustrations, Jude then gave practical
suggestions for defending the faith. He knew his readers were
vulnerable to heresies and immoral living. The first of these
admonitions is especially important—praying in the Spirit to
build up one's faith. Believers of every denomination understand this to mean praying as directed by the Holy Spirit. To
Pentecostals, this has explosive power. Praying in tongues
gives one the means of allowing his or her spirit to communicate with the Holy Spirit while bypassing the intellect.

In addition, Christians must show mercy to others, have
compassion, reach out to rescue others from error, guard
themselves against fleshly appetites, and have complete confidence in their glorious, all-powerful majestic Savior who can
keep His children from falling. Focusing on God's greatness
and striving to serve others helps believers keep their hearts
and minds where they should be.

CONCLUSION

A crossroad is a dangerous place. It's where most accidents
occur. When you reach one, you stop. You're at a standstill.
You must make a decision to go one way or another, for simply sitting there will get you run over by traffic. The Hebrew
believers had come to this point. Some had already regressed
in their faith. Hebrews 5:12 says, "Though by this time you
ought to be teachers, you need someone to teach you the elementary truths of God's word all over again. You need milk, not
solid food!" (*NIV*). Others had even quit attending church services (10:25). They were being pulled in the direction of Jewish
traditions, while the writer of Hebrews encouraged them
toward a better way. Christ is the better way.

Do you feel yourself at a crossroads spiritually? Have you
stopped growing? Make a decision to move forward. Don't go
back to the old ways. There's nothing but tragedy there. Moving
into the unknown with Christ may seem frightening and unfamiliar, but it's exciting. It's new territory! And, He'll be with you
all the way.

GOLDEN TEXT CHALLENGE

"BELOVED, WHEN I GAVE ALL DILIGENCE TO WRITE
UNTO YOU OF THE COMMON SALVATION, IT WAS NEED-
FUL FOR ME TO WRITE UNTO YOU, AND EXHORT YOU
THAT YE SHOULD EARNESTLY CONTEND FOR THE
FAITH WHICH WAS ONCE DELIVERED UNTO THE
SAINTS" (Jude 3).

The words "earnestly contend" set the stage for the certain

Talk About It:
1. What positive steps should believers take (vv. 20, 21)?
2. What should Christians hate, and how should this affect their actions (v. 23)?
3. What is Jesus able to do for His children (v. 24)?

"Prayer is not a convenient device for imposing our will on God, or for bending His will to ours, but the pre-scribed way of sub-ordinating our will to His. . . . Every true prayer is a variation on the theme, 'Your will be done.'"
—John Stott

conflict facing the committed child of God as he or she walks with God through the hostile environment of this present evil world. These words suggest an intense and momentous competition which promises the victorious Christian "an inheritance incorruptible, and undefiled, and that fadeth not away, reserved in heaven for you" (1 Peter 1:4).

It should come as no surprise that we must encounter conflict in our quest for faith in Christ today. From Genesis to Revelation, God's Word is replete with examples of stalwart spiritual giants who sought and found a faith which sustained them through floods, fires, dungeons, persecutions and even from the subtle allurements of temptation. This faith of which Jude speaks is a dynamic faith revealed in ever-increasing clarity to each successive generation of God's faithful children. It was the inner force which moved the patriarchs of old to offer acceptable sacrifices, walk in harmony with God, heed divine warnings, seek an unseen inheritance, and deny the pleasures of sin for a brief season.

This same faith moved New Testament saints to daring exploits for God. It gave the early church fathers a determination to hold fast the doctrine for which Christ died. This unseen force burned within the bosom of the Reformation leaders and the evangelists who proclaimed the glorious gospel of Christ and delivered unto us a spiritual heritage which defies comparison.

The decision we face is whether we will accept Jude's challenge and contend for this same faith today, or carelessly deny it. The culmination of centuries of divine revelation rests in our hands. Will we be as faithful as God's choice servants who have contended before us?

Daily Devotions:
M. Spiritual Life Formed
Deuteronomy 8:1-6
T. Strength for Spiritual Life
Psalm 27:1-6
W. Source of Spiritual Life
Proverbs 8:32-36
T. Spiritual Life Demonstrated
2 Corinthians 4:6-11
F. Secure Your Spiritual Life
2 Peter 1:1-11
S. Evidence of Spiritual Life
1 John 3:10-16

The Last Word (The Revelation)

Revelation 1:1-20; 12:1-17; 22:1-5

Unit Theme:
Message of the New Testament

Central Truth:
The resurrected Christ rules over history and ultimately will triumph over all evil.

Focus:
Investigate the message of Revelation and live in expectancy of Christ's ultimate victory over sin, death and hell.

Context:
The Revelation was recorded by the apostle John near the close of the first century.

Golden Text:
"Behold, I [Christ] come quickly; and my reward is with me, to give every man according as his work shall be" (Revelation 22:12).

Study Outline:
I. The Exalted Christ (Revelation 1:1-20)
II. The Victorious Christ (Revelation 12:1-12)
III. The Reigning Christ (Revelation 22:1-5)

INTRODUCTION

God's purpose for all of history, His purpose for the Bible, and His purpose for every faithful servant after Adam fell in the Garden is the establishment of the promised messianic kingdom. The Kingdom will be fully manifested only when Jesus returns, but until then, believers persevere by obedience and faith. Obedience makes hearts ready for God to act. Faith activates the power of God to manifest aspects of the Kingdom from the invisible into the visible. These come in the form of signs, wonders, miracles, answered prayers, revelations, and so on. They all prove that the Kingdom is "at hand" (Matthew 4:17).

The Book of Revelation brings God's purpose into focus. Genesis and Revelation are like bookends holding the Bible (as well as history) together. Genesis gives the origins of civilization, while Revelation records its destruction and reconstruction. In Genesis we see humanity's initial sin and the instigation of God's plan of redemption. In Revelation we see the culmination of it. Often called the Apocalypse (or *unveiling*), Revelation uncovers divine mysteries that otherwise would remain concealed.

The entire book is a recording of visions seen by John while exiled on the isle of Patmos. What comes forth is that God is sovereign over the universe. He controls history and its outcome—all for the purpose of uniting the faithful into full fellowship with Himself. Humanity was made to fellowship with God. God gave the earth to humanity to have dominion over. Satan interrupted that plan, but not permanently. The outcome is still the same. God and humanity will live and work together in unity for eternity to come. Thus, the book is meant to encourage believers. Christ will ultimately triumph over all who rise up against Him and His saints. First-century readers were facing terrible times. The persecutions under the Roman emperor Domitian were in full swing. Believers needed to be encouraged to stand firm in Christ. Those who were complacent were challenged to stop compromising with the world.

One of Revelation's key themes is the glorious second coming of Christ. At the Lord's ascension (Acts 1:9-11), clouds removed Jesus from sight, but at His second coming "every eye shall see him" (Revelation 1:7).

I. THE EXALTED CHRIST (Revelation 1:1-20)
A. Identity of the Writer (vv. 1-9)

(Revelation 1:4-9 is not included in the printed text.)

1. The Revelation of Jesus Christ, which God gave unto him, to shew unto his servants things which must shortly come to pass; and he sent and signified it by his angel unto his servant John:

2. Who bare record of the word of God, and of the testimony of Jesus Christ, and of all things that he saw.

3. Blessed is he that readeth, and they that hear the words of this prophecy, and keep those things which are written therein: for the time is at hand.

We say *writer* and not *author* because the true author of Revelation is God himself. John was simply the recipient, the scribe writing down what he saw. Revelation begins with the Trinity. The Father revealed events to the Son, who passed them to an angel to reveal to John. The term "seven Spirits" (v. 4) is another name for the Holy Spirit. The Trinity—Father, Son and Spirit—is the ultimate source of truth.

John described himself as a brother and a companion to the churches he was addressing (v. 9). His own exile to Patmos proves a dedication to spreading the gospel of Christ. After the death of Emperor Domitian in A.D. 96, he was allowed to return to Ephesus. His receiving of these visions apparently occurred while on Patmos. He was shut off from friends and fellowship. Possibly this was the very reason he was prepared for such revelation.

B. Alpha and Omega (vv. 10, 11)

10. I was in the Spirit on the Lord's day, and heard behind me a great voice, as of a trumpet,

11. Saying, I am Alpha and Omega, the first and the last: and, What thou seest, write in a book, and send it unto the seven churches which are in Asia; unto Ephesus, and unto Smyrna, and unto Pergamos, and unto Thyatira, and unto Sardis, and unto Philadelphia, and unto Laodicea.

"The Lord's day" refers to Sunday. This is the only time the term appears in the Bible. John's incarceration did not stop his zeal for serving. To say he was "in the Spirit" does not imply some high ecstatic stage. He was simply worshiping—through prayers, praise, and paying tribute to God's majesty and power. As Jesus had told the woman at Sycar: "Yet a time is coming and has now come when the true worshipers will worship the Father in spirit and truth" (John 4:23, *NIV*).

The voice John heard was like a trumpet. The voice was that of Jesus himself. He gave John a command to write "what thou seest." This command is reiterated 11 more times. In verses 8 and 11, Jesus identified Himself as the "Alpha and

Talk About It:
1. Why does John say he was a prisoner on the island of Patmos (v. 9)?
2. How did John say he was a "brother and companion" to his readers (v. 9)?
3. Identify six titles ascribed to Jesus in verses 5 and 8. What was John communicating with such a list at the beginning of Revelation?

"Many men owe the grandeur of their lives to their tremendous difficulties."
—Charles Spurgeon

Talk About It:
What did John mean by saying he was "in the Spirit" (v. 10)? What happened on that day?

Omega," the beginning and ending, the first and the last. He is the ruler of all things past, present and future.

C. The Lord's Majestic Appearance (vv. 12-16)

12. And I turned to see the voice that spake with me. And being turned, I saw seven golden candlesticks;

13. And in the midst of the seven candlesticks one like unto the Son of man, clothed with a garment down to the foot, and girt about the paps with a golden girdle.

14. His head and his hairs were white like wool, as white as snow; and his eyes were as a flame of fire;

15. And his feet like unto fine brass, as if they burned in a furnace; and his voice as the sound of many waters.

16. And he had in his right hand seven stars: and out of his mouth went a sharp twoedged sword: and his countenance was as the sun shineth in his strength.

John instinctively turned to the voice's source, and before him was the Lord standing among seven golden lampstands. He was holding seven stars in His hand and was dressed in priestly garments. As High Priest, Jesus ministers among His churches. The long robe and golden sash speak of deity in Scripture. His white head and hair speak of wisdom and purity (see Daniel 7:9). His eyes blazed like fire, His face brilliant as the sun. His feet were like the glow of bronze in a hot furnace. This intensity speaks of undeniable truth, as well as the fire of judgment. His voice sounded like "rushing waters" (v. 15, *NIV*). Anyone who has ever been to Niagara Falls can testify to such a massive sound. This indicates God's ultimate power and sovereignty. The imagery John used here was very similar to that of Daniel, Ezekiel and Isaiah. He was probably reminded of the times years earlier when he, his brother James, and Peter were with the Lord at His transfiguration (Matthew 17:1-8).

The seven stars in Jesus' right hand represent the seven angels of the seven churches in Asia (v. 20). The sword in His mouth indicates the power and force of the message being given. His words were sharp as swords, yet came from love, not anger. God's message is always based on love. Correction is given for the sake of restoring life and relationship.

D. Life and Dominion (vv. 17-20)

17. And when I saw him, I fell at his feet as dead. And he laid his right hand upon me, saying unto me, Fear not; I am the first and the last:

18. I am he that liveth, and was dead; and, behold, I am alive for evermore, Amen; and have the keys of hell and of death.

19. Write the things which thou hast seen, and the

---

paps (v. 13)— chest

girdle (v. 13)— sash

Talk About It:
1. Describe Christ's appearance (vv. 13-15) in two or three words.
2. How are Christ's words like "a sharp twoedged sword" (v. 16)?

"With His word He spoke the world into existence; and He will come again with His word to destroy all that is evil."
—David C. Cooper

The Last Word

things which are, and the things which shall be hereafter;

20. The mystery of the seven stars which thou sawest in my right hand, and the seven golden candlesticks. The seven stars are the angels of the seven churches: and the seven candlesticks which thou sawest are the seven churches.

John's reaction to the powerful vision was much the same as others in the Bible. We see such with Isaiah (ch. 6). One Hebrew word for *glory* is *kabod,* which means "the great physical weight or 'quantity' of a thing" (*Vine's Expository Dictionary of Biblical Words*). The weight of glory that was present caused John to fall. The richness of God's presence causes the body to collapse. The only body position to assume when in the presence of God's glory is on one's face in total surrender.

The phrase "fear not" occurs many times in Scripture. Such assurance is necessary before moving in God's presence. Jesus assured John that there was safety within His majesty. Fear should not overwhelm us when we willingly place our lives in the Lord's care.

Talk About It:
1. Explain John's reaction to Christ's appearance (v. 17).
2. What was John commanded to write?

II. THE VICTORIOUS CHRIST (Revelation 12:1-12)
A. Wonders in Heaven (vv. 1-6)

1. And there appeared a great wonder in heaven; a woman clothed with the sun, and the moon under her feet, and upon her head a crown of twelve stars:

2. And she being with child cried, travailing in birth, and pained to be delivered.

3. And there appeared another wonder in heaven; and behold a great red dragon, having seven heads and ten horns, and seven crowns upon his heads.

4. And his tail drew the third part of the stars of heaven, and did cast them to the earth: and the dragon stood before the woman which was ready to be delivered, for to devour her child as soon as it was born.

5. And she brought forth a man child, who was to rule all nations with a rod of iron: and her child was caught up unto God, and to his throne.

6. And the woman fled into the wilderness, where she hath a place prepared of God, that they should feed her there a thousand two hundred and threescore days.

Revelation 12—14 has been called a collection of signs (symbols, or *wonders*). Two of these appear in these verses. The first is a woman. She is clothed with the sun, the moon is her footstool, and she wears a crown with 12 stars. The only other place such symbols are used is in Joseph's dream (Genesis 37:9). Joseph dreamed that the sun, the moon, and 11 stars bowed before him. This came to pass later in Egypt

Talk About It:
1. Why does Satan always oppose God and His plans?
2. Describe the nature of Christ's future rule on the earth (v. 5).

when his brothers came to him for food. This symbolic woman, then, is likely a description of the 12 tribes of Israel. Jesus came through Israel. Paul said, "Theirs are the patriarchs, and from them is traced the human ancestry of Christ, who is God over all" (Romans 9:5, *NIV*). The male child thus would be Christ (Revelation 12:5).

Jesus Christ is the One who will rule all nations with a rod of iron, as seen in Psalm 2:9. That passage speaks of God establishing His kingdom on His holy hill of Zion. The reference to an iron rod appears again in Revelation 2:27 and 19:15. This likely will come to pass during the millennial reign of Christ, where He rules with strict justice. This is because there will be some who enter the Millennium still in mortal bodies, thus the potential for sin. When Satan is loosed near the end of the thousand years, that sin potential will express itself. It is not until the coming of the new heavens and new earth that the rod of iron can be put down and used no more.

The other wonder in this passage (v. 3) is easy to identify. The devil appears here as a "great red dragon" with seven heads and 10 horns, and seven crowns on his heads. In verses 4-6 we see a flashback to the Dragon watching intently for the birth of the long-awaited promised Son. He is ready to pounce on the Child. We also see by the stars attached to his tail that when he was expelled from heaven he took with him one-third of the angels. Satan and his entourage were cast to the earth. Verse 5 tells us that the Child was caught up to God, referring to Christ's ascension. However, because of His resurrection, Jesus was already beyond the reach of the Dragon. Thus, some see this as a picture of the church, the visible representation of Christ on the earth, being caught up in the Rapture. Thus, when the woman flees to the wilderness (v. 6), the Child is already gone. She (Israel) is taken care of for 1,260 days, indicating that the Rapture has occurred just before the first half of the seven years of Tribulation.

> "The devil is a better theologian than any of us and is a devil still."
> —A.W. Tozer

B. War in the Heavens (vv. 7-10)

7. And there was war in heaven: Michael and his angels fought against the dragon; and the dragon fought and his angels,

8. And prevailed not; neither was their place found any more in heaven.

9. And the great dragon was cast out, that old serpent, called the Devil, and Satan, which deceiveth the whole world: he was cast out into the earth, and his angels were cast out with him.

10. And I heard a loud voice saying in heaven, Now is come salvation, and strength, and the kingdom of our

God, and the power of his Christ: for the accuser of our brethren is cast down, which accused them before our God day and night.

The scene suddenly changes from earth to heaven. War has broken out between God's angels and the forces of Satan. In this war Satan and his angels are cast out of heaven, thus confining them to earth. From this we conclude that Satan will have access to heaven up to the final days. In Job he appeared before God to ask permission to harm Job. In Zechariah he accused the saints before God. At midpoint in the Tribulation, however, God sends Michael to hurl the devil and his angels down to earth. Revelation 9:1 also speaks of a star falling from the sky to earth.

Verse 10 of the text gives heaven's reaction to the devil being "cast down." This loud voice is apparently the combined voices of the martyrs of Revelation 6 who were given white robes and were seen crying out for vengeance. They now rejoice because their prayers have been answered. The saints in heaven proclaim, "Now have come the salvation and the power and the kingdom of our God, and the authority of his Christ" (12:10, *NIV*).

Talk About It:
1. What titles are given to Satan in verses 9 and 10? What is his mission?
2. How does the archangel Michael (vv. 7, 8) show forth the "salvation, and strength . . . and the power" of Christ (v. 10)?

C. Overcomers (vv. 11-12)

11. And they overcame him by the blood of the Lamb, and by the word of their testimony; and they loved not their lives unto the death.

12. Therefore rejoice, ye heavens, and ye that dwell in them. Woe to the inhabiters of the earth and of the sea! for the devil is come down unto you, having great wrath, because he knoweth that he hath but a short time.

These verses proclaim that believers in any age can overcome the attacks of Satan. Lies, false philosophies, selfish dreams and sensual temptations face the saints every day. In addition, Satan still stands in the presence of God making accusations. God has provided us ways to overcome these charges.

First, we overcome by "the blood of the Lamb." We simply remind Satan that our sins are covered by the blood of Jesus. Paul said, "There is now no condemnation for those who are in Christ Jesus, because through Christ Jesus the law of the Spirit of life set me free from the law of sin and death" (Romans 8:1, 2, *NIV*). Second, we overcome by "the word of [our] testimony." We are made stronger as we testify about our freedom in Christ to others. Third, we overcome by "loving not [our] lives unto the death." We don't permit anything to displace Christ as the center of our lives. Possession, status or position should never take priority over Christ. As we make Him our priority, we gain strength to overcome.

Talk About It:
1. How do persecuted believers overcome Satan (v. 11)?
2. Why will the time of rejoicing also be a time of woe (v. 12)?

III. THE REIGNING CHRIST (Revelation 22:1-5)

A. The Eternal City and Throne of God (vv. 1-3)

1. And he shewed me a pure river of water of life, clear as crystal, proceeding out of the throne of God and of the Lamb.

2. In the midst of the street of it, and on either side of the river, was there the tree of life, which bare twelve manner of fruits, and yielded her fruit every month: and the leaves of the tree were for the healing of the nations.

3. And there shall be no more curse: but the throne of God and of the Lamb shall be in it; and his servants shall serve him.

The angel carries John away in the spirit to view the beautiful eternal city. Starting in the previous chapter (21), John attempts a description of the New Jerusalem. His portrayal is limited in much the same way as a primitive jungle native might be today if he were suddenly transported to a major city and then back to his home. He would have no comparisons to communicate what he had seen.

John sees a glorious picture of fertility, with life radiating everywhere. He mentions both the river of life and the Tree of Life. Both are found in Old Testament passages. Psalm 46:4 says, "There is a river whose streams shall make glad the city of God, the holy place of the tabernacle of the Most High" (*NKJV*). This river symbolizes the presence of the Holy Spirit. The Tree of Life is seen in the Genesis account of Eden. The tree represents Jesus himself. He said of Himself, "I am the way, the truth, and the life: no man cometh unto the Father, but by me" (John 14:6). The total picture presented is one of saints' eternal pleasure and service to God, their intimate fellowship with Him, and a continual sense of excitement.

The description of this eternal city is somewhat like the original Garden of Eden. There were four rivers in Eden, but only one here. In Eden, Adam was prohibited from eating of the Tree of Knowledge of Good and Evil. After his sin, he was driven out of the garden to keep him from eating of the Tree of Life. Here, however, God's children will have access to the Tree of Life, for sin no longer prohibits them.

At the end of the last book of the Old Testament there is a curse. The Lord says, "Lest I come and smite the earth with a curse" (Malachi 4:6). At the end of the New Testament is a grand announcement: "There shall be no more curse" (Revelation 22:3). "Satan will be consigned to hell; all of creation will be made new; and the curse of sin will be gone forever" (*The Bible Exposition Commentary*).

Arriving at this perfect place is the hope of every believer. Paul said, "To them who by patient continuance in well doing

Talk About It:
1. Describe the "tree of life" and its purpose.
2. Why will there be "no more curse" (v. 3) in heaven?

Preview of Christ's Return

At the end of the Gospel of John, when Jesus was speaking to Peter, He alluded to the possibility that John might still be alive when He returned (John 21:22). Although tradition holds that John was eventually released from Patmos and returned to Ephesus where he died as an old man, he did, in a sense, see the Second Coming. The vision John saw in Revelation was a preview of what has yet to take place. He saw in the spiritual realm what will ultimately be seen by all believers in the natural.

seek for glory and honour and immortality, [God will give] eternal life" (Romans 2:7). Through faith, we already have a certain access to this beautiful realm. Romans 5:2 says, "Through whom we have gained access by faith into this grace in which we now stand. And we rejoice in the hope of the glory of God" (*NIV*). Paul also recognized, however, that nothing we can imagine can compare to what is coming: "I consider that our present sufferings are not worth comparing with the glory that will be revealed in us" (8:18, *NIV*).

Verse 3 of our text says "his servants shall serve him." This tells us there will be much activity throughout eternity. There will be work to do. On earth humanity has been hampered by mortality—including sin, weakness and death. In eternity there will be nothing to stop us from constant exploration, discovery and creativity.

B. The Face of God (v. 4)

4. And they shall see his face; and his name shall be in their foreheads.

According to John 1:18 and 1 John 4:12, no one has ever seen the face of God. Those who came the closest were Adam and Eve in Eden, Moses, and perhaps Enoch. Moses was only able to see Him from the backside. In heaven, however, the saints will commune with Him face-to-face. Jesus declared, "Blessed are the pure in heart: for they shall see God" (Matthew 5:8). In addition, God's people will have His name written on their foreheads. We belong to God and have been sealed. In 2 Corinthians 1:21, 22, we read, "He anointed us, set his seal of ownership on us, and put his Spirit in our hearts as a deposit, guaranteeing what is to come" (*NIV*).

In Revelation 13:16, the False Prophet puts the Antichrist's name on the foreheads of the masses during the Tribulation. This will be a satanic imitation of what God plans for the faithful.

Talk About It:
Whose name will be on the forehead of God's children, and why?

C. No More Night (v. 5)

5. And there shall be no night there; and they need no candle, neither light of the sun; for the Lord God giveth them light: and they shall reign for ever and ever.

John said in an earlier letter, "God is light, and in him is no darkness at all" (1 John 1:5). Jesus declared Himself to be "the light of the world" (John 8:12). Obviously He was speaking of spiritual light. At the same time, physical light is a manifestation of God's glory. Darkness is symbol of evil. On earth most crime is committed at night. In heaven there will be no such thing. Zechariah said, "It will be a unique day, without daytime or nighttime—a day known to the Lord. When evening comes, there will be light" (14:7, *NIV*).

Talk About It:
What will God's children reign over?

CONCLUSION

We live in a day of constant discovery. Technology is moving so fast that the body of knowledge now doubles every few years. It is impossible to keep up with every advancement taking place. However, imagine the learning curve we will experience in heaven! There is an entire universe out there to explore!

Revelation 22:3 says, "His servants shall serve him." What will this service be? Some think we may be sent to distant planets to rule and develop. Space travel from earth today is limited by time. The distance to even the nearest stars is measured in light years. A light year is the distance light travels in a year. Figure it for yourself—since light travels at the speed of 186,000 miles per second, mortal humanity can't survive the space trip, but in eternity we can. Of course, no one knows what our service to God will be like, but it certainly will be fulfilling and worshipful.

GOLDEN TEXT CHALLENGE

"BEHOLD, I [CHRIST] COME QUICKLY; AND MY REWARD IS WITH ME, TO GIVE EVERY MAN ACCORDING AS HIS WORK SHALL BE" (Revelation 22:12).

The church and the world are moving toward the climactic second coming of Christ. It will happen suddenly and decisively.

Christ's return will bring distress to the world but deliverance to the church (Luke 21:36). His coming will mean sorrow for the world but joy for the church (Matthew 25:21). The Second Coming will be a time of hopelessness for the world but will fulfill the church's "blessed hope" (Titus 2:13).

The Lord's return will bring desperation to the world but transformation to the church (1 John 3:2). His coming will pronounce doom on the earth but initiate eternal glory to the church (1 Thessalonians 4:17). It will be a time of great loss for the world but a day of rewards for believers (Revelation 22:12).

Introduction to Winter Quarter

T he first three lessons of the first unit are studies from Genesis, focusing on the Creation, the Fall, and the Flood. The fourth lesson is on the birth of Christ. They were compiled by Lance Colkmire.

Lance Colkmire (B.A., M.A.) is editor of the *Evangelical Commentary* and *Real Life* young adult curriculum for Pathway Press. His latest book, *Make a Mark,* presents 25 principles of life-shaping ministry to children.

Basic Christian doctrines are studied in the second unit. Those doctrines are the inspiration of Scripture, the Trinity, salvation, church ordinances, baptism in the Spirit, sanctification, the church, divine healing, and the return of Christ. The expositor is the Reverend Joshua Rice (B.A., M.A.Th.).

Josh Rice is regional director of youth and Christian education for the Great Lakes Region. He is a graduate of Lee University and Columbia Theological Seminary.

The World Created

Genesis 1:1 through 2:25; Colossians 2:16, 17; Hebrews 4:1-11

Unit Theme:
Beginnings (Genesis 1—11)

Central Truth:
God created all things according to His plan and purpose.

Focus:
Acknowledge and honor God as the Creator of all things.

Context:
The Book of Genesis was written between 1450 and 1400 B.C.

Golden Text:
"In the beginning God created the heaven and the earth" (Genesis 1:1).

Study Outline:
I. The Universe Created (Genesis 1:1-19)
II. Life Created (Genesis 1:20-31; 2:7-25)
III. Day of Rest Established (Genesis 2:1-3; Hebrews 4:6-11; Colossians 2:16, 17)

INTRODUCTION

In the fall quarter a broad survey or landscape view of the whole Bible was presented. Now we move into a three-lesson series called "Beginnings," focusing on the Book of Genesis. The word *Genesis* is a Greek word and means "beginning." E.J. Young says, "The word means 'origin,' 'source,' 'generation,' and has been adopted by most translations as the title of the book" (*Introduction to the Old Testament*). The Jews called the book *B'reshith*, which is the first phrase of the book in Hebrew: "In the beginning."

It is an appropriate title, as a survey of the book shows. Seven distinct "beginnings" are recorded in Genesis: (1) the beginning of the universe (ch. 1); (2) the beginning of humanity (ch. 2); (3) the beginning of sin (ch. 3); (4) the beginning of suffering (ch. 3); (5) the beginning of God's redemptive program (ch. 3); (6) the beginning of civilization (ch. 4); and (7) the beginning of the Hebrew nation (ch. 12).

In approaching today's lesson, we must rid our minds of the notion that "in the beginning" means 4004 B.C. This date is a legacy from the attempts of students of earlier years to work out from Bible references a comprehensive Biblical chronology. This has now been commonly abandoned. It is recognized by most scholars that dates before Abraham cannot be fixed with precision, due to the great probability that the genealogical records of Genesis 5 and 11 were not intended to be complete (see also Matthew 1).

"All that it states in Genesis 1:1," says Benjamin Field, "is that the act of Creation occurred at a certain point of time in past eternity, which is not chronologically fixed" (*Handbook of Christian Theology*). Thus we do not have to fight a battle with science about the date of Creation—maybe about the fact of Creation, but certainly not the date.

I. THE UNIVERSE CREATED (Genesis 1:1-19)

A. The Creator (vv. 1, 2)

1. In the beginning God created the heaven and the earth.

2. And the earth was without form, and void; and darkness was upon the face of the deep. And the Spirit of God moved upon the face of the waters.

The first sentence of the Bible asserts that at the beginning of time, which can never be dated or imagined, God was living and active. All of us, of course, have heard the question (indeed, we may have asked it): Where did God come from? Who made God?

There is only one rational answer: You cannot make God! You can make a god, or gods, but God cannot be made. Neither can He evolve or emerge. A made God, or a created God, or an evolved God, is a contradiction in terms. God is the uncaused Cause, the uncreated Creator, the unoriginated Originator. No other conception can satisfy the mind. Logically and rationally it is the God of Genesis 1:1—the eternal, the everlasting, the always-was-and-always-will-be God, or no God!

Two other basic truths about God are found in these opening verses:

God is a Person. Alan Richardson sees the personality of God in the Hebrew word for "God" (*Elohim*), which is plural in form. He says, "This is a deep Biblical insight: God is not, and never was, a lonely God. There is personality in God, and a person could not exist alone . . . a 'unitarian' or lonely God is not the God of the historic Biblical revelation." This truth is underscored in verse 26—"Let us make man." God is a Trinity—three Persons in one.

God is all-powerful, loving Spirit (v. 2). Calvin sees this activity of the Spirit as sustaining the created universe in its original formless mass until the detailed creation of verses 3-31 was performed. Others emphasize that the Hebrew word rendered *moved* has the idea of a bird brooding or hatching, therefore implying tender love.

B. The Creation (vv. 3-19)

(Genesis 1:6-19 is not included in the printed text.)

3. And God said, Let there be light: and there was light.

4. And God saw the light, that it was good: and God divided the light from the darkness.

5. And God called the light Day, and the darkness he called Night. And the evening and the morning were the first day.

These verses describe the first four of six creative days, during which the original act of creating out of nothing (v. 1) was

---

Talk About It:
1. If you don't believe Genesis 1:1, is there any point in reading the rest of the Bible? Why or why not?
2. How was the Holy Spirit involved with Creation?

"What could be more foolish than to think that all this rare fabric of heaven and earth could come by chance, when all the skill of science is not able to make an oyster?"
—Jeremy Taylor

firmament (v. 6)— expanse

Talk About It:
1. Why do you think God created light first?
2. Why did God create the world in stages?
3. According to verses 14-18, why did God create the sun, moon and stars?

expanded and developed in successive stages until the order of the universe and, especially the earth, was achieved. The work of the first four days may be lableld thus: (1) light and dark (vv. 3-5); (2) sea and sky (vv. 6-8); (3) land, sea and vegetation (vv. 9-13); (4) sun, moon and stars (vv. 14-19).

A question much debated relates to whether or not the entire work of Creation was accomplished in six literal days of 24 hours. No one who believes in an omnipotent, miracle-working God can doubt the possibility of this. Creation is a miracle, or a series of miracles, and miracles are not dependent on time. Dr. Oswald T. Allis comments, "It is a distinct feature of the miracles of the Bible that they are limited by neither space nor time. To 'evolve' water into wine could not be done any more successfully in a million years or in a thousand million than in a 'day.' Natural process could not accomplish it at all. Jesus did it apparently instantaneously (John 2:7)."

II. LIFE CREATED (Genesis 1:20-31; 2:7-25)
A. After Their Kind (1:20-25)
   (Genesis 1:21-24 is not included in the printed text.)
   20. And God said, Let the waters bring forth abundantly the moving creature that hath life, and fowl that may fly above the earth in the open firmament of heaven.
   25. And God made the beast of the earth after his kind, and cattle after their kind, and every thing that creepeth upon the earth after his kind: and God saw that it was good.

great whales (v. 21)—"great creatures of the sea" (*NIV*)
cattle (v. 24)—livestock

"Every living and moving thing with which the water teems . . . and every winged bird" (v. 21, *NIV*) were created on the fifth day. God caused "the sudden coming of hosts of winged things and fishes. They were designed to provide another visible demonstration of the Creator's power. With their appearance, there was life on the earth and also activity. And there was, furthermore, an endless succession of living creatures, all made by God's mighty hand" (Wycliffe).

Talk About It:
1. Explain the phrase "God blessed them" (v. 22).
2. What command did God give the animals? Why?

The spectacular variety of ocean life and flying creatures reflect the endless imagination and almighty power of God. Scientists have identified some 30,000 species of fish and more than 10,000 species of birds.

B. In God's Image (vv. 26-31)
   26. And God said, Let us make man in our image, after our likeness: and let them have dominion over the fish of the sea, and over the fowl of the air, and over the cattle, and over all the earth, and over every creeping thing that creepeth upon the earth.
   27. So God created man in his own image, in the image of God created he him; male and female created he them.

28. And God blessed them, and God said unto them, Be fruitful, and multiply, and replenish the earth, and subdue it: and have dominion over the fish of the sea, and over the fowl of the air, and over every living thing that moveth upon the earth.

29. And God said, Behold, I have given you every herb bearing seed, which is upon the face of all the earth, and every tree, in the which is the fruit of a tree yielding seed; to you it shall be for meat.

30. And to every beast of the earth, and to every fowl of the air, and to every thing that creepeth upon the earth, wherein there is life, I have given every green herb for meat: and it was so.

31. And God saw every thing that he had made, and, behold, it was very good. And the evening and the morning were the sixth day.

Talk About It:
1. What does it mean to be made in God's image?
2. What did God give humanity dominion over, and why?
3. What did God call His creative work (v. 31), and why?

Though man, like the land animals, was created on the sixth day, he was not placed in the sacred record in the same category or on the same level with them. A distinction was even emphasized in the divine activity. Not only did God speak and form to create man (as with other creatures), but He "breathed into his nostrils" (2:7). Thus, man is a unique part of God's creative handiwork.

This does not imply there is no similarity between humanity and animal life. Dr. A. Rendle Short says, "Without question man's body has much in common with the animals. This is obvious to everyone. The organs are much the same; the blood vessels and nerves are the same; to dissect an animal such as the rabbit is the medical student's normal introduction to human anatomy" (*The Bible and Modern Research*).

Derek Kidner shows that this is implied by the Genesis record: "He [man] shares the sixth day with other creatures, is made of dust as they are (2:7,19), feeds as they feed (1:29, 30) and reproduces with a blessing similar to theirs (vv. 22, 28a); so that he can be studied partly through the study of them; they are half his context" (*Tyndale Commentary, Genesis*).

But this is only one side of the coin. Humanity is also different from the animals, as Genesis implies and as the whole Bible teaches. Our uniqueness is summed up in the phrase "the image of God" (1:27). Not only is there in us that which makes us akin to the animals, but there is also something in us that is akin to God. Dr. R. Payne Smith says, "It [image of God] may refer to man's reason, free will, self-consciousness, and so on. But it implies something closer and more inward. It refers to man's moral powers, and especially to his capacity of attaining unto holiness" (*Ellicott's Commentary, Genesis*).

All of this means that man, as God created him, is endowed

with a capacity for fellowship with God and a potential for likeness to God, even though he has kinship to the animals (unlike the angels). We must remember, of course, that the Fall has deeply impaired this capacity and potential. Also, what was forfeited through the Fall is restored "through the redemption that is in Christ Jesus" (Romans 3:24; see also Ephesians 4:24; Colossians 3:10).

Humanity's uniqueness is further accentuated by the "dominion" that God gave him (Genesis 1:28). This, Marcus Dods says, "is not the equivalent of his being made in the image of God, but its result" (*Genesis*). This "dominion" is the subject of Psalm 8, where the comment is made, "Thou hast put all things under his feet" (v. 6). There is a quotation of this statement in Hebrews 2:8, followed by the significant statement: "But now we see not yet all things put under him." Yet, in striking contrast, "we see Jesus . . . crowned with glory and honour" (v. 9). This implies that humanity in general has never achieved this intended destiny. It was hindered by the Fall.

This does not mean that through the Fall humanity wholly lost the dominion, any more than the "image of God" was wholly obliterated. The image of God may still be seen through the ravages of sin, and the dominion is still exercised, though in distorted form. All through history, "dominion" has been turned to exploitation, misappropriation and destruction. Today humanity is reaping the harvest!

C. The Breath of Life (2:7)

7. And the Lord God formed man of the dust of the ground, and breathed into his nostrils the breath of life; and man became a living soul.

God's use of dust in creating humanity emphasizes how impermanent this human body is. When we die, the body simply decomposes back to its original material.

Second, the use of dust emphasizes how temporary this human body is. While the body is "wonderfully made" (Psalm 139:14), it is the container or temple of something of eternal value—the soul.

This brings us to the second action recorded in this verse. God breathed into this lifeless form and it became a living, spiritual being. Not only did the lungs expand, prompting steady breathing, but the spiritual aspect of being spirit and having a soul also came into existence. This reminds us that both physical and spiritual life come from God himself.

D. In the Garden (vv. 8-17)

(Genesis 2:10-17 is not included in the printed text.)

8. And the Lord God planted a garden eastward in

Talk About It:
How does this verse contradict the theory of evolution?

The World Created

Eden; and there he put the man whom he had formed.

9. And out of the ground made the Lord God to grow every tree that is pleasant to the sight, and good for food; the tree of life also in the midst of the garden, and the tree of knowledge of good and evil.

Eden was man's first environment. God himself prepared and planted this area as a "garden"; that is, cultivated land in distinction from the rest of the earth, which lay in a wild, natural state. The word *Eden* means "delight," and portrays the loveliness and charm of that first environment. Adam was given the task of cultivating it (v. 15). Eden did not mean idleness! It was by the fruit of his labor that Adam's physical life was sustained.

There were two special trees in Eden—"the tree of life" and "the tree of knowledge of good and evil." These were literal trees, but we are not to view them as having magical or even miraculous properties. More probably, as in water baptism and the Lord's Supper, they were chosen to represent spiritual realities and the sacraments of those realities.

Talk About It:
1. What was Adam's responsibility in Eden (v. 15)?
2. Why did God place the Tree of Knowledge in Eden?

E. A Perfect Match (vv. 18-25)

(Genesis 2:19, 20 is not included in the printed text.)

18. And the Lord God said, It is not good that man should be alone; I will make him an help meet for him.

21. And the Lord God caused a deep sleep to fall upon Adam, and he slept: and he took one of his ribs, and closed up the flesh instead thereof;

22. And the rib, which the Lord God had taken from man, made he a woman, and brought her unto the man.

23. And Adam said, This is now bone of my bones, and flesh of my flesh: she shall be called Woman, because she was taken out of Man.

24. Therefore shall a man leave his father and his mother, and shall cleave unto his wife: and they shall be one flesh.

25. And they were both naked, the man and his wife, and were not ashamed.

Man was made not only for dominion but for fellowship. Though he was monarch of all he surveyed, there was an aspect of his nature that could not be satisfied with power. He needed a "help meet for him" (vv. 18, 20). The idea is "one answering" to him, "a counterpart of himself," "someone with whom he could enter into responsible relations." No animal could provide this for man.

The making of woman from Adam's "rib" is deeply meaningful. Hebrew scholars point out that the Hebrew word "is never translated 'rib' except in this place, but always *side, flank*. . . . Woman is one side of man; and though he may have several sides to his nature and character, yet without woman one integral portion of him is wanting" (R.P. Smith).

Talk About It:
1. What disadvantage did Adam have compared with the animals (vv. 18-20)?
2. Explain why God created Eve as He did.
3. Whom should man *leave*, and to whom should he *cleave*? Why?
4. Why weren't Adam and Eve unashamed of their nakedness?

That man was created first and woman was taken out of man supports the Pauline doctrine of man's headship (Ephesians 5:23; 1 Corinthians 11:3). Yet because she was made of Adam's substance, woman is also equal with man—equal in essence, but different in function. Difference in function and role does not imply inferiority in nature and personality.

Having taken woman out of man, God then brought her back to man in a new way. Adam clearly recognized that his profound need was now met. His own nature could be fulfilled: "This is . . . bone of my bones, and flesh of my flesh" (Genesis 2:23). Calvin paraphrases: "Now at length I have obtained a suitable companion, who is part of the substance of my flesh and in whom I behold, as it were, another self."

III. DAY OF REST ESTABLISHED (Genesis 2:1-3; Hebrews 4:6-11; Colossians 2:16, 17)
A. Creation Completed (Genesis 2:1-3)

1. Thus the heavens and the earth were finished, and all the host of them.

2. And on the seventh day God ended his work which he had made; and he rested on the seventh day from all his work which he had made.

3. And God blessed the seventh day, and sanctified it: because that in it he had rested from all his work which God created and made.

In six days God created the earth and the heavens and everything in them. The word *host* refers to the innumerable throng of stars, plants, animals and other created things which populate the universe. God "ended" (finished) His creative work just as He had planned, in six days, and now He took pleasure in His creation.

The word *rested* (v. 2) here means "cessation of motion; peace and quiet." God rested not because He was tired, but because He had completed His task of creating the universe. God moved from the act of creating to overseeing the affairs of His creation.

God *blessed* the seventh day (v. 3), which means He bestowed good on it. "Here the good consists in the setting apart and consecrating of that day for His use" (*International Standard Bible Encyclopedia*).

Wycliffe says, "The seventh day was set apart to be hallowed and honored through the years as a reminder that God had appointed a season of rest, refreshment, and complete cessation of all ordinary work, toil, and struggle."

B. Rest Offered (Hebrews 4:6-11)
6. Seeing therefore it remaineth that some must enter

therein, and they to whom it was first preached entered not in because of unbelief:

7. Again, he limiteth a certain day, saying in David, To day, after so long a time; as it is said, To day if ye will hear his voice, harden not your hearts.

8. For if Jesus had given them rest, then would he not afterward have spoken of another day.

9. There remaineth therefore a rest to the people of God.

10. For he that is entered into his rest, he also hath ceased from his own works, as God did from his.

11. Let us labour therefore to enter into that rest, lest any man fall after the same example of unbelief.

An example is made of the unbelieving Israelites to teach us not to let life's hardships and confusions rob us of our relationship with God. Rather than entering the Promised Land at the ordained time, the Israelites' unbelief caused them to restlessly wander through the wilderness for nearly 40 years.

Unlike the Israelites, we must not harden our heart to God's voice (v. 7). Our world is filled with voices, all claiming to give expert advice, information, directions and ideas. In the midst of the babble, the voice of God does not always come through clearly—we must concentrate to get His message. Our heart must remain soft before Him.

In verse 8, the name *Jesus* actually is a reference to *Joshua*, who led the Israelites to the Promised Land. They received their physical rest, which was a symbol of the spiritual rest the Israelites had yet to experience. The Canaan rest was a break from striving, but the heavenly rest is obtained through believing.

All the people of God are promised a rest, not just the Israelites (v. 9). It is reserved for us if we will believe it and determine to qualify for it according to God's plan.

Nearly all the instances of the word *rest* in Hebrews 4 come from a Greek word meaning "cessation of labor." The one exception is in verse 9, where the word means "a religious rest or feast"—Sabbath rest. This carries a spiritual meaning that is indeed a precious promise for God's children. Nothing should distract us from entering into that rest.

When we quit trying to be righteous through our own good works and instead accept God's grace, His peace comes to our soul. Then, when our work on earth is through, we will enter our heavenly rest.

By saying we should "labour . . . to enter into that rest," verse 11 is saying our love and loyalty to our Savior will be demonstrated by our works. Just as the Israelites' lack of faith was seen in their rebellious actions, so our faith in God should be

Talk About It:
1. What things can keep us from entering into the rest God offers (vv. 6, 7)?
2. What should we "cease" trying to do (v. 10)?
3. Why and how should we "labour" (v. 11)?

seen in our service to Him. Our heart is at rest, but our hands are busy as we await our time of eternal rest.

C. Shadow Cast (Colossians 2:16, 17)

16. Let no man therefore judge you in meat, or in drink, or in respect of an holyday, or of the new moon, or of the sabbath days:

17. Which are a shadow of things to come; but the body is of Christ.

Talk About It:
How is Jesus Christ better than all the Old Testament festivals and laws?

This passage concerns Christians who were being wrongly judged by religionists who insisted they must observe all the Old Testament laws. These Christians were being condemned for not following certain dietary laws and not observing all the Jewish festivals. (Note that the term *sabbath days* is probably not a reference to the weekly day of rest prescribed by God, but to the closing days of religious festivals.)

Paul said these religious practices had served their purpose, which was to be mere *shadows* of Christ—symbols of spiritual realities which would be fulfilled in Jesus. We can now eat the living Bread and drink the living Water, and celebrate the Resurrection in our heart every day through the indwelling Holy Spirit.

CONCLUSION

Without Christ, the human heart is like the earth in its pre-Creation condition: "formless and empty, [covered by] darkness" (Genesis 1:2, *NIV*). Nevertheless, as He did once over the chaotic, dark world, the Spirit of God now moves and broods in tender love and grace over our life. His purpose is to bring light, life, order and meaning into our disordered nature.

Daily Devotions:
M. Fearfully and Wonderfully Made
Psalm 139:13-18
T. Remember Your Creator
Ecclesiastes 12:1-7
W. The Source of Strength
Isaiah 40:28-31
T. One Flesh
Mark 10:2-9
F. God's Offspring
Acts 17:22-31
S. New Heaven and New Earth
2 Peter 3:10-14

God's first creative words were "Let there be light," and light shined (v. 3). Today it is by the preaching of the gospel in the power of the Holy Spirit that the light is given. When sinners open their heart to God's light, for him or her there dawns the first new day.

GOLDEN TEXT CHALLENGE

"IN THE BEGINNING GOD CREATED THE HEAVEN AND THE EARTH" (Genesis 1:1).

Where did I come from? Why am I here? How did the earth come to exist? How did life begin? It is natural for people to ask questions like these. Someone said that a man stands upon his speck (the earth) and speculates.

Genesis is a book of answers. And it all begins with God, who was "in the beginning." The sincere seeker after God will find the answer to his or her questions.

The World Marred

Genesis 3:1 through 4:26; Romans 6:23

INTRODUCTION

The older liberals viewed the early chapters of Genesis as adaptations of ancient Babylonian traditions and stories. The newer liberals use the word *myths*, by which they mean that the Biblical accounts of Creation and the fall of man are not historical events but imaginative stories that embody spiritual truths. Because the word *myth* gives the impression of falsity, some prefer to call the Genesis narratives poems or parables.

Conservative scholars reject both the older and newer liberalism. To us these chapters are history. There are several reasons for this. One is the attitude of the Lord Jesus Christ and His apostles. It is better to follow Jesus and the apostles than either the older or newer German critics and their British and American allies. E.J. Young says of the chapter we are about to study: "That Christ and the apostles interpreted Genesis 3 as an historical document should be sufficient for the humble Christian who desires to follow in their steps" (*Genesis Three: A Devotional and Expository Study*).

Paul plainly referred to Genesis 3 in Romans 5:12-21 when he said that "sin entered into the world" by the one man Adam. He did not, however, equate this with the ultimate origin of sin. The fact that, in the Genesis narrative, the tempter appeared in the Garden deliberately set on deceiving and corrupting humanity implies that sin already existed in the tempter. Since we cannot believe that this tempter (named in the New Testament as Satan and the devil) is an eternal, changeless being, the bad equal of God, and since we cannot believe that God created him an evil being, it follows that this tempter was a created being, originally good, who became evil of his own volition in an act of arrogant rebellion against God. What we are to study, therefore, is the beginning of sin in human society.

Unit Theme:
Beginnings (Genesis 1—11)

Central Truth:
Sin and its consequences came through disobedience to God's Word.

Focus:
Investigate how sin came into our world and be aware of the effects of the Fall in our lives.

Context:
The Book of Genesis was written between 1450 and 1400 B.C. We don't know the dates of its events.

Golden Text:
"The wages of sin is death; but the gift of God is eternal life through Jesus Christ our Lord" (Romans 6:23).

Study Outline:
I. Tempted to Disobey (Genesis 3:1-7)
II. Judged for Sin (Genesis 3:8-19)
III. Consequences of Sin (Genesis 3:20—4:16, 25, 26; Romans 6:23)

I. TEMPTED TO DISOBEY (Genesis 3:1-7)

A. The Agent of Temptation (v. 1)

1. Now the serpent was more subtil than any beast of the field which the Lord God had made. And he said unto the woman, Yea, hath God said, Ye shall not eat of every tree of the garden?

Talk About It:
1. Why do you think Satan chose a serpent to speak through?
2. Why did Satan approach Eve with a question?

There are two errors to be avoided in seeking to explain the meaning of the talking serpent: (1) the serpent was not an actual snake but merely a poetic description of the woman's thoughts, and (2) the serpent was only an appearance of Satan in the form of a snake.

It is difficult to understand the curse pronounced on the serpent (v. 14) if it was merely a thought in Eve's mind, or only a spirit in physical form. The Bible taken as a whole would lead us to believe that the agent of temptation was a literal snake that became the instrument of the devil to deceive and corrupt Adam and Eve. We may wonder how a snake could be made to speak. The same problem confronts us in the story of Balaam's donkey. We cannot explain "how." But we must realize that when we are dealing with God and Satan, we are working in the realm of the supernatural, a realm that transcends natural explanations.

The important point is that the snake, which was one of God's creatures, became an agent of the devil by which Eve was deceived. Presumably, there was nothing fearful or unfamiliar about the serpent. It was a well-known creature, perhaps a pet, admired for its subtilty, which Satan used to bring about Eve's downfall.

Thus we are warned about satanic tactics. He appears, said Paul, as "an angel of light" (2 Corinthians 11:3, 14), in the guise of the familiar, the friendly, the attractive, to deceive humanity. He is still, as always, the one "which deceiveth the whole world" (Revelation 12:9).

B. The Occasion of Temptation (vv. 2-5)

2. And the woman said unto the serpent, We may eat of the fruit of the trees of the garden:

3. But of the fruit of the tree which is in the midst of the garden, God hath said, Ye shall not eat of it, neither shall ye touch it, lest ye die.

4. And the serpent said unto the woman, Ye shall not surely die:

5. For God doth know that in the day ye eat thereof, then your eyes shall be opened, and ye shall be as gods, knowing good and evil.

The occasion of temptation was "the tree of the knowledge of good and evil" (2:17). We need to be clear as to the meaning of this tree.

First, it was a literal, ordinary tree. It was not a metaphor for sexual experience, as some have imagined. Young says, "In the first chapter of Genesis, man was commanded to be fruitful and to fill the earth. Before the entrance of sin into the world, man knew about sex. He knew it was good and noble, and that he might use it for God's glory and for the fulfillment of God's command." In other words, sex could not be "the tree of the knowledge of good and evil," for God did not prohibit sexual expression, but invented it and advocated it, of course within marriage.

Second, the tree was not a magical tree, but an ordinary tree selected by God to be the means of a moral test. "There is no reason to think that there was anything in the tree itself which had power to make them wise—that was the devil's lie (v. 5) which the woman believed" (O.T. Allis, *God Spake by Moses*). It could have been any tree (the Bible does not say it was an apple tree), but God selected this particular tree as a test of obedience. The real issue was obedience or disobedience. And that meant God's will or man's will, loyalty or rebellion. The tree was the focal point for human decision on this fundamental matter.

The word *knowledge* does not mean mere intellectual knowledge, but experiential knowledge. Richardson says, "It is knowledge gained by participating actively in the affairs of life—not 'academic' or theoretical knowledge, but what in our jargon of today we might call 'existential' knowledge. A more usual English word would be 'experience'" (*Genesis I-XI*). The quest for new experiences, both good and evil, comes near to what the knowledge to be gained by eating of the tree means.

Satan, through the serpent, set out to lure Eve and then Adam to disobey God. First, he attracted Eve through the familiar serpent. Second, he engaged her in dialogue. Dialogue with the devil is always dangerous. Any answer to the devil should begin with the words "It is written." Third, he raised a doubt about the wisdom of God's commandment (v. 1). Could God make such a preposterous law? The devil is still at that game in the 21st century! Fourth, He strongly contradicted divine authority and the divine word—"Ye shall not surely die!" (v. 4). Fifth, he impugned God's motives (v. 5). Satan was saying, "God is jealous of His unlimited knowledge and power, and schemes to keep others from acquiring it. To eat the fruit of the tree will be a breakthrough of these unjust and cruel limitations into divinity."

C. The Response to Temptation (vv. 6, 7)

6. And when the woman saw that the tree was good for food, and that it was pleasant to the eyes, and a tree to be desired to make one wise, she took of the fruit thereof, and did eat, and gave also unto her husband with her; and he did eat.

Talk About It:
1. Compare Eve's version of what God said (3:2, 3) with what He actually said (2:16, 17). What's the same? What's different?
2. According to Satan, why did God not want Adam and Eve to eat from the Tree of Knowledge? What did he say would *not* happen if they did?

"The devil hath power to assume a pleasing shape."
—William Shakespeare

7. And the eyes of them both were opened, and they knew that they were naked; and they sewed fig leaves together, and made themselves aprons.

Talk About It:
1. Describe the different reasons the fruit appealed to Eve.
2. There is no record of Adam questioning Eve about eating the fruit. Why do you suppose "he did eat" (v. 6)?
3. What feelings drove the couple's actions in verse 7?

In the language of James, Eve, when seduced by the serpent, was "drawn away of [her] own lust, and enticed" (James 1:14). The suggestions and lies of the devil aroused her curiosity and awakened her desire for the fruit of the prohibited tree. The tree represented an experience that she must have, a most attractive and coveted prize.

Genesis 3:6 describes its attractiveness as threefold: (1) It was "good for food"; that is, it appealed to her sensual nature. It would give physical pleasure—even though it lay outside the will of God. (2) It was "pleasant to the eyes"; that is, it appealed to her aesthetic nature. We have to understand that both of these qualities of the tree ("good" and "pleasant") were God-created qualities, and that they were attached to all the trees in Eden (2:9). But Eve allowed herself to be deceived into thinking that because the tree was good and pleasant, therefore it was right and proper for her to have it, though God had said no. Many are still under this illusion. (3) It was "a tree to be desired to make one wise." It was this aspect of the tree, false though it was, that appealed more particularly to Eve. The serpent had created the illusion in Eve's mind that the tree had this special property. To eat of the fruit would make her "like God."

What was conceived in Eve's heart through the dialogue with the serpent was brought forth into action. What Eve did through being deceived, Adam did deliberately, following his wife's example. Thus both the woman and the man brought forth sin, willful defiance and rebellion against the Word of God. Eve and Adam made a declaration of independence from God. They set up their own kingdom and government—self-government. Such is the essence of all sin.

The immediate result of sin was so vastly different from what the serpent had promised. Derek Kinder said human depravity was "a grotesque anticlimax to the dream of enlightenment" (*Tyndale Commentary, Genesis*).

"Many of the world's most attractive temptations are like some television commercials: frequently deceptive and frightfully costly."
—**William A. Ward**

They were aware of their nakedness before (that is, of their sexuality), but now they knew with a new kind of understanding. "The sense of shame attaching to physical nakedness manifested consciousness of inner nakedness, the stripping of the glory of holiness from the soul" (M.G. Kline, *New Bible Commentary Revised*). In a word, the eye of man's soul became evil (see Matthew 6:22, 23). His nature was polluted.

II. JUDGED FOR SIN (Genesis 3:8-19)
A. Sense of Guilt (vv. 8-10)
8. And they heard the voice of the Lord God walking in

the garden in the cool of the day: and Adam and his wife hid themselves from the presence of the Lord God amongst the trees of the garden.

9. And the Lord God called unto Adam, and said unto him, Where art thou?

10. And he said, I heard thy voice in the garden, and I was afraid, because I was naked; and I hid myself.

Talk About It:
What was Adam afraid of? Why?

If we link verse 7 with verse 10, we see that the making of "aprons" and the hiding in the trees of the Garden are manifestations of the same thing—guilt-consciousness. Adam and Eve had allied themselves with God's enemy. They had preferred self-will to God's will. And conscience accused them (see Romans 2:15). They felt guilty. God became an object of terror. They abandoned their former reverential "fear of the Lord," and a sense of terror gripped them.

The fig-leaf coverings were a pathetic attempt to overcome their shame and fear, and to make themselves fit for the divine presence, a kind of do-it-yourself salvation. E.J. Young writes: "They try to do what sinners always try to do. They make an attempt at saving themselves. So perverted is their reason, so dark their light, so ignorant their knowledge, that they fall into the foolish effort of attempting to clothe their nakedness. It is the first attempt at salvation by works, and it is just as ineffectual as all such attempts" (*Genesis Three*).

Furthermore, they ran from God when He appeared. It is amazing what routes people take when they try to hide from God!

"Our age speaks of such things as error, mistake, superstition, delusion, but it does not admit such a thing as sin."
—*Quotable Quotes*

B. Evasion of Responsibility (vv. 11-13)

11. And he said, Who told thee that thou wast naked? Hast thou eaten of the tree, whereof I commanded thee that thou shouldest not eat?

12. And the man said, The woman whom thou gavest to be with me, she gave me of the tree, and I did eat.

13. And the Lord God said unto the woman, What is this that thou hast done? And the woman said, The serpent beguiled me, and I did eat.

Talk About It:
1. Why did God immediately know what they had done wrong?
2. Whom did Adam blame for his sin? Whom did Eve blame? Why didn't they take personal responsibility for their actions?

The man blamed the woman, and the woman blamed the serpent. The serpent could have blamed the devil; but as it could only talk as the devil inspired and used it, it was unable to plead, for the devil was not likely to help it put the blame on himself!

It is true that the serpent deceived Eve, as she claimed. However, she was responsible for giving in to Satan's trickery. She could have said no to his tempting.

C. Curse of Sin (vv. 14, 16-19)

14. And the Lord God said unto the serpent, Because

Talk About It:
1. Describe the curse placed on the serpent.
2. How would Eve's sin affect women's relationship with men?
3. How would motherhood become linked with sorrow?
4. How would man's life become more difficult?

enmity (v. 15)— hatred or ill will

Talk About It:
What blessing is found in the curse of verse 15?

thou hast done this, thou art cursed above all cattle, and above every beast of the field; upon thy belly shalt thou go, and dust shalt thou eat all the days of thy life:

16. Unto the woman he said, I will greatly multiply thy sorrow and thy conception; in sorrow thou shalt bring forth children; and thy desire shall be to thy husband, and he shall rule over thee.

17. And unto Adam he said, Because thou hast heark-ened unto the voice of thy wife, and hast eaten of the tree, of which I commanded thee, saying, Thou shalt not eat of it: cursed is the ground for thy sake; in sorrow shalt thou eat of it all the days of thy life;

18. Thorns also and thistles shall it bring forth to thee; and thou shalt eat the herb of the field;

19. In the sweat of thy face shalt thou eat bread, till thou return unto the ground; for out of it wast thou taken: for dust thou art, and unto dust shalt thou return.

Because of the Fall, human life and experience would hence-forth be interwoven with pain, frustration, futility, despair, and a continuous battle with physical weakness and the hard ele-ments. People would, indeed, know evil in an experiential way.

In Romans 8:18-25 Paul generalized on this aspect of judg-ment, calling it "vanity," "the bondage of corruption," and "groan[ing] and travail[ing] in pain"—a feature of all of life from which not even Christians are free until their glorification. What a legacy of sorrow and suffering has descended on humanity and creation as a result of man's attempt to equal God!

In Genesis 3:19, physical death is plainly said to be the con-sequence of the Fall. Some have tried to claim this verse implies that death is the normal and natural consequence of being constituted of dust. However, the warning that sin would lead to death (2:17), as well as the statement that man could have lived forever (3:22), imply that death was not natural but a judgment. This is how the New Testament interprets it (Romans 5:12; 1 Corinthians 15:21, 22).

D. Promise of Redemption (v. 15)

15. And I will put enmity between thee and the woman, and between thy seed and her seed; it shall bruise thy head, and thou shalt bruise his heel.

This verse is often called "The Protoevangelium" (the first gospel). Paul's allusion in Romans 16:20 encourages the belief that the serpent here is Satan; and passages like Isaiah 7:14 and Galatians 4:4 lend support to the view that "the seed of the woman" is Christ.

Thus, in the midst of decrees of judgment, God gave a hope and a promise of redemption through His incarnate Son. Satan

The World Marred

would strike Christ's "heel" through the Crucifixion, but Christ would crush Satan's head through the Cross and Resurrection (Colossians 2:15).

III. CONSEQUENCES OF SIN (Genesis 3:20—4:26; Romans 6:23)

A. Banishment From Eden (Genesis 3:20-24)

(Genesis 3:20, 21 is not included in the printed text.)

22. And the Lord God said, Behold, the man is become as one of us, to know good and evil: and now, lest he put forth his hand, and take also of the tree of life, and eat, and live for ever:

23. Therefore the Lord God sent him forth from the garden of Eden, to till the ground from whence he was taken.

24. So he drove out the man; and he placed at the east of the garden of Eden Cherubims, and a flaming sword which turned every way, to keep the way of the tree of life.

Adam and Eve had to exchange the cultivated Garden of Delight for the uncultivated wilderness. Also, they were excluded from "the tree of life," by which their immortality could be maintained. Finally, they were separated from the presence of God.

The cherubim and the flaming sword (v. 24) symbolize there is no way back to the Garden of Eden and all it meant by humanity's own effort. We are "alienated from the life of God" (Ephesians 4:18). We cannot save ourselves.

Talk About It:
1. How did God show Adam and Eve mercy despite their sin?
2. In what sense had Adam become more like God, and why was this bad?
3. Explain the significance of the statement "to till the ground from whence he was taken" (v. 23)?

B. Born Into Sin (Genesis 4:1-26)

(Genesis 4:1-26 is not included in the printed text.)

The story of Cain and Abel, the first two children of Adam and Eve, shows how terribly and rapidly Adam's posterity was affected by his sin. Allis says, "The prompt and awful working of sin is shown in the fact that the first child of the first pair becomes a murderer, the enemy of his fellowmen, while the last mentioned descendant of Cain composes a hymn of hate which glories in the sin of his ancestor" (*God Spake by Moses*).

The rest of chapter 4 describes four consequences of Cain's wickedness:

A hardened heart (vv. 9, 10). When God asks questions of man, it is not to find out answers for Himself. He knows already. He knew where Adam was hiding (3:9). He knew Cain had killed Abel. Rather, as Bennett says, "He seeks to elicit a confession" (*Century Bible*). He endeavors to bring the sinner out into the open.

When interrogated, Cain showed a truculent spirit. He deliberately lied to God and betrayed complete callousness. Instead of being shocked and horrified at the lengths to which he had gone, he was actually hardened in sin. The beast at the door had really mastered him.

Cain (v. 1)— "acquisition"
Abel (v. 2)— "that which ascends"
wroth (v. 5)— angry
Enos (v. 26)— "mortal"

Talk About It:
1. Why was Cain angry?
2. How did God warn Cain (v. 7)?
3. Describe God's punishment of Cain (vv. 11, 12).
4. How did God protect Cain, and why (v. 15)?

5. According to verse 26, what positive turn did humanity make?

The cursed ground (vv. 11, 12). The peculiar phrase "cursed from the ground" (*NASB*) is said to be capable of two meanings. Bennett comments, "Both 'so as to be driven from the ground,' and 'cursed with a curse which works from the ground'" (*Century Bible*). This implies that a twofold punishment would be inflicted upon Cain the murderer: (1) The ground which he cultivated would be blighted; (2) in consequence he would be forced to leave the territory and seek another region.

Exile (vv. 13-16). As a result of the blighted ground, Cain was driven into exile, "a fugitive and a vagabond." The word *vagabond* is better rendered "wanderer." Cain was forced to leave the area near Eden. Verse 16 says he went in the direction of the east to "the land of Nod." *Nod* is the Hebrew word rendered *vagabond* (wanderer) in verses 12 and 14. Geographically it is unknown and may be metaphorical of the life of wandering away from God to which the murderer had been banished.

What a picture of the sinner's alienation from God this is— in the present life as well as in the everlasting banishment from the presence of the Lord, which is hellfire. Every sinner lives, or rather wanders, in "the land of Nod."

A sinful progeny (vv. 17-24). Verse 14 implies that Cain's banishment would lead him, ultimately if not immediately, into contact with more people. The remaining verses of the chapter describe those people as descending from Cain himself. The question "From where did Cain get his wife?" must be given the answer "He married one of his sisters" (see 5:4). Eric Sauer shows that "with an average of only six children per family, by the time Cain was 400 years old he would have had far more than 100,000 descendants" (*The Dawn of World Redemption*).

This Cainite family developed especially in the arts and sciences. Yet interlinked with this progress was religious and moral decline. Cain's terrible example corrupted his children for many generations. Lamech is selected for special mention in this regard. He plunged headlong into polygamy and brutal murder. His statement (vv. 23, 24) is poetical in form and is permeated with bloodthirsty boasting. Another version translates it: "I have slain a man for wounding me, a young man for striking me. If Cain is avenged sevenfold, truly Lamech seventy-sevenfold" (*RSV*). In other words, for a comparatively slight attack upon him, Lamech had performed a bloody murder. If Cain could be protected for his crime, surely he (Lamech) deserved greater protection! Lamech was a terrorist who claimed the protection of the law.

C. Wages of Sin (Romans 6:23)
23. For the wages of sin is death, but the gift of God is eternal life through Jesus Christ our Lord.

"Anger is an acid that can do more harm to the vessel in which it's stored than to anything on which it's poured."
—*Quotable Quotes*

The World Marred

Sin is the condition of humanity apart from God, and its consequence is death. God's desire for all people is the opposite of death—it is eternal life.

The word *gift* in the Greek world at the time of the New Testament spoke of a favor done to someone deserving or a friend. Jesus changed the usage of that word. He taught that God's *grace gift* of eternal life is for all. The sin of humanity prompts God's grace and gift of eternal life.

While our sin earns us the death penalty, God freely offers the gift of life to all who will receive His Son.

CONCLUSION

From the very beginning, people have tried to blame their temptation and sin on others. Adam accused Eve, and Eve accused the serpent. Some in our generation blame society, circumstances, or their parents for their wicked conduct. Still others blame God for creating the appetite.

It is true that God created us with the potential for choosing right or wrong. This potential is not evil, nor is the appetite bad, until it is misdirected from a healthy fulfillment to an unhealthy abuse. The natural appetite for food, drink, sex, and achievement become sin when misdirected to gluttony, immorality, misuse of power, and greed. We are responsible for the choice.

GOLDEN TEXT CHALLENGE

"THE WAGES OF SIN IS DEATH; BUT THE GIFT OF GOD IS ETERNAL LIFE THROUGH JESUS CHRIST OUR LORD" (Romans 6:23).

By a sinful course of action we merit death, as a soldier by his service earns his rations and his pay. We disobey the law, and bring the sentence upon ourselves. But we have no power available to procure for ourselves acquittal and favor.

Human weakness has been provided for in God's plan of salvation. He who breathed natural life into man comes again graciously to inspire His creatures with spiritual life. God knows the needs of His creatures, and the gift is preeminently suitable. The Romans loved the games of the amphitheatre; but when famine threatened the city, the curses were loud and deep against Nero because the Alexandrian ships were expected to arrive with corn instead of with sand for the arena. And men like a beautiful present; let us not, therefore, hang back from accepting the royal bounty so adapted to our wants. Treat the gift with care, prize and use the treasure.

—**Excerpts from *Pulpit Commentary***

Talk About It:
Why is the result of sin called *wages*, while the response of God is called a *gift*?

Daily Devotions:
M. Flee Temptation
Genesis 39:2-10
T. God's Powerful
Forgiveness
Psalm 103:1-14
W. God Commands
Repentance
Ezekiel 18:20-
23, 30-32
T. Christ Forgives
Sin
Matthew 9:1-8
F. Promise to the
Tempted
1 Corinthians
10:6-14
S. Don't Be
Deceived
Galatians 6:3-8

The World Judged

Genesis 6:1 through 9:17

Unit Theme:
Beginnings
(Genesis 1—11)

Central Truth:
The Flood proved that God punishes the unrighteous and preserves the righteous.

Focus:
Review the story of the Flood and live righteously in an unrighteous world.

Context:
The Flood could have taken place as early as 8000 B.C. or as late as 2400 B.C.

Golden Text:
"[God] spared not the old world, but saved Noah the eighth person, a preacher of righteousness, bringing in the flood upon the world of the ungodly" (2 Peter 2:5).

Study Outline:
I. God's Case Against Humanity (Genesis 6:1-22)
II. God's Reward for Righteousness (Genesis 7:1—8:19)
III. God's Covenant With Creation (Genesis 8:20—9:17)

INTRODUCTION

The amount of space that Moses gave to his account of the Great Flood is an indication of the importance of the subject—four chapters. Its importance in the divine program is further stressed by the New Testament references to it (Matthew 24:37-39; Luke 17:26, 27; 2 Peter 3:4-6).

Before studying the story of the Flood, we should glance back to the previous two chapters of Genesis. A former lesson left us with a murdered Abel and a growing Cainite civilization. The New Testament describes Cain as "of that wicked one" (1 John 3:12); namely, a child of the devil. And the civilization that Cain fathered was also "of that wicked one." However, the fourth chapter of Genesis, which paints a horrific picture of Cainite society, ends on a happier note (4:25, 26). Another son, called Seth, was born to Adam and Eve, through whom a godly line and a righteous society came into being.

The growth of this society, sharing the same world as the Cainite, is described in chapter 5, which climaxes with the 500th birthday of Noah. It does not take many minutes to read this chapter, but it covers several thousand years of history. Most conservative scholars now believe that the 10 generations of Sethites named in the record are selective and incomplete (see also ch. 11). This means it is impossible to date either the Flood or Creation. Our lesson begins with the merging of the Cainite and Sethite civilizations.

I. GOD'S CASE AGAINST HUMANITY (Genesis 6:1-22)

A. Humanity's Corruption (vv. 1-5, 11-13)

1. And it came to pass, when men began to multiply on the face of the earth, and daughters were born unto them,

2. That the sons of God saw the daughters of men that they were fair; and they took them wives of all which they chose.

3. And the Lord said, My spirit shall not always strive with man, for that he also is flesh: yet his days shall be an hundred and twenty years.

4. There were giants in the earth in those days; and also after that, when the sons of God came in unto the daughters of men, and they bare children to them, the same became mighty men which were of old, men of renown.

5. And God saw that the wickedness of man was great in the earth, and that every imagination of the thoughts of his heart was only evil continually.

11. The earth also was corrupt before God, and the earth was filled with violence.

12. And God looked upon the earth, and, behold, it was corrupt; for all flesh had corrupted his way upon the earth.

13. And God said unto Noah, The end of all flesh is come before me; for the earth is filled with violence through them; and, behold, I will destroy them with the earth.

strive (v. 3)—"contend" (*NIV*)

The meaning of the opening verses of Genesis 6 has been debated for centuries. There are several explanations among Evangelical scholars.

One opinion is that "the sons of God" were the godly line of Seth, and "the daughters of men" were the ungodly line of Cain. The chief difficulty here is that the Biblical record de-scribes the Cainites as a strong race who could not be easily forced to bend to the will of the Sethites.

A second position is that "the sons of God" were angels who married human beings—a form of occultism that stretches the imagination. The main difficulty is that Jesus, our highest authority, implied that angels "neither marry, nor are given in marriage" (Matthew 22:30).

A third idea is that "the sons of God" were Cainite kings who claimed the divine title and forced Sethite women into polygamous marriages with them.

A fourth opinion claims that "the sons of God" means "the sons of the mighty ones," being the dominant race of Cain, and "the daughters of men" were the women of the Seth line. Thus the strong, arrogant, dominant Cainites, after the fashion of Lamech (4:19-24), brutally and arrogantly corrupted the Sethite women.

There is a close relation between opinions 3 and 4, and possibly here is the clue to the meaning of the difficult passage. In

Talk About It:
1. Why does taking "wives of all which they chose" (v. 2) indicate a problem?
2. When does God "contend" with humanity, and why did God put a limit on this?
3. Why are wicked thoughts and purposes so deadly (v. 5)?
4. How had people "corrupted his [God's] way" (v. 12)?

any case "the sons of God" are shown to be guilty of the utmost arrogance and high-mindedness. The whole passage breathes of rebellion and defiance of God.

The consequence of this intermarriage was a race of "giants" (6:4). The Hebrew word is *nephilim*, the meaning of which is uncertain. The word *giants* is rendered in the Greek Septuagint *gigantes*. However, Alan Richardson says, "The Greek word would carry a reference beyond that of our English 'giants,' who are merely very big men" (*Genesis I-XI*). Perhaps our best clue is provided by the Book of Revelation (ch. 13) in its description of the two "beasts"—political "giants" with persuasive, Hitler-like evil power.

The consequences of the union of "the sons of God" with "the daughters of men" went further than the production of super leaders. There was a more widespread consequence. The entire Sethite race became corrupted and debased. The barriers in general between the Sethites and Cainites were demolished, and all humanity became apostate. The language of Moses that describes the universal degeneracy is striking.

The word *corrupt* (vv. 11, 12) means "ruin, decay or perversion" of any kind. *Violence* means "harshness" of any kind. The *Oxford Hebrew-English Lexicon* says it describes "in general, the rude wickedness of men, their noisy, wild ruthlessness." The summing up of the worldwide condition is a horrific portrait: "Every imagination of the thoughts of his [humanity's] heart was only evil continually" (v. 5). R. Payne Smith said "a more forcible picture of complete depravity could scarcely be drawn" (*Ellicott's Bible Commentary*).

We should not fail to mark the words of Christ: "As it was in the days of Noe, so shall it be also in the days of the Son of man" (Luke 17:26). Satanic deceptions and delusions abound. The vast accumulation of knowledge and the conquests of science have fostered delusions of grandeur among humanity. There are "giants" in the earth today! Indeed, it is the age of giants today, in many ways. It is likewise an age of perversions, terrorism and violence. God is defied. Barriers of every kind are being broken. Wickedness abounds.

B. God's Concern (vv. 6-10)
(Genesis 6:9, 10 is not included in the printed text.)
6. And it repented the Lord that he had made man on the earth, and it grieved him at his heart.

7. And the Lord said, I will destroy man whom I have created from the face of the earth; both man, and beast, and the creeping thing, and the fowls of the air; for it repenteth me that I have made them.

8. But Noah found grace in the eyes of the Lord.

"A seared conscience is one whose warning voice has been suppressed and perverted habitually, so that eventually instead of serving as a guide, it only confirms the person in his premeditatedly evil course."
—Robert J. Little

perfect (v. 9)–
upright, sincere

The World Judged

We ought first to glance back at verse 3 which also express-es the divine concern over human wickedness. The passage suggests that God was weary with contending against the sin-ful human will. Luther thought that this "striving" was through prophetic witness. Calvin gives the word *strive* a more general meaning—"threats, warnings, chastisements, and so on." Another translation of *strive* is "abide." It is not the Spirit of God as a divine Person that is meant but the divine breath that animates the human body. According to this view, God decided to set a limit of 120 years on human life, instead of the hundreds of years portrayed in chapter 5.

Whichever of these explanations is correct, the divine con-cern is underscored. God's patience with the centuries of mounting rebellion and deepening wickedness was reaching its end. He was about to do something about it.

What this was is described in verses 6-13. The question is raised: If God is unchangeable (see Malachi 3:6; James 1:17), how can He repent or change His mind? While God did not change one iota in His eternal purpose for humanity, the univer-sal corruption of Noah's generation produced a change in His attitude and relations with people. Indeed, it was because He could not change in His nature and purpose that He had to change from mercy to judgment. To save humanity He deemed it necessary to destroy that generation of people. There was still one good "apple" left in the rotten basket (Genesis 6:8). God had allowed humanity to survive to the last good man, or the last good family. To save the species and thus perpetuate His benev-olent purpose, it was necessary for Him to act in judgment.

C. Place of Safety (vv. 14-22)

(Genesis 6:14-16, 20, 21 is not included in the printed text.)

17. And, behold, I, even I, do bring a flood of waters upon the earth, to destroy all flesh, wherein is the breath of life, from under heaven; and every thing that is in the earth shall die.

18. But with thee will I establish my covenant; and thou shalt come into the ark, thou, and thy sons, and thy wife, and thy sons' wives with thee.

19. And of every living thing of all flesh, two of every sort shalt thou bring into the ark, to keep them alive with thee; they shall be male and female.

22. Thus did Noah; according to all that God com-manded him, so did he.

God decided His method of judgment would be a great flood. While liberals treat the Biblical account of the Flood as a Hebrew counterpart of a Babylonian legend, and some conservatives claim the Flood was local, not universal, other conservative

Talk About It:
1. How did humani-ty's corruption affect God (v. 6)?
2. What does verse 8 mean?
3. What does it mean to *walk* with God (v. 9)?

"God is a personal Father who cares, and not a God who merely wound up the world with a key and then went away to let it run by itself. God's grace is a certainty, even amid the turmoil of today's world."
—*Quotable Quotes*

Talk About It:
1. Why was God so specific in His instructions concerning the ark (vv. 14-16)?
2. How did God explain His plan of judgment to Noah (v. 17)? How do you suppose it made Noah feel?
3. How did Noah respond to God's commands?

"Plan ahead. It was not raining when Noah built the ark."
—Unknown

scholars strongly defend the concept of a worldwide flood. H.M. Morris writes: "The entire story is filled with absurdities if the flood described were only a localized event. The elaborate provisions for the preservation of life in the ark were utterly unnecessary and unwarranted. God could merely have warned Noah to move into a region where the flood would not come, which he could have done with far less time and labor than was needed in constructing and outfitting the ark. The same is true for the animals, which the record says God caused to come to the ark; the birds especially might have flown to dry land. Finally, God's promise that there would never again be such a destructive flood would have been proved false, because there have been many floods since which were at least as great as that envisioned by the local flood theory" (*Bible and Modern Science*).

In *The Genesis Flood* the authors say, "It would not have been possible for water to cover even one high mountain in the Near East without inundating Australia and America too" (Morris and J.C. Whitcombe).

II. GOD'S REWARD FOR RIGHTEOUSNESS
(Genesis 7:1—8:19)
A. The Flood (7:1-12)
(Genesis 7:2-6, 8-10 is not included in the printed text.)

1. And the Lord said unto Noah, Come thou and all thy house into the ark; for thee have I seen righteous before me in this generation.

7. And Noah went in, and his sons, and his wife, and his sons' wives with him, into the ark, because of the waters of the flood.

11. In the six hundredth year of Noah's life, in the second month, the seventeenth day of the month, the same day were all the fountains of the great deep broken up, and the windows of heaven were opened.

12. And the rain was upon the earth forty days and forty nights.

The Bible declares that the floodwaters had two sources: "the fountains of the great deep were broken up" and "the windows of heaven were opened." The former statement means, says Morris, that "the ocean basins were fractured and uplifted sufficiently to pour waters over the continents." This would create gigantic tidal waves around the world. The latter statement is generally taken to refer to indescribable rainfall. However, some believe, on the basis of Genesis 2:5, that there was no rain before the Flood. Morris argues that in pre-Flood times a great body of water vapor surrounded the earth above its atmosphere ("the firmament" of Genesis 1), and that God caused

Talk About It:
1. Why would God protect Noah (v. 1)?
2. Why did God command that seven pairs of certain animals be taken?

this to collapse to bring colossal amounts of water upon the earth (*The Bible and Modern Science*).

B. The Way of Salvation (vv. 13-24)

(Genesis 7:17-22 is not included in the printed text.)

13. In the selfsame day entered Noah, and Shem, and Ham, and Japheth, the sons of Noah, and Noah's wife, and the three wives of his sons with them, into the ark;

14. They, and every beast after his kind, and all the cattle after their kind, and every creeping thing that creepeth upon the earth after his kind, and every fowl after his kind, every bird of every sort.

15. And they went in unto Noah into the ark, two and two of all flesh, wherein is the breath of life.

16. And they that went in, went in male and female of all flesh, as God had commanded him: and the Lord shut him in.

23. And every living substance was destroyed which was upon the face of the ground, both man, and cattle, and the creeping things, and the fowl of the heaven; and they were destroyed from the earth: and Noah only remained alive, and they that were with him in the ark.

24. And the waters prevailed upon the earth an hundred and fifty days.

In that age of universal corruption there was one man, a Sethite, who remained true to God. This man, Noah, was to fulfill a positive prophecy that his father, Lamech, had made concerning him (5:29). The Biblical portrait of Noah—"a just man and perfect in his generations, and Noah walked with God" (6:9)—is all the more beautiful when placed alongside the ugliness of his contemporaries. The New Testament broadens this portrait, describing him as a man of faith who was motivated by reverent fear of God (Hebrews 11:7), whose life and witness saved his own household and raised a standard that condemned the wicked world around him. Peter called him "a preacher of righteousness" (2 Peter 2:5). This implies that he witnessed for truth and righteousness against the permissive society of his time, and no doubt endeavored "to save some" from "the wrath to come."

God revealed to the godly Noah a plan of salvation from the coming deluge: "Make thee an ark of gopher wood" (see Genesis 6:14-22). The ark of salvation was a gigantic boxlike or bargelike vessel, constructed not for sailing but for floating, as well as for maximum capacity.

Morris and Whitcombe say that "the gross tonnage of the ark was about 13,960 tons, which would place it well within the category of large metal oceangoing vessels today" (*The Genesis Flood*). Its size was about 450 feet long, 75 feet

> "Character may be manifested in the great moments, but it is made in the small ones."
> —**Phillips Brooks**

Talk About It:
1. Explain the phrase "The Lord shut him in" (v. 16).
2. How thorough was the judgment (v. 23)?

wide, and 45 feet high. It had more space than 500 railroad cattle cars.

In this ark constructed like Moses' Tabernacle, according to a pattern given by God, Noah, his wife, his three sons and their wives were preserved from the destruction that came upon that ancient world (7:13 ff.). In addition, samples of animal life, male and female, for future breeding, were preserved.

Outside the ark, not a living creature survived. Not a frog, not a deer, not a chimpanzee—nothing. No man or woman, no boy or girl survived the Flood. There was no place to escape because the waters rose 20 feet above the highest mountain, and the earth remained flooded for months.

C. The Receding Flood (8:1-19)

(Genesis 8:5-14 is not included in the printed text.)

1. And God remembered Noah, and every living thing, and all the cattle that was with him in the ark: and God made a wind to pass over the earth, and the waters asswaged;

2. The fountains also of the deep and the windows of heaven were stopped, and the rain from heaven was restrained;

3. And the waters returned from off the earth continually: and after the end of the hundred and fifty days the waters were abated.

4. And the ark rested in the seventh month, on the seventeenth day of the month, upon the mountains of Ararat.

15. And God spake unto Noah, saying,

16. Go forth of the ark, thou, and thy wife, and thy sons, and thy sons' wives with thee.

17. Bring forth with thee every living thing that is with thee, of all flesh, both of fowl, and of cattle, and of every creeping thing that creepeth upon the earth; that they may breed abundantly in the earth, and be fruitful, and multiply upon the earth.

18. And Noah went forth, and his sons, and his wife, and his sons' wives with him:

19. Every beast, every creeping thing, and every fowl, and whatsoever creepeth upon the earth, after their kinds, went forth out of the ark.

Talk About It:
1. Explain the phrase "God remembered Noah" (v. 1).
2. What do you suppose Noah and his family's feelings were as they finally left the ark?

God caused a drying, evaporating wind to sweep the earth, helping the flood to "asswage" (recede). The same almighty power used to send the flood was now used to counteract it. It is estimated that the water went down around four inches per day until the ark rested on the mountains of Ararat in Armenia.

The entire Flood event took place over a year's time: More than 50 days were spent putting supplies and animals on the ark; it rained 40 days; the floodwaters increased for 150 days; and it took 120 days for the waters to subside.

The World Judged

Noah used birds to test the flood's decline. When Noah sent a raven out of the ark, it soon returned, for there was no place else to land. He did the same with a dove, with the same result. A week later, the dove was sent out again, and returned with an olive leaf; "then Noah knew that the water had receded from the earth" (v. 11, *NIV*). A week later, he sent out the dove yet again, and the dove did not return. Since doves won't stay in wet places, it was obvious the land was dry.

Some eight weeks after Noah took the cover off the ark, the Lord told Noah to leave the ark, along with his family and all the animals (vv. 15-17). God sent the animals to spread across the earth and multiply once again.

III. GOD'S COVENANT WITH CREATION
(Genesis 8:20—9:17)
A. Noah's Altar (8:20-22)
20. And Noah builded an altar unto the Lord; and took of every clean beast, and of every clean fowl, and offered burnt offerings on the altar.

21. And the Lord smelled a sweet savour; and the Lord said in his heart, I will not again curse the ground any more for man's sake; for the imagination of man's heart is evil from his youth; neither will I again smite any more every thing living, as I have done.

22. While the earth remaineth, seedtime and harvest, and cold and heat, and summer and winter, and day and night shall not cease.

Matthew Henry writes, "Noah was now turned out into a cold and desolate world where one would have thought his first care would have been to build a house for himself; but, behold, he begins with an altar for God. God, that is the First, must be served; and he begins well that begins with God."

It is not certain whether Noah's sacrifices were propitiatory (that is, atoning sacrifices for sin) or dedicatory. Perhaps they were both. The reference to the burnt offerings, which were a symbol of consecration to God, suggests that Noah's first act after his deliverance was to rededicate himself to God. At the same time, Noah, with his vivid awareness of the world's sin and of God's attitude to it, may have offered atoning sacrifices also.

The portrait of Noah as a man in whom the grace of God dwelt thus continues. As he was before the Flood, a man of faith and holiness, so he was as he stepped on dry land again.

B. God's Commands (9:1-7)
(Genesis 9:3-7 is not included in the printed text.)
1. And God blessed Noah and his sons, and said unto them, Be fruitful, and multiply, and replenish the earth.

Talk About It:
1. Why did Noah build an altar, and how did God respond?
2. According to verse 22, what will never change until the earth's end?

Talk About It:
1. Explain the fear and dread mentioned in verse 2.
2. Why is the shedding of blood a serious matter (v. 6)?

2. And the fear of you and the dread of you shall be upon every beast of the earth, and upon every fowl of the air, upon all that moveth upon the earth, and upon all the fishes of the sea; into your hand are they delivered.

God gave humanity a fresh start, with righteous Noah as the father of the post-Flood generations. The Lord blessed Noah's three sons—Shem, Ham and Japheth—with the ability to "increase in number and fill the earth" (v. 1, *NIV*).

The Lord renewed humanity's dominion over the animals (v. 2), and for the first time He ordained the eating of animals, with restrictions (vv. 3-5). Since the flow of blood represents life, which is sacred, people were not to use an animal for food unless it was dead.

God then put a premium on the value of human life. If an animal were to kill a person, that animal was to be killed. And if a human took the life of another person, the murderer was to be executed. Verse 6 reads, "Whoever sheds the blood of man, by man shall his blood be shed; for in the image of God has God made man" (*NIV*).

C. Divine Grace (vv. 8-17)

(Genesis 9:8-10, 14 is not included in the printed text.)

11. And I will establish my covenant with you; neither shall all flesh be cut off any more by the waters of a flood; neither shall there any more be a flood to destroy the earth.

12. And God said, This is the token of the covenant which I make between me and you and every living creature that is with you, for perpetual generations:

13. I do set my bow in the cloud, and it shall be for a token of a covenant between me and the earth.

15. And I will remember my covenant, which is between me and you and every living creature of all flesh; and the waters shall no more become a flood to destroy all flesh.

16. And the bow shall be in the cloud; and I will look upon it, that I may remember the everlasting covenant between God and every living creature of all flesh that is upon the earth.

17. And God said unto Noah, This is the token of the covenant, which I have established between me and all flesh that is upon the earth.

Talk About It:
1. With whom did God enact a covenant (vv. 9-11)?
2. Why is the rainbow an appropriate symbol of God's promise?

These verses describe the covenant God made with Noah. A divine covenant in the Bible is not a compact mutually agreed between two parties, but a sovereign enactment of God—in modern jargon, *unilateral*, not bilateral. This is clearly seen in the Noahic covenant: "I establish my covenant with you" (v. 9). It was a covenant of grace. Everything about it expresses divine grace. God graciously bound Himself to protect both humanity and "all flesh" from a further flood—disaster that had brought such terrible destruction (v. 11).

This covenant is "everlasting" (v. 16). It still continues, even though the world is sinful and rebellious (see 8:21). As a sign and pledge of His gracious covenant, God instituted the symbol of the rainbow (9:12-17). Expositors usually explain this, not as the creation of the rainbow for the first time, but as giving a special significance to a phenomenon that had existed from the dawn of Creation. However, Morris and Whitcombe claim that there was no rainfall prior to the Flood, and therefore the rainbow dates from the Flood period. It was a new creation, or a consequence of the new conditions.

In any case, the important thing is the significance of the rainbow. Richardson says, "The rainbow which appears after the storm is a fitting and beautiful symbol of God's tender mercies towards mankind" (*Genesis I-XI*).

CONCLUSION

Noah and his family were witnesses to God's first catastrophic judgment against a world so soon fallen into sin. Because of their righteousness, eight persons were allowed to enter into the ark and be saved. All others perished in the inevitable waters of the Great Deluge. We probably cannot even begin to imagine the feeling of destitution and fear that must have gripped the eight as they stepped stiffly from the ark and beheld the bleakness of a world destroyed.

According to the Bible, one of the first things they did upon disembarking was to build an altar upon which they offered sacrifices to God. Their sacrifices no doubt represented their thanksgiving to God for preserving them and, more than likely, their petition to God to save them from any future judgment. It perhaps was easy for them to wonder if God would do it again and that the next time they would be weighed in God's balances and found wanting.

God must have recognized their apprehension and came to establish a covenant with them. Said He: "Neither shall all flesh be cut off any more by the waters of a flood; neither shall there any more be a flood to destroy the earth" (Genesis 9:11). This promise was enough (God's promises are always enough), but He made it binding upon Himself by giving the people a covenant token. The token made God legally responsible to abide by His covenant. From that day, they, and all people since, have been able to fix their eyes on rainbows and know that God will not again destroy the earth by flood.

Rainbows are most gorgeous after the severest of storms. When the sun finally shines through the lingering mist, its rays are bent in unbelievable fashion, to form colors and shape no artist can set on canvas. God's promises are most real after the severest of trials. When the Son shines through the lingering mist, His true colors are molded in ways impossible to explain, to form peace and confidence no poet can describe.

GOLDEN TEXT CHALLENGE

"[GOD] SPARED NOT THE OLD WORLD, BUT SAVED NOAH THE EIGHTH PERSON, A PREACHER OF RIGHTEOUSNESS, BRINGING IN THE FLOOD UPON THE WORLD OF THE UNGODLY" (2 Peter 2:5).

It is hard to imagine only one family on earth being righteous in God's eyes, but that was exactly the case in Noah's day. Only the eight members of Noah's family were spared when God flooded the earth, while probably millions of unrighteous people were swept away in divine judgment. Noah was a "preacher of righteousness," but his warnings went unheeded in a world where everyone's desires and thoughts were focused on sin.

This reference to Noah is second in a list of three judgments recounted in 2 Peter 2:4-8. The other two are rebellious angels being sentenced to hell, and Sodom and Gomorrah being overthrown. The message is twofold: Sinners will inevitably come to judgment in God's time and way, yet faithful believers (like the obedient angels, Lot and Noah) will be spared (see v. 9).

No matter how many unbelievers populate one's neighborhood, town, state or nation, God will deliver His children from their evil influence and save them from the storm of judgment.

Daily Devotions:
M. Cry for Mercy
   Psalm 86:1-7
T. Call to Repent
   Isaiah 1:10-20
W. A New
   Covenant
   Jeremiah 31:31-34
T. All People Are
   Sinners
   Galatians 3:21-29
F. God Loves
   Sinners
   Romans 5:1-11
S. Sin No Longer
   Remembered
   Hebrews 10:11-18

The Birth of the King (Christmas)

Matthew 1:18 through 2:23

INTRODUCTION

The most significant event in the history of humanity was the birth of Jesus Christ, the Savior of the world. Had it not been for that birth, there could have been no Calvary, no resurrection, and no ascension. Indeed, "the hinge of history is on the door of the Bethlehem stable."

At first thought, it seems most unworthy that the Son of God had to be conceived, born, and to pass through all the stages of human development. But the interval between God and humanity is so vast that the difference between childhood and manhood is of little consequence. The greatest marvel is that He would consent to become man at all, not that He would consent to become an infant.

Sometime after the birth of Jesus in Bethlehem, mysterious visitors from the East arrived in Jerusalem with strange tidings. Matthew calls them "wise men," or Magi—probably priest-sages, students of astrology and religion. They had come from an eastern country, probably Persia, Arabia or Media, in quest of the "King of the Jews." Contrary to popular belief, we have no certainty as to their number or their names. But their quest was probably motivated by a holy desire and inspired by the appearance of a heavenly beacon or "star." The purpose of their coming was to pay homage to a newborn "King of the Jews," and to worship Him as a deliverer.

The Magi represent the countless hungry hearts of the heathen world who, seeing the light of God revealed in nature, yearn for the Light of the World. The Magi coming as Gentiles to pay homage in Judea is a strong proof of the messiahship of Jesus.

Unit Theme:
Christmas Lesson

Central Truth:
Because He is the King, Jesus is worthy of our adoration and praise.

Focus:
Recognize Jesus as the King and worship Him.

Context:
Jesus Christ was born in 5 B.C.

Golden Text:
"Behold, a virgin shall conceive, and bear a son, and shall call his name Immanuel" (Isaiah 7:14).

Study Outline:
I. The King Is Born (Matthew 1:18-25)
II. The King Is Sought (Matthew 2:1-8)
III. The King Is Worshiped (Matthew 2:9-12)

I. THE KING IS BORN (Matthew 1:18-25)

A. A Shocking Discovery (vv. 18, 19)

18. Now the birth of Jesus Christ was on this wise: When as his mother Mary was espoused to Joseph, before they came together, she was found with child of the Holy Ghost.

19. Then Joseph her husband, being a just man, and not willing to make her a publick example, was minded to put her away privily.

Talk About It:
1. What was Joseph's primary concern in these verses? What does this say about him?
2. How important is the doctrine of the Virgin Birth to the Christian faith? Why?

Here we have a concise and conclusive statement as to how Jesus was conceived. Matthew makes no attempt to explain how it happened, since, no doubt, he himself could not fully understand it; he makes a plain statement of the facts.

The phrase "was espoused" might better be translated "had been betrothed." In Biblical times the marriage ceremony began with a betrothal, which was almost equivalent to marriage (see Deuteronomy 22:23, 24), and which could not be broken off without a formal divorce. The betrothal ended after a period of time, generally a one-year interval, with the groom going to the bride's house and taking her home with him. During this year's interval, the betrothal was considered legal and binding on both sides, and a violation of that trust was considered as a case of adultery and was punished in that way (see vv. 25, 28).

Imagine the surprise of both Joseph and Mary when Mary "was found with child." Nothing could have been more distressing and humiliating to them. And what sustained them during this time? Adam Clarke said, "Nothing but the fullest consciousness of her own integrity and the strongest confidence in God."

Joseph now knew his wife was pregnant, but he did not know as yet that this child was conceived "of the Holy Ghost." The *Pulpit Commentary* states, "Christianity starts with a miracle. It is a miracle altogether so stupendous and so unique that its reception settles the whole question of the possibility of the miraculous. He who can believe that God shadowed Himself to our apprehension in the likeness of a man, he who can recognize in the Babe of Bethlehem, both the Son of God and the Son of Mary, will find that no equal demand is ever afterwards made upon his faculty of faith. Both Testaments begin with a miracle. A world of order and beauty arising out of chaos is a miracle as truly as is the birth of a divinely human Savior by the divine overshadowing of Mary."

What was Joseph to do? The legal penalty for Mary's supposed fault was stoning (John 8:5). Joseph loved his wife; but, as a betrothed man, he had a duty in the matter. Being just and righteous, he observed all the law of Moses, and he could not overlook the apparent fault. Yet, Joseph was motivated by a loving desire to deal with Mary as tenderly as possible. He had two alternatives: he could expose her to public repudiation and almost certain death, or he could quietly cancel the bond of betrothal without stating any reason. A Jewish husband could divorce his wife just because she did not please him; and he could do so simply by giving her divorce papers in the presence of witnesses. He did not have to specify the cause. Because of his loyal love and deep devotion, Joseph chose the latter of the two courses.

B. A Surprising Dream (vv. 20, 21)

20. But while he thought on these things, behold, the angel of the Lord appeared unto him in a dream, saying, Joseph, thou son of David, fear not to take unto thee Mary thy wife: for that which is conceived in her is of the Holy Ghost.

21. And she shall bring forth a son, and thou shalt call his name Jesus: for he shall save his people from their sins.

The processes of thought that went through Joseph's mind during these hours must have been most painful and distressing. Righteous as he was, we can be sure that he prayed. He certainly had trusted his betrothed wife, and he, no doubt, still wanted to. Yet, how could the present circumstance be explained? God, not desiring to leave His servants in perplexity any longer than necessary, sent His special representative, probably Gabriel (see Luke 1:19, 26), to appear unto and to clarify for Joseph how this situation had developed.

Perhaps desiring that Joseph be approached in his calmest moments, the angel chose to make his revelation in a dream. The angel addressed Joseph by name and identified him as "thou son of David." Joseph, no doubt, had been aware of the promise that God made to David in 2 Samuel 7:12-16, and the angel was well aware that Joseph wanted to keep the family line pure, but Joseph did not know all the circumstances of this situation. So the mission of the angel was to reveal the true circumstances of Mary's pregnancy and to urge Joseph to take her so the promise made to David might be fully carried out in his family instead of in another.

In a concise statement the angel related the greatest fact in the world's history: "That which is conceived . . . is of the Holy Ghost." This was the birth of all births; this was a truth above the reach of human thought. This was the miracle of all miracles, for the blood that was now beginning to flow through this Baby's veins would soon be made available to atone and cleanse all humanity who, born in sin, like ourselves, would accept His death for their sin and in their place.

The name *Jesus* was the personal name of our Lord and

Talk About It:
List everything you can know about Jesus from these two verses.

was derived from the Greek equivalent of the old Hebrew name of *Joshua*. It was a familiar name to the Jewish mind; other mothers had named their boys Jesus. But, from this announcement on, with every word, every act of the Savior, the name would take on a new significance and be elevated to a higher value.

And what was His mission to be? That of a great teacher? Certainly so; He became the greatest teacher that ever lived. To be a king? Most definitely, He came to set up a universal kingdom. To be a friend? Yes, in the most absolute way, one that sticks closer than a brother. But, first and foremost, He came to be a Savior. This is why, as a personal name, *Jesus* comes before His official title, *Christ*. It was, and still is, His nature to save. He came to teach in order that He might save; He came to rule over those who would be saved; and He came to establish an eternal friendship with those who were saved.

F.B. Meyer said, "This is the mission of Immanuel. He came, not as the Jews expected, to break the yoke of Caesar and to re-establish the kingdom of David; He came to break the yoke of sin, and to set up the sinless kingdom of God. The church has too often misunderstood the object of His advent, as though He meant simply to save from the consequences and results of sin. This was too limited a program for the Son of God: to cancel the results and leave the bitter cause; to deliver from the penalty, but not from the power; to rescue His people from the grasp of a broken law, but confess Himself unable to deal with the bad virus of the blood—this was to fail. No. Dare to take this announcement in its full and glorious meaning, written, as it is, on the portico of our Saviour's life."

> "In Christ two natures met to be thy cure."
> —George Herbert

C. A Fulfilled Prophecy (vv. 22, 23)

22. Now all this was done, that it might be fulfilled which was spoken of the Lord by the prophet, saying,

23. Behold, a virgin shall be with child, and shall bring forth a son, and they shall call his name Emmanuel, which being interpreted is, God with us.

Talk About It:
Explain how Jesus lives up to the name *Immanuel* in our day.

The statement "all this was done" is in the past tense, making the birth of Jesus and the saving of His people from their sins as already having taken place. This was a tool of speech to impress it upon Joseph's mind. Throughout the Old Testament this manner of speaking was used by prophets who saw the thing that was going to happen in the future with such clarity and certainty that when they uttered the prophecy, they put everything in the past tense.

The phrase "that it might be fulfilled" is one Matthew uses 10 times in his Gospel, but it is not found anywhere else in the New Testament. Matthew particularly wanted to emphasize

The Birth of the King

that the events of Christ's life were taking place in order to fulfill God's gracious promises, made in the Old Testament through the prophets.

"The prophet," to Matthew, was Isaiah; and, in many ways, Isaiah is considered the greatest of all of the Hebrew prophets. His writings are more often quoted in the New Testament than those of any other and are sometimes referred to as the fifth Gospel.

The quotation is taken from Isaiah 7:14, words that were uttered by Isaiah to King Ahaz. Ahaz was anticipating war with King Rezin of Assyria and Pekah of Israel, and was contemplating the establishment of an alliance with Assyria to effectively deal with this challenge. On command of the Lord, Isaiah went to Ahaz to try to convince him that the best course was not in a foreign alliance, but in trusting in the Lord to defeat his enemies. Isaiah tried to get Ahaz to ask for a sign from the Lord that He would do as Isaiah had said He would do, but Ahaz refused. Isaiah gave the sign anyway, which was the Virgin Birth statement, quoted here by Matthew. However, this prophecy had to wait about 700 years for its complete fulfillment, which was realized in the virgin birth of Christ.

> "God surprises earth with heaven, coming here on Christmas Day."
> —**John Bell**

D. Joseph's Acceptance (vv. 24, 25)

24. Then Joseph being raised from sleep did as the angel of the Lord had bidden him, and took unto him his wife:

25. And knew her not till she had brought forth her firstborn son: and he called his name Jesus.

Verse 25 shows Mary's pregnancy was enveloped in such sanctity that Joseph refused to normalize his marriage until after Jesus was born. At this point Catholic theologians through the centuries have declared that Joseph never did fully consummate his marriage, and that Mary lived in perpetual virginity. There is nothing here or any place in the Bible to suggest this, and the wording here intends to suggest that the marriage was fully consummated after Jesus was born.

Talk About It:
Why was Joseph so quick to obey the angel?

II. THE KING IS SOUGHT (Matthew 2:1-8)
A. The Wise Men From the East (vv. 1, 2)

1. Now when Jesus was born in Bethlehem of Judaea in the days of Herod the king, behold, there came wise men from the east to Jerusalem,

2. Saying, Where is he that is born King of the Jews? for we have seen his star in the east, and are come to worship him.

Verse 1 at once identifies the place and the time of Jesus' birth. He was born in Bethlehem ("House of Bread"), a little town about five miles south of Jerusalem. Since it was the

Talk About It:
1. Why did the wise men go to Jerusalem?
2. Why was Jesus born in Bethlehem?

Unusual Alignment

The great astronomer Kepler discovered that in Christ's birth year there was an unusual occurrence among the planets. He found that in that year Jupiter and Saturn, which are generally in remote parts of the sky, came three times so near together that to the unassisted eye the rays of one were absorbed by the other, and their combination gave an extraordinary brilliant light, which continued for some months.

—F.B. Meyer

Talk About It:
1. What does the title *Christ* mean?
2. Why was Herod "troubled"?

native town of David, it has also been called the "city of David" (Luke 2:11). Matthew omits reference to the circumstances that brought Mary and Joseph to Bethlehem, details recorded by Luke only. The time was during the reign of King Herod in Jerusalem and, according to Luke, the rule of Caesar Augustus in Rome.

The arrival of these Magi from the East very likely took place a year or so after the birth of Jesus, since the distance of travel required considerable time. Then too, Herod's decree to destroy the Bethlehem infants up to the age of 2 years seems to suggest that at least a year had passed since Jesus' birth. It was natural for the Magi to come to Jerusalem, the capital, in their quest for the infant King.

The question put by the Magi expresses the expectation prevailing throughout the East of the advent of a great king who was to rise from among the Jews. These expectations were probably based on some acquaintance with the Hebrew Scriptures, probably the Book of Daniel, and also the influence of the dispersed Jews throughout the East.

The title "King of the Jews" is applied to no one but the Messiah, and it appears later in accord with Jesus' own claims in the inscription on the cross (Matthew 27:37). What prompted the venture of these Magi at this time was the sight of "his star in the east." Although it has not been definitely ascertained whether this star was a peculiar astronomical appearance or a supernatural manifestation, it is safe to assume that it was by divine arrangement so that the Magi were thus inspired to venture out on a religious quest. Their expectations were high, for they had "come to worship him."

B. King Herod's Agitation (vv. 3, 4)

3. When Herod the king had heard these things, he was troubled, and all Jerusalem with him.

4. And when he had gathered all the chief priests and scribes of the people together, he demanded of them where Christ should be born.

The agitation of King Herod over the inquiry of the Magi was due to his jealous and suspicious nature. After his appointment to kingship by the Roman Senate in 40 B.C., he besieged Jerusalem and took it in 37 B.C., and then established his authority by force of Roman arms. His constant fear of displeasing his overlords in Rome and the suspicion of some rival to his throne made him cruel and tyrannical, and outbursts of rage and consequent massacres were not uncommon in Jerusalem. His knowledge of Israel's expectations and rumors of Messiah's nearness made him tense, so that the Magi's quest further irritated him. It is probable that Jerusalem's disturbance was due to fear of a new outbreak of violence, a revolution or a massacre.

The king at once summoned the religious leaders of the city for a consultation. It is not clear whether these chief priests and scribes of the people represented a formal meeting of the Sanhedrin or an informal gathering of religious leaders to get the desired information as soon as possible. The chief priests could have been those who had served the office of high priest, and also the heads of the 24 courses into which the priests were divided, or they could have been the Sanhedrin. The scribes were the transcribers and interpreters of the Mosaic Law. The former represented the ecclesiastical and Sadducean part, the latter the more literary and probably the Pharisaic part of the nation. With characteristic cleverness, as though he too shared the messianic hopes, he courteously inquired of them, as the authorized interpreters of Scripture, where the Christ should be born.

"He who has no Christmas in his heart will never find Christmas under a tree."
—Roy L. Smith

C. The Prophetic Light (vv. 5, 6)

5. And they said unto him, In Bethlehem of Judaea: for thus it is written by the prophet,

6. And thou Bethlehem, in the land of Juda, art not the least among the princes of Juda: for out of thee shall come a Governor, that shall rule my people Israel.

This gathering of religious leaders without hesitation informed the king that Bethlehem was the predicted birthplace of the Messiah. And they quoted from the prophet Micah (5:2) who, 700 years before the event, predicted the place and importance of the One to be born. It is recorded for us as the scribes quoted it, not as Matthew himself may have quoted the prophecy. The prophet Micah contrasts the outward insignificance of the birthplace with the spiritual and divine greatness of the One born there. And although, for some reason, they did not fully and accurately quote it, Herod got his answer. Then, too, although they knew the Scriptures, they did not act upon their knowledge. This indifference to divine truth is characteristic of many who are religious but lack in spiritual life and power.

Talk About It:
What does verse 6 reveal about Jesus' ministry? Why would this bother Herod?

D. King Herod's Hypocrisy (vv. 7, 8)

7. Then Herod, when he had privily called the wise men, enquired of them diligently what time the star appeared.

8. And he sent them to Bethlehem, and said, Go and search diligently for the young child; and when ye have found him, bring me word again, that I may come and worship him also.

Having ascertained from the Jewish theologians the prophetic information as to the place of the Messiah's birth,

Talk About It:
1. Why did Herod talk with the wise men privately?
2. What did Herod tell the wise men to do, and why?

Herod's next step in his murderous design was to determine from the Magi themselves the probable age of the infant. He supposed that the birth of the child happened simultaneously with the first appearance of the star. For this information accuracy was important and secrecy was doubly necessary, for the public must not think that Herod could give any recognition to a possible rival, nor must the parents learn of his knowledge of the event.

The unsuspecting strangers must have told the king all he wanted to know, for they now got his royal mandate to make a diligent search for the child and report back their discovery. Lest anyone, whether the Magi or the Jews, would suspect Herod's intentions, he hypocritically assured them that his desire was to join them in this reverent homage to the royal child.

III. THE KING IS WORSHIPED (Matthew 2:9-12)
A. The Guiding Light (vv. 9, 10)

9. When they had heard the king, they departed; and, lo, the star, which they saw in the east, went before them, till it came and stood over where the young child was.

10. When they saw the star, they rejoiced with exceeding great joy.

Talk About It:
How much did God want the wise men to find Jesus? Why?

It must have been a disappointing and disturbing experience for the Magi to find such ignorance and indifference in the capital city of Judaism. But having traveled so far in their quest, they must not give up now. So the weary Magi ventured forth toward Bethlehem in accord with the king's mandate. Over and above the royal direction was the sure word of prophecy that Bethlehem was the place. God's Word is a sure guide to the discovery of the Christ and His salvation (2 Timothy 3:15). But as soon as they passed the city wall, the heavenly beacon appeared again. The star which had aroused their hopes now appeared as a guide to the very place where the new King was to be found. "Its reappearance was the pledge of the full answer to their search, the full reward of their toilsome journey" (*Pulpit Commentary*). So their temporary perplexity turned to exuberant joy, and they went on their way rejoicing.

B. The Worship of the King (v. 11)

11. And when they were come into the house, they saw the young child with Mary his mother, and fell down, and worshipped him: and when they had opened their treasures, they presented unto him gifts; gold, and frankincense, and myrrh.

Talk About It:
1. How do you suppose this event affected Mary?

Upon their arrival at Bethlehem the wise men found the infant King, not in the manger where the shepherds found Him (Luke 2:16), but in the house. At the sight of the Child with His

The Birth of the King

mother, Mary, they bowed in reverent worship—not of Mary, but of the Child. For this purpose the Magi had traveled far; now the time had come for reverent homage to the divine King. Only Deity deserves our worship; and since Jesus Christ was (and is) the Son of God, He was often worshiped (Matthew 8:2; 9:18; 14:33; 28:9, 17).

Next in order was the consecration, and this was fittingly expressed by the Magi in their presentation of gifts to Christ. In full accord with Eastern usage, they opened their treasure chests and presented the three traditional gifts of homage to a ruler. As an expression of their faith in the King, these gifts gave both meaning and increase to their faith.

2. What was the significance of the wise men's gifts?

> Bring Him thy precious things
>   And lay them at His feet;
> The gold of love, the hope that springs
>   The unknown ways to meet.
>
> Bring Him thy lovely things;
>   The joy that conquers care,
> The faith that trusts and sings,
>   The frankincense of prayer.
>
> Bring Him thy bitter things;
>   The myrrh of grief and fears,
> The aching heart that stings
>   With pain of unshed tears.
>
> These for thy gifts to Him;
>   And for His gifts to thee,
> The comfort of His steadfast love,
>   His tender sympathy.
>   **—Annie Johnson Flint**

Godly Gifts
"Some gifts you can give this Christmas are beyond monetary value: Mend a quarrel, dismiss suspicion, tell someone 'I love you.' Give something away—anonymously. Forgive someone who has treated you wrong. Turn away wrath with a soft answer. Visit someone in a nursing home. Apologize if you were wrong. Be especially kind to someone with whom you work. Give as God gave to you in Christ, without obligation, or announcement, or reservation, or hypocrisy."
                    —Charles Swindoll

C. Supernatural Message (v. 12)

12. And being warned of God in a dream that they should not return to Herod, they departed into their own country another way.

It was probably during the night following their visit to the infant King that the warning dream came to these Magi. Whatever plans they may have had to return with a report to Herod were suddenly changed by divine intervention. Thus both the Magi and the Christ were protected from the immediate tyranny and wrath of Herod. Those who have found the Christ always return another way—a new and living way.

Talk About It:
How did God protect His Son?

CONCLUSION

The visit of the wise men to the Christ child in Bethlehem was motivated by a holy desire. Their own wisdom and research having failed to satisfy, they hoped for something better in Israel. They were encouraged by the heavenly light which aroused their hopes and gave guidance on the way. Although temporarily delayed in Jerusalem by human apathy, they obeyed the direction from Holy Scripture and came to Bethlehem. There they were rewarded by the holy discovery of the Christ. In faith they worshiped Him and consecrated to Him their treasures, and with confirmed faith they returned to their home.

GOLDEN TEXT CHALLENGE

"BEHOLD, A VIRGIN SHALL CONCEIVE, AND BEAR A SON, AND SHALL CALL HIS NAME IMMANUEL" (Isaiah 7:14).

King Ahaz had rejected God's offer for immediate deliverance; he also refused the sign God had promised. But Isaiah told him that in spite of his refusal, God would still give a sign to His people, and He would provide redemption for them. He was saying to the king, "By rejecting the promise, you would endeavor to overturn the decree of God; but God's purposes will remain inviolable, and your treachery and ingratitude will not hinder God from being continually the Deliverer of His people; for He will at length raise up His Messiah."

What sign would the Lord give? "Behold, a virgin shall conceive." The word *behold* was used emphatically, to denote the greatness of the event. A virgin would conceive, not by the ordinary course of nature, but by the gracious influence of the Holy Spirit (see Matthew 1:18- 25). This is the mystery Paul extolled in lofty terms, that "God was manifest in the flesh" (1 Timothy 3:16).

The prophet said that the mother would designate His name: "[she] shall call." This was contrary to custom. The father was always assigned the right of giving a name to a child. But here that responsibility was given to the mother. Therefore, it follows that this Son was to be conceived in such a manner as not to have a father on earth.

His name was to be *Immanuel*. This name indicates He was to be the only-begotten Son of God, clothed with our flesh, and united to us by partaking of our nature. *Immanuel*, which means "God with us," or "united to us," was a name that could not apply to a man who was not God. By this name He was to excel all that were before and all that were to come after Him. Immanuel was a title expressive of some extraordinary excellence and authority that He would possess above all others.

Daily Devotions:
M. Prince of Peace
   Isaiah 9:2-7
T. God Is Savior
   Isaiah 43:1-7
W. Christ's Birth
   Announced
   Luke 1:26-31
T. Sought by
   Shepherds
   Luke 2:8-18
F. The Word
   Becomes Flesh
   John 1:1-14
S. Imitate Christ's
   Humility
   Philippians 2:5-
   11

The Scriptures Are God-Inspired

Exodus 24:3-7; Jeremiah 36:2; Acts 1:15-17;
2 Timothy 3:15-17; Hebrews 4:12, 13; 1 Peter 1:22, 23;
2 Peter 1:19-21; 3:15, 16

INTRODUCTION

Imagine life in any country without written laws. When it comes to matters of governing, what if congressmen, officials and judges had no foundation from which to practice their profession? Now imagine written laws without a constitution. How confusing life would be, without a fundamental document outlining the values of a country. Even poorly governed nations that are known for oppressing their population have written laws and constitutions! Apart from these, we would be in doubt concerning our rights and our responsibilities as citizens.

In the same way that a government would cease to function without a basis for its laws, as believers in Christ we would be lost without the Scriptures. We would have nothing to guide us in the principles of living as citizens of the kingdom of God. We would be forced to figure out important questions on our own: *How should the church be led? How do we walk in the Spirit? How do we recognize sound doctrine?* In addition, we would be unfamiliar with the stories of heroes that have gone before us. Even our concept of Jesus would be distorted and incomplete. Just like the quarterback of any football team would be lost without his play book, every Christian would be aimless and unable to function without the Bible to guide them.

But what makes the Bible different from other important documents through the centuries? The answer is simple. The Scriptures are far more than inspirational stories of God's relationship with humanity—they have actually been inspired by God himself! We can trust them as reliable words of guidance, instruction and correction in our lives because of the Bible's supernatural quality. Of course, other faiths claim supernatural Scriptures as well—the Muslim Koran, the Book of Mormon, and so on. But a careful examination of what we mean by Scriptural inspiration easily proves the Bible's superiority over any other book. In a sense, everything in the Christian faith depends on a proper view of Scriptural inspiration. Without it, a multitude of issues relating to the believer would be murky. But because God has inspired it, every believer can be armed with God's truth.

Unit Theme:
Basic Christian Doctrines

Central Truth:
The Bible is God's revelation of Himself and His plan of salvation.

Focus:
Receive the Bible as inspired by God and submit to its authority.

Context:
Old and New Testament passages regarding the inspiration of Scripture

Golden Text:
"All scripture is given by inspiration of God, and is profitable for doctrine, for reproof, for correction, for instruction in righteousness" (2 Timothy 3:16).

Study Outline:
I. Given by God (Exodus 24:3-7; Acts 1:15-17)
II. Written by Men (Jeremiah 36:2; 2 Peter 1:19-21; 3:15, 16)
III. Changes Lives (Hebrews 4:12, 13; 2 Timothy 3:15-17; 1 Peter 1:22, 23)

I. GIVEN BY GOD (Exodus 24:3-7; Acts 1:15-17)

Unless God has given the Bible to humanity, it is at best just another book, and at worst the greatest hoax in history. Thankfully, there are numerous aspects of the Scriptures that point to their divine origin. Remember, in the Old and New Testaments God's people were often obstinate and skeptical. They were regularly drawn to the supposed "truths" of the idols of neighboring nations. Because of this, the words of Scriptural prophets and leaders that came to form the Bible were always clear about their source. The advantage we have is being able to see that thousands of years of history in the God-following community have proven that source dependable. The Scriptures were given to humanity from God so God might reveal who He is, and that God might reveal His sweeping plan of salvation that reaches every person, time period and nation.

A. Written Covenant (Exodus 24:3-7)

3. And Moses came and told the people all the words of the Lord, and all the judgments: and all the people answered with one voice, and said, All the words which the Lord hath said will we do.

4. And Moses wrote all the words of the Lord, and rose up early in the morning, and builded an altar under the hill, and twelve pillars, according to the twelve tribes of Israel.

5. And he sent young men of the children of Israel, which offered burnt offerings, and sacrificed peace offerings of oxen unto the Lord.

6. And Moses took half of the blood, and put it in basons; and half of the blood he sprinkled on the altar.

7. And he took the book of the covenant, and read in the audience of the people: and they said, All that the Lord hath said will we do, and be obedient.

Talk About It:
1. What did Moses write?
2. Explain the use of blood in this event.
3. What commitment did the people make?

It's hard to imagine a time when the followers of God had no written Scriptures. Scholars believe that for centuries, the Israelites depended on oral history to transmit the stories and teachings of God. Fortunately, this oral tradition continued to be dependable right into the time of the early church, given that illiteracy was the norm until modern days. Because of this, average people were known to memorize amounts of material that seem staggering to us. By the time of Christ, Jewish boys were expected to recite entire books of the Torah from memory. The incredible accuracy of this oral tradition has been confirmed time and time again, most recently with the discovery of the Dead Sea Scrolls in caves in Israel. These ancient manuscripts include every Old Testament book (except Esther), representing the earliest Biblical documents we have, and reflect incredible precision in their transmission. This discovery alone

The Scriptures Are God-Inspired

proves that the words of the Bible reach back into the earliest communities of faith.

If oral tradition worked in the days of Adam, Noah and Abraham, then why did God consider it necessary to provide His Word in written form? Several reasons can be offered. First, after 400 years of slavery in Egypt, Israel had become a large nation. They were no longer just a few clans connected to the patriarchs; they had grown into the hundreds of thousands. With so many voices, the threat of disunity was problematic. They needed the *written* Word to solve any disagreements that might arise and to serve as a concrete guide to a massive people. Second, upon being liberated from Egypt, Israel became its own nation. It needed a serious system of laws in order to survive. These are found throughout the Pentateuch, and include regulations on taxation, criminal justice and government leadership. Third, after being planted as an independent nation in between several other independent nations, it was an absolute necessity for Israel's worship to remain distinct. For this reason, the Bible provided specific instructions on worship that were constructed to serve a vast number of people, and to keep the worship of Yahweh pure from the influence of idolatrous nations. In the Books of Kings and Chronicles, we see that the children of Israel frequently fell into idol worship. However, they could always return to the sole worship of the true God because the Scriptures were preserved to guide them.

The first written Scriptures came directly from the finger of God, when Moses received the Ten Commandments (scholars often call them the "Decalogue") on Mount Sinai. However, the Bible also records God's correspondence with Moses on many other matters of Israelite worship and government. When Moses spoke these words to the people in Exodus 24, an incredible revelation from God was inaugurated. The people "responded with one voice, 'Everything the Lord has said we will do.' Moses then wrote down everything the Lord had said. He got up early the next morning and built an altar at the foot of the mountain and set up twelve stone pillars representing the twelve tribes of Israel" (vv. 3, 4, *NIV*).

The presence of the Lord was represented by the altar, and the people of Israel were represented by the 12 stone pillars. After hearing the laws of the Lord recorded in chapters 20-23, the Israelites voluntarily agreed to obey God's commands, entering into covenant with Him. To solemnize the covenant, Moses had some strong young men do the work of preparing animal sacrifices. Then Moses sprinkled half of the animals' blood on the altar, and half on the people. They were now in blood covenant with the Lord. Finally, Moses again recited the Lord's commands.

> "If we abide by the principles of the Bible, our country will go on prospering and to prosper; but if we and our posterity neglect its instructions and authority, no man can tell how sudden a catastrophe may overwhelm us, and bury all our glory in profound obscurity."
> —**Daniel Webster**

This dramatic response on the part of Moses and Israel was because they realized God was revealing Himself to them in a new way—through His *written* Word. God has always been in the revealing business. He walked in the Garden with Adam and Eve, He took the initiative in reaching out to Abraham, and He revealed His name to a terrified Moses from a burning bush. By revealing Himself in the written Word to Israel, the identity and character of God would be unquestionable for His people. They would know His unchangeable nature through His unchangeable Word.

B. Fulfilled Prophecy (Acts 1:15-17)

15. And in those days Peter stood up in the midst of the disciples, and said, (the number of names together were about an hundred and twenty,)

16. Men and brethren, this scripture must needs have been fulfilled, which the Holy Ghost by the mouth of David spake before concerning Judas, which was guide to them that took Jesus.

17. For he was numbered with us, and had obtained part of this ministry.

After Christ's ascension, while the believers waited together in Jerusalem as Jesus commanded, it was time to put someone in the place of Judas as the 12th apostle. Peter encouraged the believers by saying Judas' betrayal of Christ and subsequent death had been prophesied in the Old Testament (Psalm 69). Thus we see the early church's dependence on and confidence in the ancient Scriptures, which were used in Jewish synagogues all over the Roman Empire. The earliest Christians worshiped in these synagogues.

It took about 70 years for all of the New Testament books to be written, and probably another 100 years after that before they were considered Holy Scripture. The Old Testament was the only Scripture these early believers had, yet they certainly did not feel lacking. In fact, by examining them carefully, many Jews were converted to faith in Christ after seeing God's plan of salvation described in the Old Testament (see Acts 17:11, 12). This began with the apostles themselves, who understood that Jesus' death and resurrection had fulfilled God's plan of salvation in the Scriptures (Luke 24:44-48). Jesus did not just pop up out of nowhere! When early believers heard the gospel, they recognized it as the culmination of God's written Word that they already had.

Scholars have often called this process of God's unfurling of the plan of salvation throughout Scripture as "progressive revelation." This means that the fullness of God's plan of salvation was revealed more fully as Scripture progressed. This can be

Talk About It:
What encouraged Peter regarding Judas' betrayal?

"The Bible must be read as a whole, beginning with Genesis and ending with Revelation, letting promise and fulfillment guide our expectations for what we will find there."
—**Michael Horton**

The Scriptures Are God-Inspired

easily witnessed by looking at the Bible's first and last books. In Genesis, God creates and enters into relationship with humanity, offering a present (animal sacrifice) and future (3:15) redemption of sin. In Revelation, the risen Christ triumphs over all of the powers of sin and evil, and the community of God is restored to a place of total harmony with God's presence. God has given us a written revelation that clearly discloses His plan of salvation throughout the whole of human history.

II. WRITTEN BY MEN (Jeremiah 36:2; 2 Peter 1:19-21; 3:15, 16)

What can at first glance seem like a contradiction is really one of the most marvelous truths of Scripture. God used people to produce His timeless Word! Far from nullifying the divine origin of the Bible, man's involvement brings heavenly truth to human level, making it possible for even a child to understand its teachings. In a sense, the Scriptures mirror the incarnation of Jesus Christ. Just like God sent His Son in human form to be fully immersed in the world of humanity, the Bible comes to us as a thoroughly divine book that remains nonetheless totally connected to human experience.

A. Written by Real People in Real Times (Jeremiah 36:2)

2. Take thee a roll of a book, and write therein all the words that I have spoken unto thee against Israel, and against Judah, and against all the nations, from the day I spake unto thee, from the days of Josiah, even unto this day.

It is rare when we listen to preaching, attend Sunday school classes, or engage in personal devotions that we stop and think about a Scripture passage's original context. Of course it's important to determine what God is speaking to us now through the Scriptures, but it's equally vital that we remember the world in which they were written. In short, as we read the Bible we can't ever forget to be excited about the fact that "this stuff really happened!" The stories happened to flesh-and-blood people. Real, functioning communities of faith carried out the teachings. Incredibly, these contexts change throughout the Biblical contents. As a whole, the Scriptures span a time period of about 2,000 years, written by authors who lived in different cities and spoke and wrote in various languages. Some books, such as Proverbs, were written during prosperous times. Others, such as Daniel, were written during times of foreign oppression. Much of the New Testament was written during periods of intense persecution. The Psalms reflect ancient forms of worship. Song of Solomon celebrates marriage vows. Revelation looks forward to God's ultimate dominion. When we understand these real situations, we are able to

Talk About It:
What did the Lord command Jeremiah to do, and why?

discern much about God's revelation of Himself and His plan of salvation.

The fact that the Biblical testimonies reflect real, historical situations also allows us to fill in the background that may not be found in the Bible. Oftentimes in art work, it is the background, not the subject of the painting, that brings the subject to life. When it comes to segments of the Bible, we are fortunate to have thousands of resources readily available to provide this background. We can examine what archaeological finds have to tell us about life in ancient times. We can look at photographs or drawings of the cities we read about. Oftentimes it is this background that makes the Biblical text so applicable to our everyday lives because these things occurred in the everyday existence of ancient peoples.

This is illustrated wonderfully in the Book of Jeremiah—a rich history of the fall of Jerusalem to Babylonian siege in 587 B.C. After Jeremiah had been preaching for some time, God commanded him, "Take a scroll and write on it all the words I have spoken to you concerning Israel, Judah and all the other nations from the time I began speaking to you in the reign of Josiah till now" (36:2, *NIV*). As this passage goes on, we find out that Jeremiah actually dictated the words of God to a scribe named Baruch. After Baruch read the scroll in the Temple—urging God's people to repent or face certain judgment—the scroll was taken to King Jehoiakim and read to him by his scribe. The rebellious king burned it, but then Baruch recopied it, adding "many like words" (v. 32) that were given to Jeremiah by the Lord. In time the writings of Jeremiah encouraged the Jews who went into exile, and they still bring encouragement to us today, because they are not disconnected from authentic human suffering.

B. Inspired to Preserve Voices and Experiences
(2 Peter 1:19-21; 3:15, 16)

1:19. We have also a more sure word of prophecy; whereunto ye do well that ye take heed, as unto a light that shineth in a dark place, until the day dawn, and the day star arise in your hearts:

20. Knowing this first, that no prophecy of the scripture is of any private interpretation.

21. For the prophecy came not in old time by the will of man: but holy men of God spake as they were moved by the Holy Ghost.

3:15. And account that the longsuffering of our Lord is salvation; even as our beloved brother Paul also according to the wisdom given unto him hath written unto you;

16. As also in all his epistles, speaking in them of these

things; in which are some things hard to be understood, which they that are unlearned and unstable wrest, as they do also the other scriptures, unto their own destruction.

Two main theories have existed to describe the way in which the writings of Scripture were inspired. First, the "dictation" view holds that the writers of Scripture mechanically dictated exactly what God commanded them to say. In this view, the Biblical authors were simply note-takers, hearing from God and copying word-for-word. To some extent, this is how the Islamic world views their holy book—the Koran—and how the Mormons view the Book of Mormon. In the former, Muslim teaching states that Muhammad is the sole author of the Koran, mechanically mediating God's word to a written format. In the latter, Joseph Smith supposedly received heavenly golden plates (which no one ever saw) and translated them (though they were written in an unknown language and he was uneducated) into the Book of Mormon. If these books sound shady to you, you will be encouraged to know that the Bible was undoubtedly not written like this at all. The dictation view does not line up with the Bible. The writers of Scripture were not involuntarily led by God to write sacred words.

A second option is often called the view of "verbal inspiration." In this line of thought, the focus is still on the very words (not just the concepts) of Scripture being divinely inspired. However, the writings were inspired in such a way that the author's style, viewpoint and situation were preserved even as he wrote exactly what God desired. In some cases, even the writer's opinion remains present, as in 2 Peter 3:15, 16, where Peter refers to Paul's writings.

We know from Galatians 2 that Peter and Paul had their conflicts, and even Peter considered some of Paul's writings sometimes tough to understand. But this is expressed without in any way diminishing the authority of Paul's Scriptural letters. They reflect the very "wisdom that God gave him" (2 Peter 3:15, *NIV*).

Thinking of the context of the writers, how exactly were their words inspired? Peter explains this in 1:20, 21: "Above all, you must understand that no prophecy of Scripture came about by the prophet's own interpretation. For prophecy never had its origin in the will of man, but men spoke from God as they were carried along by the Holy Spirit" (*NIV*). The language Peter uses in this last phrase was used to describe sailing ships that were "carried along" by the wind. The words of Scripture were not mechanically dictated nor devised in the minds of people. Instead, as the writer went about his craft, the Spirit was alongside him, carrying his thoughts, concepts and words along so they became the precise message which God wanted written.

Talk About It:
1. To what are the prophetic words of the Old Testament compared in 2 Peter 2:19? Why?
2. According to verses 20 and 21, what two things did *not* happen?
3. Where does Scripture originate?
4. How do some people abuse God's Word (3:16)? Why?

"The writings of men of the Bible did not inherit the errors of their carnal minds because their writings were conceived by the Holy Spirit and born out of their personalities without partaking of their fallen nature. If we ask, how could this be . . . the answer is God says so."
—Donald Grey Barnhouse

III. CHANGES LIVES (Hebrews 4:12, 13; 1 Peter 1:22, 23; 2 Timothy 3:15-17)

Generations of believers can testify to the power of the Scriptures. In them lies the capacity to revolutionize readers of any time period, color or creed. Christian history abounds with stories of people far from God who encountered Scripture and redirected their lives. In fact, a movement of Bible study is thriving in prisons and rehabilitation centers throughout our land. The New Testament believers had only the Old Testament as their Scripture, and the New Testament writings frequently affirm their ability to transform the human heart. Now with the New Testament added, the Bible has been given that much more potency to renovate any person's sinful condition.

A. A Spiritual Transformation (Hebrews 4:12, 13; 1 Peter 1:22, 23)

Hebrews 4:12. For the word of God is quick, and powerful, and sharper than any twoedged sword, piercing even to the dividing asunder of soul and spirit, and of the joints and marrow, and is a discerner of the thoughts and intents of the heart.

13. Neither is there any creature that is not manifest in his sight: but all things are naked and opened unto the eyes of him with whom we have to do.

1 Peter 1:22. Seeing ye have purified your souls in obeying the truth through the Spirit unto unfeigned love of the brethren, see that ye love one another with a pure heart fervently:

23. Being born again, not of corruptible seed, but of incorruptible, by the word of God, which liveth and abideth for ever.

Hebrews 4 declares that the Word of God never transforms a life's surface alone. It is not content to merely change a person's outward behavior, self-esteem or thinking patterns. The Scriptures *are* the power of God to completely overhaul the sinful human heart (v. 12). The Word of God evokes a completely spiritual revolution. By "spiritual" we mean a transformation that derives from the Holy Spirit himself. The Bible does not bring about behavior modification alone—it cuts to the core fabric of sin within the self.

Nothing is hidden from God. "Everything is uncovered and laid bare" before Him (v. 13, *NIV*). The truth of this verse is realized when we read God's Word and it convicts us of our shortcomings. That's one reason some people keep their Bible on the shelf—they don't want it to expose their spiritual nakedness.

Spiritual awakening is again tied to the Word of God in 1 Peter 1:22, 23. The born-again experience stems from the

Talk About It:
1. When has God's Word been like a *two-edged sword* in your life?
2. How can we *purify* ourselves, and what is the result?
3. What is perishable? What is imperishable?

incorruptible Scriptures, which are said to be "living." Scriptures are not static words on paper, but dynamic truths lying in wait to ambush the human heart. The implanted word creates a "sincere love" that works "deeply" in believers' hearts, bringing them together in divine fellowship (v. 22, *NIV*).

B. A Practical Transformation (2 Timothy 3:15-17)

15. And that from a child thou hast known the holy scriptures, which are able to make thee wise unto salvation through faith which is in Christ Jesus.

16. All scripture is given by inspiration of God, and is profitable for doctrine, for reproof, for correction, for instruction in righteousness:

17. That the man of God may be perfect, throughly furnished unto all good works.

Not only do the Scriptures bring about a transformation of the entire self, they also are useful for daily living. They offer sound counsel on a multitude of practical needs and situations the average person faces, such as marriage, child rearing, sexuality, finances and career life.

In 2 Timothy 3, the elder Paul writes to a younger pastor he has mentored, encouraging him to continue in his knowledge of the Bible. Verse 15 proclaims that the Scriptures impart wisdom to the individual. This wisdom is *practical*, or "useful," for four distinct reasons. First, Timothy should use it for *teaching* his congregation. Any sermon without the Scripture as its center is meaningless chatter.

Second, the Scripture is useful for *rebuking* those who are errant. It convinces people of the truth, setting wrong doctrine apart from truth. The Bible is a balanced book, helping people not to fall into deadly extremes.

Third, Scripture is used to *correct us* when we are straying from a sound lifestyle. Because we will always be faced with temptations, the Bible must have the power to correct our course when necessary.

Fourth, the Biblical text *trains us* in righteousness. This verb was also used for an athlete's regular training. When we live continually in the Scriptures, we ready ourselves for important moments in our lives.

Even with this practical focus, Paul emphasizes the fact that "all Scripture is God-breathed" (v. 16, *NIV*). In the Greek language in which Paul wrote, the word *pneuma* denoted either wind, breath or Spirit. So we see again this notion of wind or breath coming from the mouth of God to *carry along* the writer. Although the Scriptures connect so easily to our human experience, we never have to doubt their divine origin.

Talk About It:
1. What had been Timothy's experience since infancy (v. 14), and why was this significant (v. 15)?
2. Why are the Scriptures so versatile (v. 16), and what do they accomplish (v. 17)?

CONCLUSION

In summary, the Bible is a book like no other. Its words have been breathed by God, but are loaded with human experience, so much so there is nothing we can experience in which its words are not applicable. We know these things not only through the testimony within Scripture itself, but also through the ability it continues to have in transforming even the most tattered lives. Its words are ancient but alive, divine but human, and always contain God's truth.

GOLDEN TEXT CHALLENGE

"ALL SCRIPTURE IS GIVEN BY INSPIRATION OF GOD, AND IS PROFITABLE FOR DOCTRINE, FOR REPROOF, FOR CORRECTION, FOR INSTRUCTION IN RIGHTEOUSNESS" (2 Timothy 3:16).

This verse dictates the authority of the Word by stating the source of inspiration to be God. The mechanics of this inspiration, or literally "God-breathed" act, are not explained. However, we should be careful not to get hung up on understanding and explaining how it happened to the extent that we miss the emphasis of the verse, which is the fact that all Scripture is God's truth communicated to us in written form.

The authority of Scripture establishes the necessity for the Word of God being a priority in our lives. This verse states that the Scriptures are *profitable*. God's Word is not just a compilation of religious writings. It is alive, powerful and sharper than a two-edged sword (Hebrews 4:12).

The Scriptures are our primary source for doctrine or teachings. Any doctrine not in harmony with the Word of God should be discarded. The role of Scripture in the act of reproof, or conviction, cannot be overemphasized. When discipline is necessary, correction is made through the guidance of the Word. In fact, the total process of instruction in righteousness, which brings us to a mature understanding of God's standard of life, is based in the Word of God.

Let us be motivated as David to hide God's Word in our hearts in order that we may enjoy the powerful benefits of every scripture.

Daily Devotions:
M. God Revealed Through His Word
1 Samuel 3:19-21
T. Changed by the Word
2 Chronicles 34:19-21, 26-33
W. Word of the Lord Recorded
Jeremiah 36:4-8
T. Responses to God's Word
Luke 8:11-15
F. Born Again by God's Word
1 Peter 1:23—2:3
S. Jesus' Testimony Is Sure
Revelation 22:13-21

The Scriptures Are God-Inspired

God in Three Persons

Deuteronomy 6:4; Isaiah 45:5, 6; Matthew 3:16, 17; John 14:16, 17; 2 Corinthians 13:14; Hebrews 9:14; 1 Peter 1:2; 3:18

INTRODUCTION

Perhaps no other subject in the history of Christianity has received so much attention as the concept of the Trinity. Scholars have spilled untold amounts of ink and preachers have given countless sermons attempting to grasp and explain this doctrine. Unfortunately, it continues to be misunderstood by many Christians today. In one sense, it is one of those deeply mysterious truths of our faith that may be impossible for our finite minds to fully understand. As Paul said in 1 Corinthians 13:12, "Now we see but a poor reflection as in a mirror" (*NIV*). That is, we exist in a dimension of earthly reality that is unable to comprehend all of God's fullness. The doctrine of the Trinity is where this fullness expresses God's existence most profoundly.

Even in the Biblical account of the Creation, we are given a hint that God exists in multiple persons. *Elohim*, a plural name for God, appears in Genesis 1:1-4. In verse 26 we see God saying, "Let *us* make man in *our* image, after *our* likeness" (italics mine).

As Scripture progresses, the picture becomes clearer. In Genesis 3:15, God himself proclaims to Satan that he will eventually be crushed through the offspring of Eve—the first prophecy of the redemptive ministry of Jesus Christ. As the Old Testament goes on, we quickly learn that God is far from alone. Angels exist to carry out His commands, frequently serving as His mediators or messengers to human beings. And the "Spirit of God" or "Spirit of the Lord" is referenced over 30 times throughout the Old Testament. It's plainly evident that hints of God's plural nature exist even from the beginning of the Scriptures.

Unit Theme:
Basic Christian Doctrines

Central Truth:
There is one God, eternally existent in three persons: the Father, the Son, and the Holy Spirit.

Focus:
Explore the doctrine of the Trinity and worship God, who is our model of loving community.

Context:
Selected Old and New Testament scriptures concerning the Holy Trinity

Golden Text:
"The grace of the Lord Jesus Christ, and the love of God, and the communion of the Holy Ghost, be with you all. Amen" (2 Corinthians 13:14).

Study Outline:
I. One God (Deuteronomy 6:4; Isaiah 45:5, 6)
II. Three Persons (Matthew 3:16, 17; John 14:16, 17; 2 Corinthians 13:14)
III. United in Redemption (Hebrews 9:14; 1 Peter 1:2; 3:18)

I. ONE GOD (Deuteronomy 6:4; Isaiah 45:5, 6)

Perhaps the most fundamental foundation of the entire Judeo-Christian worldview which has shaped the bedrock values of Western civilization is the doctrine of the oneness of God. Early Jews and early Christians alike were surrounded by polytheistic cultures that served a pantheon of gods. In fact, the Greeks and Romans constructed a divine realm in which these gods got along a lot like humans, involving themselves in marriage, socializing and procreation. When the early Christians vowed to serve only one God, they were even accused of being atheists! Within this milieu, the Judeo-Christian belief in *monotheism*, or "one God," existed as a strange abnormality, which now seems to be the predominant viewpoint among most religions of the world.

A. God Is One in Substance (Deuteronomy 6:4)

4. Hear, O Israel: The Lord our God is one Lord.

Talk About It:
1. Who is presenting this message to Israel, and what is the context (see vv. 1-3)?
2. What is the connection between verses 4 and 5?

The nature of God's oneness has been debated for thousands of years by prophets, philosophers and theologians. The issue actually stems from the difference between broad, competing views of reality in general. Scholars often divide these competing views into two main categories: monistic worldviews and theistic worldviews.

In the *monistic view*, two very different versions of reality are offered, although they both hold to one single level of reality. This level is the natural, visible world—that which can be seen, touched and/or measured. Naturalism, or atheism, teaches that this level of reality is all that exists; there is no divine realm at all. But pantheism still adheres to only one level of reality that is material, asserting that *all matter is God*. That is, there is no fundamental distinction between God and the natural world. This shows up in the present philosophy of the New Age movement, and is certainly at odds with the Scriptural viewpoint.

A *theistic view* of reality accepts the Biblical ideal that a second reality exists outside of the natural world. Although the Christian perspective certainly fits into a theistic worldview, other faiths do as well, even those who believe in multiple gods. The main characteristic of a theistic view of reality that holds to God's oneness is that as a unified whole, God exists totally independent of the natural world, so He has a choice to interact with it or not. For the deists, God simply set the world in motion and is now completely disengaged. For the Judeo-Christian worldview, God has chosen to be fully involved in the world, while remaining absolutely distinct from it.

These are some of the biggest questions of life, but why do they matter? Because the doctrine of God's oneness cannot be defended without recognizing first His independence from the natural world. In the first chapters of Genesis, God was an outside person who, by His own choice, created the universe and continued to exist distinct from it. But there is no Biblical evidence that God's distinctiveness from creation equals His lack of involvement with it. Instead, He is fully engaged with creation. God can maintain this posture because His substance is singular—He exists as a unified essence that is 100 percent divine.

It is no surprise, then, that when Moses announced the commands of God to the children of Israel in the Book of Deuteronomy, he reminded them of the oneness of God: "Hear, O Israel: The Lord our God, the Lord is one" (6:4, *NIV*). This statement reminded them that God is singular in substance and purpose. They never needed to guess about His commands—*they* are unchangeable because *He* is a unified, perfect, unchangeable whole. Therefore, His commands are timeless and perfect.

After the coming of Jesus Christ and the Day of Pentecost, the early Christians, through divine revelation, came to understand God as a Trinitarian Being, yet they maintained God's oneness. At the Council of Nicea in A.D. 325, this subject was addressed with urgency due mainly to the teaching of Arius. The dilemma had to do with the substance of the persons of the Trinity. Were they of the same substance, or only of like substance? Arius held to the latter, teaching that the Father was God and that the Son and Holy Spirit were less than God. The council recognized the clear danger of this viewpoint and held that the three persons were distinct within the Godhead but were all of the same substance. This means that the Father, Son and Holy Spirit are each fully distinct, yet all are fully unified, and fully God. God is one and at the same time existent in three Persons.

B. God Is One in Existence (Isaiah 45:5, 6)

5. I am the Lord, and there is none else, there is no God beside me: I girded thee, though thou hast not known me:

6. That they may know from the rising of the sun, and from the west, that there is none beside me. I am the Lord, and there is none else.

A second equally dangerous hazard confronted Israel's belief in one God alone. Since neighboring peoples subscribed to the notion of dozens of coexisting deities, the children of Israel might be tempted to include Yahweh in this pantheon of gods. This would allow them to continue to worship their God as one, perhaps even as the greatest of these other gods, essentially straddling the line between true monotheism and (what was at that time) culturally acceptable polytheism.

We see this phenomenon early on in the Old Testament,

Three In One

All earthly metaphors for the mystery of the Trinity are incomplete, but this doctrine of God is often explained like an egg. Although an egg has three distinct parts—a yolk, a white, and a shell—it is only as these three coexist together that an egg is formed. So also the Father, Son and Holy Spirit coexist together, forming one inseparable God in three distinguishable persons.

I girded thee (v. 5)
—God promised to strengthen Israel.

Talk About It:
1. What had the Israelites failed to acknowledge, yet what was God going to do anyway (v. 5)?
2. What did God want His people to know beyond any doubt (v. 6)?

when Yahweh is occasionally proclaimed to be the greatest among all other gods (see Exodus 18:11; 2 Chronicles 2:5). Presumably, some early believers in Yahweh also believed in a pantheon of gods with Yahweh on top. As God continued to reveal Himself, however, He silenced this notion (Isaiah 45:5, 6). God proclaimed that He was never in a place of competition with other lesser gods, because in fact, "there is no other" (vv. 5, 6, *NIV*). Again, this proclaims God's oneness. He is the one, sole Deity presiding over humanity. Though God employs ministering angels, no other being shares His divine essence. When we declare His oneness, we are also declaring the unique place He holds in the divine realm.

This doctrine has become unpopular in modern times. As our society dedicates itself to pluralism, we are led to believe that all gods of all religions are equally valid; that it is up to individuals to choose from many paths leading to many gods. The Judeo-Christian worldview stands in stark contrast to this mentality. Not only does logic tell us that things which contradict cannot all be true, but the Scriptures present an exclusive, jealous God, who scoffs at the very idea of an alternate deity. He alone claims to be the one God.

> "God is concerned with nations, but nations need to be concerned with God. No nation can have a monopoly on God, but God will bless any nation whose people seek and honor His will as revealed by Christ and declared through the Holy Spirit."
> —**John Haggai**

II. THREE PERSONS (Matthew 3:16, 17; John 14:16, 17; 2 Corinthians 13:14)

The concept that a God who is one can also exist in three persons is not easy to grasp. On first glance, the two doctrines appear to be contradictions. However, the Bible presents a harmony between them. The New Testament plainly reveals that each of the three Persons is fully God, yet there is only one God, not three.

A. The Distinct Persons of the Trinity (Matthew 3:16, 17)

16. And Jesus, when he was baptized, went up straightway out of the water: and, lo, the heavens were opened unto him, and he saw the Spirit of God descending like a dove, and lighting upon him:

17. And lo a voice from heaven, saying, This is my beloved Son, in whom I am well pleased.

The coming of Jesus Christ clarified the Old Testament references that seemed to point toward God's plural nature. However, the process by which this nature was found to be triune, or threefold, unfolded slowly. The Incarnation itself perfectly reflected God's triune identity. God the Father sent God the Son, who was conceived by Mary through God the Holy Spirit. It should not be a surprise, then, that even before Jesus began His public ministry, the Trinity was revealed (Matthew 3:16, 17).

Talk About It:
1. Why was Jesus baptized (see v. 15)?
2. Why did God do something so dramatic when Jesus was baptized?

God in Three Persons

All of the onlookers at Jesus' baptism undoubtedly knew God was revealing Himself in a unique way—in a way that had not yet occurred in human history. What they saw was clearly a manifestation of God in three persons. This initiation of Jesus' ministry brought the full attention of the Godhead, as the voice of the Father and the presence of the Holy Spirit testified to His divinity. This is especially important when we understand the concept of sonship in Jewish thought. For the voice from heaven to identify Jesus as Son was a declaration of His equality with the heavenly Father. Jewish firstborn sons were treasured by their fathers, and always received first consideration on the inheritance of the estate. They retained the same legal rights as their father, considered equal to him in every way. Therefore, even though Jesus, as the beloved and pleasing Son of God, is equal to God, the Father, Son and Holy Spirit retain distinct identities in this passage.

3. Why was God the Father "well pleased"?

The presence of the dove is identified as the Holy Spirit in each of the four Gospel accounts of Jesus' baptism. This seems like a strange way for the Holy Spirit to present Himself. It is like nothing else in the New Testament. In the Old Testament, however, remember it was a dove which indicated to Noah that a new day had dawned for the world. He sent it out of the ark the first time and it brought back the sign of an olive leaf. One week later, the dove was sent out but did not return. Noah knew then that the water had receded and that the world would be restored. This appears to be Matthew's line of thinking here: Jesus' ministry was setting the world right again, bringing humanity back into proper relationship with God.

"The word *Trinity* is not found in the Holy Scriptures, but the fact of the tri-personality of God is easily discerned."
—William Stevens

B. Distinct Roles of the Trinity (John 14:16, 17)

16. And I will pray the Father, and he shall give you another Comforter, that he may abide with you for ever;

17. Even the Spirit of truth; whom the world cannot receive, because it seeth him not, neither knoweth him: but ye know him; for he dwelleth with you, and shall be in you.

In our time, there has been renewed interest in the study of the Trinity. In the early Christian centuries, this was a vital doctrine, causing numerous councils who met for long periods of time to hash out the Scripture's teaching on God's triune nature. In the medieval church, it was often scholarly monks and nuns who committed themselves to the devotional life and thus unearthed invaluable truths about God's communal existence. In the past century, the Pentecostal Movement has underscored the importance of the Trinity, with its emphasis on the person and work of God the Holy Spirit.

Numerous scriptures indicate the distinct roles of each person in the Godhead. God the Father sent His Son into the

Talk About It:
1. How is the concept of the Trinity expressed in verse 16?
2. How does *the Spirit of truth* reveal God's three-part nature?

world. The Scriptures characterize God the Father as parent, ruler and judge. The Son came to live and die among humanity. He is therefore Redeemer and Savior. The Spirit was sent to comfort, convict and teach. He is therefore Comforter and Counselor. Perhaps these roles are best summarized by two terms: *sending* and *glorifying*. God the Father sent the Son and glorified Him. Through His death and resurrection, the Son glorified the Father and sent the Spirit. The Spirit glorifies the Son, who brings glory to the Father. And so we see unity, diversity and mutual support within God.

The Holy Spirit is given a prominent role in the teaching of Jesus. As His disciples fretted over Jesus' departure twice—before His death and then before His ascension—Jesus assured them they would not be alone. In the same way they had experienced God through Jesus' presence, God would lead them through the Holy Spirit (John 14:16-18). The Holy Spirit functions as counselor, truth-teller, and as an ever-present source of guidance and power for believers. The Day of Pentecost in Acts 2 solidified the Spirit's vital role in the life of the believer and in the church universal.

It is important to note that these distinct roles within the Trinity indicate the unity of the three persons with the closest ties in mission and purpose but clearly capable of independent action. Certain Charismatic and Pentecostal groups deny Trinitarian doctrine in favor of a "Jesus-only" or "oneness" view that explains the three persons of God as three expressions of one person. Again, we need to look no further than the New Testament for the correct view. We are also encouraged by the Nicene Creed of A.D. 325, in which the oneness of God and the distinctions between the persons of the Trinity are affirmed and explained.

C. The Trinitarian Formula (2 Corinthians 13:14)

14. The grace of the Lord Jesus Christ, and the love of God, and the communion of the Holy Ghost, be with you all. Amen.

As the early church progressed, Trinitarian formulas became standard in their writings, creeds and liturgy. We see this particularly in blessings or benedictions such as the conclusion of Paul's second letter to the Corinthians. The Corinthian believers had been saved through the gracious sacrifice of Jesus Christ, expressing the Father's awesome love, and now God the Holy Spirit was indwelling them. Here different attributes are ascribed to each individual person of the Godhead, yet God is one.

III. UNITED IN REDEMPTION (Hebrews 9:14; 1 Peter 1:2; 3:18)

Although the persons of the Trinity have distinct roles, they are

Coequal and Coeternal
Within His own mysterious being God is Father, Son, and Holy Spirit. The designations are just ways in which God is God. Within the Godhead there are three "persons" who are neither three Gods nor three parts of God, but coequally and coeternally God.
—Christian Theology in Plain Language

Talk About It:
How has your life been affected by the grace of Jesus? By the love of the heavenly Father? By the communion of the Holy Spirit?

God in Three Persons

fully united in one purpose. This overarching purpose has stayed the same throughout human history. The Trinity exists united to bring about the redemption of the world, which has been tainted by sin. The communion of the Trinity itself is the model of perfect harmony that God desires for believers and for the planet as a whole.

A. United in Community (Hebrews 9:14)

14. How much more shall the blood of Christ, who through the eternal Spirit offered himself without spot to God, purge your conscience from dead works to serve the living God?

It is important to understand the nature of the relationship between the persons of the Trinity. Misconceptions in this matter caused controversy throughout the history of the church, but its urgency also forced the issue to the forefront of early Christian theology. As previously mentioned, this question of the unity of the Trinity is associated most famously with Arius and his teaching, now commonly known as Arianism.

Arius built upon a doctrine that cropped up in the late second century A.D. called *Monarchianism*, which totally opposed the Trinitarian concept. Proponents of this view held that Jesus was inferior to God the Father, but divine power had been bestowed on Him by the Father. Arius echoed this, adding that Jesus and the Holy Spirit had been actually created by God the Father. Thankfully, Christian scholarship and history have proven these views incorrect.

Even with a Trinitarian stance, however, what is the nature of the relationships within God? Is a hierarchy, as Arius taught, implicit within their roles, in which God the Father sits on top of an organizational chart and rules over the Son, who in turn rules over the Holy Spirit? Or does a mystical equality exist within the distinct roles of the Trinity that allows them to submit, cooperate and serve one another while retaining a uniform power and substance?

Hebrews 9:14 gives us a unique glimpse into the cooperative equality of the triune God: "How much more, then, will the blood of Christ, who through the eternal Spirit offered himself unblemished to God, cleanse our consciences from acts that lead to death, so that we may serve the living God!" (*NIV*). Through the power given by the Holy Spirit, Christ offered Himself to God for the purpose of redemption. The Trinity can properly be called a cooperative community within God. Because of this cooperation within the Trinity, "divine relationality becomes the paradigm for every type of relationality in creation" (*God for Us: The Trinity and the Christian Life*, Catherine M. LaCugna). Our human relationships have an example and a model of perfect community in God himself.

Talk About It:
1. What is Christ's role in our salvation? What is the Holy Spirit's role?
2. What is the purpose of our being saved?

"God is vitally concerned with the salvation of the lost. This concern is demonstrated by the participation of all the persons of the Trinity."
—Oliver McMahan

B. Focused on Redemption (1 Peter 1:2; 3:18)

1:2. Elect according to the foreknowledge of God the Father, through sanctification of the Spirit, unto obedience and sprinkling of the blood of Jesus Christ: Grace unto you, and peace, be multiplied.

3:18. For Christ also hath once suffered for sins, the just for the unjust, that he might bring us to God, being put to death in the flesh, but quickened by the Spirit.

Talk About It:
1. Who are the *elect* (1:2)? What does God do for them?
2. How did the Holy Spirit *quicken* Christ (3:18)? How does He quicken us?

This unity within the Trinity is not just communal, it is missional, because God is on a mission together to redeem the entire world. According to 1 Peter 3:18, this redemption was eternally effected at the Cross. Each member of the Godhead had a part in the redemption at Calvary. It was Christ who died in order to pay the price of sin on behalf of humanity, and through the Holy Spirit He was raised to life so people could be restored to God the Father.

In the introduction of the same letter, Peter expresses this truth in a greeting, saying believers are "chosen according to the foreknowledge of God the Father, through the sanctifying work of the Spirit, for obedience to Jesus Christ and sprinkling by his blood" (1:2, *NIV*). This is significant because phrases like this that exist in either the greeting or closing of the letters in the New Testament were probably preexisting formulas already in use by the local churches. That is, Peter did not create this greeting, but used it because the churches would be familiar with it. If this is the case, then from its very outset the church understood God as a Trinity, and also understood His mission to be redeeming the world through the death and resurrection of Jesus Christ.

Holy, holy, holy!
Merciful and
mighty!
God in three Persons,
Blessed Trinity!
—John B. Dykes

CONCLUSION

Believing in the Trinitarian God is not optional for followers of Jesus Christ. Christ's life and teachings consistently testify to the uniqueness of God the Father and the Holy Spirit. These three persons in the Godhead function in distinct capacities, yet are of the same essence and are a mystical and equal community within themselves. In short, the members of the Trinity are eternally giving to one another in love, united to redeem a fallen world.

GOLDEN TEXT CHALLENGE

"THE GRACE OF THE LORD JESUS CHRIST, AND THE LOVE OF GOD, AND THE COMMUNION OF THE HOLY GHOST, BE WITH YOU ALL. AMEN" (2 Corinthians 13:14).

Paul began or concluded all of his epistles with an authoritative benediction. The one before us is perhaps more comprehensive than any which he wrote to the other churches.

First, observe the subject of this benediction. It is "the grace of the Lord Jesus Christ." Note the threefold title given: *Lord*—the Divine One and the Master; *Jesus*—the Savior and the Man; *Christ*—the Anointed of God, the long-promised Messiah. This grace refers to the blessings of Christ's rule as Master, of His redemption as Savior, of His boundless resources as the divine Messiah. If we are the objects of His blessings, how inestimably rich we are.

Second, the apostle refers to "the love of God." In verse 11, Paul has just spoken of God as "the God of love"; now he desires for the Corinthians the love of this God of love. The riches of divine love are the Christian's portion. The love of God as our Father is especially referred to here. It was through the Father's love that the Savior was given. However, it is through the Savior's work, and our participation in it, that we enter into the joy of God's love as the love of the Father.

Third, the apostle refers to "the communion of the Holy Ghost." This means participation in the Holy Spirit. We enjoy this through Christ. Who can estimate the value of this communion? The great work of sanctification, the constant effective teaching of the truth, preservation in times of spiritual peril, comfort in times of sorrow, ability to carry on God's work—all of these depended on our participation in the Holy Ghost. Paul told another church, "Quench not the Spirit" (1 Thessalonians 5:19). If we hinder the working of the Spirit within us, we commit spiritual suicide.

Daily Devotions:
M. Let Us Go Down
   Genesis 11:1-9
T. Who Will Go for Us?
   Isaiah 6:1-8
W. One Lord
   Zechariah 14:1-9
T. None Other God but One
   1 Corinthians 8:4-6
F. Unity of God
   Ephesians 4:1-6
S. One God, One Mediator
   1 Timothy 2:1-6

SCRIPTURE INSIGHT

Our Complete God

A triangle is a clear example of how three are required to make one, with three equal angles, each united with the other two, forming a triad of balance and strength. The primary angle of the triangle must represent the Father, for He is first of all in the Godhead; but observe that the Father alone does not constitute all there is of God.

If the Father were all there is of God, He would be complete, just as the single angle is complete. But the whole would be different from what it is—it would not be in accordance with the revelation of the Godhead as we understand it from the Scriptures.

While the Father is primary in the Godhead, and all Divinity proceeds from Him, He is united with the Son: so we draw another line, equal to the Father, and this represents the Son, "who, being in the form of God, thought it not robbery to be equal with God" (Philippians 2:6).

But the Father and the Son do not constitute the fullness of God; the Holy Spirit is also God and He is required for divine completeness. This perfection is seen in the completed pattern of the Trinity, and in the completed pattern there is strength, beauty, harmony, and purpose without end.

—**Charles W. Conn**

God in Three Persons

How We Are Saved

John 3:3-7; Acts 4:10-12; Romans 5:9-11; 10:8-13;
2 Corinthians 5:17; Ephesians 2:1-6, 8-10; Titus 3:5-7

INTRODUCTION

The question of how we are saved may seem unnecessary to some. After all, as long as we know we are saved, do the nuts and bolts of the process really matter? Remember, we are talking here not about a fringe issue in the Christian life, but of the overruling center. Because our understanding of salvation is the foundation from which all other aspects of Christian existence stem, we must comprehend it properly. Thankfully, one does not need to be a scholar to firmly grasp the principle truths of how we are saved.

It is important to realize that salvation is a concept throughout the whole of Scripture. It does not become important only with the coming of Christ. In fact, the word *salvation* occurs almost 80 times in the Old Testament. The need for divine rescue presents itself in Genesis 3, with the sin of Adam and Eve. God's response at this time predicted and set in motion the process of salvation. Speaking to the serpent in Genesis 3:15, God declares that the offspring of woman will crush the head of Satan. In chapter 4, we find the act of animal sacrifice already beginning. This made it clear that sin had created a gap between God and people. No longer did He walk with humanity in the perfect Garden. Sinful people could not live with a holy God. Therefore, the final sacrifice of the perfect Lamb of God was necessary to eternally reconcile humanity back to God.

Equally as important as how we are saved is the scope of that same salvation. First, God's salvation is *spiritual*. That is, it cuts to the very core of who we are. Second, God's salvation is *eternal*. It never loses its effectiveness or decreases its activity. Third, God's salvation is both a *moment* and a *process*. We are justified by our confession in a single moment, but are progressively saved from the old self to the Christlike self along the journey of life. This process will not be completed until we are transformed in heavenly glory.

Unit Theme:
Basic Christian Doctrines

Central Truth:
Any person can receive salvation through faith in Christ.

Focus:
Examine God's provision for salvation and believe in Jesus Christ as our Savior and Lord.

Context:
Selected New Testament passages concerning salvation

Golden Text:
"Not by works of righteousness which we have done, but according to his mercy he saved us, by the washing of regeneration, and renewing of the Holy Ghost" (Titus 3:5).

Study Outline:
I. Through Christ's Death and Resurrection (Romans 5:9-11; Titus 3:5-7; Acts 4:10-12)
II. By Grace Through Faith (Romans 10:8-13; Ephesians 2:8-10)
III. Into New Life (John 3:3-7; Ephesians 2:1-7; 2 Corinthians 5:17)

I. THROUGH CHRIST'S DEATH AND RESURRECTION
(Romans 5:9-11; Titus 3:5-7; Acts 4:10-12)

Several heresies in the early church cropped up which nullified the truth of either Jesus' death or resurrection. But a proper understanding of salvation prevailed in Christian history, and a careful study of the Scriptures confirms this understanding. Recognizing the role that both components play in the process of salvation is the first step to comprehending the majesty of God's perfect plan.

A. Christ's Death Reconciles Us to God (Romans 5:9-11; Titus 3:5-7)

Romans 5:9. Much more then, being now justified by his blood, we shall be saved from wrath through him.

10. For if, when we were enemies, we were reconciled to God by the death of his Son, much more, being reconciled, we shall be saved by his life.

11. And not only so, but we also joy in God through our Lord Jesus Christ, by whom we have now received the atonement.

Titus 3:5. Not by works of righteousness which we have done, but according to his mercy he saved us, by the washing of regeneration, and renewing of the Holy Ghost;

6. Which he shed on us abundantly through Jesus Christ our Saviour;

7. That being justified by his grace, we should be made heirs according to the hope of eternal life.

The grisly sacrificial system of the Old Testament has been preserved in great detail for us in the Book of Leviticus. For centuries God's people were required to bring bloody offerings from their flocks and herds in order to do away with their imperfection before God. These sacrifices could not be compromised in any way. The people had to follow precise rules and regulations. In this way, God communicated the seriousness of human sin and the magnificence of His holiness. The disruption of sin in the world required that death occur.

The driving concept behind these sacrifices is called *atonement*, which can be properly defined as a process of "covering over" offending sins. In the same way that the children of Israel covered their doorposts with the blood of lambs to prevent the consequence of the death angel in Egypt, sacrificing animals served to turn away the consequences of sin for the individual and the nation. This process of atonement was displayed most grandly in the annual Israelite "Day of Atonement," or Yom Kippur, outlined in Leviticus 16. On this day, which is still celebrated in the Jewish calendar, the collective sins of the nation were covered over by one sacrifice offered by the high priest. In fact, it was the

Talk About It:
1. What are we saved from, and how (Romans 5:9)?
2. What is reconciliation, why do we need it, and how can we receive it (vv. 10, 11)?
3. Why can't our "works of righteousness" (Titus 3:5) save us?
4. What does it mean to be "justified" (v. 7)?

How We Are Saved

only day of the year that the high priest entered into the most inner room of the Temple, called the Holy of Holies. There the blood of a sacrificed goat was sprinkled on the atonement cover (mercy seat) of the ark of the covenant, and the consequences of the national sins of the people were considered paid. In a symbolic gesture, a second goat (scapegoat), was sent into the wilderness as a reflection of the nation's sins being cast away.

In New Testament times, the Temple continued to operate as a place of animal sacrifice. With the death of Christ, however, early believers realized what God had done. The Cross finally and totally paid the consequence of human sin and set those who believe back in right relationship to God. In Romans 5:9-11, Paul applies the event of Christ's death in legal terms. To be *justified* in the ancient world evoked the image of a courtroom, in which a judge would find a defendant's actions either justified or unjustified depending on the evidence. Because of the death of Christ, all of our unjustified, or sinful, actions have become justified, or atoned for. We are therefore precluded from God's wrath and set in right relationship with God through faith in Jesus Christ.

In Titus 3, Paul said Christ saved us not because of any righteous acts we have done, but because of His mercy. Our sins were washed away in the new birth by the Holy Spirit, who has been generously poured out on us. Through this process we have been "justified by his grace" (v. 7), and thereby have inherited the hope of everlasting life.

> "God doesn't just patch—He renews. God doesn't just salve sins—He saves. God doesn't just reform—He transforms men by His power."
> —Merrill C. Tenney

B. Christ's Resurrection Seals God's Salvation (Acts 4:10-12)

10. Be it known unto you all, and to all the people of Israel, that by the name of Jesus Christ of Nazareth, whom ye crucified, whom God raised from the dead, even by him doth this man stand here before you whole.

11. This is the stone which was set at nought of you builders, which is become the head of the corner.

12. Neither is there salvation in any other: for there is none other name under heaven given among men, whereby we must be saved.

Without the resurrection of Christ, His death on the cross was nothing but a tragic event in history. If His bones still lay buried somewhere outside Jerusalem, He was at best a martyr, and at worst a liar. He was no more than a good teacher and a doer of great deeds. But if the Resurrection is true, then His death represents the redemption of humanity by the will and work of God himself. Like a powerful closing argument in a courtroom, the Resurrection effectively seals God's work of salvation and proclaims its truth to all of human history.

Unless the Resurrection actually occurred, belief in Christ is useless, Paul proclaims in 1 Corinthians 15. The resurrection

Talk About It:
1. How had Peter and John been able to bring healing to a crippled man (v. 10)?
2. Who are called "builders," and what had they done (v. 11)? Why?
3. What is so powerful about the name of Jesus Christ (v. 12)?

of Christ was not a spiritual or mystical occurrence. Jesus did not appear in ghostly form before His disciples. No, His discarded grave clothes and physical scars reveal that the Resurrection took place bodily. The same body that was crucified and buried also walked out of the garden tomb. Peter proclaimed the reality of Christ's resurrection powerfully in his early preaching to the Jews, as seen in Acts 4:10-12. Here, Peter was addressing the religious leaders and elders of the Jewish people in Jerusalem. They not only knew of the events surrounding Jesus of Nazareth, they had a hand in His death. This made Peter's declaration all the more shocking. The same person they had helped to kill had been physically raised back to life. Because of this, the power of Christ had been given to His followers to carry on His ministry, including that of healing. And Peter and John had just brought healing to a lame man.

More important than even miraculous works of healing is salvation itself. Peter announced to the leaders of Israel that the Resurrection sealed the act of salvation which God had performed in and through Jesus Christ. As a consequence they were without excuse, for God had clearly proven that salvation was given only through the resurrected One. Jesus is the Cornerstone, but the religious leaders had rejected Him, choosing instead to build their lives on their self-righteousness.

> "No man ever loved like Jesus. He taught the blind to see and the mute to speak. He died on the cross to save us. He bore our sins. And now God says, 'Because He did, I can forgive you.'"
> —Billy Graham

II. BY GRACE THROUGH FAITH (Romans 10:8-13; Ephesians 2:8-10)

The consequences of Christ's death and resurrection are not automatically applied to our soul. If that were so, people would have no choice. Instead, the Scriptures declare that we do have a role in effecting God's salvation. Just like a patient owns the responsibility for taking the prescription of the doctor, it is faith that attaches God's salvation to our hearts.

A. Faith Is a Confession (Romans 10:8-13)

8. But what saith it? The word is nigh thee, even in thy mouth, and in thy heart: that is, the word of faith, which we preach;

9. That if thou shalt confess with thy mouth the Lord Jesus, and shalt believe in thine heart that God hath raised him from the dead, thou shalt be saved.

10. For with the heart man believeth unto righteousness; and with the mouth confession is made unto salvation.

11. For the scripture saith, Whosoever believeth on him shall not be ashamed.

12. For there is no difference between the Jew and the Greek: for the same Lord over all is rich unto all that call upon him.

How We Are Saved

13. For whosoever shall call upon the name of the Lord shall be saved.

The act of public confession has always played a significant role in the community of faith. Jewish children have celebrated this public confession in bar mitzvah parties for centuries. When a Jewish boy turns 13 years of age, he is formally invited to be a confessing member of the faith community. This practice has its roots in the Scriptures, which are in themselves filled with public commitments to God. Joshua instructed the children of Israel to make a commitment to serve God in the Promised Land. The Psalms were constructed for use as confessions in the public worship services of Israel. So when the apostles defined the process of receiving salvation, they unsurprisingly framed it in the language of public confession (Romans 10:8-13).

In this passage, Paul is utilizing Old Testament verses in order to illustrate the concept of a righteousness that is by faith, as opposed to a righteousness earned through keeping the Law. After referencing Moses' words about God's nearness in Deuteronomy 30:14, he goes on to explain just how near God really is to humanity. Interestingly, he calls his presentation "the word of faith," indicating that this may have become an early term for the church's description of the message of the gospel. This is significant because it indicates that the earliest Christians considered faith so vital to receiving the gospel that they used the very words interchangeably!

Paul offers a dual process by which this faith is put into action. First, it requires a public confession with one's mouth. Paul is not saying that an inner belief is too weak to effect salvation, but is simply indicating the tradition of the early church that faith be verbally professed. In fact, this is similar to many Christian traditions today—asking recipients of salvation to come forward in an altar call, or to repeat a particular prayer, or to raise their hand. It is not that these things save a person, but that they allow the community of faith to acknowledge the confession of the individual. Furthermore, such practices allow the individual to take personal responsibility for acting upon their faith by expressing it outwardly. This is coupled, of course, by a belief in the inner self that Jesus was in fact raised from the dead and so lives as the Savior of the world. Paul then says God is not close only to select individuals—such as people of a certain race or social status—but to anyone who calls to Him.

Lest we believe that this confession Paul encourages is simply a routine, formulaic exercise, it's important to emphasize its content: "Jesus is Lord" (v. 9, *NIV*). The Greek word for "Lord" is *kurios*, and was regularly applied to Caesar—the leader of the Roman Empire. In fact, for any other person to claim to be the *kurios* in Roman society would have been considered high

Talk About It:
1. Why is the gospel called "the word of faith" (v. 8)?
2. Describe the confession one must make to receive salvation (v. 9).
3. What promise does verse 11 offer?

Faith Wind
When Hudson Taylor, the first missionary to China, reached the shore of the Cannibal Islands, the wind died and the ship floated near tribes looking for a human meal. When the captain asked Reverend Taylor to pray for God's help, Taylor said he would not do so until the captain unfurled the sails. When this was done, the wind picked up and they sailed to safety.
Salvation is a gift of God by grace alone, but we do need faith to make it effective in our lives.

treason punishable by death. The public confession of the early Christians was no small matter—it was scandalous toward the order of society and Caesar himself. So also, those receiving salvation by grace should understand it means committing our lives to Christ's lordship.

B. Faith Is a Gift From God (Ephesians 2:8-10)

8. For by grace are ye saved through faith; and that not of yourselves: it is the gift of God:

9. Not of works, lest any man should boast.

10. For we are his workmanship, created in Christ Jesus unto good works, which God hath before ordained that we should walk in them.

Talk About It:
1. Why shouldn't believers boast?
2. Explain the statement "We are [God's] workmanship" (v. 10).

Is the ability to have faith in Christ something we're born with, something that lies dormant in us which we have the ability to utilize when we hear the gospel? Although we certainly retain the right to choose in all situations—God does not manipulate us even for our own good—even the capacity to operate our faith is given by God. Whether He placed it in us when we were created or whether it is strength given in the moment of decision, the Scriptures point to God alone as the author of all faith.

Even the faith to receive the grace of salvation is "not from yourselves" (v. 8, *NIV*). God alone holds the rights to faith so we cannot boast about however great our measure of it might be. So we see the God-centeredness of salvation. It is God who sent His Son to provide salvation, God who extended grace to us while we were still sinners, and God who even gives us the faith to believe in the gospel of salvation. Even our responsibility to accept salvation through individual confession and personal faith is aided by the power of God.

"By grace you have been saved! Whatever else we do, praying and singing is but an answer to this word spoken to us by God himself."
—**Karl Barth**

By receiving Christ's salvation, we become His *making*. "That is, we are 'created' or 'formed' by Him, not only in the general sense in which all things are made by Him, but in that special sense which is denoted by the new creation" (Barnes). We are saved to do *good works*—to lead holy lives and serve in the ways He has preordained for us (v. 10).

III. INTO NEW LIFE (John 3:3-7; Ephesians 2:1-7; 2 Corinthians 5:17)

The most basic definition of *salvation* is "rescue." In fact, one of the earliest Christian symbols found in artwork and in caverns where believers worshiped in secret is the drawing of a ship. Scholars believe this ship signified the salvation of God that the early church believed saved people from the deep waters of evil. Scripture portrays this along with the concept of God's great ransoming of humanity through Christ. That is, just like a kidnapped person might be rescued with a ransom, God rescued us through the blood of Christ. But to be rescued from one way of life necessitates beginning a new way of life. This way of life is expounded throughout the New Testament.

A. Salvation Requires Death (John 3:3-7)

3. Jesus answered and said unto him, Verily, verily, I say unto thee, Except a man be born again, he cannot see the kingdom of God.

4. Nicodemus saith unto him, How can a man be born when he is old? can he enter the second time into his mother's womb, and be born?

5. Jesus answered, Verily, verily, I say unto thee, Except a man be born of water and of the Spirit, he cannot enter into the kingdom of God.

6. That which is born of the flesh is flesh; and that which is born of the Spirit is spirit.

7. Marvel not that I said unto thee, Ye must be born again.

Salvation requires death. In the Old Testament, followers of God killed animals to atone for their sins. In the New Testament, God offered His Son up to death. But this does not exempt us from the dying process. Instead, God requires the death of our former self to accompany the reception of His salvation. Jesus himself explains this to Nicodemus in John 3.

Talk About It:
1. "How can a man be born when he is old?" (v. 4).
2. What does it mean to be "born of water and of the Spirit" (v. 5)?

Although Nicodemus was a religious leader of Israel, he blatantly misunderstood Jesus' teaching of dying to the old self. In fact, the Greek term Jesus used for "born again" has a double meaning. It also means "born from above." Nicodemus took Jesus' statement to denote a second, chronological birth. Jesus rebutted him by launching into this second understanding of what it means to be born again. He identified it in verse 5 as the way to accomplish entrance into the kingdom of God, then broadened new birth to include two important components— *water* and *Spirit*. By "water," most scholars believe Jesus was referring to baptism, the point of public confession for the person being saved. By "Spirit," Jesus was simply highlighting the spiritual nature of this birth. It is not a fleshly or human birth, as Nicodemus suggested, but one of supernatural origins.

So we are called to a newness in salvation that mirrors the birth of a newborn baby. Salvation brings with it a life wrapped in freshness and gives us a brand-new start.

B. Salvation Produces Resurrection (Ephesians 2:1-7)

1. And you hath he quickened, who were dead in trespasses and sins:

2. Wherein in time past ye walked according to the course of this world, according to the prince of the power

of the air, the spirit that now worketh in the children of disobedience:

3. Among whom also we all had our conversation in times past in the lusts of our flesh, fulfilling the desires of the flesh and of the mind; and were by nature the children of wrath, even as others.

4. But God, who is rich in mercy, for his great love wherewith he loved us,

5. Even when we were dead in sins, hath quickened us together with Christ, (by grace ye are saved;)

6. And hath raised us up together, and made us sit together in heavenly places in Christ Jesus:

7. That in the ages to come he might shew the exceeding riches of his grace in his kindness toward us through Christ Jesus.

God views sinners as being "dead" because of their *innate corruption* ("sin") as well as their *specific acts of sin* ("trespasses"). This had once been the condition of the Ephesian Christians (as with all Christians) to whom Paul was writing. They had followed the ways of the world and Satan, its prince, filled with the spirit of disobedience, striving to satisfy their sinful nature, and therefore deserving the wrath of God.

However, by saying yes to the incomparable grace and kindness of Jesus Christ, they were no longer "dead in sins." Instead, they had been "raised up" to a new life in the heavenly realms—a new spiritual existence that would culminate with everlasting life in heaven. They had been made "alive with Christ" (v. 5, *NIV*)—as certainly as Christ's physical body had been raised from the grave, so their spiritual bodies had been resurrected from the graveyard of sin.

We are saved, or rescued, from our former way of life in which we served the sinful nature. That nature has been crucified with Christ, so that our new self can grow and develop.

C. Salvation Offers Life (2 Corinthians 5:17)

17. Therefore if any man be in Christ, he is a new creature: old things are passed away; behold, all things are become new.

The essence of salvation is newness—the brand-new life that God offers to us in Christ. Only a sinless slate can set us right in the sight of a holy God, and only a perfect sacrifice could do away with our sin. Salvation comes with a fresh set of language, new values and priorities, and a godly perspective. The joy it brings is inexpressible.

Creation itself has changed for the new believer. In 2 Corinthians 5:17 we are reminded of the great flood from which Noah was spared, as "old things . . . passed away." After the

Talk About It:
1. What does it mean to be "quickened" (vv. 1, 5), and who needs it?
2. Who is "the spirit . . . now at work in those who are disobedient" (v. 2, *NIV*)?
3. How is God shown to be "rich" and "great" (v. 4)?

"When Jesus prayed to the One who could save Him from death, He did not get that salvation; he got instead the salvation of the world."
—**Philip Yancey**

Talk About It:
What is *old* and what is *new* for the Christian?

How We Are Saved

waters subsided, creation was renewed and life was able to be fruitful and multiply. So also the new believer, whose life has been renewed, is set free to live a fruitful and abundant life in Christ. This life is lived in concert with creation as a whole, which groans for God's salvation to overtake the entire created order (Romans 8:22). How amazing is the scope of this great salvation! It is planted in the human heart, yet powerful enough to make disciples of all nations. It is best expressed in the lives of people, yet will one day reform all of creation. In all these things, Jesus Christ is our model and enabler. Through Him we are on the long road to the perfection of eternal life.

CONCLUSION

All other aspects of the kingdom of God fully hinge on a proper understanding of salvation. This includes comprehending (1) the necessity of both Christ's death and resurrection, (2) the requirement of faith alone, and (3) the provision of new life for anyone who believes. The Bible tells of God's grand vision for salvation from cover to cover. Christ's death and resurrection was God's plan for salvation "from the foundation of the world" (Revelation 13:8).

GOLDEN TEXT CHALLENGE

"NOT BY WORKS OF RIGHTEOUSNESS WHICH WE HAVE DONE, BUT ACCORDING TO HIS MERCY HE SAVED US, BY THE WASHING OF REGENERATION, AND RENEWING OF THE HOLY GHOST" (Titus 3:5).

The Greek word for *renewing* means "to make again something that is different." It signifies something different happening in our lives.

This same word is also used in Romans 12:2 concerning the *renewing* of our mind in Christ. In Titus it shows "a revival of His power, developing the Christian life" and "stresses the continual operation of the indwelling Spirit of God" (W.E. Vines).

This could never happen through our own good deeds. Stack them as high as we might, our best actions could never rebirth or renew us. That is the ministry of the Holy Spirit, who works from the inside out.

Have we been born again? Are we trusting God's mercy instead of our own efforts? Are we continually letting God's Spirit *wash* us in His renewing power as we travel through a dirty world?

Daily Devotions:
M. The Joy of Salvation
   Psalm 51:10-14
T. Praise God for Salvation
   Isaiah 12:1-6
W. Christ's Sufferings Foretold
   Isaiah 53:1-6
T. Redemption Foretold
   Luke 1:67-79
F. Jesus Seeks the Lost
   Luke 19:1-10
S. Redemption Through Christ's Blood
   Colossians 1:12-22

January 21, 2007 (Lesson 8)

Ordinances of the Church

Mark 16:16; Luke 22:19, 20; John 13:4-17; Acts 8:36-39;
Romans 6:3-5; 1 Corinthians 10:16, 17; 11:23-26;
1 Timothy 5:9, 10

Unit Theme:
Basic Christian Doctrines

Central Truth:
The church ordinances signify the relationship Christ desires with His followers.

Focus:
Explore the purposes of the ordinances of the church and appreciate their spiritual significance.

Context:
New Testament passages regarding baptism, the Lord's Supper, and footwashing

Golden Text:
"Continuing daily with one accord in the temple, and breaking bread from house to house . . . praising God, and having favor with all the people" (Acts 2:46, 47).

Study Outline:
I. Water Baptism (Mark 16:16; Acts 8:36-39; Romans 6:3-5)
II. The Lord's Supper (Luke 22:19, 20; 1 Corinthians 11:23-26; 10:16, 17)
III. Washing of the Saints' Feet (John 13:4-17; 1 Timothy 5:9, 10)

INTRODUCTION

For 20 centuries, the person of Jesus Christ and the faith surrounding Him has dominated the rise of Western culture. Without the preeminence of the church in our nation's origins and history, we would undoubtedly look like a completely different nation. In fact, much of the entire concept of democracy and individual rights is rooted in Scripture itself! In order for the universal church to thrive for so long all over the world, it has held to particular ordinances that serve to continually remind and effect in its members the basic stories and doctrines of the Bible.

The word *ordinance* is a form of the verb *to ordain*. Although we now commonly use this word to speak of the education and sending of persons into professional ministry (see 1 Corinthians 7:17; Titus 1:5), Scripture also references God's ability to ordain events (1 Chronicles 17:9; Isaiah 26:12). *To ordain* means "to set in order," and its Latin root was used in medieval times to portray troops who were arranged in ranks or rows. So then, an ordinance is something that has been orderly arranged for the good of the community.

We actually give time and esteem to ordinances throughout our lives. Birthday parties, wedding celebrations and graduation ceremonies are examples of contemporary ordinances—markers we use to set life in order, or to properly arrange the calendar of life. Do these ceremonies we observe simply memorialize and celebrate the events of our lives, or do they actually effect a change in us? To some extent they do both, which is an important point of understanding the ordinances of the church. The best metaphor for these faith ordinances is our commitment to celebrating marriage anniversaries. A couple's anniversary looks back to a single event in history and by doing so reclaims that event's potency for today.

The church's ordinances, used rightly, indicate two significant truths about the church. First, they show that the church is a historical institution. It did not recently crop up out of nowhere, but has real-life roots in the story of humanity. Second, they show that the historical truths of the Bible continue to be relevant to people today, as the Biblical story is "acted out" through ordinances as the church spreads throughout the world.

I. WATER BAPTISM (Mark 16:16; Acts 8:36-39; Romans 6:3-5)

The first ordinance of the church is water baptism. Baptism holds the most significant place among the ordinances because it is the only one directly connected with initial salvation. Each ordinance, sometimes called by the alternative name *sacrament*, represents a specific aspect of the Christian life. Through water baptism, the convert and the community of faith celebrate together God's miracle of salvation.

A. Jesus Commands Water Baptism (Mark 16:16)

16. He that believeth and is baptized shall be saved; but he that believeth not shall be damned.

damned—con-demned

There is no guesswork involved when it comes to discerning the New Testament priority of water baptism. Even at the beginning of the gospel story, before Jesus' ministry comes on the scene, the prophet John is called by his popular nickname—"the Baptist" (Matthew 3:1). Yes, John was a fiery preacher of righteousness, but he was primarily recognized as a famous baptizer. An archaeologist named Shimon Gibson has recently presented concrete evidence of John's ministry of baptism. In his book, *The Cave of John the Baptist*, Gibson lays out his findings of a freshly excavated cave with artwork and relics that identify it as an ancient baptismal site of John himself. So the cousin of Jesus is still acknowledged by history today as a proponent and practitioner of water baptism.

Before Jesus began His ministry, He was baptized by His reluctant cousin John (vv. 13-17). We are given a vital glimpse into the significance of baptism at this event, as the triune God is revealed to onlookers in the form of a dove, a light, and a voice of approval thundering from heaven. Given such a powerful illustration of the importance of baptism at the beginning of Jesus' ministry, it is no surprise that He continues to express its magnitude at His ministry's end. In Mark 16:16, Jesus said, "Whoever believes and is baptized will be saved, but whoever does not believe will be condemned" (*NIV*).

This verse is found in Jesus' final words to His disciples. He has been gloriously raised from the dead, and after rebuking the 11 disciples for their stubborn refusal to believe the testimony of the women who saw Him alive, Jesus issues His Great Commission. They are to spread out into the furthermost corners of the world and tell everyone the gospel message. If they do this faithfully, two results are to be expected. People will believe, but that's not all. Their belief will move them to publicly express their commitment to Christ in baptism. So the Great Commission has two clear parts—*to preach* and *to baptize*. One without the other handicaps the spreading of the gospel.

Talk About It:
1. According to verse 16, what would happen when the disciples carried out Christ's command in verse 15?
2. What is the connection between belief and baptism?

"On the bank of some dark river, as we are thrust backward, onlookers will remark, 'They could kill somebody like that.' To which old John might say, 'Good, you're finally catching on.'"
—William Willimon

B. An Evangelist Baptizes an Ethiopian (Acts 8:36-39)

36. And as they went on their way, they came unto a certain water: and the eunuch said, See, here is water; what doth hinder me to be baptized?

37. And Philip said, If thou believest with all thine heart, thou mayest. And he answered and said, I believe that Jesus Christ is the Son of God.

38. And he commanded the chariot to stand still: and they went down both into the water, both Philip and the eunuch; and he baptized him.

39. And when they were come up out of the water, the Spirit of the Lord caught away Philip, that the eunuch saw him no more: and he went on his way rejoicing.

Talk About It:
1. What "doth hinder" (v. 36) some people from being baptized?
2. According to Philip, what is the criteria for baptism?
3. When should a new convert be baptized?

"Most Westerners take baptism for granted, but for many in the world the act requires immense courage. In countries like Nepal it once meant imprisonment. For Soviet or Chinese or Eastern bloc believers, it was like signing their own death warrant."
—**Chuck Colson**

The Book of Acts depicts the disciples following Jesus' commandment by preaching throughout the towns and cities of Judea, Samaria, and eventually even the heart of the Roman Empire. The way in which they baptized circumcised Jews was undoubtedly controversial. In fact, what made John the Baptist such a notorious person among the Jewish religious leaders was the fact that he baptized Jews! In Judaism, Gentile converts were typically baptized in a conversion ceremony, but Jews did not see a need to baptize Jews, since they believed they were physically born into the family of God. But the apostles made no such distinction. All were sinful and needed to be redeemed by Christ, Jew and Gentile alike. This is illustrated aptly in Acts 8:36-39.

Along the road from Jerusalem to Gaza, Philip came upon a eunuch from Ethiopia who was reading the Scriptures in his horse-drawn carriage. Eunuchs served in the royal court, and were castrated for the sake of respecting the queen. This, coupled with the fact that he could read, leads us to believe this eunuch was an educated, high-ranking official. After Philip took the easy opportunity to present the message of Christ to him, the eunuch immediately declared his desire to be baptized. His driver stopped, and he was baptized on the spot before Philip was whisked away by the Spirit. This passage depicts the command of Jesus in action in the early church. And just as Jesus predicted, miracles followed the preaching *and baptizing* of the apostles.

C. Water Baptism Unites Us With Christ and His Church (Romans 6:3-5)

3. Know ye not, that so many of us as were baptized into Jesus Christ were baptized into his death?

4. Therefore we are buried with him by baptism into death: that like as Christ was raised up from the dead by the glory of the Father, even so we also should walk in newness of life.

5. For if we have been planted together in the likeness of his death, we shall be also in the likeness of his resurrection.

What exactly happens when we are baptized? Baptism is frequently defined as the outward expression of an inward faith—the way we display our newfound salvation to the church. This is certainly one of its uses, but its meaning runs a lot deeper. Paul explained each aspect of the process of baptism in Romans 6:3-5.

Primarily, the act of being placed underwater represents being united with Christ in His death. As Christ was placed underground in burial, so the convert is placed underwater. This symbolizes the death of the old nature, but also the new unity we have with Christ. But this is only half of what baptism stands for. Paul's logic is clear: the first segment of uniting with Jesus' death is followed by the second. The rising from the water portrays our unity with Christ in His resurrection in addition to His death.

In his book, *Baptism: Christ's Act in the Church*, Lawrence Hull Stookey writes: "When we understand it in this way, baptism can never again be viewed as simply an imitation of what Jesus of Nazareth experienced in the Jordan River under John the Baptizer. We are not called to be like Jesus; we are enabled to be *in* Jesus Christ by the power of the Holy Spirit. . . . Our names (that is, our whole identity, in the Biblical understanding of things) are taken up into, united with, the ineffable name of God." In this way, baptism represents a living example of joining ourselves to God.

Baptism also indicates the new believer's desire to be supported by the Christian community in his or her newfound faith. The act publicly confirms the convert's belief that they will not carry on their relationship with God in isolation, but will wholeheartedly join with the church in its mission.

So does something actually happen at baptism, or is it completely symbolic? If we compare it to a marriage ceremony, we can project that it is a symbolic ceremony which does effect something new in the life of the convert. A marriage ceremony does not fundamentally change the relationship of the wedded couple, but it does give them new rights and privileges. So also the ordinance of baptism is loaded with benefits for the individual convert and the church as a whole.

II. THE LORD'S SUPPER (Luke 22:19, 20;
1 Corinthians 11:23-26; 10:16, 17)

The Lord's Supper represents the most divisive ordinance of the church in its long history. Christian groups struggled for centuries to define what actually happens in the Communion

planted (v. 5)—united

Talk About It
1. What does it mean to be "baptized into his death" (v. 3)?
2. Describe the resurrected life Christians should live (vv. 4, 5).

Willing to Die?
Millions of people are baptized, but for many of them baptism is a completely dead form. I would advise anyone who wants to be baptized to ask himself, "Am I willing, for the sake of Jesus, to love nothing more than Him—neither wife, parents, nor children—so that He can live in me? Am I willing to give everything to Jesus and my brothers?" If you are not, don't be baptized. You must be willing to die for Him so that He himself may live in your heart. Jesus must be your only treasure.
—**Heinrich Arnold**

sacrament. Roman Catholics have traditionally held to a view called *transubstantiation*. This viewpoint proposes that the bread and wine actually, physically are transformed into the body and blood of Jesus himself. Martin Luther, the originator of the Protestant Reformation, denounced this view in favor of what he called *consubstantiation*. He taught that while the elements of the Lord's Table did not change, a spiritual presence of Christ dwelt with and in them which had great power for Communion recipients. This view is still held by many Protestants today.

A. Jesus Commands the Lord's Supper (Luke 22:19, 20)

19. And he took bread, and gave thanks, and brake it, and gave unto them, saying, This is my body which is given for you: this do in remembrance of me.

20. Likewise also the cup after supper, saying, This cup is the new testament in my blood, which is shed for you.

Talk About It:
1. Why is bread an appropriate symbol for Christ's body?
2. Why is *the cup* an appropriate symbol for His blood?
3. Explain the phrase "new testament" (v. 20).

"And even though a believer can nourish himself anytime and anywhere on the presence of Christ in His Word, there is a special nourishing offered in eating the Lord's Supper and hearing the preaching of God's Word."
—John Piper

Whereas we find the ordinance of baptism at the beginning of Jesus' ministry, the ordinance of the Lord's Supper is found at its end. Whereas the ordinance of baptism serves as the symbol of the beginning of a convert's faith, the ordinance of the Lord's Supper is one for those already believing. In the early church, particularly the second, third and fourth centuries, baptism was a prerequisite to receiving the Lord's Supper. In fact, the unbaptized were not even allowed to be present during this vital ordinance of Communion, being excused for that segment of the worship service.

Just like baptism, it is no surprise that the Lord's Supper is Jesus-focused. This observation alone gives us an excellent vantage point from which to appreciate church ordinances. They have been given to help us not only remember Jesus, but to center our lives on Him. When we continually participate in the ceremonies Jesus instituted, we are reminded of His life, His death, His resurrection, His heart, His priorities and His values. Much of this is learned and imparted by repetition, especially in the case of the Lord's Supper.

B. Paul Reiterates Christ's Command (1 Corinthians 11:23-26)

23. For I have received of the Lord that which also I delivered unto you, That the Lord Jesus the same night in which he was betrayed took bread:

24. And when he had given thanks, he brake it, and said, Take, eat: this is my body, which is broken for you: this do in remembrance of me.

25. After the same manner also he took the cup, when he had supped, saying, This cup is the new testament in my blood: this do ye, as oft as ye drink it, in remembrance of me.

Ordinances of the Church

26. For as often as ye eat this bread, and drink this cup, ye do shew the Lord's death till he come.

Several passages in the letters of the New Testament give us a unique glimpse into the way the Gospels were communicated and read in the early churches. Nowhere is this more evident than in Paul's first letter to the Corinthians, where he passed on specific teaching found in Matthew, Mark and Luke.

In 1 Corinthians 11:23-26, Paul effectively restated Jesus' instructions for honoring the Lord's Supper in a corrective way. And, in Corinth, there was much that needed correcting! Further study of this section of the chapter reveals that this church's observance of the Communion sacrament was in chaos. First, they partook of the Lord's Table divisively. Certain arrogant members used it as a time to perform, to show off their own place of supposed importance in the church. These troublemakers did not wait on the entire community to gather, but began the ceremony rashly, so that others were left out. Second, they partook of the Lord's Table disrespectfully. Apparently they had turned it into an entire meal, and some were even becoming literally drunk from drinking too much of the Communion wine.

Paul's restatement of the basic ordinance of the Lord's Supper provided just the instruction they needed to get back on track as individuals and as a community of faith. The simple tradition he received from God he passed on to the Corinthian believers, encouraging them to participate in the Lord's Supper thankfully, not competitively. In fact, this ordinance is commonly called the *Eucharist*, which derives from the Greek word *eucharisteo*, meaning "to give thanks." When rightly understood this way, the Lord's Supper truly fulfills the command of Jesus to do this "in remembrance of me" (Luke 22:19).

C. The Lord's Supper Unites Us to Christ (1 Corinthians 10:16)

16. The cup of blessing which we bless, is it not the communion of the blood of Christ? The bread which we break, is it not the communion of the body of Christ?

Just as baptism unites the new convert to the death and resurrection of Christ, the Lord's Supper unites the believer with the sufferings and provided atonement of Christ. This participation in His death is mystical and not easy to define. Martin Luther's view is helpful—that there is an inexplicable presence of Christ that always accompanies the ordinance of Communion. Throughout church history, this mystical union between Christ and the believer present in the Eucharist has been celebrated. John Chrysostom, a church bishop in the fourth century, phrased this union in this way: "How many of you say: I should like to see [Christ's] face, His garments, His

Talk About It:
1. When did Jesus institute the Lord's Supper (v. 23)? Why is this significant?
2. What should we remember when we eat the Lord's Supper (vv. 24, 25)? Why is this important?
3. How long should the church observe this ordinance (v. 26)? Why?

"What God is looking for is brokenhearted awareness of our sin. If we approach the table with this attitude, we don't have to be afraid of eating or drinking in an unworthy manner."
—Doug Goins (Discovery Publishing)

Talk About It:
Why is the Lord's Supper also called "Communion"?

shoes. You do see Him, you touch Him, you eat Him. He gives Himself to you, not only that you may see Him, but also to be your food and nourishment."

The unity that the Lord's Supper provides between Christ and the believer must not be underestimated, even if we are not part of a tradition that places a high, weekly premium on the Communion ceremony. It is not the frequency with which we receive it that matters, but the attitude in which we approach it.

In 1 Corinthians 10, Paul is combating another distortion of the Lord's Supper within the young congregation. The ceremony of the Lord's Table was being confused with, and possibly mixed together with, meals sacrificed to idols. In the ancient Greco-Roman world, community feasts were regularly given in tribute to certain gods. In fact, idol worship was so prominent that the common meat eaten by the community was often sacrificed to an idol before it went to market. This posed a complex problem for the early Christians, who stood staunchly opposed to any form of idol worship. Paul encourages believers to utilize wisdom in this regard, helping them to see it is not the meat which matters, but the avoidance of any situation that might cause the faith of a fellow Christian to falter. However, when it comes to the ordinance of the Lord's Supper, they should have nothing to do with idol feasts. Because this ordinance is not just a ceremony, but also a true *participation* (v. 16, *NIV*) in the death of Jesus Christ, it is vital that it be conducted properly and soberly.

The Lord's Supper brings us into communion with Christ, because it represents the sacrifice He made on our behalf on the cross of Calvary. Since Jesus' death was effective for all of time, there is no need for us to offer sacrifice time and time again as in the Old Testament system. The danger of the transubstantiation viewpoint is that it suggests Christ's body and blood is sacrificed over and over for the community of faith, as if the cross weren't adequate. A more Scriptural view is that Communion is a way we join ourselves to Christ, reminded that His sacrifice for our sins continues to be effectual and adequate in our lives. This sacrament is filled with Jesus through and through. As Saint Augustine, an early church father, put simply, "We do not sin when we adore Christ in the Eucharist; we do sin when we do not adore Christ in the Eucharist."

D. The Lord's Supper Unites Us With Christ's Church (v. 17)

17. For we being many are one bread, and one body: for we are all partakers of that one bread.

Just as the ordinance of baptism rallied the local church around the celebration of one's conversion, the Lord's Supper unites us with Christ's church. Paul explains this in verse 17. First, this verse gives us a window into the way the Lord's

---

Sealing Sacraments
Marriage is also an ordinance, or sacrament, of the church, and the wedding ceremony serves as an excellent illustration of the ordinances of the church. During the wedding ceremony, the couple's relationship does not fundamentally change, but their commitment to one another is sealed legally and witnessed by a supportive community. This provides encouragement and accountability in their relationship for their entire lives. So also the church ordinances allow God to seal things within us, and help us to be a part of a unified community of faith.

Talk About It:
How does the Lord's Supper unify believers?

Ordinances of the Church

Supper was received in the early church. Unlike our modern convenience of individual cups and wafers, part of the symbolism inherent in the ceremony involved the literal partaking of a single loaf. Second, this verse shows us the purpose of the Lord's Supper is not just vertical—there is more at stake here than just God and the individual. Instead, it is also horizontal—the entire community came together to celebrate what God had done for them collectively, sharing from a single loaf of bread.

III. WASHING OF THE SAINTS' FEET (John 13:13-17;
    1 Timothy 5:9, 10; John 13:4-12)
Note: Some denominations observe footwashing as a church ordinance, while others do not. This section is included for those who do.

A. Should the Church Practice Footwashing? (John 13:13-17;
    1 Timothy 5:9, 10)
John 13:13. Ye call me Master and Lord: and ye say well; for so I am.

14. If I then, your Lord and Master, have washed your feet; ye also ought to wash one another's feet.

15. For I have given you an example, that ye should do as I have done to you.

16. Verily, verily, I say unto you, The servant is not greater than his lord; neither he that is sent greater than he that sent him.

17. If ye know these things, happy are ye if ye do them.

1 Timothy 5:9. Let not a widow be taken into the number under threescore years old, having been the wife of one man,

10. Well reported of for good works; if she have brought up children, if she have lodged strangers, if she have washed the saints' feet, if she have relieved the afflicted, if she have diligently followed every good work.

When Jesus washed the feet of His disciples, He took a step that was shocking in the ancient world. There is no evidence to support that any person of superior status, with the exception of Jesus, ever voluntarily washed the feet of a subordinate. Shortly after rendering this service, Jesus gave His disciples rather explicit commands to wash one another's feet. For several reasons, it appears that Jesus' words should be taken as calling for a literal compliance.

The most natural reading of the text is one which calls for a literal fulfillment. Not only did Jesus' completely unexpected example suggest that He was serious about the practice, but He also made this intention explicit by the language He used. Jesus said that the disciples were obligated ("ought") to wash

taken into the number
(1 Timothy 5:9)—included in group of widows for which the church must provide

threescore years old (v. 9)—60 years of age

Talk About It:
1. Why did Jesus emphasize His titles of *Lord* and *Master* in John 13?
2. What makes a person truly *happy* (v. 17)?

one another's feet. Whenever this verb appears in John's writings, it indicates an obligation, not simply a suggestion or good idea (cf. John 19:7; 1 John 2:6; 3:16; 4:11; 3 John 8).

The word translated "example" in John 13:15 does not convey the idea of moral example as much as it does "prototype" or "illustration" of how something is to be done, as it meant in Greek medical manuals of the day. Jesus said those who know *and* do these things are blessed (v. 17). Amazingly, neither the rites of baptism nor the Lord's Supper are given such explicit words of institution in the New Testament.

Both the disciples described in John 13 and the readers for whom the Gospel of John was written would have had little reason to interpret the commands in anything other than a literal fashion. The Hebrew scriptures contain numerous references to footwashing. In preparation for entrance into certain sections of the Tabernacle and Temple, the priests were instructed to wash their hands and feet (Exodus 30:17-21; 40:30-32; 2 Chronicles 4:6). Several Old Testament passages present washing the feet as a part of personal hygiene and comfort (2 Samuel 11:8-11; 19:24; Song of Solomon 5:3). In other Biblical references, footwashing is offered to guests by a host/hostess as an act of hospitality (Genesis 18:4; 19:2; 24:32; 43:24; Judges 19:21; 1 Samuel 25:41).

Other evidence demonstrates that footwashing was offered to banquet guests in particular (see Luke 7:44). Ordinarily, one invited to a banquet would bathe at home, needing only to wash the feet when arriving at the home of the host/hostess to remove the dust and debris accumulated on the journey. Since footwashing was such a part of their everyday life, their most natural hearing of these words would be understood to call for a literal observance.

That the commands to wash feet were intended to be taken literally is shown by the way the earliest readers of John's Gospel interpreted the commands. In point of fact, the vast majority of the early church who commented on John 13:14-17 understood the words of Jesus as calling for a literal fulfillment.

First Timothy 5:10 demonstrates that late in Paul's life, the church had not forgotten this command of our Lord. In this passage the feet of the saints were to be washed by a group (or order) of widows. It is significant that "washing the saints' feet" is listed with other good works: child rearing, hospitality, helping those in need.

Two things of importance should be noted about this verse. First, it is the feet of the saints which were to be washed, not people in general. Second, footwashing is distinguished from hospitality in the list of 1 Timothy 5:10. These considerations seem to confirm that footwashing was no longer thought of in

> "When a footwashing occurred in the context of a meal in the ancient world, it preceded the meal, most often occurring at the door of the host. However, the footwashing which Jesus enacted interrupted the meal, rather than preceded it. Thus, this footwashing is underscored by its unusual placement."
>
> —J. Christopher Thomas

terms of hospitality but was given spiritual significance. In light of this evidence, it seems safe to conclude that Jesus intended to institute footwashing as an ongoing practice of the church.

B. What Is the Meaning of *Footwashing*? (John 13:4-12)

4. He riseth from supper, and laid aside his garments; and took a towel, and girded himself.

5. After that he poureth water into a bason, and began to wash the disciples' feet, and to wipe them with the towel wherewith he was girded.

6. Then cometh he to Simon Peter: and Peter saith unto him, Lord, dost thou wash my feet?

7. Jesus answered and said unto him, What I do thou knowest not now; but thou shalt know hereafter.

8. Peter saith unto him, Thou shalt never wash my feet. Jesus answered him, If I wash thee not, thou hast no part with me.

9. Simon Peter saith unto him, Lord, not my feet only, but also my hands and my head.

10. Jesus saith to him, He that is washed needeth not save to wash his feet, but is clean every whit: and ye are clean, but not all.

11. For he knew who should betray him; therefore said he, Ye are not all clean.

12. So after he had washed their feet, and had taken his garments, and was set down again, he said unto them, Know ye what I have done to you?

In a variety of ways John made clear that the footwashing was connected to the passion and death of Jesus. This act occurs in the first part of John 13—17, the portion of the Gospel devoted to a description of Jesus' preparing His disciples for His departure. In 13:1 the reader is told that Jesus' hour had finally come. It was His hour of exaltation on the cross, and the reader is told that He loved His own until the end. His return to the Father (v. 3) also connects the footwashing with His passion, as does the appearance of Judas the betrayer (v. 2). Finally, several scholars see a reference to the death of Jesus in verse 4, where He is described as laying aside His clothing, since when John uses the Greek term meaning "to lay aside," it ordinarily has reference to Jesus' death.

That this footwashing is unusual is indicated also by the highly deliberative way in which Jesus' actions are described. Instead of simply saying that Jesus washed the feet of the disciples, John methodically underscored the significance of Jesus' actions by specifically mentioning each step of the procedure (vv. 4, 5).

Verse 7 indicates that this footwashing was no ordinary one

Talk About It:
1. Describe the love Jesus desired to express to His disciples (v. 1).
2. What do you learn from the fact Jesus washed the feet of all 12 of His disciples?
3. Why did Peter not want Jesus to wash his feet?
4. Describe the "washing" believers need.

when Jesus himself informed Peter that he would not understand the significance of His action until after these things. Just as the disciples were unable to comprehend other events recorded in the fourth Gospel fully until after the Resurrection (2:22; 12:16), so Peter and the other disciples with him were unable to understand the full significance of footwashing until after the Resurrection.

In responding to Peter's emphatic rejection of the footwashing (13:8), Jesus informed Peter that this act is not optional and that its significance is far-reaching. "Unless I wash you, you have no part [or share] with me" (*NIV*). Simply put, Peter was told that his continued fellowship with Jesus was dependent upon his participation in the washing Jesus offers.

Finally, the primary meaning of the footwashing is given in verse 10. In response to Peter's request for washings in addition to his feet, Jesus said, "The one who has bathed has no need to wash except the feet; but is wholly clean; and you are clean, though not all of you" (writer's translation). Three things are worth noting here:

1. Two different words are used for *wash* in this verse. *Bathe* means a complete bath; *wash* is used to denote partial washings such as the hands, face or feet.

2. Jesus made reference to a bath which Peter had already received. Given the narrative of the Gospel, the only possible meaning of *bath* to this point is the water baptism administered by John the Baptist (1:26; 3:23), Jesus (3:22; 4:1), and the disciples (4:2).

3. Jesus made an identification between footwashing and the cleansing from sin which believers contract through daily life in this world. Just as a banquet guest would bathe at home and wash only the feet at the house of the host or hostess to remove the dust and debris accumulated on the road, so Peter, and the believer who experiences baptism, which signifies a complete cleansing from sin, does not need to be rebaptized but undergoes footwashing, which signifies the removal of sin that might accumulate as a result of life in this sinful world.

In a sense, then, footwashing is an extension of baptism, for it signifies the washing away of postconversion sins in the believer's life, a concern emphatically displayed in John's later epistle (see 1 John 1:8—2:2; 5:16-18).

Footwashing, then, is a sacrament on the same level as the Lord's Supper and water baptism. It is given eternal significance by Jesus, who commands that it be continued in the church. The meaning of footwashing is not to be found primarily in terms of humility or service but in the sacrificial death of our Lord.

(Section III was taken from *Ministry and Theology*, by J. Christopher Thomas, published by Pathway Press.)

Wonderful Worship

When the church participates in footwashing, a number of important aspects of worship are present:

1. There is a remembrance of Jesus' own actions in preparing the disciples for His departure.

2. Footwashing serves as a constant reminder of the continual forgiveness available to the believer.

3. Just as water baptism signifies the washing away of sin committed before conversion, so footwashing signifies the cleansing from sin that might be committed after conversion.

4. The various members of the body work together in rendering and receiving footwashing.

—**J. Christopher Thomas**

Ordinances of the Church

CONCLUSION

A vital part of the Christian experience is lost when believers overlook or disregard the importance of the church's ordinances. The faithful observance of the sacraments allows individuals the chance to experience unequaled union with Christ. They also offer an incredible opportunity for the entire community of faith to stand unified as confessors of the Christian faith. Rooted in the commands of Jesus, we must seek to interpret them Scripturally, then follow them practically.

GOLDEN TEXT CHALLENGE

"THEY, CONTINUING DAILY WITH ONE ACCORD IN THE TEMPLE, AND BREAKING BREAD FROM HOUSE TO HOUSE, DID EAT THEIR MEAT WITH GLADNESS AND SINGLENESS OF HEART, PRAISING GOD, AND HAVING FAVOR WITH ALL THE PEOPLE" (Acts 2:46, 47).

The first Christian community was known for its single-hearted devotion and was highly regarded by all the people. The common meals they had in their homes were joyful occasions and expressed their love for one another. Wholly dedicated to Christ, they continued to praise God and to worship in the Temple. The fellowship continued to grow; the Lord kept on adding to their number those who were being saved. The lifestyle of those believers was appropriate to the Holy Spirit— the Spirit of love and fellowship.—**French Arrington (*Acts of the Apostles*)**

Daily Devotions:
M. Foreshadow of the Lord's Supper
Exodus 12:21-28
T. Foreshadow of Baptism
Exodus 14:21-31
W. Example of Jesus
Matthew 3:13-17
T. Repent and Be Baptized
Acts 2:37-41
F. Christ Is Our Passover
1 Corinthians 5:6-8
S. Do Not Take Communion Unworthily
1 Corinthians 11:27-34

Baptism in the Holy Spirit

Matthew 3:11; Luke 24:49; John 7:37-39;
Acts 1:4-8; 2:1-4, 38, 39; 4:31-33; 10:44-48; 19:1-7

Unit Theme:
Basic Christian Doctrines

Central Truth:
The baptism in the Holy Spirit empowers believers to be witnesses of Christ.

Focus:
Consider the purpose of the baptism in the Holy Spirit and be continually filled with the Spirit.

Context:
Various New Testament passages on the baptism in the Holy Spirit

Golden Text:
"Behold, I send the promise of my Father upon you: but tarry ye in the city of Jerusalem, until ye be endued with power from on high" (Luke 24:49).

Study Outline:
I. The Spirit Promised
(Matthew 3:11; Luke 24:49; John 7:37-39)
II. The Spirit Received
(Acts 2:1-4, 38, 39; 10:44-48; 19:1-7)
III. Purpose of Spirit Baptism
(Acts 1:4-8; 4:31-33)

INTRODUCTION

The baptism in the Holy Spirit can be considered a gift to the church that has been reclaimed in approximately the past 100 years. As believers became disenchanted with traditional religion around the turn of the 20th century, they turned anew to the history of the early churches in the Book of Acts. Here they discovered a marked emphasis on the baptism in the Holy Spirit, with the ensuing power that spread the gospel throughout the Roman Empire. It was this experience, they decided, that was missing in the churches of their day. Their fervent seeking after God not only began to clarify this both ancient and current doctrine, but also brought revival to eastern Tennessee and southern California and place in between. One witness described one of these revival meetings:

> The people earnestly sought God, and the interest increased until unexpectedly, like a cloud from a clear sky, the Holy Ghost began to fall on the honest, humble, sincere seekers after God. While the meetings were in progress, one after another fell under the power of God, and soon quite a number were speaking in other tongues as the Spirit gave them utterance (*Like a Mighty Army: A History of the Church of God*, by Charles W. Conn).

The movement often had itinerant evangelists and were met with no small resistance by opponents—Christians and non-Christians alike. The seekers' determination to continue asking God for the experience of the baptism in the Holy Spirit as they understood it from Scripture grew into what some sociologists now say is the fastest-growing religious movement on the planet.

Unfortunately, as any movement grows, transforming from a marginalized and persecuted movement into one accepted throughout the world, misunderstandings on basic doctrinal issues can easily take place. Especially with the rise of Christian television has come the urgent need for sincere believers to watch their life and doctrine closely, as Paul encouraged Timothy (1 Timothy 4:16). It is vital that each believer embark on a clear study of what the Scriptures have to say about the promise, the reception, and the purpose of the baptism in the Holy Spirit.

I. THE SPIRIT PROMISED (Matthew 3:11; Luke 24:49; John 7:37-39)

Early Pentecostal believers experienced the baptism in the Holy Spirit in a sudden way, but not in an uninformed way. This is because they were students of the Bible, and recognized this experience with the Holy Ghost was evidenced in Scripture. So also the apostles, though being Spirit-baptized swiftly in Acts 2, knew something was coming. They did not have much information about the nature of this experience, but the Old Testament witnesses and the words of Jesus had pointed it out to them in advance.

A. Prophesied Throughout the Scriptures (Matthew 3:11)

11. I indeed baptize you with water unto repentance: but he that cometh after me is mightier than I, whose shoes I am not worthy to bear: he shall baptize you with the Holy Ghost, and with fire.

Although the doctrine of Spirit baptism as an available experience for all believers in Jesus was certainly not in existence until Acts 2, people were moved upon with supernatural power by the Spirit of God even in the Old Testament. Samson was empowered by God's Spirit to achieve extraordinary feats of human strength. Saul experienced the Spirit of God so powerfully after being anointed king by Samuel, that he prophesied. And David danced with all his might in an act of Spirit-filled worship to God. These occurrences in the Old Testament serve as signposts, or glimpses, that God was preparing His people for a powerful experience with His Spirit.

Even the one who prepared the way for Christ was waiting for the baptism of the Holy Spirit. John the Baptist boldly preached about it as he waited for the Messiah to be revealed (Matthew 3:11). Although water baptism would continue on in the Christian community, there was another baptism that John was not fit to administer. One can only imagine the anticipation that was built in the thousands of hearts who heard John's dynamic preaching. The coming King would baptize with the Spirit of God himself, allowing everyone to daily experience divine presence and power.

This broad Scriptural understanding of the work of God through the Holy Spirit is vital to Spirit baptism. Peter comprehended this on the Day of Pentecost, preaching a stunning and effective sermon based on Old Testament prophecy of the last days. Armed with proper Old Testament interpretation, the early church quickly spread the baptism of the Holy Spirit throughout the early communities of Christian faith.

B. Promised to the Apostles (Luke 24:49)

49. And, behold, I send the promise of my Father upon

Talk About It:
1. How did John compare himself with the Messiah? Why?
2. How did John's baptism compare with the baptism Jesus would perform?

Indwelling Spirit
The logical progression of the Scriptures is that of law-keeping to Spirit-indwelling. The early peoples of God principally demonstrated their relationship with Him by keeping the tenants of the Law. In Jeremiah 31:31-34, however, a new covenant is promised. In Hebrews 8 the writer proclaims this new covenant was inaugurated with Christ. Through the indwelling Holy Spirit, God's desires are written on the Christian's heart and not just on stone or paper.

Talk About It:
How were Jesus' instructions to His disciples specific, and how were they vague?

The most important proclaimer of the coming baptism in the Holy Spirit was Jesus Christ. The One who was conceived by the Holy Spirit would teach His disciples extensively about the Holy Spirit. Jesus explained that He would be departing from the earth, but He would be sending them His replacement—the Holy Spirit. The Spirit would be their Comforter, Counselor and Advocate. He would convict people of their sin when the disciples preached the gospel. He would be the eternal presence of Christ forever with them. In fact, in Luke's Gospel, Jesus' final words to His disciples before He ascended into heaven were that they should wait until the Spirit was sent. For then they would be "clothed with power from on high" to continue Jesus' ministry (24:49, *NIV*).

C. Promised to All Believers (John 7:37-39)

cried (v. 37)—"said in a loud voice" (*NIV*)

out of his belly (v. 38)—"from within him" (*NIV*)

37. In the last day, that great day of the feast, Jesus stood and cried, saying, If any man thirst, let him come unto me, and drink.

38. He that believeth on me, as the scripture hath said, out of his belly shall flow rivers of living water.

39. (But this spake he of the Spirit, which they that believe on him should receive: for the Holy Ghost was not yet given; because that Jesus was not yet glorified.)

Talk About It:
1. What kind of *thirst* was Jesus talking about?
2. Where does the Holy Spirit reside, and what does He do (v. 38)?
3. When would the Holy Spirit be *given* (v. 39)? Why then?

Christ taught the multitudes of common people about the future baptism in the Holy Spirit. The feast in John 7 is the Israelite Feast of Tabernacles, a celebration in which scores of Jews thronged to Jerusalem. The ceremonies of this feast built in scope until the final day, in which the farming harvest was celebrated with tremendous joy. The Jews had been looking for Jesus to make an appearance at this important feast, and the leaders quickly conflicted with His bold teaching. As the crowds grew more divided over who exactly Jesus was, He declared Himself to be the eternal solution to their thirst for spiritual truth. What is more, those believing in Him would experience living water flowing outward from inside of them. *Living water* was another word for water that flowed, like in a river, and was used for Jewish ceremonial baptisms. Jesus' disciples later understood that He was predicting the baptism in the Spirit that He would send to believers after His glorification through His death and resurrection.

"Water washes, and so does the Holy Spirit. It refreshes, and so does He. The Holy Spirit is represented in the eternal state as the River of Life that flows out from under the throne of God. . . . He is the River of Life now to thirsty souls."
—Ralph M. Riggs

II. THE SPIRIT RECEIVED (Acts 2:1-4, 38, 39; 10:44-48; 19:1-7)

A. The Baptism Births the New Church (Acts 2:1-4, 38, 39)

1. And when the day of Pentecost was fully come, they were all with one accord in one place.

2. And suddenly there came a sound from heaven as of a rushing mighty wind, and it filled all the house where they were sitting.

3. And there appeared unto them cloven tongues like as of fire, and it sat upon each of them.

cloven (v. 3)—divided

4. And they were all filled with the Holy Ghost, and began to speak with other tongues, as the Spirit gave them utterance.

38. Then Peter said unto them, Repent, and be baptized every one of you in the name of Jesus Christ for the remission of sins, and ye shall receive the gift of the Holy Ghost.

remission (v. 38)—forgiveness

39. For the promise is unto you, and to your children, and to all that are afar off, even as many as the Lord our God shall call.

Acts 2 is significantly more than just a display of the Holy Spirit's infilling power. The Day of Pentecost also inaugurated the birth of the church of Jesus Christ. Jesus spent three years building the foundation of His church through His band of followers, but it was not until Pentecost that they were sent forth in the power required to truly be His church in the world. This infilling was dramatic. It caught the entire city off guard (vv. 1-4).

This simple introduction is all we know about the posture of the early disciples when they received the baptism in the Holy Spirit—they "were all together in one place" (*NIV*). We assume this one place was the room where the disciples joined constantly in prayer, along with Jesus' family (see Acts 1:13, 14). They appeared to be living in this space, and they even began some of the official business of the church, appointing Matthias to replace Judas' vacant apostolic position. Perhaps they were involved in a time of corporate prayer when the Spirit filled them.

There was no question God was powerfully working. The Acts 2 experience of Spirit baptism was remarkably sensory. They heard a sound like a great wind. They saw tongues of fire that tangibly approached each of them. And they suddenly found themselves able and willing to speak out in other languages. One can only imagine the commotion this scene caused, and a crowd of Jews attending the festival of Pentecost quickly gathered. Some assumed the Christians had been partying too hard in celebrating the Jewish feast, but most of the onlookers were astonished by the languages they heard spoken. How could ordinary Galileans know languages from across the empire? After Peter offered a rousing presentation of the gospel to explain what was happening, many of his hearers were convicted and asked him what should be done. In verses 38 and 39 he commanded that they repent, be baptized in water, and then they would receive "the gift of the Holy Ghost." Incredibly, over 3,000 souls were converted that very day.

Talk About It:
1. Why do you suppose Jesus had not explained exactly when or how the Holy Spirit would come?
2. How did the believers know this was God's Spirit at work?
3. In Peter's message, what *promise* does He refer to in verse 39? Whom is the promise for?

In this chapter we see how Spirit baptism immediately empowered the community of faith to present the gospel to others. Up to this time, Peter had been a weak, self-centered disciple of Christ who had denied the Lord just weeks earlier when he was needed most. Suddenly this same Peter became a bold preacher of the gospel, helping his fellow Jews turn to God. There was an automatic connection between Spirit baptism and Christian service.

Note how the Day of Pentecost seems to be a reversal of the Old Testament story of the Tower of Babel in Genesis 11. There, God confused the languages of the people in order to prevent them from building a huge tower from which to compete with God's will. On the Day of Pentecost, the languages of the earth proclaimed a single message for all to hear—the wonders of God.

B. The Baptism Received at Cornelius' House (10:44-48)

44. While Peter yet spake these words, the Holy Ghost fell on all them which heard the word.

45. And they of the circumcision which believed were astonished, as many as came with Peter, because that on the Gentiles also was poured out the gift of the Holy Ghost.

46. For they heard them speak with tongues, and magnify God. Then answered Peter,

47. Can any man forbid water, that these should not be baptized, which have received the Holy Ghost as well as we?

48. And he commanded them to be baptized in the name of the Lord. Then prayed they him to tarry certain days.

The foremost controversy among the earliest Christian churches regarded the admission of Gentiles, or non-Jews, into the Christian faith. At first, the early believers consisted of Jews who continued to worship in the Temple and observe the Jewish laws. Christianity began as a sect of Judaism, but it did not stay that way for long. When God called a Roman centurion by the name of Cornelius to find the apostle Peter, the Gentiles were soon also swept up in the baptism with the Holy Spirit.

Simultaneous visions were given to both Cornelius and Peter at the beginning of Acts 10, preparing them for God's new work in the world. This time, Peter did not even get the opportunity to finish his message before the Holy Spirit filled his Gentile listeners. Again, this infilling was visibly evident as they spoke in tongues. Peter's amazement had to do with the fact they had not even been baptized with water, and from this point on he was a powerful influence for the full acceptance of the Gentiles into the church of Jesus Christ.

C. The Baptism Received in Ephesus (19:1-7)

1. And it came to pass, that, while Apollos was at

Corinth, Paul having passed through the upper coasts came to Ephesus: and finding certain disciples,

2. He said unto them, Have ye received the Holy Ghost since ye believed? And they said unto him, We have not so much as heard whether there be any Holy Ghost.

3. And he said unto them, Unto what then were ye baptized? And they said, Unto John's baptism.

4. Then said Paul, John verily baptized with the baptism of repentance, saying unto the people, that they should believe on him which should come after him, that is, on Christ Jesus.

5. When they heard this, they were baptized in the name of the Lord Jesus.

6. And when Paul had laid his hands upon them, the Holy Ghost came on them; and they spake with tongues, and prophesied.

7. And all the men were about twelve.

While on a missionary journey, Paul found 12 disciples in Ephesus who had never even heard of the Holy Spirit. They were remnants of those who followed John the Baptist. After Paul taught them about Jesus Christ, they were baptized in Jesus' name. When Paul placed his hands on them in prayer, they began to speak in tongues and prophesy.

Afterward, Paul spent three months ministering in Ephesus, displaying the power of the Spirit through extraordinary miracles and deliverances, thereby lifting up the name of Jesus.

III. PURPOSE OF SPIRIT BAPTISM (Acts 1:4-8; 4:31-33)

It is not Spirit baptism in and of itself that forms the present-day worldwide Pentecostal Movement, but the purpose of this blessing. In fact, there continue to be disagreements within the Charismatic and Pentecostal communities over how and when this gift is actually received. There are no differences, however, in the purpose of the baptism of the Holy Spirit. It has been given to us by God in order to build up the church for the evangelization of the world.

A. Witnessing Power (1:4-8)

4. And, being assembled together with them, commanded them that they should not depart from Jerusalem, but wait for the promise of the Father, which, saith he, ye have heard of me.

5. For John truly baptized with water; but ye shall be baptized with the Holy Ghost not many days hence.

6. When they therefore were come together, they asked of him, saying, Lord, wilt thou at this time restore again the kingdom to Israel?

> **Talk About It:**
> 1. Why had these 12 believers not yet been filled with the Holy Spirit?
> 2. What did Paul do before he prayed for them to receive the Holy Spirit, and why?
> 3. What happened when the Holy Spirit "came on them" (v. 6)?

7. And he said unto them, It is not for you to know the times or the seasons, which the Father hath put in his own power.

8. But ye shall receive power, after that the Holy Ghost is come upon you: and ye shall be witnesses unto me both in Jerusalem, and in all Judaea, and in Samaria, and unto the uttermost part of the earth.

The baptism in the Holy Spirit is not for the personal benefit of the believer, but for the progression of the mission of Jesus Christ. This mission is stated clearly in His Great Commission, that the world be reached with His message of good news. Jesus explained to His disciples that though this task was great, they would not be left alone, under their own power. Instead, the Spirit would be their energy source, their guide, and their helper in fulfilling Christ's worldwide agenda (v. 8).

Acts 1:8 represents the final words the earthly Jesus spoke to His disciples in the New Testament record. They were given to clarify the disciples' incorrect perspective that Jesus would be immediately setting up His earthly kingdom in Israel. It was the disciples who would be given the power of the Kingdom, to spread it throughout the city, the country and the empire. Their ministry follows this pattern in the Book of Acts, beginning in Jerusalem, spreading throughout the towns of the Jews and Samaritans, and finally Paul finds himself preaching at the "end of the earth" in Rome—the capital city and heart of the empire. The purpose of Spirit baptism is to give believers power to witness to those who do not know the Lord, and to lead them to God's saving kingdom.

B. Uniting Power (4:31-33)

31. And when they had prayed, the place was shaken where they were assembled together; and they were all filled with the Holy Ghost, and they spake the word of God with boldness.

32. And the multitude of them that believed were of one heart and of one soul: neither said any of them that ought of the things which he possessed was his own; but they had all things common.

33. And with great power gave the apostles witness of the resurrection of the Lord Jesus: and great grace was upon them all.

This Holy Spirit power not only drove the members of the early church to witness, it also empowered them to exist as a God-honoring community of faith. This unifying power was undoubtedly more and more necessary as disparate groups of Jews and Gentiles were brought together in local churches. Arguments and hierarchies were bound to develop, and often did, but not without the Spirit's correction. As the experience of the baptism in the Holy Spirit spread throughout the land, strong

Talk About It:
1. What did the disciples hope the resurrected Jesus would do at that time (v. 6), and how did He respond to their question (v. 7)?
2. What was God's plan for the disciples, and how would they fulfill it (v. 8)?

Talk About It:
1. How did the Holy Spirit manifest Himself in verse 31, and why?
2. According to verse 32, how should the Spirit-filled church function?
3. Describe the two uses of the word *great* in verse 33.

local churches were built who ministered the gospel to all.

In these verses we see a principal truth of the Spirit-baptized life in motion. While the experience of the baptism in the Holy Ghost is always personal, it is not individual. In fact, in almost every occurrence of Spirit baptism in Acts, it is a corporate infilling. This indicates the type of life those filled are led to live. First, Spirit-filled believers are called to lead an accountable life. The early believers were unified in their commitment to one another, both in heart and mind. Second, Spirit-filled Christians are called to lead selfless lives. In the early church, even personal possessions were given up unquestionably for the good of the community of faith. Third, those baptized in the Holy Spirit are called to live graceful lives. God's grace was with the early church as they showered their world with His message of hope, love and redemption.

The word *filled* here (v. 31) describes "the experience of somebody who is already filled with or full of the Spirit and now receives a further filling. The . . . concept that something which if full cannot be filled any further is misleading if applied to the Spirit. One filling is not incompatible with another."
—I.H. Marshall, "The Significance of Pentecost"

CONCLUSION

The baptism in the Holy Spirit is a gift offered to every believer in Jesus Christ. This gift gives us the power to break through all human barriers that divide us—barriers of race, class, gender and ethnicity. It was the power of the Holy Spirit that helped a small group of Jewish disciples form what eventually became the largest religious movement in the world. It is the power of the Spirit that will allow us to finish Jesus' mission before His second coming.

GOLDEN TEXT CHALLENGE

"BEHOLD, I SEND THE PROMISE OF MY FATHER UPON YOU: BUT TARRY YE IN THE CITY OF JERUSALEM, UNTIL YE BE ENDUED WITH POWER FROM ON HIGH" (Luke 24:49).

The occasion of these words invests them with even greater weight and solemnity. Jesus was giving His final instructions to His disciples before He was taken up into heaven. At such a time, no one, especially the risen Lord, would waste words on some frivolous subject. The last communication Christ left ringing in the disciples' ears was to wait in Jerusalem for the Holy Spirit, whom He was sending to empower them.

Although Luke 24:49 unquestionably refers to the baptism in the Holy Spirit, it is significant that the Holy Spirit is never mentioned directly. Instead, Jesus emphasized two themes which warrant closer investigation. First, He called the gift of the Holy Spirit 'the promise of the Father." Just as the coming of a Messiah had been in fulfillment of promises made long ago, so now would be the coming of the Spirit. Second, Christ spoke of "power from on high."

"The promise of the Father" means that which was promised by the Father (see Acts 1:4, 5). Jesus himself had promised the advent of the Holy Spirit in His teachings (Luke 11:13) and at the Last Supper (John 14:16-18, 26; 15:26; 16:7-15). John the Baptist preached about the baptism in the Spirit (Luke 3:16, 17; John 1:33). Peter, reaching back several hundred years, traced the promise of the outpouring of the Holy Spirit back to a prophecy of Joel (Acts 2:16-21). Finally, Paul associated the promise of the Spirit with the blessing of Abraham which is granted to believers, whether they be Jew or Gentile (Galatians 3:13, 14).

The theme of promise and fulfillment accomplishes several things. First, it establishes continuity between the Old Testament and the New Testament. Second, it demonstrates the faithfulness of God. Finally, it gives courage and faith to modern Christians who trust that what God has promised He will accomplish.

The other theme, "power from on high," stresses the need the disciples had for a power not merely outside them but above them, that is, from heaven. It is the same power believers need today.

Sanctification

John 17:14-19; Romans 12:1, 2; 1 Corinthians 6:9-11; 2 Corinthians 6:14 through 7:1; 1 Thessalonians 4:3-8; 5:23; 2 Timothy 2:20, 21; Hebrews 12:14; 13:12; 1 Peter 1:13-16; 1 John 3:1-3

INTRODUCTION

Sanctification is one of the most misunderstood and neglected doctrines of Scripture. This is shocking simply because it also represents one of the Christian faith's most fundamental and basic teachings. The word derives from two ancient Latin words—*sanctus*, meaning "holy" (the word *saint* derives from this), and *facere*, meaning "to make." Our present word *sanction* also derives from this, referring to something that is authoritatively decreed, particularly with regard to international politics (such as placing "sanctions" on an oppressive regime). However, the concept has thoroughly Biblical and theological roots, denoting the process of being made holy.

The New Testament Greek word for *sanctification* is *hagiasmos*, the noun form of its cognate verb *hagiazo* ("to sanctify") and adjective *hagios* ("sanctified"). The adjective is used to describe the Spirit of God and thus is the Holy Spirit. So the Greek and English words for *sanctification* clearly emphasize holiness as a rule. The purpose of sanctification is to make the believer holy.

But what does it mean to be holy? The answer is found in God himself. God's holiness represents two main aspects of His nature. First, God is completely set apart from all that is unholy. He is not tainted by sinful actions or attitudes in any way. Second, God is perfect, always operating in line with what is right and just. He calls believers to be set apart from sin and moving toward perfection.

John Wesley, the founder of Methodism, even renamed the doctrine of sanctification "Christian perfection." In his theology of salvation, three segments of God's grace are evident. First, *prevenient grace* prepares the heart of the unbeliever for God's invasion. Second, *justifying grace* instantaneously sets the believer right with God. Third, *sanctifying grace*, which he considered both instant and progressive, leads the believer toward Christian perfection. Of course, this final state is only reached in our heavenly bodies, but it is at work here on earth. Because God desires that we be like Christ (Romans 8:28, 29), He gives to us the experience and the process of sanctification.

Unit Theme:
Basic Christian Doctrines

Central Truth:
Every Christian is called to pursue holiness.

Focus:
Understand what sanctification is and live a holy life.

Context:
Selected New Testament scriptures concerning sanctification

Golden Text:
"Follow peace with all men, and holiness, without which no man shall see the Lord" (Hebrews 12:14).

Study Outline:
I. Sanctification Is Required (Hebrews 12:14; 1 Peter 1:13-16; 1 Thessalonians 4:3-8)
II. Sanctification Is Provided (John 17:14-19; Hebrews 13:12; 1 Thessalonians 5:23; Romans 12:1, 2)
III. Sanctification Is Life-changing (1 Corinthians 6:9-11; 2 Corinthians 6:14—7:1; 2 Timothy 2:20, 21; 1 John 3:1-3)

I. SANCTIFICATION IS REQUIRED (Hebrews 12:14; 1 Peter 1:13-16; 1 Thessalonians 4:3-8)

Sanctification is not an option in the Christian life. It is not something extra, or something added on to salvation. This may seem like common sense, but a notion prevails in many churches today that salvation is really the only necessity in life with God. The thinking goes, "Yes, it is God's will for us to be disciples, to be sanctified, and to be made holy, but these pale in comparison to being *saved*—the act that will get us into heaven." Of course, nothing could be further from the New Testament view of the Christian life. Instead, when we receive God's salvation, we receive along with it the sobering requirement of sanctification.

A. Required by the Character of God (Hebrews 12:14; 1 Peter 1:16)

Hebrews 12:14. Follow peace with all men, and holiness, without which no man shall see the Lord.

1 Peter 1:16. Because it is written, Be ye holy; for I am holy.

Talk About It:
1. What is the connection between peaceful relationships with others and holiness?
2. Why does God require us to be holy?

It is the very nature, or character, of God that sanctification be required in the first place. The Scriptures declare that because God is holy by nature, holiness is a requirement in those who draw near to Him—those who seek to live a godly life. God is so holy that Hebrews 12:14 declares holiness is the prerequisite for even *seeing* the Lord. And 1 Peter 1:16 introduces a common Old Testament refrain from the mouth of God: "Be ye holy; for I am holy." Not a few immature believers have been put off by the apparent harshness of God in this command. But it truthfully represents a beautiful invitation to join God in His state of holiness. Because God is holy, we can also learn His dynamic way of living.

As stated in the introduction, God's holiness ultimately refers to the extent to which He is set apart from all things unholy. This perfect posture of holiness that makes up the very construct of God's character is twofold.

First, *God is set apart physically*. Although He is majestically revealed in the natural world, and although His presence invades every piece of discernible and indiscernible matter, God is not equal with matter. We can certainly wonder at a stunningly bright sunset or examine a magnificent oak tree and can rightly declare how these things express the character, splendor and dignity of God. But we cannot equate any natural wonder with God, because while He expresses Himself in nature, He is set apart from it as its Creator. So we may say, "This tree reveals the detailed work of God's caring hands." But we would be completely wrong to say, "This tree is God. God is in it, and it is in God." This viewpoint has been popularized by the modern New

Age movement, but really it is the ancient theory of *pantheism*. *Pan* simply means "all," so the word denotes the worldview that "all is God." The doctrine of sanctification vigorously contests this based on God's character of holiness. Because God is holy, He is, by nature, set apart from creation, and *chooses* to create and involve Himself in the life of creation.

Second, *God is set apart morally*. The story is told of a secular college professor who loved to goad any Christian student in his classes with a simple question. After asking the Christian whether God can do anything, he invariably received an affirmative answer. The professor's next question always left the believing student speechless: "Can God create a rock that is so large He cannot move it?" Of course, this is no more than a game, a play on human words and categories that undoubtedly does not leave God stumped at all, but it does point to something deep within the nature of God. The fact is, there are some things God *cannot* do. Because He is perfectly sanctified and set apart morally, God's very character will not allow Him to sin. That option does not exist among the trillions of choices God has in any given moment. This does not restrict God's greatness; it powerfully expresses it! His holiness is such that sin never enters His mind, His motives or His choices.

So God requires sanctification for the believer because of who God is. Because He is set apart, so must we.

B. Required for Hopeful Living (1 Peter 1:13-15)

13. Wherefore gird up the loins of your mind, be sober, and hope to the end for the grace that is to be brought unto you at the revelation of Jesus Christ;

14. As obedient children, not fashioning yourselves according to the former lusts in your ignorance:

15. But as he which hath called you is holy, so be ye holy in all manner of conversation.

Peter refers to Eastern clothing when he uses the term "gird up the loins." The hot climate dictated the wearing of long, loose, flowing robes. That was fine as long as the movement of the body could be deliberate. But if there had to be movement in a hurry, then the clothing could be hampering. Therefore, they must gather up their garments so as not to impede their progress.

The apostle is admonishing us to guard our tastes, appetites, affections and inclinations. He uses the term "gird up the loins of your mind" because sin begins in the thought life. Here the idea is entertained before it becomes part of a behavior pattern. We must not let our thoughts stream as they will; we do so at our peril. F.B. Meyer put it this way: "Hold your spirit in a tight hand. Put a curb on appetite. Say no to luxurious pleasure-seeking.

> "Holiness is not hardness."
> —Charles W. Conn

manner of conversation (v. 15)— deeds and actions

Talk About It:
1. What does it mean to be spiritually *sober* (v. 13)?
2. Where must the Christian's hope be set? Why?
3. What should shape the believer's life, and what should not?

Curtail your expenditure on yourself. Do not spread yourself too widely. Watch eye and lip, thought and wish, lest any break from the containing cords of self-control" (*Tried by Fire*).

The apostle urged his readers to "be sober." The word means "temperance, self-control, and having a balanced estimate of oneself in the world." The genuinely sober individual enjoys the beautiful and innocent pleasures God has given. He uses them without abuse. He rejoices in all the good things God has blessed him with, but he never allows any of them to control him. His affections and his will are fully surrendered to God. This is why he can enjoy the life God has provided.

Peter also urges believers to "hope to the end." The hope of salvation will motivate the believer to follow after holiness. "Every man that hath this hope in him purifieth himself" (1 John 3:3). Holiness is complete separation from all that defiles. Believers must, as obedient children, forsake the lusts of the world, the flesh and the devil.

> "Christians must learn about God's holy character in order to be holy."
> —Henry Holloman

Peter says the obedient believer will not allow lust to dominate his or her life. Obedience is not holiness. Holiness is absolute surrender to God; it is the possession of the soul by God. But holiness always leads to obedience. The obedient soul is the holy soul.

C. Required by the Holy Spirit (1 Thessalonians 4:3-8)

3. For this is the will of God, even your sanctification, that ye should abstain from fornication:

4. That every one of you should know how to possess his vessel in sanctification and honour;

concupiscence (v. 5)—passionate desire

5. Not in the lust of concupiscence, even as the Gentiles which know not God:

6. That no man go beyond and defraud his brother in any matter: because that the Lord is the avenger of all such, as we also have forewarned you and testified.

7. For God hath not called us unto uncleanness, but unto holiness.

8. He therefore that despiseth, despiseth not man, but God, who hath also given unto us his holy Spirit.

Talk About It:
1. Why is sexual morality a key part of holy living?
2. Explain the warning in verse 6.

Sanctification is perhaps the most visible part of God's work in the human heart. In one respect it is the outward expression of an inner, invisible reality. This is in contrast to *justification*—that act by which God makes us righteous in His standing based on the perfect sacrifice of Jesus Christ. God himself invisibly imputes justification to our heart. However, the results of justification are never meant to stay invisible. They are purposed to be seen by all! This perfectly distinguishable aspect of salvation is sanctification, meant to be seen in the daily, practical endeavors of each individual Christian. This is clearly expressed in 1 Thessalonians 4:3-8.

Sanctification

This passage points out three ways in which we are to live out God's requirement of sanctification. First, sexual immorality must be avoided. This command is obvious throughout the Bible, but the early Thessalonian believers inhabited a sexually explicit world much like ours. Sexual promiscuity was common, accepted, and often connected to the worship of idols and false gods. These Roman Christians were not Jewish, so they did not have a faith rooted in the Old Testament. Paul had to lead them gently with simple teachings of holy living.

The second requirement of sanctification stems from the first, but broadens it. The passage calls us to be in full control of our own bodies. Does this have a sexual component? Of course! But it also calls us into account for our eating habits. It prohibits us from using our bodies to inflict harm on someone else. And since our mouths are certainly a part of our bodies, this scripture indirectly commands us to use our words in a sanctified manner. Nothing can get more practical than that.

The third requirement of sanctification is that we refrain from taking advantage of others, especially those in the household of faith. Instead, Paul encourages the Thessalonian believers to be a supportive, uplifting community. God's sanctification means we are not caught up in the worldly addiction to competition, which takes on numerous disguises, but that we build up one another. Perhaps this is the purest expression of the sanctifying work of God in our lives.

Not coincidentally, those who reject these sound principles for living sanctified daily lives are not saying "no" to the opinions of man, but to the Holy Spirit. He is called *Holy* for a reason. It is He whom Christ sent to be present with us, comfort us, convict us, and teach us. Because He exists with us in the routines of our daily lives, it is He who carries on this visible work of divine sanctification in our human vessels.

> "Morality and immorality are not defined by man's changing attitudes and social customs. They are determined by the God of the universe, whose timeless standards cannot be ignored with impunity."
> **—Dr. James Dobson**

II. SANCTIFICATION IS PROVIDED (John 17:14-19; Hebrews 13:12; 1 Thessalonians 5:23; Romans 12:1, 2)

God does not require anything that He does not provide the enabling power to achieve. Jesus Christ looked at a small group of unlearned Jewish peasants and firmly stated His requirement that they spread the gospel throughout the world, making disciples of every nation. But He did not then leave them to their own devices to get the job done. Instead, He sent them the power of the Holy Spirit, who enabled them to do His work and will. When it comes to this great challenge of sanctification, God provides the ability to achieve success from start to finish.

A. Sanctification Is God-Centered (John 17:14-19; Hebrews 13:12)
John 17:14. I have given them thy word; and the world

hath hated them, because they are not of the world, even as I am not of the world.

15. I pray not that thou shouldest take them out of the world, but that thou shouldest keep them from the evil.

16. They are not of the world, even as I am not of the world.

17. Sanctify them through thy truth: thy word is truth.

18. As thou hast sent me into the world, even so have I also sent them into the world.

19. And for their sakes I sanctify myself, that they also might be sanctified through the truth.

Hebrews 13:12. Wherefore Jesus also, that he might sanctify the people with his own blood, suffered without the gate.

Talk About It:
1. Why does *the world* hate Christians?
2. Why does God want believers living in the world?
3. How does *the truth* of God's Word sanctify believers?
4. According to Hebrews 13:12, how are believers sanctified?

Sanctification is not something we can do for and in ourselves. It is not a Biblical self-help program that teaches us to become better Christians through our own efforts. And how could we think otherwise? The basis for the New Testament gospel is that humanity is so depraved we cannot help ourselves! It is God who had to take the initiative to send His Son to purchase us, redeem us, cleanse us and free us. Should we marvel, then, at the fact it is *God* who sanctifies us?

The New Testament reveals that each person of the Holy Trinity is involved in the work of sanctifying the believer. Even our sanctifying Lamb prayed just before the time of His sacrifice that His followers would be thoroughly sanctified (John 17:17-19).

Jesus had given His disciples the words of God, calling them to follow God instead of the evil world system. As a result, the world hated them. Yet, it was not God's will to take His followers out of the world, but instead to equip them to live sanctified lives within it. They were no longer of the world even though they were still living in it.

The Word of God is one means by which God sanctifies the believer (v. 17). "Knowing that the Spirit sanctifies us through the Word does not automatically sanctify us," writes Henry Hollman. "The Spirit sanctifies us as we learn and apply the Word by His help" (*The Forgotten Blessing*).

"There are many ways to read the Bible. Such reading may be an arduous duty or a pleasant exercise, or it may become a transforming experience."
—*Christian Observer*

Jesus clearly understood that no person could or would be sanctified on his or her own. It would take God's activity in the believer's life. Jesus also understood His role in this was to *sanctify Himself*—to set Himself apart for God's purpose of the cross. Jesus suffered "outside the city gate"—outside the walls of Jerusalem—in order to sanctify people "through his own blood" (Hebrews 13:12, *NIV*).

B. Sanctification Is a Thorough Work (1 Thessalonians 5:23)

23. And the very God of peace sanctify you wholly; and

I pray God your whole spirit and soul and body be pre-served blameless unto the coming of our Lord Jesus Christ.

This verse is a benediction formula, which indicates that the theology of sanctification had grown common in the liturgy of the early church. This benediction says God wants to sanctify each part of our tri-part being—body, soul and spirit—so we will be found *blameless* at Christ's return. How can this happen? Verse 24 declares, "The one who calls you is faithful and he will do it" (*NIV*).

C. Sanctification Is the Process of Transformation
(Romans 12:1, 2)

1. I beseech you therefore, brethren, by the mercies of God, that ye present your bodies a living sacrifice, holy, acceptable unto God, which is your reasonable service.

2. And be not conformed to this world: but be ye transformed by the renewing of your mind, that ye may prove what is that good, and acceptable, and perfect, will of God.

Sanctification is God-centered because it is a thoroughly supernatural work. Under no circumstances can it be accomplished through human energy or ingenuity. In these two verses it is succinctly described as *transformation*. The Greek verb for "be transformed" is *metamorpho,* from which we received our English *metamorphosis.* So a caterpillar is said to undergo a metamorphosis that fundamentally changes it into a new creature—a butterfly. This is not by the caterpillar's own efforts. Yes, the caterpillar has the responsibility of spinning an adequate cocoon. But once inside, nature takes over its slow transformation of this creature.

In the same way, this passage declares that our response to God's mercy is simply to offer ourselves back to Him. Only He can transform, and when we allow Him the time and space to do His work, we will be slowly sanctified, or transformed. The end result of this sanctifying work is that we will learn to perfectly discern God's will in the large and small decisions of our lives.

III. SANCTIFICATION IS LIFE-CHANGING (1 Corinthians 6:9-11; 2 Corinthians 6:14—7:1; 2 Timothy 2:20, 21; 1 John 3:1-3)

Sanctification is no dull or dusty theological concept. It is not the product of scholars cooped up in ivory towers. It is not the boring remnant of an ancient religion. Instead, to undergo the process of sanctification is to experience the very life and power of God. To be sanctified is to be painfully separated from the life of the former self, and to be clothed with the righteousness of Christ. Sanctification is not only life-changing, its very definition is "life change"—to be individually set apart for God's holy purposes.

Talk About It:
Can a person be partially sanctified? Why or why not?

"Be content with no degree of sanctification. Be always crying out, 'Lord, let me know more of myself and of thee.'"
—**George Whitefield**

Talk About It:
1. What is a *living sacrifice*?
2. Why is it necessary to have a renewed mind?

"The main purpose of Christlike Christians is not to receive appreciation or to please people but to accomplish the Father's will at any cost."
—**Henry Holloman**

abusers of them-
selves (v. 9)—
homosexuals

revilers (v. 10)—
verbal abusers

Belial
(2 Corinthians
6:15)—a worthless,
lawless person

Talk About It:
1. What had the
Corinthian Christians
once been like, and
what had changed
them (1 Corinthians
6:9-11)?
2. What does it
mean to be
"unequally yoked"
(2 Corinthians
6:14), and why
must Christians
avoid this?
3. What are believ-
ers called in verse
16? What does this
mean?
4. What should
motivate us to
"cleanse ourselves"
(7:1)?

"Spirit-controlled
Christians always
advance in sanctifi-
cation."

—Henry
Holloman

A. Sanctification and the Former Self (1 Corinthians 6:9-11;
2 Corinthians 6:14—7:1)
(2 Corinthians 6:14-18 is not included in the printed text.)

**1 Corinthians 6:9. Know ye not that the unrighteous
shall not inherit the kingdom of God? Be not deceived:
neither fornicators, nor idolaters, nor adulterers, nor effem-
inate, nor abusers of themselves with mankind,**

**10. Nor thieves, nor covetous, nor drunkards, nor revil-
ers, nor extortioners, shall inherit the kingdom of God.**

**11. And such were some of you: but ye are washed, but
ye are sanctified, but ye are justified in the name of the
Lord Jesus, and by the Spirit of our God.**

**2 Corinthians 7:1. Having therefore these promises,
dearly beloved, let us cleanse ourselves from all filthiness
of the flesh and spirit, perfecting holiness in the fear of God.**

The transformative power of divine sanctification is focused
on the human sinful nature. It is this "old man" which clings to us,
attempting to drag us away from the life God has planned for us.
Oftentimes people with difficult pasts struggle to overcome the
addictions and attitudes of sin they cultivated for so long. Paul
presents a potent picture of this struggle in 1 Corinthians 6:9-11.

A chilling accusation becomes a beautiful portrait of God's
grace in the artful words of Paul. After presenting a dreadful list
of the sinners who will never inherit God's heavenly way of life,
the apostle joyfully pins it on his congregation. Yes, many of them
were caught up in sin formerly, but now they have been sanctified and cannot return to their old selves. God just won't allow it.

Yet we do have a part to play in this process. It is not "all up to
God." Paul's first letter to the Corinthian congregation did much to
correct many of their errors, but some problems still persisted. In
2 Corinthians 6:14—7:1, Paul urges them to refrain from being
unequally yoked to those who reject the faith, because God has
better things in store. They are *the temple* of God—the place in
which His Spirit dwells. He wants to "walk among them" (*NIV*),
reminiscent of Adam and Eve before the Fall. He will *receive*, or
welcome, them as His children as they walk in His purity. They will
be *sons and daughters* of the *Lord Almighty*.

The apostle concludes this truth with a gentle command:
"Since we have these promises, dear friends, let us purify ourselves from everything that contaminates body and spirit, perfecting holiness out of reverence for God" (7:1, *NIV*).

Although it is God who justifies and sanctifies, we must be
careful to keep contaminants out of our bodies and souls.
When we do this, we join God in His sanctifying work and
move toward the place of perfection.

B. Sanctification and Service (2 Timothy 2:20, 21)
20. But in a great house there are not only vessels of

---

gold and of silver, but also of wood and of earth; and some to honour, and some to dishonour.

21. If a man therefore purge himself from these, he shall be a vessel unto honour, sanctified, and meet for the master's use, and prepared unto every good work.

As in a rich man's house there are articles made of various materials, all adapted to the uses for which they are intended, so in the church of Christ there are members designed for different tasks. Though the members of a church differ in capacity, none are to be considered superior to anyone else. Any task in the service of Christ is an honorable task.

However, there are some members of the church that are not vessels of honor. Some are negligent, disobedient, and concerned more for the things of the world than for the kingdom of heaven. These must purge themselves so that they are ready for the Master's use.

C. Sanctification and the Second Coming (1 John 3:1-3)

1. Behold, what manner of love the Father hath bestowed upon us, that we should be called the sons of God: therefore the world knoweth us not, because it knew him not.

2. Beloved, now are we the sons of God, and it doth not yet appear what we shall be: but we know that, when he shall appear, we shall be like him; for we shall see him as he is.

3. And every man that hath this hope in him purifieth himself, even as he is pure.

Sin's grip is too great on this present world to hope for ultimate sanctification within its confines. Although the acceptance of salvation through Christ makes us God's children and sets us on the road to Christian perfection, it is a long road, and our sinful nature still hangs on for dear life. We still battle with nagging habits, negative attitudes and sinful tendencies. Although we are nourished by God's grace in this present life, we await another kingdom in which all struggles with sin will be concluded. In verses 2 and 3, the aging apostle John encourages his community to look forward to this day.

Our hope is set on becoming like Christ; and though we resemble Him more as our devotion to Him grows, when Christ appears to catch away His saints we shall finally be fully like Him. John says we should not wait on the second coming of Christ to make us who God wants us to be. Instead, because we have this hope, we should continue to purify ourselves from even the appearance of sin, just as God has justified us once and for all.

Talk About It:
Why does God want people to be *vessels of honor*?

Fit for Royalty
When medieval European princes sought to marry outside of royalty, they often had to convert someone in their lady's family into a *lord*. After this was done, the woman, being a sister or daughter of a "great lord," was fit to marry the prince.

The work of sanctification brings the believer to a place of readiness to be in perfect relationship with God. But remember, it is our relationship to "the Lord" Jesus Christ that makes this possible.

Talk About It:
1. Who can rightly be called *the children of God*?
2. What do God's children know about their future (v. 2)?

CONCLUSION
Sanctification is the means God uses to bring us to the place

Daily Devotions:
M. Sabbath-Keeping: Sign of Sanctification
Exodus 31:12-17
T. Be Holy, for God Is Holy
Leviticus 19:1-4
W. Be Holy
Leviticus 20:6-8
T. Servants of Righteousness
Romans 6:12-18
F. Changed Lives
Ephesians 4:17-24
S. Set Apart for God
1 Peter 2:1-10

of Christlikeness. The sacrifice of Jesus Christ on the cross was not only powerful enough to forgive our sin, it spreads God's power throughout every detail of our lives. As God invades our thinking, attitudes and actions, we find ourselves in an ongoing relationship with Him in which we both play vital roles. As we purify ourselves from sin, God causes us to live more like Christ. This process will not be finally concluded until Christ appears as judge and we go on to reign with Him forever.

GOLDEN TEXT CHALLENGE

"FOLLOW PEACE WITH ALL MEN, AND HOLINESS, WITHOUT WHICH NO MAN SHALL SEE THE LORD" (Hebrews 12:14).

To "follow" connotes an earnest and diligent pursuit. If we are following peace with all people, we are doing nothing contrary to the Word of God. We are obeying the injunction to love our neighbor as ourselves to the extent that consideration for others has become for us a way of life.

Likewise, we are pursuing the way of holiness, knowing that without it no one will see the Lord. To live and die in an unholy condition is paramount to eternal exclusion from God, for God is holy.

This is not to say, however, that we earn the right to see God by living a holy life, for only the blood of Christ entitles us to heaven. Yet, that blood is able to wash us clean from all our sin and to keep us from falling and to present us "faultless before the presence of his glory with exceeding joy" (Jude 1:24).

Peace and holiness are two objectives the believer should actively seek to cultivate. The practical living out of a life of peace toward man and holiness toward God will attract others to the way of Christ.

The Church

Matthew 28:19, 20; Acts 2:42-47; Romans 12:4, 5;
1 Corinthians 3:11; 12:12-27; Ephesians 1:22; 2:20;
4:11-16; Colossians 1:18

INTRODUCTION

People have always had options when it comes to which faith community they will join. The Old Testament is filled with the pleas of prophets begging the children of Israel to refrain from joining the faith communities of neighboring peoples who served false gods. By New Testament times, the dominant Roman culture incorporated the worship of hundreds of deities across the cities of the empire, sometimes even within the same temple. In the middle of this religious pluralism, Christ's church was born—a community paying homage to one God alone, and forsaking all others.

In modern times, the tension has shifted from Christianity versus paganism to individual faith versus church commitment. Studies show that over 80 percent of Americans claim to be Christians, yet only 40 to 50 percent of those people attend church on a regular basis. This indicates an overemphasis on individualism in our society, in which tens of millions of religious people feel they can stand alone in their faith without the support of a community of faith. As our culture embraces a postmodern worldview, which champions the religious pluralism of the ancient Greco-Roman world, the centrality of the church in Christian life must once again move to the forefront of any faith commitment.

The Greek word for *church* in the New Testament is *ekklesia*—"those called out." It is often used in classical literature to describe citizens of a town that are "called out" to serve in a town assembly. The term reflects the earliest belief of the first Christians that they had been called by God to form a community of *the called*. They were required to "come out" from the pagan way of life and join in the assembly of the saints. There was no such thing as believers who practiced their faith alone. In fact, the idea of a *personal relationship with Jesus Christ* was certainly not used in their time like it is in ours. This is not because their faith was less personal or heartfelt, but because it was deeply communal. There was an automatic connection between being a Christian and being committed to the church—both locally and universally.

Today this need exists more than ever before to reclaim our communal heritage as followers of Christ. A comprehensive understanding of the origins, the characteristics, and the purposes of the New Testament church is a vital spiritual weapon in the mind and heart of the believer.

Unit Theme:
Basic Christian Doctrines

Central Truth:
Christ is the Head of the church.

Focus:
To identify characteristics of the church and unite in fulfilling its mission.

Context:
Various New Testament passages teaching about the church of Christ

Golden Text:
"Ye are the body of Christ, and members in particular" (1 Corinthians 12:27).

Study Outline:
I. Established by Christ (1 Corinthians 3:11; Ephesians 2:20; 1:22; Colossians 1:18)
II. The Body of Christ (Romans 12:4, 5; 1 Corinthians 12:12-27)
III. Called for a Purpose (Acts 2:42-47; Matthew 28:19, 20; Ephesians 4:11-16)

I. ESTABLISHED BY CHRIST (1 Corinthians 3:11; Ephesians 2:20; 1:22; Colossians 1:18)

A. Jesus Established the Church (1 Corinthians 3:11; Ephesians 2:20)

1 Corinthians 3:11. For other foundation can no man lay than that is laid, which is Jesus Christ.

Ephesians 2:20. And are built upon the foundation of the apostles and prophets, Jesus Christ himself being the chief corner stone.

Talk About It:
1. Name some religious foundations people have laid other than Christ. How will those foundations fare? Why?
2. What does it mean to *build upon* Jesus Christ?

The church of Jesus Christ is not just the product of an efficient or productive idea. It does not represent simply a helpful way to bring believers together or the best way to pass on Jesus' message of salvation. The church does not survive as one of the most important institutions in Western culture because of the contributions it has made to the world, though it has contributed untold good among humanity for two millennia. The only reason for the church's existence is its pure and total connection to Christ. The church is not our Lord, but it has divine power because the Lord Jesus established it as the vehicle for releasing His message throughout the world, throughout time. For this reason, Paul declares in 1 Corinthians 3:11 that Christ is the only foundation upon which everything in the church hinges. When we realize that Jesus intentionally planned for the existence of a strong, enduring church, we are able to understand the incredible spiritual authority given to the church today. If we disregard this important truth, the church becomes just another social club that may bring people together with an important message, but lacks the power to transform the world.

Interestingly, Jesus utters the word *church* only twice, both in the Gospel of Matthew. First, He declares He will build the church upon Peter's confession that Jesus is indeed the Christ, the Son of God (16:18). Second, Jesus references it in a section of teaching about how to discipline errant members of the future church (18:17). Aside from these short allusions, He appears to say nothing about it. He gives us no guide for proper church government, no standard order to plan our worship services, no curriculum for new converts. All of this comes in the later letters of His followers, and even then we are given limited information (nothing about youth ministry, music ministry, etc.). Instead, Jesus' teaching is dominated by the proclamation and demonstration of the nearness of the kingdom of God. But when Jesus spoke about the kingdom of God, He was offering a blueprint for life in the future church! That is, the church would be the vehicle by which people would experience the transforming power of Jesus' kingdom even after His departure from the earth.

Since the kingdom of God—the very reign of God over any individual who would call on His name—formed the basis for the church, Jesus spent His time demonstrating Kingdom living. But His teaching was almost always on-the-job training for His apprentices, as He clearly lived out the reality of the Kingdom. By this method of teaching, Jesus trained the men who would quickly take over the helm of a new church that would later become prominent in the world.

Jesus' commitment to establishing the church in such fashion during His earthly ministry allows Paul to explain its roots in Ephesians 2:20. Calling the church "God's household" (see v. 19), he illustrates its origins. The *chief cornerstone* referred to the most vital part of ancient buildings, such as the center stone in the tall archway. If this stone was removed, the structure would literally fall apart. In the metaphor of the church, Jesus obviously serves this function. However, He chose to lay the church's foundation through His 12 apostles. The education they received from Him is almost too wonderful to comprehend! With infinite skill, Jesus trained these simple men to lead a church that would carry on His ministry, one that the gates of hell could not prevail against.

B. Jesus Leads the Church (Ephesians 1:22; Colossians 1:18)

Ephesians 1:22. And hath put all things under his feet, and gave him to be the head over all things to the church.

Colossians 1:18. And he is the head of the body, the church: who is the beginning, the firstborn from the dead; that in all things he might have the preeminence.

Jesus did not leave the work of the church to His fledgling disciples without divine assistance. He did not only give them a perfect course in leadership and then leave it to them to implement His teachings; He sent them the gift of the Holy Spirit to empower them to effectively lead the new church, and He continued to guide them. He even made a personal appearance to appoint Paul to plant churches for Gentiles throughout the Roman Empire! And Jesus' involvement in the life of the church did not cease with the close of Scripture. Today He continues to be at its helm, leading, guiding and correcting it as needed.

We find Jesus' continued position of leadership in the church lifted up throughout Paul's letters. Because Paul loves to use the metaphor of a body to describe the church, he consistently describes Jesus' status as the Head (Ephesians 1:22; Colossians 1:18). Since Jesus is alive and well, seated at the right hand of God, He gives life to the entire body of Christ. But the main point is not just that a body without a head cannot *survive*, but that it cannot *function*. Four of our five vital senses (taste, smell, vision, hearing) are housed in the head, and all are processed in the brain itself. It is the brain that sends the appropriate impulses down the spinal cord to various body

"One of the problems of the church is that it is made up of people like you and me. The church is a divine institution, founded by Jesus, but it is also a human institution. It is not a hothouse operating under ideal conditions."

—George Sweeting

Talk About It
1. What makes Jesus Christ the Head of the church?
2. How should we relate to Christ? How should we relate to fellow believers?

parts which then respond to its command. Without Jesus continuing to reign over the church from heaven, we would be incapacitated, unable to complete the work He began on earth. So then, He is truly supreme in everything having to do with the life of today's church. Each member who joins himself or herself to God's church can be assured of the ongoing leadership of Christ in their midst.

II. THE BODY OF CHRIST (Romans 12:4, 5; 1 Corinthians 12:12-27)

One of the barriers to understanding the New Testament concept of the church is our modern language surrounding it. As previously mentioned, the Greek word *ekklesia* denotes motion—those "called out" to serve God's specific purposes in the world. As the church developed from a small sect in Judaism, to growing into cross-cultural communities throughout the Roman Empire, to the official religion of that same empire, a gradual shift took place. Church began to be viewed not as a living organism, but as an institution of society. Much like we might attend a sporting event or go to a restaurant, we now speak of "going to church" without giving our words a second thought. It is certainly not the phrase alone that determines our understanding of God's church, but our words do matter. The earliest centuries of Christianity could never have used such terms because church buildings didn't exist! And millions of believers across Asia and the Middle East continue to live under governments that prohibit open Christian worship. Of course, church buildings are a great blessing to us today, but we simply cannot forget that the building does not constitute the church, but only houses it. The church exists *anywhere* two or three gather in Christ's name.

A. A Diverse Body (Romans 12:4, 5)

4. For as we have many members in one body, and all members have not the same office:

5. So we, being many, are one body in Christ, and every one members one of another.

The New Testament never describes the church of Jesus Christ in static, institutional terms. Instead, the apostle Paul coined a term for the church that captures its true essence—*the body of Christ*. This phrase captures both the position of Christ and the function of the believers in the church. Christ is the owner of the body, the invincible head of every member. The believers comprise the body through being unified in their diversity. This is not a contradiction in terms, but illustrates the core of Jesus' message concerning the kingdom of God.

In Jesus' teaching of the Beatitudes (Matthew 5:1-12),

Jesus lists those who were considered anything but blessed by the world's standards: the poor, the depressed, the hungry, the meek, the persecuted. Yet Jesus turns the world's system upside down, declaring that by receiving the kingdom of God, even the lowliest of these were eternally blessed! So His list of those with almost no status whatsoever in the world were joyfully being welcomed into God's kingdom. Jesus' ministry went on to live this out. No one was too poor, too uneducated, too ostracized, or too sinful to be denied entrance to Jesus' kingdom. He scandalously touched unclean lepers, forgave lustful prostitutes, and dined with thieves and oppressors. His ragtag bunch of disciples was certainly not great by worldly standards—fishermen, a tax collector, and a traitor. Yet even their makeup communicated the truth of Christ's great kingdom—there is plenty of room for anyone, anytime, anywhere.

Jesus' teachings on the kingdom of God set the precedent for the apostolic teachings on the church. Although many modern believers have sounded a cry to return to the days of the early church, a careful study reveals that the first-century communities were anything but perfect. The New Testament letters depict a multitude of heated disagreements among early believers (and sometimes apostles) concerning things like circumcision, eating meat, and table fellowship. This occurred because the followers of Jesus who established the early church recognized that it should be open to all people. They did not set out to build a church where everyone looked and acted the same. To some extent, it was not even vitally important that everyone in the church agreed on every detail of church law and practice. At the very least, the church was never constructed to attract perfect people. And without perfect people, conflicts and problems will always arise.

Paul effectively put this diversity to work in his description of the church in Romans 12:4, 5. A human body comprised of similar parts is just as inconceivable as a church where people are all expected to be the same. The thumb is an extremely important part of the hand, so much so that the other four fingers' usefulness would be greatly diminished without it. However, if the other four fingers were transformed into thumbs, even less could be accomplished! So it is with the members of the church. Diversity in the body of Christ is not something sentimental or optional. It is a necessity if the church is to be what Christ established it to be.

This teaching is especially powerful when we remember that Paul's congregations were typically mixed Jews and Gentiles, and thus were breeding grounds for quarrels and controversies. In fact, most of Paul's letters were written to address some conflict that had arisen within the congregation.

"The church must be one because a fragmented church is not much help to a fragmented world."
—**Justo Gonzalez**

Paul could have just as easily grouped similar types of people together and avoided such conflict. But he would not compromise the diversity of Christ's church. Without it, the church would have devolved into a social club, not a world-transforming force.

B. A Unified Body (1 Corinthians 12:12-27)

(1 Corinthians 12:14-25 is not included in the printed text.)

12. For as the body is one, and hath many members, and all the members of that one body, being many, are one body: so also is Christ.

13. For by one Spirit are we all baptized into one body, whether we be Jews or Gentiles, whether we be bond or free; and have been all made to drink into one Spirit.

26. And whether one member suffer, all the members suffer with it; or one member be honoured, all the members rejoice with it.

27. Now ye are the body of Christ, and members in particular.

A diverse group of people without a unifying set of common standards cannot accomplish anything. No society or organization can continue to exist, much less thrive, unless its constituents agree on some essential principles. In fact, some liberal church denominations today are in steep decline because of the error of over-inclusiveness. While no one—no matter how downcast, dejected or sinful—can be denied entrance into the body of Christ, there must be some criteria to join His body. Without some uniform criteria, participation in the church means nothing. Christ's church is open to *anyone*, but not *everyone*.

In order to describe Christian unity to a diverse congregation in Corinth, Paul again appealed to the concept of the human body. Since the church is a living organism, its diverse parts must be unified to perform in sync. In 1 Corinthians, Paul deals with a long list of problems in the congregation. These include conflicts over the Lord's Supper, the use of tongues and prophecy in the worship service, sexual immorality, and lawsuits between believers. For each issue, Paul responds with a different principle of the faith for the Corinthian Christians to rally themselves around. They may disagree on particulars, but they could come together on these principles. Paul's teaching on unity culminates in chapter 12, where he again picks up the body metaphor (vv. 12, 13).

No matter what disagreements the Corinthians faced, they had been unified by something far greater than church membership and someone far greater than Paul. As demonstrated by water baptism, they had received salvation through the one Holy Spirit, who does not recognize the distinctions of Jew or Greek, slave or free. These categories did not apply when they joined the body of Christ.

Talk About It:
1. How does verse 13 describe the work of the Holy Spirit in the church?
2. Does verse 26 accurately describe how our local congregation is functioning? Why or why not?
3. Explain the phrase "members in particular" (v. 27).

Broken Walls
Reverend George Whitefield sparked a revival known as the First Great Awakening. This 18th-century revival saw the salvation of tens of thousands and the planting of hundreds of new churches. As he came to America

The Church

Because God has brought unity among diversity, Paul called the Corinthians to play their specific part in the body (vv. 26, 27). The small toe may seem insignificant to the more visible or distinguished parts of the body. After all, it does not pump blood like the heart, or provide motion like the legs, or accomplish tasks like the hands. However, if one were to lose their small toe in a sudden accident, the entire body would be affected for a time. And could it not be replaced, the body's entire sense of balance would be handicapped. This describes the unity that Jesus intended for His church. The weaker, seemingly insignificant members should be included and esteemed to the same degree as the church leadership (see vv. 22-25).

III. CALLED FOR A PURPOSE (Acts 2:42-47; Matthew 28:19, 20; Ephesians 4:11-16)

God has always called and formed a community of people committed to following Him alone. This did not begin with the New Testament church. In fact, the early church did not disconnect itself from the Jewish synagogue for several decades. This illustrates the connection that existed between the communities of God both before and after Christ. In a sense, God's church has always been! In the Old Testament, it was expressed primarily through the nation of Israel—a people that God called unto Himself. Though this community often functioned as a closed, exclusive group, it was never meant to be that way. In fact, the Old Testament is full of accounts where God's power moved on non-Israelites. With the death and resurrection of Jesus, God's power became fully available to all, represented by the tearing of the Temple curtain. This indicated a new purpose for God's community that is expounded throughout the New Testament.

A. A Collective Purpose (Acts 2:42-47)

42. And they continued stedfastly in the apostles' doctrine and fellowship, and in breaking of bread, and in prayers.

43. And fear came upon every soul: and many wonders and signs were done by the apostles.

44. And all that believed were together, and had all things common;

45. And sold their possessions and goods, and parted them to all men, as every man had need.

46. And they, continuing daily with one accord in the temple, and breaking bread from house to house, did eat their meat with gladness and singleness of heart,

47. Praising God, and having favour with all the people. And the Lord added to the church daily such as should be saved.

Talk About It:
1. Describe the life of the early church, as seen in verses 42 and 46.
2. Why were "many wonders and signs" taking place (v. 43)? Should this be happening today? Why or why not?
3. How were people's needs met (vv. 44, 45)? Does this describe the church today?
4. Describe the church's relationship reputation and its growth (v. 46).

"Thanks to the Spirit, the original Christian experience of encountering the risen Jesus can always be lived anew in the worship and communion of God's pilgrim people in history, till all God's promises are fulfilled, and Christ returns in glory."
—Bruno Forte

Talk About It:
1. What lessons must the church teach?
2. Why is baptism central to the church's mission?
3. What promise does Christ give the church?

Throughout Scripture, God calls individuals to fulfill specific purposes. For Noah, it was to physically save the human race. For Abraham, it was to father a great nation. For Moses, it was to deliver the enslaved Hebrews. For Joshua, it was to conquer the Promised Land. For Paul, it was to evangelize the Gentiles. It is critical to understand that the mission of the new church was not given to just one person. From the beginning, it was to be a cooperative effort between groups of people. Of course, Jesus was careful to train and install His apostles as its first leaders, yet they do not appear to be the main catalysts of early church growth. For the most part, they remained in Jerusalem in a teaching function. So then, the majority of local church work was performed by groups of ordinary believers.

We find a beautiful portrait of the early church's collective mission in Acts 2:42-47. The "they" mentioned refers to the fellowship of early believers. The apostles are certainly highlighted as pivotal leaders of this community, yet they did not give it its distinct character. It was the devotion of the believers not only to the apostolic teaching but also to "fellowship," or relationships, that characterized Christ's first church. From the beginning, it was a relational mission, meant to include all Christians, veteran and newborn alike. The first believers ate together, prayed together, learned together, worshiped together, and thereby became a close-knit family as God worked wonders in their midst. When genuine needs arose, they pooled their resources to meet those needs.

B. A Missional Purpose (Matthew 28:19, 20)

19. Go ye therefore, and teach all nations, baptizing them in the name of the Father, and of the Son, and of the Holy Ghost:

20. Teaching them to observe all things whatsoever I have commanded you: and, lo, I am with you alway, even unto the end of the world. Amen.

The mission Christ gave His church was not only that of fellowship. Indeed, many current churches have gotten so comfortable in their internal relationships that they have neglected His overarching command to reach outside of the church community! The Great Commission was given in a group setting by none other than the risen Jesus (Matthew 28:19, 20).

The purpose of the church is primarily to be on a mission of disciple making. A disciple is an apprentice of Jesus, and He desires that entire nations should enter His school of discipleship. Notice that Jesus does not pinpoint individual converts within all nations, but targets the nations themselves. This involves bringing entire cultures under the apprenticeship of Jesus. Evangelism, baptism and teaching are part of this process. And

The Church

Jesus promised to be with His followers "always, to the very end of the age" (*NIV*).

C. A Growing Purpose (Ephesians 4:11-16)
(Ephesians 4:14-16 is not included in the printed text.)

11. And he gave some, apostles; and some, prophets; and some, evangelists; and some, pastors and teachers;

12. For the perfecting of the saints, for the work of the ministry, for the edifying of the body of Christ:

13. Till we all come in the unity of the faith, and of the knowledge of the Son of God, unto a perfect man, unto the measure of the stature of the fulness of Christ.

There are five ministry gifts mentioned in this passage. All are equally important. Each person who has one or more is a vital part of the body of Christ, an organ which is needed for the whole body to function correctly.

Apostles were men who knew Christ personally and were commissioned by Him to preach and establish churches. *Prophets* are proclaimers of spiritual truth, whether it is predicting future events or proclaiming truths received directly from God. *Evangelists* are traveling missionaries, pioneering new fields and strengthening old ones. *Pastors* and *teachers* are often the same person, being in charge of governing and building up local churches, administrating their affairs and educating believers.

The object of the church is training the saints for the work of ministry. There was no professional ministry in the church's beginning, and each mature and effective ministering saint was to help train others, just as Christ trained 12 disciples for ministering after He was gone. Perhaps we might say that the saints had a common profession—the work of the ministry. A properly functioning church, with ministering saints, builds up the body of Christ.

Talk About It:
1. According to verse 12, what is the work of church leaders?
2. What is the goal of Christian discipleship (v. 13)?

"When we describe *church*, we like to say it is a gift-evoking, gift-bearing community. . . . This is why *church* implies a people; no one enters into the fullness of His being except in community with other persons."
—**Elizabeth O'Connor**

CONCLUSION

The church's eternal significance lies in the fact it was established by Jesus himself. Christ spent the vast majority of His ministry training 12 men to take over His ministry after His departure. However, He would continue to function as the church's head, building for Himself a body of believers that were as diverse as the nations, but unified in a common purpose. This purpose is nothing less than the salvation and discipleship of all nations on earth.

GOLDEN TEXT CHALLENGE

"YE ARE THE BODY OF CHRIST, AND MEMBERS IN PARTICULAR" (1 Corinthians 12:27).

As the members in the human body, so [are] the different members of the mystical body of Christ. All are intended by Him to have the same relation to each other; to be mutually subservient to each other; to mourn for and rejoice with each other. He has also made each necessary to the beauty, proportion, strength, and perfection of the whole. Not one is useless; not one unnecessary. . . . No teacher should be exalted above or opposed to another. As the eye cannot say to the hand, "I have no need of thee," so luminous Apollos cannot say to laborious Paul, "I can build up and preserve the church without thee."

The foot planted on the ground to support the whole fabric, and the heads that swing at liberty, and the eye that is continually taking in near and distant prospects, are all equally serviceable to the whole, and mutually helpful to and dependent on each other. So also are the different ministers and members of the church of Christ.—**Adam Clarke**

Divine Healing

Exodus 15:26; Psalm 103:3; Isaiah 53:4, 5;
Matthew 8:16, 17; Mark 16:18; Acts 3:1-16; 4:23-31;
8:4-8; James 5:14-16; 1 Peter 2:24

INTRODUCTION

Miracles line the stories of Scripture throughout the Old and New Testaments, so Western society easily accepted them into its reality. However, during the period of scientific revolution called "the Enlightenment," secular thinkers began to question the possibility of miracles. As society looked to human reason to solve its problems, natural laws replaced the miraculous in the popular mind-set. Thomas Jefferson, one of the founding fathers of the United States, believed so whole-heartedly in human reason that he literally cut out every mira-cle from the Gospels. This was obviously a great deal of cut-ting, but it underscored the modern notion that miracles real-ly don't happen, and the people surrounding the earthly Jesus were just too primitive to understand what He was doing; they wrongly interpreted His actions as miraculous.

Thankfully, the doctrine of divine healing resurfaced in the 20th century as evangelical believers returned to the clear principles of Scripture. This revival of Bible study was fueled by actual revivals of healing, as "healing evangelists" traveled across the world ministering the gospel message along with opportunities for physical healing. Of course, every move-ment contains extremists on its fringes, and this one has proven to be no different. Dishonest preachers, looking to turn a profit off of people's spiritual hunger for healing, have occa-sionally tarnished the doctrine of divine healing. A number of these have been publicly exposed and humiliated. But their failure does not negate God's gift of healing. It is present throughout both Testaments of the Bible, and the Scriptures teach its relevance for the modern-day church.

The late Reverend Edwin Tull, long-time campus pastor for Lee University, told how his mother became so ill that the doc-tors could no longer help. His father had heard of that "odd" religious group that prayed for the sick. The call was made to the humble pastor and some of his congregation.

As a result of their prayer of faith, healing came immedi-ately. While still on his knees, the father called the entire fam-ily to repentance.

Unit Theme:
Basic Christian Doctrines

Central Truth:
God provides healing through the Atonement.

Focus:
Recognize that divine healing is available through Christ and pray in faith for the sick.

Context:
Selected Old and New Testament scriptures concerning divine healing

Golden Text:
"The prayer of faith shall save the sick, and the Lord shall raise him up; and if he have committed sins, they shall be forgiven him" (James 5:15).

Study Outline:
I. Provided by God (Exodus 15:26; Psalm 103:3; Isaiah 53:4, 5; Matthew 8:16, 17; 1 Peter 2:24)
II. Received by Faith (James 5:14-16; Acts 3:1-16)
III. Ministered by the Church (Mark 16:18; Acts 4:23-31; 8:4-8)

I. PROVIDED BY GOD (Exodus 15:26; Psalm 103:3; Isaiah 53:4, 5; Matthew 8:16, 17; 1 Peter 2:24)

Healing is no peculiar novelty or paranormal phenomenon. In a culture interested in extraordinary things like the existence of alien life forms, near-death experiences, and the mystical conglomeration of Eastern religions that make up the New Age movement, it is vital to carefully define the doctrine of divine healing. In fact, its definition is in its terminology. The healing the Scriptures illustrate is thoroughly *divine*! It is centered in God's nature and will, and cannot be separated from His activity. This truth explains why Peter hotly condemned Simon in Acts 8. Simon was a brand-new believer who sought to buy the ability to transfer the miraculous through the laying on of hands. His error was not just greed, but his horrible misunderstanding of Christian doctrine. Even the most pious believer cannot distribute healing as though it were his own possession. It begins and ends in the power and heart of God alone.

A. Provided in God's Nature (Exodus 15:26; Psalm 103:3)

Exodus 15:26. And said, If thou wilt diligently hearken to the voice of the Lord thy God, and wilt do that which is right in his sight, and wilt give ear to his commandments, and keep all his statutes, I will put none of these diseases upon thee, which I have brought upon the Egyptians: for I am the Lord that healeth thee.

Psalm 103:3. Who forgiveth all thine iniquities; who healeth all thy diseases.

Talk About It:
1. What was the condition of the promise God gave the Israelites in Exodus 15:26?
2. What limits are put on God's healing and forgiving ability in Psalm 103:3?

God *is* a healing God. This is such a basic and often-taught Scriptural truth that many believers likely do not completely understand its power. It is not that God *can* heal because He is God. It is not that He has the ability to provide healing and so chooses to disburse it to humanity through the church. There is likely no choice in the mind of God at all. His is a ministry of healing because He is a healer. It is in the makeup of God's nature to heal, much like it is in our makeup to breathe, think or move. Yes, we can cease these activities through the force of our will, but not for long. Our survival as human beings is dependent on them. In the same way, God's very nature constrains Him to provide divine healing to those in need.

This characteristic of God was revealed long before the healing ministry of Jesus. In fact, an incredible thing about the story of Jesus is that *even His enemies did not deny His ability to heal.* They accused Him of using demonic powers to do so, but we simply have no record of anyone in Jesus' day announcing that He was a fake healer. This is due to the fact that the people of the Old Testament came to believe firmly in God's nature to heal.

Soon after the miraculous crossing of the Red Sea, God revealed His healing nature to the children of Israel in Exodus 15:26. That verse's final phrase in Hebrew discloses a particular name of God—*Yahweh Rapha*—"Healer God." It does not denote healing as something God *does*, but as part of who God *is*. Healing is in His very name.

In this early text proclaiming God's intention to heal, it is physical healing that is in view. Of course, God's nature to heal is not constrained to physical healing alone. Throughout the Old Testament, God's healing power is applied spiritually, emotionally and even nationally. Sometimes this is to individuals who are experiencing profound depression, such as Elijah (1 Kings 19) and Jonah (ch. 4). God tenderly visits His people in their spiritual and emotional distress. Other times God embarks on healing the nation of Israel from the effects of idolatry, apostasy or military defeat. Yet even an Old Testament study of healing contains numerous references to bodily, or miraculous, healing. One is found in the psalmist's snapshot of God's nature in 103:3: "who forgives all your sins and heals all your diseases" (*NIV*).

God as forgiver applies spiritual healing, but God as healer destroys diseases. This Old Testament theology of healing stands side by side with its historical accounts of healing. God instructed the children of Israel to simply look upon a bronze serpent and their affliction was immediately vanquished. The prophets Elijah and Elisha could heal diseases and even raise the dead! By the time of Jesus, Israel had experienced and continued to celebrate a long history of God's miraculous healing power.

> "The maladies of the body, including all earthly sufferings, are associated with the soul's sicknesses ('iniquities'). Christ came as the Healer of both. By removing sin, the cause, He will finally remove sickness and suffering, the effect."
> **—Jamieson, Fausset, and Brown**

B. Provided in God's Plan of Salvation (Isaiah 53:4, 5; Matthew 8:16, 17; 1 Peter 2:24)

Isaiah 53:4. Surely he hath borne our griefs, and carried our sorrows: yet we did esteem him stricken, smitten of God, and afflicted.

5. But he was wounded for our transgressions, he was bruised for our iniquities: the chastisement of our peace was upon him; and with his stripes we are healed.

Matthew 8:16. When the even was come, they brought unto him many that were possessed with devils: and he cast out the spirits with his word, and healed all that were sick:

17. That it might be fulfilled which was spoken by Esaias the prophet, saying, Himself took our infirmities, and bare our sicknesses.

1 Peter 2:24. Who his own self bare our sins in his own body on the tree, that we, being dead to sins, should live unto righteousness: by whose stripes ye were healed.

1. How did most people respond to Christ's suffering (Isaiah 53:4)? Why?
2. According to Isaiah, what did Christ's suffering accomplish for us?
3. How should Christians be dead, how should we be alive, and how is this possible (1 Peter 2:24)?

"The expression 'his own self' (1 Peter 2:24) is emphatic, and necessary to show that Jesus verified all the ancient prophecies, to distinguish Him from the Levitical priests (who offered the blood of others, but he *by himself purged our sins,* Hebrews 1:3), and to exclude all others from participation with Him in the work of man's redemption."
—Matthew Henry

Our ultimate spiritual and emotional healing is found in God's plan of salvation. It is the greatest miracle in the world. Although salvation is invisible, all of the extraordinary visible miracles in the world cannot equal the power of one person receiving salvation. Jesus performed miracles on a regular basis, yet exclaimed it was the salvation of one sinner that caused raucous rejoicing in heaven. Because of this, we should view divine healing as something interwoven into God's plan of salvation. This is clearly illustrated by the Greek terms used in the Gospels to indicate an act of healing. Often, the term is *sozo,* meaning "to save." So the same term used for salvation is applied directly to acts of healing.

One of the clearest and most beautiful prophecies regarding God's plan of salvation through the Messiah is found in Isaiah 53. There, the prophet poetically described in advance the sufferings of Jesus. With graphic detail the sorrow of Jesus is predicted in verses 4 and 5, with this simple theological point—He willingly carried our afflictions. His hands and feet were pierced with nails, while His side was pierced with a sword. He was broken to pieces physically and spiritually for our sins, He took the punishment we deserved to buy us peace, and He was beaten to bring us healing.

Jesus' disciples understood His ministry of healing to be the fulfillment of this prophecy by Isaiah. They wanted to point out that He did not only refer to spiritual, emotional or national healing (although Jesus' ministry of healing encompassed all of these as well), but to physical, miraculous works of healing as recorded in Matthew 8:16, 17. There we see Jesus' miracles not only helping the sick, but also serving the soul. This showed what students of the Old Testament already knew—the Messiah had been sent to heal. And here we see Jesus' spoken word effecting deliverance and healing.

The secular historian Josephus (A.D. 37-100) gives us a snapshot of Jesus' reputation in the first century outside of the Biblical texts. Unsurprisingly, in his *Antiquities of the Jews,* Josephus characterizes Jesus as a healer:

Now, there was about this time Jesus, a wise man, if it be lawful to call him a man, for he was a doer of wonderful works—a teacher of such men as receive the truth with pleasure. He drew over to him both many of the Jews, and many of the Gentiles . . . and the tribe of Christians, so named from him, are not extinct at this day (*The Works of Josephus, Complete and Unabridged*).

In 1 Peter 2:24 we see the apostle reiterating Christ's fulfillment of Isaiah 53:4, 5, declaring "by his wounds you have been healed" (*NIV*). Through Christ's atonement, God has provided divine healing. At the cross He not only bore our sins, but our physical infirmities as well. Although not all physical ailments will always be miraculously eliminated in our lives on earth, we can be sure our bodies will undergo an amazing transformation in the coming age. At that time all sickness will be healed forever, because of the sacrifice of Christ.

II. RECEIVED BY FAITH (James 5:14-16; Acts 3:1-16)

Time and time again Jesus commended faith as the vehicle by which miraculous healing occurs. At times, as with the Roman centurion in Matthew 8:10, Jesus was moved by a petitioner's display of faith, while at other times He was disappointed by a lack of faith (see 13:58). It is no accident that Martin Luther's reading of Romans 1:17 sparked the Protestant Reformation: "The just shall live by faith." The rallying cry of the Reformed church became "faith alone!" as Luther declared the kingdom of God is open to all who would believe. Because divine healing is a part of God's plan of salvation, faith is needed for the believer to access it.

A. Liturgical Faith (James 5:14-16)

14. Is any sick among you? let him call for the elders of the church; and let them pray over him, anointing him with oil in the name of the Lord:

15. And the prayer of faith shall save the sick, and the Lord shall raise him up; and if he have committed sins, they shall be forgiven him.

16. Confess your faults one to another, and pray one for another, that ye may be healed. The effectual fervent prayer of a righteous man availeth much.

availeth much (v. 16)—prevails

Part of the disciples' training was to learn Jesus' ministry of divine healing. In Luke 10, 70 of Jesus' main followers were sent out not only to preach but also to heal the sick. With Jesus' departure, this ministry of healing was transferred to the life of the local church. Paul described the spiritual gift of healing in 1 Corinthians 12 among the list of gifts given by the Spirit to the church.

In James 5 we also find the liturgical use of divine healing (vv. 14-16). Here congregations are taught how to facilitate divine healing in their local worship service. The directions are so simple—so matter-of-fact—that they show how normal healing was meant to be in the New Testament church.

First, healing involved church leadership, specifically a body of elders. In the early church, elders were mature believers commissioned to enhance the spiritual life of the congregation. Their ministry involved not only teaching but also prayer. Here James instructed them to use olive oil to symbolize the application of the Holy Spirit's power when they prayed for the sick.

Talk About It:
1. Who are the church elders?
2. Why is faith a necessary element for healing?
3. What does verse 16 teach about one's character and relationships in reference to praying for healing?

Second, healing involved confession. Physical healing was viewed in conjunction with forgiveness, and therefore church members desiring physical healing were encouraged to confess their sins.

This process depicts the communal method of divine healing in the early church. The congregation at large was considered the channel of God's healing power.

B. Individual Faith (Acts 3:1-16)

(Acts 3:11-16 is not included in the printed text.)

1. Now Peter and John went up together into the temple at the hour of prayer, being the ninth hour.

2. And a certain man lame from his mother's womb was carried, whom they laid daily at the gate of the temple which is called Beautiful, to ask alms of them that entered into the temple;

3. Who seeing Peter and John about to go into the temple asked an alms.

4. And Peter, fastening his eyes upon him with John, said, Look on us.

5. And he gave heed unto them, expecting to receive something of them.

6. Then Peter said, Silver and gold have I none; but such as I have give I thee: In the name of Jesus Christ of Nazareth rise up and walk.

7. And he took him by the right hand, and lifted him up: and immediately his feet and ankle bones received strength.

8. And he leaping up stood, and walked, and entered with them into the temple, walking, and leaping, and praising God.

9. And all the people saw him walking and praising God:

10. And they knew that it was he which sat for alms at the Beautiful gate of the temple: and they were filled with wonder and amazement at that which had happened unto him.

Jesus' ministry of individual healing did not cease with the development of the church. Though healing became a liturgical function of local congregations, the apostles continued a Jesus-style healing ministry. In Acts 3:1-16, Peter's Pentecost sermon is quickly validated by a remarkable miracle at the Temple gate. Declaring the name of Jesus, Peter takes a crippled beggar by the hand and divine healing occurs. This not only gives Peter another opportunity to speak to a Jewish crowd, but also lands him before the Sanhedrin.

Peter's healing of the crippled beggar is similar to Jesus' typical healings. He first addresses the man. When the man gives him his attention, Peter gives him the opportunity to

Talk About It:
1. Why were Peter and John going to the Temple, and why was the crippled man lying there?
2. Describe the response of the people who saw the healed man (vv. 10, 11).

receive healing by speaking the name of Jesus and extending his hand. When the cripple takes Peter's hand, his legs are made whole. So we see the formula of divine healing whereby the faith of two individuals is necessary—the apostle and the cripple. The combination is the ideal.

What takes place next is often called "power evangelism." After this display of miraculous power, Peter preaches to the gathered crowd and wins converts to Christ. It should be emphasized that power evangelism is a proven evangelistic method that is still effective in many parts of the world today. It also shows that miracles are not an end in themselves. Divine healing is meant to set the stage for the delivery of the gospel.

A final point should be made in our present context. Although faith is necessary to access divine healing, this truth should be distinguished from what is commonly called the "word of faith" movement. This movement has been popularized by the unprecedented affluence in America during the past 20 years, and is almost always linked with the "prosperity gospel," which says God desires all of His followers to be materially prosperous. Using such mantras as "name it—claim it," the "word of faith" movement makes faith the prerequisite to *anything* the believer requests from God. Many go so far as to teach that faith *obligates* God to keep His promises (as if He does not obligate Himself already!). Such teaching is often applied to divine healing, but it is full of holes. It encourages people not to have faith in a God who heals, but to have faith in their faith to force God's hand. Obviously, God does not need this kind of pressure, and neither do we. He gives us the faith that we need to receive His healing.

III. MINISTERED BY THE CHURCH (Mark 16:18; Acts 4:23-31; 8:4-8)

A. Jesus Instituted Divine Healing (Mark 16:18)

18. They shall take up serpents; and if they drink any deadly thing, it shall not hurt them; they shall lay hands on the sick, and they shall recover.

A person's last words are considered sacred. We marvel at Jesus' amazing words on the cross, but let us not forget He had much to say after this. Before His ascension, Jesus effectively coached His followers on how they would take the baton of the kingdom of God and carry on His ministry. At the end of Mark's Gospel, Jesus lists several signs that will accompany His followers on their way, and will validate the message they preach.

In time, Christ-followers from many generations would be confronted with dangers involving snakes and poisons. These would come about through persecution and dangerous missionary travels, and plainly do not imitate the ministry of Jesus. We have no

3. How did Peter describe the man's healing (v. 16)?

Tumor Vanishes
In November of 2003, Kristin Connor's 2-year-old son was set to receive surgery for a deadly tumor. On the eve of the surgery, after much prayer, doctors were shocked to find that the tumor had simply vanished. This story was carried by several national news agencies, including *Newsweek*, who quoted her as saying, "It's just a miracle." This is one of thousands of modern accounts that indicate the truth of divine healing.

Talk About It:
How were two of the three promises in this verse realized in Paul's ministry (see Acts 19:11, 12; 28:1-6)?

record of Jesus encountering either. However, His followers were commanded to clearly imitate Him by healing the sick.

With this statement, Jesus effectively instituted divine healing as a basic component of the local and eternal church. His clear expectation was that His followers would heal like He did. We have every reason to take Jesus at His word.

B. Divine Healing Helped Spread the Gospel
(Acts 4:23-31; 8:4-8)
(Acts 4:23-28 is not included in the printed text.)

4:29. And now, Lord, behold their threatenings: and grant unto thy servants, that with all boldness they may speak thy word,

30. By stretching forth thine hand to heal; and that signs and wonders may be done by the name of thy holy child Jesus.

31. And when they had prayed, the place was shaken where they were assembled together; and they were all filled with the Holy Ghost, and they spake the word of God with boldness.

8:4. Therefore they that were scattered abroad went every where preaching the word.

5. Then Philip went down to the city of Samaria, and preached Christ unto them.

6. And the people with one accord gave heed unto those things which Philip spake, hearing and seeing the miracles which he did.

7. For unclean spirits, crying with loud voice, came out of many that were possessed with them: and many taken with palsies, and that were lame, were healed.

8. And there was great joy in that city.

In Acts 4:23-31, the Jerusalem congregation was understandably stressed over the sudden arrest of Peter and John by the Sanhedrin. Though the two had been released with little more than a slap on the wrist, the event did not bode well for the fledgling church. In response, they held a prayer meeting. Their request was twofold: that they would speak the Word with boldness and that miraculous healings would occur. This short but powerful prayer illustrates the link between divine healing and evangelism in the first church. When the two were joined together, a powerful kingdom force was unleashed.

God's power among the believers was in even greater need after the martyrdom of Stephen (7:59, 60). His death touched off a persecution against the Jerusalem church. Yet even this worked out for the good of the gospel, as the believers preached the message of Christ everywhere as they were scattered. Acts 8 chronicles their experiences in Samaria,

Talk About It:
1. In Acts 4, what did the church pray for, and why?
2. Why did God respond as He did?
3. In Acts 8, what was the subject of Philip's preaching, the evidence accompanying his message, and the response of the people?

beginning with Philip (vv. 4-8). The miracles were indeed astounding, but they served as mere catalysts to earn the attention and trust of the people. It is not so easy to imagine such a scene in our day. Modern peoples are taught to be skeptical of the miraculous and to search for a scientific or natural rationale for all things. Ancient peoples did not have this roadblock. The supernatural was an accepted part of their culture, and so Philip's works of healing validated his message. The result was the rapid spread of the gospel throughout Samaria.

Each of these Scriptural accounts brings the present-day church to a decisive point. Are we following in the footsteps of Jesus' healing ministry? Do we recognize the purpose and place of divine healing in the teaching of our local church? Do we practice it in our worship services, and encourage those with gifts of healing to exercise them appropriately? The Scriptures teach that Jesus desires nothing less.

> "Healing was one of the primary purposes of the ministry of Christ, and the record of His healings is almost as extensive as that of His preaching."
>
> —Charles W. Conn

CONCLUSION

God has provided healing because it is in His nature to heal. As *Jehovah Rapha*, He provides for healing in the plan of salvation unfolded throughout Scripture. This gift must be received by faith, and the Scriptures give instruction in this to both the Christian congregation and the individual Christian. The doctrine and gift of divine healing have been given to the church to cultivate and exercise as it spreads the gospel.

GOLDEN TEXT CHALLENGE

"THE PRAYER OF FAITH SHALL SAVE THE SICK, AND THE LORD SHALL RAISE HIM UP; AND IF HE HAVE COMMITTED SINS, THEY SHALL BE FORGIVEN HIM" (James 5:15).

Two things here must be given attention: the "prayer of faith" and "forgiveness of sin." Concerning the latter, the scripture says *if* he has committed sins. Some today are like Job's comforters: they believe all illness is a result of sin. While some illness comes because of sin, certainly not all can be so relegated; otherwise the text would not have said *if*.

Unconfessed known sin could surely block God's benevolent healing grace. However, the candidate for healing has God's assurance of forgiveness of sins.

By whom should the prayer of faith be made? James says the elders should pray for the sick that they may be strengthened (v. 14). This point needs our earnest attention. The church should recognize the value of its lay leaders.

Daily Devotions:
M. God Offers Healing
Numbers 21:4-9
T. Naaman Healed of Leprosy
2 Kings 5:8-14
W. Hezekiah Healed
2 Kings 20:1-11
T. Long-Term Illness Healed
Matthew 9:20-22
F. Healed in Jesus' Name
Acts 4:5-12
S. Healing Advances the Gospel
Acts 9:32-35

Things to Come

Isaiah 11:6-9; 1 Thessalonians 4:13-18; 2 Peter 3:10-14;
Revelation 3:10; 6:15-17; 19:11-21; 20:1-15;
21:1 through 22:5

Unit Theme:
Basic Christian
Doctrines

Central Truth:
God will bring His plan
for the future to fulfillment through Christ.

Focus:
To survey end-time
events and prepare
for Christ's coming.

Context:
Selected Old and
New Testament pas-
sages regarding the
last days

Golden Text:
"He which testifieth
these things saith,
Surely I come quick-
ly. Amen. Even so,
come, Lord Jesus"
(Revelation 22:20).

Study Outline:
I. The Second
   Coming of Christ
   (1 Thessalonians
   4:13-18;
   Revelation 3:10;
   6:15-17; 19:11-21)
II. The Millennium
    and Final
    Judgment
    (Revelation 20:1-
    15; Isaiah 11:6-9)
III. New Heaven and
     New Earth
     (Revelation 21:1—
     22:5; 2 Peter 3:10-
     14)

INTRODUCTION

Prophecy is central throughout the Scriptures. We claim the necessity of prophecy, especially when it comes to the person of Jesus Christ, whose coming was predicted from Genesis to Malachi in the Old Testament, including His birth-place, ministry, suffering and death. In the New Testament, prophecy was an important spiritual gift to be used during wor-ship (1 Corinthians 12; 14) and prophets such as Agabus (Acts 11:28; 21:10) functioned as vital leaders.

In this lesson, we are focusing on Biblical prophecy that specifically concerns the end times. Scholars call the study of the end times "eschatology," from the Greek noun *eschatos*, which means "end" or "last." It is impossible to be an effective student of the Scriptures without having a Biblical view of eschatology.

Eschatology is all the more important when we consider the day in which we live. It is common to the human mind to ask not only where we came from, but also where we are going. To this end, people are turning in many different direc-tions, including Scriptures, in the attempt to discern an ulti-mate plan for humanity and the cosmos. Christians and non-Christians have been captivated by the *Left Behind* book series, written by Tim LaHaye and Jerry Jenkins, which pur-ports to interpret the Book of Revelation in novel format.

On the other side of the spectrum, the study of the end times is relevant to the concept of evolution that is taught in our schools. That is, Darwin held a strong belief in *positive progress*—that our world is progressively becoming better as species learn to adapt to their surroundings. There are dozens of wilder theories about the direction our world is heading, including those that look to the existence of extraterrestrial life to give us clues as to our ultimate destiny. A Biblical view of eschatology will show all competing theories for what they are.

Eschatology is actually a recurring theme in the Old Testament (both the Law and the Major and Minor Prophets), the teachings of Jesus, and the New Testament letters. For this reason, the study of eschatology must be broad, inter-preting a range of Biblical authors and texts. Although we will certainly look to Revelation as a primary source of information on the end times, we will also turn to Paul, Isaiah and Peter for further insight.

I. THE SECOND COMING OF CHRIST
(1 Thessalonians 4:13-18; Revelation 3:10; 6:15-17; 19:11-21)

The second coming of Christ inaugurates the final stage of prophetic events in Scripture. Jesus himself spoke of His later return on numerous occasions, and the early church was spiritually and emotionally driven by a sense of Christ's coming "at any moment." Even though it has been almost 2,000 years since Christ's ascension, we must not lose heart but instead must maintain a keen understanding of the events that will surround His second coming. Only then can we watch and wait with faithfulness and devotion.

A. A Sudden Event (1 Thessalonians 4:13-18)

13. But I would not have you to be ignorant, brethren, concerning them which are asleep, that ye sorrow not, even as others which have no hope.

14. For if we believe that Jesus died and rose again, even so them also which sleep in Jesus will God bring with him.

15. For this we say unto you by the word of the Lord, that we which are alive and remain unto the coming of the Lord shall not prevent them which are asleep.

prevent (v. 15)— precede

16. For the Lord himself shall descend from heaven with a shout, with the voice of the archangel, and with the trump of God: and the dead in Christ shall rise first:

17. Then we which are alive and remain shall be caught up together with them in the clouds, to meet the Lord in the air: and so shall we ever be with the Lord.

18. Wherefore comfort one another with these words.

An early congregation with a pressing need to properly understand the end times resided in Thessalonica. Thessalonica was a booming and cosmopolitan city, filled with all the moral trappings of the Roman Empire. Convinced that the coming of Christ would take place during their lifetime, they were dismayed that some in their church had already died. This led them to fear that these deceased brothers and sisters would not get to experience the coming of the Lord, and might be left out of the future kingdom of God. Paul assured the distressed Thessalonians that the dead would not be left out of Christ's return, but would join Him even before the living (vv. 16-18).

Many scholars believe Paul is describing the rapture of the saints. After all, he clearly states we will leave the ground to meet Christ, and then spend eternity with Him. All Christians of all times will ascend with Christ to heaven, and return with Him later when He sets up His earthly kingdom.

Other scholars note that Paul doesn't say where believers will dwell with Christ after the meeting in the air. They also note

Talk About It:
1. What does it mean to "sleep in Jesus" (v. 14)?
2. According to verse 16, what sounds will be heard when Christ returns? What will be their purpose?
3. Who will be *caught up*, and why?

kept the word of my patience (v. 10)—"kept my command to endure patiently" (*NIV*)

Talk About It:
1. In the scene of 6:15, 16, why will a person's social status not matter?
2. Answer the question in verse 17.

that the word *meet* seems to reflect the ancient custom of visiting Roman officials. When a Roman emperor, governor, or other high official would visit a city, the members of that city were required to gather at the road into the city outside its walls, and thus "meet" the official in order to joyfully escort him into the city. It is certainly unclear whether or not Paul had this custom in mind, but it is an interesting possibility to consider, particularly when we discuss Christ's millennial reign and Revelation 20 and 21.

The point, of course, is not only that dead believers will participate in the rapture, but that the return will be abrupt and can take place at any moment. Given that Paul's letters were written to be read out loud to the congregation, we can only imagine the holy hush that filled the room when the Thessalonians first heard these words. Undoubtedly, they were both comforted and awed by Paul's teaching, just as we should be.

B. A Day of Wrath on Evildoers (Revelation 3:10; 6:15-17)

3:10. Because thou hast kept the word of my patience, I also will keep thee from the hour of temptation, which shall come upon all the world, to try them that dwell upon the earth.

6:15. And the kings of the earth, and the great men, and the rich men, and the chief captains, and the mighty men, and every bondman, and every free man, hid themselves in the dens and in the rocks of the mountains;

16. And said to the mountains and rocks, Fall on us, and hide us from the face of him that sitteth on the throne, and from the wrath of the Lamb:

17. For the great day of his wrath is come; and who shall be able to stand?

Many people believe that although Jesus came as a gentle lamb in the first century, He is coming as a lion with wrath and judgment at the end of the ages. There is obviously some truth to this, but we must be careful not to read the Scriptures out of their context. The Book of Revelation is primarily concerned with the overthrow of the oppressive Roman Empire. Its chapters are replete with veiled references to Rome and its rulers that first-century Christians would have quickly understood. For this reason, Saint Augustine believed the millennial reign of Christ had begun when Emperor Constantine converted the empire to Christianity in A.D. 387. With this in mind, let us summarize what Revelation has to say about Christ's coming, and the impending wrath of God with His return.

In Jesus' message to the church in Philadelphia, He promises to keep them from the ominous hour of trial about to storm the earth (3:10). In fact, many of Jesus' messages to the seven churches encourage them to persevere during the difficult days ahead. This is understandable when we realize Revelation was written during the reign of Emperor Domitian, a persecutor of Christians, and reflects back on the reign of Emperor Nero, a lunatic who blamed the Christians for the burning of Rome. Because Christians were increasingly hated by the Roman establishment, John not only encouraged them to stand strong, but also told of a coming day of judgment on all such evildoers.

Revelation 3:10 also has a broader meaning for all of God's people. The terrible persecutions which soon fell on the Philadelphia church are symbolic of "the great tribulation" (Matthew 24:21) which is yet to come upon the church, and from which God will deliver His people.

Revelation 6:15-17 specifically describes the day of judgment on Roman officials when the earth's kings, princes, generals, wealthy and powerful are first to flee to the mountains for protection from God's wrath. The Roman Empire did not consist of separate sovereign nations like we know in our day. Instead, Rome controlled everything and everyone from Britain to Russia, conquering existing nations and replacing local rulers with their own. Here again Revelation has two scenes in mind: both the overthrowing of Rome and the return of Christ in wrath. The former happened about 300 years after these words were written. The latter is certainly coming soon. All those who have rebelled against Christ—everyone from the slave to the king—will try to hide from God's judgment, but all will fail.

> "The Tribulation is not designed to chasten the saints but to punish a world that has rejected Christ."
> **—French Arrington**

C. A Final Victory (19:11-21)
(Revelation 19:17-21 is not included in the printed text.)

11. And I saw heaven opened, and behold a white horse; and he that sat upon him was called Faithful and True, and in righteousness he doth judge and make war.

12. His eyes were as a flame of fire, and on his head were many crowns; and he had a name written, that no man knew, but he himself.

13. And he was clothed with a vesture dipped in blood: and his name is called The Word of God.

14. And the armies which were in heaven followed him upon white horses, clothed in fine linen, white and clean.

15. And out of his mouth goeth a sharp sword, that with it he should smite the nations: and he shall rule them with a rod of iron: and he treadeth the winepress of the fierceness and wrath of Almighty God.

16. And he hath on his vesture and on his thigh a name written, KING OF KINGS, AND LORD OF LORDS.

At this final appearing, Christ will come from heaven in glory and power, and He will overthrow all rebellious earthly powers.

Talk About It:
1. What can we learn about Christ from His titles given in verses 11, 13, and 16?
2. What is the significance of His having a name "that no man knew, but he himself" (v. 12)?
3. What will Christ lead His armies to do (vv. 14, 15)?
4. Describe the results (vv. 20, 21).

He will come to judge the wicked of earth. As the bringer of judgment, He is pictured as riding on a white horse accompanied by the armies of heaven to exercise His authority as King of kings and Lord of lords. A great confederation of armies will gather together in a final gigantic war, the Battle of Armageddon. Demonic spirits which work miracles will be instruments in bringing together the kings of the whole earth for the final conflict, "the battle of that great day of God Almighty" (16:14). All the kings of the earth and their armies will be determined to make war against the Lamb (Christ) and His redeemed people, but they will suffer an overwhelming defeat in the Battle of Armageddon (19:19-21).

II. THE MILLENNIUM AND FINAL JUDGMENT
(Revelation 20:1-15; Isaiah 11:6-9)

The second coming of Christ is the catalyst for the culmination of end-time events. The rapture of the saints is not the end of the story of human history, but the beginning of a new story. Perhaps this is why the Second Coming played such a vital role in the theology and commitment of the early churches. They did not consider the coming Kingdom the end of their struggle for survival, but the beginning of a process that would truly set the world aright. During Christ's millennial reign, this will occur literally.

A. The Earthly Reign of Christ and His Saints (Revelation 20:1-6; Isaiah 11:6-9)

(Revelation 20:1-3 is not included in the printed text.)

Revelation 20:4. And I saw thrones, and they sat upon them, and judgment was given unto them: and I saw the souls of them that were beheaded for the witness of Jesus, and for the word of God, and which had not worshipped the beast, neither his image, neither had received his mark upon their foreheads, or in their hands; and they lived and reigned with Christ a thousand years.

5. But the rest of the dead lived not again until the thousand years were finished. This is the first resurrection.

6. Blessed and holy is he that hath part in the first resurrection: on such the second death hath no power, but they shall be priests of God and of Christ, and shall reign with him a thousand years.

Isaiah 11:6. The wolf also shall dwell with the lamb, and the leopard shall lie down with the kid; and the calf and the young lion and the fatling together; and a little child shall lead them.

7. And the cow and the bear shall feed; their young ones shall lie down together: and the lion shall eat straw like the ox.

8. And the sucking child shall play on the hole of the asp, and the weaned child shall put his hand on the cockatrice' den.

9. They shall not hurt nor destroy in all my holy mountain: for the earth shall be full of the knowledge of the Lord, as the waters cover the sea.

After the triumph of Jesus—the powerful and majestic rider on the white horse—over all evildoers in Revelation 19, Satan is confined for the specific time period of 1,000 years (20:1-3). In the next scene, John describes the reward of those who remained faithful to Jesus despite persecution (v. 4). This millennial reign appears to be an earthly reign of the saints. They will return to earth in order to officiate over it with Christ.

This earthly reign is also described by the Old Testament prophet Isaiah (11:6-9), who looked forward to a time of profound earthly peace, in which all evil has been done away with, and creation itself lives in the complete harmony enjoyed in the Garden of Eden. In fact, Isaiah's prophecy is fulfilled specifically here in Revelation 20 and 21. During Christ's millennial reign on earth, all hatred, discord and animosity will no longer exist. He will govern with peace, justice and perfection.

B. The Final Judgment (Revelation 20:7-15)

(Revelation 20:7-10 is not included in the printed text.)

11. And I saw a great white throne, and him that sat on it, from whose face the earth and the heaven fled away; and there was found no place for them.

12. And I saw the dead, small and great, stand before God; and the books were opened: and another book was opened, which is the book of life: and the dead were judged out of those things which were written in the books, according to their works.

13. And the sea gave up the dead which were in it; and death and hell delivered up the dead which were in them: and they were judged every man according to their works.

14. And death and hell were cast into the lake of fire. This is the second death.

15. And whosoever was not found written in the book of life was cast into the lake of fire.

The capstone to this incredible reign of peace, which God intended to prevail on the earth from the beginning, is the Final Judgment. Even with Jesus himself ruling the earth, human sin is not eradicated. When Satan is released from confinement, he deceptively incites a rebellion against Christ, which is quickly and easily thwarted by fire from heaven. This is certainly mysterious, but again denotes the earthly nature of the Millennium. It is not a spiritual rule, but an actual, physical rule

Talk About It:
1. What is the meaning of the *seal* in verse 3?
2. What is "the first resurrection" (v. 5)?
3. What is "the second death" (v. 6)?
4. How does Isaiah 11:6-9 picture the natural world during the Millennium?

"Satan will remain bound and inactive for the entire thousand years of Christ's reign on the earth."
—**French Arrington**

Talk About It:
1. Why will Satan be freed once more (v. 7)?
2. What is Satan's final fate (v. 10)?
3. How does everything change in verse 11?

of Jesus, which Satan attempts to overthrow. This results in the final judgments of Satan (v. 10), who is thrown into hell forever, and of lost humanity (vv. 11-15).

The Judgment appears to occur in a place beyond the reaches of the earth, and multiple books are opened. There is a distinction between a collection of "books" and the great Book of Life. The absence of a person's name from the Book of Life determines one's ultimate destination as the lake of fire. The Judgment is described in detail, and all sinners are sentenced to the lake of fire forever.

III. NEW HEAVEN AND NEW EARTH (Revelation 21:1–22:5; 2 Peter 3:10-14)

Perhaps the most beautiful scene in the Bible occurs at the end. It is quite a contrast from the simplicity and purity of the Garden of Eden, and a fitting end to God's renewal of the earth. Here the work of Christ is finally complete, as the entire creation is renewed. It is the culmination of the entire redemptive process and the fulfillment of the Scriptures themselves.

A. Fulfilling Jesus' Preaching of the Kingdom of God
   (Revelation 21:1-27)
   (Revelation 21:5-27 is not included in the printed text.)

1. And I saw a new heaven and a new earth: for the first heaven and the first earth were passed away; and there was no more sea.

2. And I John saw the holy city, new Jerusalem, coming down from God out of heaven, prepared as a bride adorned for her husband.

3. And I heard a great voice out of heaven saying, Behold, the tabernacle of God is with men, and he will dwell with them, and they shall be his people, and God himself shall be with them, and be their God.

4. And God shall wipe away all tears from their eyes; and there shall be no more death, neither sorrow, nor crying, neither shall there be any more pain: for the former things are passed away.

Central to understanding the person and work of Jesus Christ is His teaching and proclamation of the kingdom of God. This subject alone, also characteristic of the ministry of John the Baptist, dominates Jesus' preaching ministry, and gives us great insight into the new heaven and new earth depicted in Revelation. In short, Christ's basic message had to do with the nearness of God's kingdom: "The kingdom of heaven is at hand." So in the teachings of Jesus we learn that God's kingdom (rule) was present in the earthly ministry of Jesus! This is a radical truth for us to accept, given that we often think of heaven as a faraway place beyond this world, yet in Revelation the concept is driven home yet again. In fact, the coming of the New Jerusalem is undoubtedly the fulfillment of Jesus' preaching and ministry, as the distinction between heaven and earth is finally and eternally abolished. It is the ultimate answer to the Lord's Prayer, "Thy kingdom come, thy will be done on earth as it is in heaven." At the end of the age, this prayer will no longer be valid, since the two realms shall decisively be one.

The breathtaking view of the final piece in the things to come (21:1-4) includes several important characteristics. First, creation itself, including heaven, is renewed. It is unclear whether John is referring to our concept of "sky" when he mentions heaven here, but this is a possibility, as it was customary among other first-century writers. Whether or not that is the case, the renewed quality of creation is vital because it signifies the goal of the redemptive process began in the Garden has been reached.

Second, the New Jerusalem comes down to the earth. That is, it does not appear to be a place where people go one by one. Instead, the New Jerusalem comes down to them from the realm of the heavens and they enter it corporately.

Third, the New Jerusalem is an urban city. The end of human history does not take us back to the Garden of Eden, as some suppose, but places us in a physical city along with God.

Fourth, God literally lives in the city with redeemed humanity. This is not simply figurative language, for the remainder of the passage describes the wedding of the city with the Lamb himself, symbolizing the perfect union between God and people. So naturally no sanctuary is necessary for worship, as even the distinctions between sacred and secular are erased. In the New Jerusalem, God is truly all-in-all, in perfect relationship with humanity again.

The New Jerusalem is rich in symbolism. The walls of the city are made of jasper, and the foundations are decorated with every kind of precious stone. Together these stones constitute a foundation of incomparable strength and grandeur. Their splendor represents the glory of God.

The 12 gates of the city are made of 12 pearls. These pearls represent unity, purity, beauty and preciousness. There will not be a dissident voice in the Holy City. All will have the mind of Christ and unity will be perfected. This does not mean we will be robots. On the contrary, we will each be individual in character—a greater individuality than we can possibly know now—but we will also be in perfect harmony with the Lord.

The streets of the city are made of pure gold, like transparent glass. They represent the righteousness of God. That righteousness will be displayed everywhere.

B. Serving and Reigning for Eternity (22:1-5)

(Revelation 22:1, 2, 4, 5 is not included in the printed text.)

3. And there shall be no more curse: but the throne of God and the Lamb shall be in it; and his servants shall serve him.

Talk About It:
Describe *the healing of the nations* that will take place (v. 2).

The throne of God is pictured as the place from which all blessings flow. Through Christ we have present access to it. We are even encouraged in Hebrews 4:16 to "come boldly" to His throne for mercy and grace. In the eternal state, God's throne continues to be the source of our hope and help.

John saw the river of the water of life, as clear as crystal, flowing from the throne. One thinks of the function of the Holy Spirit in the present. That "living water" (John 7:38) from which we drink now is a never-ending river. For all eternity we will enjoy its nourishment.

In the Holy City, the curse of sin will be lifted. Redeemed humanity will function to our fullest potential. We will be servants who reign. Only in God's economy is such a circumstance—being a servant and a king at the same time—made possible. And this reign will never end.

C. Encouraging a Commitment to Holiness and Devotion
(2 Peter 3:10-14)

10. But the day of the Lord will come as a thief in the night; in the which the heavens shall pass away with a great noise, and the elements shall melt with fervent heat, the earth also and the works that are therein shall be burned up.

holy conversation (v. 11)—pure living

hasting (v. 12)—hastening

11. Seeing then that all these things shall be dissolved, what manner of persons ought ye to be in all holy conversation and godliness,

12. Looking for and hasting unto the coming of the day of God, wherein the heavens being on fire shall be dissolved, and the elements shall melt with fervent heat?

13. Nevertheless we, according to his promise, look for new heavens and a new earth, wherein dwelleth righteousness.

14. Wherefore, beloved, seeing that ye look for such things, be diligent that ye may be found of him in peace, without spot, and blameless.

Talk About It:
1. How will "the day of the Lord . . . come as a thief in the night" (v. 10)?
2. Why will life on earth as we know it be *dissolved*?
3. In what ways should believers be *diligent*?

The cynic or worldly person might be inclined to ask, "So what? How does this great future coming of Christ matter to our daily routines of family, work and general living?" Peter asks this very question in this passage, declaring it is vitally important for normal life. His passage also shows us that eschatology was very important to the first-century Christians. As previously mentioned, the early church lived with the expectation of this coming Kingdom, and this expectation shaped the way in which they lived their daily lives. Peter urges them toward holiness and godliness, explaining that their expectation of the great day of the Lord can actually have the effect of speeding its coming! So then, the reality of the future renewal of the heavens and the earth should never make us lazy or passive. It is not something that will allow us to rest on our laurels and wait on God to simply renew the heavens and the earth.

Yes, God will bring these things about in His own time and by His own power. Yet He still gives *us* a role to play in renewing creation. This happens anytime we invite His reign into our lives, thus placing a Kingdom "deposit" on the earth in advance. It happens anytime we devote ourselves to holy living, and thus display His beauty and order to the world. It happens anytime we commit ourselves to His causes on this earth, and thereby join Him in His ministry on earth. So in all these things, we join John in praying, "Come, Lord Jesus" (Revelation 22:20).

CONCLUSION

As 21st-century Christians, we must get beyond the notion that heaven is a far-off city waiting for our arrival at the moment of our death. Yes, the Bible teaches that our souls do depart to be in the presence of God at death, but this is not our *ultimate* destination. In fact, God's grand design to renew the heavens and the earth brings heaven *to* earth. So while we may dwell with God apart from the earth for a time, our ultimate destiny is to return here for the consummation of the kingdom of God on the earth—the arrival of the New Jerusalem. It is for this we wait in eager expectation, committed wholeheartedly to the Lord in the meantime.

GOLDEN TEXT CHALLENGE

"HE WHICH TESTIFIETH THESE THINGS SAITH, SURELY I COME QUICKLY. AMEN. EVEN SO, COME, LORD JESUS" (Revelation 22:20).

There are two speakers in this, the next-to-last verse in the Bible. First we hear from Jesus Christ himself, the inspirer of the Revelation. He declares, "Surely I come quickly," or Yes, I am coming soon" (*NIV*). This means His return is imminent—it could happen any time.

The second speaker is the recorder of the Revelation, the apostle John. John responds to the Lord's promise by saying "Amen," or "So be it." He accentuates his heart's desire by praying, "Come, Lord Jesus."

Are we longing and praying for Jesus' return?

God's City

"That is what the City of God will be like. Not a static, frozen—dead—perfection in which there is nothing more to do, think, achieve. Rather a creative, dynamic 'moving from perfection to perfection' in which there will always be new things to learn, new things to do, new tasks to perform—under the God whose own perfection is not static and lifeless, but the perfection of the God who always will be a living, active Creator."
—**Shirley Guthrie Jr.** (*Christian Doctrine*)

Daily Devotions:
M. A New World
Isaiah 65:17-25
T. Vision of the End Times
Daniel 9:20-27
W. God Will Rule
Micah 4:1-5
T. Christ Will Judge
Matthew 25:31-46
F. Proclaim Christ's Second Coming
Titus 2:11-14
S. Christ Is Coming
Revelation 22:12-17

Introduction to Spring Quarter

The teachings of Jesus as presented in the Gospel of Matthew are the focus of the first unit. The setting for the first four studies is the Sermon on the Mount, while the other teachings (lessons 5, 7 and 8) come from different settings. Lesson 6 is the Easter study. The writer of this unit is the Reverend Keith Whitt (B.A., M.Div., Ph.D. cand.).

Keith Whitt has earned degrees from Lee University and the Church of God Theological Seminary; he is completing the doctor of philosophy at the University of Nottingham (England). An ordained bishop in the Church of God, Keith has served his denomination as a pastor for 23 years, district overseer for 12 years, and as a member of various boards and committees. He has taught courses for the Church of God Theological Seminary and Lee University External Studies.

The first four lessons of the second unit deal with the Christian home. This is a topical study drawing from both Old and New Testament references. Expositions were written by Glenda Walter.

Glenda Walter is a Bible teacher and freelance writer who served as the Christian education director for Bethel Assembly of God in Sedro Woolley, Washington. She has numerous certificates of completion in Bible subjects. Glenda has also completed her certification for the Assemblies of God ACTS Training Program, specializing in Sunday school administration.

The quarter's final lesson for Pentecost Sunday explores the baptism in the Holy Spirit from Acts 1 and 2.

Christ and the Law

INTRODUCTION

The Sermon on the Mount (Matthew 5:1—7:29) is considered by many in both the secular and theological realms to be one of the best pieces of literature written and among the most profound teachings. This message of Jesus can be comforting, stimulating, informative and very challenging—challenging to understand exactly what Jesus meant, and challenging to apply the principles in our everyday lives. For example, the first response for most people is *not* to turn the other cheek when slapped (5:39)!

Readers of the Sermon on the Mount must keep in mind that Jesus intends it to be provocative in the sense that it provokes us to examine our responses and the attitudes that facilitate those responses, as well as our spiritual relationships that serve as the foundation for both the responses and the attitudes. In brief, Jesus is not looking for a change in behavior based on mindless conformity to simple principles that guide us in proper mechanical responses to all the twists and turns we encounter in life. Jesus is intentionally providing teaching that challenges our lifeless interpretations of the Old Testament, perfunctory behavior based on others' expectations, and religion without meaningful relationships. Jesus is getting to the *heart* of who we are and how that is revealed to others in everyday behavior.

As noted, the teachings can be quite difficult to understand and live. The only way we can fulfill the teaching of Jesus is through the enabling power of the Holy Spirit (John 16:13). Our will, talent and abilities are insufficient. That is the point of the sermon. It is our awareness of this that opens for us the provision of the Kingdom (Matthew 5:3).

After Jesus saw the needs of the crowd, He sat down on the undisclosed mountain and opened to them the revelation of God (v. 1). The disciplines of philosophy and theology are humanity's attempts to understand life and God. They are limited by humanity's intellectual capabilities. Revelation is God breaking through the barriers of the mind and allowing us access to things beyond our abilities that will make us more like Him.

Unit Theme:
The Teachings of Jesus (Matthew)

Central Truth:
Christ came to fulfill the Law.

Focus:
Acknowledge that Christ fulfilled the Law and submit to His authority.

Context:
Christ teaches on a high hill or mountain near Capernaum in A.D. 28.

Golden Text:
"Think not that I [Christ] am come to destroy the law, or the prophets: I am not come to destroy, but to fulfil" (Matthew 5:17).

Study Outline:
I. Salt and Light (Matthew 5:13-16)
II. Christ Fulfills the Law (Matthew 5:17-20)
III. Christ Reinterprets the Law (Matthew 5:21-32)

I. SALT AND LIGHT (Matthew 5:13-16)

A. The Versatility of Salt (v. 13)

savour—"salti-ness" (*NIV*)

13. Ye are the salt of the earth: but if the salt have lost his savour, wherewith shall it be salted? it is thenceforth good for nothing, but to be cast out, and to be trodden under foot of men.

"You [emphatic] are the salt of the earth" is the first of three metaphors used to illustrate the nature of Christianity. Salt was a necessity of life in the ancient world, serving several important functions and communicating significant concepts. First, it was used to preserve foods that tended to spoil quickly. The harmful effects of microorganisms and insects were delayed through salt. Second, it served in some places as money. Our term *salary* probably comes from this usage. A common phrase ("being worth his/her salt") follows this view. Third, salt promotes good health and has medicinal value. In suitable amounts it aids in proper circulation, muscle performance, digestion and heart function. Fourth, Job 6:6 says salt is a condiment that enhances the taste of bland food. Fifth, the Greeks associated salt with divine favor. Sixth, rabbis connected it with wisdom. Finally, in Biblical references it communicates the ideas of loyalty, faithfulness and durability (2 Chronicles 13:5); peace (Mark 9:50); judgment (Genesis 19:26); preservation and purity (Leviticus 2:13); sacrifice (Mark 9:49); healing (2 Kings 2:21); and speech that edifies (Colossians 4:6).

There is no need to limit Jesus' teaching to one aspect of salt's qualities. Christians are to serve as all of these things to the world. For example, the world is preserved by believers in at least four important ways: (1) we present hope in God's transformational abilities; (2) we preserve morality and ethics by preventing the world from instilling humanistic "values"; (3) we temporarily preserve the world from judgment (Psalm 76; 2 Thessalonians 2:6); and (4) the intercession of the saints prevents Satan from implementing all his wicked devices and plans upon an unsuspecting world.

Further, the world is influenced by the character of the church. The positive concepts of life (wisdom, faithfulness, peace, etc.) are revealed through our lifestyles, which are made possible through the provision of Jesus Christ. Thus, the world is judged by our example. We are a continual reminder of what they should be. Finally, the world is evangelized actively and indirectly through the church and its presence in the world. Evangelization takes place when we witness and when we are witnesses. That is, the church must proclaim the message of Jesus Christ, but we must also be living testimonies of His message. What we do is more powerful than what we say.

Chemically, salt cannot lose its qualities. However, outside

Talk About It:
1. How does God want you to act as salt in the lives of others?
2. Name some Christians who have "salted" your life by their influence.

"The blossom cannot tell what becomes of its odor; and no man can tell what becomes of his influence."
—Henry Ward Beecher

Christ and the Law

influences (water, contaminants) can affect its usefulness. Thus, Jesus reminds us that it is possible for His followers to become so corrupted with impurities that we lose our essential qualities and negate our function in the Kingdom (Matthew 5:13). When that happens to salt, it is thrown out and absorbed by its surroundings.

B. The Powerful Influence of Light (vv. 14-16)

14. Ye are the light of the world. A city that is set on an hill cannot be hid.

15. Neither do men light a candle, and put it under a bushel, but on a candlestick; and it giveth light unto all that are in the house.

16. Let your light so shine before men, that they may see your good works, and glorify your Father which is in heaven.

The second metaphor Jesus uses to communicate the Kingdom truths is that of light: "You are the light of the world." We are not just to be light in our homes or our church, but to a world enveloped in darkness. To illustrate this, Jesus uses a third metaphor. A city located upon a high place can be viewed from great distances during the day because of the sun that illuminates it and at night because of the light within. Such a city cannot be concealed. Calling it "a city" (not "the city") places the emphasis on the light, not the city. The focus is not on us, but on the One who illuminates us and causes His light to shine within us. Certainly, we can hinder that light, but we must not confuse His qualities with our own.

Talk About It:
1. Why would any Christian try to hide his or her "light"?
2. How is our church like "a city on a hill"?

To further illustrate our functions in the world, Jesus points out the folly of lighting a lamp in a dark house, then placing it under a basket (v. 15). The purpose of a lit candle is to provide light for its surroundings. Likewise, those who follow Jesus are to provide light in their surroundings. Our witness is not to be hid from those around us, but should shine forth as naturally as light. Earlier in Matthew's Gospel (4:16), Isaiah is quoted to illustrate how Jesus serves as light to the world. Jesus now extends His ministry and character to His followers. It is His responsibility to transform and equip us. It is our responsibility to yield to His work and let others see the fruit through our actions (5:16). We are not saved by those actions (works-righteousness); rather, our "good works" are the natural by-product of our relationship with Him, as Jesus illustrates in the Beatitudes (vv. 3-12).

"Example is not the main thing in influencing others; it's the only thing."
—Albert Schweitzer

II. CHRIST FULFILLS THE LAW (Matthew 5:17-20)

A. Fulfillment and Permanence (vv. 17, 18)

17. Think not that I am come to destroy the law, or the prophets: I am not come to destroy, but to fulfil.

jot (v. 18)—the smallest letter in the Hebrew alphabet

tittle (v. 18)—a point on a Hebrew letter

Talk About It:
1. Why did Jesus need to "fulfill" the Old Testament teachings?
2. What does verse 18 reveal about God's power?

Lots of Jots
There are 66,420 *yods* ("jots") in the Hebrew Scriptures, according to some commentators. Jesus declares that not a single one of these will fall away without the fulfillment of all things (Matthew 5:18). This should give us comfort and motivation. If He is that concerned with the things most people would not notice, then how much more is He concerned with fulfilling God's destiny for our lives? Should we not be just as concerned?

18. For verily I say unto you, Till heaven and earth pass, one jot or one tittle shall in no wise pass from the law, till all be fulfilled.

The focus shifts sharply to Jesus' authority when He declares, "Do not think that I have come to abolish the Law or the Prophets" (*NIV*). "The Law" is the first five books of the Old Testament, containing 613 commandments (248 positive and 365 negative). "The Prophets" consist of the major (Isaiah through Daniel) and minor (Hosea through Malachi) prophetical books. They are major and minor based on size, not importance. The Jews also called Joshua through 2 Kings the "former prophets." Thus, "the law and the prophets" refers to the whole Old Testament (Matthew 22:40). "I have come" speaks to His purpose and mission. It was not to do away with the Law in its entirety ("abolish"). Jesus (and the New Testament in general) quotes extensively from "the Scriptures" (the Old Testament) and uses it as a foundational authority for His message and teaching. His view of the Old Testament is positive.

Jesus states emphatically that He came "to fulfill" the Scriptures (5:17b). The language of this passage is reminiscent of Matthew 3:15, where Jesus declares He must "fulfill all righteousness." *Fulfill* can mean either "to perform" or "complete" something. Jesus fulfills the Old Testament in five distinctive ways.

First, Jesus accomplishes God's will perfectly, including the expectations of the Law and the desires of God's sovereign will. He is perfectly and faithfully obedient to all the desires of the Father. Second, Jesus accomplishes the expectations and completes the prophecies of the Old Testament. Israel failed miserably to meet God's expectations as set forth in the Scriptures. Jesus, however, succeeds in every aspect! Not only does He fulfill the prophecies concerning the Messiah, but *in him* there is the completion of all the promises and prophecies given to God's people (2 Corinthians 1:20). Third, His completion of the Law establishes a personal connection with those who need and those who seek (and struggle!) to maintain a proper relationship with God. He understands the expectations and the temptations; thus, He is able to supply whatever is needed to live in covenant with God. Fourth, Jesus fulfills the Old Testament by providing the perfect example for us, so we might conduct ourselves properly in all situations, be obedient to the Father's will, and do so with humility, gratitude, grace and love. Finally, Jesus fulfills Scripture by reinterpreting it so the original intent of God is brought back to His people.

To underscore the importance of His teaching, Jesus emphasizes His trustworthiness and authority (Matthew 5:18). "Verily, I say unto you" is the equivalent of "thus says the Lord" or "it is written," found elsewhere in Scripture. Until the completion of all created things ("heaven and earth"), not even the smallest mark used to distinguish one letter from another will disappear until all is completed. "Heaven" is not a reference to the abiding place of God, but to the skies and stars created by Him. God's purpose and will shall prevail.

B. Commandments and Responsibility (v. 19)

19. Whosoever therefore shall break one of these least commandments, and shall teach men so, he shall be called the least in the kingdom of heaven: but whosoever shall do and teach them, the same shall be called great in the kingdom of heaven.

Verse 19 emphasizes two attitudes toward the Word. *Therefore* points back to the previous two verses to emphasize the importance of these attitudes. The first attitude is one of carelessness toward even easily overlooked ("one of these least") commandments (e.g., Deuteronomy 22:6, 7). To relax the expectations and teach others through exhortation or our example to do the same is to diminish our role in the Kingdom. These, however, do not lose their right to the Kingdom. Thus, Jesus is not speaking to false teachers here. Those who deliberately pervert the Word and teach that distortion to others are strongly condemned and their eternal destiny is made certain (2 Peter 2:1). The emphasis here is on careless handling of the Word. However, an attitude of diligence in thought, actions and teaching is greatly rewarded. Jesus is not stressing a rigid fulfillment or legalistic obedience, but rather, living out the intent of God's will as revealed through the Word and the Spirit.

Talk About It:
1. Why is it important to keep the "least commandments"?
2. Who is "great" in God's kingdom?

C. Righteousness and the Kingdom (v. 20)

20. For I say unto you, That except your righteousness shall exceed the righteousness of the scribes and Pharisees, ye shall in no case enter into the kingdom of heaven.

To further emphasize and illustrate the need to examine, correct and guard our attitudes and actions, Jesus makes a startling statement—His disciples must be more righteous than even the Pharisees! He is not looking for His disciples to be more legalistic than the scribes (experts in the Scriptures) and the Pharisees (those who rigidly observed the letter of the Law, usually without concern for its intent). He is looking for a qualitative difference in His followers, not a quantitative difference. That is, Jesus is looking for a radical transformation of the heart that results in humble obedience, not a plethora of good deeds motivated by a desire to be "more holy" than everyone else.

In Matthew, righteousness includes right actions, but these

Talk About It:
Describe genuine righteousness.

actions must result from a right relationship with God, who *makes* us righteous and gives us the power to live out righteousness. This relationship must affect our attitudes and actions toward God and others. It is impossible to be right with God and wrong with others (vv. 23, 24), including those in our own household (1 Peter 3:7; Ephesians 6:4). To neglect this commandment of Jesus removes one from the Kingdom and its benefits. Ways in which this righteousness is lived out is presented in the following verses.

III. CHRIST REINTERPRETS THE LAW (Matthew 5:21-32)
A. Teaching About Anger and Relationship (vv. 21-26)

21. Ye have heard that it was said by them of old time, Thou shalt not kill; and whosoever shall kill shall be in danger of the judgment:

22. But I say unto you, That whosoever is angry with his brother without a cause shall be in danger of the judgment: and whosoever shall say to his brother, Raca, shall be in danger of the council: but whosoever shall say, Thou fool, shall be in danger of hell fire.

23. Therefore if thou bring thy gift to the altar, and there rememberest that thy brother hath ought against thee;

24. Leave there thy gift before the altar, and go thy way; first be reconciled to thy brother, and then come and offer thy gift.

25. Agree with thine adversary quickly, whiles thou art in the way with him; lest at any time the adversary deliver thee to the judge, and the judge deliver thee to the officer, and thou be cast into prison.

26. Verily I say unto thee, Thou shalt by no means come out thence, till thou hast paid the uttermost farthing.

These verses begin a section commonly known as the *antitheses* (vv. 21-48). Each passage begins with the phrase "Ye have heard that it was said," followed by an Old Testament commandment. Jesus then follows that with a reinterpretation of the Old Testament commandment, or its understanding that gets beyond legalistic obedience to the purpose behind the command and its implications for daily living ("But I say unto you . . .").

The first antithesis (v. 21) addresses the Exodus 20:13 command against murder (v. 21). The consequence of murder is judgment by humanity (Deuteronomy 16:18) and God (Romans 14:12). However, Jesus expands the commandment to address accountability for anger without cause. There are times anger can be justified (John 2:14-17). However, unjustified wrath brings us into God's judgment. Anger usually alters those involved in a negative and lasting fashion. Also, we need to discern what is and is not justified anger, based on solid

raca (v. 22)—ignorant, senseless, worthless

ought (v. 23)—a valid complaint due to offense or injury

farthing (v. 26)—coin of least value

Talk About It:
1. Why is unjust anger such a serious offense?
2. Why must believers make things right with others before approaching God?
3. Explain the statement, "Agree with your adversary quickly" (v. 25, *NKJV*).

Scriptural principles, not personal feelings or individual beliefs.

From the context, it can be surmised that inappropriate wrath is the equivalent of murdering the individual's character and destroying his or her sanctity. Telling a person that he or she is "good for nothing" ("Raca") places us in judgment by humanity (literally, the Sanhedrin or Jewish supreme court). However, to call a person a "fool," or "moron," in an angry outburst makes one angry enough to enter into eternal fire (Matthew 5:22).

The importance of right relationships for disciples is further conveyed in two examples. First, the picture is presented of a solemn worshiper presenting his gift at the altar (v. 23). If he remembers that someone has something against him, it must be corrected before approaching God. Thus, not only must we control our own anger, we must not provoke another's wrath. Our relationships with others affect our relationship with God (v. 24). Second, Jesus admonishes us to "agree" with our enemies (v. 25). The emphasis is on settling debts and disagreements with everyone—even our enemies—before they become more serious problems (v. 26). God is a God of relationship and takes all our relationships seriously.

> "An angry man opens his mouth and shuts his eyes."
> —Marcus Porcius Cato

B. Teaching About Adultery and Purity of Thought (vv. 27-30)

27. Ye have heard that it was said by them of old time, Thou shalt not commit adultery:

28. But I say unto you, That whosoever looketh on a woman to lust after her hath committed adultery with her already in his heart.

29. And if thy right eye offend thee, pluck it out, and cast it from thee: for it is profitable for thee that one of thy members should perish, and not that thy whole body should be cast into hell.

30. And if thy right hand offend thee, cut it off, and cast it from thee: for it is profitable for thee that one of thy members should perish, and not that thy whole body should be cast into hell.

Jesus quotes the commandment against adultery (Exodus 20:14), then clarifies the decree and its misinterpretation. In Jewish thought, a married man could have relations with a female slave or a Gentile and not violate the commandment against adultery. Adultery was viewed as merely violating the rights of another Jewish male by having relations with his wife. Jesus, however, reinterprets the commandment to address the issue of the heart and proper relationship with one's spouse. *To look intently with illicit desire* ("looketh . . . to lust") offends God's will as much as the physical act. Jesus is not speaking of a brief awareness of attractiveness, but a deliberate gaze motivated

Talk About It:
1. Does adultery always begin in the heart? Why or why not?
2. What do verses 29 and 30 teach about hell?
3. Describe some things believers need to "pluck out" of their lives.

March 4, 2007

by sexual desire. This can include looking in such a way that it produces desire in the person being looked upon. Looks lead to touching, and touching leads to transgression. Any thought, speech or conduct that offends the sanctity of the marriage covenant must be avoided, because it is offensive to the spouse—and to God!

To emphasize the need to remain vigilant in our awareness and actions (vv. 29, 30), Jesus uses *hyperbole*—dramatic speech designed to convey a message, but not to be taken literally. Jesus did not intend for us as His disciples to mutilate literal parts of our bodies. His point is to underscore our need to address anything that causes stumbling in or scandalizes our relationship with God. If reading certain literature, viewing some programs or movies or Web sites, visiting certain places, or keeping particular friends opens the door for temptation, then we need to sever those things from our lives before they take root and lead to eternal destruction. In brief, remove the seed before it produces fruit!

C. Teaching About Divorce (vv. 31, 32)

31. It hath been said, Whosoever shall put away his wife, let him give her a writing of divorcement:

32. But I say unto you, That whosoever shall put away his wife, saving for the cause of fornication, causeth her to commit adultery: and whosoever shall marry her that is divorced committeth adultery.

Divorce was rampant during Jesus' time on earth. There is record of a woman who had been married 21 times marrying a man with 19 previous marriages. Also, some rabbis were guilty of going out of town and marrying a woman for the day, then divorcing her before returning home in the evening. When Jesus reiterated this teaching on marital faithfulness to some Pharisees, His own disciples declared it would be better to remain single than face a life without the possibility of divorce (see Matthew 19:3-12).

Deuteronomy 24:1-4 allowed a man to divorce his wife if she became "displeasing to him because he [found] something indecent about her" (v. 1, *NIV*), while a woman could only petition a court to direct her husband to divorce her. Different rabbis interpreted "displeasing to him" in different ways: (1) Shammai viewed it as sexual impropriety; (2) Hillel taught that it meant all offensive behavior, such as burning dinner; (3) Akiba understood it as permitting divorce if another woman found more favor in a man's eyes.

Jesus challenges the rabbinic interpretations and lays down the intent of God's will—divorce is permissible only in the case of *porneia* ("fornication," KJV; "sexual immorality," *NKJV*). It is

Talk About It:
1. Why do you suppose people were taking the marriage covenant lightly?
2. Why does Jesus allow for divorce in the case of adultery?

Christ and the Law

a broad term that is generally used of "any illicit sexual behavior," including intercourse outside of marriage, lesbianism and bestiality. In 1 Corinthians 7:15, Paul allows for believers to divorce unbelievers under specific circumstances.

No one should divorce without Biblical grounds. God does not take the marriage covenant lightly, nor should we. He hates divorce and what it does to people (Malachi 2:16); He does not, however, hate divorced people—and neither should we. Again, the focus is on the motivation and condition of the heart for all involved.

> "It is not love that will keep your marriage alive. It is commitment to relationship that will keep your love alive."
> —Ian Bilby

CONCLUSION

The teaching of Jesus challenges us to examine not just our actions, but the motivation behind the actions. It has rightly been said that God is more concerned with what happens *in* us than what happens *to* us. If God knows when a sparrow falls, then He is concerned about every aspect of our lives, since we are made in His image (Genesis 1:26). God wants His best for us. That happens only when we follow His will in all aspects of our lives. If the heart is wrong, it is difficult to get His will right.

GOLDEN TEXT CHALLENGE

"THINK NOT THAT I [CHRIST] AM COME TO DESTROY THE LAW, OR THE PROPHETS: I AM NOT COME TO DESTROY, BUT TO FULFIL" (Matthew 5:17).

The words "think not" suggest the Lord's reply to implied criticism that He was destroying the Law by His teachings. He insists He did not come to contradict the law of God as given by Moses, though He opposed the legalistic religion the scribes had built upon it.

Jesus declares that the purpose of His mission was to *fulfill* the Law and the Prophets. Jesus completed the Mosaic Law by leading a sinless life, by explaining the spirit and intent of the Law, by teaching and showing how living in God's love fulfills the Law (Romans 13:10), and by bearing the curse of the Law on the cross (Galatians 3:10, 13).

It is Christ's desire that His children follow His lead by living triumphantly over sin, obeying His laws from our heart, loving God and others, and walking in the power of the resurrected Savior.

Daily Devotions:
M. God's Awesome Presence
Exodus 19:14-25
T. The Ten Commandments
Exodus 20:3-17
W. Meditate on the Law
Psalm 1:1-3
T. New Way of the Spirit
Romans 7:1-6
F. Redeemed From the Law's Curse
Galatians 3:10-14
S. Purpose of the Law
Galatians 4:21-31

Christ's Standards for Relationships

Matthew 5:33-48

Unit Theme:
The Teachings of Jesus (Matthew)

Central Truth:
Christlike love is the standard for relationships.

Focus:
Examine and accept Christ's teachings about relationships.

Context:
Christ teaches on a high hill or mountain near Capernaum in A.D. 28.

Golden Text:
"Love your enemies, bless them that curse you, do good to them that hate you, and pray for them which despitefully use you, and persecute you" (Matthew 5:44).

Study Outline:
I. Keep Your Word (Matthew 5:33-37)
II. Love Beyond Reason (Matthew 5:38-42)
III. Love Your Enemies (Matthew 5:43-48)

INTRODUCTION

"He (or she) is the kind of person only a mother could love!" This sentiment has been uttered in more languages and cultures, and more often than any of us could count. It is a fact of life that some people are easier to love than others. Some people could be classified as "relational teddy bears"; a few are "relational porcupines"; others are somewhere in between. At times, even the best of "teddy bears" can become the worst of "porcupines"! However, if God loved us when we were unlovable (1 John 4:9, 10) and He expects us to be like Him (Philippians 2:4, 5), then we must learn to love those who could be classified as "EGRs" ("extra grace required"; see Matthew 22:35-40). After all, we might be an EGR in someone else's eyes!

Relationships are vital, and they are big business in today's climate. The shelves of bookstores abound with self-help books on the subject. A search of the Internet reveals 7 million sites that offer advice on relationships. One of the most popular American daytime television programs is hosted by a psychologist who blends Biblical principles with homespun humor and psychological theory to address the needs of his guests and their relationship problems.

Proper relationships require understanding, selflessness, diligence, love, grace, making compromises, hard work and lots of forgiveness. Paradoxically, the closer we are to a person, it is easier and yet more difficult to maintain a healthy relationship with that person. Those who are closest to us understand us best, but can also hurt us the most deeply.

The main outline of this lesson focuses on three foundational relationship issues: (1) straightforward truthfulness; (2) love that is expressed in tough situations; and (3) loving when it is beyond reason to do so. Each of these issues requires the love of Christ flowing through us. The world (and our homes) will not be won to Christ just by what we say, though that is important. People are won when we allow God's love to be expressed in our lives day in and day out. We cannot win a world we do not love. We cannot love the world without Christ's love in us.

I. KEEP YOUR WORD (Matthew 5:33-37)

A. Deceit and Our Word (vv. 33-36)

33. Again, ye have heard that it hath been said by them of old time, Thou shalt not forswear thyself, but shalt perform unto the Lord thine oaths:

34. But I say unto you, Swear not at all; neither by heaven; for it is God's throne:

35. Nor by the earth; for it is his footstool: neither by Jerusalem; for it is the city of the great King.

36. Neither shalt thou swear by thy head, because thou canst not make one hair white or black.

"Again" (v. 33) connects this section with the antitheses (vv. 21-48) and Jesus' reinterpretation of the Law to reveal its true intent ("You have heard it said . . . but I say to you"). In the previous sections (covered last week), Jesus has addressed anger, adultery and divorce. Now He turns His attention to the truthfulness of one's word. Jesus does not quote one verse directly, but pulls together the teaching of several scriptures to reveal that the Old Testament teaches we should not swear falsely, but "perform [literally, "pay" or "recompense"] unto the Lord" what we declare (see Leviticus 19:12; Numbers 30:2; Deuteronomy 23:21). He states the teaching negatively ("You shall not swear falsely," *RVS*) and positively ("perform unto the Lord thine oaths").

In first-century Judaism, the making of oaths and vows was quite an elaborate and deceitful ordeal. Some oaths meant nothing, others were somewhat binding, while certain ones were very binding. There were various degrees of accountability by the oath maker. It was all in how they were phrased. For example, oaths sworn upon heaven and earth or one's own head were not binding at all. Whereas, oaths that contained a reference to God's name were very binding. Swearing "by Jerusalem" meant nothing, but swearing "to Jerusalem" was binding. It was a device to circumvent the Law and, just as importantly, one's own integrity, veracity and accountability. If a person was aware of the elaborate scheme for oaths and vows, he or she knew what to and not to believe. If not, it was quite easy to take a person at his or her word, only to find out the deceitful person never meant to keep the oath or vow. There are variations of Judaism's attempt to deceive operating in the world today.

Jesus addresses the most common forms of oaths in that day to deliver a straightforward message: we have no right to swear upon anything (vv. 34-36). Everything belongs to God, and even if His name is not uttered in the oath to avoid fulfilling one's word, He still owns everything we can swear upon. Thus, all oaths are valid.

forswear thyself (v. 33)—"break your oath" (*NIV*)

Talk About It:
1. Why do some people today make statements like, "I'll swear on my grandma's grave" and "I'll promise with my hand on a stack of Bibles"?
2. If we do make an oath, what does God require?

With Your Hat

At the county fair a distinctively dressed Quaker offered a horse for sale. A non-Quaker farmer asked its price, and since Quakers had a reputation for fair dealing, he bought the horse without hesitation. The farmer got the horse home, only to discover it was lazy and ill-tempered, so he took it back to the fair the next day. There he confronted the Quaker. "Thou hast no complaint against me," said the Quaker. "Had thou asked me about the horse, I would have told thee truthfully the problems, but thou didst not ask."

"That's okay," replied the farmer. "I don't want you to take the horse back. I want to try to sell him to someone else. Can I borrow your coat and hat awhile?"
—**Sermon Illustrations.com**

Talk About It:
Why can it be so difficult to follow Jesus' straightforward instruction in verse 37?

"It's amazing how many people are shocked by honesty and how few by deceit."
—**Unknown**

Is this a command to never take an oath or swear to tell the truth? The Essenes (an early separatist group) understood the Scriptures as prohibiting such. The Pentecostal tradition, for the most part, has held to this same understanding since its inception. Many of the early church fathers saw it as precluding any oath taking (e.g., Justin, Irenaeus, Tertullian, Origen). However, Augustine said one should try to abstain from doing so, but that it might be necessary at times. Verse 34 clearly says to abstain from swearing completely, yet Deuteronomy 6:13 allows for swearing by the name of God. Also, Jesus responded to the high priest's request to swear that He was the Son of God (see Matthew 26:63, 64). These address legal and religious situations. Thus, a person (guided by conscience) could swear in a court of law without violating the intent of Scripture. However, outside of the legal realm, oaths should be completely unnecessary.

B. Truthfulness and Our Word (v. 37)

37. But let your communication be, Yea, yea; Nay, nay: for whatsoever is more than these cometh of evil.

Jesus' teaching is simple: say what you mean. Any attempt to do otherwise finds its source in "evil." This can mean either evil as a force (a thing) or "the evil one" (the devil). The implication is that our relationships should be guided by love and God, not an evil force or yielding to the devil's nature to deceive. Jesus is not limiting our vocabulary to two words, but telling us we must mean what we say and that what we say should not be crafted to deceive—even when we tell the "truth" (cf. James 5:12).

A word of caution is in order. There are different ways to "tell the truth." The truth can be used as a weapon of destruction or an instrument of help. We must tell the truth in love, not bluntly or without grace. Our words should be "seasoned with salt" (Colossians 4:6), or spoken in such a way as to build up, not tear down. Our speech should preserve and heal. This does not mean we must remain silent when we see a person headed toward danger, but that we approach them in such a way that they are drawn closer to God. This requires the power of the Holy Spirit operating in our lives and the situation. Timing the truth can be as important as speaking the truth.

II. LOVE BEYOND REASON (Matthew 5:38-42)
A. An End of Retaliation (vv. 38, 39)

38. Ye have heard that it hath been said, An eye for an eye, and a tooth for a tooth:

39. But I say unto you, That ye resist not evil: but whosoever shall smite thee on thy right cheek, turn to him the other also.

Christ's Standards for Relationships

The law of retaliation that Jesus quotes (v. 38), also known as *lex talionis*, is in the Torah (Exodus 21:24; Leviticus 24:20; Deuteronomy 19:21). To the 21st-century reader the law of retaliation seems harsh. Deuteronomy 19:21 says that "pity" (compassion) shall not be shown (though see Leviticus 19:17, 18). The law was instituted to curb crime. Criminals knew there would be consequences for their actions. As well, this was a step toward grace. Prior to this, mercy was not shown and there was no correspondence between the retaliation and the injury. For example, if a person lost an eye, he might gouge out both eyes of the guilty party. If one person was killed, an entire family might be killed in revenge.

Jesus, however, takes it beyond the one-to-one correspondence and admonishes us to take a step back before responding to injury or insult (Matthew 5:39). This verse presents two aspects that run counter to normal human responses. First, He asserts, "Do not resist an evil person" (*NIV*). The obvious meaning is that we are not to resist the one who is doing us wrong. Second, if a person slaps us (with an open hand), we are to offer the other cheek as well. Is Jesus teaching that we must allow people to run over us? Many attempts have been made to understand this verse based on first-century customs and culture. For example, some assert that this is hyperbole, not to be taken quite so literally. Others view the slap as an accusation of heresy against the teaching of Jesus and His followers. Both of these are possible. Perhaps the best way to understand this verse is to look at Jesus' own example in difficult situations.

First, we find that Jesus defended Himself and His disciples against accusations, but did so without making the situation personal (Matthew 12:1-8). He explained the reasoning behind His actions, based on Scriptural principles. His opponents did not always receive His explanation in the same manner in which it was given, but He did His part to keep the situation from escalating, even if He had to remove Himself from the scene (John 8:59). Second, Jesus vigorously confronted accusations that arose from evil intentions and misapplied Scripture by religious leaders (Matthew 15:1-20; see also ch. 23). He opposed false teaching because He understood souls were at stake. Third, we find that when Jesus was taken before the high priest and questioned in a highly emotional situation, He remained silent (Mark 14:61). Finally, He was slapped and abused, but did not retaliate (Matthew 26:67), though He had the means to do so (v. 53).

From these examples we can draw a few conclusions. Every situation is different and should be handled in a way consistent with the situation. Jesus is not advocating that we allow

Talk About It:
1. Why did Jesus alter the "eye for an eye" approach to living?
2. Why is important for us to not retaliate when someone hurts us?

50,000 Annoying Phone Calls
Tokyo police arrested a man who was upset over being denied entrance to graduate school 14 years earlier. Since that day he averaged about 10 phone calls a night—between the hours of 8 p.m. and 2 a.m.—to the former professor whom he blamed for his lost opportunity. Those 14 years of annoying phone calls totaled up to over 50,000 calls. But they did nothing for the spurned student.
—**Sermon Illustrations.com**

people to abuse us, but that we respond in a way that will bring clarity and peace, not further discord and harm. We must think before we react in any situation. Our responses should be based on Scriptural principles and guided by the Holy Spirit (Luke 12:12). It is difficult to fight with someone who will not fight back. Also, innocence is presupposed by Jesus in Matthew 5:39, and our innocence and righteousness in themselves are a strong defense and will be vindicated by God, though we may not always like the timing (see Luke 23:47; Romans 12:17-19).

Further, there is a difference between the public and private realms. Not every insult should be addressed. Some private (and public) misunderstandings between individuals should be quickly overlooked, forgiven and put behind us. However in the public realm, we have the right to defend ourselves from false accusations and charges (Matthew 10:16-20; Luke 21:15). Again, even this defense is to be in the spirit of Christ (Philippians 2:5-11). Having the right, however, does not mean that we must act upon the right. We must not do anything to bring a reproach upon the name or work of Jesus Christ. We must be sensitive to God's guidance in each situation, even if this means suffering in silence—for great is the future reward.

B. Beyond the Expected (vv. 40-42)

40. And if any man will sue thee at the law, and take away thy coat, let him have thy cloke also.

41. And whosoever shall compel thee to go a mile, go with him twain.

42. Give to him that asketh thee, and from him that would borrow of thee turn not thou away.

We live in a world that promotes self-sufficiency, self-concern and self-preservation. This can lead to an attitude of unconcern for others. In these verses, Jesus gives three examples of reversing the expectations of the world and laying down the desire to "get even."

First, He addresses a legal situation in which a person's tunic (a linen or wool inner garment) is forcibly taken away (v. 40). Jesus says, "Give him your outer garment also" (paraphrase). Jewish males usually wore two garments—the tunic and a coat that served as protection from the elements and even a cover at night. Most people in the first century possessed only one or two tunics and one coat. Roman soldiers had the right to commandeer clothing from citizens, if necessary, though the taking of the coat was strongly discouraged. In ways that the world cannot understand, the believer knows that God clothes those who trust in Him (6:28-30), even when things are beyond our control.

Talk About It:
1. Why does Jesus want us to show kindness even to someone who sues us?
2. According to verse 42, to whom should we give and lend material things?

Christ's Standards for Relationships

Second, Jesus says that if a person is compelled to travel one mile, the response should be to accompany the person for two miles (5:41). Imperial soldiers could compel a person to carry his equipment (either on one's back or beast) for one Roman mile (1,000 paces or 4,854 feet). This was considered reasonable civic service. Epictetus, a Stoic philosopher, said it was best to be a willing participant, or a beating would motivate a person to perform the civic duty. Correctly, T.W. Manson suggests that the "first mile" be rendered unto Caesar and the second unto God.

Third, Jesus instructs His followers to "give to the one who requests of you" (see v. 42). There are no qualifications on either "give" or "requests." Thus, we are to give generously without condition. The term for "borrow" is used most often of borrowing money. The Old Testament is very specific about the generosity and compassion that God expects from His people (Deuteronomy 15:7, 8). Should we give to anyone who asks? Would we not lose everything that we have? Augustine said we are not required to give everything asked for, but to give something to everyone who asks. The implication is that we give what is needed, not necessarily what is requested, but we must do so with a right spirit. Part of being a follower of Jesus (as He illustrates here) is not fulfilling the letter of the Law, but seeking God for the right response in all situations.

III. LOVE YOUR ENEMIES (Matthew 5:43-48)

A. Blessings, Not Bitterness (vv. 43-47)

43. Ye have heard that it hath been said, Thou shalt love thy neighbour, and hate thine enemy.

44. But I say unto you, Love your enemies, bless them that curse you, do good to them that hate you, and pray for them which despitefully use you, and persecute you;

45. That ye may be the children of your Father which is in heaven: for he maketh his sun to rise on the evil and on the good, and sendeth rain on the just and on the unjust.

46. For if ye love them which love you, what reward have ye? do not even the publicans the same?

47. And if ye salute your brethren only, what do ye more than others? do not even the publicans so?

Jesus quotes scribal tradition here to correct an erroneous view of Scripture and a negative attitude toward certain people (v. 43). Leviticus 19:18 says, "You shall not take vengeance, nor bear any grudge against the children of your people, but you shall love your neighbor as yourself: I am the Lord" (*NKJV*). The scribes left out the phrase "as yourself," which probably depicts a lower expectation of love for others. Further, nowhere in Scripture are we admonished to "hate your enemy." The

Golden Giving

The story is told that one day a beggar by the roadside asked for alms from Alexander the Great as he passed by. The man was poor and wretched, yet the emperor threw him several gold coins. A courtier was astonished at his generosity and commented, "Sir, copper coins would adequately meet a beggar's need. Why give him gold?"

Alexander responded, "Copper coins would suit the beggar's need, but gold coins suit Alexander's giving."

—Sermon Illustrations.com

salute (v. 47)—
greet

1. How is it possible to love one's enemy?
2. Why does God allow both sunshine and rain in the lives of both "the just" and "the unjust" (v. 45)?
3. Answer the questions in verses 46 and 47.

Scriptural approach to one's enemies is very complex, at best. God promised to strike down Israel's enemies (Deuteronomy 33:27), yet God commanded, "If you meet your enemy's ox or his donkey going astray . . . bring it back to him" (Exodus 23:4, *NKJV*). David declared his hatred for those who hated God (Psalm 139:21, 22; *hate* can also mean "lack of favor," "disregard" or "destroy"); yet, Jesus (Luke 23:34) and Stephen (Acts 7:60) prayed for forgiveness of their enemies.

We are admonished to respond to our "enemies" in four ways (Matthew 5:44). First, we are to *love* them. This is a strong word that describes intensely warm feelings motivated by the will. We make a conscious decision to love those who oppose us. As we know, feelings follow the determination of the mind. When we declare a disposition of love toward someone, God gives us the feelings of love for him or her. Second, we are to *bless* those who attack us with their words. We do this by speaking words of blessing, commending the positive qualities of our enemies. Third, we are to *do good things* for those who despise us. Fourth, we must *pray* (intercede) for those who insult or threaten ("spitefully use") us or harass us with hostility ("persecute"). Prayer serves to help us in the situation and inject God's presence into the lives of our enemies. It has been noted that persecutors are the most difficult people to love. Prayer changes people and situations. It usually changes the one praying more than the one being prayed for—as it should.

Our love for our "Father" and the desire to be in a more complete relationship with Him motivates us to be obedient in these things (v. 45). He allows certain blessings, characterized as rain, to fall upon "the just and unjust," literally "the righteous and unrighteous" (those in relationship with Him and those who need to be in relationship with Him). We must not be guilty of dehumanizing or marginalizing our enemies. We must learn to see people the way God sees them. This means seeing their need and potential, not just what they are and how it affects us at present. Even those who do not have God can love those who treat them well (vv. 46, 47). Our response must be different; it must be motivated by eternity.

"Love means to love what is unlovable or it is no love at all."
—**G.K. Chesterton**

B. An Impossible Command? (v. 48)

48. Be ye therefore perfect, even as your Father which is in heaven is perfect.

This is one of those verses that causes the heart to beat quickly—and not usually in joy. How can we be as "perfect" as God? First, God never commands us to do something without giving us the ability to fulfill His expectations (Isaiah 40:29; Jeremiah 1:7-12). Second, we must separate the contemporary view of perfection with the Biblical sense. For most people, *perfection* means "without flaw or blemish." However, God is not looking for people who have it all together, never mess up, and are faultless in every aspect of their lives. The word translated *perfect* here means "having attained the end or desired aim." It is used to refer to the maturity of a person from infancy to adulthood.

Thus, we are to be continually growing and maturing. *Perfection* speaks to spiritual completeness. A believer is to be an undivided or whole person, made complete through the provision of our heavenly Father. All that God is that can be given to us, He imparts to those who seek Him. It starts by incorporating the teachings of Jesus into our daily lives.

CONCLUSION

Jesus challenges conventional and safe thinking in His teaching. His teaching often leads to as many questions as it does answers, just as it should! We must search our hearts and the mind of God in all of life's situations. Otherwise, personal vengeance, self-pity, bitterness and revenge will consume us—mind, body and soul. In some situations, there are no easy solutions. We must live continually in a vibrant relationship that acknowledges day-by-day dependency upon Christ. Then, others will see and desire Him!

GOLDEN TEXT CHALLENGE

"LOVE YOUR ENEMIES, BLESS THEM THAT CURSE YOU, DO GOOD TO THEM THAT HATE YOU, AND PRAY FOR THEM WHICH DESPITEFULLY USE YOU, AND PERSECUTE YOU" (Matthew 5:44).

People have basic needs that only others can fulfill. We all need love, mercy, forgiveness, fellowship. Without these, we are lonely and feel forsaken. How can we get them?

One gains friends by being friendly; a person receives forgiveness by forgiving; one receives love by loving others. This principle of the Golden Rule seldom fails.

There are some graces a person can show to others and receive in return when acting entirely on human motivation. Some non-Christians have discovered the value of this rule of life.

However, the children of God bestow these graces on others out of a heart of love. They even love their enemies from whom no grace may be returned. Yet, Christians know God loves them, and it is now their nature to do good to others. What they receive in return from other people is only a fraction of the blessings God bestows because of their faithful service. Their life is full of love.

Looking for Completeness

A Mercedes dealer once told me of a doctor who brought his new car back because it had a flaw in the paint—visible only through a magnifying glass! Often we think that God is scrutinizing us for flaws through His magnifying glass. Who could endure? God is looking for completeness in us—and we are complete only in Him. Thank God for the blood of Jesus Christ that cleanses us from our "flaws."

—Keith Whitt

Daily Devotions:

M. Treat Others Fairly
Exodus 22:21-27

T. Laws Governing Relationships
Leviticus 19:13-18

W. Friendship Covenant
1 Samuel 18:1-5

T. Christlike Love
1 Corinthians 13:1-13

F. Bear One Another's Burdens
Galatians 6:1-10

S. Don't Show Partiality
James 2:1-13

Personal Piety

Matthew 6:1-18; 9:14, 15

Unit Theme:
The Teachings of Jesus (Matthew)

Central Truth:
Believers become Christlike through developing a personal relationship with the Father.

Focus:
Study and practice Christ's teachings about personal piety.

Context:
Christ teaches on a high hill or mountain near Capernaum in A.D. 28.

Golden Text:
"Be ye therefore perfect, even as your Father which is in heaven is perfect" (Matthew 5:48).

Study Outline:
I. Selfless Giving (Matthew 6:1-4)
II. Prayer and Forgiveness (Matthew 6:5-15)
III. Fasting (Matthew 6:16-18; 9:14, 15)

INTRODUCTION

The term *piety* in English often carries with it the idea of "religious duty carried out because of a sense of obligation." This concept is foreign to this lesson and the teaching of Jesus. Genuine piety is better viewed as the way our spiritual life is lived out daily—or the way we worship God outside of the church building. Worship is not just what happens in church services. It includes how we reveal God to those around us.

Matthew 6 addresses some of the ways our righteousness is to be lived out. Righteousness finds its source in God (Psalm 97:2), issues out of holiness (Isaiah 5:16), and is a mighty force of life (Amos 5:24). It is power for living according to the desires that Almighty God has for us (Isaiah 45:8). Thus, we are expected to *have* righteousness (Psalm 40:10), *be* righteous (Revelation 22:11), and *do* righteousness (Matthew 6:1-4). Obviously, righteousness has implications for our relationship with God, who imparts His righteousness to us (Isaiah 54:17); however, righteousness also affects our relationships with those around us, as the lesson reveals.

A major portion of this lesson addresses the Lord's Prayer. Prayer was an important part of Jesus' ministry. Larry Lea says Jesus went from one place of prayer to another and did great miracles on the way (his book *Could You Not Tarry One Hour?* addresses the Lord's Prayer in a helpful, but different manner than the approach taken in this lesson). Jesus' example should serve to motivate contemporary disciples to reevaluate the importance of prayer in our busy schedules and hectic lives.

It is not just what we know—or even what we hope to accomplish—that is important. Good intentions are just that, unless they are put into action. This lesson reveals the importance of what we do and how we do it. Who we are is revealed by what we do and the manner in which we accomplish it. We must live out our righteousness with a sense of thankfulness that God has redeemed us and given us the ministry of touching the world with His love.

I. SELFLESS GIVING (Matthew 6:1-4)

A. Righteousness in Action (v. 1)

1. Take heed that ye do not your alms before men, to be seen of them: otherwise ye have no reward of your Father which is in heaven.

"Take heed" comes from a Greek word that originally meant "to bring a ship to land," a tricky endeavor in the ancient world. It was a task that required one's full attention, or one could quickly make shipwreck. Thus, it naturally came to mean "to give complete attention to." The admonition concerns the practice of our righteousness. It is putting into action in a tangible way the fruit or nature of our relationship with God and letting it benefit and bless others. It is not enough to do the right things, however. We must do so with the right intent and attitude.

This verse makes it explicitly clear that what we know affects who we are. Who we really are governs what we do, and what we do reveals to others who we are. In the end, all of these things disclose what we have with God.

As we live out our righteousness, we are not to do so in a way that calls attention to our acts of service or ministry. These are dedicated to God, who sees all. If we do ministry to be seen or recognized by people, we have already received our "reward" ("wages" or "recognition due") and dishonored the intimate nature of ministry, which is to be consecrated solely to God (see Matthew 5:12, 16). Some acts of ministry are very public and cannot be hidden. However, even these should be done in such a way that the focus is not drawn to us, but to our "Father which is in heaven." Ministry (any act of service to God) is not about reward, reputation or recompense. It is a manifested act of love dedicated to God in the service of His kingdom. The immediate reward is in the intimate nature of the fulfilling relationship we have with God. The future reward will more than make up for the private nature of our service.

B. Charitable Deeds (vv. 2-4)

2. Therefore when thou doest thine alms, do not sound a trumpet before thee, as the hypocrites do in the synagogues and in the streets, that they may have glory of men. Verily I say unto you, They have their reward.

3. But when thou doest alms, let not thy left hand know what thy right hand doeth:

4. That thine alms may be in secret: and thy Father which seeth in secret himself shall reward thee openly.

Verse 2 introduces the acts of righteousness that are expected of a believer. *Alms* are "charitable deeds" or "acts of mercy." The Biblical concept of *mercy* is love manifested in a tangible manner. God's mercy was manifested in Jesus' dying

---

alms—righteousness or piety

Talk About It:
1. When is there "no reward" from God for acts of righteousness? Why?
2. Why are some people satisfied with merely being "seen of men"?

"There are no crown-wearers in heaven that were not cross-bearers here on earth."
—**Charles Spurgeon**

Talk About It:
1. Describe the reward of hypocritical do-gooders.
2. Explain the phrase, "Do not let your left hand know what your right hand is doing" (v. 3, *NKJV*).

"Our greatest pretenses are built up not to hide the evil and the ugly in us, but our emptiness. The hardest thing to hide is something that is not there."
—Eric Hoffer

thy closet (v. 6)— your room

on the cross for us, though we did not deserve it (Romans 5:8). Thus, our acts of mercy should allow God's love to flow through us to others, even if we are not certain they deserve it. This may include giving money or goods to those in need or the poor (Deuteronomy 15:12-14; Matthew 5:42), but it is not limited to such. Mercy can take many different forms, such as mentoring a young person, assisting an overwhelmed mother of toddlers, offering words of encouragement, or standing with someone going through trying circumstances. Further, these are not to be occasional acts, but a lifestyle of service.

Again, it is an act dedicated unto God, but benefits others. Thus, it is difficult to keep entirely private. However, it is not to be done in such a way as to specifically draw attention to us or our act, as hypocrites do. The term for *hypocrite* originally was used of actors ("to play a part"), who wore masks to hide their true identity. The imagery is appropriate. Hypocrites do things to be recognized and glorified by others.

There is some debate over whether the "blowing of a trumpet" represents (1) a figurative image of calling attention to our acts of compassion, (2) a literal trumpet designed to get the public's attention, or (3) the blowing of the trumpets at the synagogue or Temple to announce the collection for the poor. Regardless of how one views the first-century interpretation, the message for the 21st century is clear—what we do must not be for our own glory. It is done in secret as much as possible and not advertised for self-promotion (v. 3). Our acts of compassion and love are dedicated to our heavenly Father alone, who takes note of our actions and our attitudes and rewards us appropriately (v. 4). Even though God will reward us "openly," our acts of mercy are motivated by love for God and humanity, not the hope of reward.

II. PRAYER AND FORGIVENESS (Matthew 6:5-15)
A. The Attitude of Prayer (vv. 5-8)

5. And when thou prayest, thou shalt not be as the hypocrites are: for they love to pray standing in the synagogues and in the corners of the streets, that they may be seen of men. Verily I say unto you, They have their reward.

6. But thou, when thou prayest, enter into thy closet, and when thou hast shut thy door, pray to thy Father which is in secret; and thy Father which seeth in secret shall reward thee openly.

7. But when ye pray, use not vain repetitions, as the heathen do: for they think that they shall be heard for their much speaking.

8. Be not ye therefore like unto them: for your Father knoweth what things ye have need of, before ye ask him.

The second example of a believer's manifested righteousness is *prayer*. "When thou prayest" (v. 5) means "at the time you pray." It does not carry the idea of "*if* you pray." There is the expectation of prayer in Jesus' teaching. Prayer is how we approach and communicate with God concerning our needs, wants, struggles, hurts and requests. The focus is not to be on grammatical construction or impressive platitudes. Prayer is intimate communication between a believer and God. Its source is to be the "heart" rather than the "head." As such, it is a private conversation, though it may be overheard by others, as in "the synagogues" (or a place of worship). Even then, the focus is to be on communicating with God, not impressing others.

Standing is one of the positions associated with prayer (Mark 11:25), though one may sit (1 Chronicles 17:16) or kneel (Psalm 95:6). In times of great brokenness, prostrating one's self before God was common (Matthew 26:39). The position of the body is not as important as the position of the heart.

Jesus is not forbidding public prayer. He prayed specifically at times so others could hear (John 11:41, 42). Here, He is addressing the issue of private prayer (Matthew 6:6). We are to find a place that allows us freedom to pray as we feel, away from the pressure of performing for others ("shut the door"), and communicate and commune with our heavenly Father. In His timing and His way, God will bless us or reward us in public for our private commitment to Him.

Prayer is not to consist of "vain repetitions" (v. 7), which comes from a word meaning "to babble thoughtlessly." In some heathen prayers, a meaningless term was taken and repeated over and over to fill the time of prayer. Jesus teaches that prayer is to be meaningful, not mindless (also see Ecclesiastes 5:2). It is the content of our prayers that is important, not the quantity of our words. This does not mean that a brief but meaningful prayer is all we should utter. Following the example of Jesus, we must have times of extended prayer with God (Luke 6:12). The Father is well aware of our needs (Matthew 6:8; also see Isaiah 65:24). He wants our presence in His presence.

B. The Application of Prayer (vv. 9-15)

9. After this manner therefore pray ye: Our Father which art in heaven, Hallowed be thy name.

10. Thy kingdom come. Thy will be done in earth, as it is in heaven.

11. Give us this day our daily bread.

12. And forgive us our debts, as we forgive our debtors.

13. And lead us not into temptation, but deliver us from evil: For thine is the kingdom, and the power, and the glory, for ever. Amen.

Talk About It:
1. How can we assure that our public prayers are sincere instead of showy?
2. Where is your "closet" of prayer? How often do you enter it?
3. What are "vain repetitions," and why is it so easy for our prayers to become full of them?
4. If the Father knows what we need before we ask Him, why ask?

"We must distinguish prayer from prayers. Saying prayers is one activity among others. But prayer is an attitude of the heart that can transform every activity."
—**David Stendl-Rast**

14. For if ye forgive men their trespasses, your heaven-ly Father will also forgive you:

15. But if ye forgive not men their trespasses, neither will your Father forgive your trespasses.

"In this manner" (*NKJV*) reveals this is a pattern to teach disciples of all ages how to pray. It is not a rigid form that must be spoken verbatim each time we pray (see Luke 11:2-4); neither is it the only prayer we are to pray (see John 17). It contains the primary areas upon which we should focus when we pray. *Pray* carries the force of a continual command. It is to be a habit that is not monotonous. That is, Jesus commands us to pray regularly, but it is not to be approached as a chore or accomplished carelessly. Prayer is an act of worship whereby one approaches God to find His heart and to reveal (lay bare) the heart of the worshiper. In prayer these two hearts are conjoined and a transformation takes place in the heart of the worshiper as it becomes more like the heart of God. It is in prayer that one loses sight of the earthly perspective and begins to see through spiritual eyes the possibilities, provision and perfection of God.

"Our Father" first reveals the interconnectedness of the believing community. He is the Father of all believers. As a prayerful worshiper, we are part of a great body of believers approaching "our" God. Second, it brings us into continuity with Christ. Only in the Lord's Prayer does He use this phrase. Elsewhere, He says "my Father" (Matthew 12:50) or "your Father" (6:1, 8, 15), not "our Father," as here and in Luke 11:2. Third, it is a reminder of our relationship with our heavenly Father. It is a relationship of love, devotion and protection. He watches over us as a parent provides for and protects his or her child. The language recalls the intimacy of the Aramaic "Abba, Father" (Mark 14:36; Romans 8:15), a reminder of the close relationship we have with God. Fourth, it is a reminder that we are the sons and daughters of God because of the Son of God (Matthew 5:9, 45; Galatians 3:26). Also, in the ancient world one's name reflected all the qualities associated with the meaning of the name. Thus, all the communicable qualities (e.g., love, holiness and life) of the Father are available to seeking believers.

The first petition of the Lord's Prayer is for His name to be *hallowed*, or "consecrated"—literally, "sanctified" or "made holy" (Matthew 6:9). How does one make God's name any more holy? After all, He is the essence of holiness! It is one of His three primary characteristics, along with love and life. As Christians, what we say and do reflects upon the world's image of God. These words and actions also reflect our own view of God. A haphazard life reveals we really do not believe that God is who He says. As we seek to live out the teachings of Jesus and

Talk About It:
1. Why is praise a critical part of prayer?
2. Explain the phrase, "Your kingdom come" (v. 10, *NKJV*).
3. Is it possible for God's will not to be done on earth? Why or why not?
4. What is God's part in leading us away from temptation, and what is our part?
5. Why is forgiving others necessary if we want forgiveness from God?

Following the Holy Spirit

Prayer can no more be divorced from worship than life can be divorced from breathing. If we follow His impulse, the Holy Spirit will always lead us to pray. When we allow Him to work freely, He will always bring the church to extensive praying. Conversely, when the Spirit is absent, we will find excuses not to pray. We may say, "God understands. He knows I love Him. But I'm tired . . . I'm so busy . . . It's just

Scripture to the best of our ability and His provision, His name is "sanctified" in our lives and the eyes of those watching us.

The second petition is literally translated "Come, Your kingdom!" It is an authoritative cry, seeking the establishment of God's kingdom in the life of the one praying. God's kingdom is not a place, though it includes heaven and earth. It is the rule and reign of God upon all creation—visible and invisible, temporal and eternal. Here, it is a cry that God will enact His power, provision and love each day in the heart and world of the disciple. Some see in this verse a declaration that believers are to establish the kingdom of God on the earth for God. Certainly, God's rule is increased on earth through the obedience of believers; however, we can only establish the Kingdom (and live obediently) through God's power. In brief, this petition is a request for God to sit upon the throne of the believer's heart and rule and reign in powerful majesty, awesome mystery, and effective accomplishment—as only God can do.

"Your will be done—on earth as it is in heaven" (v. 10, *NKJV*) is the third petition of the prayerful seeker and closely linked to the previous petition. It reflects a deep desire that the earth (especially the world of the believer) be brought into conformity with the perfect way the will of God is carried out in heaven (e.g., Revelation 4; 5). It is the desire to see God's will established now in the heart of the worshiper and the world at large, not just in the end time. It begins with a cry of desperation in the heart of the one praying, but must move from his or her mouth to the mind and the heart (determination and attitude), then to the hands and feet (character and actions). In one sense, it is a sacrificial prayer. The worshiper is laying down his or her desires, ambitions and life in order that God's will can be established personally, then the worshiper can be utilized as an instrument to help establish the divine will on the earth. It is a costly prayer.

The fourth petition moves from the grander scheme of things to the personal needs of the worshiper, "Give us this day our daily bread" (v. 11). Some see a reference here to Communion or the Word as bread. These are part of what Jesus has in mind, but not the totality. It is a recognition that anything we receive comes as a gift from God, much like the manna of the Exodus event (Exodus 16:15-32). These gifts enable us to live life now in an extraordinary fashion, not just look forward to eternal life (see John 10:10b). This declaratory petition includes both material and spiritual provision. The worshiper is seeking neither riches nor poverty, but acknowledges and embraces a day-by-day reliance upon God for all of life's needs.

The fifth petition addresses the needs of the worshiper on a relational level (v. 12). Forgiveness is foundational and essential

not convenient now. . . ." When the Spirit is absent, our excuses always seem right, but in the presence of the Spirit our excuses fade away.
—**K.T. Kendall**

Public Praying
As a student at Lee College, I was asked to pray over the class. I included all the right platitudes, delivered with a lofty tone. A good friend was sitting next to me. When I concluded, he whispered, "That was the prayer of an overseer, if ever I heard one." It was not a remark to demean those who are over us in the Lord, but was intended to question my attitude and motivation for praying. His words struck and stuck. Even public prayer should be personal communication between the person praying and the heavenly Father, who hears and answers.
—**Keith Whitt**

for the worshiper. Without God's forgiveness, we cannot become a follower of Christ (Ephesians 1:7). Without forgiveness offered to others, we cannot remain a follower (Matthew 5:23, 24). Here, again, Jesus links our forgiveness from sin with our forgiveness of others who have wronged us. The reasoning behind this is, What right do we have to ask God to forgive us, when we will not do the same for others? *Debt* can be "a sin," "something owed," or "an offense." It is an all-encompassing term. *Forgiveness* is a willful releasing of the pain, embarrassment, and desire for retaliation. It is a conscious decision to bring down the "wall" that separates us from the other person and start the relationship over on better terms—God's terms. We may be able to hide our lack of forgiveness here and now, but all things are known by the Father and will be judged in the future (Matthew 18:32-35).

The spiritual level is addressed by the sixth petition—"Lead us not into temptation, but deliver us from evil" (6:13). It reflects a desire and need for God to intervene in the spiritual struggles of the worshiper. Everyone is tempted. Scripture seems to suggest that each believer has an area of weakness or temptation, concerning which he or she must be diligent (Hebrews 12:1). Having an area of weakness does not mean that a person is destined to failure; rather, it means that he or she must rely upon the sustaining power of God and proactively flee circumstances that could lead to sin. *But* is a strong word that sets the tone for the petition and seeks deliverance from any association with "evil." God does not tempt us (James 1:13); thus, this is a plea asking God to keep us from any circumstances that may compromise our spiritual walk with Him.

The prayer ends with a doxology or declaration of praise and the foundation of this prayer (Matthew 6:13). Everything belongs to God. It is His "kingdom" of which we are members. It is His "power" and ability in which we operate. He deserves "the glory" (majesty) and honor. The prayer is punctuated with another reminder of the need for forgiveness to be offered to others and the consequences of an unforgiving heart (vv. 14, 15). Such repetition must be taken to heart.

III. FASTING (Matthew 6:16-18; 9:14, 15)
A. Appropriate Fasting (6:16-18)

16. Moreover when ye fast, be not, as the hypocrites, of a sad countenance: for they disfigure their faces, that they may appear unto men to fast. Verily I say unto you, They have their reward.

17. But thou, when thou fastest, anoint thine head, and wash thy face;

18. That thou appear not unto men to fast, but unto thy

Prayer Brings Victory

It is not preaching, teaching, singing or organizing; it is the Word of God brought against Satan's lies through prayer. Our prayers build the kingdom of God and destroy the kingdom of Satan. But where there is no prayer, there is no warfare. Where there is no warfare, there is no spiritual reality. Where there is no spiritual reality, there is no victory. Where there is no victory, there is nothing glorifying to God.

—Charles Stanley

Personal Piety

Father which is in secret: and thy Father, which seeth in secret, shall reward thee openly.

Scripture teaches corporate (Nehemiah 9:1) and private (Daniel 9:3) fasting. Here, Jesus reinforces the practice and addresses the manner in which we are to conduct private fasting. Like the previous teachings on "doing righteousness" through "acts of mercy" (see Matthew 6:1-4) and prayer (vv. 5-8), fasting (the third manifestation of righteousness in His teaching) is to be a personal matter between the worshiper and the Father (v. 18). It is not to be practiced for recognition by others. The Pharisees fasted on Mondays and Thursdays, and some made it obvious to those around them. Jesus strongly condemns this behavior. If anything, we are to go out of our way to keep it as a matter between us and the Lord (v. 17). The rabbis taught that the person fasting should wear sackcloth and place ashes upon his or her face. Believers, however, are to wash and anoint their faces with oil (see Isaiah 61:3). It is God who sees and rewards.

B. Necessity of Proper Fasting (9:14, 15)

14. Then came to him the disciples of John, saying, Why do we and the Pharisees fast oft, but thy disciples fast not?

15. And Jesus said unto them, Can the children of the bridechamber mourn, as long as the bridegroom is with them? but the days will come, when the bridegroom shall be taken from them, and then shall they fast.

Here, the disciples of John the Baptist approach Jesus with their questions concerning the supposed lack of fasting by His own disciples. Jesus explains that there are times of fasting and times of celebration. Both are part of our spiritual walk. In the Old Testament, periods of fasting were usually ended with times of celebration (see Zechariah 8:19). Jesus knew the disciples would need to fast after He was "taken from them." If the disciples needed to fast, so does the modern church. Fasting is a personal, spiritual discipline with physical and spiritual results. Although Jesus seems to be addressing personal fasting here, it is appropriate for congregations to practice periods of fasting (Acts 13:1, 2).

CONCLUSION

Living out our righteousness can be challenging at times. Jesus sets forth teaching that provides a secure foundation for effective righteousness—acts of mercy, prayer and fasting. Notice the order. Concern for others will motivate us to pray. Prayer helps us see our need to be more like Jesus. Fasting enables our hearts to be open to the necessary changes.

Talk About It:
1. Describe the fasting of hypocrites and what it accomplishes.
2. How does God want His children to fast, and why?

Talk About It:
Why should Christians practice fasting today?

"Many people would wear sackcloth and ashes to appear to others as fasting, while on the inside they were not broken, humble or mourning their sin. Consequently, Jesus . . . encouraged the people to wear their sackcloth and ashes on the inside for God to see, instead of on the outside for man to see."
—Billy Wilson

GOLDEN TEXT CHALLENGE

"BE YE THEREFORE PERFECT, EVEN AS YOUR FATHER WHICH IS IN HEAVEN IS PERFECT" (Matthew 5:48).

The absolute perfection of God is not attainable, but love, which is perfect—relative to humanity's capacity and condition—is attainable. The followers of Christ have divine capacity within them. Approach to Godlike personality is possible. The beginnings of perfection, its seeds, are already there. The aim of their life is to press on to this perfection, to allow the Holy Spirit to shape their soul into one that bears the likeness of God.

The "perfect" are not people with a conceit of perfection, but aspirants such as Paul, who seek to attain (Philippians 3:12). The perfection which would be impossible for us in and of ourselves is possible for us in and from our Christ.

Wise Living

INTRODUCTION

This lesson brings to a close the examination of the Sermon on the Mount (Matthew 5:1—7:29), which has been the focus for the previous three lessons. The Sermon on the Mount is paradoxical. Does it mean what it says (literal meaning), or does it say what it means (deeper meaning)? It contains both commands and concepts that make us uncomfortable, yet other aspects are comforting. For example, in the previous lessons we have learned that we must not shut up the doors of our hearts (or resources) to those in need (5:40-42). Trying to figure out how all this works out in practical terms can be disconcerting, to say the least. Yet it is comforting to know that God is aware of our every need (and struggle), and as we seek Him first, He supplies our needs (6:31-33).

Jesus includes intentional tension in His teaching. He purposely pushes our minds and hearts to the edge of discomfort, so that we are not dependent upon easy answers or simple formulas in our walk with Him. If the Bible addressed every situation we are likely to encounter and thoroughly answered every question we will ever have, no one would be able to read it all in several lifetimes! In fact, it seems the more time we spend in the Word, the more we realize the less we know! This tension is designed to lead us to a deeper maturity. We come to the realization that we need divine assistance in determining how the Word is to be understood and applied to our lives and circumstances. This requires a continual dependency upon and communion with the Holy Spirit (see 1 Peter 1:22).

We cannot treat others justly (Matthew 7:1-6), apply God's wisdom to our lives (vv. 7-14), or embrace the warnings of Jesus (vv. 15-29) apart from the ministry of the Spirit and the communion of the saints. The Christian way is difficult at times, but not impossible. It is challenging yet comforting. It is confusing yet simple—we must provide God a willing vessel and participate in His transformative process, accept His provision and do His will.

Unit Theme:
The Teachings of Jesus (Matthew)

Central Truth:
Christ's teachings are the foundation for wise living.

Focus:
Examine Christ's instructions for wise living and apply them to our lives.

Context:
Christ teaches on a high hill or mountain near Capernaum in A.D. 28.

Golden Text:
"Whosoever heareth these sayings of mine [Christ], and doeth them, I will liken him unto a wise man, which built his house upon a rock" (Matthew 7:24).

Study Outline:
I. Do Not Judge Others (Matthew 7:1-6)
II. Choose Wisely (Matthew 7:7-14)
III. Heed Christ's Warnings (Matthew 7:15-29)

I. DO NOT JUDGE OTHERS (Matthew 7:1-6)

A. Reciprocal Judgment (vv. 1, 2)

1. Judge not, that ye be not judged.

2. For with what judgment ye judge, ye shall be judged: and with what measure ye mete, it shall be measured to you again.

The section begins with a command—"Do not judge." The Greek can be translated correctly either as "Stop judging" or "Do not make a practice (habit) of judging." The passage makes plain that whatever judgment we make, it will be reciprocated in like manner and degree to us (v. 2).

Judge can mean several distinct things: (1) "to decide a matter in a legal proceeding"; (2) "to resolve or determine a matter based on a personal or corporate decision"; (3) "to prefer one person over another based on personal evaluation"; (4) "to evaluate a person based on personal estimation"; (5) "to criticize or judge a person's behavior or character." The first meaning is consistent with Scriptural commands and examples (Deuteronomy 1:16) and the judgment of God (2 Timothy 4:1). The second was practiced by the New Testament church (Acts 15:1-29). The third aspect can be taken in a positive or negative manner. Everyone has people with whom they prefer to spend time, based upon mutual interests and personal chemistry. However, if we begin to think of and treat some people as better than others, we are violating Scripture (James 2:1-9). This may be part of what Jesus is conveying. The fourth aspect is another Biblical concept, if used correctly. Encouragement, exhortation and edification of one another requires proper evaluation, based on Biblical criteria (Hebrews 10:24; Colossians 3:16). Thus, it is the final aspect that Jesus has in mind.

Jesus is not teaching us to stop thinking, evaluating things with critical (thorough, not negative) thinking, or ignore the presence of sin in the church; rather, He is teaching us to be considerate and generous in our evaluation of others (see Matthew 18:15-17). Rash, critical judgments are to be avoided. We do not have access to the person's inner struggles, thoughts and prayers. Judgment without knowing the heart presumes the place and function of God (James 4:11, 12), who alone knows the thoughts and intents of the person (1 Chronicles 28:9). Improper judgment will result not only in a comparable judgment by others (Job 4:8), but more importantly, God will judge us in like manner (Romans 2:5-10; James 2:13). The Biblical purpose of judgment is to right any wrongdoing. This should be our goal when evaluating a situation or person.

B. Proper Perspectives (vv. 3-5)

3. And why beholdest thou the mote that is in thy brother's

Talk About It:
1. Why is it so easy to judge others?
2. In what sense do we determine the severity of our own judgment?

"I will not judge a person to be spiritually dead whom I have judged formerly to have had spiritual life, though I see him at present in a swoon as to all evidences of the spiritual life. And the reason why I will not judge him so is this—because if you judge a person dead, you leave him, you neglect him; but if you judge him in a swoon, though never so dangerous, you use all means for the retrieving of his life."
—**John Owen**

---

eye, but considerest not the beam that is in thine own eye?

4. Or how wilt thou say to thy brother, Let me pull out the mote out of thine eye; and, behold, a beam is in thine own eye?

5. Thou hypocrite, first cast out the beam out of thine own eye; and then shalt thou see clearly to cast out the mote out of thy brother's eye.

Continuing the theme of improper judgment, Jesus illustrates the concept with a vivid and purposely outrageous analogy. He asks "why" a person feels the need to examine a small flaw in a brother (v. 3). This addresses the motivation of the examiner. Those who watch over our souls (pastors, teachers) must be diligent in keeping an eye on our lives, as they will answer to God (Hebrews 13:17). However, Jesus is addressing those whose motives and lives are impure. They carefully and specifically examine ("behold") the "speck of sawdust" (*NIV*) in a "brother's eye." *Brother* is often used in Scripture to refer to both male and female members of the church. The examiner is not looking at the world, but another person in the church. Instead of edifying, the examiner is tearing down the person for a small area of need in his or her life, but does not perceive a major flaw ("beam," or log) in his or her own life. Notice the contrasts that Jesus sets up: a carefully examined speck of sawdust in another and an unperceived beam by the one judging.

The second aspect of the analogy addresses credibility (v. 4). The language conveys the meaning, "What right do you have to even ask your brother about a small matter when you have a major problem?" The critical examiner's words carry no authority or conviction, because of the blatantly obvious (but ignored) sin in his or her own life.

Finally, Jesus addresses the arrogance of the person judging and the correction needed (v. 5). *Hypocrite* reveals that the person appears to be concerned, but in reality is critical. Jesus says the solution is to get our priorities and lives right ("first"). Before we can minister to others, we must carefully examine and address areas of sin in our own lives. We cannot lead others to a place we have not been. He does not tell us to ignore the sin in the lives of others, but to take care of our own lives before we address their needs. This results in pure motivations and Biblical methods.

C. Precious Pearls (v. 6)

6. Give not that which is holy unto the dogs, neither cast ye your pearls before swine, lest they trample them under their feet, and turn again and rend you.

Talk About It:
1. Why is it so easy to overlook the flaws in our own character?
2. Put Christ's teaching in verse 5 in your own words.

"Lord, where we are wrong, make us willing to change, and where we are right, make us easy to live with."
—**Peter Marshall**

Talk About It:
1. Whom does Christ refer to as "dogs" and "swine"? Why?
2. How does this verse call for wisdom and discretion?

This verse seems to be out of place at first glance. However, it brings perspective to the issue at hand. *Dogs* in the early world were not domesticated pets. They traveled in packs and were quite vicious; thus, they were considered unclean (see Revelation 22:15). Holy things (e.g., sacrificial meat) were reserved for priests, not for dogs (cf. Exodus 22:31). *Pigs* were also considered unclean (Leviticus 11:7), whereas *pearls* were scarce and costly. No one would think of putting pearls on a pig. They would be treated contemptuously ("trample"), because that is a pig's nature.

In brief, Jesus emphatically says we are not to be harsh in our assessment of others, without ignoring unrepentant sin. We must be discerning, without being judgmental. Further, not everyone will be open for correction and edification. If our ministry is not received, we should not waste precious time and energy with those who repeatedly reject it (unless directed by God to do so). The gospel itself, or the kingdom of heaven, is a "pearl" (Matthew 13:45, 46).

II. CHOOSE WISELY (Matthew 7:7-14)
A. Tenacity and Reward (vv. 7-11)

7. Ask, and it shall be given you; seek, and ye shall find; knock, and it shall be opened unto you:

8. For every one that asketh receiveth; and he that seeketh findeth; and to him that knocketh it shall be opened.

9. Or what man is there of you, whom if his son ask bread, will he give him a stone?

10. Or if he ask a fish, will he give him a serpent?

11. If ye then, being evil, know how to give good gifts unto your children, how much more shall your Father which is in heaven give good things to them that ask him?

Talk About It:
1. When is prayer like *asking*? Like *seeking*? Like *knocking*?
2. How is the heavenly Father like a good earthly dad? How is the heavenly Father greater?

Ask is a common term used "to make a request of" (e.g., Matthew 5:42), "to make a demand" (e.g., Luke 23:23), or "to request something in prayer" (e.g., Matthew 6:8; 21:22). The intensity of the request depends on the seriousness of the situation, much like the fervency of prayer. It can be translated, "Keep asking." Heaven can be tough to find at times! Our requests must be taken to God, who has the ability to grant requests consistent with His Word ("it shall be given you"). However, there are times when we do not know what to pray for. These times require searching for the proper words, answers from Scripture, the will of God concerning the need, and the right thing to request ("keep seeking"). Continued seeking is not in vain ("you shall find"). The last part of verse 7, again, requires action or focus on our part. When God "opens" something, it leads to the miraculous (see Matthew 3:16; 9:30; 17:27; 27:52).

A final observation is required on verse 7. Three of the verbs are active (activity by the subject, *us*: "ask," "seek" and "knock"). There are two divine passive verbs that reveal activity on God's part, not ours ("it shall be given," and "it shall be opened"). One would expect the seeking on our part to be answered by another divine passive—that is, God revealing to us what we seek. However, that is not the case. The active verb indicates that *as* we seek, we will discover experiences, wisdom and knowledge, or things that cannot be obtained quickly.

Verse 8 reinforces the teaching on prayer. The divine passive ("it shall be opened") remains the same. We cannot open it. First, we all have "doors" in our lives that refuse to open of our accord. As we persist in prayer, we are changed, listening more carefully to what God says and following where He leads; thus, we are brought to the place of readiness for the door to be opened by Him. Second, we cannot force the second coming of Jesus Christ. However, as we "knock" in prayer, God assures us that one day (though we do not know when—see Matthew 24:44) the door will be opened and we shall see our Savior. The knocking keeps us at the proper door and continually aware of His soon return.

Jesus further reinforces and expands His teaching through the use of two analogies. He asks "what man" (includes men and women) would give a stone to a son seeking a loaf of bread (v. 9). The grammar indicates that He expected a negative reply: "No one." Some of the stones in Israel are similar in appearance to a round loaf of bread. Again, He asks who would give a snake when a fish is requested (v. 10). Some suggest that the eel-like catfish of Galilee looks similar to a snake. The primary point is summed up in verse 11: God will give only good things to those who seek Him.

Three points are in order. First, Jesus recognizes the inherent sin of humanity. Apart from Him, no matter how good we are in humanity's eyes, we are still "evil" (wicked, or unprofitable). Only a right relationship with God makes us righteous in His sight. Second, if sinful parents protect their children, how much more will God protect us and lead us to "good" (beneficial) things? Third, a comparison with similar material in Luke (11:9-13, the Sermon on the Plain) discloses that Jesus taught these good things include the gift of the Holy Spirit.

B. The Golden Rule (v. 12)

12. Therefore all things whatsoever ye would that men should do to you, do ye even so to them: for this is the law and the prophets.

The Golden Rule is one of the best-known verses in the Bible. A similar saying is found in Jewish teaching (and a few other

Prevailing Prayer
God looks not at the elegancy of your prayers, to see how neat they are; nor yet at the geometry of your prayers, to see how long they are; nor yet at the arithmetic of your prayers, to see how many they are; nor yet at the music of your prayers, nor yet at the sweetness of your voice, nor yet at the logic of your prayers; but at the sincerity of your prayers, how hearty they are. There is no prayer acknowledged, approved, accepted, recorded, or rewarded by God, but that wherein the heart is sincerely and wholly. The true mother would not have the child divided. God loves a broken and a contrite heart, so He loathes a divided heart. God neither loves halting or halving.
—Thomas Brooks

Talk About It:
1. When is it most difficult to follow the Golden Rule?
2. How is this one command "a summary of all that is taught in the law and the prophets" (*NLT*)?

religions), though it is always formed in the negative: "What you hate, you should not do to anyone else" (Tobit 4:15, my translation). Jesus makes it clear we are to proactively do good to others, following the example of the Father's goodness to us.

"Therefore" can also be translated "accordingly," connecting it to God's graciousness to us in the previous verse, or even back to the teaching on judging and treatment of others (vv. 1-6). It is a comprehensive command. "Whatsoever" ("whatever things") does not seem to exclude any area of life. We are not merely to abstain from doing evil or harm to others. We must seek out ways to treat others the way we wish or desire to be treated. Obeying this commandment fulfills the Scriptures ("the Law and the Prophets," or the entire Old Testament) concerning our treatment of others. Jesus, again, rephrases this concept in Matthew 22:36-40. Repetition reinforces the teaching and the importance of the teaching to the Teacher.

C. Two Ways (vv. 13, 14)
13. Enter ye in at the strait gate: for wide is the gate, and broad is the way, that leadeth to destruction, and many there be which go in thereat:
14. Because strait is the gate, and narrow is the way, which leadeth unto life, and few there be that find it.

In the ancient walled cities, people entered and exited during the day through the main gates. Closed gates prevented enemies from entering. Usually, there was a small gate in the side wall of the city through which servants passed when the gates were closed. It was small enough that one person could pass through, but not an invading army.

Talk About It:
1. Why is the road to hell called "wide" and "broad"?
2. How responsible are we to help others "find" the narrow way?

Jesus explains in this section that there are two ways set before us: the "broad" or spacious way that brings "destruction" or eternal loss (the wide gate), or the "narrow" way that follows His teachings and results in a quality of life now and eternal life in the future (the narrow gate). Rejection of His teaching results in destruction. There is no middle ground (see Deuteronomy 11:26-28). "Few" does not limit the saved to a small number of elect. It is understood in relation to the vast number of people who have ever lived. Elsewhere, Jesus explains that "many" will come from all directions (Matthew 8:11) and, further, that His life serves as a "ransom for many" (20:28).

Some have suggested that the small servant's gate in the ancient cities was only large enough for the servant to pass through. Any load being carried had to be passed or pulled through the gate before the servant could get through—a very appropriate depiction of the disciple's life. We alone come through the door to Jesus. All burdens must be stripped off and submitted to Him, or left behind outside the gate of our journey.

"Destiny is never a matter of chance, it is a matter of choice."
—William Jennings Bryan

III. HEED CHRIST'S WARNINGS (Matthew 7:15-29)

A. Prophets and Trees (vv. 15-20)

15. Beware of false prophets, which come to you in sheep's clothing, but inwardly they are ravening wolves.

16. Ye shall know them by their fruits. Do men gather grapes of thorns, or figs of thistles?

17. Even so every good tree bringeth forth good fruit; but a corrupt tree bringeth forth evil fruit.

18. A good tree cannot bring forth evil fruit, neither can a corrupt tree bring forth good fruit.

19. Every tree that bringeth not forth good fruit is hewn down, and cast into the fire.

20. Wherefore by their fruits ye shall know them.

The prophetic anointing was known to Matthew's readers. Several times, he emphasizes Old Testament verses, applied to Jesus with a common formulary ("this was done to fulfill what the prophet spoke") to show how He fulfills the Old Testament prophecies (see 1:22; 3:3; 13:35). Further, Jesus speaks of receiving "a prophet in the name of a prophet" (10:41) and announces He is sending prophets (23:34). The problem He addresses in our text—"false prophets"—is not the office or anointing of a prophet, but those who claim to be something they are not. They come in the outer garment of domesticated sheep. In reality, they are "inwardly ravenous wolves," whose nature is to destroy and steal. We must be diligent (see Proverbs 1:32).

The function of a prophet is to speak to the people on behalf of God. A prophet may speak things that relate to the future (foretelling) or speak the things of God that edify and encourage the hearer (forth-telling). What he or she says must come true (Deuteronomy 18:18-22). Jesus assures His disciples that the true nature of a prophet (or teacher, leader, minister) will be evident by the fruit they produce (Matthew 7:16). Grapes are not found in thorn bushes, and figs are not collected from thistles. Wild weeds do not produce fruit; they hinder fruitful growth and inflict pain. Only healthy ("good") trees produce beautiful ("good") fruit (vv. 17, 18). "Every tree that does not make honest fruit is cut off and cast into fire" (v. 19, author's translation). The timing of this action is vague, but the certainty of it is not in doubt.

It is normal for us to want God to intervene immediately when we see a false prophet or someone leading others astray; however, God even loves the souls of those who destroy the people of God. Judgment will come, but before judgment an opportunity for repentance is given. God is just. His righteousness requires that He deal with sin in His time. He alone knows the hearts of those we would "cut off" immediately. Further, fire can have destructive and purifying effects. The lack of an article

Talk About It:
1. Why do false prophets wear sheep's clothing?
2. How do you distinguish a genuine prophet from a false one?

"The devil can cite Scripture for his purpose."
—William Shakespeare

("the") in the Greek indicates this fire may not be the eternal fire (though it may), but could be corrective in nature. As Jesus has pointed out, we are not to judge harshly, but examine the fruit for evidence of a person's nature and God's intervention (v. 20).

B. Works and Knowledge (vv. 21-23)

(Matthew 7:21-23 is not included in the printed text.)

Jesus builds on the previous passage with a section that teaches (1) prayer must be accompanied by doing the will of the Father to be effective (v. 21); (2) miraculous works are not evidence of right relationship with God (v. 22), as even the devil can produce deceptive miracles (2 Corinthians 11:14); and (3) only intimate knowledge of Jesus Christ (salvation) will save us from destruction (Matthew 7:23). It is not enough to know who He is and what He requires; we must *know* Him.

C. Rock and Sand (vv. 24-27)

24. Therefore whosoever heareth these sayings of mine, and doeth them, I will liken him unto a wise man, which built his house upon a rock:

25. And the rain descended, and the floods came, and the winds blew, and beat upon that house; and it fell not: for it was founded upon a rock.

26. And every one that heareth these sayings of mine, and doeth them not, shall be likened unto a foolish man, which built his house upon the sand:

27. And the rain descended, and the floods came, and the winds blew, and beat upon that house; and it fell: and great was the fall of it.

Jesus sums up and challenges the hearers with a tale of two builders, underscoring the two ways of life. A structure is only as good as its foundation. If the foundation is faulty or built upon the wrong substance, it will not stand over time, no matter how beautiful the appearance. It may look nice, but time and the elements will take their toll on what most cannot see. A proper foundation for disciples consists of *hearing* the teaching of Jesus and *doing* what He teaches (v. 24). If we do this, we are declared to be like a wise man. Failure to do so results in being declared to be like a foolish man, whose structure "will fall with a mighty crash" (v. 27, *NLT*). It will rain and the wind will "beat against" our structures. That is a fact of the fallen world in which we live. Only those who build upon the Rock will be successful.

D. Jesus and Scribes (vv. 28, 29)

(Matthew 7:28, 29 is not included in the printed text.)

The chapter closes with an observation by Matthew. The crowds were "astonished" (literally, "overwhelmed") at the authoritative

Wise Living

teaching of Jesus. It was unlike anything they had ever heard from the "scribes"—the experts in the Law.

CONCLUSION

Life is full of options and choices. We can allow our suspicions and imaginations to rule us (and destroy others), or we can choose to extend to others the same grace and consideration we need from them. We can allow the base nature of humanity to rule over us, or we can choose life in Jesus Christ. The teachings of Jesus have endured the tests of time, the scrutiny of skeptics, and the attacks of the Enemy. Two ways are set before us. Which do you choose?

GOLDEN TEXT CHALLENGE

"WHOSOEVER HEARETH THESE SAYINGS OF MINE [CHRIST], AND DOETH THEM, I WILL LIKEN HIM UNTO A WISE MAN, WHICH BUILT HIS HOUSE UPON A ROCK" (Matthew 7:24).

Jesus concluded the Sermon on the Mount with a powerful illustration which called for a personal application of the truths He taught. They must not only hear what He says, but act upon His words.

The person who builds his life on the Word is likened to the one who builds his house on a rock. In either case, there is a solid foundation. Paul had the wise builder in mind when he wrote, "For no one can lay any foundation other than the one already laid, which is Jesus Christ" (1 Corinthians 3:11, *NIV*).

When one is building on the right foundation, the house or the life withstands the severest tests. Let rain fall in torrents, let the floods rise, let the winds rage, and the house will stand. Likewise, if we have founded and grounded our life on the teachings of Jesus, we will overcome life's storms.

Daily Devotions:
M. God Blesses Wise Choices
   Genesis 13:8-18
T. Obey God's Word
   Joshua 23:1-11
W. Benefits of Wisdom
   Proverbs 3:1-10
T. Wisdom of the Gospel
   1 Corinthians 1:20-31
F. Walk Wisely
   Ephesians 5:13-21
S. Source of True Wisdom
   2 Timothy 3:10-17

The Cost of Discipleship

Matthew 10:16-42

Unit Theme:
The Teachings of Jesus (Matthew)

Central Truth:
Jesus teaches that the cost of discipleship is total submission to the will of God.

Focus:
Consider the cost of true discipleship and wholeheartedly follow Christ.

Context:
Probably took place in summer A.D. 28; location is uncertain

Golden Text:
"If any man will come after me [Jesus], let him deny himself, and take up his cross, and follow me" (Matthew 16:24).

Study Outline:
I. Count the Cost (Matthew 10:16-25)
II. Fear God, Not People (Matthew 10:26-31)
III. Follow Christ (Matthew 10:32-42)

INTRODUCTION

Turn to just about any Christian television station and there will be programs and speakers emphasizing relational issues in the family, discovering your destiny in the Kingdom, receiving the blessings God has in store for you, the need to exercise faith, the task of becoming the person God designed you to be, and why you should make a generous contribution to the ministry of the speaker. These things all have their place and are not inherently wrong, if they are based on a proper interpretation of the Word. What you are not likely to hear is much preaching or teaching on the need to expect and embrace persecution. It is one of those subjects that just does not generate much enthusiasm among speakers or hearers!

History reveals that the leaders of the world either want to control, marginalize (make it ineffective), or persecute the church. In a sense, both control and marginalization are forms of persecution. Thus, it is easy to see that the true church experiences persecution in this world (Matthew 5:10-12). In fact, persecution can even come from some regrettable sources (Galatians 1:23). However, the church has survived scandals, schisms, stupidity and suffering and still stands strong. There is no reason to believe that our place in church history will be any different.

This lesson forces us to look at our conceptions and misconceptions concerning some difficult material to understand and embrace. We understand that persecution is a part of the Christian life (John 15:20), but in this we all prefer our brother or sister have the honor!

In the early church, persecution was accepted. In fact, if a Christian was going to be martyred, fellow believers would gather at the site. This solidarity provided moral support for the martyr, but they also knew there could be a special manifestation of the Spirit poured out at the death of the saint(s). We see the Biblical support for this in the story of Stephen (Acts 7). Just before his death, he was overflowing with the Holy Spirit, looked into heaven, and saw Jesus standing at the Father's right hand (v. 55). Jesus never takes the abuse of His saints sitting down!

I. COUNT THE COST (Matthew 10:16-25)
A. Sheep, Serpents and Doves (v. 16)

16. Behold, I send you forth as sheep in the midst of wolves: be ye therefore wise as serpents, and harmless as doves.

Jesus prepares His disciples for public ministry (ch. 10) and gains our attention as He introduces new concerns. "Behold" is designed to gain the attention of the hearer and reader. He informs us that He (emphatic "I") is the One sending us with an anointing and commission. There is a divine purpose in all true ministry, and God never gives us a commission without the anointing and ability to fulfill it.

We are being sent as defenseless "sheep in the midst of wolves." This reveals there is no easy escape and little means of defense. Some suggest the disciples were already in the presence of wolves, since Jesus says "in," not "into." The wolves are not literal, however. They are vicious, aggressive rulers, leaders and false teachers, seeking to devour us and the ministry we come to accomplish (Acts 20:29). The warning should serve as a comfort: this is not an unforeseen event. Jesus is already aware of the danger.

We cannot, however, be complacent. As disciples we must ingrain into our very character ("be") the cunningness, prudence and practical wisdom associated with "serpents." Serpents are patient, crafty, and quick to assess a situation. They defend their ground when necessary and know when to slip away quietly and quickly. With these qualities, Christians must integrate the characteristics of *harmless* ("innocent" or "childlike simplicity"; literally "unmixed") doves. Doves are perceived as without guile and representing purity and integrity. As sheep in the midst of wolves, we must be submitted to our Shepherd and have integrity without a personal agenda. However, we must be smart sheep or we will be dead sheep and our ministries destroyed.

B. Coming Persecution (vv. 17-23)

17. But beware of men: for they will deliver you up to the councils, and they will scourge you in their synagogues;

18. And ye shall be brought before governors and kings for my sake, for a testimony against them and the Gentiles.

19. But when they deliver you up, take no thought how or what ye shall speak: for it shall be given you in that same hour what ye shall speak.

20. For it is not ye that speak, but the Spirit of your Father which speaketh in you.

Talk About It:
1. What "wolves" do Christians face in our community?
2. How can we obtain the wisdom Christ says we need?
3. What must Christians be "harmless"?

Faith makes a Christian.
Life proves a Christian.
Trial confirms a Christian.
Death crowns a Christian.
    —Anonymous

21. And the brother shall deliver up the brother to death, and the father the child: and the children shall rise up against their parents, and cause them to be put to death.

22. And ye shall be hated of all men for my name's sake: but he that endureth to the end shall be saved.

23. But when they persecute you in this city, flee ye into another: for verily I say unto you, Ye shall not have gone over the cities of Israel, till the Son of man be come.

Jesus makes it clear that the wolves are men and women ("men" can mean both) of whom disciples are to pay close attention ("beware," v. 17). From the context it can be surmised that they are people of authority or influence, as they "deliver" disciples to "the councils" (literally, "sanhedrins," but can include other courts) and "scourge [flog] you in their synagogues."

Synagogues ("gathering places") were instituted during the Babylonian Exile to provide places of worship for the Jews. After the Exile, not everyone could travel to Jerusalem regularly to worship at the Temple, so synagogues were set up anywhere there were 10 Jewish families, for 10 tithers were sufficient support. As the center of Jewish life, synagogues were also the place justice was administered. Offenders were flogged by a whip of four cords (often with smaller cords interwoven) while three judges were present. One judge read Scripture during the flogging; the second counted the strokes; the third gave the commands for each stroke to be administered. No more than 39 strokes could be administered. The preaching about Jesus by Jewish Christians would have been blasphemous to the Jews and worthy of scourging. Failure to stop preaching would have been considered insubordination and disruptive of public order, also a flogging offense. Disciples are further warned of persecution by Gentile authorities "for my sake," which will provide an opportunity for the disciple to give "testimony" ("bear witness" or "provide evidence") of Jesus (v. 18).

During these times of public persecution, the disciple is not to be overly concerned or anxious about the situation and *how* (the means) or *what* (the context) to "speak" (v. 19). Three things are emphasized in verses 19 and 20: (1) In the time we need it ("in that same hour"), God will provide the message and the words to deliver the message; (2) human intellect and ability are insufficient; and (3) "the Spirit of your Father" will proclaim "in ["through" or "by"] you" the message for the situation (cf. Luke 21:15). The Holy Spirit will come alongside of us and carry us through these difficult times and provide what we should speak. There are several New Testament instances of this (Acts 4:19, 20; 7; 8:35). It has been observed that we are never more true to who God called us to be than when the Holy Spirit manifests Himself in us for ministry.

Talk About It:
1. Why does Christ say to "take no thought how or what ye shall speak" in the face of persecution?
2. How does Christianity sometimes divide families?
3. What promise is given to those who faithfully endure persecution?

The Cost of Discipleship

The hatred directed against the disciple is so intense that it can involve the closest of relationships. "Brother will betray [hand over] brother to death" (Matthew 10:21, *NIV*). *Betray* is the same Greek word used of Judas handing over Jesus (26:16). Some believe Jesus is using *brother* in more than a biological sense—that a Christian brother will betray a Christian brother. Clearly, it includes biological brothers, as children and parents also will turn on each other, even resulting in death.

The hatred will be intense, persistent and widespread—"hated of all men for my name's sake" (10:22). This can mean those who preach in His name or those who are called by His name (Christians). The last half of this verse is rich. It is the one who refuses to give in, but patiently suffers and stands his or her spiritual ground, with his or her eyes upon the Savior ("endureth") that will be brought to safety, restored to health, and see Jesus ("saved").

Interestingly, Jesus instructs those persecuted to "flee" into another city (v. 23). When rejection is persistent, the disciple may escape from abuse or death, if possible. There are other places that need to hear the gospel. The last part of verse 23 concerning the coming of the Son of Man has given rise to several interpretations: (1) Jesus' return to the Father after His death; (2) His resurrection from the dead; (3) His return in judgment—perhaps the destruction of Jerusalem in A.D. 70; or (4) the Second Coming. All these views have merit, but it does seem to be a reference to the Second Coming, since Israel still is not a Christian nation.

C. Suffering by Association (vv. 24, 25)

24. The disciple is not above his master, nor the servant above his lord.

25. It is enough for the disciple that he be as his master, and the servant as his lord. If they have called the master of the house Beelzebub, how much more shall they call them of his household?

Our association as disciples, with Jesus as the Teacher, should be so strong that it is obvious to all. If the world has misunderstood the nature of Jesus' ministry and related it to false and evil religions, they will misunderstand our ministries. *Beelzebub* can mean either "lord of the flies" or "lord of the dung." It is obviously derogatory and meant to associate Jesus with Satan. This section of Jesus' teaching can best be summarized as "What I have suffered, you can expect to endure."

II. FEAR GOD, NOT PEOPLE (Matthew 10:26-31)
A. Revelation (vv. 26, 27)

26. Fear them not therefore: for there is nothing covered,

Enduring Persecution
In nations where the church is allowed to worship openly, we view persecution as an end-time event of which we should be aware, but hope to escape. Our brothers and sisters in the East and the 10-40 Window suffer terribly for the cause of Christ. Several Web sites, such as *persecution.org*, report their horrible treatment. Violence is not the only form persecution takes. In Western nations Christians are ridiculed and depicted as ignorant and prejudiced. Many attempt to marginalize the voice of the church. No matter where we serve, we must be diligent and faithful.

Talk About It:
Why should Christians expect to be persecuted?

that shall not be revealed; and hid, that shall not be known.

27. What I tell you in darkness, that speak ye in light: and what ye hear in the ear, that preach ye upon the housetops.

After an intense section detailing the persecution His disciples can expect, Jesus reassures and instills confident hope in those who follow Him. Verse 26 introduces the first of three repetitive, but important, commands in this section: "Do not be afraid" (*NIV;* see also vv. 28, 31). He is not diminishing the persecution, but emphasizing His enduring presence, sufficient provision, and soon-coming subordination of all things under His authority (28:18). The last part of 10:26 has both short-term and long-term meanings, as most prophecy does. Jesus knew the plots against Him by the Jewish leaders would soon be uncovered. Further, in the midst of our struggles and difficult times, it is difficult to see the end and make sense of it all. Jesus assures us that everything "covered" will be "revealed," and those things "hid" from our sight and understanding will be "known," or understood. Evil prefers darkness and secrecy, not openness and knowledge, but evil will be subdued by Christ.

The methodology of the disciples is contrasted sharply to that of evildoers (v. 27). We are to proclaim ("preach") in public and with boldness those things we hear in our prayer closets and quiet times with God. The wording indicates we have been given a sacred task and an official commission from the King. Many souls are depending on our obedience and faithfulness.

B. Respect (v. 28)

28. And fear not them which kill the body, but are not able to kill the soul: but rather fear him which is able to destroy both soul and body in hell.

The second directive to believers concerning fear is given by Jesus. "Fear not" can also be translated "Stop fearing!" He places *fear* ("to be frightened") in proper perspective to encourage and calm us. The "wolves" (or leaders, rulers and false teachers, v. 16) are only able to deprive a person of physical life. They do not have the power ("are not able") to deprive the "soul" of spiritual life. In theological terms, the nature of our being is body, soul and spirit. Scripture confirms this (1 Thessalonians 5:23). The *body* is the fleshy biological life form. The *spirit* is the life force from God that makes us alive. The *soul* is the center of our intellect, emotions and volition (will). It is the soul that defines who we are (character) and what we do (actions). In terms of the way we function, spirit and soul are inseparable. Both originate from God (Hebrews 12:9; Genesis 2:7) and return to Him at the death of the body (Acts 7:59;

Talk About It:
1. Why should Christians not fear persecutors?
2. In our country, when can "housetop" witnessing bring Christians trouble?

"What the world expects of Christians is that Christians should speak out, loud and clear . . . in such a way that never a doubt, never the slightest doubt, could rise in the heart of the simplest man."
—Albert Camus

Talk About It:
1. Why should Christians not be afraid of those who can "kill the body" (v. 28)?
2. Describe a proper fear of God.

The Cost of Discipleship

Genesis 35:18). Try as they may, the wolves in our lives cannot kill those things that belong solely to God.

"Rather," Jesus instructs us to "fear Him who has the continual power to utterly destroy both body and soul in Gehenna" (v. 28, author's translation). Several questions are raised by this verse. First, who is "him"? Some view this as a reference to Satan; however, the Bible instructs us to be keenly aware of his devices (1 Peter 5:8), but never tells us to fear him. Satan's reach is limited by God and his power subject to God's authority, so much so that an unnamed angel will bind him (Revelation 20:2). Only God has the power and authority to destroy body and soul. Also, *fear* can carry the connotation of "reverence" in the proper context. Finally, the grammar indicates this is a reference to God.

Second, does this verse teach *annihilationism*—the view that the soul will eventually burn up and not suffer eternally? Revelation 20:12, 13 reveals that the unrighteous dead are raised up out of Hades to stand before the Judgment seat. If they had perished, they could not be raised. Jesus is speaking of the total destruction of all that makes life meaningful, not the destruction of the soul.

Third, what is *Gehenna*? Originally, Gehenna (Valley of Hinnom) was the place children were sacrificed to Molech (2 Chronicles 28:3). Later, it became the garbage dump for Jerusalem. In Scripture, the term is often translated as "hell," as are several other terms. The different terms seem to be stylistic (preference of the writers), rather than theological. Gehenna, then, is the place of punishment for the unrighteous until the Day of Judgment. After the Judgment, it will be cast into the lake of fire, the final place of Satan and the unrighteous (Revelation 20:14, 15).

Preaching About Hell
"When I pastored a country church, a farmer didn't like the sermons I preached on hell. He said, 'Preach about the meek and lowly Jesus.' I said, 'That's where I got my information about hell.'"
—Vance Havner

C. Remembrance (vv. 29-31)
29. Are not two sparrows sold for a farthing? and one of them shall not fall on the ground without your Father.
30. But the very hairs of your head are all numbered.
31. Fear ye not therefore, ye are of more value than many sparrows.

Just as God is able to destroy the unrepentant, He is able to sustain the righteous. Nothing, no matter how insignificant, escapes His attention. We are more valuable than any other aspect of creation. Thus, Jesus reminds us that God is always in control and in everything He will take care of His children.

farthing (v. 29)— the least valuable coin

Talk About It:
How valuable are people to God, and why?

III. FOLLOW CHRIST (Matthew 10:32-42)
A. Rewarded Confessions (vv. 32, 33)
32. Whosoever therefore shall confess me before men,

him will I confess also before my Father which is in heaven.

33. But whosoever shall deny me before men, him will I also deny before my Father which is in heaven.

Talk About It
1. What can cause a Christian to deny Christ?
2. Who will testify for or against people before God? Why?

In times of persecution, it is not enough to stand strong in silence. We are not called to be unnoticed, but to be the hands, feet and voice of Jesus in our generation. He says there is a correlation between what happens when we stand before people and when we stand before God. If we "confess" (acknowledge) Jesus before others, then He will acknowledge us before the Father (v. 32). The basic meaning of *confess* is "to say the same thing." This has two implications for us. First, we must say the same thing about Christ that He says about Himself and His kingdom. Second, we must say what the Spirit gives us to speak (v. 20). To quench the Spirit is to not confess Christ (see John 16:13, 14).

Further, if we "deny" Christ, He will deny us before the Father (Matthew 10:33). *Deny* is the exact opposite of *confess*. Obviously, there are those who have (or will) verbally denied knowing Christ. It is not just a denial of Him through words; it includes activity and speech. It would be a horrible thing to stand before God in the end time and have Christ deny us. Thankfully, the example of Simon Peter reveals that even a denial of Jesus is not an unforgivable act (John 18:27; Mark 16:7).

B. Rewarded Allegiance (vv. 34-39)

34. Think not that I am come to send peace on earth: I came not to send peace, but a sword.

35. For I am come to set a man at variance against his father, and the daughter against her mother, and the daughter in law against her mother in law.

36. And a man's foes shall be they of his own household.

37. He that loveth father or mother more than me is not worthy of me: and he that loveth son or daughter more than me is not worthy of me.

38. And he that taketh not his cross, and followeth after me, is not worthy of me.

39. He that findeth his life shall lose it: and he that loseth his life for my sake shall find it.

Talk About It:
1. Describe the "sword" Christ brought to earth.
2. When do we love our family too much? How can we change?
3. How is Christian living like carrying a cross?

Jesus further illustrates the type of allegiance He expects and demands. He says, "Do not presume that I, Myself, came to throw peace upon the earth" (v. 34, author's translation). The imagery is of powerful activity. One does not bring peace by throwing it at those who need it. Peace is not the absence of all conflict or strife, but an attitude that embraces spiritual wholeness, inner harmony, and the unshakable belief that God is in control despite what we see or feel. To illustrate the nature

The Cost of Discipleship

of His ministry, Jesus says, "I came not to send peace, but a sword." Swords are used to divide, kill and conquer—a strange instrument for the "Prince of Peace" (Isaiah 9:6). However, intense spiritual warfare began at Jesus' birth. The Gospels record King Herod's attempts to kill Jesus during His infancy (Matthew 2). Sometimes, it takes the "sword" before peace can be truly established, rather than thrown into place. The Cross is evidence of that.

Again, Jesus emphasizes that the persecution and spiritual battles will involve even the closest of familial relationships (10:35, 36). Even though God instituted the family—and did so before instituting the church—our loyalty must be first and foremost to Christ (v. 37). As with any passage of Scripture, the verses here must be interpreted in light of other scriptures addressing similar subjects (e.g., Matthew 15:4-9). It is not Jesus' intention to bring conflict where there should be none. A righteous person lives in right relationship with God and others, as much as is possible (see Romans 12:18).

For the first time in Matthew (and the New Testament) the cross is introduced (10:38). Crucifixion was a common form of punishment by the Romans. Once a person was seen carrying a cross, there was no turning back to their previous conduct in life. For Christians, it is the symbol of death to sin, self-determination, and the former way of life; it represents complete surrender to God. *Take* means "to willingly receive or embrace" something, and the term for "follow" is used throughout the Gospels as a designation of discipleship (Matthew 19:21; John 21:19).

Verse 39 of the text seems contradictory, at first. It can be translated: "The one who will have discovered his existence will destroy it, and the one who will have destroyed his existence because of Me will discover it." *Life* is literally "soul," which is used to designate the totality of a person's existence, hopes, dreams and aspirations. This teaching of Jesus is found six times in the Gospels, emphasizing its importance.

Carrying the Cross

"The man with a cross no longer controls his destiny; he lost control when he picked up his cross. That cross immediately became to him an all-absorbing interest, an overwhelming interference. No matter what he may desire to do, there is but one thing he can do; that is, move on toward the place of crucifixion."

—A.W. Tozer

C. Rewarded Righteousness (vv. 40-42)

40. He that receiveth you receiveth me, and he that receiveth me receiveth him that sent me.

41. He that receiveth a prophet in the name of a prophet shall receive a prophet's reward; and he that receiveth a righteous man in the name of a righteous man shall receive a righteous man's reward.

42. And whosoever shall give to drink unto one of these little ones a cup of cold water only in the name of a disciple, verily I say unto you, he shall in no wise lose his reward.

The focus shifts from those who will persecute Jesus' disciples

1. Explain Christ's words, "He who receives you receives Me" (v. 40, *NKJV*).
2. How does Christ view ministry to "little ones" (v. 42)?

"Sometimes when I consider what tremendous consequences come from little things, I am tempted to think there are no little things."
—Bruce Barton

(and the dedication necessary for His disciples to stand strong) to those who are receptive to the gospel and its messengers (v. 40). To *receive* carries the idea of "accepting with hospitality" or "receiving in a welcoming manner." The person who receives the disciples and their message in this manner will receive the benefits of and relationship with Jesus and the Father.

Jesus teaches that those who receive "a prophet" will "receive a prophet's reward"; likewise for a "righteous" person (v. 41). *Reward* is literally "compensation for labor," in whatever form that may take. Some have understood this verse as revealing different levels of ministerial offices in the early church. However, the church was not organized into offices of ministry at this point. Jesus is teaching: (1) Those who minister will receive a reward commensurate with their labor; (2) those who assist others in fulfilling their function are full participants in that ministry; and (3) every area of ministry (seen and unseen) of the Kingdom is important and observed by God.

CONCLUSION

It is not the faint of heart who become Christians. If it required no effort or commitment, the ranks would be full of believers. Corrie ten Boom said, "The measure of a life, after all, is not its duration, but its donation."

GOLDEN TEXT CHALLENGE

"IF ANY MAN WILL COME AFTER ME [JESUS], LET HIM DENY HIMSELF, AND TAKE UP HIS CROSS, AND FOLLOW ME" (Matthew 16:24).

The requirements of discipleship are stated clearly in this verse: deny self, take up the cross, follow Christ.

Self-denial. We must renounce, forgo, or postpone any pleasure, profit, or interest which may conflict with Christ's will for our lives. Self-denial is not carelessness about one's life, health or family. It is not bodily abuse in any respect. It is simply the surrender of our will to Christ.

Cross-bearing. As Christ bore His own cross to His own crucifixion, so we must bear our cross to our crucifixion. The great crucified Leader is followed by an immense throng of crucified followers. We are crucified symbolically in all of our sufferings of mind and body in behalf of Christ and the truth.

Following Christ. The third step in Christian discipleship is to follow Christ wherever He may lead. Wilfred T. Grenfell, medical missionary to Labrador, wrote: "Feeble and devious as my own footsteps have been since my decision to follow Jesus Christ, I believe more than ever that this is the only real adventure in life." The adventure of following Christ is a supreme effort to pattern our life after His life.

Daily Devotions:
M. Jeremiah's Call
Jeremiah 1:4-10
T. Daniel's Faithfulness Rewarded
Daniel 6:10-24
W. Be Prepared for Persecution
John 15:18-27
T. Tell It Like It Is
Acts 4:13-22
F. Courage in Death
Acts 7:51-60
S. Keep the Faith
2 Timothy 4:1-8

Empty Tomb, Living Savior (Easter)

John 20:1-31

INTRODUCTION

A person once asked his pastor, "Which is greater? The Cross or the empty tomb?" The Cross and the Resurrection cannot be separated, theologically or spiritually.

The crucifixion of Jesus is attested by first-century historians (Lucian, Thallus), some of whom also mention directly or indirectly His resurrection (Tacitus, Josephus). Pliny the Younger makes reference to the large number of martyrs who were willing to die for their faith. One does not die for a myth. If the Romans could have produced Jesus' body to dispel the Resurrection and put an end to what Tacitus calls "the pernicious superstition" (*Annals* XV. 44), they would have done so.

Theologically, the death of Jesus Christ is the basis of our justification (Hebrews 9:22) and sanctification (Romans 6:6, 11), and instrumental in the baptism in the Holy Spirit (John 20:20-22). The Resurrection assures us that God's Word is true (see 1 Corinthians 15:15), our faith has a viable foundation (v. 14), and we too shall be raised, if death occurs before the Rapture (v. 22).

Spiritually, the Cross and the Resurrection represent parallel aspects of our spiritual journey. We are crucified with Christ, nevertheless we live (Galatians 2:20). We are called from darkness to light (1 Peter 2:9). We are released from the dominion of Satan into the kingdom of God (Acts 26:18). Because of Good Friday and Easter, slaves become heirs (Romans 8:17, 21). Without the effectual working of the power of Christ's crucifixion and resurrection, we would be illegitimate children, not sons and daughters of God (Hebrews 12:8). If Jesus had died and not been raised, there would be no assurance of our salvation, and there is no resurrection without death. We *must* not—no, we *cannot*—separate the two, or salvation becomes a philosophical theory, not a living event!

John's account takes a different approach from the Synoptic Gospels (Matthew, Mark and Luke; *synoptic* means "to see together"). Of course, this is true of most of his Gospel. This approach is not in disagreement with the other Gospels. The events can be reconciled. John 20 is the record of witnesses who encounter the unexpected and have their lives affected in ways they could not anticipate. It reveals their spiritual preparation for and commission to a life of telling others where they found life that others may also believe.

Unit Theme:
Easter

Central Truth:
Christ's resurrection is the foundation of Christian faith and practice.

Focus:
Review the events of Christ's resurrection and worship and serve Him as our risen Lord.

Context:
A.D. 30 in Jerusalem

Golden Text:
"Ye seek Jesus of Nazareth, which was crucified: he is risen; he is not here: behold the place where they laid him" (Mark 16:6).

Study Outline:
I. An Empty Tomb (John 20:1-9)
II. The Risen Lord (John 20:10-16)
III. The Great Commission (John 20:17-23)

I. AN EMPTY TOMB (John 20:1-9)

A. Mary's Discovery (vv. 1, 2)

1. The first day of the week cometh Mary Magdalene early, when it was yet dark, unto the sepulchre, and seeth the stone taken away from the sepulchre.

2. Then she runneth, and cometh to Simon Peter, and to the other disciple, whom Jesus loved, and saith unto them, They have taken away the Lord out of the sepulchre, and we know not where they have laid him.

Talk About It:
1. Why do you suppose Mary came to the tomb so early?
2. What did Mary think had happened to Jesus' body? Why?

All of the Gospels record that the Resurrection happened on "the first day of the week" (see Matthew 28:1; Mark 16:2; Luke 24:1), rather than the logical "on the third day" foretold by Jesus (Matthew 16:21; Mark 10:34; Luke 9:22). This is not an accident. The emphasis is on new beginnings and the newness associated with Jesus' atoning work and all it represents (see Isaiah 43:19). Because of this significance (and direction from God, no doubt), it is the day the early church chose to worship Jesus (see 1 Corinthians 16:2). Further, it represents a break from Judaism and worship on the Sabbath, for which Jesus had prepared them (see Mark 2:27).

Mary Magdalene (from the city of Magdala) made her way to the tomb "early" (probably between 3 and 6 a.m.), "when it was yet dark" (John 20:1). John does not mention other women (however, see "we" in v. 2; see also Mark 16:1ff.), probably because the others did not see the risen Lord. In the darkness, she saw the stone removed from the tomb, but did not enter the tomb. *Taken away* carries with it the idea of "lifted up," not the "rolled away" that we would expect (see Matthew 28:2). John is emphasizing the power by which the stone was moved.

Mary hurriedly made her way "to Simon Peter, and to the other disciple, whom Jesus loved" (John 20:2). Simon Peter was one of the three so-called pillar apostles (along with James and John), who often accompanied Jesus on special occasions (see Mark 5:37). "The disciple whom Jesus loved" (see John 13:23, 25) is the writer's way of referring to himself without being named. The only "John" who appears in this Gospel is John the Baptist. As well in Matthew's Gospel, Matthew is very careful to not emphasize his presence. The focus is to be on Jesus, not the instrument.

Mary told of her discovery of the empty tomb in language that revealed her deep concern. Normally, a corpse would lie on a slab in a cave tomb (sepulchre) for approximately one year. After that, all that remained were the bones, which were then placed in a small box (ossuary) and stored on a shelf to make room for another body. Burial in the ground also occurred, but was less common. Grave-robbing was very common, and this may be the source of Mary's anxiety. It is possible that the

The Third Day
My kindergarten class had been studying the Creation story for several weeks.
"What did God make the first day?" I quizzed.
"The second day?" They answered both questions correctly.
"And what happened on the third day?" I asked.
One little child, face shining, exclaimed, "He rose from the dead!"
—Michele Hardie
(*Humor for Preaching & Teaching*, Baker Books)

Empty Tomb, Living Savior

women thought the Jewish leaders had removed Him, perhaps to deny His teachings and humiliate His followers.

B. The Other Disciple's Discovery (vv. 3-5)

3. Peter therefore went forth, and that other disciple, and came to the sepulchre.

4. So they ran both together: and the other disciple did outrun Peter, and came first to the sepulchre.

5. And he stooping down, and looking in, saw the linen clothes lying; yet went he not in.

Talk About It:
1. Why did Peter and John rush to the tomb?
2. Why did John hesitate about entering the tomb?

Upon hearing the account, Peter, who seems to have taken the initiative, and "that other disciple" (John) made their way to the tomb. The younger and faster John arrived there first. John "stooped over, carefully looked in and saw the linen clothes; however, he did not enter" (v. 5, author's translation), which indicates this was a cave tomb. Linen packed with spices was wrapped (see 19:40) around the body to mask the decomposition odors, not for embalming (as the Egyptians did). The expensive linen and spices would not have been left by robbers or those moving a body.

C. Peter's Discovery (vv. 6-9)

6. Then cometh Simon Peter following him, and went into the sepulchre, and seeth the linen clothes lie,

7. And the napkin, that was about his head, not lying with the linen clothes, but wrapped together in a place by itself.

napkin (v. 7)— burial cloth

8. Then went in also that other disciple, which came first to the sepulchre, and he saw, and believed.

9. For as yet they knew not the scripture, that he must rise again from the dead.

True to his nature, when Peter did arrive, he rushed into the tomb and also observed the burial linens lying on the slab, consistent with a body that rose through them (v. 6). He observed that the head piece was "neatly rolled up in a particular place by itself" (v. 7, author's translation). This, again, confirms that it was neither robbers, who would have taken the clothes, nor those moving a body, who would not have taken the time to be neat.

Talk About It:
1. What evidence did the burial clothes give?
2. What do you think John "believed" (v. 8) at this point?

The beloved disciple, shaking off his timidity or fear, "went in also . . . saw, and believed" (v. 8). The question is, What did he believe? In light of verse 9, some say he believed that the tomb was indeed empty and Mary's account was correct. This view makes the disciples incredibly dense. Mary realizes the tomb is empty in the darkness, but they must physically enter the tomb to verify that it was indeed empty. Tombs were barely big enough for the placing of a body. One could not overlook an adult corpse, even from the outside. Rather, in spite of not fully understanding the Old Testament prophecies concerning this event, John *believed* that Jesus suffered, died, and rose again from the dead on the third day. John was a fisherman, not a scribe (expert in the Scriptures). Obviously, he had heard Jesus' prophecies concerning His death and resurrection (Matthew 16:21), but he did not have the advantage of understanding the event after the fact, as we do. He was convinced by the Living Word and would understand the written Word later (see Luke 24:46, 47). Seeing and believing is a definite theme in the fourth Gospel (John 20:29).

II. THE RISEN LORD (John 20:10-16)
A. Mary's Encounter With the Angels (vv. 10-13)
10. Then the disciples went away again unto their own home.

11. But Mary stood without at the sepulchre weeping: and as she wept, she stooped down, and looked into the sepulchre,

12. And seeth two angels in white sitting, the one at the head, and the other at the feet, where the body of Jesus had lain.

13. And they say unto her, Woman, why weepest thou? She saith unto them, Because they have taken away my Lord, and I know not where they have laid him.

The disciples left the tomb and returned home. Verses 10 and 11 also set up a contrast of reactions. The tomb was empty, so the disciples returned home. John saw the empty tomb and believed without seeing the risen Savior. At this point, the reader is unsure of Peter's reaction. Mary, however, returned to the tomb, presumably sometime after the disciples left.

Mary had been delivered from seven demonic spirits (Luke 8:2). Because of this, some view her as the unnamed prostitute of Luke 7:37. This is certainly possible, but not confirmed by Scripture. It is likely that the demonic activity severely afflicted her physically. Further, she was a woman of means and was prominent in the Gospels (see Matthew 27:55, 56; John 19:25). Jesus taught that those forgiven of much, have more reason to love Him (Luke 7:47). Mary's love for Him is certainly obvious. She returned to His last-known location, where she was overcome with grief. As she continued to weep, she "stooped down, and looked" into the tomb (John 20:11).

In the tomb, Mary saw two angels in shining garments. The language indicates it was a spiritual event. She immediately perceived they were angels, and thus, messengers of God. She was not startled, nor showed any sign of fear. Her attention was on their presence, not the grave clothes. When they addressed her politely ("Woman") and asked the reason for her

Talk About It:
Why do you suppose God sent angels to the empty tomb? What was the significance of their position in the tomb?

"Christianity is in its very essence a resurrection religion. The concept of the Resurrection lies at its heart. If you remove it, Christianity is destroyed."
—**John R. Stott**

weeping, she described the situation and expressed her deep concern and uncertainty (v. 13). She was looking for answers.

B. Mary's Encounter With Jesus (vv. 14-16)

14. And when she had thus said, she turned herself back, and saw Jesus standing, and knew not that it was Jesus.

15. Jesus saith unto her, Woman, why weepest thou? whom seekest thou? She, supposing him to be the gardener, saith unto him, Sir, if thou have borne him hence, tell me where thou hast laid him, and I will take him away.

16. Jesus saith unto her, Mary. She turned herself, and saith unto him, Rabboni; which is to say, Master.

Suddenly Mary became aware of someone outside the tomb, for she turned around and saw Jesus standing, but did not recognize that it was Him (v. 14). The Gospel accounts reveal this was not an unusual situation for those encountering the risen Jesus (see Luke 24:13-35). It is possible that her tears hindered her vision. Jesus asked her two distinct questions. First, He asked, "Why are you weeping?" Jesus was not expecting an answer. This was a mild rebuke. Jesus was alive! There was no need to weep. Second, He asked, "Whom do you seek?" Some believe Jesus was asking Mary to reflect on who she needed Him to be for her. If so, she missed it at first and assumed He was a caretaker. Her focus was still on His body, not His presence—until He called her by name. Immediately, she knew who He was and responded with the Aramaic "Rabboni!" John explained the meaning of this term of respect for his Greek readers.

It is interesting that Jesus' first appearance was not to Pilate, Herod, or one of the high priests. It was not to one of the pillar apostles or the remainder of the Twelve. It was to a woman delivered of seven demons! Contrary to some beliefs, women are highly regarded in the New Testament, as this event reveals (also see Romans 16). God refuses to be put into our boxes and molds. In fact, He seems more concerned about breaking our molds than fitting into them.

III. THE GREAT COMMISSION (John 20:17-23)

A. Message From Jesus (vv. 17, 18)

17. Jesus saith unto her, Touch me not; for I am not yet ascended to my Father: but go to my brethren, and say unto them, I ascend unto my Father, and your Father; and to my God, and your God.

18. Mary Magdalene came and told the disciples that she had seen the Lord, and that he had spoken these things unto her.

Talk About It:
1. Why didn't Jesus immediately reveal Himself to Mary?
2. Describe a time when you thought Jesus was not present, but then you discovered He actually was there.
3. Why did Mary address Him as "Master"?

1. Why do you suppose Jesus first appeared to Mary Magdalene instead of to one of His disciples?

2. What did Jesus tell Mary to do, and how did she respond?

You Must Choose

"'I'm ready to accept Jesus as a great moral teacher, but I don't accept His claim to be God.' That is the one thing we must not say. A man who was merely a man and said the sort of things Jesus said would not be a great moral teacher. He would either be a lunatic—on a level with the man who says he is a poached egg—or else he would be the Devil of hell. You must make your choice. Either this man was, and is, the Son of God; or else a madman or something worse."
—**C.S. Lewis**

Verse 17 is viewed as one of the most difficult verses in Scripture to interpret. The traditional translation of "Touch me not," in the sense of not initiating an action, fails to reveal the full meaning of the Greek. It is better understood as, "Do not cling to Me," or "Do not prolong an action already begun." Mary would certainly have run to the One who delivered her from bondage! This may be assurance from Jesus that He was not going anywhere just yet, so there was no need to cling to Him. Further, Matthew 28:9 indicates the women "held" ("seized with enthusiasm") Him briefly after His resurrection. Considering the other Gospels' accounts, it is difficult to reconcile the idea of her not touching Him at all.

The second difficulty involves the assertion that Jesus could not be touched until He had ascended to the Father. Proponents of this idea contend that Jesus ascended to the Father for glorification immediately after this appearance and before any others, then ascended again publicly in Acts 1. However, the translation above precludes the need for Him to do so. Further, there is no record of this clandestine ascension or hint that it ever happened. John seems clear that Jesus was active and revealed Himself to many on that day. A slightly expanded translation may be helpful in understanding this verse: "There is no need to cling to Me! I have not yet ascended to My Father and your Father, to My God and your God, but I certainly will. Go to My brothers and tell them these things you have witnessed." The following verse reveals this is exactly what Mary did (v. 18).

The third difficulty is the meaning of the term "brethren" (v. 17). Some believe Jesus was referring to His siblings, not His disciples. It is possible that His siblings were convinced of Jesus' true identity, but the reader has not been told that at this point. Jesus does not normally use this term for disciples, but He has paved the way for it (see Matthew 12:50). Therefore, it is best viewed as a term of close relationship to His disciples.

B. Assurance, Commission and Preparation (vv. 19-23)

19. Then the same day at evening, being the first day of the week, when the doors were shut where the disciples were assembled for fear of the Jews, came Jesus and stood in the midst, and saith unto them, Peace be unto you.

20. And when he had so said, he shewed unto them his hands and his side. Then were the disciples glad, when they saw the Lord.

21. Then said Jesus to them again, Peace be unto you: as my Father hath sent me, even so send I you.

22. And when he had said this, he breathed on them,

and saith unto them, Receive ye the Holy Ghost:

23. Whose soever sins ye remit, they are remitted unto them; and whose soever sins ye retain, they are retained.

John makes it clear that the events thus far occur on the day of Jesus' resurrection (v. 19). It is natural, given the events they had experienced in a brief period of time, that they would be fearful for their own lives. "Disciples" could be the 10 (Thomas is absent, v. 24), or it could include all those who followed Him, including the women. Given Mary's experience, it seems logical that many of the faithful would gather to hear the story. Regardless, they were behind "shut doors," which could refer to double doors or, more likely, to a locked door at the entrance of the house and another into the room.

Suddenly and unexpectedly, Jesus appears in their midst and comforts them, "Peace be with you." John seems to be communicating that Jesus did not open the doors. For someone who conquered death, doors would not be a problem! His words reflect the usual Hebraic greeting (*shalom*); however, here they take on a greater significance (as in v. 21). "Peace" is not the absence of conflict in our lives, but spiritual health and comfort that derive from the provision and presence of God. Their fears of the Jewish leaders, and of their own fates, were quieted by Jesus' sudden appearance. To further convince them of His identity and reality, Jesus reveals the wounds in His hands and side (v. 20). Their tattered and strained nerves were calmed with an abundance of joy.

In verse 21, He repeats the greeting in the course of His commission. It is a formal commission, to send them forth in the same manner in which the Father sent Him. What they have seen in Jesus they are to do.

The next two verses have elicited a plethora of interpretations. A literal translation says, "And when Jesus said these things, He breathed and said to them: 'Receive the Holy Spirit!'" (v. 22). It does not say directly that He breathed on the disciples. So what does this mean?

An examination of the viable interpretations is required. First, it is asserted that this is the point at which the disciples actually got saved. Against this is all the language of Jesus that reveals they were His (John 17:9, 10). The terminology of *discipleship* indicates they were following their Messiah with body, soul and spirit. Second, this is seen as a separate Pentecost, meaning His disciples received the Spirit here *and* in Acts 2:1-4. Scripture is clear that the Holy Spirit would not come until Jesus resumed His place in heaven (John 7:39). Third, a very unlikely view is that the disciples were receiving the breath of God, not the Spirit. How this differs is unclear. Fourth, this is best viewed as a preparation for Pentecost. This fits what we

Talk About It:
1. What were the Lord's first words to His disciples, and why?
2. What did the Father send Jesus to do, and what does Jesus commission His followers to do?
3. Why did the disciples need the Holy Spirit?

Bewildered Believer
Several years ago in *Christianity Today*, a popular columnist wrote under the pen name of Eutychus (see Acts 20:9). In one column he responded to a letter he supposedly received from "Bewildered," who said their church's preacher claimed Jesus just fainted on the cross and the disciples brought Him back to health. Here's how Eutychus replied:

"Dear Bewildered: Beat your preacher with a cat-of-nine-tails with 39 heavy strokes, nail him to a cross; hang him in the sun for six hours; run a spear through his heart; embalm him; put him in an airless tomb for three days and see what happens."

find in the Gospel of John, where the giving of the Spirit is promised throughout (7:37-39; 14:16, 26; 15:26; 16:7, 13). The writer is building anticipation and expectancy. Further, there is no evidence of any change following this event, which one would expect if this was anything other than preparation for the promised outpouring.

Verse 23 of the text is best understood as giving this power to the church (see Matthew 18:15-18 and Lesson 7), not to the apostles—or those "designated" as their descendants. As noted, there were probably more than the 10 disciples present at this event, yet Jesus does not exclude them or include Thomas (who is not present) later (see vv. 24-28). In Matthew 18 this teaching occurs within the context of church discipline. If the offender does not repent, the church can exclude him or her from fellowship, thus, their sins are retained. Here, the context is mission. If the church does not preach Christ to sinners, their sins will not be forgiven. Believers have an awesome responsibility. Souls *are* in our hands.

CONCLUSION

The atoning work of Jesus Christ affects us all differently. Each of us wants God to touch us on the basis of our needs and desires. Just as John reveals an Easter event that was personal to those whose stories he records, God will make this event personal for us. He lives! And because He lives, we shall live!

GOLDEN TEXT CHALLENGE

"YE SEEK JESUS OF NAZARETH, WHICH WAS CRUCIFIED: HE IS RISEN; HE IS NOT HERE: BEHOLD THE PLACE WHERE THEY LAID HIM" (Mark 16:6).

The women, like so many people today, were seeking a dead Christ. Some still confine Him to a cross or a shrine. The angelic message was that Jesus is alive and that the gospel is the message of a living Savior triumphant over death and the grave. Notice that the angel reminded them, "He is risen, as he said" (Matthew 28:6). It is perfectly natural that the women would be fearful because what they were observing was a supernatural manifestation, and their reaction to it was typically human.

They discovered their fears about removing the stone were needless; for, when they got there, they found it had already been rolled away by the Lord. How often we worry unnecessarily over things that never happen! We could save ourselves a lot of anxiety if, as we will go through life, we would exercise a little more implicit trust in God.

Empty Tomb, Living Savior

Jesus Teaches to Value Others

Matthew 18:1-35

Unit Theme:
The Teachings of
Jesus (Matthew)

Central Truth:
A Christian is to love
every person as
much as he loves
himself.

Focus:
Recognize the value
of others and demon-
strate respect in rela-
tionships.

Context:
A.D. 29 in Galilee

Golden Text:
"All things whatsoev-
er ye would that men
should do to you, do
ye even so to them"
(Matthew 7:12).

Study Outline:
I. Humble Yourself
(Matthew 18:1-14)
II. Seek
Reconciliation
(Matthew 18:15-
20)
II. Show Mercy
(Matthew 18:21-
35)

INTRODUCTION

A person receives all kinds of advice when he or she is facing life-changing circumstances. It seems that everyone has an opinion or feels the need to share their wisdom and experiences. However, we listen very carefully when someone shares advice, who has gone through the same thing we face. For example, the loss of a child is something no parent should ever face. Those who have faced the deaths of other close family members (parents, siblings) think they know how a grieving parent feels—and they mean well. However, it takes another grieving parent to truly know what the loss of a child is like. From this person comes authoritative encouragement and wisdom that speaks directly to the heart.

The teachings and example of Jesus reveal a deep concern and compassion for people. Jesus came to die for our sins, but He also came to experience the things we experience. The Gospels record several instances where Jesus "was moved with compassion" when He saw the needs of people (e.g., Matthew 9:36; Mark 6:34). The word used conveys the idea that He feels what we feel. He speaks to us out of experience *and* wisdom.

In this lesson, we examine the teaching of Jesus concerning life in His community, the church. The church is not a building or a denomination. It is the living body of Christ, composed of every blood-washed believer of every age: Old Testament saints, who looked forward to the Cross and the redemption promised by God, even if they did not know the specifics of the plan; New Testament saints, who looked back at the Cross and embraced the redemption provided by Jesus; and modern saints, who know that their Redeemer lives because of the power of the Spirit.

Jesus addresses the treatment and acceptance of others, as well as the proper attitude toward them and ourselves when sin arises. The themes of forgiveness and reconciliation are revisited in the Gospel of Matthew. Jesus strongly emphasizes these areas because He understands the power of and need for unity in the Body. A congregation divided is no threat to the devil. In fact, they are doing Satan's work for him.

I. HUMBLE YOURSELF (Matthew 18:1-14)

A. The Value of Children (vv. 1-5)

1. At the same time came the disciples unto Jesus, saying, Who is the greatest in the kingdom of heaven?

2. And Jesus called a little child unto him, and set him in the midst of them,

3. And said, Verily I say unto you, Except ye be converted, and become as little children, ye shall not enter into the kingdom of heaven.

4. Whosoever therefore shall humble himself as this little child, the same is greatest in the kingdom of heaven.

5. And whoso shall receive one such little child in my name receiveth me.

In a brief period of time, the disciples heard Jesus' affirmation that He was the Messiah, who would suffer, die, and be raised from the dead (Matthew 16). They witnessed (or heard from those who did) the Transfiguration, Jesus' power over demonic possession, and His ability to fund ministry from a fish, if need be (ch. 17). They knew the coming of His kingdom was near. It is only natural for them to wonder about the nature of the Kingdom. Most likely, a natural concern for their place in the Kingdom motivated the question concerning the "greatest in the kingdom of heaven" (18:1). It is also possible they were concerned with Simon Peter's growing prominence (see chs. 16, 17). There is no strong rebuke from Jesus, however, which suggests this is a general inquiry, not one motivated by illicit ambition (cf. 20:20-24).

Rather, He answers the question through an illustrated teaching moment. He called a little child to Him and stood him (or her) in their midst. Thus, there were more than the Twelve listening to the Master. Emphasizing the importance of His words, Jesus says, "Truly I say to you" (18:3a, *NASB*). *Truly* is generally translated "Amen," the usual response of a worshiping community to words of truth. Here it emphasizes the importance and gravity of what follows. He continues, "Unless you change . . . you will never enter the kingdom of heaven" (v. 3b, *NIV*). The grammar indicates that the disciples' concern for prominence was not yet a problem, but that Jesus knew it could soon be. Further, it is a call to the others ("whosoever") listening to be converted and come to God in the humility (voluntary submission), trustfulness, innocence and dependence of a little child (v. 4). This is true greatness. As well, our treatment and acceptance of others is directly linked to our relationship with Jesus (v. 5). *To receive* means "to embrace with hospitality," or it can mean "to take someone by the hand."

In the course of this teaching, *child* ("little ones") has a twofold meaning. First, it speaks about the value of actual chil-

Talk About It:

1. Do you think the disciples were surprised by Jesus' answer to their question, "Who is the greatest in the kingdom of heaven?" Why or why not?

2. What does it mean to "become as little children"?

3. What does it mean to "welcome" a child, and why is it so important to do so?

"The size and power of adults impress young children. Realizing their own smallness and powerlessness, they need the protection and care of parents. Jesus says, be like a child in your relationship with God."

—Catherine Stonehouse

Jesus Teaches to Value Others

dren to God and His kingdom, as well as our need to consider their place and prominence in the Kingdom. Second, it reminds all disciples that we are "little ones," or children of God. God is not looking for childish behavior, but a childlike attitude from His children.

B. The Seriousness of Sin (vv. 6-9)

6. But whoso shall offend one of these little ones which believe in me, it were better for him that a millstone were hanged about his neck, and that he were drowned in the depth of the sea.

7. Woe unto the world because of offences! for it must needs be that offences come; but woe to that man by whom the offence cometh!

8. Wherefore if thy hand or thy foot offend thee, cut them off, and cast them from thee: it is better for thee to enter into life halt or maimed, rather than having two hands or two feet to be cast into everlasting fire.

9. And if thine eye offend thee, pluck it out, and cast it from thee: it is better for thee to enter into life with one eye, rather than having two eyes to be cast into hell fire.

Verse 6 is a transitional verse ("but") that connects and redirects the flow of the teaching from the example of children to the issue of obstacles that cause sin in others and ourselves. Jesus warns that anyone who shall "offend one of these little ones which believe in me" will suffer severe consequences. *To offend* means "to stumble." It is the mental and moral corruption of a person through misinformation that causes them to lose their standing with God. That misinformation is most likely intentional, though it can be through inferior knowledge. Jesus says that anyone who causes a person to sin against God would be better served if a large millstone were hung around his or her neck and drowned in the depths of the sea. Jesus is not speaking of heavy stone used by individuals to ground grain, but one so large that it requires a beast of burden to turn it. We cannot cause others to stumble without causing ourselves to do the same. Thus, it serves as a severe and sobering warning to those who lead and instruct others to be diligent in the Word and ways of the Spirit. Jesus previously said that a person cannot just sit back and refrain from evil, but must be actively involved in doing good (Matthew 6:1; 7:19); thus, teachers, ministers, parents and others who have influence with people do not have the option of just sitting back to make sure we do not cause others to stumble. We must be led by the Spirit.

In 18:7 there are two expressions of "woe," a term that communicates regret for sin, compassion for the sinner, and the

Talk About It:
1. Describe ways that "little ones" are being led astray from Christ in our society. What should the church do about it?
2. Why does Jesus take spiritual offenses so seriously?
3. What are some things a believer might have to "pluck out" or "cut off" from their lives in order to please God?

Drowning by wearing a millstone "was one mode of capital punishment practiced by the Greeks, Syrians, Romans, and by some other nations. The meaning is, it would be better for him to have died before he had committed the sin. To injure, or to cause to sin, the feeblest Christian, will be regarded by Christ as a most serious offence, and will be punished accordingly."

—Albert Barnes

Talk About It:
1. What special attention do "little ones" receive from the heavenly Father? Why?
2. Why did Jesus tell this parable at this point in His teaching?

promise of judgment. There is no delight in the punishment, but it is certain because of the "stumbling" caused. Because of the fallen state of the world, it is inevitable that enticement to sin occurs, but "woe" to the one through whom it comes, for that person will be punished, unless he or she repents. Those who promote sin in our world, either actively or through the gradual desensitization of people and society, should be trembling.

Jesus moves from those who instigate sin to the examination of our lives to look for things that promote sin (vv. 8, 9). It is material He included in the Sermon on the Mount (5:29, 30), thus, the repetition serves to underscore the importance of removing the source of sin from our lives. Jesus is not advocating the literal cutting off of a limb or the self-infliction of blindness. He is saying it is better to limit our actions, perceptions, and personal liberty on earth, than suffer eternally. If it requires that our personal convictions be more stringent than those of others, the outcome is worth it. However, we must remember that personal convictions are just that—personal—and should not be imposed on others.

C. The Value of Every Person (vv. 10-14)
(Matthew 18:10-14 is not included in the printed text.)

To emphasize the value of every person to God, Jesus tells the parable of the lost sheep. Seven things are clearly communicated in this passage: (1) We must take great care that we do not "despise," or treat anyone (child or believer) with anything less than full respect. (2) Angels, who have access to the throne of God, are assigned to individuals and active in their lives. (3) Jesus wants *everyone* to be saved, even those who cause others to sin. (4) Every person is valuable, even those who sin. (5) God searches out those who stray from His fold. (6) The salvation of every soul should be celebrated. (7) It is not God's will for anyone to suffer eternally.

II. SEEK RECONCILIATION (Matthew 18:15-20)
A. Righting Wrongs (vv. 15-17)

15. Moreover if thy brother shall trespass against thee, go and tell him his fault between thee and him alone: if he shall hear thee, thou hast gained thy brother.

16. But if he will not hear thee, then take with thee one or two more, that in the mouth of two or three witnesses every word may be established.

17. And if he shall neglect to hear them, tell it unto the church: but if he neglect to hear the church, let him be unto thee as an heathen man and a publican.

In many congregations and among too many Christians, Jesus' teaching concerning reconciliation and church discipline is forgotten at best, or deliberately ignored at worst. He is very specific in how those who are in serious disagreement should handle the situation. First, it deals with members of the church (v. 15), both male and female ("brother" can apply to both), though it is an excellent procedure for addressing issues with those outside the church (family, coworkers, neighbors). Second, it concerns serious issues, not differences of opinion, slighted feelings, or minor grievances where grace, forgiveness, and an attitude of leaving these things in the past should flow abundantly. As Christians, we should be so in love with Christ and His followers that we intentionally choose to exercise forgiveness and mercy (love in action)—with or without being asked. This is an attribute of spiritual maturity.

What should not be ignored are serious offenses—*trespasses*, which literally means "missing the mark." This term represents a violation of God's will and Word. If an offending sin is committed—or an offense (major or minor) concerning which the offended cannot get over after prayer—then the next step is to (1) go with the determination to bring the matter into control (idea behind "go" in the Greek); (2) bring the situation to light ("tell"), as the offender may not be aware of the seriousness of the situation; and (3) do so in private ("alone"—literally, "only"). It is a time for honesty and forthrightness in love and an attitude of reconciliation (see Leviticus 19:17). The process is to be relational; that is, one must not lose sight of the relationship and how its breech would affect all involved (God, offended and offender) and others in the congregation. If he or she comprehends your concerns ("hears"), then you have "gained [literally, "to make a profit"] your brother."

If the brother or sister does not "hear," or comprehend the severity of the matter and his or her responsibility, *then* the offended is to share the matter with "one or two" mature and objective believers (Matthew 18:16a; see also Deuteronomy 19:15). If they agree it is an issue to be addressed, then meet together and review the situation, so that "every fact may be confirmed" (Matthew 18:16b, *NASB*). As they listen to both sides, they may see more than the two people involved perceive.

If this does not resolve the matter, because the offender refuses to listen (or hears without heeding) and accept responsibility, the next step is to "tell it" (lay the matter out) to the church (v. 17a). This should be done in a private session of the body of believers that compose the congregation. Again, the goal is not to choose sides, but to establish Biblical justice—right the wrong, or with love to bring reconciliation between all involved. If he or she refuses the counsel of the church (directly or indirectly), the absolute last resort is to treat the person as one who is not a member of the congregation or a believer

Talk About It:
1. Why is it important to keep an offense between the two parties, if at all possible?
2. When should a dispute be brought before "two or three" believers, and why?
3. Why is Christ's pattern for reconciliation not followed more frequently today?

Forgiveness Frees
A pastor friend of mine received a call from a former member, who had treated him terribly at a particular church. She told him that she had suffered horribly, both physically and spiritually, since that time and that every time she prayed, she saw his face. Over the phone, forgiveness flowed and reconciliation was made. Forgiveness is necessary for the present and the future.
—**Keith Whitt**

("Gentile and a tax collector," v. 17b, *NASB*). Remember, however, Jesus came to save the lost (v. 11); thus, the church cannot give up on the offender.

B. The Power of Determination and Unity (vv. 18-20)

18. Verily I say unto you, Whatsoever ye shall bind on earth shall be bound in heaven: and whatsoever ye shall loose on earth shall be loosed in heaven.

19. Again I say unto you, That if two of you shall agree on earth as touching any thing that they shall ask, it shall be done for them of my Father which is in heaven.

20. For where two or three are gathered together in my name, there am I in the midst of them.

Verse 18 (see also 16:19) has elicited a number of interpretations through the years. A few of the more feasible interpretations include: (1) In many Pentecostal/Charismatic circles, it is understood as giving the believer authority *to bind* ("to tie up" or "to seek in prayer") or *loose* ("set free" or "release") things in or through the spiritual realm. (2) It is viewed by some as giving the church the authority to declare what is forbidden (bind) and allowed (loose) for believers to do, based on the written and discerned will of God (a rabbinic teaching). (3) The church, through the Holy Spirit, has the authority to bind and loose sins (see John 20:23). (4) The church has the authority to include people in and excommunicate persons from its ranks. One can argue passionately for any of these interpretations, but not all will be convinced. Any interpretation should not be separated from the context of church discipline.

The teaching illuminating the power of determination (the resolve to do God's will) through intentionality (a made-up mind) and unity (a heart for God and people) continues with a verse on prayer. Jesus says "if two believers can *agree* ["be of one mind" or "be determined in harmony"] concerning every matter for which they pray, God will establish it" (v. 19, author's translation). The power of and emphasis upon unity should not be ignored. As with all scriptures, this one should be understood in light of other verses on prayer; such as, we should pray with faith (Mark 11:24) and on the basis of God's will (James 4:3).

Jesus moves from prayer to the community gathered. He says it only takes "two or three" gathered in His name for His presence to be manifested in their midst (Matthew 18:20). Traditionally, this has been understood as two or three gathered together to worship. The verse clearly confirms this, for to be gathered in Christ's name is to be a worshiping community. We gather because we want to experience Him. However, it should not be limited to the confines of a building. An old rabbinic tradition says that if two people are reading the Scriptures together, God is between them. Whenever and wherever we gather in His name, we should plan for, welcome, and anticipate His presence. When Jesus comes, He comes as King, Redeemer, Transformer and Comforter.

III. SHOW MERCY (Matthew 18:21-35)
A. Forgiveness (vv. 21, 22)

21. Then came Peter to him, and said, Lord, how oft shall my brother sin against me, and I forgive him? till seven times?

22. Jesus saith unto him, I say not unto thee, Until seven times: but, Until seventy times seven.

Upon hearing the teachings concerning discipline, unity and forgiveness, Peter asks Jesus how often he should forgive an erring brother or sister. Generously, he asks, "Seven times?" (v. 21). The term for *forgive* means "to release a person from a debt or burden," with the idea of leaving it in the past. It is the primary word used of God's forgiving us. In verse 22, Jesus responds with a phrase that means either "seventy-seven times" (77) or "seventy times seven" (490). Either is a significant number of times. Further, Jesus is not suggesting that on the 78th or 491st time, we cease to forgive. His emphasis is that we forgive as many times as is needed.

B. The Unforgiving Servant (vv. 23-35)

(Matthew 18:28-34 is not included in the printed text.)

23. Therefore is the kingdom of heaven likened unto a certain king, which would take account of his servants.

24. And when he had begun to reckon, one was brought unto him, which owed him ten thousand talents.

25. But forasmuch as he had not to pay, his lord commanded him to be sold, and his wife, and children, and all that he had, and payment to be made.

26. The servant therefore fell down, and worshipped him, saying, Lord, have patience with me, and I will pay thee all.

27. Then the lord of that servant was moved with compassion, and loosed him, and forgave him the debt.

35. So likewise shall my heavenly Father do also unto you, if ye from your hearts forgive not every one his brother their trespasses.

Jesus illustrates for the disciples the importance and nature of forgiveness through the parable of the unforgiving servant, a parable that should be read by every believer on a regular basis. A servant who owes an outrageous amount of money (each talent represents 15 years of wages for a laborer) is forgiven by the king (vv. 24, 27); but when encountering a fellow

Talk About It:
1. What does it mean to genuinely forgive someone?
2. Why must we be willing to forgive someone repeatedly?

Talk About It:
1. What does it mean to be "moved with compassion" (v. 27)? Why should this be a characteristic of all Christians?

2. According to verse 35, what should unforgiving people expect from God the Father? Why?

Daily Devotions:
M. Reconciliation Achieved
   Genesis 33:4-16
T. Revenge Resisted
   1 Samuel 24:1-12
W. Follow Righteousness and Mercy
   Proverbs 21:20-26
T. Comfort One Another
   2 Corinthians 1:1-7
F. Minister Reconciliation
   2 Corinthians 5:17-19
S. Submit to God
   James 4:6-10

servant who owed him a fairly significant amount of money (100 denarii, or 100 days' wages), he did not extend the forgiveness he just received (v. 28).

From this parable, we can glean: (1) A day of reckoning will come for all of us (vv. 23, 28). (2) We will stand before God one day (vv. 24, 32). (3) We owe a debt because of sin that we can never hope to repay (vv. 25, 34). (4) Our cries for forgiveness are met by the compassion and provision of Jesus Christ (vv. 26, 27). (5) When we are released from our sins, we are truly released (v. 27). (6) As we have been forgiven, we must forgive others (v. 33). (7) Failure to forgive *from the heart* (v. 35) will result in punishment we do not want to suffer (v. 34). Forgiveness of others is as much (or more!) for us as it is for them (vv. 33, 35).

CONCLUSION

Matthew 18 is a weighty chapter that addresses our attitudes toward servanthood, treatment of others, and the need to address sin. Sin creates more problems than the sinner ever imagined. Few people set out to destroy their lives, families or churches; yet, sin affects more than just the sinner. Jesus set out several principles that we would do well to follow.

GOLDEN TEXT CHALLENGE

"ALL THINGS WHATSOEVER YE WOULD THAT MEN SHOULD DO TO YOU, DO YE EVEN SO TO THEM" (Matthew 7:12).

Speaking from his bitter experience as a slave and crippled person, Epictetus said, "What you avoid suffering yourself, seek not to inflict on others."

To desist from harming others is the less important aspect of Christ's teaching. Just as Jesus spent His life doing good to others, so we must do the same.

Jesus Teaches About the Last Days

Matthew 24:1-51

INTRODUCTION

The evangelist Matthew, under the inspiration of the Holy Spirit, chose to compose his Gospel around five major discourses or blocks of teaching/preaching by Jesus. These include the Sermon on the Mount (chs. 5-7), the Missionary Discourse (ch. 10), the Parables (ch. 13), Church Discipline (ch. 18), and the Eschatological Discourse (chs. 24, 25). Some would add to this list Jesus' scathing denunciation of the Pharisees in chapter 23.

Today, the lesson examines Matthew 24 and the signs of the last days and issues related to the return of Jesus. There seems to be a universal (and understandable) need in new converts to start their Biblical journey by studying prophecy and end-time events. They are not alone. There is a universal curiosity about what the Bible has to say concerning the end of time, especially when our world of comfort becomes threatened (such as September 11, 2001). Preachers of prophecy scramble when catastrophic events take place to see how they fit into our understanding of the last days. Talking about end-time events can be a productive method of witnessing to unsaved people.

Prophecy can be difficult to understand, and end-time events even more frustrating to integrate with the myriad of eschatological verses in Scripture. *Eschatological* (dealing with end-time events, such as Matthew 24) and *apocalyptic* (catastrophic changes in world order, such as the Book of Revelation) literature utilize a significant portion of the Old Testament as foundational material. The understanding of prophecy requires that one be well-versed in the Bible. Even then, there are some things we just do not know. To further complicate the examination of Matthew 24, one must remember that prophecy usually has a short-term (the destruction of Jerusalem in A.D. 70) and long-term meaning (the end of time) and the prophecies are not necessarily in chronological order. Elmer Odom, who taught for many years at Lee University before receiving his heavenly reward, prefaced his lectures on prophecy with this appropriate admonition: "The surest way to understand prophecy is to wait until it is fulfilled!"

In the end, God's plan will be fulfilled. The future is related to the present; there is a day of reckoning coming in the future for unrepentant deeds done in the present; and, we know God is in control, even when our world looks out of control!

Unit Theme:
The Teachings of Jesus (Matthew)

Central Truth:
Jesus warns people to be ready for His return.

Focus:
Explore Christ's teaching about the last days and anticipate His return.

Context:
Jesus teaches at the Mount of Olives in spring A.D. 30.

Golden Text:
"Then shall appear the sign of the Son of man in heaven: and then shall all the tribes of the earth mourn, and they shall see the Son of man coming in the clouds of heaven with power and great glory" (Matthew 24:30).

Study Outline:
I. Signs of the Last Days (Matthew 24:1-20)
II. The Great Tribulation (Matthew 24:21-28)
III. The Second Coming of Christ (Matthew 24:29-51)

I. SIGNS OF THE LAST DAYS (Matthew 24:1-20)

A. Prophecy Concerning the Temple (vv. 1, 2)

1. And Jesus went out, and departed from the temple: and his disciples came to him for to shew him the buildings of the temple.

2. And Jesus said unto them, See ye not all these things? verily I say unto you, There shall not be left here one stone upon another, that shall not be thrown down.

Talk About It:
What tone of voice do you suppose Jesus used in this statement about the Temple? Explain your response.

Immediately following Jesus' denunciation of the Pharisees (23:1-36) and His lament (expression of deep grief) over Jerusalem (vv. 37-39), He leaves the Temple, and the disciples ask about the fate of the center of the Jewish faith (24:1). Herod I decided to remodel and enlarge the second temple of Zerubbabel in 19 B.C. The work was not completed until a few years before its destruction. Therefore, the construction continued during the ministry of Jesus. This may account for the disciples' question (v. 3). According to the first-century historian, Josephus, the Temple was constructed of massive white polished marble stones with sections of gold overlay. He says that from a distance the sun's rays upon the gold looked like flashes of fire on a mountain of snow (*War* 5.222-223). Jesus tells them of the Temple's total destruction, which was to be fulfilled in A.D. 70 (v. 2). No stone would be untouched.

B. Signs of the End (vv. 3-14)

(Matthew 24:10-14 is not included in the printed text.)

3. And as he sat upon the mount of Olives, the disciples came unto him privately, saying, Tell us, when shall these things be? and what shall be the sign of thy coming, and of the end of the world?

4. And Jesus answered and said unto them, Take heed that no man deceive you.

5. For many shall come in my name, saying, I am Christ; and shall deceive many.

6. And ye shall hear of wars and rumours of wars: see that ye be not troubled: for all these things must come to pass, but the end is not yet.

divers (v. 7)—various

7. For nation shall rise against nation, and kingdom against kingdom: and there shall be famines, and pestilences, and earthquakes, in divers places.

8. All these are the beginning of sorrows.

9. Then shall they deliver you up to be afflicted, and shall kill you: and ye shall be hated of all nations for my name's sake.

Jesus and the disciples move to the Mount of Olives (probably across from the Temple), where the disciples ask Him about (1) the timing of His prophecies; (2) the sign of His return (*parousia*, the visit of royalty); and (3) the completion of the age. The New Testament teaches there are two ages (eons or epochs)—this present evil age and the age to come (Matthew 12:32). The ministry of Jesus initiated the age to come, the reclaiming of the world order and instituting the kingdom of God over all creation. Thus, as Christians we live in the overlap of these two ages. We are *in* this evil world, but not *of* this world (John 17:15, 16).

Jesus, as usual, addresses the real concern before addressing the disciples' questions (Matthew 24:4-8). He warns, "Take heed that no one leads you astray" (v. 4, *RSV*). The idea is of someone wandering around without direction or understanding, or because they have been deceived. It is a solemn warning for all disciples. He identifies three ways this can happen: (1) many individuals falsely, deceptively, and somewhat successfully claiming to be the Messiah; (2) being deeply and emotionally troubled by necessary reports of "wars and rumors of wars"; and (3) catastrophic world events, both because of and beyond human control. "All these things are merely the beginning of birth pangs" (v. 8, *NASB*). "Birth pangs" is used of the physical travail and pain involved in birthing a child, but it also speaks of the messianic woes, or the travail involved in "the birthing" of the kingdom of the Messiah and the new age.

The effect of all this for disciples is sobering (v. 9): First, those in authority will "deliver" ["hand over"] you up to be afflicted [literally, "pressed together under pressure"]." Second, some believers will be put to death for their faith and witness. Finally, the universal hatred by "all nations" because of Christ's name will be incurred. History reveals there are always segments of the church suffering persecution, though the entire church may not be affected. It also reveals, however, that there are times when the entire body comes under persecution. Jesus seems to have both aspects in mind.

The tumultuous times and severe persecution will adversely affect believers (vv. 10-12). It will cause "many" (1) to stumble and fall away ("be offended," or be entrapped like an animal); (2) to "betray," or hand one another over to the persecutors; (3) to "hate" other Christians; (4) "false prophets" to arise with effectively deceptive teaching that ensnares many; (5) to be affected by the rampant "iniquity," or lawlessness (the practice of sin) and allow their love to gradually grow cold.

All is not bleak, however. "Whoever stands his or her ground and refuses to give in shall be delivered and made whole" (v. 13, author's translation). Unfortunately for some saints, this will occur in the age to come, not this one. Tertullian (A.D. 200) said, "The blood of martyrs is the seed of the church." This fits well with Jesus' declaration that the "gospel" (good news)

Talk About It:
1. Why have so many false messiahs arisen over the centuries? Why is it still happening today?
2. List the "beginning of sorrows" (v. 8) given in verses 6 and 7. How relevant are they to our day?
3. What can Christians expect from "all nations" (v. 9), and why?
4. Explain the phrase "the love of many shall wax cold" (v. 12). How can Christians avoid this fate?

Easy Targets
One morning in the 1920s in London, Arthur Ferguson saw a wealthy American admiring the statue of Admiral Lord Nelson and the column it rested on. Suddenly inspired, Ferguson put his selling ability to work and "sold" Nelson's column to the American for $30,000! Ferguson later "sold" the famous clock Big Ben to another American for $5,000 and took $10,000 from another as down payment on Buckingham Palace.
By the time he was arrested, Ferguson had

---

announcing the coming of Jesus Christ and His kingdom will
be "preached" (made known) in a public, extensive and effective manner in the inhabited earth as a successful "witness," or
testimony (from the Greek word for "martyr") to "all nations" (v.
14). When these things are fulfilled—through the design of the
Father, the preaching of the Cross and the provision of the effi-
cacious blood of Jesus Christ, and the empowering and sustaining of the Holy Spirit—"then shall the end come."

C. The Abomination of Desolation (vv. 15-20)
(Matthew 24:15-20 is not included in the printed text.)
Jesus continues to address end-time events with a reference to the "abomination that causes desolation" (v. 15, *NIV*),
prophesied by Daniel (9:27; 11:31; 12:11). This phrase can
mean: (1) something similar to the offering of swine in the
Temple by Antiochus Epiphanes during the period between the
Old and New Testaments; (2) the utter desolation of the land;
or (3) the participation of the Antichrist in the rebuilt Temple. In
light of the phrase "stand in the holy place" and the admonition
for the reader to be careful in considering this, it seems to refer
to a combination of the first and last. However, the warning for
those in Judea to flee to places of safety (Matthew 24:16-20)
does speak to the desolation of Jerusalem in A.D. 70.

II. THE GREAT TRIBULATION (Matthew 24:21-28)
A. The Great Tribulation (vv. 21, 22)
**21. For then shall be great tribulation, such as was not
since the beginning of the world to this time, no, nor ever
shall be.**
**22. And except those days should be shortened, there
should no flesh be saved: but for the elect's sake those
days shall be shortened.**
Daniel 12:1 serves as the Old Testament foundation for
this passage. Jesus says there will be "great tribulation" (v.
21). *Tribulation* is great distress that is caused from external
and internal pressure. It is so severe that it means "to the
point of bursting." There is a twofold meaning here. Believers
of all ages have and will face great distress. It is part of being
a sojourner in a foreign land. We long for the release from this
world, but suffer its injustices until that time. Yet, Jesus adds,
this tribulation will be unlike anything that ever has been or
will be. This also points to what is commonly known as the
Great Tribulation, a seven-year period between the two
events of the Second Advent, that is, after the Second Coming
(1 Thessalonians 4:13-18) and before His return to bring judgment (Revelation 19:11-16).
Matthew 24:22 can be understood as a continuation of the

previous verse or as resuming the line of thought in verse 14. It seems to be a commentary on the end-time events as a whole and not one specific event, such as the Tribulation. The severity of the events, at times, will be such that the time will necessarily be shortened or no one will survive ("no flesh would have been saved," ASV). "But, because of the chosen ones ["elect"], those days have already been decreased" (author's translation). This can be interpreted two ways: (1) Those days have already been shortened in the plan of God to spare those who are believers; or (2) because of the believers' desire to be with Him, the end-time events have been shortened and the world will be spared prolonged judgment.

> "Most of us are optimists, and it is not easy for some to believe that catastrophe awaits the world. Nonetheless, that is exactly what God's Word foretells."
> —Clyne Buxton

B. The Rise of Antichrists (vv. 23-26)

23. Then if any man shall say unto you, Lo, here is Christ, or there; believe it not.

24. For there shall arise false Christs, and false prophets, and shall shew great signs and wonders; insomuch that, if it were possible, they shall deceive the very elect.

25. Behold, I have told you before.

26. Wherefore if they shall say unto you, Behold, he is in the desert; go not forth: behold, he is in the secret chambers; believe it not.

In the last days, "then" many will be deceived by and chase after false messiahs and false prophets, who produce fantastic signs and miraculous wonders in an attempt to deceive even believers. It is not within human capabilities to do these things. The source of the power is evil and has evil intent.

Talk About It:
1. What do you think the "great signs and wonders" of the false Christs are? What makes them so effective?
2. Where should we *not* look for the Messiah, and why not?

C. Concerning Lightning and Vultures (vv. 27, 28)

27. For as the lightning cometh out of the east, and shineth even unto the west; so shall also the coming of the Son of man be.

28. For wheresoever the carcase is, there will the eagles be gathered together.

Verse 27 is picturesque and fairly straightforward: the coming of the Son of Man will be quick, obvious and extraordinary. Verse 28 presents several possible interpretations: (1) It was a well-known proverbial saying in Jesus' day. (2) It teaches that the spiritually dead ("carcase") attract judgment (gathered vultures). (3) The coming of Jesus will be as visible and public as vultures circling their next feast. In light of the context, this third one seems the best interpretation.

Talk About It:
Why will Jesus return "as the lightning" (v. 27)?

III. THE SECOND COMING OF CHRIST (Matthew 24:29-51)
A. The Coming of the Son of Man (vv. 29-31)

29. Immediately after the tribulation of those days shall

the sun be darkened, and the moon shall not give her light, and the stars shall fall from heaven, and the powers of the heavens shall be shaken:

30. And then shall appear the sign of the Son of man in heaven: and then shall all the tribes of the earth mourn, and they shall see the Son of man coming in the clouds of heaven with power and great glory.

31. And he shall send his angels with a great sound of a trumpet, and they shall gather together his elect from the four winds, from one end of heaven to the other.

"Immediately after the tribulation of those days," several celestial catastrophes will occur, affecting the light from the sun, moon and stars (v. 29). These events recall the prophecies of Ezekiel 32:7 and Joel 2:10. It is not unusual for each of these sources of direct or indirect light to be eclipsed or hidden at different times; however, here the sun is unable to give light, the moon cannot give her radiance, and the stars will fall in ruins from the sky at the same time. Further, Jesus says the very powers of the heavens will be unexpectedly and disastrously shaken. "The heavens" are not identified, but probably refer to the first (celestial realm) and second (the realm of evil powers; see Ephesians 6:12) being subject to the power of God, whose abiding place is the "third heaven" (2 Corinthians 12:2).

The image is that of the heavens being emptied to emphasize and make room for "the sign of the Son of man in heaven" (Matthew 24:30). Some view the sign as a supernatural outward sign, such as a cross in the sky (Chrysostom), while others see it as speaking of His return itself. Still others understand *sign* to mean "a standard" or "banner" of some sort. Isaiah 18:3 speaks to this and seems to serve as the foundation of these verses (also see Zechariah 9:14). Whatever it is will cause all the nations of the earth to "mourn." *Mourn* means "deep grief caused by remorse." Here, it carries with it a sense of being "cut off" from the coming of the Son of Man in majesty and power—in stark contrast to His humble first appearing on earth (see Luke 2:1-38).

At that time, His "angels," or messengers, will be sent with authority at the "mighty trumpet blast" (Matthew 24:31, *TLB*; cf. 1 Corinthians 15:52; 1 Thessalonians 4:16). Their purpose is to gather together in one place His "chosen ones" (*TLB*) from the "four winds, from the farthest point of heaven to the other farthest point of heaven" (author's translation). First, the "four winds" is a way of saying from every direction of the earth (see Revelation 7:1). Second, "from farthest point . . . to farthest point" is a way of communicating the comprehensiveness of the gathering. No saint of God will be overlooked or left behind.

B. Learning From Nature (vv. 32-35)

(Matthew 24:32, 33 is not included in the printed text.)

34. Verily I say unto you, This generation shall not pass, till all these things be fulfilled.

35. Heaven and earth shall pass away, but my words shall not pass away.

Jesus instructs us to "learn the parable from the fig tree" (v. 32, *NASB*). The fig tree is one of the few trees in Israel that sheds its leaves in winter. When spring arrives, the twigs become "tender" and leaves spring forth, a sure sign that summer is eminent. *Learn* is a cognate (related word) of the word *disciple* in the Greek. The parable probably speaks on at least three levels: (1) learn to read the signs pointing to His coming (v. 33); (2) the appearance of the fig tree's leaves point to, but do not cause, summer (some things we respond to, but do not control); and (3) the winter of distress should not prevent a personal preparation for His return (continued faithful discipleship).

The next verse presents difficulties (v. 34). Jesus' affirmation of truth and importance ("I tell you the truth"; also see v. 35) is followed by the statement that "this generation will certainly not pass away until all these things have happened" (*NIV*). Who is "this generation," and what are "all these things"? First, some assert (wrongly) that Jesus thought He would return shortly after His death and is saying He will return before the death of the generation that composed His first-century audience. However, Jesus says that even He does not know (at this point) "the day or the hour" of His return (see v. 36). Second, a more popular view is that "all these things" refers to the destruction of Jerusalem; however, Jesus speaks of much more than the prophecies concerning Jerusalem. Third, "generation" refers to the Jewish people or the human race in general. This is a viable understanding. Fourth, the early church fathers understood "generation" as a reference to the church, which will prevail against the gates of Hades and endure to the end. This is also a possible understanding. Jesus was not a false prophet; thus, He could not have meant the physical generation to which He was speaking. The fourth option, connecting the "chosen ones" with "this generation," seems to fit best.

Talk About It:
1. How do we know when the end of time is "at the door" (v. 33)?
2. Explain the statement "Heaven and earth shall pass away" (v. 35a).
3. Explain the statement "My words shall not pass away" (v. 35b).

"The word of Christ is more sure and lasting than heaven and earth."
—**Matthew Henry**

C. The Day and the Hour (vv. 36-51)

(Matthew 24:43-51 is not included in the printed text.)

36. But of that day and hour knoweth no man, no, not the angels of heaven, but my Father only.

37. But as the days of Noe were, so shall also the coming of the Son of man be.

38. For as in the days that were before the flood they were eating and drinking, marrying and giving in marriage, until the day that Noe entered into the ark,

39. And knew not until the flood came, and took them all away; so shall also the coming of the Son of man be.

40. Then shall two be in the field; the one shall be taken, and the other left.

41. Two women shall be grinding at the mill; the one shall be taken, and the other left.

42. Watch therefore: for ye know not what hour your Lord doth come.

No human nor angel knows the "day and hour" of His coming, but the Father alone (v. 36). First, this suggests that believers should not become ensnared in trying to determine the date of Christ's coming. The phrase "that day and hour" refers to specific dates and times. Oftentimes, preachers of prophecy declare that trying to determine the year does not violate this verse. Certainly, we all have opinions. However, those who have attempted to determine the year and stated that Jesus would return in a specific year (some so bold as to give the day!) have been sorely embarrassed. We are to be wise concerning the signs, live in a state of continual preparedness, and not grow weary.

Second, Jesus willingly restrained His deity while on the earth (see Philippians 2:5-8). There is no reason to believe He is still unaware of the timing of end-time events and His return, now that He has picked back up the mantle of His divineness, so to speak. He is fully God. As such, He is omniscient (or knows all things), including the time of the Second Coming.

Jesus gives several examples to illustrate the suddenness of His return (Matthew 24:37-51). First, He compares His return to "the days of Noah" (vv. 37-39). It took Noah as long as 120 years to build the ark, based on Genesis 6:3. Jesus' intent here is to emphasize the parallel between the two events, such as the spiritual dullness caused by daily living, the long period of preparation, and the sudden occurrence of the event.

Second, He uses the example of workers in the field (men) and the mill (women) to reveal that some will be "taken" and others will not (vv. 40-42). Both the men and the women were fulfilling their expected duties in life. Two were prepared beforehand; two were not. Jesus commands us to "watch" (be vigilant) spiritually, because we do not know when He will return (v. 42).

Third, Jesus tells a story of "the goodman" (the head of the house), who would have stayed awake if he had known when the thief was coming (v. 43). As with the other examples, it closes with the admonition to be ready at all times, for Jesus will return in an unexpected and even unlikely time (v. 44).

The teaching then shifts from an emphasis on watchfulness to preparedness (vv. 45-51). The first servant is "faithful and wise" (opposite of foolish) and carries out his duties as he

Talk About It:
1. Why does God keep the date of Christ's coming "top secret"?
2. How is our day like Noah's day?
3. How do we live in readiness for Christ's return?

Wrong Dates

A particular minister spent a great deal of time and money publishing and distributing books to other ministers, giving 88 reasons Jesus would return on a specific date. When he missed it, he republished the book with the reason he missed the date by one year and a day. That date did not produce the return of Christ either. Sadly, this gifted and dedicated person drifted into oblivion. He did not heed Jesus' admonition concerning dates, and the church lost a gifted prophecy preacher.

Jesus Teaches About the Last Days

should, whether the master is there or not (vv. 45-47). This servant is "blessed" (a privileged recipient of God's favor) and rewarded with caring for more of the master's possessions. It is an excellent blessing and awesome responsibility to be entrusted with the things of God! The second servant is concerned with appearances and is selfish, rather than faithful (vv. 48, 49). The master will return, and the consequences for unfaithfulness and the lack of preparedness will be severe (vv. 50, 51).

CONCLUSION

Jesus will return for His church! It may not happen when we think it should, or even the way we think. Our responsibility is not to focus solely on the event, but rather, our responsibilities until the time that He comes. We must be faithful in His kingdom; be determined to endure the persecution; watch the signs, not only for our sake, but also for those around us who need salvation; and be prepared for His return in every moment of our lives.

GOLDEN TEXT CHALLENGE

"THEN SHALL APPEAR THE SIGN OF THE SON OF MAN IN HEAVEN: AND THEN SHALL ALL THE TRIBES OF THE EARTH MOURN, AND THEY SHALL SEE THE SON OF MAN COMING IN THE CLOUDS OF HEAVEN WITH POWER AND GREAT GLORY" (Matthew 24:30).

Some of all the tribes and kindreds of the earth shall mourn; for the greater part will tremble at His approach, while the chosen remnant, one of a family and two of a tribe, shall lift up their heads with joy, knowing that their redemption draws nigh, and their Redeemer. Note, sooner or later, all sinners will be mourners. Penitent sinners look to Christ, and mourn after a godly sort; and they who sow in those tears, shall shortly reap in joy. Impenitent sinners shall look unto Him whom they have pierced, and, though they laugh now, shall mourn and weep after a devilish sort, in endless horror and despair.

The Son of Man will be the Judge, that He may be seen, that sinners thereby may be the more confounded. [They will say,] "Is this He whom we have slighted, and rejected, and rebelled against; whom we have crucified to ourselves afresh; who might have been our Savior, but is our Judge, and will be our enemy forever?"—**Matthew Henry**

God's Design for the Home

**Genesis 2:18-25; Deuteronomy 6:1-9;
Psalm 128:1-6; Matthew 19:3-6**

Unit Theme:
The Christian Family

Central Truth:
Following God's design for the home brings His blessings.

Focus:
Affirm and follow God's plan for the family.

Context:
Selected passages revealing God's plan for the family.

Golden Text:
"Choose you this day whom ye will serve . . . but as for me and my house, we will serve the Lord" (Joshua 24:15).

Study Outline:
I. God Establishes Marriage (Genesis 2:18-25; Matthew 19:3-6)
II. God's Foundation for the Home (Deuteronomy 6:1-9)
III. God Blesses the Family (Psalm 128:1-6)

INTRODUCTION

The starting point for discovering God's design for marriage is found in His Word with His creation of the first two human beings. The Hebrew word *ish*, meaning "male," is the same root word for "husband." The Hebrew word *isha*, meaning "woman" or "female," is the same word for "wife."

Clearly, according to Scripture, God designed and established marriage to be a covenant union between a man and a woman. By His divine providence, this sacred union begins with a couple's mutual attraction and growing affection for each other prior to marriage. God uses the strength of the couple's love to seal their hearts as one as they enter into a covenant vow of commitment through the rite of marriage.

From the beginning, God decreed that the intimate union of every husband and wife become the foundation of the home and family. In fact, it is through their sacred intimate union that God's own wedding gift to every couple is revealed. He allows both husband and wife to share in His creativity. He ordained that both, through the union of their love, bring forth children.

Is it any wonder that God, who so beautifully designed, established and ordained marriage, would also perform the first human wedding?

In the Old Testament, we read how God viewed marriage with such special significance that He lovingly spoke of the spiritual relationship between Himself and the Israelites as one of betrothal or marriage (see Isaiah 62:4, 5; Hosea 2:19). In the New Testament, Christ is identified as the Bridegroom and the believing church as His beloved bride (Matthew 9:15; Revelation 21:9). In John 17, Christ prayerfully reveals His divine desire for a relationship of oneness with His bride.

The Scriptures also reveal to us why marriage holds a unique place in God's heart. His own character is built into His design for marriage. His love is marriage's foundation of purity, selflessness, fidelity and permanence. God still continues today to call forth these same qualities from every couple He joins together in marriage.

I. GOD ESTABLISHES MARRIAGE (Genesis 2:18-25; Matthew 19:3-6)

A. Adam's Need (Genesis 2:18-20)

18. And the Lord God said, It is not good that the man should be alone; I will make him an help meet for him.

19. And out of the ground the Lord God formed every beast of the field, and every fowl of the air; and brought them unto Adam to see what he would call them: and whatsoever Adam called every living creature, that was the name thereof.

20. And Adam gave names to all cattle, and to the fowl of the air, and to every beast of the field; but for Adam there was not found an help meet for him.

In this passage we gain insight into God's character by seeing His compassion and concern for man's need. And it is evident that even from the beginning, God's sympathy toward man moves Him to meet Adam's need.

The first chapter of Genesis provides us with an overview of all of God's creative work. In verse 31, Moses (the author) tells us how God viewed His work with great satisfaction. God declared that everything He had made was "very good" and, therefore, His creation of history's first couple was "very good."

In chapter 2 the author draws us away from all of God's other creative works to focus specifically on His involvement with humanity, the crown of His creation. Verse 18 reveals that after God had created the first man, Adam, He acknowledged there was yet one aspect of His human creation which He considered "not good": Adam was alone.

God purposely chose not to create both man and woman at the same time as He had created all other male and female creations. He wisely planned for Adam to experience loneliness in his life. God allowed Adam to discover for himself his own need for companionship by giving him the task of naming all of the animals and birds that He brought before him. God then stood back, watching Adam carefully study every creature's nature, habits and movements. Adam then named each parent species accordingly. Adam observed that every species had an opposite counterpart with many similarities. Yet there was not even one found among any of God's creation that matched his own physical being. Under God's divine plan, Adam was first made aware of his loneliness. Only then could he experience and fully appreciate God's provision for his need.

It is interesting that long before the fall of man, God perfectly planned for marriage and the family. Genesis 1:26, 27 reminds us God created both male and female in His own image or likeness. This includes the engrafting of His providing and protective nature as our heavenly Father and His nurturing nature of a mother.

an help meet (v. 18)—"a suitable helper"

Talk About It:
1. Do you suppose God didn't realize Adam would feel "alone" until after He created him? Explain your answer.
2. What responsibility did God give to Adam, and why (v. 19)?

"A successful marriage is always a triangle—a man, a woman, and God."
—Cecil Myers

God blessed our first parents, commanding them to be fruitful, multiply and fill the earth (v. 28). Adam could not fulfill this command alone. He needed the help of a lifelong female companion. The verses from Genesis 2 prove man's need is often rooted in God's sovereignty.

B. God's Provision (Genesis 2:21-25; Matthew 19:3-6)
  (Genesis 2:24, 25 is not included in the printed text.)
  Genesis 2:21. And the Lord God caused a deep sleep to fall upon Adam, and he slept: and he took one of his ribs, and closed up the flesh instead thereof;
  22. And the rib, which the Lord God had taken from man, made he a woman, and brought her unto the man.
  23. And Adam said, This is now bone of my bones, and flesh of my flesh: she shall be called Woman, because she was taken out of Man.
  Matthew 19:3. The Pharisees also came unto him, tempting him, and saying unto him, Is it lawful for a man to put away his wife for every cause?
  4. And he answered and said unto them, Have ye not read, that he which made them at the beginning made them male and female,
  5. And said, For this cause shall a man leave father and mother, and shall cleave to his wife: and they twain shall be one flesh?
  6. Wherefore they are no more twain, but one flesh. What therefore God hath joined together, let not man put asunder.

put asunder (Matthew 19:6)— separate

Talk About It:
1. Why was Eve's creation so different from Adam's?
2. What question did the Pharisees pose in Matthew 19:3?
3. What problems are created when a married man doesn't "leave" Mom and Dad?
4. Why is divorce so common? What is God's opinion of it?

God had taken special care to psychologically prepare Adam for the reception of his own female companion. He then caused Adam to succumb to His divine anesthetic. While he slept, God supernaturally reached into Adam's side and removed one of his ribs. The Bible tells us God closed up the outer flesh and from the rib He created the first woman.

God, by His sovereign choice, did not create woman from the dust of the ground as He had created Adam. Instead, He created woman from man's flesh and bone, allowing both to be of "one flesh." In so doing, God expressed His divine will for oneness in marriage.

In this passage from Genesis 2, we see God's deep concern for man's incompleteness. God's concern led to three distinct acts: (1) God acknowledged man's need for a companion. (2) God went to great lengths in preparation to meet man's need. (3) God himself brought Adam His divine provision in answer to man's need.

Adam immediately recognized a shared identity between himself and the female God had created for him. He jubilantly

God's Design for the Home

declared, "This is now bone of my bones, and flesh of my flesh" (v. 23). The progression of this Hebrew expression, which serves to indicate family kinship, begins here with Adam's declaration and courses its way throughout the Old Testament (e.g. Genesis 29:14; 2 Samuel 5:1). Finally, Adam could name one of God's female creations who was comparable to himself intellectually, physically and emotionally. Because she was created from man, Adam chose to call her "woman."

The story of man's creation cannot be told without also telling the Biblical account of the first marriage. The two accounts are inseparable. God's perfect design of history's first couple proves that neither man nor woman is complete without the other. As stated earlier, it is God's desire for "oneness" to be the foundation of all marriages.

In Genesis 2:24 and Matthew 19:5, God says, "A man [shall] leave his father and his mother, and shall cleave unto his wife." The word *leave* speaks of complete departure, while *cleave* expresses the idea of being *joined* or *glued* together. Both words are used to describe a married couple's sacred obligation of absolute commitment to each other.

Figuratively speaking, Christ left His heavenly Father to join Himself to His bride—the church. The Bible assures us that Christ has lovingly committed Himself to every Christian for eternity. In turn, those who are willing to leave all worldly ways behind through salvation are cleaving to Christ as His bride. Thus, the first recorded marriage in the Bible is also symbolic of the marriage relationship between Christ and the church.

> "It is not marriage that fails; it is people that fail. All that marriage does is show people up."
> —**Anonymous**

II. GOD'S FOUNDATION FOR THE HOME
(Deuteronomy 6:1-9)
A. Fear God (vv. 1-3)
1. Now these are the commandments, the statutes, and the judgments, which the Lord your God commanded to teach you, that ye might do them in the land whither ye go to possess it:

2. That thou mightest fear the Lord thy God, to keep all his statutes and his commandments, which I command thee, thou, and thy son, and thy son's son, all the days of thy life; and that thy days may be prolonged.

3. Hear therefore, O Israel, and observe to do it; that it may be well with thee, and that ye may increase mightily, as the Lord God of thy fathers hath promised thee, in the land that floweth with milk and honey.

Nearly four decades had passed since God, through His servant Moses, delivered the Israelites from Egyptian bondage. Under God's direction, Moses led the Israelites through the desert to Mount Sinai. There, the chosen nation gratefully vowed

Talk About It:
1. What did God command His people to do?
2. What is God's desire for future generations?

their loyalty and obedience to God in a covenant (see Exodus 24:7, 8). The nation's covenant allegiance, however, was short-lived. The desert years of chronic disobedience, disloyalty and faithlessness toward God prevented the Israelites from taking possession of His promise of a new and prosperous land. Instead, their lifestyle choices set into action sin's consequences. Tragically, nearly all of God's chosen people who originally experienced His miraculous deliverance from Egyptian slavery had perished in the desert wilderness.

The Book of Deuteronomy presents us with a new generation of Israelites who, as babes and children, were reared in the desert. The Israelites' years of aimless desert wanderings had finally come to an end, and this new generation of Israelites stood before Moses at the borders of Canaan eager to enter the land promised to their ancestors.

Moses was fully aware that this new generation was about to embark on a whole new life under new leadership in a new land. Once there, they would also face many new temptations and challenges. So Moses exhorted the Israelites to hear and obey God's divine instructions for maintaining a covenant lifestyle in the Promised Land they were about to possess.

In Deuteronomy's previous chapters, Moses reminded this new Israelite generation of God's miraculous interventions in Israel's history. Moses carefully rehearsed God's command-ments, cautioning His chosen people to obey all of them, regard-less. God's laws were His divine instructions to guide them in their new life ahead. Moses also warned the Israelites against forgetting God in the new land and disobeying His command-ments. Moses used this final opportunity to exhort God's peo-ple to keep their renewed covenant vows to God through love and obedience toward God. He assured them of God's promised blessings for doing so, which included prolonged life and prosperity.

In verses 1 and 2, Moses emphasized the fact that obedi-ence to God's covenant commandments comes from pos-sessing an attitude of a holy fear of the Lord. He was not speaking about obeying God through a terror-ridden submis-sion. Rather, he purposed to impart to the Israelites his own attitude of reverential love toward God. By laying a firm foun-dation of obedience toward God through a healthy fear of the Lord, Moses paved the way for the new Israelite generation to experience much more of God's divine interventions in the land He promised them.

"The most impor-tant thought that ever occupied my mind is that of my individual responsi-bility to God."
—Daniel Webster

B. Love God (vv. 4-6)
4. Hear, O Israel: The Lord our God is one Lord:
5. And thou shalt love the Lord thy God with all thine

heart, and with all thy soul, and with all thy might.

6. And these words, which I command thee this day, shall be in thine heart.

Moses' first four books of the Old Testament provide us with detailed acts of God's love for the nation of Israel. His fifth book, Deuteronomy, however, is the first Old Testament book to record God's expressed love for His chosen people. In the chapters that fill Deuteronomy's pages, Moses reminds the new Israelite generation of their special relationship with God—how God especially chose them to be His own treasured possession (see 7:6; 14:2). God separated the nation to Himself for His holy purpose of bringing forth the world's future Savior.

The emphasis of God's love for His chosen people is expressed not only through His servant Moses but also through many other prophets and Biblical writers. For example, Hosea spoke of God's love for Israel as the love of a parent for a precious child (see Hosea 11:1, 4). Hosea explained how God took hold of Israel's childlike arms and drew the nation out from Egypt into His own holy arms with gentle cords of love.

In these verses from Deuteronomy 6, Moses stresses to the new Israelite generation the importance of responding to God's unfailing love for them with a mutual love and loyalty toward God. It is only from genuine love for God ingrained in the believer's heart that a wholesome fear of the Lord emerges. Such a union of love and reverence for God always results in an attitude of joyful obedience to His law. Jesus emphasized this truth more fully in the New Testament. In John 14:15, 21, He declared to His followers, "If you love Me, keep My commandments. . . . He who has My commandments and keeps them, it is he who loves Me" (*NKJV*).

If we truly love God, we will also love His commandments. In Biblical times, as well as modern, any governing law reveals the character and personality of the lawgiver who has the authority to enforce the commandments of the law. This is why David could so easily express his love for God's commandments in Psalm 119:47, 48. The commandments embodied the nature of God, who wrote them. For this reason, David delighted in God's law.

In verse 38, David described himself as being "devoted to fearing" God (*NKJV*). His reverential love for God served as his guide to keep him from grieving God's Spirit through disobedience. In Deuteronomy, Moses' greatest desire for the Israelites was that they would possess a similar attitude of holy reverence and devotion toward God. He exhorted them to love God with all their heart, with all their soul, and with all their strength. A personal love for God alone and for His commandments would, in turn, inspire the Israelites to also teach their children

Talk About It:
1. Why the emphasis on God being "one" (v. 4)?
2. Why are "heart," "soul," and "might" mentioned separately (v. 5)? Why not just say "with your all"?
3. How can God's Word be in "thine heart" (v. 6)?

"The intrinsic drive to please the significant people in our lives reflects the fact that we were built to bring pleasure to someone outside of ourselves—God. The highest satisfaction of life is knowing in our spirits that He indeed is pleased with us."

—Joseph Stowell

how to experience an intimate love for God through their example of obedience to His law.

The Hebrew word for *law* means "instruction." God designed His covenant commandments to instruct and guide His people in all aspects of their everyday lives, including moral, civil and ceremonial matters. These verses reveal it was God's desire that even the children be diligently taught how to love and reverence Him through their parents' examples of loving obedience. A prayerful reading of Deuteronomy 6 provides today's Christian parents with godly instructions for parenthood.

C. Teach Your Children (vv. 7-9)

7. And thou shalt teach them diligently unto thy children, and shalt talk of them when thou sittest in thine house, and when thou walkest by the way, and when thou liest down, and when thou risest up.

8. And thou shalt bind them for a sign upon thine hand, and they shall be as frontlets between thine eyes.

9. And thou shalt write them upon the posts of thy house, and on thy gates.

Keeping God's law in constant attention would require some method. Verses 7-9 suggest practical measures to make this possible. They are still relevant today.

Truths to be taught should be made conspicuous. The Hebrews were aware of the fact that their law was to be kept before them. All about them they provided reminders of the reality of the unseen God. On small parchment rolls were written four passages of Scripture: Deuteronomy 6:4-9; 11:13-21; Exodus 13:1-10, 11-16. These were placed in small containers worn on the arm and forehead. They were called *phylacteries* (Hebrew, *tefillin*) in the New Testament (Matthew 23:5). There is considerable argument concerning whether the instructions in Deuteronomy are intended to be taken literally, but the answer seems obvious. The instructions are definite. The teaching method was excellent. The danger lay not in the physical reminders but in their becoming a superstitious object considered valuable in themselves rather than as reminders. Truly devoted Jews always found them helpful.

The real point of the instruction was not physical but symbolic: God's laws are meant to affect both the person and his home day in and day out. The setting for these famous verses is important; this passage is part of the long preface to the detailed law code which begins in chapter 12, and it seeks to bring home to the reader the importance of reading, learning, obeying, and applying not only the Ten Commandments of chapter 5 but all the lesser rulings of later chapters.

The word for *doorpost* (v. 9, *NKJV*) has gained usage in its

Talk About It:
1. Who bears the primary responsibility for providing spiritual training to children, and when should they teach children (v. 7)?
2. How can we put God's Word before the eyes of our children?

God's Design for the Home

own right. *Mezuzah* is the name that is now given to a small box containing a parchment inscribed with Deuteronomy 6:4-9 and 11:13-21, along with the name *Shaddai*, and fixed to the doorposts of orthodox Jewish homes as a reminder of their faith. Whether taken literally or metaphorically, the signs described in 6:8, 9 indicate that the individual, his home, and his community were to be distinguished in their character by obedience to the commandments as a reason of love for God.

Yet, even in Judaism, man's love for God could not reach its highest expression or fulfillment. It took Jesus Christ's coming to realize the meaning of such affection.

III. GOD BLESSES THE FAMILY (Psalm 128:1-6)
A. Essentials of Worship (v. 1)

1. Blessed is every one that feareth the Lord; that walketh in his ways.

All through Scripture we see evidence of the family's symbolic meaning. The Old Testament begins with the history of the first marriage and family, and then continues with God's divine interventions in families thereafter. The New Testament emphasizes our Christian status as the bride of Christ, as well as our spiritual relationship with our heavenly Father.

In this opening verse from Psalm 128, God reveals the two essential elements that invoke God's blessings on the family—reverence for Him and obedience to His Word. It is noteworthy that all of the family's members are to be continually nurtured in these two essential elements.

The *fear of the Lord* speaks of a life of reverence toward God. Much like the relationship of love and companionship between a husband and his wife, so God desires an intimate relationship of love and companionship with each one of us. A human heart that is bound to God's heart with a strong love is ever conscious of His abiding presence and is also conscious of offending Him through sin.

Both the fear of the Lord and love for God speak of the believer's worship of God. To fear the Lord is to reverence His divine being and majesty in an attitude of holy adoration. This kind of wholesome fear flows from a deep and abiding love for God.

Loving God with our all motivates us as Christ's followers to respond to every situation with Christlike behavior. To put it another way, there is a definite spiritual connection between the Christian's inward life and his outward actions. When the fear of the Lord and love for God abounds, Christlikeness is inevitable.

This brings us to the second essential element for a blessed family life. To *walk in God's ways* means uncompromising obedience to His Word. Our Christianity is meaningless unless we

I saw tomorrow look at me
From little children's eyes;
And thought how carefully we'd teach
If we were really wise.
—Anonymous

Talk About It:
Can a person fear the Lord without walking in His ways? Why or why not?

"One of the reasons people find it hard to be obedient to the commands of Christ is that they are uncomfortable taking orders from a stranger."
—Gary Gulbranson

are serious about obeying God. The Christian family's lifestyle choices, based on the Word of God, may also become witnessing tools to help others around them learn of God's all-encompassing love.

B. God's Model Family (vv. 2-6)

2. For thou shalt eat the labour of thine hands: happy shalt thou be, and it shall be well with thee.

3. Thy wife shall be as a fruitful vine by the sides of thine house: thy children like olive plants round about thy table.

4. Behold, that thus shall the man be blessed that feareth the Lord.

5. The Lord shall bless thee out of Zion: and thou shalt see the good of Jerusalem all the days of thy life.

6. Yea, thou shalt see thy children's children, and peace upon Israel.

Talk About It:
1. According to verse 2, what brings happiness? Why?
2. How does God promise to bless the person "who fears the Lord" (v. 4)?
3. How does the family influence the nation?

This particular psalm was a personal favorite of Martin Luther. In fact, he often referred to it as the "Wedding Psalm for Christians." Matthew Henry titled it "A Psalm for Families." Others throughout history have affectionately named it "The Believer's Marriage Song."

No matter how it's referred to, this psalm presents the reader with one of the most beautiful portrayals of the family whose members worship God together through reverential love and obedience. It encourages family members to nurture a wholesome fear of the Lord and to wisely choose to live by God's Word. In reality, this passage mirrors the heart of God for all Christian families throughout the church.

This psalm reveals that God blesses family members who live out God's love and respect for one another in the home, and that these same family members are more likely destined to become model citizens in the community. In other words, the family who makes God the focus of their lives glorifies God by making a spiritual impact on neighboring families. As previously stated, the Christian family's lifestyle choices reflect the Biblical standards by which they live. Such families are assured of many blessings both in the natural and in the spiritual.

One of the many blessings God promises includes prosperity in labor. Throughout Scripture we read that prosperity is linked to both reverence for God and obedience to His Word. God's promise of prosperity applies to physical labor as well as to blessing in Christian ministry work.

A second area of blessing concerns the family's bonding of love and loyalty. The phrase "a fruitful vine" (v. 3) speaks of a wife who draws her inner strength and support from her husband's deep love for her. She returns her love with joyful giving of herself to her husband and her children in ways that enrich their lives.

In verse 3, we read that the children of a godly home are said to be "like [fine] olive plants." Olive trees are known for being practically indestructible. New plants grow from even the seemingly lifeless root of the olive tree running along the ground. The children of God-fearing parents represent God's unhindered blessing of longevity which continues on in the new life through reproduction.

The entirety of this psalm opens our eyes to the central truth that every Christian family can have a major influence on the ushering in of God's divine blessing of peace and prosperity on their cities and even their nations. God hears the prayers of His people everywhere. It is His desire to answer such prayers of faith with the blessings recorded in His Word for every nation who worships Him through reverential love and obedience.

"Let France have good mothers and she will have good sons."
—Napoleon Bonaparte

CONCLUSION

Someone has said, "God created the family before He birthed the church." Trying to build a successful church without focusing on ministry to families will lead to failure. It is God's plan for parents to love God supremely and for their children to follow their example. Healthy families build strong churches.

GOLDEN TEXT CHALLENGE

"CHOOSE YOU THIS DAY WHOM YE WILL SERVE . . . BUT AS FOR ME AND MY HOUSE, WE WILL SERVE THE LORD" (Joshua 24:15).

The power of choice is tremendous—indeed, sometimes frightening—in its implications. By it destinies are settled. God respects that power as a sacred room in the home of human personality. He will not invade it. He never compels anyone to serve Him. Will it be God or the devil? Heaven or hell? It is up to us.

Whether we like it or not, we *must* choose. The neutralists of Joshua's day, intent on evading their responsibility, were actually deciding against the Lord. Their procrastination was fatal. "Choose you *this* day . . ." was the wise admonition of their aged leader. Their habit of halting between two opinions was ruining them.

Joshua and his family, thank God, had decided long since. He had chosen his Lord while still a youth. And how signally God had honored him! Have you decided to serve Him? If not, choose today to serve Jesus Christ. Set the example for your family.

Daily Devotions:
M. God Institutes Marriage
Genesis 1:26-28
T. Serve the Lord
Joshua 24:14-24
W. Consequences of Disobedience
Judges 2:6-15
T. The Sanctity of Marriage
Mark 10:1-12
F. Husband and Wife Relationship
1 Corinthians 7:1-9
S. Mutual Submission in Marriage
Ephesians 5:22-33

Responsibilities to Children

Deuteronomy 4:1-10; Psalm 127:1-5; Proverbs 22:6; 23:13-16; Mark 10:13-16; Ephesians 6:1-4

Unit Theme:
The Christian Family

Central Truth:
Christian parents have a responsibility to nurture and train their children.

Focus:
Acknowledge that children are a blessing from God and accept our responsibilities to them.

Context:
Selected Scripture passages on ministering to children

Golden Text:
"Provoke not your children to wrath: but bring them up in the nurture and admonition of the Lord" (Ephesians 6:4).

Study Outline:
I. Children Are a Blessing (Psalm 127:1-5; Mark 10:13-16)
II. Importance of Godly Instruction (Deuteronomy 4:1-10; Proverbs 22:6)
III. Value of Godly Discipline (Proverbs 23:13-16; Ephesians 6:1-4)

INTRODUCTION

In Biblical times, it was commonly believed that children were a mark of God's special favor on the parents. Because children were viewed as gifts from God himself, each child that was added to the Hebrew family greatly increased the parents' joy. Simply put, the more children, the merrier!

This was especially true if the expectant child turned out to be a son. The Scriptures reveal two primary reasons for this. First, in Genesis 3:14, 15, God voiced His promise to the serpent of sending a Savior through a woman. Since that time, every woman of Hebrew descent desired to be the chosen mother of God's promised Savior. Second, as a rule, the male child carried on the family name, heritage and traditions. Adult males also provided financial and military support for their aged parents.

God's precious gift of children, however, obligated parents with the responsibility of instructing and training their young in accordance with His divine Law. This not only included diligently teaching children how to observe all of God's commandments and statutes, but also how to faithfully serve Him throughout their lives with a reverential fear.

I. CHILDREN ARE A BLESSING (Psalm 127:1-5; Mark 10:13-16)

A. Building the House (Psalm 127:1, 2)

1. Except the Lord build the house, they labour in vain that build it: except the Lord keep the city, the watchman waketh but in vain.

2. It is vain for you to rise up early, to sit up late, to eat the bread of sorrows: for so he giveth his beloved sleep.

Just as a carpenter needs the right tools to build physical houses, so God requires the right tools to build us into His spiritual houses. One of the tools needed is found in these first two verses of Psalm 127—we must be consciously dependent on God in all things.

Three times the psalmist uses the word *vain* in these two verses to describe the heart and the life of the person who chooses to place his or her trust in their own efforts to meet life's needs rather than trusting God. *Vain* literally means "empty," "fruitless" and "unsatisfying." This word aptly describes the empty, fruitless and unsatisfied life without God. The psalmist says that choosing to lead a vainglorious lifestyle, putting excessive pride in one's own achievements, leads to anxiety, sleeplessness and much sorrow.

A parallel Scripture passage on the importance of trusting God is Proverbs 3:5, 6. These verses reveal there is a unique path of life divinely carved out for every Christian. God's promises are recorded in His Word for our assurance. Whenever we encounter obstacles blocking life's path, we only need to trust His promises to clear the way. God gives us His assurance that His presence will always go before us to guide us through life. Parents who prayerfully look to God in all things set the example for their children to learn how to do the same.

Conscious dependency on God, even in the little things, is a constant theme found in the Old and New Testaments. One of the many Scripture passages that express God's desire for complete trust in Him is Matthew 6:31-34, part of Christ's Sermon on the Mount. Here, the Lord exhorts His followers not to be overly anxious about anything in this life. Instead, He emphasizes the importance of seeking the kingdom of God and His righteousness above all else. He encourages believers not to place their trust in the things of the world to meet their needs. Rather, they are to trust in both His divine ability and willingness to fulfill His promises.

All of God's promises are as unalterable as is His nature. It is often while waiting before Him in prayer that the Holy Spirit gives direction by bringing to mind one or more of the promises found in the Word. It is up to us to give God the tool of our faith He requires. Those who choose to partner with God by completely trusting Him in all areas of their lives are assured of His divine blessings of fruitful lives, peace of mind, and much joy.

B. Children—God's Offspring (Psalm 127:3-5)

3. Lo, children are an heritage of the Lord: and the fruit of the womb is his reward.

4. As arrows are in the hand of a mighty man; so are children of the youth.

5. Happy is the man that hath his quiver full of them: they shall not be ashamed, but they shall speak with the enemies in the gate.

The only secure way of life is the household of faith whose builder is God. A godly family firmly established on a divine foundation is one whose members, like those of Noah's family, are assured of surviving life's storms through God's power. With this in mind, the psalmist next turns our attention to the children in the home, saying that they are truly God's offspring. As previously mentioned, Hebrew parents considered each additional child a reason for great joy and celebration. Daughters were special jewels who crowned the hearts of their parents. However, sons were even more highly valued. Many sons, in fact, symbolized the family's strength. For this reason, a father of several sons was viewed as a great asset to the community.

During peaceful times, both elders and younger citizens, including adult sons from large families, congregated at the city's gate. During war times, this same gate was a place where Israel's enemies would often contend with God's people in hopes of taking possession of the city and its inhabitants. Here, sons would fight to protect their beloved families as well as the communities in which they lived. Sons reared to reverence God in all things would also look to Him for victory in battle. Thus, rearing children to honor God produced material and physical benefits.

C. Blessing the Children (Mark 10:13-16)

13. And they brought young children to him, that he should touch them: and his disciples rebuked those that brought them.

14. But when Jesus saw it, he was much displeased, and said unto them, Suffer the little children to come unto me, and forbid them not: for of such is the kingdom of God.

15. Verily I say unto you, Whosoever shall not receive the kingdom of God as a little child, he shall not enter therein.

16. And he took them up in his arms, put his hands upon them, and blessed them.

Catherine Stonehouse said: "Jesus valued children and took time for them. Parents wanted Jesus to bless their children. It was not enough for them to bring the boys and girls to see and hear Jesus from a distance, parents wanted Jesus to touch their children, to hold them in His arms, to look into their eyes, and to speak a blessing. Something about Jesus caused parents to assume He would bless their children. However, the disciples saw children as less important than adults; they did not want them bothering Jesus and taking His precious time and energy" (*Joining Children on the Spiritual Journey*).

When the disciples tried to prevent the parents from bringing their little ones to Christ to receive His personal blessing for them, He became sorely displeased. The word *displeased* is a compound word meaning "much anguish," signifying that the incident caused Christ deep emotional hurt. He justly rebuked His disciples for their insensitivity. It is from the example of these parents in Christ's day that today's Christian parents find encouragement to prayerfully seek God's blessing and guidance for their children.

Christ went further, teaching that a child's absolute dependency and trusting faith in his or her parents mirrors the exact absolute faith God desires from His children.

II. IMPORTANCE OF GODLY INSTRUCTION
(Deuteronomy 4:1-10; Proverbs 22:6)

A. Love Manifested Through Obedience (Deuteronomy 4:1-8)
(Deuteronomy 4:3, 4, 7, 8 is not included in the printed text.)

1. Now therefore hearken, O Israel, unto the statutes and unto the judgments, which I teach you, for to do them, that ye may live, and go in and possess the land which the Lord God of your fathers giveth you.

2. Ye shall not add unto the word which I command you, neither shall ye diminish ought from it, that ye may keep the commandments of the Lord your God which I command you.

5. Behold, I have taught you statutes and judgments, even as the Lord my God commanded me, that ye should do so in the land whither ye go to possess it.

6. Keep therefore and do them; for this is your wisdom and your understanding in the sight of the nations, which shall hear all these statutes, and say, Surely this great nation is a wise and understanding people.

In the previous chapters of Deuteronomy, Moses used the Israelites' historical background to lay a foundation for his farewell address. He carefully reminded the Israelites of God's divine interventions in setting them apart to be His chosen people. He also reminded them of God's faithfulness in miraculously supplying

Talk About It:
1. Why did the disciples rebuke the parents, and why did Jesus rebuke the disciples?
2. In what sense does the kingdom of God "belong" to little children?
3. How must people "receive" God's kingdom if they want to inherit it? Why?

"Christ loves little children because He loves simplicity and innocence; He has sanctified their very age by passing through it Himself—the holy Jesus was once a little child."
—**Adam Clarke**

diminish ought (v. 2)—"take away" (*NASB*)

Baal-peor (v. 3)—a false god of the Moabites

Talk About It:
1. What is the con-
nection between
"listen" (*NKJV*) and
"possess" (v. 1)?
2. Why do some
people try to add to
or take away from
God's Word?
3. What made
Israel a "great
nation" (vv. 7, 8)?
What makes a
nation great today?

Revival or Ruin?
 Babylon, Persia,
Greece, Rome,
Spain and France
all had their turn in
being the richest in
the world. And
instead of saving
them, their so-
called prosperity
proved to be the
ruin of them. Our
nation is now the
richest, but it could
easily become a
second-class
nation and head
downward. Money
will not save us.
Only a sane, spiri-
tual revival which
changes the
desires of people
will save us.
—**Roger Babson**

all of their needs throughout their previous 40 years of desert wanderings.

Drawing upon God's covenant faithfulness as an incentive, Moses issued a powerful appeal in chapter 4 to the newest generation of Israelites for devotion to God through obedience to His law. The Hebrew word for *law* is *torah*, which means "instruction." The Torah was literally God's instruction book to the Israelites, showing them how to live a devoted and obedient life toward Him. Initially it consisted only of the first five books of the Old Testament, containing all of God's divine statutes, commandments and ordinances given through Moses.

The Hebrew word for *statutes* (v. 1) comes from a root word meaning "to engrave," and carries with it the idea of permanency. In other words, God's statutes were meant to be engraved on the hearts of His people as a permanent aid in guiding their individual, social and religious way of life. The word *ordinances* ("judgments"), on the other hand, referred to the nation's judicial matters. God's ordinances guided Israel's judges in all of their decisions.

Moses exhorted the new Israelite generation to listen to God's instructions with their hearts and obey His Word with an attitude of reverential love and gratitude. The Israelites' obedience and reverence toward God meant the fulfillment of His divine blessings in their new life ahead.

In verse 2, Moses cautioned the Israelites against adding to or subtracting from God's Word. In other words, they were not to rationalize away God's commands to justify their sins. Nor were they permitted to add their own false interpretations to the Law, which God had clearly spoken through Israel's great leader.

Moses confirmed his cautionary instructions with a reminder in verse 3 of God's recent wrath and judgment on the Israelites for their disloyalty and utter wickedness in worshiping the Baal Peor. Because of their idolatry, 24,000 Israelites were killed in a plague (see Numbers 25:1-9).

In verses 6-8 of the text, Moses says that a people abundantly blessed by God because of their love and obedience toward Him would stand out as a bright light to all other nations darkened by sin. Worshipers of false gods would see the blessings of answered prayers in response to the obedience and devotion of God's people. They too would have an opportunity to repent and reverence the only true God.

B. Wisdom for Parents (Deuteronomy 4:9, 10; Proverbs 22:6)
    Deuteronomy 4:9. Only take heed to thyself, and keep thy soul diligently, lest thou forget the things which thine eyes have seen, and lest they depart from thy heart all the days of thy life: but teach them thy sons, and thy sons' sons;

10. Specially the day that thou stoodest before the Lord thy God in Horeb, when the Lord said unto me, Gather me the people together, and I will make them hear my words, that they may learn to fear me all the days that they shall live upon the earth, and that they may teach their children.

Proverbs 22:6. Train up a child in the way he should go: and when he is old, he will not depart from it.

Moses cautioned the Israelites not to ever forget God in their new land, especially in times of plenty. They were to live with the intimate knowledge of God's covenant love for them as their guide. Moses exhorted the chosen nation to respond to God's love by expressing an attitude of gratefulness and reverence toward Him in their daily living, including their personal conduct, treatment of others, and their devotion and worship toward God.

In verses 9 and 10, Moses expresses God's desire for preservation and keeping of His law from one generation to the next. It is for this reason that God gave parents the responsibility of instilling into their children's minds and hearts reverence for God through obedience. Impressionable young children learn best by repetition, observation and example. Therefore, the most effective way for children to learn to obey God is by watching and following their parents' godly examples in everyday living.

Moses' instruction to parents is applicable to all parents of every generation. It is a special ministry as well as a God-given responsibility to teach children to revere God by obeying His Word. In order to assist parents in this challenging task, God enforces His truths through teachers, pastors, and many other Christian leaders.

Moses made it clear to the Israelite parents of his day that each successive generation's reverence and obedience toward God meant His continued blessings and protection. However, he made it equally clear that defiance through unrepented sin and disobedience meant the eventual lifting of God's grace and favor from the Israelites. The Bible reveals that God desires to bless every generation of those who reverence Him with love and obedience. However, this can only happen as each generation learns to revere God.

In Proverbs 22:6, we read of God's encouraging word to parents who raise their children on the firm foundation of His Word. In the Hebrew, the phrase "in the way he should go" speaks of progressive child training. In other words, parents are encouraged to train their children according to their developmental growth and age-level understanding. A person's formative years of wholesome Christian nurturing will have a major influence on his or her decisions and actions all through life. They will never be able to fully escape their spiritual training. Thus many prodigal adults eventually come back to Christ.

Talk About It:
1. What must God's people *not* "forget" (Deuteronomy 4:9)?
2. What is God's plan for passing on faith in Him (vv. 9, 10)?
3. How can we effectively "train up" children in the way they should go (Proverbs 22:6)?

Powerful Proverb
A problem with claiming Proverbs 22:6 as a guaranteed truth is that we can't interpret a proverb as a promise. Biblical promises are considered to be truisms rather than promises from God. Yes, they are true, but they are not guarantees. What this proverb does say to us as parents is that we may do everything right and our children will still go astray, *but* they probably won't.
—**Christine Yount** (*With All Their Heart*)

III. VALUE OF GODLY DISCIPLINE (Proverbs 23:13-16; Ephesians 6:1-4)

A. Withhold Not Correction (Proverbs 23:13-16)

13. Withhold not correction from the child: for if thou beatest him with the rod, he shall not die.

14. Thou shalt beat him with the rod, and shalt deliver his soul from hell.

15. My son, if thine heart be wise, my heart shall rejoice, even mine.

16. Yea, my reins shall rejoice, when thy lips speak right things.

hell (v. 14)—
Sheol, the world of the dead

reins (v. 16)—
heart or inmost being

Talk About It:
1. Why do many parents fail to properly discipline their children?
2. What brings parents the greatest joy (vv. 15, 16)? Why?

Parents reading these verses from Proverbs for the first time might ask themselves if God is condoning child abuse. The answer is emphatically *no*. Nowhere in Scripture does God condone abuse of any kind. On the other hand, as these and other similar verses on the subject of discipline prove, neither does God condone unrestrained and unruly behavior in children. What these verses tell us is that a total lack of discipline can, and often does, lead to a child's eventual ruin and possibly even premature death.

A significant example of excessively permissive parenting is found in 1 Samuel 2:22-25. Here, we read how Eli, the high priest of Shiloh, raised his two sons, Phinehas and Hophni, without proper disciplining. In time, the corrupt deeds of both sons brought ruin and shame on the family name and, more importantly, on the ministry of the priesthood.

Through His prophet Samuel, God rebuked Eli for favoring his sons above Him by allowing them to do whatever they pleased, including eating the choicest part of the sacrificial offerings (ch. 3). Later, in chapter 4, both of Eli's sons were slain in battle on the same day. The shock of losing both of his sons as well as the ark of the covenant (which Phinehas and Hophni had stolen from Shiloh) also cost Eli his own life.

Another Scriptural example of a parent who refused to discipline his child is King David. In 1 Kings 1:6, we read how David never brought the hand of discipline down on his royal son, Adonijah. Prince Adonijah was King David's fourth surviving and eldest son who grew up used to getting whatever he wanted. At one point, he set his desires on obtaining the throne and being crowned king of all Israel. However, God had previously chosen Solomon, Adonijah's half-brother, as successor to the throne after King David's death. In spite of this, Adonijah exalted himself against God's will and twice attempted to seize the throne. His actions led to an early death (see story in 1:5–2:25).

As children of God, even our heavenly Father disciplines us out of His immeasurable love (Proverbs 3:11, 12). He disciplines us with a rod of correction suited to the sin. Similarly, parents are advised to discipline their children with a "rod of correction" that matches the misbehavior according to the age level of the child.

Godly parents know the truth of Proverbs 23:15—nothing makes the parents' heart happier than the wise decisions and choices of their children. And when their children speak wise words issuing from a discerning heart, the parent is "thrilled" (see v. 16, *TLB*).

> "Too many parents are not on spanking terms with their children."
> —**Anonymous**

B. Love Encourages Relationship (Ephesians 6:1-4)

1. Children, obey your parents in the Lord: for this is right.

2. Honour thy father and mother; (which is the first commandment with promise;)

3. That it may be well with thee, and thou mayest live long on the earth.

4. And, ye fathers, provoke not your children to wrath: but bring them up in the nurture and admonition of the Lord.

God designed the home to be the perfect environment for young children to learn to obey His will by first learning to obey their parents' will. God's sovereign plan for developing a child's Christian character includes, among many things, both parental love and purposeful discipline.

The tender and nurturing care of a mother exemplifies our heavenly Father's tender and nurturing care of each one of us. Fathers, on the other hand, characterize our heavenly Father's attributes of sovereign protection and provision for His children. The combined love of both parents provides the Biblical mentoring needed to open a child's heart within, allowing the love and knowledge of God to grow as he or she grows.

Though the exact methods of child training and discipline may vary from family to family, the ultimate goal of every Christian parent is to lead their children into an eternal relationship with Christ. They are to use every opportunity to teach their children to make lifestyle choices that please the heavenly Father. As a child grows with a reverence for God, he or she is far more likely to make a personal decision to accept Christ, the Son of God's love, as his or her personal Savior.

There are two commands in Ephesians 6 which, if obeyed, will aid a child in making that most important of all life's decisions. The first command is given to children: they must obey their parents, and for good reason. A lack of obedience toward parents often leads to lawlessness in society. To be lawless in society, more often than not, means becoming a slave to worldly vices and criminal activities that so often lead to death. Therefore, it is out of God's protective love that He gives this command to children.

Talk About It:
1. What does it mean to obey one's parents "in the Lord" (v. 1)?
2. What benefits come with honoring one's parents, and why (vv. 2, 3)?
3. What can cause children to be filled with resentment and anger, and what is the cure?

His second command is directed to Christian fathers: they are not to provoke their children to anger as some worldly parents may do. Rather, they are to discipline their children in such a way that the child's attention is directed on the heavenly Father's displeasure of his or her bad behavior as well as His love for them. It is important that children learn to seek God's forgiveness, too.

The word *admonition* (v. 4) means "put in mind." This indicates Christian fathers and mothers are to counsel their children with the Word of God, giving reproof and correction for bad behavior and wrong attitudes. Also, they are to acknowledge a child's good behavior and encourage him or her to continue pleasing God with right choices.

A child's upbringing of such balanced discipline by the loving example of their parents carries much weight in instilling the concept that *love* is an action word. As Christ's life example reveals, those who truly love God obey Him.

CONCLUSION

In his book *Transforming Children Into Spiritual Champions*, George Barna writes, "I have been discouraged to discover that most American adults—including most parents—see spiritual development of children as a value-added proposition rather than the single-most important aspect of children's development." He challenges the church to "reconsider the priority of spiritual growth in the lives of children and to accept it as being more important than intellectual, physical and emotional development."

GOLDEN TEXT CHALLENGE

"PROVOKE NOT YOUR CHILDREN TO WRATH: BUT BRING THEM UP IN THE NURTURE AND ADMONITION OF THE LORD" (Ephesians 6:4).

Constant corrections—without commendations—can greatly discourage children, as Paul indicated here. The Greek work rendered *exasperate* (*NIV*) means "to provoke, to anger." A father's unreasonable demands, petty rules, or unjust treatment, can lead children to be angry, which is an undesirable trait. *Embitter* (Colossians 3:21, *NIV*) means "to be aroused or provoked." Such agitation by constant criticism and unreasonableness can readily cause boys and girls to be discouraged— "to lose heart" or "to be without enthusiasm."—Roy B. Zuck (*Precious in His Sight*)

> "Rather than engaging in a war to break the child's 'sinful will,' Christian nurture must seek to strengthen the will for obedience by building personal responsibility."
> —Lawrence Richards

Daily Devotions:
M. A Child Committed to God
   1 Samuel 1:20-28
T. A Father Judged
   1 Samuel 3:10-14
W. A Model Family
   Jeremiah 35:12-19
T. A Father's Love
   Luke 15:11-24
F. Legacy of Faith
   2 Timothy 1:1-7
S. Discipline With Love
   Hebrews 12:5-11

Responsibilities to Children

Foundations for Family Finances

Proverbs 3:9, 10; Malachi 3:8-11; Luke 12:13-21; 1 Corinthians 16:1-3;
2 Corinthians 9:6-8; 1 Timothy 6:6-10, 17-19; Hebrews 13:5, 6

INTRODUCTION

God sometimes allows His children to experience financial problems. Note that the key word here is *allow*. One of the spiritual benefits of this is that our faith increases as we learn to focus on God's faithfulness to keep His word rather than on the situation.

Focusing on God's covenant promises during trying times allows His peace to see us through them. It is important to keep in mind that it was only when Peter stopped looking to Christ in faith that he began to sink with fear. In Psalm 73, we read how the psalmist experienced a similar situation. He too took his eyes off God's past faithfulness and was flooded with bitterness and frustration over the seemingly prosperous life of the wicked.

The psalmist chose to take his doubts and frustrations to God in prayer. As he waited before God, he gained insight into the "end" of those who trust in their wealth rather than in God (v. 17). Therefore, in the presence of God's hearing ear, the psalmist repented of his bitter attitude and, like Peter, he also realized that his true source of hope and help is in God alone.

Unit Theme:
The Christian Family

Central Truth:
Christians should use Biblical principles to manage money.

Focus:
Examine Biblical principles regarding money and manage our resources wisely.

Context:
Selected Scripture passages regarding material possessions

Golden Text:
"Seek ye first the kingdom of God, and his righteousness; and all these things shall be added unto you" (Matthew 6:33).

Study Outline:
I. Avoid Materialism (Luke 12:13-21)
II. Give Faithfully (Malachi 3:8-11; Proverbs 3:9, 10; 1 Corinthians 16:1-3; 2 Corinthians 9:6-8)
III. Trust in God (1 Timothy 6:6-10, 17-19; Hebrews 13:5, 6)

I. AVOID MATERIALISM (Luke 12:13-21)

A. Beware of Covetousness (vv. 13-15)

13. And one of the company said unto him, Master, speak to my brother, that he divide the inheritance with me.

14. And he said unto him, Man, who made me a judge or a divider over you?

15. And he said unto them, Take heed, and beware of covetousness: for a man's life consisteth not in the abundance of the things which he possesseth.

divider (v. 14)— arbiter

The literal translations in both Hebrew and Greek for the word *covet* mean "to desire." Desire itself is not wrong. In fact, God tells us in His Word that if we delight ourselves in Him, He will fulfill the desires of our hearts (Psalm 37:4). The fault lies, however, in allowing desire to turn into a consuming passion or obsession. It is then that desire becomes covetousness. A covetous person is like one who has an unquenchable thirst that can never be satisfied.

Talk About It:
1. Why do you suppose this man went to Jesus about the inheritance?
2. Why did Jesus refuse to intervene in the dispute?
3. How does Jesus' statement in verse 15 compare with the world's view?

The author of the Book of Hebrews reminds us that our Christian conduct must always be without covetousness (13:5). There are many Biblical illustrations which reveal that covetousness and greed are twin evils that every Christian must avoid. The commandment against coveting traces back to the time of Moses when he brought God's commandments down from Mount Sinai (see Exodus 20:17).

In Luke 12, Christ quickly draws our attention to this command. Here we read how a man from the crowd to whom He was ministering came to Him with a specific request. The man asked Christ to tell his brother to divide an inheritance with him. Christ immediately recognized that the man in question had a covetous spirit, which prompted him to make such a request. After sternly rebuking the man, Christ warned His listeners against covetousness. He told them that abundant life is more than having an abundance of worldly possessions. It is life filled with the eternal things of God.

The apostle Paul points out in Colossians 3:5 that covetousness is actually idolatry. Idolatry is a spiritual sin which rejects God and His Word and allows someone or something else to occupy the heart's throne. Idols come in many shapes and sizes, including money, work, entertainment, or even a ministry. The list is endless.

In the case of the man who made the request in Luke 12:13, he was coveting an inheritance. Christ harshly rebuked the man. In doing so, He also indirectly rebuked the man's brother who refused to divide the inheritance, proving that he too was equally guilty of material thinking.

The Scriptures show that God is not against His people

"The man who covets is always poor."
—Claudian

Foundations for Family Finances

being wealthy or owning valuable possessions. After all, it is the blessing of the Lord that makes one rich (see Proverbs 10:22). However, He does not want His people fooled into believing that wealth and valuable possessions bring true peace, contentment or security. Peace is found only in the eternal riches of God's kingdom. This is why we are told to seek His kingdom first. Only then does God promise to add everything else we need in accordance with His will for us (Matthew 6:33). God's kingdom is the only source of "righteousness, and peace, and joy in the Holy Ghost" (Romans 14:17).

> "Envy is thin because it bites but never eats."
> —*Spanish proverb*

B. Be Rich in God (vv. 16-21)

16. And he spake a parable unto them, saying, The ground of a certain rich man brought forth plentifully:

17. And he thought within himself, saying, What shall I do, because I have no room where to bestow my fruits?

18. And he said, This will I do: I will pull down my barns, and build greater; and there will I bestow all my fruits and my goods.

19. And I will say to my soul, Soul, thou hast much goods laid up for many years; take thine ease, eat, drink, and be merry.

20. But God said unto him, Thou fool, this night thy soul shall be required of thee: then whose shall those things be, which thou hast provided?

21. So is he that layeth up treasure for himself, and is not rich toward God.

Christ often used parables to illustrate a spiritual truth. In this case, He arrested the attention of His listeners by telling them a parable to illustrate how covetousness and greed can separate a person from God.

The man in Christ's story was rich with material abundance. In contrast, however, this man's soul was spiritually impoverished. Everything the man thought and planned pointed to himself. For example, in this short parable the man used the word *I* six times, which is the number symbolizing man; also, the rich man used expressions such as "all my crops," "my barns," and "my goods" to reveal how he wrongfully claimed sole ownership of what came from God.

We read in Psalm 24:1 and 50:12 that God alone is the ultimate owner of the earth and everything in it. In 1 Chronicles 29:14, King David acknowledged that "all things" come from God and are therefore His possessions. By His sovereign grace, we are made caretakers of His possessions as He blesses.

In light of this, God's Word teaches us to seek His will for the best way to honor Him with the material and financial blessings

Talk About It:
1. Name reasons why the rich man's soil was "very productive" (v. 16, *NASB*).
2. Why did he choose to hoard his goods?
3. According to this parable, who is a *fool*?

He generously entrusts to our care. Because it is Christ's nature to give, we are to follow His example of giving to help those in need. In fact, one of the main reasons God blesses His people materially and financially is to enable us to bless others (see 1 John 3:17). It is His desire that we prayerfully seek His will for the amount and the distribution of His possessions.

The rich farmer in Christ's parable chose to commune with himself rather than to commune with God concerning the best use of his material blessings. Anytime we choose to leave God out of our plans and decisions, it is a sure sign we are not seeking to fulfill His will but only our own. This man's love for his abundant material possessions caused his heart to harden toward any thought of honoring God. He chose to look for ways to store up earthly treasures for himself rather than give even a tithe of what was entrusted to him by God.

The rich farmer suddenly discovered, to his surprise, that though he gained much materially, he lost his soul eternally, which is the greatest of all losses. He learned too late that covetousness is a serious sin with deadly consequences.

For this reason, Christ exhorts us in Luke 12:15 to keep ourselves free from all covetousness. He explains in Mark 7:20-23 that covetousness is an evil that defiles the heart. Rather than allowing possessions to possess us, we are to seek to be possessed with a divine spirit of giving.

> "He who lives to benefit himself confers on the world a benefit when he dies."
> —**Tertullian**

II. GIVE FAITHFULLY (Malachi 3:8-11; Proverbs 3:9, 10; 1 Corinthians 16:1-3; 2 Corinthians 9:6-8)

A. Tithes: Show of Honor (Malachi 3:8-11; Proverbs 3:9, 10)

Malachi 3:8. Will a man rob God? Yet ye have robbed me. But ye say, Wherein have we robbed thee? In tithes and offerings.

9. Ye are cursed with a curse: for ye have robbed me, even this whole nation.

10. Bring ye all the tithes into the storehouse, that there may be meat in mine house, and prove me now herewith, saith the Lord of hosts, if I will not open you the windows of heaven, and pour you out a blessing, that there shall not be room enough to receive it.

11. And I will rebuke the devourer for your sakes, and he shall not destroy the fruits of your ground; neither shall your vine cast her fruit before the time in the field, saith the Lord of hosts.

Proverbs 3:9. Honour the Lord with thy substance, and with the firstfruits of all thine increase:

10. So shall thy barns be filled with plenty, and thy presses shall burst out with new wine.

Malachi, God's last Old Testament prophet, opens our eyes

to see both God's love and His deep sorrow over the unholy actions of His chosen people of Israel. Clearly, Malachi expressed the dominant emotion weighing heavy on God's heart: "I have loved you." God's beloved people responded with great skepticism. From the hardness of their hearts they asked, "In what way have You loved us?" (1:2, *NKJV*).

The apostasy of the chosen nation of Israel was so widespread in Malachi's day that God found almost no love or honor for Him from His people. All but a tiny remnant had long since turned their backs on Him to follow other gods. Even the priests of Malachi's day had abandoned their devotion toward God. So God vividly described, through His prophet, the sore abuse of their sacred temple duties. He rebuked the priests for treating their ministry obligations with such contempt that they continually offered Him stolen, blind, lame and sick animal sacrifices (vv. 7-14). They even neglected their duties of regularly supplying the table of showbread with fresh bread. The ancient Hebrews knew this particular bread represented the Bread of His presence, figurative of God's intimate fellowship with them.

God next turned His attention on the rest of His people. He openly charged them with the sin of robbing Him of His tithes and offerings (3:8). According to Leviticus 27:30, a tithe (or one-tenth of all God blessed His people with) was to be returned to Him.

Proverbs 3:9, 10 reveals that giving tithes is a display of honor toward God. The first example of one who honored God in this manner is recorded in Genesis 14:18-20. Here, Abraham gratefully offered tithes after his victory from war with the Mesopotamian kings (see Hebrews 7:4). Later in Genesis we read that Jacob honored God by vowing to give Him a tithe of his possessions (28:22).

Unlike their ancestors, Abraham and Jacob, the Israelites of Malachi's day kept for themselves the tithes that rightfully belonged to God. Their unwillingness to honor God through giving proved their loss of heart devotion toward Him.

It is interesting that God charged His people of robbing Him of both tithes and offerings. The word *tithe* means "tenth," and that is all God requires from His people. An offering, on the other hand, is an amount freely given above the tithe; it is offered as an even greater show of honor. It is given willingly from the heart and not out of duty. The practice of giving tithes and offerings continued throughout the New Testament (e.g., Mark 12:41-44; Luke 18:12).

The Scriptures exhort us to follow Christ's example of honoring God through giving. We read in Luke 20:20-26 that the Pharisees attempted to test Jesus with a question concerning paying taxes. He responded with a word for believers of every generation. He said to give unto Caesar what belongs to him and give to God what belongs to God.

Talk About It:
1. What does God consider "robbery"? Why?
2. What can result from refusing to give to God?
3. How does God promise to bless people who tithe to Him?

"Sixteen out of 38 of Jesus' parables deal with money. More is said in the New Testament about money than about heaven and hell combined."
—**Roby Walker**

Blessings are promised to tithers. In Malachi 3:10, God says He will "open the windows of heaven," blessing tithers with overabundance. To an agriculturally based people, He added, "I will prevent pests from devouring your crops" (v. 11, *NIV*). Testimonies of 21st-century tithers who don't live off the land declare that God rebukes other types of "devourers" in response to their obedience.

B. Giving: the Measuring Rod of Love (1 Corinthians 16:1-3; 2 Corinthians 9:6-8)

1 Corinthians 16:1. Now concerning the collection for the saints, as I have given order to the churches of Galatia, even so do ye.

2. Upon the first day of the week let every one of you lay by him in store, as God hath prospered him, that there be no gatherings when I come.

3. And when I come, whomsoever ye shall approve by your letters, them will I send to bring your liberality unto Jerusalem.

2 Corinthians 9:6. But this I say, He which soweth sparingly shall reap also sparingly; and he which soweth bountifully shall reap also bountifully.

7. Every man according as he purposeth in his heart, so let him give; not grudgingly, or of necessity: for God loveth a cheerful giver.

8. And God is able to make all grace abound toward you; that ye, always having all sufficiency in all things, may abound to every good work.

The first three verses from 1 Corinthians 16 give us a glimpse of the tithing practices of the early church. The apostle Paul instructed the Corinthian churches to follow through with the same instructions he had previously given to God's people in the Galatian churches. He encouraged these believers to make it a practice of regularly setting aside a portion of their financial blessings on the first day of the week to give toward fulfilling the will and work of the Lord. In verse 3, Paul referred to their giving as a "gift" (*NKJV*). This word *gift* literally means "grace." He continued with his theme on the grace of giving in 2 Corinthians 8 and 9.

By pointing out that giving is an act of grace, Paul also directed the believer's attention to "the Spirit of grace," which is one of the Holy Spirit's many titles (see Zechariah 12:10). It is the indwelling Holy Spirit who gently persuades the believer to honor God by giving to others out of his or her abundance. For this reason, Paul exhorts all believers to obey the Holy Spirit's inner promptings and excel in the grace of giving (2 Corinthians 8:7).

All through Scripture, we see evidence of God's giving nature.

bring your liberality unto Jerusalem (v. 3)—send your gifts to poor Christians in Jerusalem

Talk About It:
1. How frequently did Paul say offerings should be received (1 Corinthians 16:2)? Why so often?
2. Explain the phrase "as God hath prospered him" (v. 2), as it relates to giving.
3. Explain the law of the harvest given in 2 Corinthians 9:6.
4. How can a grudging giver become a cheerful one?

Foundations for Family Finances

No life, however, exemplifies this more than Jesus Christ's. The Gospels prove He was passionate about revealing God's giving nature through the example of His own selfless life. It is from His life's example of cheerfully giving from the heart that we, in turn, also learn how to be "cheerful givers" (9:7). The Greek translation for the word *cheerful* is *hilaros*, from which we get our English word *hilarious*. Paul chose this word to describe what our attitude should be when we give tithes and offerings. We are not to give grudgingly out of some sense of duty. Rather, we are to give with an attitude of great joy.

The Hebrew translation for the word *cheerful* means "to cause to shine." Paul desired that all Christians give from hearts overflowing with the joy of the Lord, evidenced by faces shining with the oil of gladness. Such givers bring their gifts "bountifully" instead of "sparingly" (v. 6).

Albert Barnes wrote, "Money given in alms, money bestowed to aid the poor and needy, or to extend the virtue and peace of religion, is money bestowed in a way similar to the act of committing seed to the earth. It will be returned again in some way with an abundant increase. The seed may be buried long. But in due time it shall spring up and produce an ample increase."

Verse 8 says God will meet the needs of the cheerful, generous giver. And beyond that, "you will always have . . . plenty left over to share with others" (*NLT*).

III. TRUST IN GOD (1 Timothy 6:6-10, 17-19; Hebrews 13:5, 6)
A. Great Gain (1 Timothy 6:6-10, 17-19)

(1 Timothy 6:17-19 is not included in the printed text.)

6. But godliness with contentment is great gain.

7. For we brought nothing into this world, and it is certain we can carry nothing out.

8. And having food and raiment let us be therewith content.

9. But they that will be rich fall into temptation and a snare, and into many foolish and hurtful lusts, which drown men in destruction and perdition.

10. For the love of money is the root of all evil: which while some coveted after, they have erred from the faith, and pierced themselves through with many sorrows.

In his first letter to Timothy, Paul warns believers against putting their trust in anything other than God. The essential theme of Paul's message is godly contentment. *Godliness* refers to Christ's nature manifested in us through the indwelling power of the Holy Spirit. *Contentment*, on the other hand, speaks of us allowing our heart to be captured by Christ's peace. In other words, godly contentment is the result of following the heart and

raiment (v. 8)— clothing

perdition (v. 9)— destruction

Talk About It:
1. Paul says godliness should not be seen as a "means of gain" (v. 5, *NKJV*), yet "godliness with contentment is great gain" (v. 6). Explain this.

2. According to verse 8, what should we be content with? How common is such contentment in the church today?
3. What dangers are inherent with a "desire to be rich" (v. 9, *NKJV*) and a "love for money" (v. 10)? Why?
4. Describe the "riches" Christians should seek after (vv. 17-19).

"Be happy with what you have and are, be generous with both, and you won't have to hunt for happiness."
—**William Gladstone**

conversation (v. 5)—character and lifestyle

mind of Christ by trusting in God's sovereign will for the sufficiency of His provision.

This passage also calls to mind a portion of Christ's Sermon on the Mount. Our Lord cautioned against accumulating riches for security reasons (Matthew 6:24-34). He was not against Christians possessing material wealth. He warned believers, however, against trusting in material possessions, which are at best temporary and corruptible. Christ's desire is for all believers to fill their hearts with the eternal treasures of heaven. We accomplish this by first seeking God's kingdom.

This is possibly what Paul had in mind when he made his impressive statement in 1 Timothy 6:6. Here, he declared that godliness combined with contentment is "great gain." The opposite of godly contentment is covetousness. Paul forewarns believers that those who shun faith in God's covenant promises to supply their needs and instead place their faith in their own self-sufficiency are in danger of facing destruction and utter ruin. In fact, the Greek translation for the words *destruction* and *perdition* (ruin) in verse 9 implies irretrievable loss.

Those who stray from trusting God to trusting in riches have "pierced themselves with many griefs" (v. 10, *NIV*). The wounds suffered from materialism are self-inflicted. Those who decline in their love for God, more often than not, excel in a love for money. Though this is not the only root of evil, love of money produces many other kinds of evils.

Paul encourages those whom God has especially blessed with material wealth to give from their abundance to others who are in need (vv. 17, 18). By doing so they are storing up "treasure for themselves as a firm foundation for the coming age, so that they may take hold of the life that is truly life" (v. 19, *NIV*).

No matter what our financial situation may be, giving to others who are in need unleashes a spiritual freedom which is found only in Christ's Spirit who dwells in us. Through our giving we are made His witnesses of His giving nature.

B. Christlike Trust (Hebrews 13:5, 6)

5. Let your conversation be without covetousness; and be content with such things as ye have: for he hath said, I will never leave thee, nor forsake thee.

6. So that we may boldly say, The Lord is my helper, and I will not fear what man shall do unto me.

The Christian who allows covetousness to possess his or her heart and mind also allows the Holy Spirit to withdraw His presence and power from their lives. The spiritual value of the Holy Spirit's abiding presence in the Christian's life far outweighs the monetary value of all the world's treasures.

For this reason, the author of the Book of Hebrews exhorts

all Christians, "Let your conversation be without covetousness" (v. 5). God's servant-writer is not speaking about the Christian's manner of speech; instead, he is referring to the Christian's manner of life. Every Christian's conduct is to be without covetousness of any kind—especially the love of money.

The Greek word translated as *covetousness* often refers to an arrogant greediness. The word used here suggests an aggressive attitude of one who seeks to take advantage of the unsuspecting for personal gain. The aggressive action is so overpowering that it renders its victim helpless and hopeless.

Christ lived out His earthly life contented to trust the heavenly Father to meet His every need, paving the way for every believer to follow His example. While covetousness feeds on selfishness, Christlike contentment feeds on selflessness. A truly contented Christian looks to God as the supplier of all his or her needs. He or she trusts that God's sovereign provision is sufficient. The Greek word for *content*, in fact, translates to mean "sufficient for one's self." It suggests the idea of possessing enough so there is no need for any other additional outside aid to what God supplies.

CONCLUSION

Paul testified of experiencing a life of true contentment (see Philippians 4:11). He was not speaking arrogantly. He was emphasizing the fact that he trusted solely in God for his provisions. Paul rooted his contentment in God's sovereign ability and grace. He affirmed, "My God will supply every need of yours according to his riches in glory in Christ Jesus" (v. 19, *RSV*).

GOLDEN TEXT CHALLENGE

"SEEK YE FIRST THE KINGDOM OF GOD, AND HIS RIGHTEOUSNESS; AND ALL THESE THINGS SHALL BE ADDED UNTO YOU" (Matthew 6:33).

If we want our mundane needs to be met, we should *not* make those needs the top priority in our life. Instead, our main pursuit should be God's kingdom and His righteousness.

The word *seek* means to "covet earnestly; strive after" (Vines). Most people spend their lives striving after material things, and they never find lasting satisfaction. Instead, we should follow hard after God, trusting Him to meet our needs.

We pursue *righteousness*, which is "holiness of heart" and "purity of life." It is the character of God's kingdom, which He is building in the lives of all who love Him supremely. "Heaven is the end, and holiness is the way," said Matthew Henry. Along the way, God will add "all these [material] things" as a testimony to His love and power.

Talk About It:
1. How can we overcome covetousness?
2. What is our source of confidence?

"Someone who's obsessed with making money to the exclusion of other goals in life has likely foregone the possibility of the acceptance in God's kingdom."
—**Jimmy Carter**

Daily Devotions:
M. Blessings of Obedience
Deuteronomy 28:1-13
T. Proper Priorities Please God
1 Kings 3:3-14
W. The Joy of Trusting God
Psalm 21:1-7
T. Invest Wisely
Matthew 25:14-30
F. A Sacrificial Gift
Luke 21:1-4
S. Love in Action
1 John 3:16-24

Good Communication Is Essential

Proverbs 18:13; Ecclesiastes 5:1-3; Ephesians 4:25-29; James 1:19-21; Romans 12:9-21

Unit Theme:
The Christian Family

Central Truth:
Communicating with love is essential to healthy family relationships.

Focus:
Realize the importance of effective communication and practice it in family relationships.

Context:
Selected Scripture passages on effective communication

Golden Text:
"Let no corrupt communication proceed out of your mouth, but that which is good to the use of edifying, that it may minister grace unto the hearers" (Ephesians 4:29).

Study Outline:
I. Be a Good Listener (Ecclesiastes 5:1-3; James 1:19-21; Proverbs 18:13)
II. Communicate With Truth and Affirmation (Ephesians 4:25-29)
III. Communicate With Love (Romans 12:9-21)

INTRODUCTION

You do not have to be an eloquent speaker to be an effective communicator. Moses learned this when God called him to lead the Israelites. His inability to speak clearly prompted him to tell God, "I have never been eloquent, neither in the past nor since you have spoken to your servant. I am slow of speech and tongue" (Exodus 4:10, *NIV*).

In response to Moses' concern, God gave His assurance that He would not only be with Moses, but also He would teach him what to say. For Moses to be God's spokesperson, however, he had to first master the art of listening.

Listening to God does not mean trying to hear verbal expressions with the human ear. It means listening as God's Spirit speaks to our heart, and then responding with loving submission. The boy Samuel discovered how to respond to God's voice. When the Lord called him into ministry, Samuel replied, "Speak, for your servant is listening" (1 Samuel 3:10, *NIV*).

Mastering the art of hearing from God begins primarily in the home. As young children, we learn to listen to and obey our parents. And it is the responsibility of parents to help their children learn how to talk with God through prayer.

Effective Christian communicators are those who have mastered the art of listening to God with the heart's ear. They then can communicate well with fellow Christians within their home and elsewhere.

I. BE A GOOD LISTENER (Ecclesiastes 5:1-3; James 1:19-21; Proverbs 18:13)

A. Listen and Obey (Ecclesiastes 5:1-3)

1. Keep thy foot when thou goest to the house of God, and be more ready to hear, than to give the sacrifice of fools: for they consider not that they do evil.

2. Be not rash with thy mouth, and let not thine heart be hasty to utter any thing before God: for God is in heaven, and thou upon earth: therefore let thy words be few.

3. For a dream cometh through the multitude of business; and a fool's voice is known by multitude of words.

The writer of Ecclesiastes tells us we are not to take the blessed privilege of prayer and worship lightly. We are instructed to walk prudently (or wisely) when we enter into the presence of God. In other words, before we utter one word of prayer, it is wise to first honor God by acknowledging His presence in reverent silence.

The Lord reigns in heaven as the all-knowing, all-powerful and all-present God. We, on the other hand, are His children who dwell on earth. For this reason, He is worthy of our utmost reverence and respect. By allowing for a time of reverential silence, our worship of Him can fill our hearts with praise and thanksgiving for who He is and for all He has done for us. In the words of Christ, "Out of the abundance of the heart [the] mouth speaks" (Luke 6:45, *NKJV*).

Perhaps the most important reason we have for drawing near to God is to hear His counsel. Christ, whose prayers arrested the attention of His disciples, warns us in Luke 8:18 to take heed "how" we hear. This means we are to listen to God and respond with eagerness to obey whatever He says to do.

The author of Ecclesiastes emphasizes the foolishness of irreverently going before God, rushing through a list of requests and leaving His presence in haste. According to 5:1-3, such one-sided prayers are uttered with many words without any reverence for the very God to whom the prayers are made. Such irreverent prayers are equivalent to "the sacrifice of fools" (v. 1)—sacrifices made to God by individuals whose heart is not right with God.

Romans 12:1, 2 teaches us that when we enter God's presence, we are to present ourselves as "living sacrifices." In other words, we are to come before the Father as Christ did with a readiness to hear and obey. First Samuel 15:22 says, "To obey is better than sacrifice."

Our heavenly Father's heart of immeasurable love yearns for His children to come into His divine presence through prayer. Christ's death on the cross made this possible in "a new and living way" (Hebrews 10:20). When Christ died, God reached

---

keep thy foot (v. 1)—guard your steps

through the multitude of business (v. 3)—"when there are many cares" (*NIV*)

Talk About It:
1. What kind of sacrifice should a Christian offer God?
1. Why is it important not to "be hasty to utter anything before God" (v. 2)?
2. Why does a "multitude of words" (v. 3) often mark a foolish person?

---

down from heaven and ripped the Temple's thick veil that separated the Holy Place from the Holy of Holies, forever symbolizing humanity's new access to Almighty God. By God's covenant design, we are made partakers of Christ's righteousness through salvation. Because of our relationship with the Father through Christ, we are privileged with immediate access to the Father's throne room.

B. Receive the Engrafted Word (James 1:19-21)

19. Wherefore, my beloved brethren, let every man be swift to hear, slow to speak, slow to wrath:

20. For the wrath of man worketh not the righteousness of God.

21. Wherefore lay apart all filthiness and superfluity of naughtiness, and receive with meekness the engrafted word, which is able to save your souls.

James also calls our attention to the importance of hearing and obeying God. Just as children must learn early in life to listen to and obey the voice of their parents, so every one of God's children must learn to listen to and obey God's voice as He gives instruction from His Word.

In verse 19 James teaches us, "Be swift to hear." Christ tells us repeatedly in the Gospels that He did only those things His Father instructed Him to do (see John 10:25). We also learn from the Gospels that He spent significant time in prayer where He received His Father's instructions. It is from His example of prayerfully listening to God and obeying His will that we learn to do the same.

In John 10, Christ calls us His sheep. He explains that just as sheep recognize their leader's voice, His spiritual sheep recognize His, the Good Shepherd's, voice. Because it is the Shepherd's voice, we are to quickly obey whatever He says to do. He will never ask us to do anything contrary to His written Word.

In James 1:19 we are also told to be "slow to speak." God gave us two ears but only one tongue. This means we are designed for listening, especially to God. This does not mean we should not pray all that is on our hearts. It does mean, however, that we are to allow for a time of reverential listening.

This same verse instructs Christians to be "slow to wrath," for "the wrath of man" does not produce "the righteousness of God" (v. 20). We are to lay aside all filthiness and abundant wickedness, which bursts forth when a person's anger is out of control. Because we are new creatures in Christ through salvation, our old way of dealing with life's problems is to be a thing of the past.

Christianity does not exempt any of us from problems in life.

However, when we are faced with trials, we have new and better weapons for dealing with them, including prayer and faith in God's promises. Situations happen that can lead to anger, bitterness, frustration and hurt. Our thoughts can become so fixed on the incident that mental arguments run rampant. When this happens, we cannot hear God's counsel on the matter. It is only when we yield ourselves to the Holy Spirit's influence that we can embrace God's Word for every situation.

Finally, James tells us the manner in which we are to receive God's Word—in humble submission toward God. The phrase "engrafted word" in verse 21 translates to mean "implanted or rooted." As we look to God in prayer, He counsels us from His Word. The Holy Spirit plants the seed of the Word deep in the soil of our hearts. It is up to us to nurture His Word with study and faith so it takes root and grows to bear the fruit of righteousness. The living "seed-Word" that falls on this type of good soil roots, grows and reproduces new life in others as we give testimony to God's ministry in our life.

> "Many have fallen by the edge of the sword, but not so many as have fallen by the tongue."
> —*The Apocrypha*

C. Hold Your Tongue (Proverbs 18:13)

13. He that answereth a matter before he heareth it, it is folly and shame unto him.

Some people picture themselves as experts in everything. Whenever a subject comes up, they are quick to offer their opinion and advice. Even before an issue is fully developed, such a person jumps in and begins talking. Many times, his or her rashly spoken comments only make the person look foolish. Others sometimes feel ashamed and embarrassed for this person, yet the foolish one is often oblivious to this! To avoid such a condition, we should often pray the words of Psalm 141:3: "Set a guard, O Lord, over my mouth, keep watch over the door of my lips" (*NASB*).

Talk About It:
Why is it foolish to answer without first listening?

> "The trouble with a fellow who talks too fast is that he is liable to say something he hasn't thought of yet."
> —**Don Radde**

II. COMMUNICATE WITH TRUTH AND AFFIRMATION (Ephesians 4:25-29)

A. Be Angry at Sin (vv. 25-27)

25. Wherefore putting away lying, speak every man truth with his neighbour: for we are members one of another.

26. Be ye angry, and sin not: let not the sun go down upon your wrath:

27. Neither give place to the devil.

The Ephesians' recent conversion to Christianity inspired the apostle Paul to instruct the young converts in the Christian way of life. His chief aim was to help them make the transition from their former lifestyle of sin and rebellion against God to leading new lives in Christ. The new Ephesian believers were

Talk About It:
1. According to verse 25, why should Christians "put away lying"?
2. How can we become angry without sinning?
3. What does it mean to "give place to the devil" (v. 27)?

Leveling With Others

On the whole, people go around not only with two faces, but with two tongues; one that speaks directly to others, and one that speaks about them. The rationalizations flow easily: "It would be unkind to be frank." "Why should I stick my neck out?" "What is the truth?"

The truth is that we are frightened to behave naturally because we are scared to acknowledge the good and the bad in ourselves. . . . [But] only if we know ourselves can we risk being honest with others.

—Alma Birk

---

struggling with many of the sins from their former life, including lying. So, Paul challenged the young converts to put away lying once and for all and to speak the truth to one another. Lying was an acceptable practice among the pagans from which the Ephesian believers came, so they had to be taught it was totally unacceptable for followers of "the truth" (John 14:6).

Paul's exhortation to the Ephesians is just as crucial for today's Christians as it was for the Ephesian believers of his day. Like all other types of sin, lying and its effects are universal. Humanity's first encounter with lying occurred in the Garden of Eden when Satan deceived Eve. The primary reason for telling a lie is to deceive.

Christ said in John 8:44 that Satan is incapable of telling the truth because there is no truth in him. He is not only a liar, but also the father of lies. It is imperative, therefore, that Christians resist every temptation to lie. Rather, we are to yield ourselves to "the Spirit of truth" (16:13) on every occasion.

In Ephesians 4:25, Paul especially emphasized the importance of Christians speaking the truth to one another, echoing the passage in Zechariah 8:16, 17. All through Scripture, we find references to the fact that lying is a sin. In fact, according to Proverbs 6:16-19, lying is one of the seven sins God hates. The practice of lying results in separation from God. Lying also breaks the bond of Christian fellowship and unity. Solomon warns in Proverbs that lying not only causes hurt but is also evidence of hatred toward the one being deceived (see 10:18; 26:24).

Echoing the passages in Psalms 4:4 and 37:8, Paul exhorts believers to reject the thought of committing an angry act of sin toward another. It is normal to feel anger when another person wrongs us. However, Paul warns of the danger of Christians harboring anger for an extended length of time. He urges believers, "Don't let the sun go down with you still angry—get over it quickly" (Ephesians 4:26, *TLB*).

Nursing anger leads to bitterness, which is the seed of revenge. Any vengeful action toward another is a sure sign of unforgiveness. Our Lord reminds us in His Sermon on the Mount that being unforgiving toward others will hinder our finding forgiveness from God (Matthew 6:12, 14, 15).

The true test of Christianity is forgiveness and love. The two are inseparable. Choosing to forgive and to love is the only way to heed Paul's counsel not to give place to the devil.

B. Impart Grace (vv. 28, 29)

28. Let him that stole steal no more: but rather let him labour, working with his hands the thing which is good, that he may have to give to him that needeth.

29. Let no corrupt communication proceed out of your

---

mouth, but that which is good to the use of edifying, that it may minister grace unto the hearers.

Only when the heart has experienced the Holy Spirit's transforming power can there be a desire for practicing a new lifestyle. References to some of the wickedness the Ephesians were accustomed to are recorded in Acts 19:19, 23-41. Idolatry, occultism and immorality filled everyday life. Besides lying, another specific sin Paul pointed out was stealing. Going a step further, Paul urges the new converts to seek out honest employment that will not only benefit their own needs but also bless those in need. Paul's reference to "good" work (Ephesians 4:28) speaks of labor that in no way harms others. In other words, Paul advises these and all Christians never to accept employment that is immoral or criminal.

Another point Paul elaborates on is the Christian's manner of speech. In verse 29, he tells Christians to watch what they say. He specifically states believers are not to engage in "corrupt" conversation. The Greek translation for the word *corrupt* suggests a state of putridness as that of decaying or rotting food. What Paul is saying here is that Christians are to keep themselves from speaking things that will bring contamination to another's soul. Such speaking would include profanity, off-color stories, offensive language, and talk that undermines another person's faith in God's promises by speaking words of doubt and discouragement.

Paul's words are a reminder to all Christians that the things we say reflect the condition of our heart. The only way for others to acknowledge a transformation in our lives is by the observance of our conduct and manner of speech. Our godly lives are the best tool for testifying of God's forgiveness and the transforming power of the Holy Spirit.

In Philippians 4:8, Paul says every Christian heart is to be filled with an abundance of thoughts that are true, noble, just, pure, lovely and of good report. We are only to meditate on victorious and praiseworthy thoughts. It is only out of the abundance of these in the heart that Christians can impart "edifying . . . grace" (Ephesians 4:29) to others.

III. COMMUNICATE WITH LOVE (Romans 12:9-21)
A. Love Without Hypocrisy (vv. 9-16)

9. Let love be without dissimulation. Abhor that which is evil; cleave to that which is good.

10. Be kindly affectioned one to another with brotherly love; in honour preferring one another;

11. Not slothful in business; fervent in spirit; serving the Lord;

12. Rejoicing in hope; patient in tribulation; continuing instant in prayer;

Talk About It:
1. How does Paul balance a negative command with a positive one in verse 28?
2. What kind of talk is "edifying," and what benefit does it have (v. 29)?

"Cold words freeze people, and hot words scorch them, and bitter words make them bitter, and wrathful words make them wrathful. Kind words also produce their image on men's souls; and a beautiful image it is. They soothe, quiet, and comfort the hearer."
—Blaise Pascal

dissimulation (v. 9)—hypocrisy

business (v. 11)—diligence

---

13. Distributing to the necessity of saints; given to hospitality.

14. Bless them which persecute you: bless, and curse not.

15. Rejoice with them that do rejoice, and weep with them that weep.

16. Be of the same mind one toward another. Mind not high things, but condescend to men of low estate. Be not wise in your own conceits.

Talk About It:
1. What does it mean to "prefer one another" (v. 10)?
2. Why can Christians not be lazy?
3. What does it mean to be "instant in prayer" (v. 12), and why is this important?
4. When is it hardest to obey the commands in verse 15?
5. What one word best captures the Christian attitude seen in verse 16?

Paul's message to the Roman believers is that sincere love is to be the motivating force behind the Christian's every action. Our love must be "without hypocrisy" (v. 9, *NKJV*).

To have full spiritual insight into Paul's admonition, we must also read his Spirit-inspired definition of love recorded in 1 Corinthians 13. Here Paul offers a striking contrast of hypocritical love, which is not really love at all, with the genuiness of godly love. By substituting the word *love* throughout this chapter with the name *Christ*, we clearly see the nature of His being. First John 4:8 declares that "God is love."

This is the principle that lies at the root of Paul's message. He urges Christians to imitate Christ's loving nature in every way and in every circumstance. Most of us will admit this is not always easy. It is comforting to know that the indwelling Holy Spirit makes this possible, for it is His ministry to glorify Christ in all things (John 16:14).

It is for this reason that God's chosen apostle elaborates for us in these verses what it means to be a Christian. The word *Christian* is not just a title given to those who accept Christ as their Savior. Christianity is a way of life!

Children often exhibit character traits and physical features that are like their parents'. In a spiritual sense, God's children are designed to exhibit similarities of His nature and character in their Christian lives. The sincere love of God demonstrated through the believer's actions is proof of a life wholly yielded to the Spirit's will. To put it another way, allowing love to guide our actions is the same as choosing to be Christlike.

Christlikeness, according to Paul, means abhorring all that is evil and clinging to only what is good (Romans 12:9). In the original, the word *abhor* means "turn in horror." Christians are to turn away in horror at the very thought of doing anything sinful to another. Rather, we are to *cleave* (be glued to) whatever results in goodness.

Sincere love and humility are inseparable (v. 10). One cannot exist without the other. The word *love*, as is used in verse 10, speaks of the same type of love family members have for one another. In other words, Paul encourages all believers to treat each other with brotherly love and respect at all times.

> "The service we render to others is really the rent we pay for our room on this earth. It is obvious that man is himself a traveler; that the purpose of this world is not 'to have and to hold' but 'to give and to serve.' There can be no other meaning."
> —Wilfred Grenfell

Paul's message also suggests nurturing a spirit of equality among believers. No believer is to think of himself or herself as better or more spiritual than any other Christian. Just as Christ did, Paul admonishes Christians to share each other's tragedies and triumphs (v. 15), and minister to one another's needs (v. 13). Often, it is through such bonding that we communicate love to a world greatly lacking in love. The goodness of God's love expressed through us leads sinners to repentance.

The *New Living Translation* renders verse 16, "Live in harmony with each other. Don't try to act important, but enjoy the company of ordinary people. And don't think you know it all!"

B. Love Overcomes (vv. 17-21)

17. Recompense to no man evil for evil. Provide things honest in the sight of all men.

18. If it be possible, as much as lieth in you, live peaceably with all men.

19. Dearly beloved, avenge not yourselves, but rather give place unto wrath: for it is written, Vengeance is mine; I will repay, saith the Lord.

20. Therefore if thine enemy hunger, feed him; if he thirst, give him drink: for in so doing thou shalt heap coals of fire on his head.

21. Be not overcome of evil, but overcome evil with good.

Rather than repaying evil for evil, Paul instead charges Christ's followers to be careful to do what is "honest"—right and praiseworthy—in the sight of others. In verse 18, Paul says that, as much as possible, Christians are to "live peaceably with all men." A willingness to change the way we think of someone, especially a difficult person, is one way to achieve peaceful relations. This may mean spending time in prayer, asking God to open our eyes to see that person as He sees them.

Paul's message expresses his desire for all Christians to use every opportunity to exhibit Christ's virtues of love and forgiveness. It is in these virtues that peace exists. Christlikeness is always to be the Christian's highest aim.

This passage hints of a sense of personal satisfaction that might be gained by avenging ourselves when we are wronged. However, Paul proclaims there is a far better solution. Instead of stooping to the offender's level, Paul stresses the truth that vengeance belongs in God's holy hands and not in ours. We should subdue any inclination of revenge by doing good to those who have caused hurt. Although Jesus Christ had every right to retaliate, instead "he humbled himself, and became obedient unto death" (Philippians 2:8). Paul urges all believers to follow Christ's example.

In verse 20 of our text, Paul offers specific advice on how to

honest (v. 17)—
honorable

Talk About It:
1. According to verse 17, what kind of reputation should believers have?
2. How far should a Christian go to "live peaceably with all men" (v. 18)?
3. What overcomes evil? Why?

deal with the unkind actions of others. He assures us that none of our good deeds offered to those who have harmed us go unnoticed. All of our good deeds offered in love, forgiveness and peace are like hot coals heaped upon the offender's head. Many have testified of their own conversion experiences because of these virtuous embers burning in their hearts.

Finally, in verse 21, Paul cautions believers not to allow evil to overtake and conquer their Christian spirit. He encourages the maintenance of Christlikeness, especially in opposing situations. Yielding to the power of the Spirit of love dwelling within enables believers to love the unlovely even when they are at their worst. Christians who practice overcoming evil with good make the best communicators of God's love.

> "The best way to destroy your enemy is to make him your friend."
> —**Abraham Lincoln**

CONCLUSION

Christianity is a practical religion. We cannot be genuine believers by simply performing a set of religious rituals at church Sunday after Sunday. Instead, Christianity is fleshed out in day-to-day living—at home, on the job, in the neighborhood and around town. And Christlike communication is part of that process. We must "talk the talk" even under pressure situations when we are tempted to spew out words that tear down, cause pain, and undermine our witness. May God sanctify our tongues!

GOLDEN TEXT CHALLENGE

"LET NO CORRUPT COMMUNICATION PROCEED OUT OF YOUR MOUTH, BUT THAT WHICH IS GOOD TO THE USE OF EDIFYING, THAT IT MAY MINISTER GRACE UNTO THE HEARERS" (Ephesians 4:29).

Satan is the corrupter of words, of lives, of truth. The Enemy corrupts God's own words by distortion and by misuse, even as he did in the Garden of Eden and at the temptation of our Lord. And when our own words begin to reflect his ideas and his message of doubt, we spread words which are corrupted. Corrupt communication spreads doubt. Corrupt communication breeds distrust and destroys reputations. Corrupt communication comes from the heart where a devilish attitude is entertained.

Heated words and spiteful verbal thrusts always destroy communication. They act as a barrier to harmony and love. The Word teaches that these enemies of harmony and good communication come from the heart which is filled with self-pity or selfish desires. How much sweeter would be the peace in our homes, and how much better would be the understanding which we would share, if we prayed the psalmist's prayer, "Let the words of my mouth, and the meditation of my heart, be acceptable in thy sight, O Lord, my strength, and my redeemer" (Psalm 19:14).

Daily Devotions:
M. Come to an Agreement
   Genesis 31:43-55
T. Communicate Clearly
   Nehemiah 2:1-8
W. Wholesome Speech
   Proverbs 15:1-7
T. Communicate With Boldness
   Ephesians 6:18-24
F. Purity in Word and Conduct
   1 Timothy 4:6-16
S. Power of the Tongue
   James 3:1-12

Good Communication Is Essential

Baptism in the Holy Spirit (Pentecost)

Acts 1:1-8; 2:1-39

INTRODUCTION

In the Old Testament the Feast of Pentecost was also known as the Feast of Firstfruits. It was the celebration of the firstfruits of the wheat harvest. *Pentecost* means "fiftieth." It was so named because the feast took place 50 days after the Passover. The Feast of Pentecost marked the completion of the wheat harvest.

Christ was crucified at the time of the Passover and arose the Sunday after Passover. Correspondingly, the coming of the Spirit was 50 days later, on Pentecost. Pentecost was the time when the offering of Christ, the sacrificial Lamb, was manifested through the power of the Holy Spirit. The account of this manifestation is found in the text of today's lesson.

Pentecost was the time when the effects of Christ's death and resurrection were poured out upon the disciples. The living presence of Christ through the power of the Spirit was manifested. The presence of Christ through the Spirit made possible the proclamation of salvation to the entire world. It empowered the disciples with the living presence of the risen Lord.

There are many themes which can be covered in this lesson, but the emphasis is on the Spirit's empowering believers to carry out Christ's mission in the world. The purpose of the outpouring of the Spirit was not merely the edification of the recipient. Rather, the purpose goes beyond the individual. The person receiving the Spirit becomes a witness and an instrument. The outpouring of the Spirit empowers the believer to be a witness of Christ.

Unit Theme:
Pentecost

Central Truth:
God gave the Holy Spirit so every believer in Christ may be filled with the Spirit.

Focus:
Understand that the fulfillment of God's promise to give the Holy Spirit in abundance began on the Day of Pentecost, and be filled with the Spirit.

Context:
The city of Jerusalem on the Day of Pentecost in A.D. 30

Golden Text:
"The promise is unto you, and to your children, and to all that are afar off, even as many as the Lord our God shall call" (Acts 2:39).

Study Outline:
I. Baptism in the Spirit Foretold (Acts 1:4-8)
II. Baptism in the Spirit Received (Acts 2:1-13)
III. Spirit Baptism for All Believers (Acts 2:14-18, 37-39)

I. BAPTISM IN THE SPIRIT FORETOLD (Acts 1:4-8)

In Acts 1:1-3 Luke summarized the record of his Gospel. In the Book of Luke he had written to Theophilus about the events of Jesus' ministry. He now intended to tell him in the Book of Acts about the things Christ had continued to do.

Luke emphasized that Jesus was not dead. He said in verse 3 that Jesus "shewed himself alive after his passion." The intent of Luke in Acts was to tell the reader about the acts Christ continued to do through the church. Rather than being dead, Christ is alive and ministering through the power of the Spirit.

The outpouring of the Spirit at Pentecost was the demonstration of Christ's continuing presence. This is what thrilled the disciples at Pentecost. The outpouring of the Spirit revealed to them that the Jesus who was crucified, was resurrected, and had ascended was still present with them through the power of the Spirit.

A. Spirit Baptism (vv. 4, 5)

4. And, being assembled together with them, commanded them that they should not depart from Jerusalem, but wait for the promise of the Father, which, saith he, ye have heard of me.

5. For John truly baptized with water; but ye shall be baptized with the Holy Ghost not many days hence.

"The promise of the Father" was the coming of the Spirit. Jesus had discussed the coming of the Spirit with the disciples. For example, in John 14:25, 26, He said the Holy Spirit would come. He would teach them and bring to their remembrance the things Christ had taught. Christ encouraged the disciples in Acts 1:4 to wait in Jerusalem until this promised One would come to them.

Verse 5 illustrates the manner in which the promise would come. It would be a baptism, that is, an immersion in the Spirit, which would empower them and initiate them for witness throughout the world.

The disciples believed on Christ and had even ministered in His name, but this baptism would be distinctive because of the indwelling presence of the Spirit. John's baptism had been with water and represented cleansing and consecration. However, the baptism with the Holy Spirit would mark the actual infilling of the presence of Christ by the power of the Spirit. As a result, they would be empowered for a dynamic witness.

B. Powerful Witness (vv. 6-8)

6. When they therefore were come together, they asked of him, saying, Lord, wilt thou at this time restore again the kingdom to Israel?

Talk About It:
1. What did Jesus command His disciples to do? What promise would they receive for obeying the command?
2. How is Spirit baptism similar to water baptism? How is it different?

"There are two basic ingredients involved in the baptism in the Holy Spirit: the readiness of our Lord Jesus Christ to baptize the believer, and the desire and readiness of the Christian to receive the baptism."
—Don Basham

Baptism in the Holy Spirit

7. And he said unto them, It is not for you to know the times or the seasons, which the Father hath put in his own power.

8. But ye shall receive power, after that the Holy Ghost is come upon you: and ye shall be witnesses unto me both in Jerusalem, and in all Judaea, and in Samaria, and unto the uttermost part of the earth.

Luke had mentioned in verse 3 that Jesus had taught His disciples about the "kingdom of God." The disciples now asked in verse 6 if "the kingdom" would soon be restored to Israel. Jesus answered their political question about Israel with a spiritual statement concerning the kingdom of God.

Jesus' response to the disciples highlights the sovereignty of God. He responded in verse 7 by saying the times and seasons of the restoration were not for them to know. *Times* comes from the Greek word *chronos*, indicating general stretches of time. *Seasons* comes from the Greek word *kairos*, indicating specific periods of time.

The phrase "not for you to know" indicates that the disciples did not know and would not know these general or specific times regarding the exact and full establishment of the Kingdom. The latter part of the verse emphasizes that at that time God had reserved for Himself the knowledge of these times and seasons. The word *own* emphasizes God's unique rule and authority in the establishment of the Kingdom.

The rule and power of God would be expressed by the coming of the Spirit. The Spirit would not reveal the times or seasons, but He would provide them with the presence and power of Christ. This would make them witnesses for Christ, and God would thereby establish His kingdom.

Verse 8 is very important because it communicates the nature and result of the baptism in the Spirit. Through this baptism they would receive the power of the Spirit. *Power* comes from the Greek word *dunamis*. Essentially, it means "to be able." It indicates power which enables someone to accomplish a specific task.

As a result of this baptism, the disciples would be witnesses. The word translated as *witness* means "to confirm something that you know on the basis of a certain authority." The authority for the disciples' witness would be the baptism in the Holy Spirit. Their witness would testify of the presence and ministry of Christ in the world.

Christ then ascended into heaven, and the disciples obediently returned to Jerusalem (vv. 9-26). There they waited for the Spirit. Verse 14 describes what they did while they waited— they remained in a spirit of unity centered on "prayer and supplication."

Talk About It:
1. What is different between the "power" in verse 7 and the "power" in verse 8?
2. What is the primary purpose of the baptism in the Holy Spirit?

"The basic reason for the coming of the Spirit was to enable the church to carry out the Great Commission. Having 'the ends of the earth' as its evangelistic goal protects the church from becoming introverted and turned in on its own life."
—**French Arrington**

II. BAPTISM IN THE SPIRIT RECEIVED (Acts 2:1-13)

A. Unity (v. 1)

1. And when the day of Pentecost was fully come, they were all with one accord in one place.

Talk About It:
What does it mean for a group of Christians to be in "one accord," and how can this happen?

The background for the Feast of Pentecost was discussed earlier in the introduction to today's lesson. However, by the time of Luke, the Feast was also used by the Jews to commemorate the giving of the Law at Sinai. This was because the Pharisees and other teachers of the Law had placed the date of the giving of the Law on the same day as the Feast of Pentecost.

The reference to unity in verse 1 is not a casual reference. Those gathered in the Upper Room did not just happen to be in the same place. Rather, the notation marks the unity of their fellowship. Luke intentionally notes that the disciples placed a priority on gathering together and fostering unity ("with one accord"). This is the second time he identified this characteristic (see 1:14). Their unity was an expression of readiness as well. They were all anticipating the coming of the promise of the Spirit.

The baptism in the Spirit has been promised to believers today. This empowerment of the Spirit is fostered in the gathering and unity of believers.

B. Wind and Fire (vv. 2, 3)

2. And suddenly there came a sound from heaven as of a rushing mighty wind, and it filled all the house where they were sitting.

3. And there appeared unto them cloven tongues like as of fire, and it sat upon each of them.

Talk About It:
1. Why do you suppose the signs of fire and wind accompanied the outpouring of the Holy Spirit?
2. Why aren't the signs of wind and fire a normal part of the manifestation of God's Spirit today?

Verses 2 and 3 give a graphic description of the coming of the Spirit. These verses provide the only direct description of this initial baptism in the Holy Spirit. This description is brief by comparison with other events described in Acts. Luke's brevity may have been an effort to highlight the most important aspects of the event.

Verse 2 identifies the source of the manifestations that follow. The source was heaven. A sound "as of a rushing mighty wind" was heard, and it was divine in origin. A corresponding appearance was "cloven tongues" (v. 3), which had the same origin as the sound. The manifestation of the divided tongues was seen by the disciples, and they appeared to be like fire.

These manifestations were signs of the presence and activity of the Spirit. They marked the sovereign action of God among them. Just as with the giving of the Commandments on Sinai, these were outward manifestations which could be seen and heard (Exodus 19:16-20). There are many outward manifestations recorded in Scripture. God used these to bring people to the recognition of His presence. The burning bush in the wilder-

"In Ezekiel's vision of the valley of the dry bones, the wind symbolized the life-giving, energizing power of the Holy Spirit. In His conversation with Nicodemus, Jesus used the wind as a symbol of the life-giving work of the Spirit."
—Homer Rhea

Baptism in the Holy Spirit

ness (Exodus 3) and the brightness over the Tabernacle in the wilderness (Numbers 14:10) are examples.

The manifestations of the wind and fiery tongues were not repeated in Acts. This does not diminish the authenticity of their appearance. They served the special purpose of accompanying the move of the Spirit in this initial baptism in the Holy Spirit.

C. Tongues (v. 4)

4. And they were all filled with the Holy Ghost, and began to speak with other tongues, as the Spirit gave them utterance.

Verse 4 reveals yet another manifestation that was present at Pentecost, "speaking with other tongues." This was not only an external evidence but one which affected the disciples personally. Speaking in tongues was of divine origin—"the Spirit gave them utterance."

Talk About It:
What happened to all the believers, and what was the immediate result?

They were filled with the Holy Spirit. *Filled* in this context indicates an empowering experience marked by the manifestation which follows, speaking in other tongues. Tongues was the outward sign of this baptism in the Spirit.

Other comes from the Greek word *heteros*. It means a language that is "different" or "unknown." The languages were known to visitors in Jerusalem during the feast; however, the languages spoken were unknown to the disciples.

Neither here nor in the two other similar occurrences in Acts (10:46; 19:6) do the words "other tongues" imply the ability to speak a foreign language. Rather, it is speaking in a tongue unknown to the speaker. This was, and is, the initial evidence of the baptism in the Holy Spirit. In none of the three occurrences mentioned is the identification of the foreign languages a concern or a criterion of the experience. Only in Acts 2:6-11 is understanding of the languages mentioned. What is significant in these three passages is that the recipients spoke in languages unknown to them.

Jesus had already declared that power for being a witness would be the result of the experience. Peter also preached in Acts 2 that the Spirit was being poured out for greater proclamation of the gospel.

"Tongues are the evidence of the Pentecostal dimension of the work of the Spirit, not the gift itself. The gift is the Spirit's power that strengthens the believer's commitment to evangelism and intensifies devotional and worship life."
—French Arrington

D. Questions (vv. 5-11)

(Acts 2:9-11 is not included in the printed text.)

5. And there were dwelling at Jerusalem Jews, devout men, out of every nation under heaven.

6. Now when this was noised abroad, the multitude came together, and were confounded, because that every man heard them speak in his own language.

7. And they were all amazed and marvelled, saying one

to another, Behold, are not all these which speak Galilaeans?

8. And how hear we every man in our own tongue, wherein we were born?

The initial reaction of the crowd was marked confusion. Luke said they "were confounded" (v. 6). *Confounded* literally means "to be poured together or mixed." The crowd was "mixed up" (bewildered) by what they were witnessing.

Their confusion stemmed from the fact they heard these disciples speaking in different languages. Each of them heard their native language. They were amazed that the disciples from Galilee were speaking in so many different languages that could be understood by those present.

Their message was about the "wonderful works of God" (v. 11). The text does not clearly say they heard the message of salvation in their own language, although that could have been the case. The gospel certainly was proclaimed later by Peter. The difference that the baptism in the Spirit made in Peter's life was not the ability to speak a foreign language. The difference was that he was now empowered by the infilling of the Spirit.

Some scholars have taught that speaking in other tongues was merely for the purpose of declaring the gospel in different languages on the Day of Pentecost. However, the gospel was proclaimed that day by a Spirit-filled believer, Peter, speaking in his own native tongue.

Speaking in different languages that were understood by the foreigners present was a miraculous sign similar to the sound of the rushing wind and the appearance of divided tongues. The different languages were manifestations to the hearers of the sovereignty, power, authority and presence of God. They witnessed the move of God and marveled at the results.

E. Doubts (vv. 12, 13)

12. And they were all amazed, and were in doubt, saying one to another, What meaneth this?

13. Others mocking said, These men are full of new wine.

In these two verses Luke identified the sentiments of the crowd. They were all amazed. Some were skeptical. Some doubted. Some mocked. *Doubt* comes from a Greek term which means "to be perplexed." It represented a deeper level of anxiety than just mere confusion. *Mocked* was a more serious term, indicating "ridicule toward another." Whereas some were mixed up and others were anxious about the outpouring of the Spirit, the mockers were seriously ridiculing the experience.

These different responses mirror those of many today toward the Pentecostal experience. Some are simply confused

Baptism in the Holy Spirit

about the meaning of the experience, but are open to receiving a message that declares the wonders of the Lord. Others may have personal struggles and perhaps anxiety about accepting the message of the baptism in the Holy Spirit. But some openly ridicule the experience. Peter stood and declared the Pentecostal message in the next few verses, addressing all three categories of responses.

III. SPIRIT BAPTISM FOR ALL BELIEVERS (Acts 2:14-18, 37-39)

A. Declaration of Pentecost (vv. 14, 15)

14. But Peter, standing up with the eleven, lifted up his voice, and said unto them, Ye men of Judaea, and all ye that dwell at Jerusalem, be this known unto you, and hearken to my words:

15. For these are not drunken, as ye suppose, seeing it is but the third hour of the day.

Despite the reaction of the crowd, Peter stood up, declaring the message of the gospel and the coming of the Spirit. He addressed the false interpretations and accusations of the crowd. He clarified that these Spirit-filled believers were not drunk. "The third hour of the day" (9 o'clock in the morning) was not the time when people usually became inebriated. It was usually a time of religious sacrifice.

Talk About It:
Why was Peter able to speak to the crowd with such boldness?

Peter defended the conduct of the disciples under the influence of the Spirit by clarifying, not ignoring, the accusations of the crowd. Bold witnessing is not ashamed, nor does it hide from ridicule. By the power of the Spirit, the believer can use times of criticism as opportunities for witness.

B. Fulfillment of Prophecy (vv. 16-18)

16. But this is that which was spoken by the prophet Joel;

17. And it shall come to pass in the last days, saith God, I will pour out of my Spirit upon all flesh: and your sons and your daughters shall prophesy, and your young men shall see visions, and your old men shall dream dreams:

18. And on my servants and on my handmaidens I will pour out in those days of my Spirit; and they shall prophesy.

In further response to the crowd, Peter declared the Biblical truth of the outpouring of the Spirit. He cited the prophecy recorded in Joel 2:28-32. Joel was a familiar prophet to the Israelites and proselytes gathered in Jerusalem that day. Prophecy concerning the last days should have been especially important to them. They were under Roman occupation. They awaited the Messiah and the establishment of God's kingdom on earth.

The prophecy of Joel indicated three essential elements.

Talk About It:
1. Why did Peter quote from the prophet Joel?
2. Describe the various things Joel said would happen as a result of the Holy Spirit's outpouring.

First, the Spirit would be abundantly poured out so the word of the Lord might be proclaimed (Acts 2:17, 18). Second, there would be signs and wonders, especially of judgment (vv. 19, 20). Third, those who would believe on the Lord would be spared that judgment (v. 21).

These elements highlight the importance of the Spirit's outpouring and the subsequent power to witness. The world is destined for the Judgment, the "great and notable day of the Lord" (v. 20). The baptism in the Holy Spirit has been given so the witness of Christ may be heard and redemption made available. Peter proceeded with the message of salvation. He was now empowered by the infilling of the Spirit to boldly proclaim this witness.

C. Conviction of Hearts (vv. 37-39)

37. Now when they heard this, they were pricked in their heart, and said unto Peter and to the rest of the apostles, Men and brethren, what shall we do?

38. Then Peter said unto them, Repent, and be baptized every one of you in the name of Jesus Christ for the remission of sins, and ye shall receive the gift of the Holy Ghost.

39. For the promise is unto you, and to your children, and to all that are afar off, even as many as the Lord our God shall call.

Peter's powerful sermon was based on the Word of God and revealed the person and work of Jesus Christ. The message was heard with faith by many, and they desired to be saved.

The phrase "pricked in their heart" (v. 37) is better translated "they were cut to the heart." The hearers were "pierced," or "stabbed." Peter's sermon stirred strong emotions that brought life-changing power. It was not a mere recitation of facts; he preached with anointing, and thus they were deeply moved in their hearts and saw the need for repentance.

Peter had a ready answer to the repentant heart's question, "What shall we do?" The answer was quite simple: "Repent and be baptized . . . for the forgiveness of your sins" (v. 38, *NIV*). This needs to be remembered by every Christian. We do not come to Christ by our own efforts or self-achievement. To repent means to actually turn from the way of sin. To be baptized in water is a public sign that forgiveness of sins has taken place in the heart. It is an outward symbol of an inner reality of forgiveness experienced.

The receiving of "the gift of the Holy Ghost" is closely related to repentance and water baptism. Tragically today many Christians think they can pick and choose at a spiritual smorgasbord. But God wants every believer to be filled with the Spirit!

CONCLUSION

Christians have been commanded to be a witness and proclaim the message of salvation. However, the command has not been given without the power to fulfill it. God has given the outpouring of the Spirit so His message might be carried forth. As a result, we should never feel the call to witness is beyond us.

The task of winning the lost is great, but the power given to carry out the task is just as great. If the lost are not won, it is not because God has failed to provide the power to proclaim His salvation. The task is not carried out when His children fail to obey the command or fail to accept the power of the Holy Spirit's baptism.

GOLDEN TEXT CHALLENGE

"THE PROMISE IS UNTO YOU, AND TO YOUR CHILDREN, AND TO ALL THAT ARE AFAR OFF, EVEN AS MANY AS THE LORD OUR GOD SHALL CALL" (Acts 2:39).

This verse gives us some far-reaching insights concerning the promise of the Holy Spirit. Let us consider them.

1. *The Maker of the Promise*—The Scripture passage quoted by the apostle Peter on the Day of Pentecost indicated that God himself would pour out the Holy Spirit upon believers as a vital part of the future deliverance. The promise was confirmed by Jesus Christ as He prepared His disciples for His departure (Luke 24:49; Acts 1:8). Also the Holy Spirit for believers was, and still is, a vital part of the divine intercession of Jesus on our behalf (John 14:16, 17).

2. *The Meaning of the Promise*—The promise of the outpouring of the Holy Spirit included several spiritual enablements for the recipients: inspiration for worship (John 4:23, 24); power for preaching, prophesying and witnessing (Acts 1:8; 2:17, 18); help in prayer (Romans 8:26, 27); and the Comforter to teach, guide and equip the believer (John 16:7-15).

3. *The Measure of the Promise*—The Holy Spirit was poured out upon the disciples and followers of Jesus, but the outpouring did not stop there. The Spirit was promised to their descendants and to the "far-off" people, meaning the Gentiles. The Spirit also was promised to all the people of the world who would ever hear the call of God and respond to Him in repentance and faith.

Thus, we can see that Acts 2:39 gives us divine assurance of spiritual comfort and enablement because of the One who promised, because of the unlimited potential of power by the Holy Spirit, and because of the unlimited number of people who can receive the Holy Spirit.

Daily Devotions:
M. Spirit-Filled Elders
Numbers 11:24-29
T. Anointed by the Spirit
Isaiah 61:1-11
W. The Holy Spirit Promised
Joel 2:28-32
T. John Prepared the Way
Matthew 3:1-9
F. Baptism in the Holy Ghost
John 1:29-34
S. Baptism Into Christ
1 Corinthians 12:12-18

Introduction to Summer Quarter

God's Providence in Salvation History" is the theme of the first unit. It explores various individuals who played a key role in God's unfolding plan of redemption: Moses, Ruth, David, Esther, John the Baptist, Mary, and Paul.

The expositions were written by the Reverend Rodney Hodge (see biographical information on page 16).

The second unit is "Prayers and Exhortations in the Psalms." The six psalms studied have a variety of themes: praising God, feeling forsaken, having confidence in God, living right, praying for deliverance, and celebrating God's justice.

Reverend Lance Colkmire (B.A., M.A.) wrote the expositions for these lessons. He is editor of the *Evangelical Sunday School Lesson Commentary* and young adult curriculum for Pathway Press. Lance is a graduate of Lee University and the Church of God Theological Seminary. He has taught courses at both of those schools, and he serves the South Cleveland Church of God as ministries coordinator.

God Delivers His People (Moses)

Exodus 1:22 through 2:10; 3:1-22; 16:1 through 17:6; 20:1-17; Deuteronomy 6:1-5; 8:3; 34:1-12; Joshua 1:1-5

INTRODUCTION

The lessons of our unit comprise a backward look at God's hand of providence in bringing salvation to humanity. Another word for *salvation* is *redemption*. In a purely spiritual sense, salvation has to do with restoration to relationship with God. Why is there a need for such restoration? Because Adam fell in the Garden, broke his perfect relationship with God, and thus lost his original purpose. What was that purpose? We find it in Genesis 1:28: "Be fruitful and multiply; fill the earth and subdue it; have dominion over the fish of the sea, over the birds of the air, and over every living thing that moves on the earth" (*NKJV*). In other words, God created man as His steward over the earth.

After restoration, the ultimate plan for humanity is that we partner with God and be steward over all things He created. We see this in Hebrews 2:7: "Thou crownedst him [man] with glory and honour, and didst set him over the works of thy hands." The "works of thy hands" comprises all of creation. In giving Adam the power of choice, God knew he would fall and have to be restored. The history of the last several thousand years is the story of God's working to bring His plan to fruition.

In order for fallen humanity to be restored to God's purpose, we would have to be redeemed from our sinful state. How would this be done? By the shedding of a perfect blood sacrifice. Why a blood sacrifice? Simply because life is in the blood, and God ordained that this be the means. There is perfect order in everything God does. He has ordained that salvation, or redemption, be by the shedding of innocent blood to cover sin (in the Old Testament) and remove sin (in the New Testament). Through salvation, people are thus restored and can work with God.

In the story of salvation, Moses played a key role. Redemption would have to come through a Redeemer. That Redeemer would have to be born into a family—the family of Abraham. The Redeemer would have to come through a specific people dedicated to God's purposes. That people was the Israelites, or the nation of Israel. Moses was their first leader.

In today's lesson we find the nation of the Redeemer caught in a 430-year bondage to Egypt. Moses was to be their deliverer. It has been said that Genesis lays the foundation for our understanding creation and a personal God. Exodus follows by laying the foundation for understanding salvation.

Unit Theme:
God's Providence in Salvation History

Central Truth:
God delivers His people from oppression and provides a rich inheritance.

Focus:
Recognize the providence of God in the life of Moses and trust God as our Deliverer.

Context:
Selected texts regarding the life of Moses

Golden Text:
"I am come down to deliver them [my people] out of the hand of the Egyptians, and to bring them up out of that land unto a good land and a large, unto a land flowing with milk and honey" (Exodus 3:8).

Study Outline:
I. Promise: Deliverance (Exodus 1:22 through 2:10; 3:7-10)
II. Provision: Essentials for Living (Exodus 3:12-15; 16:4, 5; 17:1-6; Deuteronomy 6:1-5; 8:3)
III. Purpose: Provide an Inheritance (Deuteronomy 34:1-12; Joshua 1:1-5)

I. PROMISE: DELIVERANCE (Exodus 1:22—2:10; 3:7-10)
A. Pharaoh's Fear (1:22)

22. And Pharaoh charged all his people, saying, Every son that is born ye shall cast into the river, and every daughter ye shall save alive.

Talk About It:
Why did Pharaoh want the newborn boys murdered, but not the girls?

This last verse of Exodus 1 shows the culmination of resentment the Egyptians felt toward the immigrant Israelites. Until Joseph had died, the descendants of Abraham were treated well in Egypt. Joseph had single-handedly (through God's intervention) saved Egypt from death through famine. However, after Joseph's death, the mind-set in Egypt changed, eventually bringing enslavement of Israel. Oppressed to the ultimate degree, the people reached a state of hopelessness, but God heard their cry and now would bring them out of slavery into their own land.

Though the Israelites were enslaved, the Pharaoh still feared them. "There was a very real danger that the Hebrews, dwelling in Goshen, on the northeast border of the land, might join any invaders that might attack Egypt" (*The Wycliffe Bible Commentary*). This fear led Pharaoh to try to destroy every male Israelite at birth. One that he failed to destroy was the infant Moses, whom God protected.

B. Divine Preservation (2:1-10)

(Exodus 2:1-10 is not included in the printed text.)

Talk About It:
1. From what you learn in these 10 verses, list three adjectives describing Moses' mother.
2. Since Pharaoh's daughter knew this was a Hebrew boy, why didn't she have him killed?

Moses was born to Levite parents. Centuries earlier, Jacob had pronounced a curse on Levi because of cruel actions he and Simeon had taken in vindicating their sister Dinah. Moses' descent from Levi perhaps helps typify him as a portrait of Christ, "who came in the likeness of sinful flesh and was made a curse for us" (*Matthew Henry's Commentary*). The fact that Moses descended from Levi did much to lift that tribe from its curse.

The story of Moses' mother placing him in a basket and leaving him in the bulrushes would today make for a crime of abandonment. However, this certainly was not the case. She had already hid him for three months, probably with frequent close calls of being discovered. She likely placed him in the river's edge, knowing that Pharaoh's daughter bathed there. Moses' mother prayed he would be found and rescued. The whole act on her part was one of faith. "Just as the ark of Noah had been the means by which a family was saved from a watery death, so this ark in which she placed her baby would be the means of saving him" (*The Nelson Study Bible*).

"Knowing that I am not the one in control gives me great encouragement. Knowing the One who is in control is everything."
—Alexander Michael

Though only his sister (Miriam) is mentioned here, Moses had an older brother, Aaron, who would play a major role in the deliverance of the Israelites. Also, we see irony in the fact that Moses would be raised and preserved by the very people from whom he would lead his people's deliverance.

God Delivers His People

C. Moses' Encounter (3:7)

7. And the Lord said, I have surely seen the affliction of my people which are in Egypt, and have heard their cry by reason of their taskmasters; for I know their sorrows.

The remaining verses of chapter 2 partially fill in the blanks as to Moses' upbringing in Pharaoh's court. Since his real mother became his nurse, it is likely that he maintained some contact with his own people. However, we do not know whether he fully understood the circumstances of his birth and adoption. Did he recognize early on a mighty hand and calling on his life? It is impossible to tell. What we do see, however, is his sense of injustice at the Egyptians' treatment of the enslaved Israelites. Stephen's sermon in Acts 7 gives us more clues. Verse 23 says when Moses was 40 years old, he was moved to "visit his brethren, the children of Israel" (NKJV). Verse 25 indicates he knew his people would be delivered through his hands. What Moses did not understand was that he could not accomplish this on his own. The murder of an Egyptian sealed his identity with the Israelites, but postponed their deliverance by 40 years. Since his crime was a capital offense, he had to escape, and likely in his own mind, put away the thought that he would be a deliverer.

Moses' 40 years on the backside of a desert brought him to the age of 80. No longer was he the brash young warrior who felt he could accomplish much by his own energies. He had to come to the end of himself before God could use him. The encounter with God at the burning bush brought into focus all that Moses had thus far been unable to understand on his own. Here he met the God of the universe (as well as being the God of the Israelites) and learned that his own passion for his people had been God's passion as well. Moses learned that the God who had made covenant with Abraham was still committed to that covenant.

D. Promised Deliverance (vv. 8-10)

8. And I am come down to deliver them out of the hand of the Egyptians, and to bring them up out of that land unto a good land and a large, unto a land flowing with milk and honey; unto the place of the Canaanites, and the Hittites, and the Amorites, and the Perizzites, and the Hivites, and the Jebusites.

9. Now therefore, behold, the cry of the children of Israel is come unto me: and I have also seen the oppression wherewith the Egyptians oppress them.

10. Come now therefore, and I will send thee unto Pharaoh, that thou mayest bring forth my people the children of Israel out of Egypt.

The burden of deliverance was no longer (nor had it ever been) on Moses' back. Moses' role was simply to lead the people. Here

Talk About It:
What had God *heard* and *seen*, and what did He *know*?

"God delights in spreading His protective wings and enfolding His frightened, weary, beaten-down, worn-out children."
—Bill Hybels

Talk About It:
1. Where did God say He wanted to bring His people "out of," and where did He want to take them "unto" (v. 8)? Which action would be more challenging?
2. According to verse 10, what was the first step in God's deliverance plan? Why was this so intimidating?

God says He had come down to bring the people out of Egypt. To bring the Israelites into a *land*—the land of Canaan—would be a fulfillment of the pledge made to Abraham (Genesis 12:7; 15:12-21). That promised land was "flowing with milk and honey," indicating that it would sustain their physical needs. The land was also spacious, judging from the fact that six different nations presently possessed it.

All of this likely came as a great shock to Moses, who had given up on the larger dreams of life. "God often comes for the salvation of his people when they have done looking for him" (*Matthew Henry's Commentary*).

Whereas Moses had heard the cry of the people some 40 years earlier, it is now apparent that God had heard it as well. Verse 9 of the text summarizes all that God has said to Moses with two main points: (1) Israel is in need, and (2) God will meet it. Verse 10 then begins God's commission of Moses to be the instrument for that deliverance.

II. PROVISION: ESSENTIALS FOR LIVING (Exodus 3:12-15; 16:4, 5; 17:1-6; Deuteronomy 6:1-5; 8:3)
A. A Promised Sign (Exodus 3:12)

12. And he said, Certainly I will be with thee; and this shall be a token unto thee, that I have sent thee: When thou hast brought forth the people out of Egypt, ye shall serve God upon this mountain.

Talk About It:
What "token" did God give Moses, and why?

God promised Moses a sign that He would be with him. Interestingly, Moses had not asked for such a thing (as did Gideon and others later to follow). In most cases, a sign is given *now* as assurance of something to come. However, the sign given to Moses was one of faith. Moses was simply to believe God and see great things happen. Once out of Egypt, he was to lead the people to the same mountain where he now was standing and have them worship God. "The promise that God would have the people serve Him in that place was an assurance, if fully believed, that all intervening obstacles would be removed by His power" (*Barnes' Notes*).

The burning bush and the direct conversation with God himself were also confirmation signs Moses could rely on. As their meeting continued, the rod changing into a serpent and Moses' hand becoming leprous were added signs as well (4:2-7).

B. The God of Your Fathers (vv. 13-15)

13. And Moses said unto God, Behold, when I come unto the children of Israel, and shall say unto them, The God of your fathers hath sent me unto you; and they shall say to me, What is his name? what shall I say unto them?

14. And God said unto Moses, I AM THAT I AM: and he

> "Let all men know how empty and worthless is the power of kings. For there is none worthy of the name but God, whom heaven, earth and sea obey."
> **—King Canute**

God Delivers His People

said, Thus shalt thou say unto the children of Israel, I AM hath sent me unto you.

15. And God said moreover unto Moses, Thus shalt thou say unto the children of Israel, The Lord God of your fathers, the God of Abraham, the God of Isaac, and the God of Jacob, hath sent me unto you: this is my name for ever, and this is my memorial unto all generations.

Moses fully anticipated that when he went to the people saying the God of their fathers had sent him, they would ask who this "God" was. Why? Because they had little understanding of their own ancestry. By now, after all the years in bondage, they were much steeped in Egyptian superstition and idolatry. There were gods for various needs and manifestations. The Israelites only vaguely knew their history and what God was like. The Book of Genesis had not yet been written down by Moses, or at least not yet read to them. To want to know God's name was thus a natural question.

How much did Moses himself understand of God? He had been educated in Egypt, and likely had learned much about Joseph and the God he had served. Also, some believe that Genesis was written during the 40 years Moses spent in Midian. Still, Moses himself was going through an amazing revelation, so the question he posed here may have been for his own understanding as well.

God gave Moses two answers to his question. The first was His name. To call Himself "I Am That I Am" may seem a vague answer to modern minds, but He was expressing a totality of deity—the highest and fullest expression that can be made. The next answer was to identify Himself as the God of Abraham, Isaac and Jacob. This identification with Israel's forefathers would immediately set Him apart in their minds from all the gods of Egypt. The people would have to be brought out of Egypt, but Egypt would have to be extracted from them as well. The first extraction they needed was any sense of affinity to Egyptian idolatry.

God also called himself *Lord,* representing the Hebrew name *Yahweh.* This name indicated His character, authority, power and reputation, and gave the people a third-person form to use. "This name was to be a 'memorial'; it was to be for the act of uttering the mighty deeds of God throughout all generations" (*The Zondervan NIV Bible Commentary*).

C. Bread From Heaven (16:4, 5)

4. Then said the Lord unto Moses, Behold, I will rain bread from heaven for you; and the people shall go out and gather a certain rate every day, that I may prove them, whether they will walk in my law, or no.

5. And it shall come to pass, that on the sixth day they

Talk About It:
1. What was Moses' first concern about God's orders (v. 13)?
2. What is the significance of the name "I AM"?
3. Who is "the God of Abraham . . . Isaac, and . . . Jacob"?

shall prepare that which they bring in; and it shall be twice as much as they gather daily.

Talk About It:
How did God want to "prove" His people, and why?

We now jump a number of chapters to a point after Israel has come out of Egypt. God's track record of faithfulness has been perfect, but the Israelites' faith was still lagging. They had not learned from the 10 plagues suffered by the Egyptians while they remained immune. They had not learned from the destruction of the Egyptian army in the Red Sea, and they forgot the song they had sung to God after crossing that sea on dry land. They had not learned from God making the bitter waters of Marah sweet. In modern terminology we might say this was a people who could not "see beyond their noses" nor "think past lunch."

The Israelites had been incredibly blessed. They were even promised to be free of all diseases that had plagued the Egyptians—if they would only obey God (Exodus 15:26). Still, all they knew how to do was complain. Is this really so uncommon? Don't we today see individuals who spend their lives complaining, and even when their needs are met they continue their complaint? They are cursed by what they have habitually spoken. We are all a product of what we speak.

The point at which the people complained about a lack of food came one month after they left Egypt, likely when their stored supplies they had brought were running out. They did not deny God's sovereign hand and ability, yet chose to criticize His faithfulness.

God responded by raining bread from heaven miraculously. Included in this provision, however, would be another test—to see if the people would trust God. There would be no manna on the Sabbath. On the sixth day, the people were to gather enough for two days. It was not to be left in its gathered form, but rather prepared by milling and baking.

D. Water From the Rock (17:1-6)
(Exodus 17:1-4 is not included in the printed text.)
5. And the Lord said unto Moses, Go on before the people, and take with thee of the elders of Israel; and thy rod, wherewith thou smotest the river, take in thine hand, and go.

6. Behold, I will stand before thee there upon the rock in Horeb; and thou shalt smite the rock, and there shall come water out of it, that the people may drink. And Moses did so in the sight of the elders of Israel.

Talk About It:
1. To whom did the people complain, and to whom were they really griping (v. 2)?

We see here a repeat performance of Israel's complaining when a fresh test came their way. God had directed that they go to Rephidim. When they arrived, they fully expected to find water, but the riverbed had already dried up. Rather than reminding themselves of God's past faithfulness, they instead quarreled

God Delivers His People

with Moses. They were like spoiled children, always demanding instant answers to their needs. God had directed them to move from the Wilderness of Sin, where they had faced hunger, to this place where they faced thirst. Instead of passing the test, they tested God's patience. God filled their need each of these times, but it did not result in any change of attitude or heart.

The Israelites' hunger and thirst was selfishly oriented; in contrast, Jesus said, "I am the bread of life: he that cometh to me shall never hunger; and he that believeth on me shall never thirst" (John 6:35). Jesus is saying we must come to Him in faith, believing He will be faithful.

E. The Greatest Commandment (Deuteronomy 6:1-5)

(Deuteronomy 6:1-5 is not included in the printed text.)

Though verses 1-3 contain a single commandment, we can dissect it into three parts: (1) Fear God. (2) Keep His commandments. (3) Teach your children to do the same. The fear of the Lord is an understanding of God's greatness, holiness, faithfulness and worthiness. Out of that fear the other two parts will come. People begin to disobey God when they lose their reverential fear. Certainly the Israelites never lost their terror at seeing the mighty works God did, but they never fully revered Him either. Only if the people kept this commandment, however, could they expect God to prosper them or the succeeding generations. The phrase "that it may be well with thee" (v. 3) indicates a full range of God's blessings: lives of peace, meaningful work, health, happiness, blessed children, and more. If God was at the center, all would be well: "Love the Lord your God with all your heart, with all your soul, and with all your strength" (v. 5, *NKJV*).

F. Not by Bread Alone (8:3)

3. And he humbled thee, and suffered thee to hunger, and fed thee with manna, which thou knewest not, neither did thy fathers know; that he might make thee know that man doth not live by bread only, but by every word that proceedeth out of the mouth of the Lord doth man live.

The Book of Deuteronomy is a farewell address by Moses where he reminded the people of all that had happened during the 40 years of wilderness wandering. The word *bread* is an all-inclusive term for physical provision. This second generation Moses was addressing had seen their parents fail because they only wanted God's hand without His heart. Beyond food and water, they had been free of disease, their clothes and shoes had not worn out, and they had been protected from the harsh elements of the desert. God had provided, but He wanted His people to live by the words He gave them. In other words, He wanted relationship. He wanted their trust and hearty obedience to all that He commanded.

2. What made the complainers' question in verse 3 so ridiculous?

3. What are the similarities and differences in how God miraculously used Moses' rod before (v. 5) and how He would use it now (v. 6)? Why did God involve a rod in these mighty acts?

Talk About It

1. Why did God give His people His commands *before* they went into the Promised Land (vv. 1, 2)?

2. How did God promise to bless His people in the new land (v. 3)?

3. Explain the importance of verse 4.

Talk About It:

What was God trying to teach His people by His provision of manna?

III. PURPOSE: PROVIDE AN INHERITANCE
(Deuteronomy 34:1-12; Joshua 1:1-5)

A. View of the Promised Land (Deuteronomy 34:1-4)
(Deuteronomy 34:1-3 is not included in the printed text.)

4. And the Lord said unto him, This is the land which I sware unto Abraham, unto Isaac, and unto Jacob, saying, I will give it unto thy seed: I have caused thee to see it with thine eyes, but thou shalt not go over thither.

Moses was now 120 years old. Except for his one episode of disobedience, he had faithfully carried out all that God had called him to do. That one frustrating moment, however, had cost him an entrance into the Promised Land. God carried him up from the plains of Moab to the highest point of Mount Nebo. From this vantage point, Moses could see Jericho, the first city in Canaan the invading Israelites would have to conquer. Moses could see the land, but he could not enter it. This was not just a cruel joke God played on Moses, but was symbolic of something much greater.

"Moses must die without entering the typical rest because as the Old Testament mediator he had by official transgression disqualified himself for completing the mission which prefigured that of the sinless Son of God" (*Wycliffe Bible Commentary*). Moses was a type of Christ, but he was not perfect. Only Jesus was perfect and could perfectly complete all that God sent Him to do.

B. The Death of Moses (vv. 5-9)
(Deuteronomy 34:5-9 is not included in the printed text.)

Moses did not die because of old age, sickness or injury, but by the command of God. Verse 7 says "his eyes were not weak nor his strength gone" (*NIV*).

Even though Moses' one act of unbelief—striking the rock instead of speaking to it (Numbers 20:6-12)—had long since been forgiven, Moses still suffered the temporal penalty of not being allowed to lead Israel into Canaan. Still, we note that verse 5 of the text begins by calling Moses "the servant of the Lord."

Moses died and was buried in some way unknown to us. Israel mourned for him for 30 days.

C. None Like Moses (vv. 10-12)

10. And there arose not a prophet since in Israel like unto Moses, whom the Lord knew face to face,

11. In all the signs and the wonders, which the Lord sent him to do in the land of Egypt to Pharaoh, and to all his servants, and to all his land,

12. And in all that mighty hand, and in all the great terror which Moses shewed in the sight of all Israel.

Moses carried the distinct quality of knowing God "face to

face." No other person had known such a close relationship with God nor performed the wonders Moses did. In addition, Moses was wise enough to mentor his successor, a quality rarely found in Biblical leaders. Joshua was ordained by Moses, and that ordination filled him with the spirit of wisdom (v. 9). This was an administrative wisdom, empowering Joshua to govern the nation.

D. The New Leader (Joshua 1:1-5)

1. Now after the death of Moses the servant of the Lord it came to pass, that the Lord spake unto Joshua the son of Nun, Moses' minister, saying,

2. Moses my servant is dead; now therefore arise, go over this Jordan, thou, and all this people, unto the land which I do give to them, even to the children of Israel.

3. Every place that the sole of your foot shall tread upon, that have I given unto you, as I said unto Moses.

4. From the wilderness and this Lebanon even unto the great river, the river Euphrates, all the land of the Hittites, and unto the great sea toward the going down of the sun, shall be your coast.

5. There shall not any man be able to stand before thee all the days of thy life: as I was with Moses, so I will be with thee: I will not fail thee, nor forsake thee.

The Book of Joshua picks up where Deuteronomy ends—with the death of Moses. Again we see Moses called the "servant of the Lord." From Exodus through Deuteronomy, Moses had been the central figure, but now that leadership shifts to Joshua. In these verses we see God promise Joshua the same protection, care and presence that Moses had known.

Joshua had the distinct advantage of having watched Moses face frightening situations, and then see how God had intervened. He learned by watching and supporting Moses. Joshua's challenge would be as daunting as his mentor's had been. The crossing of the Jordan would mark the entrance into the Promised Land, but next they would have to take the land God had promised to them. All Joshua needed to do, however, was "be strong and very courageous" (v. 7).

CONCLUSION

In Exodus 3:11, we see Moses ask God a question that has been asked countless times since by men and women responding to the divine call on their lives. That question: *Who am I?* Often the question is asked in doubt, likely because many simply don't want the responsibility and sacrifice that the call requires. Others ask the question out of abject humility. This was the case with Moses. He was an aging and broken man.

Earlier in life he had thought himself ready of his own might to be Israel's deliverer, but 40 years of lonely schooling in the land of Midian had wrenched him of personal strength.

God waited 40 years for Moses to come to this position. Now, all that was left for Moses to learn was faith. Each of his objections and questions was met by assurance that God would not fail. God was a God who could be trusted. Finally, Moses submitted to the role he had been preparing for all his life.

GOLDEN TEXT CHALLENGE

"I AM COME DOWN TO DELIVER THEM [MY PEOPLE] OUT OF THE HAND OF THE EGYPTIANS, AND TO BRING THEM UP OUT OF THAT LAND UNTO A GOOD LAND AND A LARGE, UNTO A LAND FLOWING WITH MILK AND HONEY" (Exodus 3:8).

The Lord had come down to earth planning personally to intervene in Israel's behalf. He was going to rescue them from the Egyptians and lead them to a land flowing with milk and honey. This latter description is one used frequently in the Bible for the land of Canaan. It probably reflects the pastoral background of these people, in whose diet milk was essential. *Honey* probably included not only the honey of bees, but also grape juice, boiled down into a dark, golden-brown syrup, very sweet, and much used in Palestine as a condiment (*Cambridge Bible*).

The "Egypt" in our day is the sinful world in which we live. While we must live *in* this world, God can deliver us *from* its control. In fact, He wants us to enjoy the "milk and honey" of spiritual abundance right now. God's Spirit flows in us, empowering us to lead godly lives until we inherit the eternal promised land of heaven.

God Rekindles Hope (Ruth)

Ruth 1:1 through 4:22

INTRODUCTION

The story of Ruth is a vital one in the history of salvation. Ruth is a picture of a Gentile being grafted into the family of God in redemption. Redemption is the central theme throughout this love story, with the kinsman-redeemer, Boaz, symbolizing Christ mediating salvation for us.

Historically, the Book of Ruth is a wrenching narrative of the difficulties an Israelite family faced during the chaotic times of the Judges. Israel as a whole was far from God during this time, as reflected by the famine the land was going through. Elimelech and Naomi left Bethlehem to go to Moab to escape the difficulties. This proved to be an unwise move, for while there, their two sons and Elimelech himself died. Ironically, the place they had left (Bethlehem) meant "house of bread," which might be interpreted to mean "place of provision." In other words, despite hard times, one needs to stay where God has promised him blessing (bread). Bethlehem was in the Promised Land; Moab was not. We are reminded that Elimelech and Naomi made the same mistake Abraham had made when he went to Egypt after famine came to the land (Genesis 12:10). It is noteworthy that when Naomi returned home with Ruth, those people who had remained during the famine were once again prospering, while she had lost everything. To leave the inheritance God had given and go to live in a heathen place was certainly not an act of faith. Still, God displayed a mighty hand of mercy in the events that later took place.

The love story that develops between Ruth and Boaz is an encouraging one for all. Ruth was a Moabite, while Boaz was a descendant of Rahab, a prostitute who was saved from the fall of Jericho. Despite their dubious ancestries, they were destined to be part of the family line that produced King David, and ultimately Jesus himself. This shows us God's plan of salvation is for all people, the past doesn't matter, and we all become equals at the foot of the Cross.

In the later years of Israel's history, the story of Ruth was read at the annual Jewish feasts. Since the bulk of the drama occurs during harvest time in Bethlehem, it was usually read during the Feast of Pentecost. The encouraging outcome to Ruth's story gave balance to the dreary centuries of decline during the period of the Judges. Also, the conversion of Ruth to the God of Israel gives a picture both of God's plan for all people, as well as what blessings could have come to every Israelite, had they been as committed and loyal as Ruth was.

Unit Theme:
God's Providence in Salvation History

Central Truth:
God restores hope to those who remain faithful to Him.

Focus:
Observe the providence of God in the life of Ruth and hope in Christ as our Redeemer.

Context:
During the time of the judges, probably between 1360 and 1060 B.C.

Golden Text:
"Blessed be the Lord, which hath not left thee this day without a kinsman" (Ruth 4:14).

Study Outline:
I. Plan: Preserve a Family (Ruth 1:1-22)
II. Provision: Protection and Resources (Ruth 2:1-18)
III. Purpose: Prepare a Royal Line (Ruth 4:13-22)

I. PLAN: PRESERVE A FAMILY (Ruth 1:1-22)

A. Self-Imposed Tragedy (vv. 1-13)

(Ruth 1:1-13 is not included in the printed text.)

In the Book of Ruth, one never sees anyone call on God directly. Rather, what we discover early on is Naomi's lament over the circumstances God had allowed into her life. This is found in verse 13, where she says, "The hand of the Lord is gone out against me." Likely, Naomi realized profoundly the mistake she and Elimelech had made in leaving Bethlehem for Moab. She assumed God was disciplining her. She also does mention God as having "visited his people" (v. 6), indicating that she had heard the famine was over in Bethlehem.

Moab is located east of the Dead Sea. The Moabites were descendants of Moab, who was a product of incest between Lot and one of his daughters (Genesis 19:36, 37). There was a long history of ill will between Israel and Moab. Moabites had hired the prophet Balaam to curse Israel (Numbers 22:1-8) during the wilderness experience. Moabites generally were not allowed to take part in corporate life in Israel, though intermarriage with them was not specifically prohibited. Later, however, David found a friend in the king of Moab during his years of running from Saul (1 Samuel 22:3, 4). This is likely attributed to his ancestry from Ruth.

Crops in Palestine were dependent on specific seasons of rainfall (former and latter rains). Bethlehem was a fertile area, but needed the precious rain to live up to its meaning—"house of bread." Moab, though not all that far geographically from Bethlehem, had large fertile areas that must have received more rain during the regional famine. The adage "The grass looks greener on the other side" aptly fits the situation. Due to the famine, Elimelech and Naomi decided to go to Moab. Symbolically, this would have put them out of God's will. Their inheritance was in the Promised Land, not in a foreign place. However, the two sons' names give us some insight into the parents' thinking. *Mahlon* means "sickly," while *Chilion* means "wasting." Apparently, both boys carried some physical weakness or infirmity, and the move to Moab was at least partially out of concern for their health. Would they have died anyway, had the family remained in Bethlehem? We don't know.

Elimelech means "God is king," or "my God is king." He likely had no intention of keeping his family in the foreign land, but meant only a temporary move. However, when one goes to the foreign land, very quickly it is easier to compromise further. When both sons took Moabite wives, the enticement to stay there solidified. It is plausible to assume that Naomi would never have returned to Bethlehem had her husband and two sons lived. It took the humbling experience of successive

---

Talk About It:
1. List all the difficulties that came to Naomi, as seen in verses 1-5.
2. Describe the relationship between Naomi and her daughters-in-law, as seen in verses 9 and 10. What does this reveal about Naomi?
3. How did Naomi try to convince her daughters-in-law to stay in Moab (vv. 11-13)?

"I take refuge in the Lord. Unashamedly I run to Him. . . . I hide myself away with Him. I crawl into a corner and talk to Him. When the pressure is on, I pull the drapes and commune with Him."

—**Stuart Briscoe**

tragedies to bring her back to the place of God's provision.

In verse 8 Naomi encourages the two young women to stay in Moab, pronouncing a blessing of Jehovah over them by saying, "The Lord deal kindly with you." The word *kindly* means "loyal, covenantal love." Despite the sorrows and bitterness she has faced, she still sees God as the means of hope.

B. Ruth's Pledge (vv. 14-18)

14. And they lifted up their voice, and wept again: and Orpah kissed her mother in law; but Ruth clave unto her.

15. And she said, Behold, thy sister in law is gone back unto her people, and unto her gods: return thou after thy sister in law.

16. And Ruth said, Intreat me not to leave thee, or to return from following after thee: for whither thou goest, I will go; and where thou lodgest, I will lodge: thy people shall be my people, and thy God my God:

17. Where thou diest, will I die, and there will I be buried: the Lord do so to me, and more also, if ought but death part thee and me.

18. When she saw that she was stedfastly minded to go with her, then she left speaking unto her.

In the ancient world the plight of a widow was difficult. The plight of three widows would be even worse. For Naomi to be left without her husband and two sons while in a foreign land complicated her situation even more. It was inevitable that she try to return to her own people. We see that neither daughter-in-law "questioned their duty to accompany their mother-in-law, though it meant leaving their own land" (*Zondervan NIV Bible Commentary*). Their relationship with Naomi was strong. We know nothing of their families in Moab, but Naomi logically saw more benefit for them to stay there. She had no idea what she would be facing back in Bethlehem. Also, she knew that as foreigners in Israel, the two young women would be socially disadvantaged.

Orpah made the logical decision to stay in Moab. This should not cast any shadow over her, for Naomi truly thought this was best. Ruth made the harder decision. She was leaving her family, her culture, and her religion behind. The chief deity of Moab was Chemosh (see Numbers 21:29). To go on with Naomi meant conversion to serving the God of Israel.

Ruth 1:16, 17 is seen as one of the most beautiful and self-denying statements of the entire Bible. It is the epitome of dedication. Ruth renounced her past to go with her mother-in-law, and this was an expected journey into poverty. She had no idea of what good the future held for her. She only knew her love for (and trust in) Naomi. In essence, she made a vow of dedication,

Talk About It:
1. List each of the commitments Ruth made to Naomi in verses 16 and 17.
2. How did Naomi respond to Ruth's vow (v. 18)?

Unbreakable Commitment
Often, two people's names are linked because their stories and destinies are so interwoven. For instance, great twosomes of the Bible would include David and Jonathan, Adam and Eve, Mary and Joseph, Ananias and Sapphira, Peter and John, and so on. No two are more interlinked, however, than Ruth and

which can be paraphrased as "May a severe judgment fall upon me if I am not true to my vow" (*Wycliffe Bible Commentary*). Naomi accepted her decision as final without further debate, and likely with relief. Having a strong, young daughter-in-law as a companion would make life easier to face. Also, since travel was dangerous in those times, two women on a journey were not as vulnerable as one.

C. Return to Bethlehem (vv. 19-22)

19. So they two went until they came to Bethlehem. And it came to pass, when they were come to Bethlehem, that all the city was moved about them, and they said, Is this Naomi?

20. And she said unto them, Call me not Naomi, call me Mara: for the Almighty hath dealt very bitterly with me.

21. I went out full, and the Lord hath brought me home again empty: why then call ye me Naomi, seeing the Lord hath testified against me, and the Almighty hath afflicted me?

22. So Naomi returned, and Ruth the Moabitess, her daughter in law, with her, which returned out of the country of Moab: and they came to Bethlehem in the beginning of barley harvest.

The fact that all the city was stirred over Naomi's return indicates the position that Elimelech's family had once held there. They apparently had been prominent citizens. Perhaps many were overjoyed at unexpectedly seeing Naomi again, or they were shocked at her pitiful appearance. It is obvious that no one had been aware of her plight. Naomi's name means "pleasantness" or "my joy." That joy she had known in earlier years had now turned to sadness. The change bewildered all who saw her.

Naomi had definitely gone through hardships—but so do most people at some point in life, so why should she be bitter? Grief is understandable, yet Naomi changed her name to *Mara* ("bitterness") to reflect the pain she felt. That pain included having unwisely left home for a foreign land. As Naomi looked at the renewed prosperity those who had "stuck it out" were now experiencing, she had to have realized that some of her suffering had been of her own doing.

We see a glimmer of hope expressed in verse 22 in that Naomi returned home at the beginning of barley harvest. The barley harvest began right after Passover, which was held on the 15th day of the month Nisan. This roughly corresponds with our April/May springtime. In classic storytelling fashion, we have seen the bottom of the despair section. Next we will see the turnaround. "The Moabite experience had proved tragic, but the fields of Bethlehem were now full" (*Wycliffe Bible Commentary*).

Talk About It:
1. Why did the people of Bethlehem ask, "Is this Naomi?" (v. 19).
2. How had the Lord "testified against" Naomi, according to her thinking (vv. 20, 21)?

"Few things are more bitter than to feel bitter. A man's venom poisons himself."
—*Quotable Quotes*

God Rekindles Hope

II. PROVISION: PROTECTION AND RESOURCES
(Ruth 2:1-18)

A. Ruth Gleans in the Fields of Boaz (vv. 1-4)
(Ruth 2:1-4 is not included in the printed text.)

These four verses set up the love story that is about to unfold. There are some details which we must conjecture. Where did the two women live? Apparently in a house on land Elimelech had owned. Elimelech and Naomi had not meant to stay in Moab, but rather to return after the famine ended. The property was still his; however, because of his and his two sons' deaths, Naomi would not be able to transfer it to her ownership. "According to law, land passed from a man to his son or to his kinsman; property could pass from father to daughter if there was no son, but the law did not make specific provision for passing an inheritance from husband to wife" (*Zondervan NIV Bible Commentary*).

This would necessitate a kinsman-redeemer. It was important that land remain within the family or clan. A close male relative needed to be found to marry Ruth and sire a child in behalf of her deceased husband, Mahlon. As the story continues, we see that Boaz was not the closest male relative eligible for this role, but certainly was the one of Naomi's choosing. Likely, this was because she had begun to see the hand of God operating in the matter.

This brings us back to our present verses. It is obvious that Boaz providentially came into the picture. He owned land, was a successful farmer with a number of hired workers, and had excellent reputation and character. We also catch a glimpse of ancient means of caring for the poor. The Law expressly allowed for gleaning, where the poor could follow the harvesters and pick up any grain that was left behind. However, all farmers were not always cooperative. Ruth could only hope that she would find a field where the owner would not drive her away. We also see here the destitute situation. Ruth had to do something in order that the two women have anything to eat. Respectfully, she asked Naomi's permission to go to the fields and find leftover grain.

The subsequent meeting between Ruth and Boaz was only coincidental from their perspective, but was providential from God's. When Boaz came to the field to check the progress of the work, he greeted his workers with an Israelite blessing, "The Lord be with you" (v. 4). This gives clear insight into his godly character.

B. Ruth Meets Boaz (vv. 5-10)
5. Then said Boaz unto his servant that was set over the reapers, Whose damsel is this?

"her hap" (v. 3)—
"as it turned out" (*NIV*)

Talk About It:
1. What role does coincidence play in these verses? What role does providence play?
2. Why do you suppose Ruth grabbed Boaz's attention?

"Sometimes when I consider what tremendous consequences come from little things—a chance word, a tap on the shoulder, or a penny dropped on a newsstand—I am tempted to think . . . there are no little things."
—Bruce Barton

---

6. And the servant that was set over the reapers answered and said, It is the Moabitish damsel that came back with Naomi out of the country of Moab:

7. And she said, I pray you, let me glean and gather after the reapers among the sheaves: so she came, and hath continued even from the morning until now, that she tarried a little in the house.

8. Then said Boaz unto Ruth, Hearest thou not, my daughter? Go not to glean in another field, neither go from hence, but abide here fast by my maidens:

9. Let thine eyes be on the field that they do reap, and go thou after them: have I not charged the young men that they shall not touch thee? and when thou art athirst, go unto the vessels, and drink of that which the young men have drawn.

10. Then she fell on her face, and bowed herself to the ground, and said unto him, Why have I found grace in thine eyes, that thou shouldest take knowledge of me, seeing I am a stranger?

Talk About It:
1. What request had Ruth made of the head servant (vv. 6, 7)?
2. Name three kindnesses Boaz showed to Ruth (vv. 8, 9).

"A bit of fragrance always clings to the hand that gives you roses."
—Proverb

Boaz questioned the foreman as to the identity of the young woman (v. 5). Already a spark of attraction is noted. He had certainly heard about the return of Naomi with a widowed Moabite daughter-in-law, but he apparently had not seen either of them. The foreman told him of her polite request to glean in the field. He even described her diligent work. The positive words of the foreman served to further increase Boaz's interest. As the story progresses, we see that Boaz was much older. There is no indication that he might already have had another wife (or wives). It appears that he simply had never married. He immediately began conversation with Ruth and encouraged her not to glean in any other fields but his. He also made sure that she had adequate drink to combat the hot sun.

Ruth's response to Boaz was very thankful and humble, but shows no particular spark of love interest on her part. She was simply amazed that he would express such favor to her, a foreigner.

C. Boaz Compliments Ruth (vv. 11, 12)

11. And Boaz answered and said unto her, It hath fully been shewed me, all that thou hast done unto thy mother in law since the death of thine husband: and how thou hast left thy father and thy mother, and the land of thy nativity, and art come unto a people which thou knewest not heretofore.

12. The Lord recompense thy work, and a full reward be given thee of the Lord God of Israel, under whose wings thou art come to trust.

Boaz had already heard of Ruth's noble actions and loyalty to Naomi. He complimented her willingness to abandon her own life and people to come to a foreign place. Then he pronounced a blessing on her for believing in the God of Israel. The phrase "under whose wings thou art come to trust" presents a metaphor of a baby bird snuggling under its mother's wings.

Ruth responded to Boaz with both surprise and humility. She was no more than a poor servant girl. He was a rich farmer. She did not expect such excellent treatment. Perhaps now she recognized a spark of interest in herself.

Talk About It:
1. What had Boaz learned about Ruth (v. 11)?
2. What blessing did Boaz pronounce on Ruth (v. 12)?

D. Ruth Finds Favor (vv. 13-18)

(Ruth 2:13-18 is not included in the printed text.)

Boaz in these verses becomes more than casually interested. After Ruth went back to work, gleaning, he ordered his reapers to leave extra sheaves for her, but not so much as to embarrass her in her humble situation. He also provided that she eat with the workers. We see that after satisfying her own hunger, she kept some back—to take to Naomi. This showed her continued respect and care for her mother-in-law. When the day ended, Ruth proudly carried her day's reward of grain to show Naomi. Upon finding out who the landowner was that had been so generous, Naomi's "matchmaker" instincts quickly fired up (see vv. 19-23; 3:1-18). Her faith in God's providence was quickly restored as well.

Talk About It:
1. Describe Ruth's work ethic.
2. What were the "handfuls of purpose" (v. 16)?

III. PURPOSE: PREPARE A ROYAL LINE (Ruth 4:13-22)

A. Birth of a Son (vv. 13, 14)

13. So Boaz took Ruth, and she was his wife: and when he went in unto her, the Lord gave her conception, and she bare a son.

14. And the women said unto Naomi, Blessed be the Lord, which hath not left thee this day without a kinsman, that his name may be famous in Israel.

We jump past the details to see that Boaz did become the kinsman-redeemer for Ruth and Naomi. The nearer relative who was in line to be the redeemer willingly gave up his rights, because he would have endangered his own estate. "Perhaps the kinsman was aware that he would be paying part of what should be his own children's inheritance to buy land that would revert to Ruth's son as a legal heir of Elimelech" (*Zondervan NIV Bible Commentary*). There is also the possibility that he was not willing to intermarry with a Moabite woman. Though such intermarriage was not forbidden between Israelites and Moabites, it was frowned upon, and social problems would have had to be dealt with. Boaz, on the other hand, showed no reluctance in taking Ruth. Any reservations he might have had

Talk About It:
1. Why did the women bless the name of the Lord?
2. What was their desire for Obed?

were more than relieved by the humility and loyalty Ruth had shown to Naomi.

Both Naomi and Ruth found redemption in the marriage. Elimelech's name was preserved in that Naomi was given a grandson. Widowhood had deprived both Ruth and Naomi of a son, but Ruth and Boaz now had a boy. The women of Bethlehem who had earlier seen Naomi's bitterness now gathered to see her happiness. They praised God for providing a redeemer for Naomi. It would appear that they saw the child as the kinsman-redeemer, but Boaz was the true redeemer. The baby was the result of the redemption. Still, in a sense, the child changed everything. They blessed him, praying that his name would become famous. And famous it did become, because he later became the grandfather of David, the greatest king of Israel.

B. Sovereign Restorer of Life (vv. 15-22)

(Ruth 4:18-22 is not included in the printed text.)

15. And he shall be unto thee a restorer of thy life, and a nourisher of thine old age: for thy daughter in law, which loveth thee, which is better to thee than seven sons, hath born him.

16. And Naomi took the child, and laid it in her bosom, and became nurse unto it.

17. And the women her neighbours gave it a name, saying, There is a son born to Naomi; and they called his name Obed: he is the father of Jesse, the father of David.

The women of Bethlehem not only recognized this child as a redeemer, but as a restorer of life for Naomi. They had seen her bitterness. They now saw her change of countenance. She would have an heir to take care of her in her old age. The women also had wonderful compliments for Ruth, saying she was better as a daughter to Naomi than seven sons could have been. This is important, because sons were considered so much more important than daughters.

In the genealogy beginning in verse 18, we find Pharez, who was the son of the relationship between Judah and Tamar (Genesis 38). Tamar was Judah's daughter-in-law and had been left as a childless widow twice (having been married to both Er and Onan, sons of Judah). Judah's refusal to provide his third son as another kinsman-redeemer led to her portraying herself as a harlot. She hid her identity, prostituted herself to Judah, and became pregnant. Thus, Judah himself became an unwitting redeemer.

Through this genealogy we see the difference between disobedience and obedience. Judah would have left his daughter-in-law destitute, had she not reverted to deceit. The sad story that resulted was not a pretty one. On the other hand, the humble

---

"Joys are always on the way to us. They are always traveling to us through the darkness of the night. There is never a night when they are not coming."
—Amy Carmichael

Talk About It:
1. How would Obed minister to Naomi (v. 15)?
2. How did Naomi serve her grandson (v. 16)?
3. What role would Obed play in Israel's history (v. 17)?

"Jesus Christ is everywhere; He is behind everything we see if only we have eyes to see Him; and He is the Lord of history if only we penetrate deep enough beneath the surface."
—Charles Malik

God Rekindles Hope

and beautiful story of Ruth presents an entirely different picture. We see that the hand of God ultimately controls the direction of history. We also note that Boaz is named in the genealogy rather than Mahlon or Elimelech, even though his kinsman-redeemer role was to give an heir to the dead men. Perhaps this is simply to highlight the beauty of the story. Two people living in different lands were divinely brought together under very unusual circumstances to become ancestors of the greatest king of Israel, David (v. 17). And in the centuries to come, the Messiah himself was born through their ancestral line.

CONCLUSION

Pastor Carter Conlon of Times Square Church in New York City once preached a powerful sermon titled "When God Brings You Home Empty." Using the story of Naomi's plight, he showed how we must come to end of our own solutions to life's problems before God can intervene. We must be empty before God can fill us. We must be devoid of any hope in human means before divine means takes over. Naomi ultimately recognized that the tragedies she had faced were not accidental. They were caused by misjudgments and lack of faith, but still God had a hand in their outcome. The story of Ruth ends with a wonderfully happy Naomi enjoying the life of a grandmother.

GOLDEN TEXT CHALLENGE

"BLESSED BE THE LORD, WHICH HATH NOT LEFT THEE THIS DAY WITHOUT A KINSMAN" (Ruth 4:14).

Right after Ruth married Boaz, she conceived and had a son. The celebrating neighbor women called this newborn baby a *redeemer* ("kinsman") because of the role he would play in the life of Naomi, the boy's grandmother. "As the son of Ruth he was also the son of Naomi (v. 17), and as such would take away the reproach of childlessness from her, would comfort her, and tend her in her old age, and thereby become her true deliverer" (Keil & Delitzsch). The women named the baby *Obed*, meaning "serving one" (v. 17), as one who would take care of his grandmother, bringing joy to her heart. No longer would Naomi call herself *Mara*, for her bitterness was taken away.

The amazing turn of events in Naomi and Ruth's story displays the great love and sovereignty of God, and it is a story God is repeating again and again in our day. When we as God's people are hopelessly bound by bitter circumstances, God delights in birthing unexpected blessings in our lives.

Daily Devotions:
M. Hope Reinforced
   Judges 6:33-40
T. Hope Rewarded
   Job 42:10-17
W. Hope in the Lord
   Psalm 31:19-24
T. Hope of Future Glory
   Romans 8:18-25
F. Hope as an Anchor
   Hebrews 6:13-20
S. Hope of Christ's Return
   Revelation 21:1-7

God Chooses a King (David)

1 Samuel 16:1-13; 17:33-58; 2 Samuel 2:1-7; 7:8-16

Unit Theme:
God's Providence in Salvation History

Central Truth:
God selects leaders based on the condition of their hearts.

Focus:
Review the providence of God in David's life and submit to God our King.

Context:
Studies from the life of David (11th century B.C.)

Golden Text:
"The Lord seeth not as man seeth; for man looketh on the outward appearance, but the Lord looketh on the heart" (1 Samuel 16:7).

Study Outline:
 I. Plan: Anoint a King
 (1 Samuel 16:1-13)
 II. Provision: Power of God's Name
 (1 Samuel 17:33-52)
 III. Purpose: Establish a Kingdom
 (2 Samuel 7:8-16)

INTRODUCTION

Israel had wanted a king so that they could be like the nations surrounding them. Because of their disobedient hearts, living under a theocracy with an invisible God seemed too intangible, too uncertain. However, their very first taste of monarchy proved quickly that they did not know what they were asking for. Saul manifested all the terrible things Samuel had predicted in 1 Samuel 8:11-17. These included: (1) drafting young men into military service; (2) drafting young women to serve in the palace and court; (3) taxing people's crops and flocks; (4) appropriating properties of private citizens; (5) eroding personal freedoms. Unless a leader's heart is under submission to God, these are the natural by-products of power. Saul simply did not have the heart qualifications for kingship. By the end of 1 Samuel 13, God had given up on him and was seeking out "a man after his own heart" (v. 14). Of course we know that God already knew what would happen with Saul, and had been preparing David all along.

To have a heart after God is not the normal human proclivity. This must be learned, but it also must be learned willingly. The individual must desire change in his or her innermost being so they can please God. Saul never captured this mind-set, though at first it seemed he might. When he learned he was to be the ruler over Israel, he actually hid behind a pile of refuse. Someone had to find him and bring him out into the public. Early in his reign, however, his deeper nature surfaced. He was impetuous, unwilling to receive instruction, and proud. In short, he was resistant to God working in him.

Interestingly, early on in his reign, before his actual coronation, Saul gathered a group of brave men around him "whose hearts God had touched" (1 Samuel 10:26, *NKJV*). These were men who had been willing to let God mold them. Paradoxically, Saul understood the need for being malleable before God, but himself could not enter into the process. In other words, He wanted God, but without relationship.

In contrast to Saul, David was the opposite. Born somewhere around 1085 B.C., he was the classic throwaway child. His mother had been married before, bearing two daughters who became his half-sisters. She then bore seven sons to his father, Jesse, before he was born. David was relegated to handling the family's flock of sheep when he was still very young. Somehow, perhaps out of his loneliness, he learned an amazing dependence on God during this time.

I. PLAN: ANOINT A KING (1 Samuel 16:1-13)
A. Samuel Sent to Bethlehem (vv. 1-3)
    (1 Samuel 16:3 is not included in the printed text.)

1. And the Lord said unto Samuel, How long wilt thou mourn for Saul, seeing I have rejected him from reigning over Israel? fill thine horn with oil, and go, I will send thee to Jesse the Bethlehemite: for I have provided me a king among his sons.

2. And Samuel said, How can I go? if Saul hear it, he will kill me. And the Lord said, Take an heifer with thee, and say, I am come to sacrifice to the Lord.

Samuel had done his best to keep hope alive in behalf of Saul. He had seen potential in the man from the moment he had met him. Among his first words to Saul were these: "I . . . will tell thee all that is in thine heart" (9:19). God had not chosen Saul to be king just to prove to the people the futility of a monarchy. No, there had been great possibilities in the heart of Saul. The dreams he had for his life were likely noble. But dreams are not achieved without distress. Distress should bring a humble dependence upon the Lord, as can be seen in the life of the patriarch Joseph. Instead of humbling himself, however, Saul hardened as he faced tougher circumstances. God saw this and, in our text, gently chastised Samuel for his misplaced hopes. This is a rarity in the history of humanity. Out of His mercy and grace, God usually is the last to give up on an individual. We note, however, that Saul still was given many opportunities to repent and change, but instead more deeply hardened his heart.

When Samuel had first anointed Saul as king, we read that "God gave him another heart . . . and the Spirit of God came upon him, and he prophesied among them" (10:9, 10). Many have debated as to whether the Spirit moved on Saul with a heart for God and regeneration, or merely with qualifying anointing for kingship. The actions of Saul testify that the "another heart" he received was one for dispensing civil government and other kingly duties, but did not seem to impact his moral character.

B. Samuel Announces a Sacrifice (vv. 4, 5)

4. And Samuel did that which the Lord spake, and came to Bethlehem. And the elders of the town trembled at his coming, and said, Comest thou peaceably?

5. And he said, Peaceably: I am come to sacrifice unto the Lord: sanctify yourselves, and come with me to the sacrifice. And he sanctified Jesse and his sons, and called them to the sacrifice.

Samuel was concerned for his own life, as well as the Lord's

horn (v. 1)—a ram's horn used for holding olive oil

Talk About It:
1. In verse 1, what did God tell Samuel to stop doing? What two things did God tell him to do?
2. What was Samuel's dilemma (v. 2)?
3. Why do you suppose God did not name the one to be anointed before Samuel went to Jesse's house (v. 3)?

Hardened Heart
There are times in Scripture when God hardens people's hearts, but He only does so to those who have already set themselves on such a course. This was true with the Pharaoh in Egypt (Exodus 4:21; 7:3; 14:4, 17). It was also true with the entire Jewish people when they refused Jesus as Messiah. They could not believe because, as Isaiah had prophesied, "their eyes were heavy, their ears

were closed, and their heart did not understand" (see 6:10).

When God hardens a heart, it is for the greater good of humanity. Saul would be replaced by David, who became Israel's greatest king and ancestor to the Messiah. Israel's hardness opened the way for salvation to be brought to the Gentiles. Jesus lamented that the Jews "did not know the time of [God's] visitation" (Luke 19:44, *NKJV*), but recognized this as necessary in the larger scope of redemption.

Talk About It:
1. In verses 6 and 7, what characteristics did God tell Samuel to ignore? What did God tell him to consider?
2. How do you suppose God was speaking to Samuel through this selection process?

reputation, when God sent him to Bethlehem. To publicly anoint a new king was, on the surface, an act of treason. Not only that, this could cause the people to question Samuel's honor. Had he not anointed Saul upon God's instruction? Hadn't Saul been the right choice? Also, was God so capricious that He would change His mind so quickly? And if so, could God's integrity be questioned? God told Samuel to cloak the purpose of his mission in a legitimate opportunity to go to Bethlehem. Samuel apparently "was in the habit of holding religious gatherings in different provincial towns from time to time" (*The Wycliffe Bible Commentary*).

The fact that the elders of Bethlehem trembled at Samuel's coming indicates their fear of him. Samuel was the true representative of God in the land. His integrity was above reproach, and what he said was seen as law. He held court regularly at various places as a type of circuit judge, and the officials feared that his unexpected coming might be to expose sin among them. Also, word was likely out among the people that there was a breach between Samuel and Saul. The officials certainly would not want to get entangled in that. Samuel quickly laid their fears to rest. Even though the Law provided for sacrifices to be made at the Tabernacle, Samuel customarily did so at different places to encourage the worship of the Lord.

We see here as well the view that most Israelites had toward God. They missed His love and desire for fellowship with them. Instead, all they saw was His justice. "They knew [Samuel] was a prophet of the Lord, and they were afraid that he was now come to denounce some judgments of the Most High against their city" (*Adam Clarke's Commentary*).

C. The House of Jesse Recognized (vv. 6-10)
(1 Samuel 16:6-10 is not included in the printed text.)

God had already told Samuel that he was to anoint one of the sons of Jesse as king. It is not clear as to whether Samuel knew Jesse. Neither is it clear as to Jesse's social and financial status in Bethlehem. That David shepherded over the family flock by himself seems to indicate the family was neither wealthy nor prominent. Even though Samuel's true mission was concealed by a public sacrifice, the ceremony was open to only the elders and a select few others. We do not know whether the townspeople's curiosity was aroused, but Samuel had the status to invite whom he pleased without question.

Samuel naturally assumed that the eldest son of Jesse would be God's choice for king. Eliab likely had all the appearances of a good candidate, but God had a different plan. Eliab was immediately eliminated. Verse 7 reminds us that outward impressions are often misleading, so believers must have spiritual discernment to look beneath the surface. As happened to

God Chooses a King

Eliab, all of David's brothers were divinely rejected. None of them were acceptable.

D. Samuel Anoints David (vv. 11-13)

11. And Samuel said unto Jesse, Are here all thy children? And he said, There remaineth yet the youngest, and, behold, he keepeth the sheep. And Samuel said unto Jesse, Send and fetch him: for we will not sit down till he come hither.

12. And he sent, and brought him in. Now he was ruddy, and withal of a beautiful countenance, and goodly to look to. And the Lord said, Arise, anoint him: for this is he.

13. Then Samuel took the horn of oil, and anointed him in the midst of his brethren: and the Spirit of the Lord came upon David from that day forward. So Samuel rose up, and went to Ramah.

Samuel knew he had heard accurately from God that one of Jesse's sons was to be anointed, so he had to be puzzled at this point. Instead of questioning God, as we so often do, he wisely questioned the information he had at hand. Many times when we think God has failed, we simply do not have all the facts, or God's plan has not yet sufficiently unfolded. That David had not been called from the field indicates a possible disobedience on Jesse's part. Samuel had instructed him to bring his sons to the sacrifice, and that presumably meant all his sons. If the elders trembled at the sight of Samuel coming to their town, Jesse might well now tremble for not having been forthright about his children. At the same time, Jesse likely had no knowledge of what was happening, and the sequence of events occurred so quickly that he simply had forgotten or been unable to send someone for David. Also, we see the possibility that David was not well regarded among the sons of Jesse. Instead of being loved as the baby of the family, perhaps he was a forgotten child.

It was probably an awkward wait while someone was sent for David. When he arrived, Samuel was immediately at peace. David presented a striking appearance. The word *ruddy* is only used for one other man in the Old Testament, and that was Esau. It probably refers to a clear, rosy complexion reflecting vigorous strength. "God made it clear to Samuel that He did not choose David on the basis of his good looks. This was a bonus to David's inner worth" (*The Nelson Study Bible*).

David's brothers were witnesses to his anointing but likely were not told the full implication of what was taking place. "Probably they understood by the anointing that David would become a disciple of Samuel, or in time might become a prophet in Samuel's stead, as later Elisha became the ministering servant

Ramah (v. 13)— Samuel's hometown

Talk About It:
1. What is the significance of Jesse's description of David?
2. What happened when Samuel anointed David?

"Do you wish to rise? Begin by descending. You plan a tower that will pierce the clouds? Lay first the foundation of humility."
—Augustine

of Elijah" (*The Wycliffe Bible Commentary*). The anointing with oil symbolized anointing with the Holy Spirit. Isaiah 61:1 begins by saying, "The Spirit of the Lord God is upon me; because the Lord hath anointed me . . ." Anointing with oil appears to have been done only on the first of a royal dynasty, since here Samuel anoints David just as he had Saul in 1 Samuel 10:1.

II. PROVISION: POWER OF GOD'S NAME (1 Samuel 17:33-52)
A. Saul's Reluctance and David's Willingness (vv. 33-37)

33. And Saul said to David, Thou art not able to go against this Philistine to fight with him: for thou art but a youth, and he a man of war from his youth.

34. And David said unto Saul, Thy servant kept his father's sheep, and there came a lion, and a bear, and took a lamb out of the flock:

35. And I went out after him, and smote him, and delivered it out of his mouth: and when he arose against me, I caught him by his beard, and smote him, and slew him.

36. Thy servant slew both the lion and the bear: and this uncircumcised Philistine shall be as one of them, seeing he hath defied the armies of the living God.

37. David said moreover, The Lord that delivered me out of the paw of the lion, and out of the paw of the bear, he will deliver me out of the hand of this Philistine. And Saul said unto David, Go, and the Lord be with thee.

When we reach this defining moment in David's life, it is easy to forget that he had already been a regular visitor to the king's household. His reputation as a handsome young warrior who could play the harp had reached the troubled king, and he had been brought in to soothe away the distressing spirits that came over Saul (16:14-23). Likely, some months or even years had already passed since David's anointing by Samuel. What is apparent is that the Holy Spirit had left Saul and had come upon David.

Saul was not impressed with David's willingness to fight Goliath, but he didn't know the "God factor" that was on David's side. David showed no fear, having earlier killed both a lion and a bear. His was not a youthful showing off, but rather a practical evaluation of how God would use him to destroy Israel's enemy. "Saul and his people were in despair as the consequence of their being occupied with the things of sight; the man of faith had a contemptuous disdain for Goliath because he viewed him from God's viewpoint—as His enemy, as 'uncircumcised'" (Pink).

David gave all the credit for his past feats to God alone. Those victories would provide him the faith to trust God to help him defeat Goliath. He saw the situation correctly as a spiritual

Talk About It
Why and how had David been faithful to his flock of sheep? What lessons did he learn from these experiences?

"God wants us to be victors, not victims; to grow, not grovel; to soar, not sink; to overcome, not to be overwhelmed."
—William A. Ward

God Chooses a King

one and not a military one. There was no reason for God's people—in this case the army of Israel—to be intimidated by a heathen giant.

B. Armor and Stones (vv. 38-40)

38. And Saul armed David with his armour, and he put an helmet of brass upon his head; also he armed him with a coat of mail.

39. And David girded his sword upon his armour, and he assayed to go; for he had not proved it. And David said unto Saul, I cannot go with these; for I have not proved them. And David put them off him.

assayed (v. 39)—
tried to walk

40. And he took his staff in his hand, and chose him five smooth stones out of the brook, and put them in a shepherd's bag which he had, even in a scrip; and his sling was in his hand: and he drew near to the Philistine.

scrip (v. 40)—
pouch

Next came an exercise in futility. Saul determined to help David as best he could—if the young man was determined to put himself in harm's way—by lending him his own personal armor. Of course, this would have been the best armor available to the Israelite army. David probably tried on the armor simply out of respect for the monarch. However, David said he had not *proved* this armor, meaning he had never used it.

Talk About It:
Why did David feel safer without armor than with it?

Insisting he could not use such heavy armor with which he was unfamiliar, David took the pieces off and selected five smooth stones from a stream bed for his slingshot. His only other weapon was his shepherd's staff. The question arises as to why he picked up five stones. Certainly his confidence in God was strong enough to believe he could kill the giant with just one. The answer is possibly found in 2 Samuel 21:15-22. Here we are told that four other giants eventually came against David. These enormous humans were not uncommon in the land at the time. David might have sensed that slaying Goliath would incite others to fight him. In this light, the gathering of five stones was an act of faith for the future. Personally, this writer believes there was something prophetic taking place as well. The four other giants came many years later, and it was actually David's mighty men who killed them, though David still got the credit (see v. 22). The picking up of five stones symbolically assured that David would be victorious for all of his life. He was God's man. All five giants were doomed when he picked up five stones.

"We can retreat from life or meet it head-on. God has a plan for each life, but we'll never find that plan or victory by a head-in-the-sand approach to life. When it comes to problems, the only way out is through them."
—Al Bernstein

C. No Fear (vv. 41-47)

(1 Samuel 17:41-44 is not included in the printed text.)

45. Then said David to the Philistine, Thou comest to me with a sword, and with a spear, and with a shield: but I

staves (v. 43)—
sticks

come to thee in the name of the Lord of hosts, the God of the armies of Israel, whom thou hast defied.

46. This day will the Lord deliver thee into mine hand; and I will smite thee, and take thine head from thee; and I will give the carcases of the host of the Philistines this day unto the fowls of the air, and to the wild beasts of the earth; that all the earth may know that there is a God in Israel.

47. And all this assembly shall know that the Lord saveth not with sword and spear: for the battle is the Lord's, and he will give you into our hands.

Talk About It:
1. What was Goliath's attitude toward David, and why (vv. 42-44)?
2. Compare Goliath's weapons with David's chief weapon (v. 45).
3. In what sense was this a spiritual battle?

Though Goliath *disdained* David and cursed him (vv. 42, 43), David was not discouraged. He had earlier been taunted by his own brother Eliab, but still held his resolve (vv. 28, 29). David had his attention set on the Lord, not on the enemy. He revealed his confidence in the Lord by the words he spoke here. Defying the armies of Israel was equivalent to defying God himself. Anxious to complete his task, David proclaimed that the giant would be killed that very day and his head cut off. "Faith having brought God into the scene could announce the victory in advance. One stone in its hand was worth more than all the Philistine's armor on the giant of unbelief" (Pink).

D. Amazing Victory (vv. 48-52)

(1 Samuel 17:48-52 is not included in the printed text.)

David did exactly as he said he would do. One accurately placed stone killed the giant. David cut his head off with the giant's own sword. This was considered the absolute indignity to a fallen foe. The death of Goliath produced such panic in the Philistine ranks that they fled in complete disorder. The Israelites chased them all the way to Gath, which was ironically the hometown of Goliath.

Talk About It:
1. Describe David's approach to the fight (v. 48). What does this say?
2. Why did David use Goliath's own sword?
3. How did David's victory affect the Israelites? The Phillistines?

III. PURPOSE: ESTABLISH A KINGDOM (2 Samuel 7:8-16)

A. Rest From His Enemies (vv. 8, 9)

8. Now therefore so shalt thou say unto my servant David, Thus saith the Lord of hosts, I took thee from the sheepcote, from following the sheep, to be ruler over my people, over Israel:

9. And I was with thee whithersoever thou wentest, and have cut off all thine enemies out of thy sight, and have made thee a great name, like unto the name of the great men that are in the earth.

sheepcote (v. 8)—pasture

We move to a time much later in David's life. At this point he was firmly established on the throne of a united Israel. Many of his enemies had been conquered, and he unexpectedly had a restful interlude. We say interlude, because much more fighting still lay ahead of him. His years since the anointing by Samuel

God Chooses a King

had been full of stress, but for a brief season he now had time to reflect on God's goodness toward him. In this, David was no different from believers today. We are constantly battling a triple-threat enemy—the world system, the flesh, and the devil. Seldom do we see times that we can relax from our wars. We know that every victory means new skirmishes lie around the next corner. Yet, God grants every Christian moments of peace.

During this time (v. 1ff.) David was humbled by the fact that he lived in a grand house, while the ark of the covenant was still housed in a tent. He suddenly had the grand idea of building a dwelling place for the ark. Instead of moving impulsively, however, he called on the prophet of God to get affirmation for his plans. Nathan was quick to see David's noble intentions, and assured him of God's approval without first seeking the Lord. That night, however, the Lord gently chastened the prophet for having spoken hastily.

The next day, the Lord used Nathan to remind David of God's amazing calling on his life. God had found him in a pasture and placed him in a palace. God had given him "a great name" (v. 9).

Talk About It:
Describe all the things God had done for David (vv. 8, 9).

B. God's Plan (vv. 10-16)
(2 Samuel 7:14-16 is not included in the printed text.)

10. Moreover I will appoint a place for my people Israel, and will plant them, that they may dwell in a place of their own, and move no more; neither shall the children of wickedness afflict them any more, as beforetime,

11. And as since the time that I commanded judges to be over my people Israel, and have caused thee to rest from all thine enemies. Also the Lord telleth thee that he will make thee an house.

12. And when thy days be fulfilled, and thou shalt sleep with thy fathers, I will set up thy seed after thee, which shall proceed out of thy bowels, and I will establish his kingdom.

13. He shall build an house for my name, and I will stablish the throne of his kingdom for ever.

Nathan was David's personal adviser, speaking for God on all spiritual matters. He would later confront David over his murder of Uriah and sin with Bathsheba. When he initially gave David the affirmation to build a temple, he had been speaking from a general understanding, and not specifically from the Lord. God let Nathan know that a physical dwelling place was not important. What was important was that He be the center of the people's hearts.

God gave Nathan a fresh message for David. That message contained a covenant. God would build a house for David, just

Talk About It:
1. What did God promise to do for the Israelites?
2. What did He promise to do for David?

as David had desired to build a house for Him. He would provide a place for David and his countrymen, a place free from oppression. God would make David's name great, and his successor (son) would be allowed to build a temple for the Lord. More importantly, God would be a Father to this son. This would come as a great comfort to David, who by this time was already well aware of the many problems among his children. Every man wants to believe that good will come through his offspring.

If David's descendants committed iniquity, God would use the "rod of men" (v. 14) to discipline them. David could be assured that God cared for his descendants, and that his throne would last forever. This promise, nevertheless, was still conditional. David's descendants could not use the covenant to justify wickedness. David's throne being in place "forever" refers ultimately to Christ, whose kingdom never ends.

CONCLUSION

One might ask why a lesson on God's choice of a king would be important. The answer is simple. David was both the ancestor and a foreshadow of Christ, our King.

Every kingdom has three elements—a king, subjects, and a domain. Jesus rules as King, and lived humanly on earth as a direct descendant of David. Those who accept Jesus are the subjects in this Kingdom, and His domain is all of creation. Hebrews 2:8 describes it this way: "Thou hast put all things in subjection under his feet. For in that he put all in subjection under him, he left nothing that is not put under him." David's greatest honor was being the mortal king through which the divine King of kings would be born.

GOLDEN TEXT CHALLENGE

"THE LORD SEETH NOT AS MAN SEETH; FOR MAN LOOKETH ON THE OUTWARD APPEARANCE, BUT THE LORD LOOKETH ON THE HEART" (1 Samuel 16:7).

David was not a perfect man. In fact, he was just as flawed, if not more so, than Saul. However, David recognized his dependence on God, whereas Saul consistently held to an independent spirit. David was contrite when faced with his sins, while Saul whitewashed his. David strove to be obedient, while Saul never was willing to face himself. David knew his own pitfalls and asked for God's help. This is epitomized in the words he wrote: "Let the words of my mouth and the meditation of my heart be acceptable in Your sight, O Lord, my strength and my Redeemer" (Psalm 19:14, *NKJV*).

This is what God is looking for in every believer. He is concerned with heart attitudes as opposed to outward show of obedience. He is interested in character, not image. This is extremely

God Chooses a King

important in a day when people are caught up in how they project themselves as opposed to who they really are.

"Character is what God knows we are, what we are like when no one is watching. We can package, we can perform, we can project, we can promote, and we can pretend. What is scary is that when we are through, we have something in which God has no interest." David was truly concerned about his character in God's sight, while Saul was only interested in his projected reputation (Stuart Briscoe, *David, A Heart for God*).

Daily Devotions:
M. God Called
   Abraham
   Genesis 12:1-9
T. God Called
   Samuel
   1 Samuel 3:1-10
W. God Called
   Isaiah
   Isaiah 6:1-8
T. Christ Called
   Levi
   Luke 5:27-32
F. Christ Called
   Zacchaeus
   Luke 19:1-9
S. The Spirit Called
   a Team
   Acts 13:1-5

God Preserves His People (Esther)

Esther 1:1 through 10:3

Unit Theme:
God's Providence in Salvation History

Central Truth:
God places His followers in positions of influence to advance His purposes.

Focus:
Discover the providence of God in the Book of Esther and follow His plan for our lives.

Context:
Esther was written between 485 and 435 B.C.

Golden Text:
"Who knoweth whether thou art come to the kingdom for such a time as this?" (Esther 4:14).

Study Outline:
I. Plan: Save a Nation
(Esther 3:8-14; 4:1-16)
II. Provision: Access and Favor
(Esther 5:1-8; 7:1-10)
III. Purpose: Guarantee a Heritage
(Esther 8:3-13; 9:18, 19, 27, 28)

INTRODUCTION

Like David, Esther was a person who willingly put her life on the line in behalf of the people of God. She was a beautiful young Jewish girl who became the queen of Persia. She used her position to save the Jews in Persia from annihilation. Scripture says, "Esther obtained favor in the sight of all who saw her" (Esther 2:15, *NKJV*). *Favor* means "positioned for divine blessing." Proverbs 16:15 says, "In the light of the king's face is life, and his favor is like a cloud of the latter rain" (*NKJV*). Zechariah 10:1 says, "Ask . . . the Lord [for] rain in the time of the latter rain." We see, therefore, that rain symbolically equates to favor, and thus, in the season of favor, one should ask for more favor. In other words, use favor for the good of others. Esther had the favor of everyone, including the king; but more importantly, she had the favor of God. She pressed the favor that she had gained with the king, making a commitment to give her all, even if it cost her life. Her words of resolve speak for her: "And so will I go in unto the king, which is not according to the law: and if I perish, I perish" (Esther 4:16).

The lesson of Esther is a rich one. Had she not seized the moment of destiny, God would still have found someone to save His people, but she would have missed the opportunity to make history. God will always raise up the people He needs to accomplish His purposes. However, every one of us reaches a crossroad at which we must decide whether we will achieve our destiny or squander it. The following summarizes this well: "If you're stuck in a moment, turn around, stop looking backward, and dare to look forward. This is an adventure that awaits you, an opportunity to explore and even create a future. Time was not created with the power to hold you back. And if the future terrifies you, then just take it one moment at a time" (Erwin McManus, *Seizing Your Divine Moment*).

Why is Esther important in the history of salvation's story? Because in Esther, God provided a deliverer. She was a precursor to the great Deliverer, Jesus himself. We also see several basic principles which operate in the lives of God's people:

1. God is always in control. Haman's plan to destroy the Jews was no problem for the Almighty.

2. There are no coincidences in the lives of God's people. Romans 8:28 says, "All things work together for good to them that love God, to them who are the called according to his purpose."

3. God has set a destiny for each of His children. Destiny is the planned purpose for one's life. This plan, however, does not take away the power of choice. Had Esther not accepted her destiny, He would have had someone else ready.

I. PLAN: SAVE A NATION (Esther 3:8-14; 4:1-16)

A. Hatred Aroused (3:8)

8. And Haman said unto king Ahasuerus, There is a certain people scattered abroad and dispersed among the people in all the provinces of thy kingdom; and their laws are diverse from all people; neither keep they the king's laws: therefore it is not for the king's profit to suffer them.

In a time period from 605 B.C. until 586 B.C., the Babylonian Empire invaded Judah and took many thousands of Jews into captivity. The prophet Jeremiah prophesied this would be a 70-year captivity. By the end of the period, Babylon herself had been defeated and replaced by the Persian Empire (539 B.C.). Thus, the government over Jewish exiles also was transferred. Cyrus the Great of Persia (559-530 B.C.) allowed Jewish captives to return to their homeland in Jerusalem. "He is praised most highly . . . in Isaiah 44:28 and 45:1, where he is called God's *shepherd* and His *anointed"* (*Nelson's Illustrated Bible Dictionary*). Probably another 50 years or more had passed before the story of Esther occurred. Though no one knows who wrote the book, or the exact time of its composition, it is likely to have been written in the last half of the fifth century B.C., after the reign of Ahasuerus (Xerxes I, 486-465 B.C.). This is a pre-Islamic story that took place in ancient Iraq. Most likely, the dramatic events we see unfold in Esther occurred around 473 B.C.

Herodotus described Xerxes as one of the most powerful Persian kings, but also said he was handsome, ruthless and brilliant. At the same time, "according to rabbinic tradition, Esther was one of the four most beautiful Jewish women of all time—the others were Sarah, Rahab and Abigail" (Tommy Tenney, *Finding Favor With the King*). The story of Esther explains the origin of the Feast of Purim, the last festival of the Jewish year. Esther is one of two books in the Bible named for women, the other being Ruth. Also, it is one of several not quoted in the New Testament. It is a story of God's love and protection for His people.

Our immediate text takes us to the heart of the story where the antagonist, Haman, is introduced. Jewish tradition identifies him as a descendant of the Amalekites (who were descendants of Esau), though this is uncertain. Haman had been promoted to prime minister of Persia. Mordecai, the cousin of Queen Esther, had come to the attention of Haman because he had refused to kneel before him. Mordecai had bowed respectfully many times before other government officials. This was not against Jewish law. However, the "reverence" (3:5) Haman demanded bordered on idolatry, and Mordecai refused to worship anyone except the living God. Mordecai "told them that he was a Jew . . . wherefore Haman sought to destroy all the Jews that were throughout the whole kingdom" (vv. 4, 6).

Ahasuerus (*uh-haz-you-EH-rus*)—The Hebrew form of the name *Xerxes*, who reigned over Persia from 485 to 465 B.C.

Talk About It:
What was Haman's accusation against the Jews?

"If only there were evil people somewhere, insidiously committing evil deeds, and it were necessary only to separate them from the rest of us and destroy them. But the line dividing good and evil cuts through the heart of every human being. And who is willing to destroy a piece of his own heart?"

—Alexandr Solzhenitsyn

B. Plot Proposed (v. 9)

9. If it please the king, let it be written that they may be destroyed: and I will pay ten thousand talents of silver to the hands of those that have the charge of the business, to bring it into the king's treasuries.

Talk About It:
How did Haman say the king would benefit from his plan?

Haman did not at first identify which people he was talking about, but simply described them as aloof foreigners who refused to obey the king's laws. Appealing to the emperor's nationalist sense of superiority, Haman convinced him that a *pogrom* ("an organized massacre of people") would be of benefit to the nation. He offered to spend a personal fortune—worth millions of dollars today—to carry out his mission. This amounted to literally tons of silver. Where would he come up with these resources? Perhaps by taking over the property of the slaughtered, for many Jews were wealthy. Note, however, that Haman did not mention Mordecai's name specifically, yet this man was the focus of his wrath. To have said such would have brought a more careful scrutiny of his motives.

C. Pogrom Set in Place (vv. 10-14)

(Esther 3:10-14 is not included in the printed text.)

Talk About It:
1. How did the king respond to Haman's request (vv. 10, 11)?
2. According to verse 13, what did the new law say?

The king bought the idea without examination. Haman was given total authority to carry out his scheme. Unknown to either man, however, the death sentence would include the queen. Verse 11 seems to indicate the king rejected Haman's offer to pay the expenses. This was likely a diplomatic politeness on the king's part. Scribes put the plan into documentation, and copies of the decree were sent across the land with the king's signet ring imprint, something like a notary seal we see today. The 13th day of the month of Nisan was set for the order to be executed. This turned out to be almost a year later. No reason is given for the time lapse, but many Jews would certainly have had time to escape the land. Permission to plunder the possession of the Jews is indicated in verse 13, and "all who helped to exterminate them would gain spoil, but a portion would be turned over to Haman" (*The Wycliffe Bible Commentary*). This entire scheme "perplexed" (v. 15) the city of Shushan, likely because so many Jews lived here, but also because they had many friends in that city.

D. Grief Expressed (4:1-12)

(Esther 4:2, 3, 5-12 is not included in the printed text.)

Mordecai *(MAWR-duh-ki)*—v. 1—The adoptive father of Esther, his young cousin

1. When Mordecai perceived all that was done, Mordecai rent his clothes, and put on sackcloth with ashes, and went out into the midst of the city, and cried with a loud and a bitter cry;

4. So Esther's maids and her chamberlains came and told it her. Then was the queen exceedingly grieved; and

she sent raiment to clothe Mordecai, and to take away his sackcloth from him: but he received it not.

Mordecai's reaction was typical of Oriental grieving. Sackcloth and ashes are spoken of many times in the Bible as a visible sign of mourning and anguish. Despite the death sentence, Mordecai was certainly not ashamed to make his feelings known publicly. Perhaps in part, this was to get Esther's attention. He made his grief an open spectacle at the king's palace gate. There apparently was no easy direct communication between him and Esther, especially since she had earlier been instructed by him to hide completely her Jewishness. Mordecai did have normal access to the king's court, since he himself was a government official, but because he was wearing grieving clothes, he could not enter.

Esther's maids and attendants saw what was happening with Mordecai and brought it to her attention. Likely, those closest to her knew at least something of her relationship with him. Not comprehending a reason for his grief, Esther sent clothes to him, but he would not accept them. He knew he had to communicate with her more directly. She then sent Hathach, a eunuch assigned to her, to find out more. Mordecai informed him of everything, including how much money Haman had agreed to pay into the treasury for his evil plot. Hathach must have had Mordecai's full confidence, as well as that of the queen. He asked the eunuch to relay a complete explanation to Esther and plead with her to go before the king. His request would thus require that she reveal her Jewish identity.

Esther responded by reiterating the difficulty she would have in approaching the king. No one could enter the inner courts without royal summons—lest he or she be ready to face execution. Since she had not been before him in the last 30 days, she was unsure of his affection for her. Though she was the queen, there were many other wives and concubines in the court that may have been satisfying his sexual appetites. She could easily assume that she had lost favor with him. Hers may not have been so much a fear of losing her life as it was a futility in even trying to persuade him. At the same time, she may initially have been more concerned for her own well-being than that of her people. For some time she had been removed from the culture and relationships within the Jewish community.

E. Esther Challenged (vv. 13-16)

13. Then Mordecai commanded to answer Esther, Think not with thyself that thou shalt escape in the king's house, more than all the Jews.

14. For if thou altogether holdest thy peace at this time, then shall there enlargement and deliverance arise to the

chamberlains (v. 4)
—Eunuchs who were serving in the king's court

Talk About It:
1. How and why did Mordecai show his grief so publicly?
2. What made Mordecai's request (v. 8) seem foolish (v. 11)?

"The only cure for grief is action."
—**George Henry Lewes**

Jews from another place; but thou and thy father's house shall be destroyed: and who knoweth whether thou art come to the kingdom for such a time as this?

15. Then Esther bade them return Mordecai this answer,

16. Go, gather together all the Jews that are present in Shushan, and fast ye for me, and neither eat nor drink three days, night or day: I also and my maidens will fast likewise; and so will I go in unto the king, which is not according to the law: and if I perish, I perish.

The entire Jewish population was about to be destroyed. Someone would have to risk all to save this people. Whether or not Esther had the favor of the king, she still was the obvious choice. Her call for the people to fast is the closest hint of any reference to God in the entire book. Yet we see God's mighty hand at work behind the scenes, orchestrating situations and events to protect His people.

Mordecai laid out an ultimatum to Esther. If she didn't go before the king but instead tried to hide her identity, she certainly would eventually be found out, and still would lose her life. Also, he insisted that someone else would rise to the occasion to deliver the Jewish people. Esther's was more of a personal challenge. Would she seize the divine moment life had prepared her for, or would she default?

Esther's response—"If I perish, I perish"—forever immortalized her as being willing to give her life. This was a yielded submission to providence. She would go to the king, even if it meant her instant execution. "The fasting for three days implies a period of earnestly seeking God in prayer at this critical juncture" (*The Nelson Study Bible*).

II. PROVISION: ACCESS AND FAVOR (Esther 5:1-8; 7:1-10)
A. Plan Conceived (5:1-8)
(Esther 5:3-8 is not included in the printed text.)

1. Now it came to pass on the third day, that Esther put on her royal apparel, and stood in the inner court of the king's house, over against the king's house: and the king sat upon his royal throne in the royal house, over against the gate of the house.

2. And it was so, when the king saw Esther the queen standing in the court, that she obtained favour in his sight: and the king held out to Esther the golden sceptre that was in his hand. So Esther drew near, and touched the top of the sceptre.

During the three days of fasting, which Esther and her maids also participated in, a plan was birthed. Esther dressed in her royal robes and went before the king as Mordecai had instructed.

Talk About It:
1. Name two things Mordecai said would happen if Esther did *not* act (vv. 13, 14).
2. Why did Esther call the Jews to fasting?
3. When is it right to break the law?

"Courage is being scared to death—and saddling up anyway."
—John Wayne

"Courage is fear that has said its prayers."
—Dorothy Bernard

Likely, she exercised everything she knew to make herself as attractive to him as possible. Her beauty impressed the king, and instead of rebuking her, held out his scepter to signal her approach. The word *favor* here is extremely important. The first time it is used in the Bible is when three divine visitors (one of which was the Lord himself) came to see Abraham. Abraham entreated, "If I have found favor in your eyes, my lord, do not pass your servant by" (Genesis 18:3, *NIV*). To have favor means to be positioned for divine blessing. The psalmist speaks of God's favor toward Israel: "Thou shalt arise, and have mercy upon Zion: for the time to favour her, yea, the set time, is come" (102:13). Also, Jesus quoted the prophet Isaiah when He declared of Himself, "The Spirit of the Lord is on me . . . to proclaim the year of the Lord's favor" (Luke 4:18, 19, *NIV*).

So we see that Esther had the king's favor. Obviously he wanted to know why she would make such a brave appearance—she must have a pressing need. He assured her that she could have anything she desired. However, his offer to give her half his kingdom (vv. 3, 6) was likely an exaggeration.

Instead of immediately giving her Jewish identity away, Esther laid out an invitation to a banquet she had prepared. Inviting Haman as well would give her the opportunity to have the criminal on hand when she made her accusations. However, at that banquet she still did not make her motive known, but invited the two men to another meal the next day. Building heightened interest, as well as possibly beguiling her lover/husband with her beauty, she said she would make her request known at that time.

B. Plan Carried Out (7:1-10)

(Esther 7:7-10 is not included in the printed text.)

1. So the king and Haman came to banquet with Esther the queen.

2. And the king said again unto Esther on the second day at the banquet of wine, What is thy petition, queen Esther? and it shall be granted thee: and what is thy request? and it shall be performed, even to the half of the kingdom.

3. Then Esther the queen answered and said, If I have found favour in thy sight, O king, and if it please the king, let my life be given me at my petition, and my people at my request:

4. For we are sold, I and my people, to be destroyed, to be slain, and to perish. But if we had been sold for bondmen and bondwomen, I had held my tongue, although the enemy could not countervail the king's damage.

5. Then the king Ahasuerus answered and said unto

Talk About It:
1. Why do you suppose Esther wore "her royal apparel" when she appeared before the "royal throne" (v. 1)?
2. Why did Esther go to the trouble of preparing two banquets?

"True faith does not attempt to manipulate God to do our will; it positions us to do His will."
—**Philip Yancey**

countervail (v. 4)—"compensate for" (*NKJV*)

Esther the queen, Who is he, and where is he, that durst presume in his heart to do so?

6. And Esther said, The adversary and enemy is this wicked Haman. Then Haman was afraid before the king and the queen.

At the second banquet the king, whose interest now was peaking, again assured Esther that she had his *favor,* thus making it easy for her to bring accusation against Haman. She explained that her people had unjustifiably been set up for extermination. She gave "an impassioned plea to the king in which she also disclosed her true identity to him for the first time" (*The Nelson Study Bible*). She then unmasked Haman as the perpetrator of the evil. She went on further to explain that if her people had simply been sold as slaves, she would not have brought the issue to him. However, their destruction would be a terrible blow to the economy of the nation.

The king's response was one of astonishment and fury. Verse 7 tells us that the king rose and went into the palace garden, perhaps seeing that he was caught in a terrible dilemma and needed to think through his response. He was wrathful toward Haman, but had himself given the man orders that bore his royal seal. Meanwhile, Haman, knowing that his own life was likely over, grasped at Esther to implore her mercy. This was poor timing, for the king returned and assumed that Haman was trying to molest the queen. Immediately the servants covered Haman's face, assuring his sentence of death. Haman was hanged on the gallows that had been prepared for Mordecai. Esther apparently made no verbal response to what transpired.

III. PURPOSE: GUARANTEE A HERITAGE (Esther 8:3-13; 9:18, 19, 27, 28)

A. Haman's Decree Nullified (8:3-13)

(Esther 8:4-10, 12, 13 is not included in the printed text.)

3. And Esther spake yet again before the king, and fell down at his feet, and besought him with tears to put away the mischief of Haman the Agagite, and his device that he had devised against the Jews.

11. Wherein the king granted the Jews which were in every city to gather themselves together, and to stand for their life, to destroy, to slay, and to cause to perish, all the power of the people and province that would assault them, both little ones and women, and to take the spoil of them for a prey.

On that same day Esther received from the king everything that belonged to Haman's estate. Persian law allowed for the estate of a traitor to become custody of the crown. Esther also revealed her

Talk About It

1. How did Esther describe the condition of herself and her people (vv. 3, 4)?

2. Why was the king so furious?

3. Describe the sudden reversal in Haman's feelings and fortune.

Real Repentance?

God is a merciful God, and true repentance will always touch His heart. When Haman entreated Esther for mercy, it was not out of any change of heart toward the Jews, but simply to stay alive. His hatred of the Jews had not changed. His heart had not been affected, only his circumstances.

Talk About It:

1. What was Haman's fate, and why (v. 7)?

God Preserves His People

relationship to Mordecai, and the king immediately invited Mordecai into his presence. "Xerxes removed from his finger the signet ring that he had 'reclaimed' from Haman and gave it to Mordecai, thereby making him prime minister with power to act in the king's name" (*Zondervan NIV Bible Commentary*). Esther immediately gave Mordecai charge of Haman's estate.

Still not sure about the edict condemning the Jewish people, Esther pleaded for their lives before the king. She indeed pressed the favor she had earned. He responded by extending the golden scepter to her. He then instructed that another decree be written in behalf of the Jews. While a royal decree could not be changed, a second one could be written to counter the first. Royal secretaries were summoned, and they wrote out Mordecai's orders in every language used throughout the empire. No one would be able to plead ignorance of this massive change of policy. Couriers on horseback were sent out to carry the proclamation as fast as possible.

The Jews in Persia were given extraordinary rights to protect themselves and take vengeance on those who might attack them. On the day when "the enemies of the Jews had hoped to overpower them . . . the tables were turned and the Jews got the upper hand over those who hated them" (9:1, *NIV*). The Persian leaders in every province stood with the Jews because of their "fear of Mordecai" (v. 3), who had been promoted to a high position in the king's court. The various ethnic groups who came against the Jews were soundly defeated.

B. The Feast of Purim Established (9:18, 19, 27, 28)

18. But the Jews that were at Shushan assembled together on the thirteenth day thereof, and on the fourteenth thereof; and on the fifteenth day of the same they rested, and made it a day of feasting and gladness.

19. Therefore the Jews of the villages, that dwelt in the unwalled towns, made the fourteenth day of the month Adar a day of gladness and feasting, and a good day, and of sending portions one to another.

27. The Jews ordained, and took upon them, and upon their seed, and upon all such as joined themselves unto them, so as it should not fail, that they would keep these two days according to their writing, and according to their appointed time every year;

28. And that these days should be remembered and kept throughout every generation, every family, every province, and every city; and that these days of Purim should not fail from among the Jews, nor the memorial of them perish from their seed.

These verses explain the Feast of Purim on the Jewish

---

2. How complicated was it to enact the new law (vv. 9, 10)?
3. What right were the Jews given (v. 13)?

Letting God Be Judge

From our perspective of history, it seems cruel that the Jews in Persia were given such rights of vengeance, especially when Scripture says, "Dearly beloved, avenge not yourselves, but rather give place unto wrath: for it is written, Vengeance is mine; I will repay, saith the Lord" (Romans 12:19, Paul quoting Deuteronomy 32:35). We have to remember, however, that the times in Persia were extraordinarily cruel, and human life was worth little. Jesus came to elevate mankind above the terrible harshness of the Old Testament concept of an "eye for an eye" (Matthew 5:38). Paul encourages believers in the new covenant to commit their lives to the Lord and let Him handle retribution.

"In remembrance of how God remained hidden throughout the Purim miracle, Jews dress up on Purim and many hide their faces."
—*Wikipedia*

calendar. This feast celebrated the victory of the Jews over their enemies in Persia. The Jews living in Shushan (Susa) were given two days to destroy their enemies (the 14th and 15th of the month of Adar), and then celebrated on the 15th. Jews in other parts of the empire had only one day to kill their enemies, and thus celebrated on the 14th.

The name *Purim* comes from the word *pur,* meaning "lot." This refers to the lot that was cast to determine the day for the Jewish execution by Haman. "On both days of the feast the modern Jews read the Book of Esther in their synagogues. Whenever Haman's name is pronounced, they make a terrible noise in the synagogue. Some drum with feet on the floor, and the boys have mallets with which they knock and make a noise" (*Jamieson, Fausett, and Brown Commentary*). Today the feast is observed in February or March.

CONCLUSION

The great moral of the story of Esther is that she put her life on the line in behalf of others. Self-sacrifice is a worthy trait we find throughout the stories of great heroes. They forget themselves and think of others first. Also, we know that God is always at work in the world and has a plan. His plan will always excel and succeed. It started in eternity past when He chose us to be His people. As Paul said, "According as he hath chosen us in him before the foundation of the world, that we should be holy and without blame before him in love" (Ephesians 1:4).

Esther gives hope to those who are wrongly accused. Even Hitler and the Nazis were frightened of people reading the Book of Esther. It was banned in their death camps. Jewish prisoners saw her story as a hope of future deliverance. There are still heroes being created every day. They see the wrong being committed, and put themselves in the line of fire so others might be saved.

GOLDEN TEXT CHALLENGE

"WHO KNOWETH WHETHER THOU ART COME TO THE KINGDOM FOR SUCH A TIME AS THIS?" (Esther 4:14).

Mordecai's language to Esther was positive and confident amid a severe situation. Why did he not say, "You are the only hope. You are the only one who can save the nation"? The reason behind Mordecai's persuasion was his knowledge of God and also of Esther. She responded with an affirmative action.

Similar incidents have occurred many times before and are destined to occur many times again. Only the names and places have been changed. The opportunity and gravity of the hour for the work in the kingdom of God continually poses itself to Christians.

This scripture has a fourfold admonition for Christian living:

1. Regardless of the circumstances, God's providence will never fail. God cares and He will provide.

2. Preparation for crisis must be made in the normal routine of life if these moments are to become opportunities instead of disasters. With each crisis, opportunities unfold to the believer.

3. Purposefulness is exemplified in the lives of all people committed to God.

4. Personal responsibility must be accepted. If one refuses to yield, another will take his or her place. God desires every person to learn, at that juncture in their personal history, that they have come to the Kingdom "for such a time as this."

Daily Devotions:
M. God Gives Victory
Exodus 17:8-16
T. Guarded by an Angel
Exodus 23:20-30
W. Deliverance Through a Prophetess
Judges 4:4-15
T. God Preserves His Deliverer
Matthew 2:11-23
F. Death Defeated
Romans 5:12-21
S. God Preserves His Saints
Revelation 19:1-9

God Calls for Repentance (John the Baptist)

Isaiah 40:3-5; Matthew 3:1-3; Luke 1:5-25; 3:1-6, 15-18

Unit Theme: God's Providence in Salvation History

Central Truth: Repentance prepares hearts for Christ's presence.

Focus: Examine the providence of God in John the Baptist's ministry and prepare our hearts for Christ's rule.

Context: Various passages regarding repentance

Golden Text: "Repent ye: for the kingdom of heaven is at hand" (Matthew 3:2).

Study Outline:
I. Plan: Prepare for Christ's Mission (Isaiah 40:3-5; Matthew 3:1-3)
II. Provision: Power From God (Luke 1:5-25)
III. Purpose: Proclaim the Savior (Luke 3:1-6, 15-18)

INTRODUCTION

In the last book of the Old Testament the prophet Malachi declares, "Behold, I will send you Elijah the prophet" (4:5). He goes on to say that this *Elijah* would turn the people's hearts (fathers to children and children to fathers). People's hearts are not changed unless God draws them. Jesus said, "No one can come to me, except the Father which hath sent me draw him" (John 6:44). He also said, "And I, if I be lifted up from the earth, will draw all men unto me" (12:32). Since both the Father and the Son are in heaven, this *drawing* is accomplished by the Holy Spirit, the third person of the Trinity, who is active on the earth right now. However, the Holy Spirit uses human vessels to accomplish His purpose.

This brings us to John the Baptist. Luke tells us he was full of the Holy Spirit from his mother's womb (Luke 1:15), and that he would operate "in the spirit and power of Elias [Elijah] . . . to make ready a people prepared for the Lord" (v. 17). Notice that John was not Elijah, but operated with the same power and spirit. There is no such thing as reincarnation. John called people to repentance, opening their hearts for the first coming of Jesus. Most of the people who later followed Jesus had first been influenced by the preaching of John.

John electrified people. They saw in his message that God was about to finally do something on earth. After all, there had been a 400-year period when He had seemed silent. The last words of the last prophet, Malachi, had promised that one would come preparing the way for the Messiah. John fit the bill exactly.

However, Malachi went on to speak of the "great and dreadful day of the Lord" (Malachi 4:5), something that is yet to occur. Interestingly, as they were coming down from the Mount of Transfiguration, Jesus said something puzzling to Peter, James and John: "Indeed, Elijah is coming first and will restore all things, but I say to you that Elijah has come already, and they did not know him but did to him whatever they wished" (Matthew 17:11, 12, *NKJV*). Moses and Elijah had appeared from heaven at the Transfiguration. Note that John the Baptist had already been beheaded at this time, indicated by the words "did to him whatever they wished." Jesus was stating that an "Elijah" had already come, meaning John the Baptist, but also prophesying that another Elijah is yet to come. Just as John heralded the first coming of Jesus, there will be another who will herald His second coming, at which time will also occur the "great and dreadful day" spoken of by Malachi.

I. PLAN: PREPARE FOR CHRIST'S MISSION (Isaiah 40:3-5; Matthew 3:1-3)

A. Forerunner of Christ (Isaiah 40:3-5)

3. The voice of him that crieth in the wilderness, Prepare ye the way of the Lord, make straight in the desert a highway for our God.

4. Every valley shall be exalted, and every mountain and hill shall be made low: and the crooked shall be made straight, and the rough places plain:

5. And the glory of the Lord shall be revealed, and all flesh shall see it together: for the mouth of the Lord hath spoken it.

Isaiah prophesied some 700 years earlier that there would be a forerunner to the Messiah. He spoke his words as a message of *comfort* (v. 1) to the exiles living in Babylon. Interestingly enough, this was some 150 to 200 years before the Captivity even began. He promised that the exiles would return to Jerusalem, and that the "glory of the Lord" would be revealed. This would be personified in the appearance of the Lord himself, or at least someone powerfully representing Him.

The forerunner would preach a message of preparation, crying out in a wilderness. This has a double meaning. Isaiah speaks of a physical preparation of the land routes by which the Lord would arrive. This comes from the ancient practice where road workers were sent ahead of an important official to clear the way for his caravan to travel through. The more important the official visiting, the more preparation that must be made. "The implication here is that Jehovah was to return to Jerusalem through the desert route by which the exiles would return from Babylon, and that a fitting preparation for his advent would be the removal of obstacles and the smoothing out of a highway" (*The Wycliffe Bible Commentary*). We know that John did preach in the wilderness, but "it was in the moral wilderness that the way of the Lord was to be prepared" (*Jamieson, Fausset and Brown Commentary*). In other words, his message was directed to the valleys, rough places, mountains of sin, and crooked ways that pervert men's hearts. Also, Isaiah's message is one of "coming back," meaning both the coming back of people from physical bondage and from spiritual exile. If we look at Isaiah 60:1-3, we see that the prospects for this revelation went well beyond just the Jews, but to all humanity (Gentiles) as well.

Isaiah's words about preparing a place in the desert point to a necessity in all who want to serve the Lord. The desert experience is a prerequisite to fulfilling God's call. If we don't humble ourselves, the wilderness becomes all the more difficult. If we have given ourselves to Christ, then we have no rights of our

Talk About It:
1. What does it mean to "make straight . . . a highway for our God" (v. 3)?
2. Describe the impact of John's ministry, according to verse 4.
3. How would "the glory of the Lord . . . be revealed" (v. 5)?

Called to Preach?
  "The one thing no church can stand is a pastor who really wants to be something else. The men who really want out ought to be helped out, for the Christian ministry is no place for a man who wants to be something else. It is a place for men who can give counsel, not the place for men who need counsel."
—Duke McCall

own. Paul said, "You are not your own; you were bought at a price" (1 Corinthians 6:19, 20, *NIV*). It is difficult enough to go through a wilderness in submission as John did. We hear of no complaints from him. What happens when we get there kicking and screaming? When Isaiah speaks of valleys being filled and mountains brought low, this indicates the hold that sin has over us being broken. Everything that is of pride must be leveled in us. If we fight against God's work in us, it becomes a *sifting*. This is what Jesus told Peter would happen to him (Luke 22:31).

It is only after pride is broken that we can truly cry out to God. Valleys speak of humility. The wilderness humbles us and makes us ready to hear from God. The Prodigal Son did not humble himself until he had lost all his money and his pride, and was left eating pig's food. Then he came to his senses. The wilderness is a time to cry out to God. When we seek Him there with all our hearts, then we become the voice "crying out in the wilderness" to our generation.

B. Preacher of Repentance (Matthew 3:1-3)

1. In those days came John the Baptist, preaching in the wilderness of Judaea.

2. And saying, Repent ye: for the kingdom of heaven is at hand.

3. For this is he that was spoken of by the prophet Esaias, saying, The voice of one crying in the wilderness, Prepare ye the way of the Lord, make his paths straight.

Talk About It:
1. Why did John preach in the wilderness instead of the city?
2. Restate the phrase "Repent ye" in your own words.

As the forerunner to Jesus, John the Baptist preceded Christ in birth, ministry and in death. His role was to convince Jews to repent of their sins (and show such by water baptism), so that they would be ready to receive the imminent coming of the Messiah. Despite his strange manner and lifestyle, the people heartily welcomed his message. They saw him as a real prophet (the first in 400 years), and anticipated that a new age was about to dawn. That John was full of the Holy Spirit gave great power to his words, convicting people of their sins. John proved to be the last of the Old Testament prophets, even though his story is written in the New Testament. Jesus said, "The law and the prophets were until John: since that time the kingdom of God is preached, and every man presseth into it" (Luke 16:16). The crowds that came to hear John immediately associated him with the words of Malachi 4:5, 6, which compared this forerunner to the ancient prophet Elijah. They saw the visible similarity to Elijah, who is described in 2 Kings 1:8 as "an hairy man, and girt with a girdle of leather about his loins." Some even asked John if he was Elijah somehow reincarnated, which of course he denied (John 1:21).

One has to wonder how John's message initially found an

audience. The location of his ministry stayed in the Judean wilderness, a barren area extending along the western shore of the Dead Sea. His ministry was short-lived, coming to a close soon after Jesus appeared on the scene. His execution at the hand of Herod was around A.D. 27-28. Since his mother, Elizabeth, was a cousin to Mary, he and Jesus were also distant cousins. They likely knew each other during their youthful years, but John probably did not realize Jesus' true identity until He came to be baptized (Matthew 3:16, 17).

John's message was twofold. The first part was to *repent*. This means "a change of mind which issues in regret and in change of conduct" (*Vincent's Word Studies*). Repentance carries the idea of both turning from sin and turning to God. Without the working of the Holy Spirit through John, this would have been a very hard sell (and still was with self-righteous religious leaders). Most Jews already considered themselves to be the people of God living in covenant relationship.

The second part of his message was the nearness of the kingdom of heaven. Use of the word *heaven* here indicates the Jewish hesitancy to speak the name of God. However, there is no difference between "kingdom of heaven" and "kingdom of God." There are 32 references to the "kingdom of heaven" in the New Testament, and 69 to the "kingdom of God." Either way, there was a rising expectation among the Jews of a fresh visitation from heaven that would change every known paradigm.

Just what is the Kingdom? It is the sum total of all that was lost when Adam sinned in the Garden of Eden. God gave Adam and Eve dominion over the earth (Genesis 1:28). The psalmist said, "The heaven, even the heavens, are the Lord's; but the earth hath he given to the children of men" (Psalm 115:16). God intended that humanity multiply, fill the earth, subdue it, and be steward over it. However, Adam forfeited that right and authority, giving it away to Satan. God knew humanity would fail. Even before the earth was created, He had an eternal plan in place to restore all that we would lose. We see this as early as Genesis 3:15. When Jesus came to the earth, He had one central purpose—to restore the Kingdom to humanity. He said, "For the Son of man is come to seek and to save that which was lost" (Luke 19:10). Jesus also said, "It is your Father's good pleasure to give you the kingdom" (12:32). Both John and Jesus began their ministries by proclaiming that the Kingdom was "at hand." Everyone thought Jesus meant the nation of Israel. They wanted to see their prestige restored to what it had been. They did not comprehend the Kingdom.

Thus, the Kingdom is the realm of domain over the earth that Christ restored to His children. Primarily, it is still in the invisible realm, but it is accessible. That's why Jesus taught the

Radical Change
"The New Testament word for *repentance* means changing one's mind so that one's views, values, goals, and ways are changed and one's whole life is lived differently. The change is radical, both inwardly and outwardly; mind and judgment, will and affections, behavior and lifestyle, motives and purposes, are all involved. Repenting means starting a new life."

—J.I. Packer

disciples to pray, "Thy kingdom come. Thy will be done in earth, as it is in heaven" (Matthew 6:10). All we have to do is raise our eyes to a higher level and *see* it, as Jesus told Nicodemus (John 3:3).

II. PROVISION: POWER FROM GOD (Luke 1:5-25)
A. Angelic Visitation (vv. 5-12)

(Luke 1:5-12 is not included in the printed text.)

Talk About It:
1. Describe the character of Zacharias and Elizabeth (v. 6).
2. What was Zacharias' response to the angel, and why (v. 12)?

Zacharias and Elizabeth were a godly couple who were barren and well advanced in age. He was among the many priests (possibly as many as 18,000) who served in rotation at the Temple for one week twice a year. The offering of incense was something only a priest could do, and "each morning, one of the priests would enter the Holy Place in the Temple (the sanctuary) to offer incense. Incense was burned in the Temple twice daily. Lots were cast to decide who would enter the sacred room, and one day during that week Zacharias was chosen by lot" (*The Life Application Commentary Series*). Although this was a great honor to have drawn the lot, there was nothing to indicate that Zacharias would be visited by an angel. He was immediately overwhelmed with fear, and yet ultimately awed that he and Elizabeth were included in the sovereign plan of God.

B. Birth Announcement (vv. 13-17)

13. But the angel said unto him, Fear not, Zacharias: for thy prayer is heard; and thy wife Elisabeth shall bear thee a son, and thou shalt call his name John.

14. And thou shalt have joy and gladness; and many shall rejoice at his birth.

15. For he shall be great in the sight of the Lord, and shall drink neither wine nor strong drink; and he shall be filled with the Holy Ghost, even from his mother's womb.

16. And many of the children of Israel shall he turn to the Lord their God.

17. And he shall go before him in the spirit and power of Elias, to turn the hearts of the fathers to the children, and the disobedient to the wisdom of the just; to make ready a people prepared for the Lord.

Talk About It:
1. Describe the guidelines given for bringing up John (v. 15).
2. What impact would John have (vv. 15-17)? How?

Angels are scary creatures. Virtually every time anyone in the Bible received such a visitation, it provoked a reaction of great terror. The phrase "Do not be afraid" appears often in Scripture when fears had to be calmed. It was not by chance that Zacharias was the priest on duty that day. God was orchestrating history.

The angel said that Zacharias' prayers had been heard. What prayers? They were not likely for a child at this late date in life. More likely he was praying for the coming of the Messiah

God Calls for Repentance

and the deliverance of Israel from her oppressors. Yes, these prayers would be answered, but also prayers that were prayed (for a son) early in life. No prayer is ever lost to the Almighty. The name to be given to the child was *John*. "When God names a child, a greatness usually follows" (*Nelson Study Bible*). The angel also identified this son as being a direct fulfillment of the prophecies of Malachi.

C. Zacharias' Doubt (vv. 18-25)
  (Luke 1:18-25 is not included in the printed text.)
  It is not a good thing to talk back to an angel. Zacharias expressed doubt by his question. His asking for a sign showed a lack of faith. "Instead of looking to God by faith, the priest looked at himself and his wife and decided that the birth of a son was impossible. He wanted some assurance beyond the plain word of Gabriel, God's messenger, perhaps a sign from God" (*The Bible Exposition Commentary*). This was a different reaction from the one Abraham gave when he was promised a son. Scripture says, "Abraham believed God, and it was accounted to him for righteousness" (James 2:23, *NKJV*). The angel now identifies himself as Gabriel, one of only two angels named in the Bible. As a result of his doubt, Zacharias was struck dumb until the birth of John. He was not even able to pronounce the priestly blessing to the crowd that had gathered outside. All they could do was deduce that he had experienced a vision.

  Very quickly, however, Elizabeth did become pregnant. Why she hid herself for five months is not known, unless there was a measure of modest embarrassment at her condition so late in life. Perhaps, as well, she wanted this time to reflect on the fact that her child would be the very one to herald the coming of the Messiah.

III. PURPOSE: PROCLAIM THE SAVIOR (Luke 3:1-6, 15-18)
A. The Word Unto John (vv. 1, 2)
  1. Now in the fifteenth year of the reign of Tiberius Caesar, Pontius Pilate being governor of Judaea, and Herod being tetrarch of Galilee, and his brother Philip tetrarch of Ituraea and of the region of Trachonitis, and Lysanias the tetrarch of Abilene,
  2. Annas and Caiaphas being the high priests, the word of God came unto John the son of Zacharias in the wilderness.
  John's role was to prepare the hearts of the Jewish people for the first coming of Jesus. As we have seen, he spent a number of years in the desert letting God wrench *self* out of him, and then at the appointed time, the message came "unto him" (v. 2). To have the word of God revealed to us, we have to die to ourselves

"Christian holiness, whether for the church or for the individual, can never be a static thing, something gained once for all. It has to be maintained amidst conflicts and perils that are renewed day by day."
—Stephen Neill

Talk About It:
1. What surprising sign did Gabriel give to Zacharias, and why (vv. 18-20)?
2. How did Zacharias communicate with the waiting people, and what did they think had happened to him (v. 22)?
3. How did Elizabeth view her pregnancy (v. 24, 25)?

tetrarch (v. 1)—a prince who governs one-fourth of a kingdom or country

Talk About It:
Contrast John with Annas and Caiaphas.

in the desert experience. This is affirmed by what Paul said: "For if we would judge ourselves, we would not be judged" (1 Corinthians 11:31, *NKJV*). The first word for *judge* here means "to separate oneself thoroughly." The second means "to punish or condemn." If we lose our lives in Christ, we will not be judged for disobedience, and the word can come *unto* us. Even though John had an amazing anointing and call on his life, he still had to separate himself unto God so the message of God could come to him. The same is true for us.

Notice to whom the message of God did not come—"Annas and Caiaphas . . . the high priests" (Luke 3:2). Caiaphas was the high priest, with his father-in-law, Annas, "still a sort of 'high-priest emeritus'" (*Zondervan Pictorial Bible Dictionary*). Those two held their religious positions by political appointment of the Roman government. They later played leading roles in Christ's crucifixion.

B. The Word Proclaimed (vv. 3-6)

3. And he came into all the country about Jordan, preaching the baptism of repentance for the remission of sins;

4. As it is written in the book of the words of Esaias the prophet, saying, The voice of one crying in the wilderness, Prepare ye the way of the Lord, make his paths straight.

5. Every valley shall be filled, and every mountain and hill shall be brought low; and the crooked shall be made straight, and the rough ways shall be made smooth;

6. And all flesh shall see the salvation of God.

Baptism is an outward sign of something that has happened inwardly. As people were convicted by the message John preached, they repented and demonstrated that repentance by baptism. It is hard to trace exactly where John came up with the idea of baptizing people, but it appears not to have taken anyone by great surprise. "Converts from pagan religions were admitted to Judaism only after fulfilling certain obligations, which included the study of the Torah, circumcision, and a ritual bath to wash away the impurities of the Gentile background" (*Life Application Commentary Series*). What does appear to have been new was for Jews themselves to be baptized as a sign of repentance. "John's baptism looked forward to the coming of the Messiah, while Christian baptism looks back to the finished work of Christ" (*The Bible Exposition Commentary*).

It is not clear whether John ever identified himself as a fulfillment of Isaiah's prophecy, or whether the Gospel writers did so in retrospect, but everyone who came to hear him saw the obvious. The times were ripe for the Messiah to appear. Luke here concludes by declaring, "All flesh shall see the salvation of God" (v. 6).

"Prayer is putting oneself in the hands of God, at His disposition, and listening to His voice in the depths of our hearts."
—**Mother Teresa**

Talk About It:
1. Why was baptism central to John's ministry?
2. Explain the statement "All flesh shall see the salvation of God" (v. 6).

"I preached as never sure to preach again, And as a dying man to dying men."
—**Richard Baxter**

God Calls for Repentance

C. A Prophet or the Christ? (v. 15)

15. And as the people were in expectation, and all men mused in their hearts of John, whether he were the Christ, or not.

The people could not help but see that John was a prophet. Some even wanted to believe he might be the Christ. In the next verse John dispelled those notions. However, we also need to look at the qualifications of a prophet. From an Old Testament perspective, Deuteronomy 18:22 indicates that everything a prophet speaks in the name of the Lord must come true. However, that is impossible in the short run, for much of Biblical prophecy is still to be fulfilled. This is typified in that Malachi spoke of Elijah coming before the "great and dreadful day of the Lord" (Malachi 4:5). Obviously, this has not yet occurred. No, the true test of a prophet is given by Jesus when He spoke of false prophets: "Ye shall know them by their fruits" (Matthew 7:16). John the Baptist was full of the Holy Spirit. Paul said the fruit of the Spirit is "love, joy, peace, long-suffering, kindness, goodness, faithfulness, gentleness, self-control" (Galatians 5:22, 23, *NKJV*).

Talk About It:
Why did people think John might be the Messiah?

D. One Mightier to Come (vv. 16-18)

16. John answered, saying unto them all, I indeed baptize you with water; but one mightier than I cometh, the latchet of whose shoes I am not worthy to unloose: he shall baptize you with the Holy Ghost and with fire:

17. Whose fan is in his hand, and he will throughly purge his floor, and will gather the wheat into his garner; but the chaff he will burn with fire unquenchable.

18. And many other things in his exhortation preached he unto the people.

This is the first direct mention by John of the One to come after him. Jesus had not yet appeared. John saw his own ministry and efforts as minor compared to what would follow. His water baptism would pale when compared to baptism by the Holy Spirit. That baptism would have the same effect as fire. Fire is a symbol of judgment, purification and refinement. The Holy Spirit had been prophesied as coming with the Messiah (Isaiah 11:2). Jesus, at His baptism by John, would be filled with the Spirit. Also, He said, "He who has seen me has seen the Father" (John 14:9, *NKJV*). We can also tie this to what God said through Ezekiel: "And I will not hide My face from them anymore; for I shall have poured out My Spirit on the house of Israel" (39:29, *NKJV*). Jesus was the visible representation of the Father. The Holy Spirit represents the face of God. No wonder John was overwhelmed at the prospect of what was coming. John could not envision himself of being worthy enough to even tie the Messiah's sandals.

Talk About It:
1. How did John compare himself and His ministry with the Messiah's (v. 16)?
2. How did John describe the Messiah's ministry (v. 17)?
3. How do you know John's message was not one-dimensional?

"Men are never duly touched and impressed with a conviction of their insignificance until they have contrasted themselves with the majesty of God."
—**John Calvin**

CONCLUSION

We have a tendency to think of John the Baptist in superhuman terms. Yes, he was filled with the Holy Spirit while still in his mother's womb, but he had to face struggles like everyone else. I doubt that he particularly enjoyed growing up in the desert wilderness, but he was inwardly compelled to do so. He probably didn't enjoy living like a madman when he preached his message of repentance and water baptism. Also, John 10:41 says he performed no miracles. There was no supernatural affirmation to his ministry. These were tough prices for him to pay.

John was of a priestly lineage. He could have spent his youthful years in rabbinical school *preparing* for the priesthood. There was a level of affluence he could have enjoyed growing up in his father's house. Instead, he chose the difficult path of obedience. He paid the price of going through a desert experience. We also know how human he was, because when imprisoned, he sent word to Jesus asking if He really was the Messiah (Matthew 11:3). He went through his own period of doubt brought on by severe testing. Yet, he was declared by Jesus to have been the greatest of the prophets (v. 11).

GOLDEN TEXT CHALLENGE

"REPENT YE: FOR THE KINGDOM OF HEAVEN IS AT HAND" (Matthew 3:2).

John never traveled to Jerusalem to speak. The crowds came to him as he stayed in areas around the Jordan River. When the anointing truly comes over a person, the people will come. Hungry people will go to where they can hear God speak. John never took an offering, never worried about how he could support himself. He had nothing but the message of God on his mind. There was also no candy-coating of the message. He even called some a "brood of vipers" (v. 7, *NKJV*). His message was tough, but the anointing and power of the Holy Spirit was upon him—and people repented of their sins. The kingdom of heaven advanced through his ministry.

Daily Devotions:
M. Repentance
   Needed
   Deuteronomy
   31:24-30
T. Repent of
   Disobedience
   Judges 2:1-7
W. Repent of
   Idolatry
   Ezekiel 14:1-8
T. Jesus Preached
   Repentance
   Matthew 4:12-
   17
F. The Disciples
   Preached
   Repentance
   Mark 6:10-13
S. Godly Sorrow
   Leads to
   Repentance
   2 Corinthians
   7:6-11

God Calls for Repentance

God Chooses a Vessel (Mary)

Isaiah 7:14; Luke 1:1-56; Hebrews 9:1-15

INTRODUCTION

God never abdicated His throne over any part of creation, especially the earth. Psalm 24:1 says, "The earth is the Lord's, and all it contains, the world, and those who dwell in it" (*NASB*). Even before humanity fell in the Garden of Eden, God had a plan in place for redemption. It would be through His Son coming to earth and restoring what Adam had lost to the devil. The Old Testament contains a gradual unfolding of one theme—a Redeemer is coming. Along the way we see God working: "For the eyes of the Lord run to and fro throughout the whole earth, to shew himself strong in the behalf of them whose heart is perfect toward him" (2 Chronicles 16:9). We also see the futility of those who oppose Him: "The wicked plots against the just, and gnashes at him with his teeth. The Lord laughs at him, for He sees that his day is coming" (Psalm 37:12, 13, *NKJV*).

Thus far in our unit we have looked at individuals who played key roles in the unfolding story of salvation. Moses delivered Israel and gave her the Law, demonstrating God's demand for a holy people through which the Messiah could come. Ruth was a Gentile grafted into the royal line of Israel to show the inclusiveness of God's plan. David was a man after God's heart, and provided a kingly dynasty through which the ultimate King would come. Esther showed God's care and faithfulness to those people who are His own. John the Baptist called people to repentance from sin so their hearts would be prepared for the Savior.

God governs the affairs of humanity. Whenever He purposes to advance His plan, He shares His heart with individuals who are in tune. Amos 3:7 says, "Surely the Lord God does nothing, unless He reveals His secret to His servants the prophets" (*NKJV*). Some 700 years before Jesus was born, He told Isaiah that He would be born to a virgin. Micah was given the place where Jesus would be born—Bethlehem. Other prophets were given bits and pieces of the big picture. John the Baptist was sent to the world as the Messiah's forerunner.

And now we come to Mary, the mother of Jesus. When God was finally ready to send His Son into the world, He spoke to a simple virgin in the town of Nazareth, a village far off the beaten path of divine expectations.

Unit Theme:
God's Providence in Salvation History

Central Truth:
Salvation requires our continuing submission to Christ's indwelling presence.

Focus:
Reflect on the providence of God in choosing Mary as the mother of Jesus and evidence His presence to the world.

Context:
Various passages concerning Mary, the mother of Jesus

Golden Text:
"To whom God would make known what is the riches of the glory of this mystery among the Gentiles; which is Christ in you, the hope of glory" (Colossians 1:27).

Study Outline:
I. Promise: God With Us
  (Isaiah 7:14; Luke 1:26-33)
II. Provision: Miraculous Conception
  (Luke 1:34-38)
III. Purpose: A New Covenant
  (Luke 1:46-55; Hebrews 9:11-15)

I. PROMISE: GOD WITH US (Isaiah 7:14; Luke 1:26-33)
A. An Incomparable Sign (Isaiah 7:14)

14. Therefore the Lord himself shall give you a sign; Behold, a virgin shall conceive, and bear a son, and shall call his name Immanuel.

Talk About It:
1. Why was it important that Jesus be born to a virgin?
2. Would God's Son have been called *Immanuel* before coming to earth? Why or why not?

We must put this verse in historical context. It is interesting to see how God sometimes gave long-range prophecies right in the middle of short-range immediate circumstances. Isaiah 7:1–12:6 is a section of the prophetic book that deals primarily with wars between the alliance of Syria and Israel against Judah. The prophet Isaiah's words were aimed at turning the hearts of people in Judah back to the Lord. He was anxious to touch Ahaz (king of Judah) and bring him to repentance and faith in Jehovah.

The immediate framework of our text is a conversation between Isaiah and Ahaz. Isaiah tells him not to be afraid of Israel and Syria. The arrogant kings of those nations were nothing more than "smoking firebrands" (v. 4) drawn from a fire. Their plans were futile, and they could not stand against the Lord. Isaiah then offered Ahaz a chance to ask the Lord for a sign demonstrating what he had just spoken (vv. 10, 11). This was a very gracious offer. "Reinforcement of such an overflowing gesture of grace hardly seems conceivable, and yet it is secured by the possessive pronoun *your*, reminding him (Ahaz) of his special relationship to God as the chosen king" (*Zondervan NIV Bible Commentary*). Out of arrogance and hypocrisy, Ahaz refused, saying he would not *test* the Lord. This was not a statement of faith, but one of rejection of God's help. Despite his attitude, Isaiah then addressed Ahaz as the "house of David" (v. 13), suddenly speaking to the broader context of God's promises to the royal line. Whether Ahaz's ears understood or not, what was now being said was a sign given to all humanity of things to come.

If one were on the scene listening to Isaiah's words, the logical immediate interpretation would be this: A young unmarried woman would give birth to a son. Before this son was old enough to know right from wrong, the kings of Syria and Israel would be defeated and destroyed (see vv. 14-16). The Hebrew word used for *virgin* here could simply mean a young woman of marriageable age. However, most prophecies contained both an immediate and an ultimate fulfillment. That later fulfillment is the one of momentous importance. Matthew draws the conclusion in his Gospel (1:22-25) that Isaiah was speaking of Mary. Mary was a virgin at the time of Jesus' conception and remained so until after His birth. The conception was a miracle of the Holy Spirit rather than a sexual act with a man. The fact that Isaiah called this child's name *Immanuel,* meaning "God

"God walked down the stairs of heaven with a Baby in His arms."
—**Paul Scherer**

God Chooses a Vessel

with us," added tremendous depth to his words. If this child was to be "God with us," then He had to be God himself.

In summarization we can say this: There was likely an initial prophetic fulfillment that somewhat gave immediate validity to Isaiah's words. However, the greater fulfillment came 700 years later when the virgin Mary conceived Jesus, the true *Immanuel,* through the power of the Holy Spirit coming over her.

B. An Angelic Visit (Luke 1:26-28)

26. And in the sixth month the angel Gabriel was sent from God unto a city of Galilee, named Nazareth,

27. To a virgin espoused to a man whose name was Joseph, of the house of David; and the virgin's name was Mary.

28. And the angel came in unto her, and said, Hail, thou that art highly favoured, the Lord is with thee: blessed art thou among women.

Already in Luke's Gospel we have seen a visitation by the angel Gabriel. This was described in Zacharias' encounter in our last lesson. When Zacharias innocently expressed doubt by his questioning, we caught the powerfully negative reaction of the angel. This was not arrogance on Gabriel's part, but heavenly visitation requires a response of faith. Now, with his visit to Mary, we see that faith beautifully expressed. The mention of the *sixth* month establishes a link between Elizabeth and Mary. A casual reading would infer that this was the sixth month of the Hebrew year, but what is meant is the sixth month of Elizabeth's pregnancy.

That Mary was already engaged to Joseph does not mean she was a mature adult. Betrothals were often set soon after a girl reached puberty (age 12 or 13). A betrothal was legally binding, but sexual intimacy was not allowed until marriage. It took divorce or death to end a betrothal. After a betrothal was established, the groom could claim his bride at whatever point he chose, but wisdom would suggest waiting a while. The wedding was simply an affirmation of what had already been established legally. In addition to his initial disbelief of her story, Joseph's distress may have been over Mary being pregnant so young. A quick marriage would dispel questions, but it could also raise others, that is, if she was still barely past childhood. Common sense would generally assume that the bride have some growing years to prepare for the responsibilities of marriage.

Both Matthew and Luke include a genealogy of Jesus. It is usually thought that Matthew's is traced through Joseph, while Luke's is through Mary's family, although it is never stated as such. What is important is that Jesus was in both genealogies a legitimate member of the royal line of David.

Talk About It:
1. Which three words in verse 26 capture the ministry of all angels?
2. What were the three encouraging messages Gabriel gave Mary in verse 28?

Another contrast between the two visits of Gabriel is seen in the fact that Mary is greeted with an affirmation of her character. Zacharias received no such words. The phrase "The Lord is with thee" is identical to the Lord's salutation to Gideon many centuries earlier (Judges 6:12). Note, as well, that Zacharias was of an affluent priestly household in Judea, while Mary was from a common home in Galilee. "The people in Judah disdained the Jews in Galilee and claimed they were not *kosher* because of their contacts with the Gentiles there (Matthew 4:15). They especially despised the people from Nazareth (John 1:45, 46)" (*The Bible Exposition Commentary*). God constantly thwarts the expectations of humanity. Here He did so by choosing a girl from a despised community to be the mother of His Son.

C. Mary's Reaction (vv. 29, 30)

29. And when she saw him, she was troubled at his saying, and cast in her mind what manner of salutation this should be.

30. And the angel said unto her, Fear not, Mary: for thou hast found favour with God.

Talk About It:
Why are people fearful when an angel appears?

Mary's reaction to the sudden visitation was that of "Why me?" She immediately questioned in her mind what she had done to earn the divine blessing of God. The word *favour* appears 70 times in the King James translation of the Bible, and is generally used to express God's approval of an individual. Favor is the unseen hand of endorsement by the Holy Spirit over a life. One who is in favor is trusted by God to use the blessings coming his or her way for divine good. "That the Lord was with Mary indicates that God would give her His help in the privilege and responsibility she was about to receive" (*The Life Application Commentary Series*).

D. Son of the Highest (vv. 31-33)

31. And, behold, thou shalt conceive in thy womb, and bring forth a son, and shalt call his name Jesus.

32. He shall be great, and shall be called the Son of the Highest: and the Lord God shall give unto him the throne of his father David:

33. And he shall reign over the house of Jacob for ever; and of his kingdom there shall be no end.

Talk About It:
Describe all the qualities in these three verses that apply to Jesus Christ and to nobody else.

While Zacharias had been terrified at Gabriel's appearance, Mary's troubling had to be more at the message given to her. To become pregnant miraculously and carry the very Son of God carried tremendous consequences for her future. The name to be given this boy was *Jesus,* which means "Yahweh saves," and was a common rendition of the name *Joshua.* As Joshua had led the Israelites from the wilderness into the

God Chooses a Vessel

Promised Land, her son would lead God's people from sin into eternal life. Somehow Jesus would be both human (Mary's son) and divine ("the Son of the Highest").

God had promised David a throne that would last forever. However, history had seemed to prove otherwise. Descendants of David had ruled in Judah all the way to the Captivity, but post-exilic Palestine had not even included a monarch. Mary was now being promised that her ancestor's royal line would be reestablished, and would reign forever. This had to be mind-boggling to the young girl. The covenant with David, as well as the covenant with Israel as a people, would be renewed. As young as she was, Mary was well-steeped in her heritage. The Savior of Israel was to be born from her body! The implications were enormous.

II. PROVISION: MIRACULOUS CONCEPTION (Luke 1:34-38)

A. Mary's Question (v. 34)

34. Then said Mary unto the angel, How shall this be, seeing I know not a man?

Mary, like Zacharias, asks a question, but not for a sign. She only wants light shed on the situation. How could she give birth to a son without having had sexual relations with a man? As a betrothed bride, she knew she would eventually be in sexual union with her husband, but what kind of impregnation could the angel be suggesting? She apparently assumed something would happen immediately. But how could a virgin become pregnant?

The region of Galilee had strong Roman and Greek influence. Mary was possibly aware of pagan legends of offspring between gods and humans, but those stories intimated gods having sex with humans. This was by no means what Gabriel was suggesting. He had said she would simply conceive (v. 31). Thus, Mary's question can be reduced to one word: *How?* "Accordingly, instead of reproof, she receives an explanation on that very point, and in mysterious detail" (*Jamieson, Fausset and Brown Commentary*).

> "The hint half guessed, the gift half understood, is Incarnation."
> **—T.S. Eliot**

> "If you want to get the hang of it [the Incarnation], think how you would like to become a slug or a crab."
> **—C.S. Lewis**

B. Gabriel's Answer (v. 35)

35. And the angel answered and said unto her, The Holy Ghost shall come upon thee, and the power of the Highest shall overshadow thee: therefore also that holy thing which shall be born of thee shall be called the Son of God.

Matthew's recording of this wonderful story says, "When as his mother Mary was espoused to Joseph, before they came together, she was found with child of the Holy Ghost" (1:18).

The invisible Holy Spirit is the person of the Trinity operating on the earth. There is a delicate, modest, mysterious lack of

Talk About It:
1. Explain the
two uses of the
word *holy* in this
verse.
2. What can "the
power of the
Highest" *not* do?

explanation as to how this was accomplished. No livid sexual encounter need enter anyone's mind. Gabriel simply told Mary that the Holy Spirit would accomplish the matter. "It was not by ordinary generation; but, as the Messiah came to redeem sinners—to make atonement for 'others,' and not for himself—it was necessary that his human nature should be pure, and free from the corruption of the fall. God therefore prepared him a body by direct creation that should be pure and holy" (*Barnes' Notes*).

Gabriel uses the word *power,* or *dunamis,* the miracle-working power of God Most High. Note that this is the root of the modern word *dynamite.* "Since Jesus existed before His mother, He could not be conceived in the womb in the normal way. The virgin birth is a miracle of God that brought the eternal Son of God into the world without any taint of sin in His human nature" (*The Bible Exposition Commentary*). Peter would later write of Christ that He "did no sin, neither was guile found in his mouth" (1 Peter 2:22). Gabriel said this child would be "that Holy One" (*NKJV*) both because of His connection with the Holy Spirit and because He would live a life of absolute purity.

We should not suppose Mary was sinless. Though she was young, humble and pure, she still carried the curse of Adam. Rather, she was the vehicle through which God could legally enter the world and redeem lost people. Jesus' sinlessness was because He was the Son of God. He was God come to earth housed in human flesh. Unlike Adam, who failed God, Jesus would always obey His Father. His perfection would allow Him to suffer on behalf of sinners and make them acceptable to God.

"The Incarnation would be equally a miracle however Jesus entered the world."
—P.T. Forsyth

C. Elizabeth's Child (vv. 36, 37)

36. And, behold, thy cousin Elisabeth, she hath also conceived a son in her old age: and this is the sixth month with her, who was called barren.

37. For with God nothing shall be impossible.

Though they were cousins, it is not likely that Mary had any prior knowledge of Elizabeth's pregnancy, even though the older woman was now in her sixth month. Communications and travel were very slow. Even though there were three festivals each year that the Jews attended in Jerusalem, only the men were required to go. Also, part of the reason Nazareth was lowly regarded was that the people there were not as faithful to make the pilgrimages regularly.

Both pregnancies were miraculous—one to a very old woman and one to a virgin. Although Mary had not asked for a sign, she was now being granted one. As we see the story further unfold, we note that Mary would desperately need someone with whom she could relate. Joseph did not believe until

Talk About It:
1. How would the
news about
Elisabeth encourage Mary?
2. Restate verse
37 in words a
small child would
understand.

he received a visitation in a dream, and we have no recording as to how either family responded. Elizabeth was the truest friend Mary would have during this time. Questions did apparently follow Mary for many years. It is intimated in John 8:41 that some thought Jesus was born of *fornication.*

D. Mary's Submission (v. 38)

38. And Mary said, Behold the handmaid of the Lord; be it unto me according to thy word. And the angel departed from her.

Mary responded by willingly submitting to God's plan for her. She believed the angel's message, understood the negative implications of what she might have to endure, and gave herself to be God's vessel. She surrendered all—body, mind and spirit—to the Lord. She was the perfect example for us to follow, similar to what Paul urged: "I beseech you therefore, brethren, by the mercies of God, that ye present your bodies a living sacrifice, holy, acceptable unto God, which is your reasonable service" (Romans 12:1).

Talk About It:
How did Mary describe herself, and why?

III. PURPOSE: A NEW COVENANT (Luke 1:46-55; Hebrews 9:11-15)

A. Mary's Song (Luke 1:46-49)

46. And Mary said, My soul doth magnify the Lord,

47. And my spirit hath rejoiced in God my Saviour.

48. For he hath regarded the low estate of his handmaiden: for, behold, from henceforth all generations shall call me blessed.

49. For he that is mighty hath done to me great things; and holy is his name.

Mary quickly left Galilee to journey to Judea, to the home of Zacharias and Elizabeth (vv. 39, 40). This was a difficult journey of at least three days (between 50 and 70 miles), and a very dangerous one for a woman to make alone. No details are given of how it was planned or accomplished. Possibly she accompanied a caravan of traders, or some other commercial travelers of the day. We are not told as to whether Joseph had yet received the vision in a dream that changed his mind. Did she go with his blessing, or was this escape an opportunity for him to decide what he was going to do? Did she overrule parental objections to such travel? We don't know. All we know is that Mary left her home to find the one household that could best understand her situation.

Talk About It:
What do these poetic words reveal about Mary's faith in God?

The meeting of Mary and Elizabeth was a spiritual one (vv. 41-45). Note that Elizabeth had no prior knowledge of what had happened to Mary. Although she was by far the older woman, she quickly acknowledged the superiority of the child Mary was carrying over hers. She also blessed Mary for having believed what the angel had told her. God often confirms through others the messages He speaks to our hearts. John, now possibly a seven-month unborn, literally leaped within his mother's womb at the nearness of the One for whom he would one day prepare the way. Elizabeth declared that Mary was blessed *among* women. Note that she did not say *above* women. Verse 15 declares that John would be filled with the Holy Spirit "even from his mother's womb." It is likely this was the occasion when he was filled. Notice that his mother was filled as well. It was the Holy Spirit who showed Elizabeth that Mary was pregnant with the Messiah.

Mary responded to this greeting by lifting her voice in a hymn of praise, known as the Magnificat. It was a recital of things God had done for her, as well as for others in the past. It contained tidbits of quotations from Old Testament passages. The phrase "great things" appears in 1 Samuel 12:24; 2 Samuel 7:21-23; and Psalm 126:2, 3. The phrase "my Saviour" is reminiscent of the words of Habakkuk 3:18: "I will rejoice in the Lord, I will joy in the God of my salvation." The essence of her words was that God had performed a miracle in her life, one which would bring the Savior to the earth.

Some commentators suggest that Mary had a deep knowledge of the Scriptures. This would not have been unusual for a devout person like Mary. Yet, this is not necessarily so. The prophetic aspect of God speaking directly to her heart is not only possible, but likely, giving words to her lips that she had not formed in her mind until they were spoken. Note that she prophesied that all generations to come would call her blessed. Obviously, this has been a prophecy fulfilled!

B. God's Mercy (Luke 1:50-55)
(Luke 1:51-55 is not included in the printed text.)
50. And his mercy is on them that fear him from generation to generation.

In the second part of her song, Mary expands the theme from personal blessings to those blessings which God extends to all who fear Him "from generation to generation," but especially of her own time. Included here are three distinct groups: the helpless (v. 51); the lowly, or humble (v. 52); and the hungry (v. 53). In the process, the *proud,* the *mighty,* and the *rich* are brought low. "The common people of that day were almost helpless when it came to justice and civil rights. They were often hungry, downtrodden, and discouraged (Luke 4:16-19), and there was no way for them to 'fight the system'" (*The Bible Exposition Commentary*). From her womb would come One who would truly lift those who had been persecuted and oppressed. Mary saw the entire world being turned upside down.

Talk About It:
1. How does God respond to those who are *proud* and *exalted*? Why?
2. What did God's promise to Mary have to do with her nation (vv. 54, 55)?

God Chooses a Vessel

C. A Better Covenant (Hebrews 9:11-15)

(Hebrews 9:11-14 is not included in the printed text.)

15. And for this cause he is the mediator of the new testament, that by means of death, for the redemption of the transgressions that were under the first testament, they which are called might receive the promise of eternal inheritance.

Mary saw prophetically that her Son would bring great change, a reversal of fortunes. One of those changes was a better covenant. The old covenant had come through Moses, and included a priesthood which was limited and only symbolic of redemption. The blood of animal sacrifices could only temporarily cover the sins of people. There was nothing there to remove the sinful heart. People were doomed to repeat their vile acts and saw no hope of change. Jesus, however, brought a new tabernacle—a heavenly one—when He entered the Holiest of Holies, the very presence of God the Father. There He presented His own blood as a once-and-for-all sacrifice for humanity's sins. By this He obtained eternal redemption. His sacrifice would never have to be repeated because it was perfect. Thus, He is the mediator of an entirely new way—a way of mercy, as Mary saw in her song—for all of us to come to renewed relationship with God.

Talk About It:
1. When did Christ become our "high priest," and why (vv. 11, 12)?
2. What can Christ do for our conscience, and how?

CONCLUSION

Mary has been viewed from two perspectives down through the last 2,000 years. Some magnify her to the point of idolatry, placing her above Jesus himself. Others forget her and seem to think that any young girl could have been the Lord's mother.

Mary certainly deserves respect. Elizabeth, filled with the Holy Spirit, called her "blessed . . . among women" (Luke 1:42). Gabriel called her "highly favoured" (v. 28). There is nothing in Scripture to indicate that she ever exalted herself. She endured the shame Jesus had to face by staying at the foot of His cross. She was also among the 120 believers who waited in the Upper Room for the outpouring of the Holy Spirit (Acts 1:14). She apparently viewed herself as simply another follower of the Savior, and for that we can admire her all the more.

GOLDEN TEXT CHALLENGE

"TO WHOM GOD WOULD MAKE KNOWN WHAT IS THE RICHES OF THE GLORY OF THIS MYSTERY AMONG THE GENTILES; WHICH IS CHRIST IN YOU, THE HOPE OF GLORY" (Colossians 1:27).

The apostle Paul is excited that a *mystery*—a truth understandable only by divine revelation—has now been made known. This truth was hinted at in the Old Testament, but was put into effect when Christ completed His mission on earth.

Here's the revelation: Eternal salvation is available to all people regardless of their nationality. It's for Jew and Gentile alike.

And there's more to the mystery. Not only are believers *in Christ* (saved and safe), but Christ is *in them* (in full union with God). The indwelling Christ is the believers' "hope of glory" both now and eternally.

God Calls an Apostle (Paul)

Acts 7:54 through 8:1; 9:1-22; 13:46-49;
Romans 11:13-16; Galatians 1:1-24

INTRODUCTION

At some point during his youth (probably around age 13), Paul was sent to Jerusalem by his family to study at the feet of Gamaliel, the great teacher-rabbi of the day. Paul's family held Roman citizenship, and used the benefits that came with such as they needed. They were by far more dedicated, however, to their Jewish heritage as members of the tribe of Benjamin. In effect, they lived the best of both worlds. Being Pharisees, Paul's family in Tarsus had maintained strict Jewish traditions. His years of study in Jerusalem only added to his intense orthodoxy.

It is possible that Paul was in Jerusalem during the years of Jesus' ministry, but no hint is given in any of his writings that he ever had contact with the Lord. Ancient tradition places his birth date as two years after Jesus was born. A lowly itinerant Rabbi in trouble with the authorities likely would not have caught the attention of the intense divinity student. Only after Jesus' resurrection and the rapid spread of Christianity did Paul have to get involved, and that because his own traditions were being threatened. At whatever point followers of Christ came to his attention, he gave himself to a cause he saw as righteous—to persecute and destroy them. The idea that Jews had crucified their Messiah was anathema to Paul.

Even though he was a dedicated student, practical teaching of the day demanded that he also learn a trade. His was that of tentmaking. He was well-rounded, except for his close-mindedness to what the Old Testament really taught about the Messiah. The cross of Jesus was a "stumblingblock" for him (1 Corinthians 1:23).

From our contemporary perspective we would think that the resurrection of Jesus would have been sufficient proof to the Jews in Jerusalem, but this was not the case. They simply believed this was a hoax perpetrated by loyal followers. If we look at the many appearances Jesus made during those 40 days (and despite the fact that as many as 500 saw him at one time, 1 Corinthians 15:6), we have to realize that these were all sympathetic *brethren.* Jesus was not seen by those who hated Him. Consequently, their unbelief was only deepened and their prejudices further cemented.

One moment, however, in the manifest presence of the risen Lord is enough to change a life forever. Paul's meeting with Jesus changed him from being the faith's great persecutor to its greatest defender, and this happened almost in an instant.

Unit Theme:
God's Providence in Salvation History

Central Truth:
God's transformed people are called to evangelize the lost.

Focus:
Consider the providence of God in Paul's life and answer God's call to evangelism.

Context:
An overview of the life of Paul

Golden Text:
"The Lord commanded us, saying, I have set thee to be a light of the Gentiles, that thou shouldest be for salvation unto the ends of the earth" (Acts 13:47).

Study Outline:
I. Plan: Redirect a Life
(Acts 7:54—8:1; 9:1-5)
II. Provision: Confirm an Apostle
(Acts 9:6-22; Galatians 1:1, 11-17)
III. Purpose: Evangelize All People
(Acts 13:46-49; Romans 11:13-16)

I. PLAN: REDIRECT A LIFE (Acts 7:54—8:1; 9:1-5)

A. Paul's Role in Stephen's Death (7:54—8:1)

(Acts 7:54—8:1 is not included in the printed text.)

Talk About It:
1. What was Stephen filled with, and what were the religious leaders filled with?
2. How did Stephen's death influence Saul?

Paul's quest to obliterate the spread of Christianity had to be frustrated by the fact that Stephen was doing amazing "wonders and miracles" (6:8). The young deacon was full of "wisdom and the Spirit" (v. 10, *NKJV*), and was a powerful witness for the faith. Until he became active in ministry, the signs and wonders had all been done by the apostles. Stephen now set the standard for many others to follow. We might ask, Just what were the miracles he was doing? Likely they were healings of every manner of disease. Also, as a deacon serving the poor, he may have solved economic, spiritual and social problems among the people he served. God is interested in every facet of our lives, so the miraculous can take many forms. Stephen's brilliance (reflecting the Holy Spirit) made the Jewish religious establishment look like the selfish power-mongers they were. Stephen pressed the envelope even further. His "powerful testimony would be the climax of the church's witness to the Jews. Then the message would go out to the Samaritans and then to the Gentiles" (*The Bible Exposition Commentary*).

At what point Paul noticed Stephen is not known, but somehow he was present when the members of the Synagogue of the Freedmen seized the evangelist and dragged him before the high priest and council. The treatment Stephen received—false witnesses, false accusations, stirring up of a mob against him, and an unjust inquisition before the Sanhedrin—were a duplication of what Jesus had undergone. Acts 6:15 says his face shone like that of an angel, not unlike the way Moses' face had shined when he came down from Mount Sinai (Exodus 34:29, 30).

Stephen's sermon drove his antagonistic listeners into a rage. Religion can evoke the most horrifying of emotions. How many lives have been lost in bombings, assassinations, and terrorist attacks—because of religious bigotry! For Stephen, his gaze looked past the death sentence to the presence of Jesus, who was standing at the Father's right hand ready to welcome him. When all was finished, Stephen was dead—something Paul had stood by and lent his assent to. However, an indelible image was painted in Paul's mind that day. "The church father Augustine wrote that the church owes Paul to the prayer of Stephen" (*Nelson Study Bible*). Paul would later reflect at how he had "beyond measure . . . persecuted the church of God, and wasted it" (Galatians 1:13).

"I would rather have the whole world against me but know that the Almighty God is with me, be called an apostate but know that I have the approval of the God of glory."

—**Mehdi Dibaj**
(an Iranian who, in 1993, was executed for becoming a Christian)

B. Paul's Threatenings (9:1, 2)

1. And Saul, yet breathing out threatenings and slaughter against the disciples of the Lord, went unto the high priest,

2. And desired of him letters to Damascus to the synagogues, that if he found any of this way, whether they were men or women, he might bring them bound unto Jerusalem.

The word *yet* seems to indicate that Stephen's death had brought certain pause among the Jews. Some sort of conscience-driven reflection may have told most people there had been a major injustice here, no matter their feelings about *disciples* of Jesus. Notice that this was the term given to believers. The term *Christian* had not yet been coined.

Even though the death of Stephen was on his conscience, Paul convinced himself that he was defending historic Judaism. He refused to consider the possibility that Jesus was alive and was all He had claimed to be. In Paul's mind, Jesus was a dead rabbi, and his followers were a dangerous sect. He saw their power (and obviously there had been powerful displays) as from Satan, not from God. Miracles are never a proof to the unbelieving heart. Remember all the wonderful acts God performed on behalf of the Israelites coming out of Egypt, yet they died in the desert because of unbelief. Miracles are confirmations for those who will believe.

After Stephen's death, Paul took center stage in persecuting believers. The Jewish leaders were happy to let him do their dirty work. Just as they were happy for the Romans to crucify Jesus, they were now content to let someone else enforce their impassioned hatred. Paul heard of believers who had scattered to Damascus and were infiltrating the synagogues there. Damascus was 175 miles northeast of Jerusalem. Paul planned to arrest those followers of Jesus and bring them back to Jerusalem to stand trial before the Sanhedrin. Bearing this in mind, the entourage with Paul had to be quite large, making his conversion experience one witnessed by many.

C. Jesus' Appearance to Paul (vv. 3-5)

3. And as he journeyed, he came near Damascus: and suddenly there shined round about him a light from heaven:

4. And he fell to the earth, and heard a voice saying unto him, Saul, Saul, why persecutest thou me?

5. And he said, Who art thou, Lord? And the Lord said, I am Jesus whom thou persecutest: it is hard for thee to kick against the pricks.

Paul was on the way to Damascus, where there was a Jewish community numbered in the thousands. It is a credit to the early believers that they had already infiltrated the synagogues there with the gospel. Remember that they still considered themselves Jews, and it was natural for them to worship in the synagogues. Paul had authorization from the high priest,

Talk About It:
Compare Saul's passion to destroy Christianity with our church's passion to spread the gospel.

"It is still one of the tragedies of human history that 'the children of darkness' are frequently more determined and zealous than 'the children of light.'"
—**Martin Luther King Jr.**

Talk About It:
1. In what sense was Saul actually persecuting Jesus?
2. How was Saul "kicking against the *pricks* [pointed sticks]" (v. 5)?

and this was likely for several reasons: (1) to stop the spread of Christianity; (2) to seize believers; and (3) to keep Rome from being stirred.

The midday sun in Palestine is extremely bright and hot. For a light to capture Paul, it would have to be even brighter than the sun. Paul's testimony in Acts 26:14 tells us Jesus spoke to him in Hebrew, possibly in the Aramaic dialect that He had used while on earth. In 9:17 we read that Paul actually saw Jesus. An unspoken requirement for apostleship was that they all had seen Jesus. Paul confirmed this to the Corinthians when he said, "Am I not an apostle? am I not free? have I not seen Jesus Christ our Lord?" (1 Corinthians 9:1).

The encounter knocked Paul to the ground. Those with him could not interpret this as heat stroke or some type of seizure, for they also fell and heard a sound (Acts 26:14), and were left speechless (9:7). While Paul didn't know who was speaking, he understood that it was an exalted person worthy of great respect. What a shock it was to discover that Jesus himself was really alive, and was speaking to him directly! Paul knew he had to change his entire mind-set, as well as the policies he had been pressing. Without such a visitation, it would have been almost impossible to change the mind of a self-righteous Pharisee. Compared to the brilliance of the light and power of the glorified Christ, Paul's good works and legalistic self-righteousness looked like filthy rags. He later counted all of his former life as "dung, that I may win Christ" (Philippians 3:8).

II. PROVISION: CONFIRM AN APOSTLE (Acts 9:6-22; Galatians 1:1, 11-17)

A. First Instructions (Acts 9:6-9)

(Acts 9:6-9 is not included in the printed text.)

Paul's first question after realizing he had just met the King of kings was, "What do You want me to do?" (v. 6, *NKJV*). Though he thought he had been only persecuting believers in Christ, he was now aware that he was persecuting Christ himself. Likely he already realized there was a mission for his life. Jesus didn't reveal that mission immediately, but instead sent him into Damascus, where someone would give the now blind man further instructions. Years later Paul reflected on this event, saying that he had been "apprehended of Christ Jesus" (Philippians 3:12).

B. Reluctant Ananias (vv. 10-14)

10. And there was a certain disciple at Damascus, named Ananias; and to him said the Lord in a vision, Ananias. And he said, Behold, I am here, Lord.

11. And the Lord said unto him, Arise, and go into the

God Calls an Apostle

street which is called Straight, and enquire in the house of Judas for one called Saul, of Tarsus: for, behold, he prayeth,

12. And hath seen in a vision a man named Ananias coming in, and putting his hand on him, that he might receive his sight.

13. Then Ananias answered, Lord, I have heard by many of this man, how much evil he hath done to thy saints at Jerusalem:

14. And here he hath authority from the chief priests to bind all that call on thy name.

Ananias was a devout Jewish believer who had apparently earlier gone to Damascus to escape persecution. He was "highly respected by all the Jews living there" (22:12, *NIV*). Somehow, word of Paul's coming to round up renegade followers of Christ for trial had already reached his ears. This tells us something of the unity among believers at this phase of the early church, since the grapevine was well organized. The trip to Damascus from Jerusalem could take up to a week's travel. Believers here were already preparing to hide from their number one enemy.

When Ananias heard the Lord instruct him to go find Paul, his first impression must have been that certain death was waiting on him. He perhaps assumed he would be the next martyr after Stephen. According to Greek church tradition, Ananias was eventually martyred. "It has been further stated that his house was turned into a church, which remains to the present day, though now occupied as a Turkish mosque; but even the Mohammedans have the tradition, and treat his memory with great respect" (*Adam Clarke's Commentary*).

There is much indicated in the statement, "behold, he prayeth" (v. 11). "Instead of trusting himself, Saul was now trusting the Lord and waiting for Him to show him what to do" (*The Bible Exposition Commentary*). Paul had even been given a picture in his mind of Ananias coming to him and restoring his sight. The great persecutor recognized his own need, and was praying earnestly. This revelation was apparently enough to change Ananias' mind about doing the Lord's bidding.

C. First Announcement of Paul's Commission (vv. 15, 16)

15. But the Lord said unto him, Go thy way: for he is a chosen vessel unto me, to bear my name before the Gentiles, and kings, and the children of Israel:

16. For I will shew him how great things he must suffer for my name's sake.

This is the first indication of the thrust of Paul's future ministry to the Gentiles. Ananias knew the reputation of Paul as a

Talk About It:
1. Describe the reputation of Ananias (v. 10).
2. Why was the phrase "he is praying" (v. 11, *NKJV*) significant?
3. What had Ananias heard about Saul?

"Do the thing you fear most and the death of fear is certain."

—**Mark Twain**

Talk About It:
1. What did God call Saul in verse 15, and why?
2. What great challenge faced Saul if he accepted God's calling (v. 16)? Why do you suppose God revealed this to him now?

Pharisee. From a human perspective, Paul seemed the least likely candidate for such a work. Even Paul would later marvel at having been chosen. That he would go to Gentiles, kings and Jews proved to be prophetically correct. The rest of Acts, and his own letters, confirm his calling. Also, the very notion of the gospel being preached to Gentiles would have taken Ananias by surprise. At this point all believers were Jewish. Even when Jesus sent out the 12 disciples, He had told them to go only to Jews (Matthew 10:5, 6).

In retrospect, Paul was the perfect candidate for preacher to the Gentile world. He had a thorough understanding of Judaism and Jewish traditions, but grew up a citizen of Rome, and knew the Greek culture as well. He could fit in anywhere. He was "all things to all men so that by all possible means I might save some" (1 Corinthians 9:22, *NIV*).

D. Filled With the Holy Spirit (vv. 17-22)
(Acts 9:18-22 is not included in the printed text.)

17. And Ananias went his way, and entered into the house; and putting his hands on him said, Brother Saul, the Lord, even Jesus, that appeared unto thee in the way as thou camest, hath sent me, that thou mightest receive thy sight, and be filled with the Holy Ghost.

Talk About It:
What did Ananias call Saul, and how did Ananias prove his sincerity?

As an act of inclusion in the body of Christ, Ananias called Paul a *brother*. Paul had certainly been humbled at this point. He was no longer an arrogant Pharisee, but a blind beggar. Being addressed as a brother now identified him as a member of the sect he had heretofore despised. The laying on of hands was what might be termed a "point of contact" for Paul to receive the Holy Spirit. Immediately Paul regained his sight, and he "arose, and was baptized" (v. 18).

It is important that God used Ananias to minister to Paul, as he was not one of the original apostles. "It is likely that he was a Christian of note at Damascus; and as no organized church had probably been formed there as yet, he probably took a leading part in the private meetings of the disciples for 'reading, exhortation and prayer'" (*Jamieson, Fausset and Brown Commentary*).

When Paul began preaching that "Christ . . . is the Son of God" (v. 20), everyone who heard him was amazed. Why would the man who came to Damascus to arrest Jesus' disciples now be promoting His cause? Yet Paul grew stronger, confounding the local Jews, "proving that this Jesus is the Christ" (v. 22, *NKJV*).

E. Paul's Appointment as an Apostle (Galatians 1:1, 11-17)
(Galatians 1:1, 11-17 is not included in the printed text.)

God Calls an Apostle

Paul often had to defend his apostleship. He was not one of the original disciples, yet his conversion had been far more dramatic than any of the others. Many Judaizer believers disliked him because of his ministry to Gentiles. Their distaste was primarily caused by their own prejudices. As we see in verse 1, Paul defended his message and ministry as coming directly from the risen Lord. "If the Judaizers had any apostleship, it was from men. Paul's was not. It had a higher source. Nor was it through man. No person, apostle or other, had mediated Paul's authority. It came instead through the intervention in his life of Jesus Christ" (*The Wycliffe Bible Commentary*). Christ had personally appeared to Him after His ascension. No other apostle could claim such a visitation.

Paul saw no reason to conform to what other people thought an apostle should be. He knew he had received his commissioning, his message, and his ministry directly from Christ. To validate his calling, he could simply point to what he had been before Christ appeared to him. His past was well known, and no one could deny that a divine intervention would have been required for such a change in him to have occurred.

III. PURPOSE: EVANGELIZE ALL PEOPLE (Acts 13:46-49; Romans 11:13-16)

A. Paul Turns to the Gentiles (Acts 13:46-49)

46. Then Paul and Barnabas waxed bold, and said, It was necessary that the word of God should first have been spoken to you: but seeing ye put it from you, and judge yourselves unworthy of everlasting life, lo, we turn to the Gentiles.

47. For so hath the Lord commanded us, saying, I have set thee to be a light of the Gentiles, that thou shouldest be for salvation unto the ends of the earth.

48. And when the Gentiles heard this, they were glad, and glorified the word of the Lord: and as many as were ordained to eternal life believed.

49. And the word of the Lord was published throughout all the region.

Paul had felt it necessary to first offer the gospel to the Jews everywhere he went. This was possibly based on something deeply embedded in him, going all the way back to Genesis 12:2, 3. Here, God had told Abraham, "I will bless those who bless you, and whoever curses you I will curse; and all peoples on earth will be blessed through you" (*NIV*). Through the Jews, God had revealed Himself, so that the whole world would come to know Him. The message that Jesus taught had its basis in Judaism. When asked what the greatest commandment was, Jesus responded by quoting Deuteronomy 6:5: "Love the Lord

Talk About It:
1. How did Paul explain his calling and education (vv. 1, 11, 12)?
2. Before his conversion, how had Paul treated Christ's church (v. 13), and why (v. 14)?
3. Explain Paul's use of the term *separated* ("set apart") in verse 15.

"God doesn't call people who are qualified. He calls people who are willing, and then He qualifies them."
—**Richard Parker**

published (v. 49)—" spread" (*NKJV*)

Talk About It:
1. What was Paul's mission (vv. 46, 47)?
2. What does it mean to "glorify the word of the Lord" (v. 48)?

your God with all your heart and with all your soul and with all your strength" (*NIV*). He then added, "Love your neighbor as yourself" (Matthew 22:39, *NIV*). The promises of a Redeemer/Messiah were sprinkled throughout the Old Testament. In fact, for us as modern Christians, it would be difficult to understand the faith without the Old Testament.

Paul desperately desired that the Jews receive the gospel message. They should be the people most ready to hear. However, as is typical of humanity, those who should see the truth often do not. Instead of believing, the Jews were contentious and saw themselves as God's chosen ones. When Gentiles eagerly embraced the message of salvation for all, the Jews were angered all the more, feeling that their religion had somehow been infected by evil. Everywhere Paul went, they stirred up hatred against him. No wonder he was finally ready to wash his hands of the matter. This was not to say he would refuse to share the message with the Jews, but rather that "their rejection of it . . . opened the way for its being carried to the Gentiles" (*Jamieson, Fausset and Brown Commentary*).

B. Israel's Future Restoration (Romans 11:13-16)

13. For I speak to you Gentiles, inasmuch as I am the apostle of the Gentiles, I magnify mine office:

14. If by any means I may provoke to emulation them which are my flesh, and might save some of them.

15. For if the casting away of them be the reconciling of the world, what shall the receiving of them be, but life from the dead?

16. For if the firstfruit be holy, the lump is also holy: and if the root be holy, so are the branches.

In the verses prior to our text, Paul had just gone about to prove that the Jews were guilty of sin, having rejected the Savior. Their great sin was simply unbelief in their Messiah. The results of this provided a great benefit to the Gentiles. They were offered the gospel and salvation. (Of course, God had planned the inclusion of Gentiles all along.) However, if these new believers were to expect God to be faithful to them, would He not also be faithful to the Jews, with whom He had the first covenant? They would rise again, much like a resurrection from the dead. "The failure of Israel in rejecting Christ will make their eventual acceptance as vivid and wonderful as the resurrection that all believers will experience; it will be as if they had come back from the dead" (*Nelson Study Bible*). Paul was certain of a noble future for Israel. She would not always reject Christ. One day she will come to her senses and recognize what she has missed.

emulation (v. 14)—jealousy

Talk About It:
1. Who was Paul's "flesh," and why did he want to provoke them to jealousy (v. 14)?
2. Who makes up the "root," and who are the "branches" (v. 16)? What does this mean?

God Calls an Apostle

CONCLUSION

There are spiritual truths that can be understood in earthly terms; but when heaven invades earth, these principles simply don't apply anymore. A perfect illustration is the cleansing of the Gadarene demoniac in Mark 5. If we were to deal with a person so troubled, we would expect to spend years (even after casting out the demons) discipling the man before giving him responsibility. Yet, perhaps just an hour later the man returned to Jesus asking to follow Him. Jesus said no, but instead, "Go home to your family and tell them how much the Lord has done for you" (v. 19, *NIV*).

Jesus had transformed him from a demoniac to a preacher of the gospel almost instantaneously. This is the power of His manifest presence. It is the same power that changed Paul on the road to Damascus. From hater to defender, Paul was transformed immediately. We need to seek this same power working in our lives today.

GOLDEN TEXT CHALLENGE

"THE LORD COMMANDED US, SAYING, I HAVE SET THEE TO BE A LIGHT OF THE GENTILES, THAT THOU SHOULDEST BE FOR SALVATION UNTO THE ENDS OF THE EARTH" (Acts 13:47).

"God commissioned Jesus, the Servant of the Lord, to bring the light of salvation to the Gentiles. The [first] missionaries [Paul and Barnabas] were to take the torch of the gospel to 'the ends of the earth.' By turning to the Gentiles they fulfilled the prophecy of Isaiah 49:6.

"Upon hearing Isaiah 49:6 from the lips of Paul [quoted in Acts 13:47], many of the Gentiles joyfully accepted the gospel. The Jews could make it difficult for the missionaries, but they could not keep the word of God from spreading throughout the region" (French Arrington, *Acts of the Apostles*).

This gospel torch has now been passed to our generation. Are we shining it brightly, praying and looking for opportunities to spread the good news?

Daily Devotions:
M. Abram's Life Redirected
Genesis 17:1-9
T. Jacob's Life Redirected
Genesis 32:24-30
W. Aaron Confirmed as Priest
Exodus 40:12-16
T. Jeremiah Confirmed as Prophet
Jeremiah 1:1-10
F. Target: All the World
Mark 16:15-20
S. No Respecter of Persons
Acts 10:34-43

Prayer of Praise

Psalm 18:1-50

Unit Theme:
Prayers and Exhortations in the Psalms

Central Truth:
God our deliverer is worthy of our praise.

Focus:
Acknowledge the sufficiency of God and praise Him for victory.

Context:
Written near the end of David's 70 years of life on earth

Golden Text:
"The Lord is my rock, and my fortress, and my deliverer; my God, my strength, in whom I will trust; my buckler, and the horn of my salvation, and my high tower" (Psalm 18:2).

Study Outline:
I. Praise for Deliverance (Psalm 18:1-19)
II. Praise for Direction (Psalm 18:28-36)
III. Praise for Dominion (Psalm 18:43-50)

INTRODUCTION

David "served his own generation by the will of God," and then passed away (Acts 13:36). What greater comment could be made in summary of a person's life?

It was in the latter part of his life that David penned Psalm 18. In its introduction, he is called "the servant of the Lord." He is the first person after Moses and Joshua to have been specifically called the Lord's servant.

The introduction says David "spake unto the Lord the words of this song." In other words, David penned its words as a private expression of praise to God. However, its universal theme of God's deliverance made this a psalm that became part of Israel's "hymnbook."

David wrote Psalm 18 "in the day that the Lord delivered him from the hand of all his enemies," the introduction continues. This does not mean God delivered David from all his opponents on a single day, for as we read about his life, we see a series of battles and victories taking place over many years. Instead, David is an old man now, and he is reflecting on all the ways God had rescued him through the years.

The introductory phrase "from the hand of Saul" probably signifies that King Saul was David's worst enemy, pursuing David with his army but never defeating him. David was particularly thankful for his divinely enabled escapes from Saul's hand.

Like David, it is most important for us to praise God in the private place when He acts on our behalf. Yet it is exciting when God's intervention for us becomes an anthem of praise for an entire congregation! We should determine to worship God privately for answered prayer and to praise Him publicly with our testimony.

I. PRAISE FOR DELIVERANCE (Psalm 18:1-19)

A. My Rock (vv. 1-3)

1. I will love thee, O Lord, my strength.

2. The Lord is my rock, and my fortress, and my deliverer; my God, my strength, in whom I will trust; my buckler, and the horn of my salvation, and my high tower.

3. I will call upon the Lord, who is worthy to be praised: so shall I be saved from mine enemies.

David recognized God as his power source, delivering him from evil and evildoers. And he was unashamed to declare his love for the Lord in intimate terms (v. 1). He was saying he loved God from his inmost being. In verse 2, David listed titles for God that sparked such love in David's heart:

- *My rock:* In Palestine's hills there were many rocky crags that became shields as people hid under them.
- *My fortress:* A place of defense often built on rocks or hills
- *My deliverer:* Providing escape from enemies
- *My strength:* God is the fountain and origin of help.
- *My buckler:* A shield covering one's head and heart
- *The horn of my salvation:* As an animal's horn protects it from enemies, so God protects His children from their enemies.
- *My high tower:* A place above the battle where new perspective can be gained

"I will call upon the Lord" (v. 3) indicates a continuous action. By living in a state of dependence on God, the psalmist knew he could trust Him for deliverance. Therefore the Lord was "worthy to be praised."

B. My Life-Giver (vv. 4-6)

4. The sorrows of death compassed me, and the floods of ungodly men made me afraid.

5. The sorrows of hell compassed me about: the snares of death prevented me.

6. In my distress I called upon the Lord, and cried unto my God: he heard my voice out of his temple, and my cry came before him, even into his ears.

Here David used strong imagery to summarize his various life-threatening experiences. *The Living Bible* paraphrases verses 4 and 5 like this: "Death bound me with chains, and the floods of ungodliness mounted a massive attack against me. Trapped and helpless, I struggled against the ropes that drew me on to death."

As David was pulled into the waters of darkness, he *called* upon the Lord, and then he *cried* unto God. He was desperately seeking deliverance.

Talk About It:
1. What do all the descriptions for God in verse 2 have in common?
2. What does it mean to "call upon" the Lord, and what benefit does it bring (v. 3)?

"We sometimes fear to bring our troubles to God, because they seem small to Him who sits on the circle of the earth. But if they are large enough to vex and endanger our welfare, they are large enough to touch His heart of love."
—**R.A. Torrey**

sorrows (vv. 4, 5)—cords or ropes

prevented (v. 5)—confronted

Talk About It:
1. Describe David's desperate situation in your own words (vv. 4, 5).
2. Why does God hear our calls and cries?

The Lord answered David "out of his temple" (v. 6). This does not indicate the earthly temple in Jerusalem, for it would not be built until the reign of David's son, Solomon. Instead, the Lord heard David from heaven. "His exaltation there does not lift Him above the reach of our cry, but enables Him the more effectually to 'come down' for our relief" (*Jamieson, Fausset and Brown Commentary*).

C. My Savior (vv. 7-15)

7. Then the earth shook and trembled; the foundations also of the hills moved and were shaken, because he was wroth.

8. There went up a smoke out of his nostrils, and fire out of his mouth devoured: coals were kindled by it.

9. He bowed the heavens also, and came down: and darkness was under his feet.

10. And he rode upon a cherub, and did fly: yea, he did fly upon the wings of the wind.

11. He made darkness his secret place; his pavilion round about him were dark waters and thick clouds of the skies.

12. At the brightness that was before him his thick clouds passed, hail stones and coals of fire.

13. The Lord also thundered in the heavens, and the Highest gave his voice; hail stones and coals of fire.

14. Yea, he sent out his arrows, and scattered them; and he shot out lightnings, and discomfited them.

15. Then the channels of waters were seen, and the foundations of the world were discovered at thy rebuke, O Lord, at the blast of the breath of thy nostrils.

Talk About It:
1. What moves God to "part the heavens and come down" to earth (see v. 9, *NIV*)?
2. How can God speak through thunderstorms?

When God answered the psalmist's desperate cry for help, it was a majestic wonder to David, and a nightmare to His enemies. "The earth shook and trembled," and the foundations of the mountains were shaken because of God's anger (v. 7). Smoke and fire were said to come out of the Lord's nostrils. This is not a literal description, but a symbolic picture of God's wrath toward David's enemies.

The Lord was so concerned with David's situation that He figuratively "came down" from heaven, riding on the back of heaven's angels, soaring on the wind. He came to David's aid rapidly and majestically, hidden in the darkness of clouds. Lightning flashed before Him, hailstones rained down, and "the Lord thundered from heaven; the voice of the Most High resounded" (v. 13, *NIV*).

God's actions "discomfited" (v. 14) David's enemies. In other words, they were confused and confounded as God laid bare the foundations of the sea and the earth in His wrath.

Prayer of Praise

D. My Rescuer (vv. 16-19)

16. He sent from above, he took me, he drew me out of many waters.

17. He delivered me from my strong enemy, and from them which hated me: for they were too strong for me.

18. They prevented me in the day of my calamity: but the Lord was my stay.

19. He brought me forth also into a large place; he delivered me, because he delighted in me.

David pictured himself as a man drowning, helplessly tossed about by the waves and going under. But then the Lord reached down His hand and drew David out. It's like a second Moses story. Just as Israel's deliverer was named *Moses* (meaning "to draw out") because he was pulled from the Nile River, so David was drawn out from the dark waters of his enemy's attack.

David admitted that his hate-filled enemy was "too strong" for him to defeat on his own. This was true when Goliath stood before him and when Saul's 3,000 soldiers pursued him. The enemy confronted ("prevented," v. 18) David on a day that seemed marked for disaster, but David leaned on the Lord, and the result was miraculous. Whereas David had been trapped in a tight place with no way out, God reached down and placed him in a "large place" (v. 19)—a place of freedom. This happened because God "delighted in" David—God stood up for him because David and his cause were both righteous.

II. PRAISE FOR DIRECTION (Psalm 18:28-36)

A. Over a Wall (vv. 28-31)

28. For thou wilt light my candle: the Lord my God will enlighten my darkness.

29. For by thee I have run through a troop; and by my God have I leaped over a wall.

30. As for God, his way is perfect: the word of the Lord is tried: he is a buckler to all those that trust in him.

31. For who is God save the Lord? or who is a rock save our God?

The "candle" in verse 28 refers to an oil lamp that is symbolic of prosperity and blessing. David believes God will not allow dark experiences to snuff out his lamp, but will keep it continually burning, and will guide David's life. This scripture may also have reference to the Messiah eventually being born through David's descendants. David's ancestral line would not be cut off; indeed, the Savior would be born through it (Jeremiah 23:5, 6).

Through divine enablement, the psalmist said he had violently confronted and defeated bands of soldiers, and he had successfully scaled the wall of an enemy city. David was referring to a literal military victory, or maybe more than one.

Talk About It:
1. What are the "many waters" (v. 16) David describes?
2. How was hatred influencing David's enemies (vv. 17, 18)?
3. What does it mean to be in "a large place" (v. 19)?

The Greatest Lesson
The last and greatest lesson that the soul has to learn is the fact that God, and God alone, is enough for all its needs. This is the lesson that all His dealings with us are meant to teach; and this is the crowning discovery of our whole Christian life. God is enough!
—Hannah Whitall Smith

Talk About It:
1. How is God like a light?
2. What physical feats had God enabled David to perform (v. 29), and why?
3. Explain the phrase "the word of the Lord is tried" (v. 30).
4. Answer the questions in verse 31.

girdeth (v. 32)— "arms" (NIV)

Talk About It:
1. Describe the path God prepares for His children (vv. 32, 33, 36).
2. God is noted for His "gentleness" (v. 35), yet He skilled David's "hands to war" (v. 34). How can this be?

In 2 Samuel 5, we read how David and his men captured the city of Jerusalem, "and called it the city of David" (v. 9).

In crisis after crisis the psalmist had "tried" the Lord God (Psalm 18:30), and found that his trust had never been misplaced. He discovered that the ways of God are "perfect"— pure, unfailing, totally different than the idol gods served by other nations. That's why he had been able to run through a troop and leap over a wall: the perfect God had been his "buckler," or defense shield, the "rock" on which he triumphed.

B. Under My Feet (vv. 32-36)

32. It is God that girdeth me with strength, and maketh my way perfect.

33. He maketh my feet like hinds' feet, and setteth me upon my high places.

34. He teacheth my hands to war, so that a bow of steel is broken by mine arms.

35. Thou hast also given me the shield of thy salvation: and thy right hand hath holden me up, and thy gentleness hath made me great.

36. Thou hast enlarged my steps under me, that my feet did not slip.

The perfect God had made David's way *perfect*—"absolutely smooth, free from stumblings and errors, leading straight forward to a divine goal" (Keil and Delitzsch)—and armed him with strength (v. 32). The Lord made him quick and fleet like a deer so he could travel in the "high places" where safety and nourishment are found (v. 33).

However, when David had to face his enemies, the Lord equipped him with the skill and strength he needed to succeed (v. 34). The Lord had dealt with him *gently* (favorably and kindly), and that was the source of David's greatness (v. 35). God's "right hand"—perceived as the hand of strength—had supported and sustained him in every situation.

In verse 36, the psalmist said the Lord had made his path wide so his feet would not "slip." "The reference here is to the ankle, the joint that is so useful in walking, and that is so liable to be sprained or dislocated. . . . Before, he had been like one whose ankles are weak or sprained; now he was able to tread firmly. The divine favor given to him was as if God had given strength to a lame man to walk firmly" (Albert Barnes).

III. PRAISE FOR DOMINION (Psalm 18:43-50)
A. Fading Strangers (vv. 43-45)

43. Thou hast delivered me from the strivings of the people; and thou hast made me the head of the heathen: a people whom I have not known shall serve me.

Prayer of Praise

44. As soon as they hear of me, they shall obey me: the strangers shall submit themselves unto me.

45. The strangers shall fade away, and be afraid out of their close places.

David praises God for the establishment and spread of his kingdom. The king had faced the "strivings" (attacks and contentions) of his own people, including the rebellion of his own son Absalom (2 Samuel 15–18), yet God had delivered and established him. Moreover, God had given David victory after victory over the foreign ("heathen") nations surrounding Israel (see 8:1-14).

Some nations, hearing of David's conquests, willingly submitted themselves to Israel's rule. Even if they did so deceitfully, acting only out of terror and hoping one day to rebel, it would not matter. All were losing heart and came "trembling from their strongholds" (v. 45, *NIV*). Like dying flowers, the enemy nations were wilting, fading and falling away.

B. Exalted God (vv. 46-50)

46. The Lord liveth; and blessed be my rock; and let the God of my salvation be exalted.

47. It is God that avengeth me, and subdueth the people under me.

48. He delivereth me from mine enemies: yea, thou liftest me up above those that rise up against me: thou hast delivered me from the violent man.

49. Therefore will I give thanks unto thee, O Lord, among the heathen, and sing praises unto thy name.

50. Great deliverance giveth he to his king; and sheweth mercy to his anointed, to David, and to his seed for evermore.

Psalm 18 closes with a hymn of praise that summarizes the entire song. In contrast to all other gods, which "have mouths, but they speak not: eyes have they, but they see not" (115:5), the Lord Almighty *lives*. So we should bless Him for being the "rock" who speaks and sees and hears, and we must exalt His name for being the God who saves (18:46).

Many enemies did "rise up" against David, yet the Lord lifted him to a higher place (v. 48). It is critical to remember than when people and spiritual forces arise against us, they are no match for the God who is within us. He can always take us higher, because "greater is he that is in you, than he that is in the world" (1 John 4:4).

David had discovered that rather than trying to get revenge on his enemies, it was wiser to let God *avenge* His cause (Psalm 18:47). If David was in the right and his enemy was wrong, in time the God of justice would handle matters in His perfect fairness. This happened in David's life when God finally

Talk About It:
1. Why did David need deliverance from his own people?
2. How did David's reputation influence people from other nations?

Talk About It:
1. What is the connection between the words *avenge* and *subdue* in verse 47?
2. Why would David "give thanks . . . among the heathen" (v. 49)?
3. Who was David referring to as "anointed" (v. 50), and why?

put all of Israel under David's reign, though it took many years of trials and tests for it to come to pass.

The psalmist said he would praise the Lord "among the Gentiles" (v. 49, *NKJV*). This was a prophetic declaration that not just Jewish people would know and worship God, but that Gentile nations would sing His praises as well. When we and other Gentile believers use the Psalms in our worship of God, we are fulfilling David's word.

The psalm concludes by David glorifying God for His mercy and anointing on his life, but then again anticipates the coming of the Messiah. It echoes the prophecy given to David in 2 Samuel 7:12, 13: "When your days are fulfilled and you rest with your fathers, I will set up your seed after you, who will come from your body, and I will establish his kingdom. He shall build a house for My name, and I will establish the throne of his kingdom forever" (*NKJV*).

CONCLUSION

David's song in Psalm 18 is also found in 2 Samuel 22, with very little variation. It begins, "And David spake unto the Lord the words of this song in the day that the Lord had delivered him out of the hand of all his enemies, and out of the hand of Saul" (v. 1).

The previous chapter (21:15-22) describes some of David's most formidable enemies. David and his men killed four Philistines of giant stature, including one man who had 12 fingers and 12 toes. In one of those battles, David had become exhausted. A giant named Ishbi-benob, wielding a new sword, was ready to kill David, but one of David's men stepped in and rescued him.

In our daily lives, we may not face literal giants, but we do run into overwhelming situations from time to time. If our trust and hope is in God, He will deliver us in whatever way and through whatever means He deems best.

GOLDEN TEXT CHALLENGE

"THE LORD IS MY ROCK, AND MY FORTRESS, AND MY DELIVERER; MY GOD, MY STRENGTH, IN WHOM I WILL TRUST; MY BUCKLER, AND THE HORN OF MY SALVATION, AND MY HIGH TOWER" (Psalm 18:2).

The psalmist calls God several descriptive names in this verse. *The Living Bible* renders them like this: "my fort . . . a rugged mountain where I hide . . . my Savior . . . a rock where none can reach me . . . a tower of safety . . . my shield . . . the strong horn of a mighty fighting bull."

It all boils down to one fact: God is the Almighty Deliverer in every situation, and this should cause us to praise Him.

Daily Devotions:
M. Song of Moses
Exodus 15:1-11
T. Song of Hannah
1 Samuel 2:1-10
W. Song of David
1 Chronicles 29:10-19
T. Song of Mary
Luke 1:46-55
F. Song of Zacharias
Luke 1:67-79
S. New Song
Revelation 5:8-14

Prayer of Forsakenness

Psalm 22:1-31

INTRODUCTION

Many of the Psalms are messianic, meaning that they speak of Christ, the Messiah, in prophetic terms. The Psalms were written as expressions of worship and centered on contemporary themes; it was in a prophetic manner that they spoke of the Messiah.

Psalm 22 foretold in amazing detail the suffering of Christ. Perhaps He meditated on its words as He, the Innocent One, died for us, the guilty ones. Our guilt became His; His innocence, ours. His sacrificial death in substitution for ours is recognized by the Father when we repent of our sins and by faith accept the Savior and His sacrifice.

C.I. Scofield, in the edition of the Bible that bears his name, says, "Psalms 22, 23 and 24 form a trilogy. In Psalm 22 the *good* Shepherd gives His life for the sheep (John 10:11); in Psalm 23 the *great* Shepherd, brought again from the dead through the everlasting covenant (Hebrews 13:20), tenderly cares for the sheep; in Psalm 24 the *chief* Shepherd appears as King of glory to own and reward the sheep (1 Peter 5:4)."

When sung in sequence, these psalms gave an impressive picture of the ministry of the Messiah. The people of Israel were able to see Him suffering for them, caring for them, and reigning over them. If the Hebrew worshipers sang these songs with joy at the anticipation of the Messiah, how much more meaningful they are to us, who know the Savior of whom they speak!

Unit Theme:
Prayers and Exhortations in the Psalms

Central Truth:
God hears the cries of those who feel forsaken.

Focus:
Empathize with those who feel forsaken by God and find hope in His care.

Context:
A messianic psalm composed by David

Golden Text:
"He [God] hath not despised nor abhorred the affliction of the afflicted; neither hath he hid his face from him; but when he cried unto him, he heard" (Psalm 22:24).

Study Outline:
I. Experience of Abandonment (Psalm 22:1-8)
II. Affirmation of God's Care (Psalm 22:9-21)
III. Proclamation of Hope (Psalm 22:22-31)

I. EXPERIENCE OF ABANDONMENT (Psalm 22:1-8)

A. Feeling Forsaken (vv. 1, 2)

1. My God, my God, why hast thou forsaken me? why art thou so far from helping me, and from the words of my roaring?

2. O my God, I cry in the daytime, but thou hearest not; and in the night season, and am not silent.

roaring (v. 1)—
groaning

Talk About It:
1. Why did God the Father seem so far away in Jesus' worst hour?
2. How did Jesus' suffering occur both in the daytime and the night (see Matthew 27:45)?

Psalm 22 is known as the Psalm of the Cross. "The fact that Jesus uttered from His cross the words of bitter woe that begin this poem, has given and must ever give it a special interest and importance. It is natural that Christian sentiment should fasten lovingly on it, and almost claim it, not only as a record of suffering typical of our Lord's suffering, but as actually in every detail prophetic of Him" (*Ellicott's Commentary*).

The immediate circumstance out of which this psalm arose seems to be a personal crisis of David, or perhaps the suffering of the nation of Israel. In either case, the plaintive cry in verse 1 can come only from one who has prayed earnestly for divine assistance without seeing the answer to that prayer. Although this is a typical experience of most Christians, the greatest example of it in history was when Jesus, dying on the cross, spoke these very words (see Matthew 27:46).

These agonizing words marked Christ's first and only experience of separation from the Father. Jesus was bearing our sins to His death, and God in His holiness could not look upon sin. He, the innocent One, died for us, the guilty ones.

It is a fearful experience to pray and sense that no answer comes back. Jesus prayed in the night in the Garden of Gethsemane, and He prayed in the daytime on the cross, but seemingly God did not answer. Likewise the psalmist poured his heart out to God day and night, but the Lord did not answer him.

It is important that the psalmist continued to pray even when it seemed God did not hear him. So did Jesus. In this, the believer is wiser than the worldly—for the typical person would cease to speak to one who seemed not to answer. In His parable of the unjust judge, Jesus taught us to pray even when it seems our prayers are unanswered (Luke 18:1-8).

"One of the prominent symptoms of our times . . . is loneliness. Isn't it ironic that in an age of the greatest population explosion the world has ever known, more people are desperately lonely than ever before?"
—**Paul Little**

B. Recalling God's Record (vv. 3-5)

3. But thou art holy, O thou that inhabitest the praises of Israel.

4. Our fathers trusted in thee: they trusted, and thou didst deliver them.

5. They cried unto thee, and were delivered: they trusted in thee, and were not confounded.

The holiness of the Lord makes Him worthy of our prayers, our trust and our worship. The picture in verse 3 shows our prayers forming the throne room of God. As we send our praises heavenward, we provide the foundation for His glory and majesty upon the earth. He *inhabits* our praise.

In verses 4 and 5, the psalmist looked over the record of God's dealings with Israel and reminded Him of how He had delivered the Israelites from their trouble. We need to remember that throughout human history, God has brought deliverance to those who seek Him. Deliverance has not always come in the *way* people expected it, not even *when* expected, but it has always come. Sometimes the Lord does not answer a prayer immediately because of the greater glory of answering later in ways people cannot even imagine. God could have helped Israel to escape unnoticed out of Egypt, but it was more glorious to deliver them even as Pharaoh pursued them. God the Father let the Son die on the cross, but then He performed the most glorious act in history—bringing Jesus back to life.

Almost always, when we imagine God is not answering prayer, it is because He does not answer in the way we expected or desired. But the psalmist declares how God cooperates with us. We ask, trust and wait. God delivers and enlightens in His time. The examples of the past serve as guideposts for today.

C. Surviving Ridicule and Hate (vv. 6-8)

6. But I am a worm, and no man; a reproach of men, and despised of the people.

7. All they that see me laugh me to scorn: they shoot out the lip, they shake the head saying,

8. He trusted on the Lord that he would deliver him: let him deliver him, seeing he delighted in him.

Here we see how Christ, the "man of sorrows" (Isaiah 53:3), suffered utter humiliation. He felt lower than a man, beneath the dignity of humanity, and felt that all people despised Him. This emphasized and intensified His sense of aloneness. He felt God had forsaken Him and that He was despised by the world.

The crudeness and cruelty of the mob had its day in the crucifixion of Christ. The insults were complete. Name it—Christ suffered it on the cross:

> And those who passed by blasphemed Him, wagging their heads and saying, "You who destroy the temple and build it in three days, save Yourself! If You are the Son of God, come down from the cross." Likewise the chief priests also, mocking with the scribes and elders, said, "He saved others; Himself He cannot save" (Matthew 27:39-42, *NKJV*).

The mob that jeered at Christ knew not how well the Lord would deliver Him. He could have saved Christ from the cross, but He waited to deliver Him from the grave—a much greater deliverance.

Talk About It:
How can we find deliverance from trouble?

"Troubles are often the tools by which God fashions for us better things."
—**Henry Beecher**

shoot out the lip **(v. 7)**—shaking one's head

Talk About It:
1. What does it mean to be "a reproach of men" (v. 6)?
2. What was the main message in the people's mockery of Christ?

The world hated Jesus because of His confidence in God (Psalm 22:8). The same truth is valid today. Unbelievers despise Christians for reasons they do not themselves understand. There is an unavoidable tension between those who follow God and those who reject Him. Righteous people are, by their very lives, a rebuke to people of sin. These sinners took delight in scorning Jesus as having an ill-placed trust in God.

II. AFFIRMATION OF GOD'S CARE (Psalm 22:9-21)

A. From Birth (vv. 9, 10)

9. But thou art he that took me out of the womb: thou didst make me hope when I was upon my mother's breasts.

10. I was cast upon thee from the womb: thou art my God from my mother's belly.

The psalmist recognized that God was watching over him at the moment of his birth. While he was unaware of God's presence and help when he was an infant, David could look back and say God had enabled him to survive and thrive in an era when babies easily died through disease or sickness.

David may have felt God's hand was on his life in a distinctive way, being "cast upon" God's protection and care from birth. When we read of the dangers young David faced and overcame while watching over his father's sheep, we see God's providence in action.

When we think of these verses also being prophetic, we recall the hazards of Christ's early years: the unborn Child surviving Mary's risky journey to Bethlehem; the Savior being born in a cave where animals were kept; the persecution by Herod; the sudden trip to Egypt to spare Jesus' life. Perhaps these events flashed through Christ's mind as He suffered on the cross—the horror He did not escape.

B. On the Cross (vv. 11-18)

11. Be not far from me; for trouble is near; for there is none to help.

12. Many bulls have compassed me: strong bulls of Bashan have beset me round.

13. They gaped upon me with their mouths, as a ravening and a roaring lion.

14. I am poured out like water, and all my bones are out of joint: my heart is like wax; it is melted in the midst of my bowels.

15. My strength is dried up like a potsherd; and my tongue cleaveth to my jaws; and thou hast brought me into the dust of death.

16. For dogs have compassed me: the assembly of the wicked have inclosed me: they pierced my hands and my feet.

17. I may tell all my bones: they look and stare upon me.

18. They part my garments among them, and cast lots upon my vesture.

As Christ hung on the cross, there truly was no one to help Him. He alone was bearing the sins of the world. But after His six hours of hell on earth, death did come; and two days later He was resurrected as the eternal Savior who would never again be separated from His Father.

Verses 12-18 describe Christ's suffering with amazing accuracy, especially when we realize there is no historical record of crucifixion until some five centuries after the writing of this psalm. The enemies of Christ surrounded Him like strong, violent bulls (v. 12). Like hungry, roaring lions encircling their prey, they tore at Christ, devouring Him (v. 13). Matthew 27:26 records that the Roman soldiers tore apart Christ's flesh with the scourge of their whip. "Then the governor's soldiers took Jesus into the Praetorium and gathered the whole company of soldiers around him. . . . They spit on him, and took the staff and struck him on the head again and again" (vv. 27, 30, *NIV*).

The psalmist describes the Savior's suffering in stark detail (22:14-17):

- His hands and feet were pierced.
- He was "poured out like water."
- His bones were "out of joint" as He hung there.
- His heart "melted away" (*NIV*) as death drew near.
- His tongue stuck to the roof of His mouth in His horrific thirst.
- His strength was completely gone, so that He was no longer able to gasp for breath.
- As people stared at Him and His enemies gloated over Him, His body was exposed to them.

Verse 18 even describes how Christ's clothing would be divided and gambled over. Four Roman soldiers did just that, dividing one part of His clothing into quarters, and gambling over the seamless second piece (John 19:23, 24).

C. In Despair (vv. 19-21)

19. But be not thou far from me, O Lord: O my strength, haste thee to help me.

20. Deliver my soul from the sword; my darling from the power of the dog.

21. Save me from the lion's mouth: for thou hast heard me from the horns of the unicorns.

The picture here is of an imposing collection of forces, each capable of inflicting death, coming upon one person. First, there's a man-made weapon—the sword—ready to take the person's "soul" or life. Then there's the power of ferocious, filthy, vicious dogs. This pack of dogs is surrounding "my darling"—the one and

Talk About It:
1. Describe some situations where no one but God can help.
2. How was Christ "poured out like water" (v. 14)?
3. How did onlookers respond to the suffering Christ (v. 17)?

"The cross of Christ must be either the darkest spot of all in the mystery of existence or a searchlight by aid of which we may penetrate the surrounding gloom."
—**Burnett Streeter**

my darling (v. 20) —my precious life
unicorns (v. 21)— wild oxen

Talk About It:
What is God called in verse 19, and why?

only Son of God. Verse 21 is a plea for salvation from the deadly teeth of lions and the deadly horns of wild beasts.

Surrounded by such formidable foes, the psalmist (and the Christ) prays, "O Lord, be not far off; O my Strength, come quickly to help me" (v. 19, *NIV*). While Christ would die, in accordance with God's plan and not because of the force or will of the Enemy, He would break the sword, silence the dogs, break the lions' teeth, and dehorn the wild beasts in His resurrection. And now His salvation and deliverance can be ours!

III. PROCLAMATION OF HOPE (Psalm 22:22-31)
A. God Hears (vv. 22-25)

22. I will declare thy name unto my brethren: in the midst of the congregation will I praise thee.

23. Ye that fear the Lord, praise him; all ye the seed of Jacob, glorify him; and fear him, all ye the seed of Israel.

24. For he hath not despised nor abhorred the affliction of the afflicted; neither hath he hid his face from him; but when he cried unto him, he heard.

25. My praise shall be of thee in the great congregation: I will pay my vows before them that fear him.

When God answers someone's prayer after a season of suffering or anguish, it is a time of celebration. With verse 22 the psalm of suffering and woe is transformed into a psalm of victory and praise.

The psalmist said he would lift up the name of the Lord in the place of worship among his brothers. He was now on the victory side of suffering, and he would praise God for it in the sanctuary. Verse 22 is quoted in Hebrews 2:12, where Jesus is speaking. Jesus became "the author of . . . salvation . . . through suffering" (v. 10, *NIV*). Thereby He brings people into His family, and "is not ashamed to call them brothers" (v. 11, *NIV*). When we who are God's children gather for corporate worship, we should lift up His name with exuberant praise.

In Psalm 22:23, we see the psalmist was not satisfied with praising the Lord by himself. Instead, He urged His fellow Jewish believers to fear the Lord and praise Him. Why? Because in the middle of their trials, God did not despise nor abhor them because of their suffering, nor did He turn His back on Him. Instead, the Lord listened to their cry for help. In His perfect timing, He answered them.

B. God Satisfies (vv. 26-31)

26. The meek shall eat and be satisfied: they shall praise the Lord that seek him: your heart shall live for ever.

27. All the ends of the world shall remember and turn unto the Lord: and all the kindreds of the nations shall worship before thee.

Talk About It:
1. Why is it important to worship with other believers?
2. What does it mean to "fear the Lord" (v. 23)?
3. How does God *not* respond to the "despised or disdained" (v. 24, *NIV*)? How *does* He respond?
4. How serious does God take the vows we make to Him?

"God knows the best possible thing for us is to be absolutely taken up and obsessed with Him. He knows that He's the ultimate source of all joy and comfort, and He wants us to come to the source."
—Mike Taylor

Prayer of Forsakenness

28. For the kingdom is the Lord's: and he is the governor among the nations.

29. All they that be fat upon earth shall eat and worship: all they that go down to the dust shall bow before him: and none can keep alive his own soul.

30. A seed shall serve him; it shall be accounted to the Lord for a generation.

31. They shall come, and shall declare his righteousness unto a people that shall be born, that he hath done this.

"The call to thanksgiving is now ended; and there follows a grateful upward glance towards the Author of the salvation; and this grateful upward glance grows into a prophetic view of the future" (Keil & Delitzsch). It speaks of a time when "the meek" (v. 26)—here meaning the wretched, the poor and the miserable—who seek the Lord will have their needs abundantly met through Jesus Christ. They will find satisfying nourishment that lasts forever.

The psalmist foresaw the time when "all the ends of the world" (v. 27)—people from every nation—would turn to the Lord. This time is now, when anyone anywhere who answers God's call will be saved. Yet this time is also futuristic, when the Lord sets up His kingdom on earth and rules over every nation. On that day, not just the poor will bow before the Lord, but also the wealthy. Those who die will "go down to the dust" worshiping God (v. 29).

The *seed* in verse 30 refers to the people of God. The psalmist prophesied that all kinds of people would become part of God's family, and the gospel would be passed on from generation to generation.

"He hath done this" (v. 31) glorifies the coming Messiah for fulfilling the divine plan of salvation. Today, however, we can look back on Christ's finished work on the cross and His final words of victory—"It is finished" (John 19:30)—and receive all the blessings of Christ's atonement. "He has done it" and "It is finished," and we are the benefactors!

CONCLUSION

Our prayers can go out to God, and we can know He hears our cry, that He understands and cares, and will give us the help we need in the hour of trouble. Why? Because He has gone along the way before us and has suffered and endured every trial known to humanity. "Let us therefore come boldly unto the throne of grace, that we may obtain mercy, and find grace to help in time of need" (Hebrews 4:16).

GOLDEN TEXT CHALLENGE

"HE [GOD] HATH NOT DESPISED NOR ABHORRED

Talk About It:
1. What is true satisfaction?
2. Compare the world's future relationship with God (vv. 27-29) with the world's present relationship with Him.
3. How can we positively influence generations yet to be born?

"I've read the last page of the Bible. It's all going to turn out all right."
—Billy Graham

THE AFFLICTION OF THE AFFLICTED; NEITHER HATH HE HID HIS FACE FROM HIM; BUT WHEN HE CRIED UNTO HIM, HE HEARD" (Psalm 22:24).

God graciously accepted it [Christ's sacrifice] as a full satisfaction for sin, and a valuable consideration on which to ground the grant of eternal life to all believers. Though it was offered for us poor sinners, God did not despise nor abhor Him that offered it for our sakes. . . . But when Jesus cried unto Him, when His blood cried for peace and pardon for us, God heard Him. This, as it is the matter of our rejoicing, ought to be the matter of our thanksgiving. Those who have thought their prayers slighted and unheard, if they continue to pray and wait, will find they have not sought in vain.—**Matthew Henry**

Have Confidence in God

Psalms 27:1-14; 29:1-11

INTRODUCTION

The words of Psalm 27 give us some insight into the spiritual life of the psalmist David during some difficult days. The formula expressed still brings deliverance and victory just as it did for David. In this psalm he declares his confidence in the Lord. He calls the Lord his light, his salvation, and his strength. He affirms his confidence in God to keep him, although he is aware of his many enemies. David's attitude can be summed up in the words of Paul: "If God be for us, who can be against us?" (Romans 8:31).

The fellowship and guidance of the Lord mean more to David than anything else in life. Over and over he asked the Lord to never turn away His listening ear and His comforting arm.

In the second psalm being studied in today's lesson, we see David lifting up the glory and majesty of God, and urging his readers to hear God's voice. The psalmist's words bring to mind a modern hymn titled "Glory to His Name":

Hail the Son of Righteousness, Creator, Lord and King,
  Let the nations of the earth, His praises loudly sing.

Come before His presence, let His praises loudly ring,
  With a shout of exaltation, let His people sing.

Bow in humble adoration, on your faces fall,
  Then be quick to answer when you hear the Savior call.
—Joe E. Parks

Unit Theme:
Prayers and Exhortations in the Psalms

Central Truth:
With God as our companion, we have confidence for living.

Focus:
Discover and follow the path to confidence in God.

Context:
Two psalms attributed to David

Golden Text:
"The Lord is my light and my salvation: whom shall I fear? The Lord is the strength of my life; of whom shall I be afraid?" (Psalm 27:1).

Study Outline:
I. Depend on God's Help (Psalm 27:1-6)
II. Seek God's Face (Psalm 27:7-14)
III. Hear God's Voice (Psalm 29:1-11)

I. DEPEND ON GOD'S HELP (Psalm 27:1-6)
A. In the Light (vv. 1-3)

1. The Lord is my light and my salvation; whom shall I fear? the Lord is the strength of my life; of whom shall I be afraid?

2. When the wicked, even mine enemies and my foes, came upon me to eat up my flesh, they stumbled and fell.

3. Though an host should encamp against me, my heart shall not fear: though war should rise against me, in this will I be confident.

If you've ever been in an underground cave without any light, you can relate to David's situation. In a cave you cannot even see your hand in front of your face. You can almost feel the darkness. You can quickly become disoriented, losing your sense of direction and time.

While David was not in a literal cave, he was surrounded by dark foes and enemies. They were ready to "eat up" his flesh. No, they were not cannibals. But they were like ravenous beasts anxious to destroy David. Into this seemingly hopeless situation a light began to shine—the light of the Lord, which caused David to sing in the midst of his enemies: "The Lord is the stronghold of my life—of whom shall I be afraid?" (v. 1, *NIV*). In the brightness of the Lord's light, the attack by David's enemies turned into a farce: "they stumbled and fell" (v. 2).

David had such confidence in the Lord that even if an army lined up against him, he said he would not be fearful. Even if war broke out against him, he would not lose hope. This was more than just talk, for there was a time when David was actually pursued by the army of jealous King Saul. David's trust in the Lord was so great that when he twice had the opportunity to take Saul's life, he resisted the temptation. On the second occasion, David told Saul, "As surely as I valued your life today, so may the Lord value my life and deliver me from all trouble" (1 Samuel 26:24, *NIV*). The Lord did just that.

B. On a Rock (vv. 4-6)

4. One thing have I desired of the Lord, that will I seek after; that I may dwell in the house of the Lord all the days of my life, to behold the beauty of the Lord, and to enquire in his temple.

5. For in the time of trouble he shall hide me in his pavilion: in the secret of his tabernacle shall he hide me; he shall set me up upon a rock.

6. And now shall mine head be lifted up above mine enemies round about me: therefore will I offer in his tabernacle sacrifices of joy; I will sing, yea, I will sing praises unto the Lord.

The psalmist zeroed in on the "one thing" that was most important to him: living in the presence of the Lord all the days of his life—"to have a perpetual enjoyment of God's realized grace and presence. All other blessings are included in this, so that this one thing is, and shall always be, the psalmist's ruling desire. The Tabernacle, and subsequently the Temple, symbolized the union between God and His true worshippers, dwelling in spirit with Him there" (*Jamieson, Fausset and Brown Commentary*).

David yearned to gaze upon the grace, beauty and wisdom of the Lord, and to find answers to life's questions from Him. As we read David's many psalms of worship (e.g., Psalms 29 and 30), we realize he did "behold the beauty" of the Lord's character; and as we read the various psalms (e.g., Psalms 13 and 15) in which he raised critical questions, we realize he did seek and find the wisdom of God.

Because his trust was in the Lord, David knew God would give him refuge from trouble in His *pavilion* (27:5), or "tent," referring to the Tabernacle. God would not hide him just anywhere in the Tabernacle, but specifically in the "secret" place—the Holy of Holies—the place of intimate communion with God. David's feet would be established "upon a rock" (v. 5)—a place inaccessible to his enemies. In Psalm 61:2, David prayed, "From the end of the earth will I cry unto thee, when my heart is overwhelmed: lead me to the rock that is higher than I."

Standing on that rock of safety, David's head would be "lifted up" above all his enemies around him. So when he came to the Tabernacle sacrifice unto the Lord, he would not do so quietly. Instead, he would sing and shout to the Lord.

II. SEEK GOD'S FACE (Psalm 27:7-14)
A. Never Unheard (vv. 7, 8)

7. Hear, O Lord, when I cry with my voice: have mercy also upon me, and answer me.

8. When thou saidst, Seek ye my face; my heart said unto thee, Thy face, Lord, will I seek.

"This earnest prayer seems to have been prompted by a returning sense of danger. He had had assurance of the divine favor. He had found God ready to help him. He did not doubt but that He would aid him; yet all this did not prevent his calling upon Him for the aid which he needed, but rather stimulated him to do it. With all the deep-felt conviction of his heart that God was ready and willing to assist him, he still felt that he had no reason to hope for His aid unless he called upon Him. The phrase 'when I cry with my voice' refers to the fact that he prayed audibly or aloud. It was not mental prayer, but that which found expression in the language of earnest entreaty" (Barnes).

Talk About It:
1. What "one thing" did the psalmist desire, and how did he act on it?
2. How did the psalmist worship God, and why?

"The chief end of man is to glorify God and enjoy Him forever."
—*The Shorter Catechism*, 1646

Talk About It:
1. What is "mercy," and why did David need it?
2. What does it mean to answer God with one's heart?

The psalmist hears the Lord tell him, "Seek My face" (v. 8, *NKJV*). This is both an invitation and a command. It is God holding the door of favor open to David. Without hesitation, David replies from his heart, "I will." This verse reminds us of God's command invitation to His people in 2 Chronicles 7:14: "If my people, which are called by my name, shall humble themselves, and pray, and seek my face, and turn from their wicked ways; then will I hear from heaven, and will forgive their sin, and will heal their land."

B. Never Forsaken (vv. 9, 10)

9. Hide not thy face far from me; put not thy servant away in anger: thou hast been my help; leave me not, neither forsake me, O God of my salvation.

10. When my father and my mother forsake me, then the Lord will take me up.

The psalmist felt alone and appealed to God not to forsake him. The extremity of all loneliness is to feel that one has been forsaken by the Lord. It is the feeling of ultimate rejection and despair. This accentuated the suffering that Jesus endured on the cross when He felt for a moment that the Father had forsaken Him (Mark 15:34). One of the prices of Jesus' incarnation was His experiencing all human emotions. So, for a brief time, He was partaker of an intensely human sense of loneliness.

Verse 10 declares that mothers and fathers can desert their own children. This is an all-too-true reality in our society. Some parents neglect, abandon or abuse their own children. Yet the psalmist says even if we are estranged from our closest human ties, we can always count on the Lord to be with us and strengthen us. We are never alone, for the Lord is always with us. He provides believers the sustaining grace they need for every situation.

C. Never Disappointed (vv. 11-14)

11. Teach me thy way, O Lord, and lead me in a plain path, because of mine enemies.

12. Deliver me not over unto the will of mine enemies: for false witnesses are risen up against me, and such as breathe out cruelty.

13. I had fainted, unless I had believed to see the goodness of the Lord in the land of the living.

14. Wait on the Lord: be of good courage, and he shall strengthen thine heart: wait, I say, on the Lord.

The psalmist was in a hostile and dangerous situation. His enemies were telling lies and making threats against him. So David prayed that the Lord would be his teacher and guide. He prayed for a straight and discernible path that would lead him out of enemy territory and into a place of safety.

Talk About It:
1. What was David's concern in verse 9?
2. Explain the phrase "take me up" (v. 10).

"Let a man go away or come back: God never leaves. He is always at hand, and if He cannot get into your life, still He is never farther away than at the door."
—Meister Eckhart

Talk About It:
1. What is a "plain path" (v. 11), and how do we find such?
2. Compare "the will of [David's] enemies" (v. 12) with "the goodness of the Lord" (v. 13).
3. What is promised those who "wait on the Lord" (v. 14)?

Have Confidence in God

In verse 13 we see that David "believed"—he had confidence—that the goodness of the Lord would be poured out on him "in the land of the living," or during his days on the earth. Just as there are dangers and enemies and trials on the earth, there are also blessings. While the greatest treasures of all are waiting in heaven, God also provides divine favors in this life. "He lavished on us" the "riches of God's grace" through Jesus Christ (Ephesians 1:7, 8, *NIV*).

Many times the key to receiving God's answer is waiting. Not waiting idly, like someone sitting on a bench hoping the bus will come soon. Instead, we should "be strong and take heart" (Psalm 27:14, *NIV*), recalling the times He has ministered to us in the past, and seeking His face. Charles Spurgeon said, "Wait at His door with prayer; wait at His foot with humility; wait at His table with service; wait at His window with expectancy."

III. HEAR GOD'S VOICE (Psalm 29:1-11)

A. His Mighty Name (vv. 1, 2)

1. Give unto the Lord, O ye mighty, give unto the Lord glory and strength.

2. Give unto the Lord the glory due unto his name; worship the Lord in the beauty of holiness.

Who can "give" Almighty God "glory and strength"? Absolutely no one. The idea here is for the glory and strength that God possesses to be recognized and honored. "O ye mighty" are called to do this. This phrase might refer to angels, or it could refer to the chosen people of God.

The mighty ones are called to "worship the Lord in the beauty of holiness." This refers either to the worshipers arraying themselves in holy attire or coming into God's glorious sanctuary to worship. Either way, they are to ascribe to God the glory that His name deserves, which is *all* glory. In Psalm 24:10, David wrote, "Who is he, this King of glory? The Lord Almighty—he is the King of glory" (*NIV*).

B. His Mighty Voice (vv. 3-9)

3. The voice of the Lord is upon the waters: the God of glory thundereth: the Lord is upon many waters.

4. The voice of the Lord is powerful; the voice of the Lord is full of majesty.

5. The voice of the Lord breaketh the cedars; yea, the Lord breaketh the cedars of Lebanon.

6. He maketh them also to skip like a calf; Lebanon and Sirion like a young unicorn.

7. The voice of the Lord divideth the flames of fire.

8. The voice of the Lord shaketh the wilderness; the Lord shaketh the wilderness of Kadesh.

the hinds to calve
(v. 9)—"the deer
give birth" (*NKJV*)

Talk About It:
1. How is thunder like the voice of God?
2. How do the forces of nature influence people's response to God?

"A philosopher once asked, 'Where is God?' The Christian answered, 'Let me first ask you, Where is He not?'"
—**John Arrowsmith**

Talk About It:
1. How does Genesis 8:1-3 confirm Psalm 29:10?
2. How can we receive God's strength and peace?

"We are a long time in learning that all our strength and salvation is in God."
—**David Brainerd**

9. The voice of the Lord maketh the hinds to calve, and discovereth the forests: and in his temple doth every one speak of his glory.

The occasion of this psalm is a mighty thunderstorm. Seven times the phrase "the voice of the Lord" is used to describe the thunder of the storm. While we know that thunderstorms occur from natural causes, the awesomeness of thunder reminds us of God's greatness. And God does speak to people through thunderstorms, earthquakes, hurricanes and other "loud" natural forces. But He also speaks through the gentle wind, the beautiful rose and the beautiful sunshine. Paul said, "Since earliest times men have seen the earth and sky and all God made, and have known of his existence and great eternal power" (Romans 1:20, *TLB*).

"It is not God's anger but his majestic power which makes the storm move. It begins out over the Mediterranean Sea with power and majesty. It then moves in over the mountains to the north of Palestine and over the wilderness to the south. The description of the effect upon trees, mountains, wilderness and animals is followed by the chorus of 'glory' which comes from man's worship" (Wycliffe).

Mighty cedars are broken in the storm, and are tossed around like animals at play. Lightning is sent forth like divided flames of fire, and thunder echoes through the wilderness. Trees are stripped bare, and animals give birth. In response to all this, God's people shout, "Glory to the Lord!"

C. His Eternal Reign (vv. 10, 11)
10. The Lord sitteth upon the flood; yea, the Lord sitteth King for ever.
11. The Lord will give strength unto his people; the Lord will bless his people with peace.

When the floodwaters raged over the earth in the days of Noah, God was enthroned above them, orchestrating their path. And the Lord continues to preside over every storm, reigning as the eternal King.

Because God is above the storm, we who are under the storm have hope. The God who has all strength gives His people strength to make it through any storms that arise, whether they are physical or spiritual storms. And in the middle of the storm, God will give His people the peace they need. He will either give us peace to survive the battle or He will tell the storm, "Peace, be still" (Mark 4:39).

CONCLUSION

The three main points in today's lesson are these: Depend on God's help, seek God's face, and hear God's voice. Are you following these directives?

1. Are you depending more on God or your own ideas?
2. Are you seeking God's face with all your heart?
3. Are you listening for God's voice and following His ways?

GOLDEN TEXT CHALLENGE

"THE LORD IS MY LIGHT AND MY SALVATION: WHOM SHALL I FEAR? THE LORD IS THE STRENGTH OF MY LIFE; OF WHOM SHALL I BE AFRAID?" (Psalm 27:1).

Fear of failure keeps more people from accomplishing things than perhaps all other emotional forces combined. There would be few limits to the feats most of us would attempt if somehow we could be assured before we began that our efforts would succeed.

Psalm 27:1 refers to many different kinds of fears: fear of dying, fear of injury, fear of financial need, fear of rejection, and so on. But the fear that holds back many would-be witnesses from doing God's will is the fear of failure.

The psalmist encourages us to let God handle our fears. Let us allow His Spirit to fight and overcome the fear in us.

Daily Devotions:
M. Be Strong
  Joshua 1:3-9
T. Be Courageous
  2 Chronicles
  15:1-8
W. Be Fearless
  Isaiah 35:3-10
T. Have Faith
  Matthew 8:5-13
F. Trust God
  Acts 27:22-35
S. Stay Confident
  Hebrews 10:23-35

Encouragement to Righteous Living

Psalm 37:1-40

Unit Theme:
Prayers and Exhortations in the Psalms

Central Truth:
God punishes the wicked but honors those who live to please Him.

Focus:
Contrast the behavior of the wicked and the righteous and commit our lives to God.

Context:
Written by David, probably between 1000 and 980 B.C.

Golden Text:
"Commit thy way unto the Lord; trust also in him; and he shall bring it to pass. And he shall bring forth thy righteousness as the light, and thy judgment as the noonday" (Psalm 37:5, 6).

Study Outline:
I. Commit to God (Psalm 37:1-8)
II. Trust God for Protection (Psalm 37:11-20)
III. Wait on the Lord (Psalm 37:34-40)

INTRODUCTION

Regardless of age, personality, maturity, education or spiritual condition, all people experience anxiety at some time. This unpleasant emotion can overshadow and sour even the most pleasant environments. Our present time has often been referred to as the "age of anxiety," in spite of all the modern conveniences and scientific technology at our disposal.

Let's compare the definitions of *fear* and *anxiety*. Fear comes most often from realistic threats such as storms, air and water pollution, or an increased violent crime rate. Definite visible or discernible threats stimulate fear. Anxiety, however, is a feeling of tension, apprehension, or worry that isn't necessarily tied to or stimulated by any specific realistic threat. It develops or rises from a perceived danger to either oneself or one's valued treasure.

There are two basic forms of anxiety. The first form, *state anxiety*, is short-term. It occurs from time to time in a variety of settings but isn't a regular characteristic of the individual's life. Though momentary, this form can be just as intense and worrisome as the more extended type.

The second form, known as *trait anxiety*, can be described as chronic or as being ingrained in an individual. The individual with this form of anxiety appears to have adopted an anxious lifestyle, seemingly needing to have to worry or be in a state of tension in order to feel normal.

Since Christians are also subject to anxiety, there are two interrelated questions that need to be considered: (1) What is the Biblical position concerning anxiety? (2) How should the believer deal with anxiety? This lesson deals specifically with the second question and will also incorporate some scriptures concerning the first one.

Psalm 37 is one of three psalms that deal with the perplexing problem of the prosperity of the wicked or unbelievers (see also Psalms 49; 73). The God-fearing individual reviews the prosperity of those who disregard God and wonders how it can be. In further contemplation of this apparent inequity, anxiety may arise in the believer's spirit. Responding to this situation, David wrote wonderful words of comfort, while at the same time indicating several specific steps that can be taken to quiet the anxiety.

I. COMMIT TO GOD (Psalm 37:1-8)

A. Trust and Delight (vv. 1-4)

1. Fret not thyself because of evildoers, neither be thou envious against the workers of iniquity.

2. For they shall soon be cut down like the grass, and wither as the green herb.

3. Trust in the Lord, and do good; so shalt thou dwell in the land, and verily thou shalt be fed.

4. Delight thyself also in the Lord; and he shall give thee the desires of thine heart.

The key to handling anxiety is seen in the first line of the psalm. Everything else an individual may try will be unsuccessful unless this action is fulfilled. There has to be a conscious effort to stop anxiety-producing actions. "Fret not" can be phrased in a variety of ways: "Stop worrying," "Don't allow yourself to be disturbed," "Get rid of uneasy feelings." This emphasizes that anxiety flows from within and is a personal matter for us to deal with. No one else can eradicate it.

Successful handling of anxiety demands right thinking. For that reason David gave a reminder of the future of those evildoers who are the source of our frustration. They are temporary. In a short time their lives will end and their bodies decay just like grass or a plant. Such people's lives often fade quickly from memory and the works of their hands disintegrate. Those who appear so mighty and prosperous today may be gone tomorrow. Knowing this, why should we be anxious over issues so unsure and temporal?

What we think affects our feelings. Our feelings in turn affect our actions. Unless our thought life operates with the proper information, the other steps for overcoming anxiety can be only partially successful at best.

The negative reactions we avoid are to be replaced with positive actions. Verse 3 tells us to begin by trusting in the Lord. Trusting God means putting our complete confidence in Him. This ranges from expecting small provisions all along the way to taking refuge and hiding in Him during major crises.

While trusting in Him we are to *delight* in Him. This means to take pleasure in our relationship with the Lord. As we trust, we experience satisfaction and enjoyment. Complete trust overcomes the anxiety, which has already become part of us, or prevents it from entering our thinking. Trusting in the Lord creates for us a happy, fulfilling relationship, not one of grudging acceptance.

B. Commit Your Way (vv. 5, 6)

5. Commit thy way unto the Lord; trust also in him; and he shall bring it to pass.

Talk About It:
1. How can evildoers cause believers to be fretful and envious?
2. What is the connection between *trusting* and *doing* in verse 3?
3. What does it mean to *delight* in the Lord, and what is the benefit?

"Envy takes the joy, happiness and contentment out of living."
—**Billy Graham**

judgment (v. 6)—
"the justice of your
cause" (*NIV*)

Talk About It:
1. What will God
"bring to pass" (v.
5) for people com-
mitted to Him?
2. What will God
"bring forth" (v. 6),
and why?

Total Trust
"Last night in the
wee hours a
thought came to
me, to trust God
beyond my own
understanding of
God. . . . . I shared
it [the thought] with
two friends my own
age, and one said
to trust God beyond
our own under-
standing is what is
required of us in
dying, for our own
understanding can-
not penetrate the
veil of death."
—John S. Dunne

wicked devices
(v. 7)—"evil
schemes"

Talk About It:
1. What happens to
a believer who
doesn't "rest in the
Lord" (v. 7)?
2. What results
from anger and
fretting (v. 8)?
Why?

6. And he shall bring forth thy righteousness as the light, and thy judgment as the noonday.

The second part of trusting is committing our way to the Lord. We make His path our path. We surrender our wishes. We give up our methods. We say, "God, You're in the driver's seat, and I'm in the backseat. Any way or place You choose to take me is fine with me."

Trust cannot exist without the committing of our way. All attempts to retain our authority or sovereignty immediately lessen or even destroy the trust relationship. Trust by its nature necessitates giving up our will in order to receive the benefits of the one on whom we are depending.

Verses 4 and 5 indicate how trust brings desired results. Hearts' desires and life needs come to those who trust in the Lord. God wants to and loves to provide for His children. One caution does need to be given, however. Although God pro-vides for us on the basis of our need, He also takes into con-sideration the attitude in which we ask. And He is also mindful of what will benefit us most in the long run. So if, in a given sit-uation, we have trusted and not received, we need to first eval-uate our desire. Then we must consider that God may want to provide for us some future blessings.

Verse 6 reminds us that trusting in the Lord results in our vin-dication as time passes. This may include a general concept of the rightness and benefits of being a Christian. Or more specif-ically, God may bring to light that one's actions and attitudes were correct, though misinterpreted or completely disregarded.

C. Rest in the Lord (vv. 7, 8)

7. Rest in the Lord, and wait patiently for him: fret not thyself because of him who prospereth in his way, because of the man who bringeth wicked devices to pass.

8. Cease from anger, and forsake wrath: fret not thyself in any wise to do evil.

The third part of trusting in the Lord logically follows the pre-vious two; however, at times it can be difficult to accomplish. We are to rest in the Lord. This is more than simply relaxing. It means to be still before the Lord. We are to stop striving to accomplish our desire by means of our own activity. We can-not claim trust in the Lord until we stop and wait in quietness and patience for the Lord to accomplish what the situation demands. That doesn't mean trust is synonymous with idle-ness or inactivity. It does mean that we need to be willing to cease with our own efforts when there is nothing more we can do, and rest in confidence that God is in control.

We are to be still before the Lord not only in actions but also in our emotions. Anger at someone's prosperity in spite of their spiritual wickedness cannot be allowed to continue to burn. As we take away the fuel for the fire of anger, then anxiety will also die within.

II. TRUST GOD FOR PROTECTION (Psalm 37:11-20)
A. Fate of Evildoers (vv. 12-15, 17, 20)

12. The wicked plotteth against the just, and gnasheth upon him with his teeth.

13. The Lord shall laugh at him: for he seeth that his day is coming.

14. The wicked have drawn out the sword, and have bent their bow, to cast down the poor and needy, and to slay such as be of upright conversation.

15. Their sword shall enter into their own heart, and their bows shall be broken.

17. For the arms of the wicked shall be broken: but the Lord upholdeth the righteous.

20. But the wicked shall perish, and the enemies of the Lord shall be as the fat of lambs: they shall consume; into smoke shall they consume away.

Talk About It:
1. Why do wicked people plot against the righteous?
2. What will eventually happen to the plots of evil people?

The answer for anxiety includes waiting for God's justice. God by His nature is just and deals accordingly with all people. So the future of evildoers, or the wicked, is predicted. Their prosperity and the inequity between them and the righteous is only temporary. Verse 9 states they "shall be cut off." Verse 10 says "yet a little while." There will be a change in their status, but we need to wait for God to exercise His justice.

In verses 12 and 14 we see why anxiety may develop in some individuals as they watch the progress and prosperity of the wicked. Even when the wicked are quiet and appear disinterested in the righteous, the potential for conflict is evident. They may secretly be plotting harm while on the outside appearing calm and complacent.

Anxiety may arise as a person dwells on the callousness of evildoers. They have no concern for the poor and needy. Instead of offering compassionate help to lift and minister, they are prepared to hurt and destroy. The same attitude is directed to those who are upright. Their moral, godly lifestyle offers a contrast the evildoers desire to destroy. Their intent to do harm can be seen in the unsheathed sword and the pulling back of the bow to release the arrow. Their weapons of death and destruction are evident.

Anxiety does not need to dominate since we know justice will prevail. Instead of victory and domination, destruction is the fate of evildoers. The weapons intended to bring harm will either be broken or used to bring about their own death. The scene described in verse 15 reminds us of the story of Haman, as recorded in the Book of Esther. In spite of all his sinister plotting and evil intentions, he was put to death on the gallows he had built for Mordecai (Esther 7:10).

Verse 17 of the text indicates specifically how their strength and ability to do harm will be overcome. The arms are a symbol of strength. With the arms the sword is wielded and the bow drawn. However, if the arms are broken, the person loses his ability to handle weapons and engage in warfare. He becomes a defeated, helpless foe. That is the fate of the evildoers as God's justice prevails. They shall be burned up and, like smoke, "they shall vanish away" (v. 20, *NKJV*).

B. Future of the Righteous (vv. 11, 16, 18, 19)

11. But the meek shall inherit the earth; and shall delight themselves in the abundance of peace.

16. A little that a righteous man hath is better than the riches of many wicked.

18. The Lord knoweth the days of the upright: and their inheritance shall be for ever.

19. They shall not be ashamed in the evil time: and in the days of famine they shall be satisfied.

The future of the righteous is a marked contrast to the fate of the evildoers. The righteous look forward to an inheritance and peace, while the wicked can expect only death and destruction. For that reason the limited material resources of the righteous are far better and more greatly to be desired than all the wealth accumulated by the wicked (v. 16). Earthly little with a heart of righteousness will produce an abundance of eternal possessions.

The future of the righteous includes an inheritance—we will inherit the earth. Though now dominated by evil, the earth will become the domain of the righteous. And the distinct atmosphere will be one of peace. The conflict and strife of this world will not be known then. Verse 18 reveals the time frame for the benefits hinted at in verse 16. The inheritance and also the time of peace will be forever. There will be no need to worry that it will be broken or brought to an end.

A second benefit of the righteous is being able to stand strong in times of disaster. Instead of withering when confronted by crises, the righteous don't have to hang their heads either in shame for who they are or in defeat because of the opposition. The Lord provides strength and sustenance. This is not only the hope but also the assurance of the righteous.

III. WAIT ON THE LORD (Psalm 37:34-40)

A. Powerful but Evil (vv. 34-36, 38)

34. Wait on the Lord, and keep his way, and he shall

Encouragement to Righteous Living

exalt thee to inherit the land: when the wicked are cut off, thou shalt see it.

35. I have seen the wicked in great power, and spreading himself like a green bay tree.

36. Yet he passed away, and, lo, he was not: yea, I sought him, but he could not be found.

38. But the transgressors shall be destroyed together: the end of the wicked shall be cut off.

In verse 34, God's people are urged to keep their hope in Him, follow His ways, and stay rooted in the land He has provided. In time they will see God's disfavor fall upon the wicked people who reject Him and His ways. This does not mean the righteous should celebrate when the ungodly are "cut off," but simply that they can be certain this will happen.

"Like a green bay tree" (v. 35) refers to a tree growing up in its native soil, as opposed to its being transplanted to another place. There the tree can grow strong, wide, deep and tall. The phrase *great power* means "terrible; inspiring terror." The psalmist had seen such people—terrible in their evil, yet growing in their prosperity and influence. We too have seen ungodly people flourish like this, whether they are crooked politicians, godless entertainers or athletes, or heartless millionaires.

The psalmist was saying, "I have had an opportunity, in my long life, of witnessing the accuracy of the statement just made, that a righteous man may live to see a confirmation of the truth that wickedness, however prosperous the wicked man may be, will lead to ultimate ruin" (*Barnes' Notes*).

"The transgressors shall be destroyed together" (v. 38) indicates there will be no exceptions. All sinners are bound for mutual destruction. Each one will be "cut off."

B. Challenged but Rewarded (vv. 37, 39, 40)

37. Mark the perfect man, and behold the upright: for the end of that man is peace.

39. But the salvation of the righteous is of the Lord: he is their strength in the time of trouble.

40. And the Lord shall help them and deliver them: he shall deliver them from the wicked, and save them, because they trust in him.

We need to observe and take careful notice of the *perfect* person—the blameless man or woman who serves and obeys God; the one who is *upright*, or righteous. The psalmist urges us to compare that person's future with the wicked person's. Not only does the "perfect man" have peace in his present life, but his future really will be a "happily ever after" story. That person will die a peaceful death and then be ushered into an eternity of peace.

Talk About It:
1. What does it mean to "wait on the Lord" (v. 34)?
2. Why does God sometimes allow "the wicked" to gain "great power" (v. 35)?
3. Whom could David not find, and why not (v. 36)?

"Patience is the greatest of all shock absorbers. The only thing you can get in a hurry is trouble."
—Thomas Dewar

Talk About It:
1. Why is it important to observe the upright person's life?
2. Describe the relationship between the righteous person and the Lord (vv. 39, 40).

Of course, no one can be called "upright" or "perfect" through his or her own doings, nor can they deliver themselves from their difficulties. Instead, the same Lord who enables them to be righteous will be "their strength in the time of trouble" (v. 39). He will do that because their trust is in Him. He will help them, deliver them and save them.

CONCLUSION

While the godly person is to "fret not" because of the way in which the wicked prosper and carry out their evil devices, he is to keep silent and wait for God. In so doing he is neither troubled by their actions nor tempted to copy them, and he creates the patience so necessary to be a mature Christian.

Patience is life's hardest lesson. Learning it once is not sufficient, for all of life is a practice in patience. We must learn to operate on God's timetable.

Daily Devotions:

M. The Wicked Will Perish
   Psalm 1:1-6
T. The Kingdom of Righteousness
   Isaiah 32:1-8
W. Fear and Honor the Lord
   Malachi 3:16 through 4:3
T. Separating Sheep From Goats
   Matthew 25:31-46
F. God's Righteous Judgment
   Romans 2:1-10
S. Redeemed by the Blood
   Ephesians 2:11-18

GOLDEN TEXT CHALLENGE

"COMMIT THY WAY UNTO THE LORD; TRUST ALSO IN HIM; AND HE SHALL BRING IT TO PASS. AND HE SHALL BRING FORTH THY RIGHTEOUSNESS AS THE LIGHT, AND THY JUDGMENT AS THE NOONDAY" (Psalm 37:5, 6).

To commit our ways unto the Lord is to commit to Him everything of which we are masters (our futures, our desires, our achievements) and likewise, those things that we cannot master (our failures, our mistakes, and the circumstances in which we find ourselves). Commitment means the dethronement of our selfish wills as we completely turn our lives over to Him who is able to accomplish all things.

Trusting implicitly in His greatness, we find that the burdens of life cease to be ours and become His. We are changed from prisoners shackled by life's problems to soldiers who see their captain doing battle for them. Trusting God is simply taking Him at His Word and believing He will do that which He has promised. It is faith in action. The effectiveness of trust depends on the object of trust. But He who created us and sustains our existence will certainly bring to pass within us the promises of His Word.

Prayer for Deliverance

Psalm 40:1-17

INTRODUCTION

It is generally agreed that David was the author of Psalm 40; perhaps it was occasioned by his restoration to the throne after the brief usurpation of Absalom (2 Samuel 19). David opens the psalm with thanksgiving to God for His deliverance. He then passes on to a more general praise of God for all His glorious manifestations of Himself in the history of His people.

The psalmist next wonders how he is to manifest his gratitude, and this leads to the outburst that he can do this only by a complete dedication of himself and constant proclamation of God's loving care. Although recently delivered from peril, the psalmist is still encompassed by sufferings and dangers; and he declares his trust in God—that He will be his helper and defender.

The word *trust* has been defined as "firm belief or confidence in the honesty, integrity, reliability, justice, and so on, of another person or thing; faith; reliance." The Word of God has much to say about the need of trust in the life of an individual. We are told, "Trust in the Lord with all thine heart; and lean not unto thine own understanding" (Proverbs 3:5).

Trust in God is never misplaced; for He has promised, "Lo, I am with you alway, even unto the end of the world" (Matthew 28:20).

Unit Theme:
Prayers and Exhortations in the Psalms

Central Truth:
The Lord is faithful to hear our cries for deliverance.

Focus:
Acknowledge our need for deliverance and rejoice in God's mercy.

Context:
Either just before David became king or at Absalom's rebellion

Golden Text:
"I am poor and needy; yet the Lord thinketh upon me: thou art my help and my deliverer; make no tarrying, O my God" (Psalm 40:17).

Study Outline:
I. Divine Rescue (Psalm 40:1-4)
II. Heartfelt Gratitude (Psalm 40:5-12)
III. Celebration of Deliverance (Psalm 40:13-17)

I. DIVINE RESCUE (Psalm 40:1-4)

A. The Wisdom of Waiting (vv. 1, 2)

1. I waited patiently for the Lord; and he inclined unto me, and heard my cry.

2. He brought me up also out of an horrible pit, out of the miry clay, and set my feet upon a rock, and established my goings.

Talk About It:
1. What does it mean to "wait patiently" for the Lord?
2. What did the Lord do for David?

One of the most difficult things to endure in life is a period of waiting. It is a natural characteristic of humanity that we want immediate action. We don't like to wait.

The psalmist here indicates that he had cried out to the Lord for help, and then had waited patiently for an answer. This expression would suggest that he confidently and persistently waited, fully expecting divine intervention.

In the letter to the Hebrews we are reminded that patience is essential if we are to inherit the promises of God: "That ye be not slothful, but followers of them who through faith and patience inherit the promises" (6:12). "For ye have need of patience, that, after ye have done the will of God, ye might receive the promise" (10:36).

Patience is a necessary ingredient in the Christian life. We are to run the race with patience (Hebrews 12:1); we are to be patient in well-doing (Romans 2:7; Galatians 6:9); we can be patient in tribulation (Luke 21:19; Romans 12:12); and we are to await patiently God's answer (Psalm 37:7; 2 Thessalonians 3:5).

Patience is an attitude that produces the fruit of godliness, self-control, and unselfish attitudes toward others. Often when we rush ahead without waiting, we will make grave mistakes. The psalmist advises over and over that it is best to wait on the Lord. He promises that while we wait, the Lord will strengthen our heart.

Waiting brings deliverance. In verse 2 of the text, the psalmist gives the account of his own deliverance. The Lord brought him up "out of an horrible pit, out of the miry clay, and set [his] feet upon a rock, and established [his] goings." Pits or cisterns in Palestine were often filled, during the wet season, with water to be used during the dry season. As the water level would fall, the soaked earth at the bottom of the pit would become deep mud, or "miry clay." These were often used as prisons. Jeremiah was kept as a prisoner in such a place (Jeremiah 38:6).

This verse is a type of the sinner bogged down in the miry clay of sin, a prisoner of Satan, who is brought out of the "horrible pit" and has his feet set firmly on the Rock, Christ Jesus, who establishes his goings.

"The faith of Christ offers no buttons to push for quick service . . . and that is too much for the man in a hurry. He just gives up and becomes interested in something else."
—A.W. Tozer

B. The Joyful Results (vv. 3, 4)

3. And he hath put a new song in my mouth, even

Prayer for Deliverance

praise unto our God: many shall see it, and fear, and shall trust in the Lord.

4. Blessed is that man that maketh the Lord his trust, and respecteth not the proud, nor such as turn aside to lies.

Deliverance always brings joy. The prisoner brought from the horrible pit into the light of a new day would feel gladness in his heart. Likewise, the soul who has been brought out of the horrible pit of sin and has had his sins forgiven becomes a new person, with gladness in his heart. A song of praise to God bursts forth from the heart made new, and those who see the evidence of this change may come to fear God and put their trust in Him also.

How happy is that man who trusts in God! He is not influenced by those with honeyed words or lying tongues. He keeps his eyes on the Lord regardless of the circumstances, for he knows that from Him alone come deliverance, guidance and strength.

The promises of people are often empty; the happiness of the world is superficial. But the song that God places in our soul flows deep within. We cannot find true happiness and blessing until we make the Lord our trust.

II. HEARTFELT GRATITUDE (Psalm 40:5-12)
A. Counting Your Blessings (vv. 5, 6)

5. Many, O Lord my God, are thy wonderful works which thou hast done, and thy thoughts which are to us-ward: they cannot be reckoned up in order unto thee: if I would declare and speak of them, they are more than can be numbered.

6. Sacrifice and offering thou didst not desire; mine ears hast thou opened: burnt offering and sin offering hast thou not required.

"It is not only for His recent deliverance that the psalmist owes thanks and gratitude to God. God's mercies in the past had been countless, and have laid him under unspeakable obligations.

"God's thoughtfulness for man, His consideration and providential care, deserve praise and thanks equally with His wondrous acts. They are so numerous that it is impossible to reckon them up. Many of them, moreover, are secret, and escape our notice. Words, therefore, are insufficient; and some better return than mere words must be found.

"Will the right return be by sacrifices and burnt offerings? 'No,' the psalmist answers to himself; it is not these which God really 'desires.' . . . The one thing needed is obedience—a cheerful, willing obedience to all that God reveals as His will" (*The Pulpit Commentary*). We learn from this passage that

Talk About It:
1. What does it mean to have a "new song" in one's mouth?
2. Whom does the Lord bless, and why?

A friend asked the great composer Hadyn why his church music was so full of gladness. Hadyn said, "When I think upon my God, my heart is so full of joy that the notes dance and leap from my pen."
—**Henry Van Dyke**

reckoned (v. 5)—recounted

Talk About It:
1. What does the psalmist say are "more than can be numbered" (v. 5)?
2. God required "sacrifice and offering" in the Old Testament, but what does He really "desire" (v. 6)?

"Our heavenly Father wants nothing but the best for any of us, and only He knows what that is, for He is all-wise, the Omniscient."
—**Elisabeth Elliot**

Jehovah values far more the obedience of the heart than all the imposing performances of ritualistic worship.

B. Delighting in God's Will (vv. 7, 8)

7. Then said I, Lo, I come: in the volume of the book it is written of me,

8. I delight to do thy will, O my God: yea, thy law is within my heart.

the volume of the book (v. 7)—the scroll

Talk About It:
Explain the phrase "Thy law is within my heart" (v. 8).

Whether consciously or unconsciously, David speaks as a type of Christ. This segment of Psalm 40 (also quoted in Hebrews 10:5-7) without a doubt points to Christ for its fulfillment, for it was He who was so eager to accomplish the will of God as the prophets had foretold. Over and over in references concerning the life of Jesus, the phrase is used, "This was done that the scriptures might be fulfilled."

John Flavel wrote, "Be ready to do the will of God; be also ready to suffer. And as to sufferings for Christ, they should not be grievous to Christians that know how cheerfully Christ came from the bosom of the Father to die for them.

"What have we to leave or lose in comparison with Him? What are our sufferings to Christ's? There is no comparison; there was more bitterness in one drop of His suffering than in a sea of ours" (*The Treasury of David*).

> "The man or woman who is wholly or joyously surrendered to Christ can't make a wrong choice—any choice will be the right one."
> **—A.W. Tozer**

C. Spreading the Message (vv. 9, 10)

9. I have preached righteousness in the great congregation: lo, I have not refrained my lips, O Lord, thou knowest.

10. I have not hid thy righteousness within my heart; I have declared thy faithfulness and thy salvation: I have not concealed thy lovingkindness and thy truth from the great congregation.

Talk About It:
What should not be "hid" or "concealed" by believers (v. 10)?

David sang the praises of God and extolled His righteousness and truth. He did not preach in the modern sense of the word, since preaching was reserved for the priests and Levites. The words he penned have reached as deep into hearts as any sermon ever preached, for his psalms glorify God and exalt Him in all His greatness.

The great theme of his proclamation in public was the righteousness of God. God is righteous; He wants His people to be righteous and has provided a way for them to be so. David has declared God's faithfulness to His word, His salvation for all, His loving-kindness and His truth (see Psalms 25:5, 10; 36:5-7, 10).

That David did not refrain from telling of God's righteousness, faithfulness, salvation, loving-kindness and truth is evidenced throughout his psalms. These psalms, while given to the Israel of David's day, have come down to us swelling the audience of "the great congregation" (40:10).

> "Witnessing goes far beyond what we say at certain inspired moments. So the question is not *will* we witness (speak), but *how* will we witness?"
> **—Paul E. Little**

D. Praying for Preservation (vv. 11, 12)

11. Withhold not thou thy tender mercies from me, O Lord: let thy lovingkindness and thy truth continually preserve me.

12. For innumerable evils have compassed me about: mine iniquities have taken hold upon me, so that I am not able to look up; they are more than the hairs of mine head: therefore my heart faileth me.

compassed (v. 12)—surrounded

taken hold (v. 12)—overtaken

David has confidence that the God who has delivered him in the past will continue to deliver him now and in the future.

It is true that past experiences are extremely valuable to us. Regardless of the disappointment or suffering involved, if we can look back and see how God brought to us deliverance, comfort, or strength in the hour when it was needed, past experiences perform a great service. Trust in God, which is rewarded by answers to prayer, produces faith for future trials. If we trust the Lord, we can have faith for any situation.

Although David is asking for God's help, he acknowledges his own unworthiness. The dark pages of David's life seem to haunt him here, and he feels a deep and bitter consciousness of sin.

None of us are worthy of God's blessings. Whether our lives have been sinful or morally good, there is nothing we can do to merit the wondrous salvation purchased by the shed blood of our Savior. "Our own righteousness is as filthy rags" (see Isaiah 64:6). The only righteousness that will count is His righteousness which He gives to us when He is in us and through us in a daily walk with Him.

Talk About It:
1. What had overtaken David, and how was this affecting him (v. 12)?
2. In verse 11, what did David request from the Lord?

"Looking at the wound of sin will never save anyone. What you must do is look at the remedy."
—D.L. Moody

III. CELEBRATION OF DELIVERANCE (Psalm 40:13-17)
A. Deliver Me (v. 13)

13. Be pleased, O Lord, to deliver me: O Lord, make haste to help me.

The remaining verses of this psalm are almost identical with Psalm 70. "There are many psalms which begin in a sigh and end with a song, showing us that even in the act of waiting before God and of waiting on God, the darkness often passes away. We find our burden rolling off in the very act and energy of prayer. In this psalm, however, matters are reversed; and immediately following on a song of triumph and a vow of surrender, there is a piteous wail. This dissimilarity . . . has led to a very general opinion that what here seems to be the latter part of this psalm is actually another psalm. . . . The probability of this is confirmed by the fact that Psalm 70 is the same as the close of Psalm 40" (*The Pulpit Commentary*).

However, it is true in the Christian life that after a person has experienced the glorious salvation, he often becomes the object

Talk About It:
Was David right to ask God to "make haste"? Why or why not?

Aha, aha (v. 15)—a gleeful exclamation of ill-wishing at another's misfortune

Talk About It:
1. Whom did David want God to *confound* and *shame*, and why?
2. What did David want his enemies to discover about him?

Talk About It:
What was the psalmist's desire for all who seek God?

Talk About It:
How did David view himself? How did he see the Lord? Why does this matter?

of Satan's attacks. These attacks may come in many forms. They may come from unsaved friends or relatives; they may be physical afflictions; they may consist of times of mental stress; or they may be fears and doubts. We do know that God's people are going to be a tried people; and there are times when our faith seems to shrink, and we feel surrounded by trouble.

B. Confound Them (vv. 14, 15)

14. Let them be ashamed and confounded together that seek after my soul to destroy it; let them be driven backward and put to shame that wish me evil.

15. Let them be desolate for a reward of their shame that say unto me, Aha, aha.

The psalmist now prays that all his enemies may be thwarted in their evil designs against him. They are not only attacking him outwardly but also seeking the destruction of his soul.

David wants God to vindicate him; he wants God to let his enemies see that he is in the right. David wants his enemies to be put to shame for desiring that evil come to him.

When evildoers shall some day see the result of their malicious deeds forever turned against them, then they shall be ashamed. When the wicked gleefully scorn the righteous, and when in affliction they awake someday to their utter destruction, they will know that God surely avenges His own. God will always have the last word, not wicked people.

C. Rejoice in Him (v. 16)

16. Let all those that seek thee rejoice and be glad in thee: let such as love thy salvation say continually, The Lord be magnified.

That God in His righteous sovereignty shall in the end prevail over all adversaries causes those who seek Him now to rejoice and be glad in Him. That God's great, eternal purposes are being fulfilled and will ultimately triumph causes such as love His salvation to say, "The Lord be magnified." So now let us make Him great in the eyes of men and women, boys and girls.

D. Believe in Him (v. 17)

17. But I am poor and needy; yet the Lord thinketh upon me: thou art my help and my deliverer; make no tarrying, O my God.

The psalmist returns to his own immediate need, but with it all he is assured that God understands and will deliver. He, as Habakkuk facing the appalling condition of the nation, kept his feet on the ground and his head in the heavens and declared, "We shall not die. O Lord, thou hast ordained them for judgment. . . . But the just shall live by his faith" (Habakkuk 1:12; 2:4).

Faith abides over the wrecks of time! So David cries out, "Yet the Lord thinks upon me." How precious!

CONCLUSION

David began this psalm with praise and gratitude (vv. 1-10). His mind and heart then turned to the merciful goodness of God (v. 11). He appealed also to the retributive justice of God (vv. 14, 15). Confidence in Jehovah is sensed in the beginning and ending of the psalm. "Thou art my help and my deliverer"—that is, confidence. "Make no tarrying, O my God"—that is trustful asking (v. 17).

GOLDEN TEXT CHALLENGE

"I AM POOR AND NEEDY; YET THE LORD THINKETH UPON ME: THOU ART MY HELP AND MY DELIVERER; MAKE NO TARRYING, O MY GOD" (Psalm 40:17).

How often have you seen a man or woman standing by the road holding a cardboard sign reading, "Stranded: Need Help," or something similar? You wonder if the need is legitimate, or if the person is too lazy to get a real job.

In Psalm 40:17, it's as if David is holding a sign reading "I am poor and needy." But instead of begging from passersby, he is aiming his message to heaven. And his need is legitimate.

The word *poor* here means "afflicted; greatly distressed." *Needy* means "utterly destitute; a beggar." David was in desperate need, and he knew people could not supply his need. So he turned to God, knowing the Lord was thinking about him. It's amazing to know that David was on the Lord's mind, and that we too are in His thoughts at every moment.

Of course, just being in God's thoughts is not enough in itself; the reason He keeps us in mind is so He can be our helper and deliverer in time of need. David said, in effect, "I am greatly distressed, but God is *my* help; I am destitute, but God is *my* deliverer."

David desperately needed rescue, and he knew God was his rescuer. So he boldly prayed, "Do not delay, O my God" (*NKJV*). He needed help—and he needed it then—and he knew God would not fail him. Nor will He fail us.

Daily Devotions:
M. Deliverance From Oppression
   Exodus 3:15-22
T. Rejoice in God's Mercy
   Judges 5:1-11
W. Gratitude for Restoration
   Joel 2:21-27
T. Thankfulness for Healing
   Luke 17:11-19
F. Celebration of Healing
   Acts 3:1-10
S. A Miraculous Deliverance
   Acts 9:36-43

Celebrate God's Justice

Psalm 68:1-35

INTRODUCTION

We live in a world where injustices are common. In the United States, a convicted criminal—even a murderer—can be set free because of a legal technicality, giving him or her the opportunity to hurt others. Meanwhile, a person can be found guilty of a crime and serve years in jail, only for the legal system to finally discover this person was innocent after all.

Imagine how a person who was wrongly convicted or wrongly accused must feel when justice is carried out, and that person is found innocent. How the exonerated person must celebrate justice!

Today's lesson focuses on celebrating the justice of God. This is something we can do every day, because God *never* acts unjustly. In Isaiah 45:21, the Lord says, "There is no God else beside me; a just God and a Saviour; there is none beside me." Psalm 89:14 declares, "Righteousness and justice are the foundation of Your throne; mercy and truth go before Your face" (*NKJV*).

To say God is *just* means He is "perfect, righteous and holy." Deuteronomy 32:4 says, "He is the Rock, His work is perfect; for all His ways are justice, a God of truth and without injustice; righteous and upright is He" (*NKJV*).

One person said, "God is *just*, meaning He is no respecter of persons in the sense of showing favoritism. . . . God is *omniscient*, meaning He knows the past, present and future, even what we are thinking at any given moment; since He knows everything, His justice will always be administered fairly" (*gotquestions.org*).

I. REJOICE IN GOD'S JUSTICE (Psalm 68:1-6)

A. Let God Arise (vv. 1-3)

1. Let God arise, let his enemies be scattered: let them also that hate him flee before him.

2. As smoke is driven away, so drive them away: as wax melteth before the fire, so let the wicked perish at the presence of God.

3. But let the righteous be glad; let them rejoice before God: yea, let them exceedingly rejoice.

During Israel's wilderness wanderings, whenever it was time to break camp and move forward, the priests carrying the ark of the covenant would lead the way. Moses would say, "Rise up, O Lord! Let Your enemies be scattered, and let those who hate You flee before You" (Numbers 10:35, *NKJV*), and the procession would begin.

David echoes the words of Moses in Psalm 68:1. Since the ark represented the presence of the Lord, the belief was that wherever the ark went, the enemies of God would be scattered and run away. That's one reason why the return of the ark to Jerusalem under David's leadership resulted in such a mighty celebration of praise and thanksgiving (2 Samuel 6). "David and all the house of Israel brought up the ark of the Lord with shouting, and with the sound of the trumpet" (v. 15).

Before the Lord's presence, God's enemies vanish like smoke being blown away by the wind; they melt away like wax on a burning candle (Psalm 68:2). That's because unholy people cannot abide in the presence of a holy God.

However, the righteous have nothing to fear. Instead, they should rejoice "exceedingly" (v. 3)—with a celebration that is multiplied and prolonged. King David did this when the ark was returned to Jerusalem. He whirled and leaped in dance, celebrating with his entire being (2 Samuel 6:16), though his wife, Michal, harshly criticized his actions (v. 20).

Things have not changed much in our day. Exuberant worshipers still get criticized by pew-warming critics.

B. Sing Unto God (vv. 4-6)

4. Sing unto God, sing praises to his name: extol him that rideth upon the heavens by his name JAH, and rejoice before him.

5. A father of the fatherless, and a judge of the widows, is God in his holy habitation.

6. God setteth the solitary in families: he bringeth out those which are bound with chains: but the rebellious dwell in a dry land.

The name *Jah* is a contraction of *Jehovah*, the name of God revealed to Moses at the burning bush (Exodus 3:14). It means "I am who I am," or "I will be who I will be."

Talk About It:
1. Contrast God's enemies (v. 1) with the righteous (v. 3).
2. If the wicked are like smoke and wax (v. 2), what are the righteous like?

"God is no greater if you reverence Him, but you are greater if you serve Him."
—Augustine

Talk About It:
1. To whom does God give special attention (vv. 5, 6), and why?
2. What does it mean to "dwell in a dry land" (v. 6)?

The picture here in Psalm 68:4 is of Jehovah riding at the front of a march. Many translators say the Hebrew word rendered as *heavens* is better translated as "an arid tract" or "desert." So Jehovah is leading the children of Israel on their march through the wilderness.

God's people are twice urged to sing unto God, indicating the intensity with which they should praise Him. They are told to *extol* Him, which means "to lift or raise a level path for God," who will lead them. They extol Him through wholehearted devotion and worship.

The character of God is seen in verses 5 and 6. First, He cares for orphans, and will be a father to them. In 10:14, the Lord is called "the helper of the fatherless."

Second, He gives justice to widows. From His "holy habitation" in heaven, God reaches down to them in their need. "The Lord is in his holy temple; the Lord is on his heavenly throne. He observes the sons of men; his eyes examine them" (11:4, *NIV*).

Third, "God sets the lonely in families" (68:6, *NIV*). There are two possible interpretations. This verse might be saying that the Lord brings lonely people into marriage relationships, or it could mean that the Lord provides a comfortable dwelling place for people who have no home. Whatever the exact original meaning, testimonies of modern believers tell us God does both.

"He who has God and many other things has no more than he who has God alone."
—C.S. Lewis

Fourth, God brings justice to those who have been unjustly sentenced and condemned. Peter calls the Lord "him who judges justly" (1 Peter 2:23, *NIV*). Of course, the other side of His justice means that "the rebellious"—those who refuse to submit to His lordship—will live in dryness and barrenness, separated from the blessings of God.

II. REJOICE IN GOD'S SALVATION (Psalm 68:18-22)
A. Gifts Received (v. 18)

18. Thou hast ascended on high, thou hast led captivity captive: thou hast received gifts for men; yea, for the rebellious also, that the Lord God might dwell among them.

Talk About It:
1. In what sense are all people "captives"?
2. Where does the Lord desire to "dwell," and why?

This verse is a continuing picture of the God-led march taking the ark of the covenant to Jerusalem. The Lord God had come down to lead His people to victory, and then had ascended back to heaven. "Captivity captive" indicates that people who had been under the control of other nations had now become Israel's prisoners, defeated on the Israelites' march to Jerusalem. The "gifts" were the spoils of victory that were distributed both among the conquering Israelites as well as among "the rebellious" (the captives themselves), declaring the grace of God.

There is also a prophetic element to this verse, as explained by Paul in Ephesians 4:9, 10: "Now this, 'He ascended'—what does it mean but that He [Jesus Christ] also first descended into the lower parts of the earth? He who descended is also the One who ascended far above all the heavens, that He might fill all things" (*NKJV*).

Through the resurrection of Jesus, He was empowered to set free the rebellious captives of sin and make them His servants instead. From His place of exaltation in heaven, He now empowers His church with spiritual gifts—"to prepare God's people for works of service, so that the body of Christ may be built up until we all reach unity in the faith and in the knowledge of the Son of God and become mature, attaining to the whole measure of the fullness of Christ" (vv. 12, 13, *NIV*).

B. Salvation Promised (vv. 19-22)

19. Blessed be the Lord, who daily loadeth us with benefits, even the God of our salvation. Selah.

20. He that is our God is the God of salvation; and unto God the Lord belong the issues from death.

21. But God shall wound the head of his enemies, and the hairy scalp of such an one as goeth on still in his trespasses.

22. The Lord said, I will bring again from Bashan, I will bring my people again from the depths of the sea.

A distinct second part of this psalm begins in verse 19, with the psalmist calling Israel to take a hard look at its present situation. Most commentators agree that the phrase "with benefits" was not in the original text. Instead, the middle part of the verse more accurately reads, "who daily bears our burdens." The Lord God allows burdens to come our way, yet as "the God of salvation," He enables us to carry that load. He can even deliver us from death (v. 20).

In verse 21 we see that the same God who can prevent injury and death from overtaking His children will also crush those who "go on in their sins" (*NIV*). "Hairy scalp" refers to the crown of the rebellious person's head, which will be fatally wounded when God brings final judgment.

The references to "Bashan" and "the depths of the sea" (v. 22) refer to two great victories in Israel's history. Numbers 21:33-35 records Israel's victory over King Og of Bashan and his army, while Exodus 14:21, 22 describes how God enabled Israel to walk through the Red Sea in their exodus from Egypt. The psalmist was reminding his readers that the same God who saved Israel *then* would deliver them *now*.

III. REJOICE IN GOD'S POWER (Psalm 68:28-35)
A. Kings Worship the King (vv. 28-31)

28. Thy God hath commanded thy strength: strengthen, O God, that which thou hast wrought for us.

> "When he abandoned all attempts to save himself, Jesus Christ saved him. This was all he knew about it. And more, this was all there was to it."
> —Ichabod Spencer, *of a friend*

issues (v. 20)—escapes

Bashan (v. 22)—territory east of the Jordan River and the Sea of Galilee

Talk About It:
1. Why does God sometimes allow His people to be "loaded" with burdens?
2. Why is the word *again* used twice in verse 22?

> "Don't try to defend what God does. What He does is right because He does it."
> —Henry Jacobsen

29. Because of thy temple at Jerusalem shall kings bring presents unto thee.

30. Rebuke the company of spearmen, the multitude of the bulls, with the calves of the people, till every one submit himself with pieces of silver: scatter thou the people that delight in war.

31. Princes shall come out of Egypt; Ethiopia shall soon stretch out her hands unto God.

In verse 28 we see a call for Israel to display its strength. In reality, however, this was a display of God's strength, for it was only through God that Israel had been birthed and brought into a position of power. But what God had done in the past was not enough. So the psalmist declared, "Show us your strength, O God, as you have done before" (v. 28, *NIV*).

In verse 29, attention is drawn to "thy temple at Jerusalem." This literally refers to a palace overhanging Jerusalem. No palace had yet been built for the human king, but the Lord himself was reigning over Jerusalem, letting His presence dwell in the Tabernacle. This verse speaks of foreign kings bringing gifts to the Lord in Jerusalem, which would happen during the reign of David's son, Solomon. However, this verse will be completely fulfilled when God sets up His earthly kingdom and all the kings of the earth bow to His lordship.

There is a call for God to "rebuke" and "scatter" fierce and warmongering kings ("bulls") and armies ("calves") of the earth (v. 30). The time is foreseen when these enemy nations will bow before God, willingly paying tribute at the Temple with pieces of silver. The psalmist envisioned Egypt and Ethiopia—representing the mightiest nations of that day—as coming to Jerusalem to reverence the Lord God.

B. God Provides Power (vv. 32-35)

32. Sing unto God, ye kingdoms of the earth; O sing praises unto the Lord; Selah.

33. To him that rideth upon the heavens of heavens, which were of old; lo, he doth send out his voice, and that a mighty voice.

34. Ascribe ye strength unto God: his excellency is over Israel, and his strength is in the clouds.

35. O God, thou art terrible out of thy holy places: the God of Israel is he that giveth strength and power unto his people. Blessed be God.

After declaring that all the nations of the earth will bow before God (vv. 30, 31), the psalmist calls people from every nation to sing praises to the Lord (v. 32). He urges them to sing to the One who is enthroned above the heavens, where He reigns in His sovereignty over all of nature (v. 33). He should be praised for His power and majesty (v. 34).

---

spearmen (v. 30)—wild beasts of the reeds (perhaps crocodiles), representing the strongest of armies

Talk About It:
1. What would God's strength do for Israel (vv. 28, 30)?
2. What would foreign kings do, and why (v. 29)?

Right Worship
Remember the perfections of God whom you worship, that He is a Spirit, and therefore to be worshipped in spirit and truth; and that He is most great and terrible, and therefore to be worshipped with seriousness and reverence, and not to be dallied with, or served with lifeless toys of lip-service; and that He is most holy, pure, and jealous, and therefore to be purely worshipped; and that He is still present with you, and all things are naked and open to Him.
—Richard Baxter

terrible (v. 35)—awesome